American–East Asian Relations: A Survey

Harvard Studies in American–East Asian Relations 1

The Harvard Studies in American–East Asian Relations are sponsored and edited by the Committee on American–Far Eastern Policy Studies of the Department of History at Harvard University.

Contributions by

Burton F. Beers   Kwang-Ching Liu
Robert Dallek   Louis Morton
Roger Dingman   Charles E. Neu
Raymond A. Esthus   Jim Peck
John K. Fairbank   Robert S. Schwantes
Edward D. Graham   Peter W. Stanley
Morton H. Halperin   James C. Thomson Jr.
Waldo H. Heinrichs, Jr. Marilyn Young
Akira Iriye

American–East Asian Relations:

A Survey

Edited by Ernest R. May and James C. Thomson Jr.

Harvard University Press, Cambridge, Massachusetts, 1972

Contents

From Pearl Harbor to the Present

ERNEST R. MAY

Foreword

For nearly two centuries now Americans have traveled to the western shores of the Pacific—to "East Asia," that arc of cultures extending from Korea and Japan in the north, through China at its center, to Indochina in the south. In reverse flow, East Asians have come to America. American and Asian governments have treated with one another. Millions of Americans who have never seen the region at first hand have meanwhile developed images of East Asia, ranging from "light of the East" through "400 million customers" to "Yellow Peril." Asians have entertained equally varied images of America. These many interactions—American–East Asian relations —form a distinct and important area for scholarly exploration.

The importance of this field of scholarship may be self-evident. Since the beginning of the 1940's, the United States has engaged in three major wars in Asia. Until very recently, the United States and the People's Republic of China, both nuclear powers, have seemed on a dangerous collision course. Meanwhile, economic ties have multiplied bewteen America and non-Communist Asia. Politically and economically Americans and Asians have become almost as interdependent as Americans and Europeans.

Americans and Asians do not, however, have any understanding of one another comparable to the understanding—faulty though it often is—between Americans and Europeans. To be sure, America is an offshoot of Europe. Americans and Europeans share a heritage and certain values and ways of thinking. Americans and Asians, on the other hand, have little common background. They find it hard to comprehend one another's languages, concepts, and beliefs. Although Asia has occasionally had significant influence on the arts in the United States, appreciation of Asian cultures among the wider American public has rarely risen above faddish interest in mah-jongg, Zen Buddhism, and, most recently, the thought of Chairman Mao.

We lack adequate knowledge about political, economic, and cultural relationships between America and Asia. Such knowledge must be gathered by scholars who can work expertly at both ends of these relationships. Among them must be historians trained in the highly sophisticated field of U.S. history and equally well trained in the history of Japan, China, Korea, Indochina, or aspects of Southeast Asia. Knowing the necessary languages and using first-hand sources, these historians can reconstruct the evolution of linkages.

Such reconstruction may improve understanding not only of past interaction but also of the societies engaged in this interaction, for one large hypothesis deserving exploration is that Americans and Canadians in the eastern Pacific and the Japanese, Chinese, Koreans, and Indochinese in the western Pacific have many experiences in common and many common problems, not least of which is their relationship to each other. Given enough groundwork, social scientists may be able to compare modernization in the eastern and western Pacific areas, processes of revolutionary change, or processes of "imperialism." At an even higher level, they may become able to generalize more confidently about cross-cultural influences. As the cycle of learning runs, new theories by social scientists should raise still other new questions for historians.

Seeing a possible opportunity to stimulate a major advance in scholarship, the American Historical Association in 1968 established a Committee on American–East Asian Relations. Subsequently the Ford Foundation gave this committee funds for a modest program of scholarships, research grants, and conferences.

Once formed, the AHA Committee decided that a first necessary step was the preparation of a historiographical survey, for the history of American–East Asian relations, while a frontier zone, is not *terra incognita;* and the first step for organizers of any new exploration must be examination of reports by scouts who have gone before.

Although most past work might have been one-sided, or at least based only on sources in Western languages, there existed a good many books, articles, and theses that brought together information about aspects of the field. The committee asked a number of American scholars to prepare essays on relatively limited topics or periods, identifying important writings about them, saying something about changing fashions in interpretations, and, if possible, pointing out subjects which seemed prime targets for research by a new breed of historians equipped with dual competence in American and East Asian history. This volume consists of the essays thus commissioned.

The various authors prepared their essays during 1969. Each contributor received copies of all other drafts. Then in January 1970, all authors met together for three days at the Posada Jacarandas in Cuernavaca, Mexico. (Since then, the essays have sometimes been labeled "the Cuernavaca papers." When hearing the phrase, some have expressed puzzlement that work on American–

East Asian relations should have been discussed at a meeting in Latin America. Those doing so betray lack of familiarity with Cuernavaca. No one who has stood, short-sleeved in winter, on the balcony of Cortéz's palace and seen the morning sun brighten the snow of Popocatepetl and Ixtaccihuatl can wonder for a moment at the choice.)

In addition to the authors of essays, eight other scholars attended the three-day meeting and offered comments or critique. Alexander De Conde of the University of California (Santa Barbara), Norman Graebner of the University of Virginia, and Richard W. Leopold of Northwestern University attended as members of the AHA Committee. Professors De Conde and Leopold have both written textbooks surveying American diplomatic history. The former has written, in addition, major monographs on the Washington and Adams administrations, and Professor Leopold has written on the twentieth-century secretary of state, Elihu Root. Professor Graebner has published studies dealing with mid-nineteenth century expansionism and post-World War II U.S. foreign policy.

Two other historians of the United States attending as commentators were Dorothy Borg of Columbia and Josefina Knauth of El Colegio de México. Miss Borg, a member of the AHA Committee, is author of two distinguished monographs on U.S. relations with China in the 1920's and 1930's. Professor Knauth brought to bear on the subject matter of the conference the perspective of a specialist on U.S.–Latin American relations. Similarly, Bernard Cohen of the University of Wisconsin and William W. Lockwood of Princeton University contributed insights from the fields, respectively, of political science and economic history, Professor Cohen being the author of two works analyzing relationships between public opinion and foreign policy and Professor Lockwood the author of a history of the economic development of Japan.

The eighth commentator was James W. Morley of Columbia University, a political scientist by trade but also a member of the AHA Committee, author of an important monograph on modern Japanese history, and from 1968 to 1969 special assistant to the U.S. ambassador to Japan.

After the Cuernavaca meeting, the essays were revised. Since the table of contents specifies their respective subjects and an appended roster identifies the contributors, no more need be said here to introduce the essays themselves. Together, they provide a portrait of existing historical writing about American–East Asian relations.

A few more introductory words are in order, however, about the state of the field as a whole:

For practical purposes, two books have heretofore defined it: Tyler Dennett's *Americans in Eastern Asia* (New York: Macmillan, 1922) and A. Whitney Griswold's *The Far Eastern Policy of the United States* (New York: Harcourt, Brace, 1938). Other general works exist. Lawrence H. Battistini's *The United States and Asia* (New York: Praeger, 1955) is an example. Textbooks on American diplomatic history necessarily treat American–East Asian relations, and there are many such textbooks. Nevertheless, Dennett and Griswold have dominated. Almost all other writers have borrowed from them judgments about the relative importance of events and individuals. Most have taken the questions raised by Dennett and Griswold as those central to the field. One general point demonstrated by the essays in this volume is that this framework needs modernization.

Dennett wrote soon after World War I. The publication of his book followed only by months the Washington Conference of 1921–22. There, the American, British, French, and Japanese governments had signed three treaties. One set limits on battleship building. The second dissolved the twenty-year-old Anglo-Japanese alliance, substituting an Anglo-Japanese-American-French agreement to consult in case of trouble in the Pacific. The third treaty committed all signers to respect China's territorial integrity and to refrain from seeking unfair advantages in China. Japan and China signed still a fourth treaty, providing for return of certain territory to China. These treaties symbolized the hope that the Pacific powers would cooperate in preserving peace and achieving progress.

In *Americans in Eastern Asia,* Dennett sought to prove that the United States had benefited in the past from a policy of cooperation. He described the development of American trade in Asia and argued that from this trade had followed the one interest of the U.S. government—to ensure that Americans could carry on their business without suffering discrimination. "The tap-root of American policy has been demand for most-favored-nation treatment," declared Dennett. "One frequently meets the assumption that the Open Door Policy was invented by John Hay and first applied in 1899. The Open Door Policy is as old as our relations with Asia." (p. *v*)

In Dennett's view, U.S. objectives in Asia had not been in question during the nineteenth century. At issue had been only strategy. In seeking most-favored-nation treatment, should the government act alone or in concert with others?

As Dennett saw it, the United States had originally followed in the wake of Britain. In the Cushing treaty of 1844, the United States

obtained from China concessions identical with those extorted by
the British as a result of the Opium War. Similarly, the American-
Chinese treaty of 1858 copied an Anglo-Chinese treaty which was a
product of Palmerstonian gunboat diplomacy. In the meantime,
however, the United States grew concerned lest the British acquire
territory or privileges from China. During the civil wars of 1850–
1864 set off by the Taiping uprising, American Commissioner
Humphrey Marshall lent support to the imperial Chinese authorities.
"To Marshall," wrote Dennett, "the United States owed the discovery
of the truth that the weakness, or dissolution, of China, was a matter
of national concern . . . , and that the true policy of the American
Government must be to strengthen and sustain the Chinese Government against either internal disorder or foreign aggression." (p.
206) Recognizing this truth but recognizing also that the United
States could not protect China alone, Secretary of State Seward
sought to make the Open Door and the preservation of Chinese
integrity objects of cooperation among all the powers.

With regard to Japan, the United States initially acted independently. Commodore Perry forced the opening of trade. Townsend
Harris, however, negotiated a treaty which gave the United States
no exceptional rights. His sole objective was a mutually beneficial
trade relationship. Harris's efforts, wrote Dennett, were in entire
accord with what was already traditional American policy in China:
"The United States . . . desired for its citizens an open door to trade,
and the surest way to open this door and to keep it open, was on the
one hand to persuade the sovereign states of Asia to open their doors,
and then to strengthen these states so that they themselves would
be able to keep them open." (p. 358)

From 1870 to 1899, according to Dennett, the American government lost sight of the corollary need for cooperation among occidental states sharing an interest in the Open Door. The United States
tended to become more and more a backer of Japan. In Dennett's
view, this was a mistake. The right course for America was even-
handed cooperation with all states willing to support the most-
favored-nation principle, and John Hay's Open Door notes of 1899
and 1900 returned the United States to this historic course.

Griswold's *Far Eastern Policy* took up where Dennett's book left
off. It started with the War of 1898 and continued through the outbreak of the Sino-Japanese War in 1937. For Griswold the major
events were the annexation of the Philippines, the issuance of the
Open Door notes, mediation in the Russo-Japanese War, the Taft
administration's effort to create a loan consortium in China, Wil-

son's opposition to the twenty-one demands made upon China by Japan in 1915, the treaties emerging from the Washington Conference, the 1924 ban on Japanese immigration, and the so-called Stimson Doctrine of 1931. Although Griswold published his book three years before Pearl Harbor, he saw as of greatest significance those developments leading to war between the United States and Japan.

Griswold saw these developments as not only regrettable but also unnecessary. He attributed the annexation of the Philippines to the zeal of a small group of well-placed expansionists, envisioning both a vast future of trade with China and a much enhanced world political role for the United States. He saw the Open Door notes as a product of the same forces, supplemented by sentimental pro-Chinese opinion and crafty diplomacy on the part of Englishmen eager to involve the United States in defense of British interests both in Asia and elsewhere.

Subsequently, argued Griswold, the Open Door and territorial integrity principles had the power of shibboleths. Each successive administration felt bound to uphold them. This made correspondingly easier the task of those who continued to argue that the China trade would gain importance, that the United States had a duty to act as a great power in Asia, and that Americans owed a moral obligation to the Chinese. It also made easier the task of Englishmen and Anglophiles who wished to entangle the United States in European politics. Griswold wrote: "From 1900 to 1932 American efforts in behalf of China's integrity had passed through a number of cycles, all ending in failure. With what consequences? Jeopardizing the security of America's own territorial integrity (by antagonizing the most likely attacker of the Philippines). Encouraging Chinese patriots to hope for, if not to count on, a type of American support that never materialized. Obstructing the most profitable trend of American commerce and investment in the Far East which, since 1900 had been toward Japan and not China . . . Stimulating naval rivalry between the two nations. Involving the United States in European politics *via* the back door of Eastern Asia." (p. 467)

As essays in this volume testify, Dennett and Griswold have been corrected or amplified by many subsequent writers. Moreover, historians have treated many events occurring later. Almost a third of the essays in this volume deal with writings on American–East Asian relations since 1938. Even so, the impress of Dennett and Griswold is present. The reason is that most historians regard the questions pursued by Dennett and Griswold as the central questions in the field. What were the interests of the United States? Did the American government correctly perceive those interests? If not, why not? What policies did the government pursue? Why? Were those policies successful or unsuccessful?

If the essays in this volume establish any one point, it is that these are no longer the questions most likely to stimulate creative scholarship. Future research needs to explore subjects neglected or unperceived by Dennett and Griswold and others in their mold. On the American side, one such subject is the activity of Americans in Asia. For Dennett and Griswold the major actors were consuls, diplomats, and State Department officials. They asked what these officials did to protect trade or missionary activity. They did not look at traders and missionaries themselves or ask: What led them to Asia? What did they do there? And what about other types to whom the diplomats paid less attention—tourists, journalists, teachers, adventurers, and vagabonds?

The State Department concerned itself with other governments. From a State Department perspective, Asia consisted of China, Japan, and Korea. The remainder, being colonial territory, was part of Europe. Hence, Dennett and Griswold and writers in their tradition paid minimal attention to Southeast Asia. Even the Philippine Islands cut a small figure, showing up only as a subject of diplomatic controversy in 1898–1900 and later as a point of possible pressure by the Japanese. In this volume, Peter Stanley's essay on the Philippines stands in isolation, for the history of American governance of that country has not been incorporated into the conventional framework for understanding American–East Asian relations. Similarly, mainland Southeast Asia receives mention principally in essays on the 1950's and 1960's when it becomes a focus of high-level American diplomacy.

If the economic rather than the diplomatic record provided the basis, we might have a rather different conventional framework. (See table.) The figures support Griswold's thesis that China should have been of less interest than Japan to the United States. In the decades of the twentieth century covered by his volume, American trade with Japan more than quadrupled. By the late 1930's it was almost three times the trade with China. Even more striking, however, is the fact that trade with Southeast Asia steadily constituted one quarter to one third of all American trade with Asia, including that with Turkey, the Middle East, and India; and from 1900 onwards trade with Southeast Asia exceeded trade with China by a wide and increasing margin. If economic statistics dictated propor-

U.S. trade totals (imports plus exports) for various parts of Asia (in millions of dollars)

Decade	China[a]	Japan[b]	Southeast Asia[c]	Other Asia[d]
1870–9	195.8(33%)	96.6(16%)	189.0(28%)	108.6(23%)
1880–9	290.6(33%)	179.4(20%)	271.1(31%)	152.9(16%)
1890–9	331.5(28%)	320.0(27%)	330.6(28%)	201.9(17%)
1900–9	616.8(24%)	813.6(32%)	700.1(27%)	430.6(17%)
1910–9	1,221.4(16%)	2,891.4(36%)	2,147.1(27%)	1,595.1(21%)
1920–9	2,991.3(17%)	6,477.9(38%)	4,012.5(24%)	3,545.3(21%)
1930–9	1,414.5(13%)	3,757.9(36%)	3,753.5(35%)	1,583.1(16%)
1940–9	2,768.3(13%)	1,887.3(9%)	6,371.4(30%)	9,113.0(48%)
1950–9	2,052.9(5%)	12,026.2(28%)	13,830.8(29%)	14,644.1(38%)
1960–9	9,171.1(9%)	45,844.8(44%)	16,977.0(17%)	27,041.8(30%)

Source: U.S. Bureau of the Census. Statistical Abstract of the United States, 1878–
a Includes leased territories, 1900–19, and Taiwan 1950–69
b Includes Korea 1910–45
c Estimate, 1870–1919; actual, 1919–69
d Includes Western Asia

tions, a twenty-chapter history of American–East Asian relations, 1870–1970, would devote ten chapters to Japan, seven to Southeast Asia, and only three to China.

While no one would argue that a history of American–East Asian relations should actually give Southeast Asia more than twice as much space as China, the trade statistics do suggest that histories in the Dennett–Griswold tradition err in looking only at those parts of Asia which were major concerns of the State Department. Not only do these statistics register mutual interests to which diplomats perhaps paid too little heed, but they reflect movements of goods and people as well as dollars. Future histories plainly ought to take more account of Americans in Asia who escaped the notice of diplomats. They also ought to assess the impact of Asia on the minds of these Americans and their impact in turn on the minds of less cosmopolitan fellow citizens.

Yet another broad area needing more attention is the Asian side of the American–East Asian relationship. For the most part, we do not even have evidence from Chinese, Japanese, and Korean sources relating to the types of questions that Dennett and Griswold asked. We do not know whether American diplomats were right or wrong in judging the intentions and behavior of the Asians with whom they dealt. That is, however, only the first frontier of ignorance. Beyond lie more difficult questions concerning relations between Asians and the thousands of Americans who traded, preached, taught, lived or traveled among them, and relations between Asians who had traveled to or read about America and those who had not.

Of necessity, the essays in this volume deal primarily with works in the Dennett–Griswold mold. They thus provide a faithful representation of the literature on American–East Asian relations as of the end of the 1960's. Also, however, they note studies that have begun to chart a larger field, and many point to specific patches of wilderness that seminars or doctoral theses or monographs might explore.

The authors and sponsors of this volume hope that it will encourage new work, fresh thought, and new syntheses. The sooner the present work becomes obsolete, the more gratified we all will be.

From the Empress of China to

the First Open Door Notes,

1784–1899

Early American–East Asian Relations

Two facts dominate the historiography of the 1784–1839 period: works are limited in number, and relatively few of those which do exist have been written in the past forty years. The scarcity and age of materials give the field a peculiar coloration for the student approaching it for the first time, for much of it appears to be the remote study of a remote period. Why this is so must be viewed at the outset because the relevance of the pre-treaty period to an understanding of subsequent history is one of the major interpretive issues which the topic presents.

The dramatic reawakening of American interest in the Far East at the end of the nineteenth century provided the impetus for scholarly description of the course of American–East Asian relations up to that time and developments in American diplomacy in the East through the 1920's kept interest in the topic alive. The preponderance of what are now the standard secondary works dealing with early East Asian relations were written in the first three decades of this century. Some of these were summary works which treated the early period as a preface to the era of formal diplomatic relations. Written by diplomatic historians stimulated by diplomatic events, these works frequently reflected the assumptions that treaties and agreements were the most fruitful material for describing the relationships between peoples and that, in its East Asian dealings at any current point, American ideals and conduct could better be understood by types of American action in the past.

After 1930 interest in the pre-treaty period declined markedly. The most obvious reason for this was the shift in attention to more contemporary issues and the attempt to understand them through analysis of twentieth-century phenomena. The "old China trade" slipped into the background, whence the aspects of it most frequently discerned were the quaint, the romantic, and the legendary. At the same time certain purely academic considerations worked toward the dampening of scholarly interest in the field. Kenneth

Scott Latourette[1] and Foster Rhea Dulles[2] in their respective treatments of the pre-treaty era and Tyler Dennett[3] in the relevant chapters of his general survey had thoroughly mined out much of the primary data to be obtained from published sources of the period itself. For a long time there was uncertainty as to what unpublished material was available and at all times there was the problem that the bulk of such material was deposited in about half a dozen libraries on the east coast. These facts, in addition to the number and urgency of more recent topics for which documents were available, led to the practical discouragement of graduate level historical research. Curtis W. Stucki's *American Doctoral Dissertations on Asia, 1933–1958,*[5] for example, lists forty-six dissertations on Sino-American relations, of which only seventeen touch upon the period before the twentieth century and only four deal with the period before the Cushing treaty.

This long neglect of the pre-treaty era may be at an end. The bibliographical discussion below cites several recent studies whose authors find the origins of their respective themes in the period before 1840. But the question remains: what does the study of this era contribute to an understanding of the overall problem of American–East Asian relations? And this, of course, is the particularized version of the old question of change versus continuity in history.

The case for continuity is easier to perceive from the sinocentric viewpoint. Chinese historical thought, stressing cyclical and typological phenomena, enables one to see the Americans as another group of outsiders, "barbarians." The period of their presence at the gates has not been long in comparison with others, even those from the West, and within that period variations in the tactics of the barbarians' approach and of China's response are less significant than the overall correspondence of this phenomenon to others for which there is historical precedent. Even if one deals with Sino-American and more generally Asian-American contact in a more pragmatic way, the designation of an "old China trade" as a qualitatively different period makes only limited sense. The economic cir-

1. *The History of Early Relations between the United States and China, 1784–1844* (New Haven: Yale University Press, 1917), Transactions of the Connecticut Academy of Arts and Sciences, XX, 1–209 (August, 1917).

2. *The Old China Trade* (Boston: Houghton Mifflin Co., 1930).

3. *Americans in Eastern Asia: A Critical Study of United States' Policy in the Far East in the Nineteenth Century* (New York: The Macmillan Co., 1922).

4. A situation now remedied by Kwang-Ching Liu's *Americans and Chinese: A Historical Essay and a Bibliography* (Cambridge, Mass.: Harvard University Press, 1963).

5. Ithaca: Southeast Asia Program, Department of Far Eastern Studies, Cornell University, 1959.

cumstances of the trade were changed less by treaties than by purely economic factors and, although the missionaries gained a limited legal footing by the first treaties, their methods and motives changed only subtly and mainly in response to alterations in the intellectual climate in which they were formed. If one raises the question, an important one to some Americans then and now, of whether these outsiders were significantly different from others in their behavior toward Asian peoples and states, the American notion of periodization of this history contributes little toward an answer.

These lines of analyses may not be wholly satisfactory to Americans dealing with this history but they offer valuable insights. The notion of a confrontation between radically dissimilar cultures in which the incidents may differ in time but in which the fundamental configurations of assumption and attitude remain much the same may in the end be the most fruitful way of understanding the whole course of American–East Asian relations. If this is so, the first half century of a period not yet two centuries old might logically be viewed as the time when those configurations were first revealed in action. Even the more pragmatic view suggests that this was in fact a period in which many typical aspects of the relationship appeared, at least in embryo—the growing scope and complexity of American interest, Chinese and later Japanese resistance to ideas and values which Americans thought the hallmarks of their society, the ambivalence which Americans came to feel as a consequence, the division between those Americans whose interest in East Asia was mainly exploitive and those whose interest was ameliorative. Certainly these are among the major themes to be seen across the whole spectrum of Asian–American relations. Just as certainly their development will more clearly be understood if their roots in the early decades are seen for what they really are: not merely "background" but an integral part of the whole.

American writing on the early period of relations with East Asia has been dominated for nearly fifty years by Tyler Dennett's *Americans in Eastern Asia*. Odds are very strong that an undergraduate approaching the field will read this book first, probably as the text for a survey course, and rare is the graduate student who writes a dissertation without Dennett at his elbow. Despite its datedness, it remains the only summary work which gives extensive treatment to the pre-treaty period while establishing a sense of continuity with the phases of American–East Asian relations which followed. Inevitably Dennett's interpretive themes have influenced, if they have not dominated, most subsequent writing of specialized works and of general diplomatic history. Though he argued that the pre-treaty era was "without political significance," he felt that American merchants' adaptation to the peculiar circumstances at Canton formed a matrix in which subsequent national policy was formed, particularly in the matter of the Open Door doctrine and American respect for the integrity of China.[6]

In this and in related interpretive matters Dennett drew upon a body of American writing stretching well back into the nineteenth century, the bulk of which tended toward the congenial conclusion that Americans had most characteristically behaved responsibly and respectfully toward East Asian peoples and governments. This tradition began with works which are, technically, primary sources. But this is a peculiar historiography in which the traditional line between primary and secondary material is often difficult to draw. The modern scholar will find, as did Dennett, that many nineteenth century first-hand accounts are not only invaluable repositories of detailed information, but that they embody those statements of attitude toward Far Eastern peoples upon which traditional interpretation has been based.

The works of three men suffice for brief consideration, not only because they were central to Dennett's research but because they are still useful sources of fact and opinion for any student of the period. Samuel Shaw, the first American to trade at Canton and the first American consul there, left a careful account of his experiences, which was published more than sixty years later.[7] Robert Bennet Forbes, who was the unofficial spokesman for American traders at Canton during the years of the opium crisis (1839–1842), published an apologia at the time[8] and an autobiography some three decades later.[9] William C. Hunter, associated with the firm of Russell and Company at Canton between 1829 and 1842, subsequently wrote two chatty accounts of the pre-treaty era.[10] Certain themes run through

6. See Ernest R. May, "Factors Influencing Historians' Attitudes: Tyler Dennett," Dorothy Borg, comp. *Historians and American Far Eastern Policy* (New York: Occasional Papers of the East Asian Institute, Columbia University, 1966).

7. Josiah Quincy, ed., *The Journals of Major Samuel Shaw, the First American Consul at Canton, with a Life of the Author* (Boston: W: Crosley and H. P. Nichols, 1847).

8. *Remarks on China and the China Trade* (Boston: S. N. Dickinson, 1844).

9. *Personal Reminiscences* (Boston: Little, Brown, and Co., 1878).

10. *Bits of Old China* (London: Kegan Paul, Trench, & Co., 1855) and *The "Fan Kwae" at Canton before Treaty Days, 1825–1844* (London: Kegan Paul, Trench, & Co., 1882). Ch'eng-wen Publishing Company, Taipei, reprinted *"Fan Kwae"* in 1965 and *Bits of Old China* in 1966. The works were critically discussed in Philip de Vargas' "Hunter's Books on the Old Canton Factories," *Yenching Journal of Social Studies*, 2.1 (July 1939), 91–117.

the writing of all three men, particularly the facility of commercial dealings at Canton and the pleasantness of the life there. Forbes was the most critical in his attitudes toward the Chinese. Hunter was an unabashed sinophile and therein lies his importance for the whole sweep of subsequent American writing on this period, because his circumstantial accounts of pre-treaty Canton were the chief source for what have become the standard secondary works. The consistent body of assumptions about American respect for the Chinese and about a normative relationship of amity which runs through much of this writing can be traced to a reliance on Hunter.

Such assumptions were important aspects of two genreal works on Asian-American relations written in response to America's re-awakened interest in the Far East at the turn of the century. James Morton Callahan's *American Relations in the Pacific and the Far East*[11] and John W. Foster's *American Diplomacy in the Orient,*[12] as diplomatic histories, slighted the pre-treaty era and overstated the importance of its one diplomatic event, the Edmund Roberts mission of 1832–1834. Both works now make disappointing reading except for their interpretive statements. Callahan developed the theme of America's early contact with the Far East as part of an unfolding national involvement in the whole Pacific region, a natural consequence of continental expansion. Foster wrote that he was concerned to prove that American conduct in the East "reflect[s] credit upon his country." These assumptions of a virtual manifest destiny in the East and of the excellence of American intentions there have remained very much a part of the landscape in most subsequent treatments of this period.

The first study to deal exclusively with the pre-treaty era was the work of a returned China missionary who was to become one of the giants of Sino-American studies. Kenneth Scott Latourette's *History of Early Relations between the United States and China, 1784–1844* was written under the direction of Frederick Wells Williams at Yale. The research was careful and extensive, embracing "practically all known available material," and the result was an excellent account of these early years of American trade analyzed by its subperiods. This system of topical division still serves well and Latourette's bibliography is still useful for its coverage of published nineteenth-century sources.

The year following the publication of Latourette's *Early Relations*

11. Baltimore: Johns Hopkins Press, 1901: Johns Hopkins Studies in Historical and Political Science, series 19, nos. 1–3.
12. Boston: Houghton Mifflin Co., 1903. A new, revised edition was issued in 1926.

saw the completion of the first of Hosea Ballou Morse's great studies bearing on China's relations with the West, *The International Relations of the Chinese Empire*.[13] The first volume, *The Period of Conflict*, appeared in 1910. Despite the concentration in this volume on the period 1843–1860, it dealt in some detail with earlier Sino-Western contact and among its many merits was that of breaking away from the diplomatic historian's definition of "relations" to perceive that China had an important relationship with the trading nations of the West, even though it was not defined by treaties. The aspects of Morse's work which put it outside the tradition of American studies of the East are precisely those which make it still basic reading and an even better starting point than Dennett's book. His view of the whole topic was basically sinocentric and related more closely than any of the works discussed above to the earlier efforts of such missionary scholars as S. Wells Williams and W. A. P. Martin to see the world by looking outward from China. Moreover, Morse's knowledgeable interest in the British experience in China[14] led him to see as few other American writers have that the history of the old Canton trade was dominated by British business and politics.

The decade following the publication of Dennett's *Americans in Eastern Asia* was one of the most productive periods for works dealing with the pre-treaty era. In 1929 Kenneth Scott Latourette published *A History of Christian Missions in China*,[15] an extensive survey of the entire field from the earliest missionary arrivals to the time of writing. Although the pre-treaty era was one of severe limitations on American evangelical work in China, Latourette's discussion of it was excellent in its detail, in its analysis of the attitudes and expectations of the first missionaries, and in its placement of of this segment of the history in the context of the whole movement.[16] Two years later George H. Danton in *The Culture Contacts of the United States and China: The Earliest Sino-American Culture Contacts, 1784–1844*[17] made the first sustained effort to deal with the fact that the evangelical penetration of China produced a clash between two markedly different cultures. Missionary writers of the nineteenth century had been aware of this and some of them,

13. 3 vols., London: Longmans, Green, and Company, 1910–18.
14. Morse, The *Chronicles of the East India Company, Trading to China, 1635–1834*, 5 vols. (Oxford: Oxford University Press, 1926–29).
15. New York: The Macmillan Co., 1929.
16. Kenneth Scott Latourette, *History of the Expansion of Christianity*, 7 vols. (New York: Harper & Brothers, 1937–45), also contains an excellent but more generalized discussion of the topic. Most pertinent is vol. VI (1944).
17. New York: Columbia University Press, 1931.

Williams and Martin especially, had treated the theme with considerable sophistication. But Danton urged the claims of cultural history and its insights as a key to understanding Sino-American relations as a whole. His work was especially sound in the treatment of American attitudes and the manner of their formulation.

One of the most popular of all books on the pre-treaty era, Foster Rhea Dulles' *The Old China Trade*, also appeared in these years. The work is open to criticism on the grounds that its economic analysis was superficial, that it failed to relate the Canton trade adequately to larger patterns of world trade, and that it treated the whole topic in a romantic fashion.[18] It nonetheless contained a colorful description of the hong system and of the life at Canton based on primary sources and no secondary work has ever succeeded so well in conveying a feeling for the quality of this life.

A more analytical approach to the economic history of the period characterized the first of two studies of major figures of American business, Kenneth Wiggins Porter's *John Jacob Astor: Business Man*[19] Porter examined Astor's motives and expectations in entering the trade and the interrelationship between his China business and his interests in the fur trade and European commerce. Nowhere, prior to this time, had there been such an extensive treatment of the activities of a single China merchant and the result was a clarity and a sense of the specific in matters previously treated only through generalizations. Six years later, in 1937, Porter produced a business history of the Jackson and Lee families of Boston through their two most active generations.[20] Like Astor, these men were also engaged in a complex structure of maritime enterprises linking Canton, India, the United States, and Europe. This study displayed the same careful, detailed analysis as the Astor biography and added to it the dimension of the development of China trade interest in time. Both of Porter's works have additional value for the scholar by dint of the inclusion of a number of pertinent documents not elsewhere available in print.

One of the important themes which ran through all discussions of the Canton trade form Latourette's *Early Relations* onward was American participation in the opium trade. This has been analyzed in two journal articles, the first by Charles C. Stelle late in 1940, the second by Jacques M. Downs in 1968, and in a recent work of

18. Dulles wrote that he had "attempted to capture the spirit of adventure and daring" of the early trade.

19. 2 vols., Cambridge, Mass.: Harvard University Press, 1931.

20. Kenneth Wiggins Porter, *The Jacksons and the Lees: Two Generations of Massachusetts Merchants, 1765–1844*, 2 vols. (Cambridge, Mass.: Harvard University Press, 1937).

British scholarship, Austin Coates' *Prelude to Hong Kong*.[21] Despite the limitation of his study to the trade before 1820, Stelle managed to get well beyond traditional generalizations about American opium dealing in China and made clear the connection between the traffic in Turkey opium and the American trading position in the Mediterranean, as well as the complex economic effects of opium smuggling on the whole pattern of commerce at Canton. Downs carried this work forward, describing in considerable detail the initial processing of the drug in the eastern Mediterranean, indicating the way in which opium trading ran as a strong thread through virtually all American trading at Canton, and bringing the analysis of the trade down to the Opium War. Coates, as his title indicates, was primarily interested in the events which made Great Britain a colonial power on the China coast in the wake of the Opium War. But as part of the prelude he established the involved situation of Anglo-American rivalry and cooperation in all trading, opium prominently included.

These studies by Downs and Coates are products of a recently revived interest in the pre-treaty period among both European and American scholars. The past decade has seen a number of works which deal with the old China trade, frequently as part of a perspective more broadly inclusive in time. Most imposing of the new books is Louis Dermigny's *La Chine et l'Occident: Le commerce à Canton au XVIIIe Siècle, 1719–1833*,[22] a massive study of Chinese trade with the West which represents the most exhaustive utilization to date of European sources. This will be essential reading for the economic historian, not only for the completeness of the data presented but for the analysis of the changing nature of the trade and its wider implications, especially in the development of Britain's economic empire. It will be of value to all students, however, for its discussion of the divergence between myth and reality which Chinese and Westerners, respectively, held of one another.

Among scholars more specifically concerned with Sino-American relations, Arthur M. Johnson and Barry E. Supple in *Boston Capitalists and Western Railroads: A Study in Nineteenth-Century Invest-*

---

21. Charles C. Stelle, "American Trade in Opium to China, Prior to 1820," *Pacific Historical Review*, 9.4 (December 1940), 425–444; Jacques M. Downs, "American Merchants and the China Opium Trade, 1800–1840," *Business History Review*, 42.4 (Winter 1968), 418–442; Austin Coates, *Prelude to Hong Kong* (London: Routledge & Kegan Paul, 1966).

22. Louis Dermigny, *La Chine et l'occident: Le Commerce à Canton au XVIIIe Siècle, 1719–1833*, 3 vols. plus vol. IV ("Album") (Paris: S. E. V. P. E. N., 1964). Reviewed by John K. Fairbank in *Harvard Journal of Asiatic Studies,* 27 (1967), 286–290.

ment Process[23] have contributed an analysis of the kinship structure linking Boston's China merchants, the sources and extent of profit in the trade, and the role which these relationships and this capital played in the early financing of railroads to and in the western United States.

Other recent studies concern the related areas of missionary history and the definition of American attitudes toward China and toward itself in relation to China. Kwang-Ching Liu's *American Missionaries in China*[24] deals largely with the later period in which Protestant work flourished but it contains valuable reflections on the thought patterns which characterized American evangelical work in China throughout the century. Relevant portions of Clifton Jackson Phillips' *Protestant America and the Pagan World: The First Half Century of the American Board of Commissioners for Foreign Missions, 1810–1860*[25] are useful on the same point and on the specific process by which Americans became interested in and committed to the conversion of China.

One of the most provocative new studies, Stuart C. Miller's *The Unwelcome Immigrant: The American Image of the Chinese, 1785–1882*,[26] has opened the question of America's image of the Chinese and the effect of this image on the mistreatment of Chinese in this country. Miller contends that, from the beginning of contact with China, Americans developed a set of preponderantly negative views which played a significant part in the dark chapter of discrimination and violence directed against Chinese immigrants later in the century. His research into missionary and secular documents of the pre-treaty period was careful and extensive, giving his study value not only for its thesis but for its bibliography. My own dissertation, "American Ideas of a Special Relationship with China, 1784–1900,"[27] based on much the same sort of material Miller employed, dealt with the notions of particular promise and particular responsibility which Americans thought they perceived even in their early dealings with China.

Studies on early American relations with Japan are even more scarce than those on China but they form an important prelude to understanding the more active period of that relationship which began in the 1850's. The principal thematic concern of this literature is whether the infrequent instances of Japanese-American con-

23. Cambridge, Mass.: Harvard University Press, 1967.
24. Cambridge, Mass.: Harvard University Press, 1966.
25. Cambridge, Mass.: Harvard University Press, 1969.
26. Berkeley: University of California Press, 1969.
27. Ph.D. diss., Harvard University, 1968.

tact in these years was fundamentally amicable or hostile. The most extensive treatment of the topic is Sakamaki Shunzo's *Japan and the United States, 1790–1853*,[28] a work valuable for its thoroughness and because it is one of the very few in the corpus of American–East Asian studies on the early period which are written from an Asian perspective. Shunzo argued from Japanese archival evidence that early contact with Americans had been guarded on the part of the Japanese but not, as popularly supposed, characterized by hostility or by mistreatment of shipwrecked sailors. He further demonstrated that the Japanese had considerable information about the United States and a fair perception of its place in the world well before the arrival of Commodore Perry. An earlier work, Harry Emerson Wildes' *Aliens in the East*,[29] had argued the opposite thesis. Wildes examined the Western approach to Japan down to the 1860's, set the American experience in this larger context, and stressed the continuity of Japan's resistance to foreign encroachment both before and after the Perry expedition as an explanation for Japan's position and attitudes in the 1930's. More recently William L. Neumann's article on the background of the Perry expedition[30] discussed the growth of an expansive, optimistic mood which informed the business and evangelical communities in the United States in the 1850's and prompted their support of an aggressive policy toward Japan. Early contacts by traders and whalers are discussed in the early chapters of Foster Rhea Dulles' *Yankees and Samurai*.[31] Dulles argued that mutual curiosity and interest between Japanese and Americans has been their normative relationship since the beginning and that the period of mistrust and hostility culminating in World War II was an aberration.

The limitations of extant studies have the merit of leaving the field open for new scholarship. Material is there aplenty in the vast collections of merchant and missionary papers, government documents and contemporary periodicals.[32] What follows is a series of

28. *Japan and the United States, 1790–1853: A Study of Japanese contacts with and conceptions of the United States and its people prior to the American expedition of 1853–54*, Transactions of the Asiatic Society of Japan, 18, 2nd ser., 1939.

29. *Aliens in the East: A New History of Japan's Foreign Intercourse* (Philadelphia: University of Pennsylvania Press, 1937).

30. "Religion, Morality, and Freedom: The Ideological Background of the Perry Expedition," *Pacific Historical Review*, 23.3 (August 1954), 247–257.

31. *Yankees and Samurai: America's Role in the Emergence of Modern Japan* (New York: Harper & Row, 1965).

32. Kwang-Ching Liu, *Americans and Chinese*, is the best guide to this material and Liu's introductory essay contains many excellent suggestions for future study.

suggestions for work which needs to be done if early American–East Asian relations are to be understood as they ought. These suggestions are limited to American problems which can be dealt with through available American sources. This is a limitation in light of the practical, not of the ideal, however. It should be remarked at the outset that the best studies, whatever problem they undertake to examine, will be those which reflect the broadest acquaintance with China itself and with the British domination of the international trading community at Canton in the pre-treaty era. Nearly every one of the issues treated below has a Chinese aspect or even a Chinese counterpart and, for the student who knows the language or who has competent translation facilities at hand, the possibilities are vast despite the difficulties of access to Chinese materials.[33] The prominence of the British in the old China trade and the American consciousness of playing a secondary role, whether in trade or evangelization, can no longer be ignored or underestimated as it has been in so much earlier writing. This point has been most forcefully stated by John K. Fairbank in an article entitled " 'American China Policy' to 1898: A Misconception."[34] It has already been suggested that one might well start his secondary reading with the works of H. B. Morse and Louis Dermigny which establish this British context. It is appropriate here to suggest that American scholars in future should include prominently in their research programs an extensive examination of public and private documents available in Great Britain.

Economic History

The very term "old China trade" indicates that its salient feature was maritime commerce. There is a great field for new research here, both by dint of the questions to be answered and the untapped source material available for answering them. There is need for a comprehensive economic history of the American trade. Such a work and the more specialized research leading up to it and flowing from it should undertake to deal with the following problems:

What was the nature and extent of the American commercial connection with China and the Far East in general prior to the voyage of the *Empress of China* in 1784, which opened the direct

33. See "Symposium on Chinese Studies and Disciplines," *Journal of Asian Studies*, 23.4 (August 1964), 507–538. An example of this sort of scholarship is W. E. Cheong's "Trade and Finance in China: 1784–1834," *Business History*, 7.1 (January 1965), 34–56.

34. *Pacific Historical Review*, 39.4 (November 1970), 409–420.

trade? Merchants of the post-Revolutionary years obviously expected to resume commercial activities whose patterns were already well established. Not enough is known of those patterns. What was the nature of the tea and China and India goods businesses in the colonies? Did any Americans go to China or the Indies before the Revolution under East India Company auspices, or did any have private investments in these trades through Company ship officers or supercargoes? If so, were any of these Americans active in opening the direct trade after the Revolution? In short, what were the lines of continuity linking the periods before and after the break with England?

What was the relationship, both in anticipation and in the actual conduct of the trade, between commerce with Canton and that with the vast area between Cape Horn and the Cape of Good Hope? It is a commonplace of the standard secondary works that the Canton trade was but a part of a larger configuration collectively referred to as the Indies trade. This truism needs to be fleshed out and analyzed for the information which more detailed study will supply on the true importance of the Canton trade itself and on the development of American interest in Japan and the Far East generally. This line of analysis should logically lead on to the larger question of the place of the early China trade in America's development as a maritime power. The rather high percentage of tea and other goods reexported to Europe suggests that the China trade may have facilitated the conduct of a much broader American commerce. Since Porter's studies of Astor, the Lees, and Jacksons, however, no one has applied to this complex phenomenon the sort of sophisticated analysis which G. C. Allen and Audrey G. Donnithorne[35] and Michael Greenberg[36] have more recently brought to bear on the British China trade.

Through the first four decades of direct commerce the most often and most warmly debated public question connected with it was whether this trade brought health or harm to the national economy. Some of the economic notions of that day now seem naive but the fears that a luxury trade might be an extravagance the nation could ill afford and that badly needed specie was being drained away were genuine. A new economic analysis should deal with the myths which grew up in connection with the trade, including that which credited

35. *Western Enterprise in Far Eastern Economic Development, China and Japan* (London: Allen & Unwin, 1954).

36. *British Trade and the Opening of China, 1800–42* (Cambridge, England: Cambridge University Press, 1951).

Canton commerce with saving the infant republic from economic collapse.

The role of special federal regulations designed to aid direct trade to Canton was never far from sight in any contemporary debate over the merits of this business. As late as 1922 Tyler Dennett could describe these early acts of Congress as granting "such favors as now seem almost incredible." The subject is important not only for its bearing on economic development but because it was the most significant instance of political activity connected with the China trade before the dispatch of the Cushing mission. The argument of the free trade polemicists that these acts were a fraudulent exercise of mercantile political power were extreme[37] but they suggest the extensive influence of China merchants on public policy.

The economic and technological impact of the China trade on shipbuilding and ancillary industries needs study. This is touched upon in such general works as John G. B. Hutchins' *The American Maritime Industries and Public Policy, 1789–1914: An Economic History*[38] and William Armstrong Fairburn's *Merchant Sail.*[39] The development of the clipper ship has been discussed quite as much as it needs be but relatively little has been done on the evolution of the American East Indiaman as a distinct type of vessel.

Diplomatic and Political History

The period 1784–1839 has been described as being without political significance. The judgment is arguable. It was, in fact, a time which presented some interesting political phenomena which have gone largely ignored:

The China trade and the nature of America's relationship with the Far East were issues in domestic politics. When the Tyler administration requested an appropriation for the Cushing mission, the debate revealed well-developed party positions for and against opening formal diplomatic relations. The evolution of these positions can be traced back through events earlier in the century and its investigation should reveal the origins of a certain ambivalence in American thinking about China as a place with which America should, or should not, maintain diplomatic relations.

37. See Matthew Carey, *The New Olive Branch*, 2nd ed. (Philadelphia: M. Carey & Sons, 1821).

38. Cambridge, Mass.: Harvard University Press, 1941.

39. 6 vols., Center Lovell, Maine: Fairburn Marine Educational Foundation, 1945–55.

The merchant consuls at Canton were in a unique position because of the Chinese fiction of not recognizing them as officials of another state. Was there, nonetheless, a de facto political relationship built up over the years? What leadership did the consul exercise over his countrymen at Canton? To what extent was American consular practice consciously or unconsciously shaped by the policy and experience of the British and continental trading companies? What sorts of people wanted this apparently unlovely job? Was the position abused for private advantage, as some claimed at the time?

The tendency since Dennett's time has been to regard the relative absence of naval activity in the East in these years as a matter of foreign policy dictated by mercantile interest—a desire not to upset the delicate situation of Americans at Canton. It may have been quite as much a matter of naval policy arising out of wholly different considerations. How did officers look upon cruises to the Far East? Was this a place where command reputations could be won or was it a potential graveyard for careers? How much reliance was consciously placed on the British navy to do what the U.S. navy was not doing?

Missionary History and Cultural Influence

Missionary activity may be linked to a study of the process of cultural interchange on the assumption that missionaries formed the principal channel for a two-way process of cultural influence between East and West. In some ways this is the most difficult area of prospective scholarship because the issues are the most elusive of precise definition and treatment. But for an overall understanding of American–East Asian relations this may ultimately be the most fruitful field, as John K. Fairbank argued in his presidential address to the American Historical Association in 1968.[40]

The early work of evangelical missionaries in China has been extensively described, despite the fact that these men were on Chinese ground only during the last decade of the pre-treaty era. Moreover, enough his been written about evangelical denominations and of the formation and growth of mission societies to permit the scholar to acquire a reasonable sense of the American religious context in which the China work began. In these respects the historiography of this topic is the exception to the general rule of sparseness. Motivation and attitudes among missionaries and their supporters are central questions. A good start was made by Oliver

40. "Assignment for the '70's," *The American Historical Review,* 74.3 (February 1969), 861–879.

Wendell Elsbree in *The Rise of the Missionary Spirit in America, 1790–1815*[41] and has been carried onward by Phillips in his *Protestant America*. A challenging analysis of America's missionary self-image in these years is also found in James A. Field's *America and the Mediterranean World, 1776–1882*.[42]

As of 1784, what did Americans actually know about China and the Far East? From what sources and through what channels had they their information? William C. Appleton in *A Cycle of Cathay: The Chinese Vogue in England During the Seventeenth and Eighteenth Centuries*[43] has demonstrated that the English craze for things Chinese was on the wane in these years, and Dermigny, in the first volume of his study, discusses the successive development of new European images of China. Were those who made American opinion, or those who typified it, moving with the times in this respect? Or was the framework of American notions about China more dated, hence more flattering? Did the attitudes of the late eighteenth century become a mold in which nineteenth century experience was perceived, or were these attitudes abandoned in the light of what may have seemed contrary evidence? And what of American knowledge and assumptions about East Asian peoples other than the Chinese?

In the early phase of their contact with East Asia, Americans used an imprecise vocabulary to differentiate among Far Eastern peoples and cultures. The interchangeable use of the terms "China trade," "East Indies trade," "India trade" suggests that such discrimination was minimal and ill-informed. Akira Iriye has opened a fruitful line of inquiry in his "East and West in Nineteenth Century American Thought."[44] This sort of conceptual analysis should be applied to American views of the distinctive elements among East Asian peoples. Moreover, a study of American conceptions of interest or prospective interest within different East Asian nations should lead to a better understanding of the early period itself and of the development of persistent American attitudes. America's tendency in later years to subordinate interest in Japan to that in China, even when Japanese relations were more valuable by any objective measure, may have its roots in the early concentration on the China trade.

Finally, whether one admired the Chinese or any other East Asian people, one had at any rate to deal with them in the process of trade

41. Williamsport, Pa.: The Williamsport Printing and Binding Co., 1928.
42. Princeton: Princeton University Press, 1969.
43. New York: Columbia University Press, 1951.
44. *Papers on China*, 14 (Cambridge, Mass.: East Asian Research Center, Harvard University, 1960), 70–86.

or evangelization. The tactics or style of this dealing would always have been in some measure a function of personality but would also have reflected certain general assumptions about the sort of folk one dealt with. It is possible that these tactics would reveal more about the actual relationship between East Asians and Americans than any formal diplomatic acts. It is also possible that this is one of the more enduring aspects of the relationship.

America and China:

The Mid-Nineteenth Century

The American view of American–East Asian relations has suffered from the same myopia that has afflicted American studies of China —the self-congratulatory belief that the subject is unique, in a class by itself. This happy thought derives from the traditional Chinese view of China and Chinese history—that it has been unparalleled and is therefore incomparable. The Chinese sense of central uniqueness, so implicit and indeed explicit in the Chinese record, has rubbed off on Western students of that record. Reinforced by the special charm and difficulty of the Chinese writing system, this sense of uniqueness has pervaded the Western view of all things Chinese, even including China's contact with the United States, which has been seen as a "special relationship."[1]

I do not mean to knock the idea. It was standard procedure for Chinese diplomats to develop special relationships with all the outside barbarians. Take just one example out of a myriad: in 1843 the high Manchu negotiator, Ch'i-ying, developed a personal relationship with Sir Henry Pottinger, who had just concluded the diplomatically devastating Opium War; among many other expressions of special esteem for his arch-enemy, Ch'i-ying even proposed that since he had no son himself he should adopt Sir Henry's eldest boy, who should thenceforth be named "Frederick Ch'i-ying Pottinger."[2]

No one who has lived in China will deny that the art of personal relations has been more highly developed and more subtly utilized there than in raw America. And since relations depend on feelings, a special Sino-American relationship has no doubt existed whenever it has been felt to exist. Our myopia consists only in assuming that this attitude, true of one era of Sino-American contact, was neces-

1. See Edward Dewey Graham, "American Ideas of a Special Relationship with China: 1784–1900" (Ph.D. diss., Harvard University, 1968).

2. J. K. Fairbank, *Trade and Diplomacy on the China Coast* (Cambridge, Mass.: Harvard University Press, 1953), p. 110. See also Fairbank, ed., *The Chinese World Order: Traditional China's Foreign Relations* (Cambridge, Mass.: Harvard University Press, 1968), pp. 13, 31, and passim.

sarily true of other eras. We need to study the gradual development of the American image of China by stages from its inception.

This growth begins from almost nothing. If we go back to the founding fathers, we find that the best private libraries of colonial America barely touched on China, while men like Hamilton, John Adams, Franklin, and Jefferson evidently "stumbled upon the subject of China late in their careers, and found it a new and unstructured topic." George Washington in 1785 "expressed great surprise to learn that the Chinese were not white, although he had known that they were 'droll in shape and appearance.' "[3]

In short, China was still in the "Far East," still approached intellectually by way of Europe. The early American trading vessels got to Canton more easily by way of the Cape and the Indian Ocean than by the Straits of Magellan and the Pacific. But even after the Pacific route was used, American thinking about the Far East continued to be informed mainly by European views. The primacy of Europe in learning about China went back to the sixteenth century, when East Asia and the Americas had been opened to contact respectively by Portugal and by Spain. Especially in the era of Jesuit reporting on China, before and after 1700, Paris had become the chief source of publications. A rough indication of this European dominance and American backwardness in book publication about China can be seen from an analysis of the Widener Library shelflist for China, Japan, and Korea, which provides a chronological listing.[4] Hardly any books on East Asia seem to have originated in the United States and Canada before 1830, and rather few before the 1880's. Only from the 1890's does American publication become extensive. (It surpasses that of Europe only from the 1940's.) Our first conclusion is that the American image of China in the eighteenth century was a transplanted and assimilated version of the European image.[5] It differentiated only slowly, as American experience and interests accumulated.

Our second conclusion must be that to study the place of China

3. Stuart Creighton Miller, "The Chinese Image in the Eastern United States, 1784–1882" (Ph.D. diss., Columbia University, 1966, University Microfilms ed., 1967), pp. 26–30, citing library lists examined by Louis Wright, Carl Bridenbaugh, Frederick Tolles, and Daniel Boorstin.

4. The following table, constructed by Linda Marks, groups some 10,000 works by decade and place of publication. "East Asia" here includes India, Australia, New Zealand, and Southeast Asia as well as Hong Kong, China, Japan, etc. Later editions of a work are counted as separate works. So are American editions of books first published abroad.

5. Donald Lach is appraising the early European knowledge of East Asia in concrete detail: *Asia in the Making of Europe*, vol. 1, 2 books, *The Century of Discovery* (Chicago: University of Chicago Press, 1965).

on the American horizon requires a comparison with the place of other areas on that same horizon. It is all very well to trace the growth of the China trade or Protestant missions in concrete, absolute terms, but what was their importance in comparative terms?

The Precedence of the Near East

Here we are immensely aided by a recent study by James A. Field, Jr., *America and the Mediterranean World 1776–1882*,[6] a brilliant synthesis of American thought and action—commercial, naval-diplomatic, and missionary. Without attempting a detailed comparison of the Levant with China and Japan, this work makes it very plain that the Mediterranean and the Near East not only preceded the Far East as a focus of American attention overseas but also bulked larger until rather late in the nineteenth century, certainly up to its mid-point. Thus the American Near Eastern expansion helped formulate the rationale and set the style and even trained some of the personnel for the later Far Eastern expansion. Mr.

Widener Library Holdings on China, Japan, and Korea
(Categorized according to place of publication)

	Europe	United States	Russia	East Asia
1700–1799	133	2		1
1800–1809	15	1		1
1810–1819	21	3		
1820–1829	41		3	
1830–1839	47	10	2	6
1840–1849	78	11	2	7
1850–1859	93	26	1	10
1860–1869	139	22	2	11
1870–1879	96	14	2	58
1880–1889	180	55	8	45
1890–1899	242	157	15	103
1900–1909	670	318	27	78
1910–1919	338	277	10	119
1920–1929	420	333	41	223
1930–1939	603	495	75	450
1940–1949	207	521	31	100
1950–1959	422	586	291	396
1960–1967	368	614	241	270

Source: Widener Library Shelflist, 14: China, Japan and Korea (Cambridge, Mass.: Harvard University Library, 1968), "Chronological Listing by Date of Publication," pp. 374–494.

6. Princeton, N.J.: Princeton University Press, 1969.

Field's work can be used to illustrate this thesis all along the line.

First of all, he analyzes the early republic's liberal-commercial ideology and its expression in policy (this needs doing for the Far East and the mid-century in a similar fashion): "As the aim in constitution making was to insulate the citizen from the enemy within, the power of the state, so in foreign policy it was to insulate him from the threat posed by the great monarchies of Europe. Political isolationism was thus the external counterpart of the Bill of Rights, seeking to limit the capabilities of governments in the interest of the liberties of individuals." In this spirit the young republic both at home and abroad backed the free enterprise of trade as the mechanism of inevitable progress and believed also in the advancement of scientific technology—"the omnipotence of applied knowledge."[7] The army was to be a frontier police and an engineering agency, the navy a sea police force to protect the freedom of the seas for commerce by individuals. The navy was not for power politics. It advanced science through hydrography and exploration. In general, "the government was to hold back, the individual to go forward, but the responsibility of both was to lead by example and precept toward the better world."

As to the American strategy in foreign relations—at the birth of the republic Britain held Canada, and Spain held the trans-Mississippi region and Florida. Africa was a mystery, the Pacific almost unexplored, China still isolated except at Canton, and Japan completely isolated except for the Dutch. Europe was small, compressed by the Moslem conquest which left the Turks still in the Balkans and the Moslem states in North Africa. The Mediterranean thus remained "a frontier between two civilizations,"[8] and the American aim there was to get around the imperial monarchies of Britain, France, and Spain with their oppressive governments and religious establishments and deal with the smaller states on the fringe of European expansion. We could even deal with the Russian empire and the Ottoman Empire on the other side of Western Europe as possible friends.

As to the primacy of Near East over Far East—both the American navy and the missionary movement got their start in the Mediterranean and became active in the Far East only later. As an incentive to research, let us note the dates of service of leading naval officers on the Barbary Coast and in East Asian waters. (See table.) The precedence in time of Mediterranean experience over East Asian experience forms an obvious pattern awaiting exploration. In both

7. Ibid., pp. 7, 20.
8. Ibid., pp. 26, 27.

Service of certain American naval officers in the Mediterranean and the Far East

Officer	Mediterranean	Far East
James Biddle	1802–03,	1807,
(1783–1848)	1826–32	1846
George C. Read	1815, 1826,	1838–40
(1787–1862)	1832–34	
Lawrence Kearny	1825–29	1840–42
(1789–1868)		
Matthew C. Perry	1825–26,	1852–54
(1794–1858)	1831–32	
John Rodgers	1828,	1852–56,
(1812–1882) Son of	1845–48	1870–72
John Rodgers		
(1773–1838), who		
had trained Perry		
Robert W. Shufeldt	1846–48,	1869,
(1822–1895)	1872?	1880–82

Source: *Dictionary of American Biography,* passim. Some dates are uncertain.

cases the young American navy was much indebted to the British empire for safe harbor and bases for refitting and supplies, and even for financial facilities via London. Hong Kong became the counterpart of Gibraltar, Malta, and Port Mahon (on Minorca, used with Spain's permission ca. 1815–48). Gunboat diplomacy of course had its first heyday against Tripoli, Tunis, Algiers, and Morocco in the decades just before the opening of the treaty ports in China and Japan. It lived on in the "Perry tradition," according to which American naval officers by a combination of skills and qualities could succeed in "opening" secluded countries of East Asia—a model that influenced both John Rodgers the younger and Robert Shufeldt in the case of Korea.

The same pattern of Near Eastern precedence applies to Protestant missions. After its founding in 1810, the American Board of Commissioners for Foreign Missions sent its first missionaries to India in 1812 and to "western Asia" (actually Smyrna) in 1819. By 1824 the mission at Beirut had opened a school and by 1827 the Protestant press at Malta was printing the scriptures in four languages.[9] The first American missionary to China, E. C. Bridgman,

9. Ibid., pp. 93–102; Clifton Jackson Phillips, *Protestant America and the Pagan World: The First Half-century of the American Board of Commissioners for Foreign Missions, 1810–1860* (Ph.D. diss., Harvard University, 1954; Cambridge, Mass.: Harvard University Press, 1969).

was sent in 1829, a full decade after the pioneers to the Near East and his printer-colleague, S. W. Williams, joined him only in 1833. Meanwhile the ABCFM by 1823 had undertaken to educate some Greek boys in Cornwall, Connecticut, and a few Chinese boys were brought there too. But it was another half century before the Chinese government's Educational Mission came to the Connecticut Valley in 1872, with similar results—deracination of the students. Again, the kingpin of ABCFM operations during four decades, Rufus Anderson, visited the Mediterranean in 1829 and 1844 (as well as India and Ceylon in 1854, and Hawaii in 1862) but never got to China or Japan.

It seems fairly plain that for the early missionaries, as for the G.I.'s of World War II, China was the "end of the line," the theater of operations farthest away and last to be opened up. This suggests that the institutional structures and practices as well as the ideology of Protestant missions, already much influenced by the British example, had been largely shaped outside China in the decades from 1810 to 1840, before the Sino-American confrontation in the treaty ports really began. For example, by the time of the first American treaty with China in 1844, some sixty American missionaries had been sent to the Middle East,[10] hardly more than twenty to the Far East. Their experiences, reported in channels like the *Missionary Herald,* no doubt contributed to the China missionaries' self-image and influenced their conduct. One is reminded of the Franciscan and Dominican friars of the sixteenth and seventeenth centuries who approached China from the Philippines with special preconceptions about the desirability of preaching in the streets, or of the British merchants of the eighteenth and nineteenth centuries, who approached China from the background of their specific experience as the upper class rulers of India.

There is even a Near Eastern aspect to the old China trade, for the American supply of Turkey opium to China began from Smyrna as early as 1804[11] and continued to be important throughout the pre-treaty period. Until the end of the East India Company monopoly of British East Asian trade in 1834, the Company's policy operated to keep British competitors out of the Turkey opium trade and so

10. David H. Finnie, *Pioneers East: The Early American Experience in the Middle East* (Cambridge, Mass.: Harvard University Press, 1967), p. 118.

11. Ibid., pp. 30–31. S. E. Morison, *The Maritime History of Massachusetts, 1783–1860* (Boston: Houghton Mifflin, 1921), p. 181, states that the American opium trade at Smyrna began before the end of the eighteenth century. The pioneer study by the late Charles C. Stelle (from his University of Chicago Ph.D. diss.), "American Trade in Opium to China Prior to 1820," *Pacific Historical Review,* 9.4 (December 1940), 425–444; and his "American Trade in Opium to China, 1821–1839" in 10.1 (March 1941), 57–74, has now been

leave it to the Americans, principally Perkins and Company of Boston. When Turkey opium increasingly was taken from Smyrna to London by English merchants to supply the American China trade, this merely illustrated the intertwined relationships of the Anglo-American trade expansion. After Russell and Company succeeded Perkins and Company in 1830, it continued to develop its business as consignee in China of opium from India, even though American vessels were still barred from the Indo-Chinese carrying trade. Certainly, as Louis Dermigny so eloquently argues, the growth of the Canton trade was an international phenomenon in which American activity was inextricably tied in with British, in many parts of the world.[12] It cannot be studied in isolation. Another exhaustive, and comparative, vacuum-cleaner type of study, in the Dermigny manner of the French school of Professor Fernand Braudel, is needed for the China trade in the three decades 1834–1864, the transition from the Canton system to the treaty port system.

Even a very brief look at the subject matter of American journals in the mid-nineteenth century suggests the continued primacy of the Near and Middle East over the Far East as foci of public interest. For example, *Littell's Living Age* in the year 1845–46 selects newsworthy topics concerning the Near and Middle East over the Far East at the rate of four or five to one. In 1860 the preponderance is still roughly two to one.[13] No doubt it is to be expected that India and the Islamic world including Turkey and Egypt should have bulked larger in American news channels at mid-century than the Pacific world including Southeast Asia, China, and Japan, where contact was as yet less well established. On the other hand, a glance at *Hunt's Merchants' Magazine* for the same periods provides a striking contrast. Commercial news from East Asia (from Singapore to the Pacific) predominates almost two to one over such news from the Near and Middle East.[14] One may hypothesize that at mid-cen-

---

supplemented and filled out by Jacques M. Downs, "American Merchants and the China Opium Trade, 1800–1840," *Business History Review* 42.4 (Winter 1968), 418–442.

12. *La Chine et l'occident: Le commerce à Canton au XVIIIe siècle, 1719–1833*, 4 vols. (Paris: S.E.V.P.E.N., 1964), esp. pt. 3, chap. 3, "L'expansion Yankee," pp. 1161–1198. Thirty years ago Eldon Griffin compiled some of the basic data for such a study concerning the consular service in his privately printed volume, *Clippers and Consuls: American Consular and Commercial Relations with Eastern Asia, 1845–1860* (Ann Arbor, Mich.: Edwards Brothers, Inc., 1938).

13. (Boston, 1844–), vols. 6–9 (July 1845–June 1846), vols. 64–67 (January-December 1860).

14. Freeman Hunt, ed. (New York: 1839), vols. 14–16 (January 1846–June 1847), vols. 42–43 (January–December 1860).

tury the trade was ahead of the news, or more specifically that the American world of foreign news had a far different shape from the American world of overseas trade. Studies are needed to define for mid-century not only the make-up of the "foreign policy public"[15] but in particular the make-up of two major interest groups, the "foreign trade public" and the "foreign missions public."

What Ever Happened to the Old China Trade?

We are indebted to Arthur M. Johnson and Barry E. Supple for the first major study of the impact of Far Eastern trade on the American economy.[16] The Forbes group of Boston capitalists that led the way in building up the Chicago, Burlington, and Quincy and other railroad systems had its roots in the China trade, specifically in Thomas Handasyd Perkins. He visited Canton in 1789, and with his brother James set up the Boston firm of J. and T. H. Perkins in 1792. They had three nephews: William Sturgis, John Perkins Cushing, and John Murray Forbes. J. P. Cushing (1787–1862) lived and traded in Canton and Macao during the twenty-five years from 1803 to 1828 and developed a close, rather filial relationship with the leading hong merchant Houqua II (Wu Ping-chien, 1769–1843), for whom he carried on an English-language correspondence and invested large funds in international trade on a profitable commission basis.[17] John Murray Forbes (1813–1898) was in Canton only in the period 1830–1836. But he inherited the commission business that Cushing had carried on for Houqua as well as the chief role in the American opium trade, and after he returned to Boston and became a railway entrepreneur, he continued to draw capital from Russell & Co.'s trade in China.

In short, the China trade of the period down to mid-century created an in-group, mainly from Boston, often related by family ties, whose trading experience in China had given them confidence in one another, capital to invest, skill in doing so over extended periods and at a distance, and worldwide connections to facilitate it. J. M. Forbes was only *primus inter pares* among Russell and Co. partners who made money in China and then invested both it and their managerial talent in American railways: for example, John C.

15. See Ernest R. May, *American Imperialism: A Speculative Essay* (New York: Atheneum, 1968).

16. *Boston Capitalists and Western Railroads: A Study in the Nineteenth-Century Railroad Investment Process* (Cambridge, Mass.: Harvard University Press, 1967).

17. Ibid., p. 23. Kwang-Ching Liu has collected from archives a manuscript volume of Houqua's English correspondence.

Green, Joseph Coolidge, Jr., John N. Alsop Griswold, George Tyson. There were many others who combined the roles of early trader to China and later financier in America's westward expansion: John Bryant, William Sturgis, William Appleton, Augustine Heard, Russell Sturgis, Samuel Hooper, Edward Cunningham, to scratch only the surface and say nothing of John Jacob Astor. Many of them seem worth studying along the lines developed by Johnson and Supple. No doubt we shall find that the opium trade built a good deal more than the C. B. and Q.

Why did the Boston traders forsake opium, tea, and silk in order to invest in America's railways and industrial development? The answer seems self-evident—the superior profitability of investment in the United States. But there is a Chinese side to the story—the increasing competition of Chinese merchants in China and the limited possibilities for long-term industrial investment there. You could make money on the China coast and in the treaty ports, but you couldn't put your money to work there. As China's domestic trade revived after the mid-century rebellions, for example, the great British house, Jardine Matheson and Company, found its branches squeezed out of the smaller ports by Chinese competition in the late 1860s just as it was forced out of the Indo-China opium trade by Indian (Parsee) competition a few years later.[18] Russell and Company, in the J. P. Cushing tradition, had worked closely with Chinese merchants and merchant-officials at Shanghai, and Edward Cunningham pioneered in securing Chinese capital to help inaugurate the American-managed steamboating on the Yangtze.[19] But the railway age in America had no counterpart in China, which remained a place for trade but not for industrial growth. Russell and Company sold their China steamship fleet in 1877. The tea trade gravitated to India and Japan. Opium became a domestic Chinese product. The clipper ship, an American specialty, gave way to steam. The conjunction of opportunities and capacities that had fostered America's China trade disintegrated, and the trade lost importance.

The old China trade had helped to build America, but what it left behind was not a great American vested interest still present in East Asian trade and power politics—like the British position in Jardine's, the Imperial Maritime Customs and the Shanghai Municipal Council—but rather a nostalgic sentiment, a New England tradition

18. Edward LeFevour, *Western Enterprise in Late Ch'ing China: A Selective Survey of Jardine, Matheson and Company's Operations 1842–1895* (Cambridge, Mass.: Harvard University Press, 1968), chap. 3.

19. Kwang-Ching Liu, *Anglo-American Steamship Rivalry in China 1862–1874* (Cambridge, Mass.: Harvard University Press, 1962).

represented by Brattle Street chinoiserie, a sense of the "special relationship" described by Professor Graham. We may hypothesize that the trade of the early nineteenth century, in retrospect, contributed to an image of China that encouraged missionary interest later in the century.[20]

It takes two to trade but only one to preach. The anomaly of our early China relations is that both the flag and the missionaries followed the trade but the treaty privileges that were designed principally to help trade became eventually the bulwark, even more, of the mission enterprise.

The Two Faces of the China Missionary

The missionary movement, since it is carried on by a self-selected and embattled in-group, leaves a record primarily of in-group effort and accomplishment. The missionary is constantly struggling on two fronts, to change the heathen abroad and to maintain his support from home. Philistines, doubters, and backsliders confront him on both fronts, and both must be dealt with by constant witness. This produces two flows of written matter—the tracts, translated scriptures, and other Chinese-language writings with which to build the church in China and the English-language reports, circular letters, lectures, articles, and books with which to encourage and mobilize the constituency at home. The literature now available in our libraries represents both these flows of written matter, but neither has been much studied for purposes of academic research. The first necessity has been to compile the in-group record, in itself a vast undertaking, for which Kenneth Scott Latourette has blazed the trial and left us all in his debt. Yet the structure of mission societies, stations, personnel, and institutions, still only dimly perceived, is merely the framework within which this major strand of American–East Asian relations developed.

On the Chinese-language front, almost nothing has been done to analyze Christian writings in Chinese and see how their foreign ideas were presented to Chinese readers and often unavoidably modified in the process. Considerable bodies of these materials are available[21] and more may be expected to turn up in our libraries as

20. The influential little book by William C. Hunter of Russell and Company, *The "Fan Kwae" at Canton before Treaty Days 1825–1844,* by "an old Resident," published in London in 1882, was an "eye-witness" account forty years after the fact; its tendency to idealization was pointed out long ago by Professor Philip de Vargas, "William C. Hunter's Books on the Old Canton Factories," *Yenching Journal of Social Studies* 1.2 (July 1939), 91–117.

21. The volume compiled by Robert L. Irick, Ying-shih Yü, and Kwang-

their crucial importance becomes more widely recognized. But few researchers have as yet addressed themselves to the basic question: what did the Christian literature mean in Chinese? Surely this is the first question to ask.[22]

A comparably elementary point has been demonstrated for China's diplomatic history by Professor Sasaki's publication of the Chinese versions of British communications to the Chinese authorities in the period 1834–1859 as found in the Public Record Office in London.[23] These were the documents read by the Chinese diplomats, who did not read the English-language versions later published in the Blue Books. Yet it has taken more than a century for anyone to note this basic fact. Historians East and West have been unconscious cultural imperialists in this respect, not bothering even to ask: what was the action document on the Chinese end of Anglo-Chinese relations? Even today, no one has as yet published a study of these Chinese documents that represented the British approach to China. There are rumors that certain bundles of incomprehensible Chinese documents have been observed in the National Archives in Washington, but no one has as yet pursued this obvious lead.

The literature of the home front of American missions is of course very extensive but few have looked at it with the China front in mind. Academic studies of overseas missions are amazingly few.[24] Biographies, surveys of major movements and the work of mission boards, and large bodies of mission records are of course available, but not case studies of mission stations and how they functioned

---

Ching Liu, *American-Chinese Relations 1784–1941: A Survey of Chinese-Language Materials at Harvard* (Cambridge, Mass.: Harvard University Press, 1960, in the series "Research Aids for American Far Eastern Policy Studies" issued by the Harvard History Department committee on that subject) lists 63 items of pamphlets, books, and periodicals produced by Protestant missionaries and their Chinese colleagues, plus 73 items in Chinese produced as textbooks or by educational institutions, and a variety of other materials, many as yet uncatalogued in 1960. See pp. 113–135.

22. For one beginning, see Douglas G. Spelman, "Christianity in Chinese: The Protestant Term Question," *Papers on China*, 22A (Cambridge, Mass.: East Asian Research Center, Harvard University, May 1969), 25–52.

23. Sasaki Masaya, comp., *Ahen sensō zen Chū-Ei kōshō bunsho* (Materials on Chinese-English negotiations before the Opium War; Toyko, 1967–; *Ahen sensō no kenkyū shiryō hen* (A volume of historical materials for research on the Opium War; Tokyo, 1964); *Ahen sensō go no Chū-Ei kōso shiryō hen kō* (Draft volume of historical materials on Chinese-English disputes after the Opium War; Tokyo, 1964). These three volumes cover the period 1834 to 1859.

24. At least if we judge by Nelson R. Burr, *Critical Bibliography of Religion in America*, 2 vols. (Princeton, N.J.: Princeton University Press, 1961). For a brief diatribe on this topic, see John K. Fairbank, "Assignment for the '70's," *American Historical Review* 84.3 (February 1969), 861–879.

or of how missionaries approached their home constituencies. This is a field of enormous potentialities at the levels of biography and institutional history, leading on into realms of national psychology, thought, and policy.

It may be suggested that many missionaries of the mid-century, lacking converts, felt a considerable strain in facing two ways: encountering hostility and apathy in China yet obliged to convey a message of hope and progress to the folks back home. What frame of mind did this experience create?—certainly an ambivalence between the China mission as unappreciated and unrewarding locally yet constantly worthy and deserving of continued support from a distance. At any rate, the remarkable nonsuccess of the early decades of Protestant missions in China presumably contributed to the rather bitter, pejorative, and "anti-Chinese" attitudes so often expressed in America by missionaries of this early period. As Stuart Miller has noted, the Protestant pioneer, Robert Morrison, when he felt discouraged, could see the Chinese as "specious, insincere, jealous, envious, distrustful . . . Sadducean, atheistic in spirit, selfish, cold-blooded, and inhumane," while the great early interpreter of China to America, S. Wells Williams, had to confess the Chinese people were "vile and polluted in a shocking degree."[25] Miller's quotations cover a broad range: in 1824 Ralph Waldo Emerson referred to China as "that booby nation"; by 1846 the pioneer female missionary, Mrs. Henrietta Shuck, denounced Chinese "pride, self-righteousness, blind inconsistency, shameful dissoluteness, lurking atheism, and hungering and thirsting after unrighteous gain." This early disenchantment gradually wore off, but even in 1880 an American Board pamphlet described the Chinese as "cunning and corrupt, treacherous and vindictive."[26]

Plainly the missionary role is psychologically complex and deserving of very intensive study. Abstract love and particular hates, professional optimism and personal frustration, religious devotion and practical fears—to be a missionary is not a simple thing. The result is that the rational Confucian anti-Christian resistance seems often more intelligible to modern students than does the culturally aggressive righteousness of the foreign evangelist.

In the American view of China, it may be suggested, this extreme ambivalence of the early missionary experience reinforced both the self-righteousness of our Hopkinsian "disinterested benevolence," as applied to the masses of China living in darkness, and the natural

25. Miller (see note 3 above), pp. 170 and 151, quoting *The Middle Kingdom* (1848), 2.96.

26. Miller, pp. 153, 157, 181.

aggressiveness of the American idealist-reformer who sees a human scene in dire need of practical improvement. The natural result was that the evangelist soon moved into good works—medicine, education, reform in general. Protestant missions thus found their mode of cultural accommodation in China, which may be compared with the doctrinal accommodation worked out by Matteo Ricci and his followers for their Catholicism 250 years earlier.[27]

The Hegemony of Britain

One further theme calls for revision—the idea of the American diplomatic approach to China as independent of the British, less imperialistic, more friendly and egalitarian and yet enterprising and decisive. This view as to the facts is actually a reflection of the attitudes eloquently expressed in the American record. By dealing so fully with the American record, and not with the more informative British records, Tyler Dennett's *Americans in Eastern Asia* set a nationalistic style in 1922 which has persisted ever since and still needs correction. A classic example of this Americanistic approach was the filial effort of a New York lawyer, Thomas Kearny, in 1932 to prove that his distinguished forebear, Commodore Lawrence Kearny, had played an essential role in securing most-favored-nation treatment for the United States in 1842. Professor T. F. Tsiang could only conclude in reply that British and Chinese ideas, for different reasons, converged in making the treaty ports "open equally to all nations;" and Kearny's request was not decisive.[28] As of 1964 it was still possible to publish a study of Sino-American relations based on the Sino-American record alone, disregarding the British.[29] Such work may be intensively researched and highly informative, yet achieve no greater objectivity or perspective than Dennett had fifty years ago.

In fine, it must be recognized as a major premise that China's nineteenth-century foreign relations constitute a multi-archival

27. See George H. Dunne, S.J., *Generation of Giants: The Story of the Jesuits in China in the Last Decades of the Ming Dynasty* (Notre Dame, Ind.: University of Notre Dame Press, 1962). This is the best-researched study of the subject.

28. See Thomas Kearny, "Commodore Kearny and the Open Door and Most Favored Nation Policy in China in 1842 to 1943," *New Jersey Historical Society Proceedings*, 50 (1932), 162–190; Kearny, "The Tsiang Documents . . . An American Viewpoint," *Chinese Social and Political Science Review*, 16.1 (April 1932), 75–104; T. F. Tsiang (Chiang T'ing-fu), "A Note in Reply," in ibid., pp. 105–109.

29. Te-kong Tong, *United States Diplomacy in China, 1844–1860* (Seattle: University of Washington Press, 1964).

field, that Sino-American relations are only a subsection of this field, that American activity in China, especially in the early decades, was that of "minor barbarians," who might be played off against the major and more bellicose aggressors, principally the British. Anglo-American fraternization and cooperation in both trade and evangelism, British leadership and American acceptance of it, form the general pattern. In the last analysis, "Sino-American relations" as seen in China from the Chinese end are not a meaningful field of study; they must always yield to "Sino-British-American relations" as a more meaningful field of study. Thus in his very useful volume, *China's Management of the American Barbarians: A Study of Sino-American Relations, 1841–1861, with Documents,* Earl Swisher makes the point that "the United States played a very minor role . . . [but] was the most important neutral state during this period . . . more available for Chinese 'management' than [the] French or Russians," to say nothing of Great Britain as Peking's "principal antagonist."[30]

If we approach nineteenth-century China from the outside view of world trade and politics, perhaps this point can be symbolized by tagging the "opened" portion of China, the treaty ports and trading and preaching areas made accessible by the unequal treaty system, as part of Britain's "informal empire,"[31] a concept of some qualitative value even if rather difficult as yet to quantify. On the other hand if we approach it through the Chinese tradition in foreign relations, the British leadership in the joint administrative arrangements of the treaty system as consummated in 1860—including the administration of Shanghai and other ports and the Maritime Customs—may also be linked to a tradition of "synarchy"—non-Chinese participation in the government of China.[32] Whichever way one approaches treaty port China, from outside or inside, it is essential that American activity there be fitted into an international, predominantly British-colored, milieu. In this sense there are no pure "Sino-American" relations in China. The Americans are part of a

30. Far Eastern Association, now Association for Asian Studies, monograph no. 2, 1953, intro., pp. xvi–xvii.

31. Edmund S. Wehrle, *Britain, China, and the Antimissionary Riots, 1891–1900* (Minneapolis: University of Minnesota Press, 1966, see pp. 6–7) borrows this concept for the Chinese case from John Gallagher and Ronald Robinson (see their article, "The Imperialism of Free Trade," *Economic History Review,* 2nd ser., 6 (1953), 13.

32. See John K. Fairbank, "Synarchy under the Treaties" (in Fairbank, ed., *Chinese Thought and Institutions,* Chicago: University of Chicago Press, 1957, pp. 204–231), and Fairbank, "The Early Treaty System in the Chinese World Order" (in Fairbank, ed., *The Chinese World Order,* Cambridge, Mass.: Harvard University Press, 1968, pp. 257–275).

"foreign" community which they by no means dominate, members of a class of privileged "foreigners" who form an additional stratum of the local ruling class.

This situation, only in small part of American creation, gives the American experience in China an ambivalence, an innate tension or contradiction, that plagues the conscience and no doubt produces guilt feelings. The American in his self-image until late in the century is an anti-imperialist (and therefore anti-British) democrat, but he cannot live in China except as the British do, as a member of the elite, a superior person by every standard, material, intellectual, political. Judging from examples of a later day, we can imagine how a typical American tenderfoot would often express the egalitarianism of the open frontier by disrupting the boundaries of class status and becoming great friends with the houseboy, the cook, and the chair-coolie. This attack on the Chinese social hierarchy naturally would threaten the integrity of each servant's role, offend his self-respect, and show that the American lacked a cultural sense of propriety, could not be respected, and so was fair game for deceit and manipulation. Innumerable small cases added up to international contact. The American in China was obliged to be a democrat manqué, a ruler with qualms of conscience, in a world he never made but found seductively enjoyable. Insofar as he had a different social ideal than his British cousin, China was frustrating. The Englishman fitted into China's ruling class with less tension between his ideals and his actions.

These various approaches—by way of the Near Eastern precedents, the impact of the China trade on America, the psychological stress of evangelism, the American subordination to Britain in the treaty ports—could be supplemented by many more topics awaiting reevaluation. Even the briefest exploration indicates that American–East Asian relations are an almost untouched field.

America and China:
The Late Nineteenth Century

Until the acquisition of the Philippines, there was no American territorial possession in Asia. The American "empire," if this term can be appropriately used at all for the period 1850–1898, lay in the vast expanse between the Missouri and the Pacific (and in Alaska), where wilderness was being conquered, where cities grew, and where various forms of injustice were being committed and slowly being corrected. Yet across the Pacific, in the lands of East Asia, the Americans had also acquired certain influence and interests. Through the "unequal treaties," which the United States, along with other powers, had concluded with China, Japan, and Korea, Americans in each of these countries participated in an international arrangement that has sometimes been described as "semi-colonial." There was never any question of American colonization or territorial expansion in these countries: before 1898 the total number of Americans in East Asia, at any given time, was never more than several thousand. Yet the activities of these men—including diplomats and consuls, merchants and entrepreneurs, technicians and adventurers, missionaries and educators—represented a dimension of the national experience that should be given its due in the history of the United States. Long before America became a world power, many Americans had had contact with the East Asian peoples and had even contributed to their development.

In assessing America's relations with East Asia, the historian of the United States would undoubtedly concentrate on those contacts that had an impact on America itself, and especially on her foreign policy. But in a broader perspective, should we not include in the inquiry the impact of America on other lands? The American civilization has been a complex one. It has been distinguished by economic and technical achievements as well as a sense of mission, by callousness as well as good will, by extreme pragmatism as well as the belief that our basic values are applicable to all mankind. Through the long contacts between the Americans and the East

Asian peoples, did the American civilization—its technology and institutions, ideas and values—leave no lasting influence? If America's "manifest destiny" stopped at the waters of the Pacific, at least until 1898, did the "mission" of the American people (to borrow Professor Merk's dichotomy) extend across that ocean in the preceding decades?

In East Asia, the Americans had encountered, of course, sophisticated civilizations of ancient origin which were to develop principally according to the dictates of internal forces. Instead of wilderness, Americans found themselves amidst mature societies, distinguished by virtues of their own as well as by weaknesses. "We are the newest, as China is the oldest, empire of the world. Our institutions are but the raw experiments of yesterday." Thus wrote William Speer, a missionary who had worked among the Chinese in both China and California, in a book published in 1870. Speer was intensely sympathetic toward the Chinese and critical of the treatment they received in the United States. Yet despite the kind words he had for the "institutions of China," he predicted that "they will be changed; the time has come for that change." Looking toward the future, he hoped for "the regeneration of this Newest Empire of the world as the chief human means of effecting that of its Oldest Empire."[1]

A survey of the existing studies on America's relations with China between 1850 and 1895 indicates that scholarship on this subject has barely begun. One facet of the field, the story of the Chinese in this country, has received comparatively more attention. The record of Americans in China, however, has been neglected. Despite the existence of the extremely competent survey by Tyler Dennett, American policy toward China in this period so far has not received adequate monographic coverage; and even fewer works have been published on the activities of the Americans at the nongovernment level.[2] This survey of works currently available is therefore limited

1. William Speer, *The Oldest and the Newest Empire: China and the United States* (Cincinnati: National Publishing Co., 1870), pp. 6, 23, and 552–553.

2. For the second half of the nineteenth century, the only systematic study of the American trade with China, and that merely a statistical analysis, is found in Shü-lun Pan, *The Trade of the United States with China* (New York: China Trade Bureau, 1924). Two monographs which utilize the archives of the American firms in China are Kwang-Ching Liu, *Anglo-American Steamship Rivalry in China, 1862–1874* (Cambridge, Mass.: Harvard University Press, 1962), and Stephen C. Lockwood, *Augustine Heard and Company, 1858–1862: American Merchants in China* (Cambridge, Mass.: East Asian Research Center, Harvard University, 1971). For a general view of Christian missions in China beyond the period of Clifton J. Phillips, *Protestant America and the Pagan*

to two portions of the field—American contacts with the Chinese who came to the United States, and the American policy toward China.

The history of Chinese in nineteenth-century America—especially in regard to their reception by the American people and government —was given a remarkable pioneering survey as early as 1909. Well-documented and lucidly written, Mary R. Coolidge's *Chinese Immigration*[3] brings out aspects of American social and legislative history that even today have not been treated adequately in general surveys. Coolidge's facts have been on the whole confirmed by monographs. Ping Chiu's careful statistical study, *Chinese Labor in California, 1850–1880: An Economic Study,* supports Coolidge's claim that between 1854 and 1870, the Foreign Miners' Tax, paid largely by the Chinese, provided nearly half of all the revenue of the state of California and its counties and that it was the Chinese who provided the crucial labor force for the Western sections of the transcontinental railroads.[4] Coolidge's insistence that the Chinese laborers, despite their willingness to accept low wages, did not really offer serious competition to the white workers in the Far West seems also to have been proven. Ping Chiu has shown that the Chinese in California (according to census figures a total of 34,933 in 1860 and 75,132 in 1880, at the last date constituting 8.7 per cent of the state's population), besides working in the inferior placers, in railroad construction, and in agriculture, were concentrated in such noncompetitive low-wage and low-price fields as the textile, clothing, shoe, and cigar industries. The fluctuating wage rates in California during this period were caused, in fact, not by Chinese competition, but by such general factors as the inflow of industrial manufactures from the eastern United States. Coolidge's analysis of the anti-Chi-

World: The First Half-century of the American Board of Commissioners for Foreign Missions, 1810–1860 (Cambridge, Mass.: East Asian Research Center, Harvard University, 1969), one must still turn to Kenneth S. Latourette, *A History of Christian Missions in China* (New York: Macmillan, 1929). A few excellent Ph.D. dissertations on missionary topics are, however, at this writing, being prepared for publication.

3. New York: Henry Holt, 1909.

4. Madison: University of Wisconsin Press, 1963. Many aspects of the subject can of course be explored in human and social terms. Available documentation on Chinese labor engaged in the construction of Pacific railroads, for example, is indicated in Alexander Saxton, "The Army of Canton in the High Sierra," *Pacific Historical Review,* 35 (1966), 141–152. Among social and economic studies of the Chinese in the United States, valuable especially for the period after 1880, the following may be recommended: Rose Hum Lee, *The Chinese in the United States of America* (Hong Kong: Hong Kong University Press, 1960) and S. W. Kung, *Chinese in American Life: Some Aspects of Their History, Status, Problems, and Contributions* (Seattle: University of Washington Press, 1962).

nese movement in California and in Congress has also been proven accurate by later writers. Elmer C. Sandmeyer's *The Anti-Chinese Movement in California*[5] tells essentially the same story without some of Coolidge's details. Tien-lu Li's *Congressional Policy of Chinese Immigration*[6] adds almost nothing to Coolidge's account of how the legislation for the exclusion of Chinese laborers was deliberated, passed, and repeatedly augmented, although Li does provide further insight into how the series of laws were enforced. So far there has been no extended study on the treatment the Chinese received outside California during the nineteenth century.[7] But at least a few of the sanguinary anti-Chinese riots that spread from California to Washington and Wyoming, have been the subject of scholarly articles.[8]

While the several phases of the American anti-Chinese movement are now known, the question is, of course, how to explain it and assess its general significance. In the works of Coolidge and Sandmeyer, the basic interpretation has emerged that it was the unstable frontier society of California—and by inference, that of the other western states and territories—that produced the movement and that it was the crucial position California occupied in the presidential-election politics of the last three decades of the nineteenth century that persuaded Congress to adopt the sweeping and unprecedented immigration laws applicable to the Chinese. Coolidge emphasizes the color prejudice of the large number of southern and foreign-born citizens in California, especially the Irish, who in 1877 provided the chief support for Denis Kearney's anti-Chinese Work-

5. Urbana: University of Illinois Press, 1939.

6. Nashville, Tenn.: Publishing House of the Methodist Episcopal Church, South, 1916.

7. Gunther Barth's monograph cited in note 10, below, has an excellent section on Chinese workers at North Adams, Mass., and other eastern communities in 1870 and the few years thereafter. Barth also gives fascinating details of the unrealized plans of the southern planters in the late 1860's "to substitute Chinese hands for negro slaves."

8. Paul M. DeFalla [DeJalla], "Lantern in the Western Sky," *Southern California Quarterly*, 42 (1960), 57–58, 161–185; William R. Locklear, "The Celestials and the Angels: A Study of the Anti-Chinese Movement in Los Angeles to 1882," ibid., 42 (1960), 239–256; Lynwood Carranco, "Chinese Expulsion from Humboldt County," *Pacific Historical Review*, 30 (1961), 329–340; Jules Alexander Karlin, "The Anti-Chinese Outbreak in Tacoma, 1885," ibid., 23 (1954), 271–283, and "The Anti-Chinese Outbreaks in Seattle, 1885–1886," *Pacific Northwest Quarterly*, 39 (1948), 103–130; Paul Crane, "The Chinese Massacre," *Annals of Wyoming*, 12 (1940), 47–55 and 153–161. Chinese documents in Chu Shih-chia, *Mei-kuo p'o-hai Hua kung shih-liao* (Historical materials on American persecution of Chinese laborers; Peking: Chung-hua, 1958), including the reports of the Chinese consul in San Francisco and of the Chinese minister in Washington (mostly dated the 1880's), have so far not been studied by scholars in the United States.

ingman's Party. Sandmeyer is more inclined to trace the anti-Chinese feeling to the offense given by the Chinese themselves—their failure to adopt American dress, their acting like servile labor gangs, the dirt and the alleged immorality of Chinatown. Like Coolidge, however, Sandmeyer also emphasizes the weaknesses of the young California society—the smallness of the settled populations, the boom and bust economy which produced particular stress in the 1870's, and the precarious balance of strength between the two major political parties. These generalizations have been accepted by the authorities on California history and on American ethnic problems.[9] But as indicated in two recent monographs, the subject could and should be viewed in broader perspective.

In his extremely well-researched *Bitter Strength: A History of the Chinese in the United States, 1850–1870*,[10] Gunther Barth brings out the cultural conflict that lay behind California's encounter with the Chinese. Barth sees the unfortunate confluence of two historical forces—the one the agricultural population of south China, with its ingrained way of life and its seemingly peculiar institutions; and the other the social vision of the new state of California, in a country torn by the slavery issue. Barth's vivid reconstruction of peasant life in the Pearl River delta and of certain practices concerning Chinese emigration to Southeast Asia provides the essential perspective to the history of the Chinese in America. He emphasizes the fact that the Chinese who came to this country were "sojourners" and not immigrants; their goal was always to return to their native land as soon as they had accumulated a modest competence.[11] And he compares the early Chinese in California to the "indentured laborers" of America's colonial past. While they were not "coolies" in the sense of having been induced or forced to sign away their lives for many years—as were most Chinese laborers in Peru or Cuba in the middle decades of the nineteenth century—most Chinese who came to California appear nevertheless to have pledged their service to Chinese merchants in San Francisco who had either financed their passage to the United States or arranged their employment here. The exact relationship between the laborer and the merchant, including the length of indenture and the kinship and *Landsmann* ties that may have ameliorated the obligation, is im-

9. John Walton Caughey, *California*, 2nd ed. (Englewood Cliffs, N.J.: Prentice-Hall, 1953), pp. 383-388; Oscar Handlin, *America: A History* (New York: Holt, Rinehart and Winston, 1968), pp. 563–564.

10. Cambridge: Harvard University Press, 1964.

11. On this point, see also Lee, *The Chinese*, pp. 69–76.

possible to document.[12] It is a fact, however, that the Chinese Six Companies in San Francisco had the power to prevent individual Chinese from returning to China, and there must also have been an inescapable "web of control" formed by the merchants in Chinatown and their agents in the mining camps. Chinese miners and workmen were so dependent on their gang-leader or foreman in their dealings with the Californians that the latter could not but be impressed by their "docile servitude."

Though the appearance and habits of the Chinese inspired hostility, in Barth's view, it was the belief that they were slaves that particularly irked the Californians—not just politicians and journalists but also the respectable miners and farmers. Agreeing with Rodman Paul,[13] Barth believes that the Californians of those days, in their concern for the state's future, were possessed by a "diseased local exaggeration of our common national feeling towards foreigners." Barth argues, however, that the young California's intent was not so much to exclude all foreigners as to eradicate any taint of slavery. With Leonard Pitt,[14] he believes that nativism in California, at least in the early 1850's, which saw the beginning of the anti-Chinese movement, was not instigated by rabble or dissolute men but by those "possessed by and acting from a zeal for order." Although *Bitter Strength* closes with the year 1870, the author suggests that California's aversion to slavery, no less than the "filth and immorality" associated with Chinatown, was behind the anti-Chinese movement that continued for many decades. Without exonerating bigotry, Barth nevertheless believes that anti-Chinese politics did reflect certain ideals and experiences that characterized the American civilization of that time.

In the perspective of a century later, one can see that the large-scale transplantation of the Chinese peasantry to the newly conquered American frontier was bound to create an agonizing

12. Barth has used the few extant Chinese-language sources of Californian origin that pertain to this period, including the Chinese sections of the *Tung-ngai san-luk* (The Oriental), a paper published between 1855 and 1857 under the guidance of William Speer. Whatever doucments there were in the San Francisco Chinatown as of 1906 seem to have been destroyed by the great fire of that year. More information may perhaps be gleaned from the magazine *Hsia-erh kuan-chen* (The Chinese serial), a Chinese-language magazine published by the British missionaries in Hong Kong, 1853–1856. See Chu, *Mei-kuo p'o-hai Hua-kung shih-liao*, pp. 73–74.

13. Rodman W. Paul, "The Origins of the Chinese Issue in California," *The Mississippi Valley Historical Review*, 25 (1938), 181–196.

14. Leonard Pitt, "The Beginnings of Nativism in California," *Pacific Historical Review*, 30 (1961), 23–38.

situation. But the Barth thesis also provokes questions about American idealism itself.[15] It is true that the Chinese sojourner had but little interest in acculturation and that the system that grew out of the debtor-usurer relationship bore resemblance to servitude, but should the Americans have expressed their disapproval by imposing discriminatory taxes on the Chinese; by committing violence against them; and by prohibiting their coming altogether?

To the inflamed masses of the sandlot meetings, the Chinese were, of course, beyond redemption. But even the respectable Californians, including the railroad builders and factory owners who hired Chinese workers and defended them before the government committees, actually did very little to improve their condition—whether they were in bondage or free. The public at large merely applauded the anti-Chinese bills and editorials. In the end, it was not the vaunted ideals of the new state, but certain more prosaic and unsung forces that offset to some degree the society's indifference. The California courts did not entirely neglect what was due the Chinese. Although they could not become naturalized, their right to work and to own property was respected by the courts, if not by all the people. The discriminatory taxes levied on foreign (mostly Chinese) miners were declared unconstitutional by the state supreme court in 1870, and three years later, Chinese testimony was declared admissible in the trial of lawsuits.[16] The American legal system at least afforded the Chinese minimum protection, and there was one group among the Americans who worked to meet their needs. Beginning with the establishment of the Presbyterian Mission to the Chinese in San Francisco in 1852, work among California Chinese was developed by several churches, which in turn solicited public support. The Presbyterian William Speer and the Methodist Otis Gibson were only the most famous among the Protestant clergymen who defended the Chinese before government committees and before the public.[17] Despite the not untypical belief of Frank M. Pixley, the San Francisco publisher, that "the Chinese have no souls to save, and if they have, they are not worth saving," the missionaries hoped to spread

15. Alexander Saxton's "The Indispensable Enemy: A Study of the Anti-Chinese Movement in California" (Ph.D. diss., University of California, Berkeley, 1967) explores the implications of the anti-Chinese movement in the ideology of the labor unions and in Democratic Party politics in California through 1886. The study is being prepared for publication.

16. Coolidge remains the best account on the legal status of the Chinese in nineteenth-century California.

17. Robert Seager II, "Some Denominational Reactions to Chinese Immigration to California, 1856–1892," *Pacific Historical Review*, 28 (1959), 49–66. The Baptists began work among California Chinese in 1854, the Episcopalians in 1855, the Methodists in 1868, and the Congregationalists in 1870.

the gospel to China itself through the Chinese that came to this country (although by 1885, the Protestant churches are known to have won only 673 Chinese converts in California).[18] The missionaries also promoted the education of the Chinese. As early as 1854, a night school for San Francisco Chinese was established by the Presbyterians, teaching among other subjects "astronomy, geometry, chemistry and other sciences." This example was followed by other churches, but only very slowly by the government.[19] John Swett, a New Englander who became California State Superintendent of Public Instruction in 1866, wanted Chinese children to attend white schools, but he succeeded in changing the statutes only so far as to allow the admission of Chinese pupils to regular public schools when "the parents of white children made no objection." The petition of J. Lewis Shuck, the Baptist missionary, that there should be a public Chinese school in Sacramento was repeatedly denied, and it was not until 1885 that a public school for the Chinese was established in San Francisco. The Chinese themselves were responsible in a large measure for the slowness of their acculturation, but existing evidence—which needs to be more fully understood—does indicate equal slowness on the part of the general public and the government to extend a helping hand.

If California's treatment of the Chinese thus seems to point to certain weaknesses in American idealism, what then about the nation as a whole, which eventually sanctioned the sweeping exclusion bills? Coolidge has ascribed this development to the expediency resorted to by both major parties in currying the favor of the California electorate, the strength of the two parties being so closely matched in this period. Recent writers have added further insights. Oscar Handlin has stressed the extension of the color line from the Negroes to the Chinese, as well as increasing public awareness of racist theories. Carey McWilliams is struck by the conspicuous southern-western alliance in Congress after 1876, when the anti-Chinese movement made headway there; Carl Wittke and Lawrence Brown point to the roles of organized labor and of the Irish in nation-

18. Ibid., p. 60, n. 48. Pixley's statement, made in 1876, is quoted in Coolidge, *Chinese Immigration*, p. 96.

19. Speer, *The Oldest and the Newest Empire*, pp. 659–661; Barth, *Bitter Strength*, pp. 170–173. At the urging of churchmen, a public day-school was organized for the Chinese in San Francisco in 1859, but it was discontinued at the end of the year because the 77 students registered, nearly all over eighteen, could not attend regularly because of employment. Reestablished as a night school, the school appears to have been discontinued in 1861 "either from motives of economy or because of the protests of the parents of white children." Coolidge, *Chinese Immigration*, p. 435.

alizing the Chinese issue.[20] But the most provocative thesis is presented by Stuart C. Miller in his recent *The Unwelcome Immigrant: The American Image of the Chinese, 1785–1882.*[21] Like Barth, Miller points to a profound cultural gap between Americans and Chinese—not in reference to California's experience, but as evidenced by an alleged unfavorable impression the Americans had long had of China and the Chinese. Miller emphasizes the emergence of the so-called scientific racism in the 1870's; he has new material on the anti-Chinese stand of the Irish labor leaders. He believes, however, that these factors are not as fundamental to the explanation of the anti-Chinese movement as a deep-rooted sinophobia that has been traced to the writings of the Americans in the old China trade, to books written by British and American "diplomats" who had visited Canton before the Opium War, and to the prolific diatribes of Protestant missionaries. While the traders, on the whole, confined themselves to "good-natured derision" of the Chinese, the diplomats found the Chinese to be "depraved," and the missionaries condemned their "spiritual and moral turpitude." Through such books as Sir John Barrow's *Travels in China* and magazines such as the American Board's *Missionary Herald,* many Americans, even at mid-nineteenth century, had become aware of Chinese "deceit, cunning, idolatry, despotism, xenophobia, cruelty, infanticide, and intellectual and sexual perversity." With the rise of the mass media in the third quarter of the century, this Chinese stereotype indeed became even more widely known—thanks, according to Miller, not to events in California but to those in China that got into the newspapers. China's "cunning and treacherous" conduct during the *Arrow* War of 1856–1860 and, especially, the anti-Christian riots that culminated in the Tientsin Massacre of 1870 (in which ten French nuns were killed, as well as a dozen other Europeans) all created an indelible impression. Miller believes that the unfavorable image of the Chinese was so generally accepted that by the 1870's, it could not but affect the thinking of the anthropologists measuring the "brain capacity" of the "coolies" or senators pondering a Chinese exclusion bill.

20. Oscar Handlin, *The American People in the Twentieth Century* (Cambridge: Harvard University Press, 1954), pp. 36–39; *The Americans: A New History of the People of the United States* (Boston: Little Brown, 1963), p. 304; Carey McWilliams, *Brothers Under the Skin,* rev. ed. (Boston: Little, Brown, 1951), pp. 97–98, 100–104; Carl F. Wittke, *We Who Built America: The Saga of the Immigrant,* rev. ed. (Cleveland: Press of Case Western Reserve University, 1967), pp. 472–479; Lawrence G. Brown, *Immigration: Cultural Conflicts and Social Adjustments* (New York: Longmans, Green, 1933), p. 266.
21. Berkeley: University of California Press, 1969.

Miller's work raises more questions than it settles, for it may be argued, in the first place, that there never was a single American image of the Chinese. Merchants, diplomats, and even missionaries often had kindly things to say about this people. Books by William C. Hunter, Sir John Davis, Abbé Évariste Huc, and Samuel Wells Williams did not convey a mere picture of darkness. Indeed, the industry and civility of the Chinese, their veneration for learning, and the alleged "popular government" of Chinese villages were often praised, even by the missionaries.[22] Miller has left unanswered the question of whether the opinion leaders of the east coast were more influenced by the anti-Chinese folklore that originated in California —regarding "the immorality, crime, and disease of the Chinatowns" —than by whatever impression they might have formed of the Chinese in China. Miller does offer evidence that the Tientsin Massacre moved a small-town New York newspaper to ask editorially whether the Chinese should be encouraged to come to this country and that as late as 1877 the scholar Edwin Meade referred to this massacre when he asked the Social Science Association of America: "Can the injection of such a race into the body politic be viewed by any thinking American without anxiety and alarm?"[23] Yet Miller has not succeeded in linking this view with the wavering stand of the east coast newspapers on the issue of Chinese exclusion; neither

22. The broad question of the missionary view of the Chinese cannot be argued here. Even S. W. Williams, whom Miller frequently cites as evidence of the missionary's extreme disdain for the Chinese, acknowledges the positive side of the latter's character and civilization. He writes in the 1848 edition of his book in reference to the Chinese people: "Some of the better traits of the character have been remarkably developed. They have attained, by the observance of peace and good order, to a high degree of security for life and property; the various classes of society are linked together in a homogeneous manner by the diffusion of education and property, and equality of competition for office; and industry receives its just reward of food, raiment, and shelter, with a uniformity which encourages its constant exertion." Again, "the non-existence of caste, the weakness of the priesthood which cannot nerve its persecuting arms with the power of the state . . . ; the popular origin of the officers of government, and lastly, the degree of industry, loyalty, and respect of life and property characteristic of this people; all of these furnish some ground for thinking that the regeneration of China will be accomplished, like the operation of leaven in meal, without shivering the vessel." See his *The Middle Kingdom: A Survey of the Geography, Government, Education, Social Life, Arts, Religion, &c., of the Chinese Empire and Its Inhabitants,* 2 vols. (New York: Wiley and Putnam, 1848), II, 95 and 602. See also a later edition of the book (New York: Charles Scribner's, 1883), I, 519 and II, 742. Attention should be drawn to two other works on the American image of the Chinese: James M. McCutcheon, "The American and British Missionary Concept of Chinese Civilization in the 19th Century" (Ph.D. diss., University of Wisconsin, 1959), and John B. Foster, "China and the Chinese in American Literature, 1850–1950" (Ph.D. diss., University of Illinois, 1952).
23. Miller, *The Unwelcome Immigrant,* p. 141.

has he studied the motivation of those eastern and midwestern congressional leaders who voted for the exclusion acts of 1882 and after. Numerous factors must be considered in the background of such legislation; there is opportunity for a splendid monograph that would weigh such factors as party politics, pressure groups, racial predilections, the California anti-Chinese folklore, and even the scandals originating from the tiny Chinatown in New York. But the unfavorable image of the Chinese in China—reinforced as it was by the fear of the Yellow Peril,[24] and the fact that there were four hundred million Chinese—may well be one of the principal factors, although this is not as yet proven by Miller. While not conclusive, his study nevertheless serves as an indispensable starting point for any future work on the American anti-Chinese movement.

But Miller also raises questions for the study of American–East Asian relations in general. If a large number of Americans, owing to impressions that had long been building, regarded the Chinese as depraved and unfit for civilized life, were there not at least some, even including leaders of opinion, who were stimulated to feel that Americans could contribute to the uplift of the Chinese in their own country? If the Chinese in the United States were to be restricted to the one hundred thousand or so that were already here in 1882, were the Americans then not to be concerned at all with the four hundred million Chinese in China? As far as is known, the general public accepted, with almost complete indifference, the increasingly harsh Chinese exclusion bills that passed Congress, just as the same public was apparently undisturbed by the spate of anti-Chinese riots in the western states and territories in the mid-1880's that were reported in the newspapers. Yet this was also a period of rapid growth in the United States of the Christian missions to China, and just as the Congressional anti-Chinese movement came to a height in the 1890's, American diplomatic interest in China—which was not completely identified with economic interest—was also growing.

The same decades that saw the development of anti-Chinese politics in the United States also saw many Americans go to China—not so many as the Chinese who came here but representing more diverse motives and social origins. The record of the Americans in China is, however, very imperfectly known. There is as yet no all around factual survey of American activities in China during the nineteenth century, let alone an interpretive history that would bring out the full implications of the subject. The diplomatic side

24. See the introductory chapters of Richard Thompson, "The Yellow Peril, 1890–1925" (Ph.D. diss., University of Wisconsin, 1958).

of the story has been given a pioneering survey in Tyler Dennett's *Americans in Eastern Asia: A Critical Study of United States' Policy in the Far East in the Nineteenth Century*.[25] But good as it is, there is the question whether this book offers sufficient perspective as an assessment of American-Chinese political relations. There are on our library shelves, alas, too few monographs on American policy in China before 1895. But books done by historians of China and her foreign relations, as well as dissertations in American history, already serve to provoke new questions.

Although written in the perspective of Far Eastern problems on the eve of the Washington Conference of 1922,[26] *Americans in Eastern Asia* makes a signal contribution by tracing the origins of the Open Door policy, as defined by John Hay in 1899–1900, in the preceding century. Dennett saw the "taproot" of this policy to be the insistence that the Americans should enjoy "most-favored-nation treatment" in China or elsewhere in East Asia—in other words, opportunities for trade and for proselytizing equal to those obtained by European nations. This objective was already discernible in Canton before the treaties. New England traders, some serving as "merchant consuls," tried as best they could to get the Chinese to treat Americans at least as favorably as other Western traders. The formal beginning of this policy was, however, Daniel Webster's instructions to Caleb Cushing,[27] who concluded in 1844 America's first treaty with the Celestial Empire. From the instructions to American representatives in China issued by Webster's successors down to the time of John Hay, Dennett has shown that through the century, the United States consistently claimed for American traders and missionaries the same rights as were obtained by other nations. While the Hay notes were addressed to the changed situation of the European powers seeking leaseholds and exclusive spheres of influence and while assurance from other powers was, in this new context, more important that the commitment from China, the major aim of these notes was nevertheless equal opportunity for the Americans. There were, moreover, other elements of the Open Door doctrine that had nineteenth-century precedents. The desire

25. New York: Macmillan, 1922.
26. See Ernest R. May, "Factors Influencing Historians' Attitudes: Tyler Dennett," in Dorothy Borg, ed., *Historians and American Far Eastern Policy* (New York: East Asian Institute, Columbia University, 1966), pp. 32–37 and Dorothy Borg, "Two Historians of the Far Eastern Policy of the United States: Tyler Dennett and A. Whitney Griswold" (Paper prepared for Conference on Japanese-American Relations, 1931–1941, Hakone, Japan, July 1969).
27. This and other key documents are conveniently collected in Paul H. Clyde, *United States Policy Toward China: Diplomatic and Public Documents, 1839–1939* (Durham: The Duke University Press, 1940).

to "sustain China" and especially to support her "territorial and administrative entity" was traced by Dennett to the anti-British fulminations of Humphrey Marshall, the U.S. commissioner in China, 1852–1854, and to the pronouncements of Anson Burlingame, the American minister to Peking, 1861–1867, and of secretary of state, William H. Seward. Beginning with Seward, however, the United States had generally favored a "cooperative policy" in China—that is, concerted action with the European powers, short of a formal alliance, for the purpose of securing the treaty rights of all and of sustaining China. Although neglected by the immediate predecessors of McKinley, cooperation among the powers in regard to China was in Dennett's view nonetheless a traditional policy.

Despite his stressing the provenance of the Open Door concept, Dennett may be criticized for being preoccupied, after all, with the issues of his day and not having considered sufficiently other American overseas interests during the nineteenth century. He mentions only casually that the most-favored-nation policy was "as old as the Declaration of Independence" and that it had in fact been "enunciated on the coast of Africa in 1832."[28] One should add, of course, that the demand for most-favored-nation treatment had characterized American relations with Spanish and Portuguese America and with the new states that emerged therefrom in the 1820's, and, in an even closer parallel, this treatment, as well as extraterritoriality, had been written into the first American treaty with the Ottoman Porte (1830).[29] Moreover, Dennett has neglected the forces on the American scene that compelled greater interest in Asia during the second half of the nineteenth century—the increasing interest in markets overseas for products of American industry and agriculture and the persistence and growth of the Christian mission-

28. However, a year after he published *Americans in Eastern Asia,* Dennett wrote: "The most-favored-nation clause is a characteristically American doctrine. It appeared in the first commercial treaty ever negotiated by the United States and all subsequent commercial treaties retained it. It was the most fundamental American commercial policy." See his introduction to Mingchien J. Bau, *The Open Door Doctrine in Relation to China* (New York: Macmillan, 1923), p. xiii. In an essay written in the 1930's, Dennett enlarges on these thoughts: "[The doctrine of the Open Door] had a close affinity with the doctrine of the Rights of Man which infused the Declaration of Independence. It had been asserted hundreds of times outside of China in odd corners of the world not alone by the United States but also by England after the latter became the mechanized workshop of the world." Dennett, "The Open Door," in Joseph Barnes, ed., *Empire in the East* (New York: Doubleday, Doran, 1934), p. 271.

29. The provisions regarding extraterritoriality were somewhat unclear in the Turkish text of the treaty, however. See Nasim Sousa, *The Capitulatory Régime of Turkey: Its History, Origin, and Nature* (Baltimore: The Johns Hopkins Press, 1933), pp. 130–132.

ary movement. Although he makes a contribution toward analyzing William H. Seward's vision of an American commercial empire in the Pacific basin,[30] he has not examined the outlook in this regard of the secretaries of state from Fish to Olney—an inquiry now to be found in Walter LaFeber's *The New Empire: An Interpretation of American Expansion, 1860–1898*.[31] One should note that for his facts on the American policy in East Asia before 1895, LaFeber relies heavily on Dennett. Moreover, in his preoccupation with the economic forces, LaFeber has dealt only peripherally with the American sense of mission, either in its secular or religious form. While *American in Eastern Asia* must now be read together with works by LaFeber and others,[32] new research and synthesis are still needed before the full background of America's ninteenth-century policy toward China can be brought out.

Americans in Eastern Asia is not only inadequate in its coverage of the American background. What is perhaps an even more serious defect, it has not put American policy in the East Asian context either. Valuable though it is, as a study of American diplomatic objectives in nineteenth-century China, it has not stressed the Chinese and European diplomacy in the background; nor has it inquired into the operations of American policy in China—the degree to which, through whatever means, the United States actually gained control over the country for the sake of trade and missionary activities. Furthermore, Dennett has not made an attempt to assess the effects of America's policy and action on the Chinese scene. Although followed by many writers and summarized in textbooks,[33]

30. See in addition to *Americans in Eastern Asia,* his article "Seward's Far Eastern Policy," *American Historical Review,* 28 (1922), 45–62.

31. Ithaca: Cornell University Press, 1963, esp. chaps. 1–5.

32. See Marilyn B. Young, "American Expansion, 1870–1900: The Far East," in Barton J. Bernstein, ed., *Toward a New Past: Dissenting Essays in American History* (New York: Random House, 1967; Vintage edition, 1969), pp. 176–201. William Appleman Williams, *The Roots of the Modern American Empire: A Study of the Growth and Shaping of Social Consciousness in a Marketplace Society* (New York: Random House, 1969) emphasizes the desire of the farm interest-groups for overseas markets, including those in Asia.

33. Among the important books which accept the main thesis of *Americans in Eastern Asia* are Foster Rhea Dulles, *China and America: The Story of Their Relations since 1784* (Princeton: Princeton University Press, 1946) and Thomas A. Bailey, *A Diplomatic History of the American People,* 5th ed., (New York: Appleton-Century-Crofts, 1955). Aspects of Dennett's book even had an influence on Chinese authors. Li Ting-i, *Chung-Mei wai-chiao shih, 1784–1860* (A History of Chinese-American diplomatic relations; Taipei: Li-hsing, 1960), although using Chinese sources, relies heavily on Dennett for facts. Ch'ing Ju-chi, *Mei-kuo ch'in Hua shih* 2 vols. to date (A history of American aggression against China; Peking: San-lien, 1952, 1956), while using Chinese sources and adding the typical condemnation of the Americans, frequently cites Dennett and other American works.

Americans in Eastern Asia must be regarded as having told only a ·
segment of the story.

For the fuller diplomatic background, the work done by historians
of China's foreign policy is helpful. From the research of Earl
Swisher and John K. Fairbank, two highly relevant facts have
emerged: that it was the Chinese policy to accord most-favored-
nation treatment to the United States; and that it was chiefly the
British who created the conditions under which the American
treaty rights in China came to be of any substance. Swisher's impressive volume of Chinese diplomatic documents, translated into
English,[34] indicates the feasibility of studying the other side of
American-Chinese relations. Despite his importance as a representative of American desires and sentiments, Caleb Cushing, who
signed the Treaty of Wang-hsia in 1844, has undoubtedly been
overrated for the success of his diplomatic strategy and acumen.
American traders had been allowed by the Ch'ing officials to trade
in the same manner as the British, even before Cushing arrived in
Macao in February 1844;[35] and despite his claim that it was his
threat of going to Peking that won him the treaty, Chinese records
suggest that the Ch'ing negotiators at Canton had accepted the
treaty of their own accord. Fairbank, in his *Trade and Diplomacy on
the China Coast: The Opening of the Treaty Ports, 1842–1854*[36]
inaugurates a basic inquiry into Ch'ing foreign policy that has led
him to explore its many cultural roots. The Chinese had so easily
conceded their first treaty with the British (1842–1843, including
the supplementary treaty of the latter year) not only because China
had been subdued in war but also because there were definite
precedents since the T'ang dynasty for the Middle Kingdom's allowing the "barbarians" to administer their own merchant colonies at

34. Earl Swisher, *China's Management of the American Barbarians: A
Study of Sino-American Relations, 1841–1861, with Documents* (New Haven:
Far Eastern Association, 1953). See also his "The Management of the Ameri-
can Barbarians: A Study in the Relations between the United States and
China from 1840 to 1860" (Ph.D. diss., Harvard University, 1941), pp. 60
and 172–173.

35. On this point, see also T. F. Tsiang, "The Extension of Equal Commercial Privileges to Other Nations Than the British After the Treaty of
Nanking," *Chinese Social and Political Science Review*, 15.3 (1931), 422–44;
and "A Note in Reply [to Thomas Kearney]," ibid., 16.1 (1932), 105–109.

36. 2 vols., Cambridge: Harvard University Press, 1953. See also Fairbank,
"Synarchy under the Treaties," in Fairbank, ed., *Chinese Thought and Insti-
tutions* (Chicago: University of Chicago Press, 1957), pp. 202–231; and "The
Early Treaty System in the Chinese World Order," in Fairbank, ed., *The
Chinese World Order* (Cambridge: Harvard University Press, 1968), pp. 257–
275.

the seaports—the onerous regulations that the Ch'ing dynasty imposed in Canton notwithstanding. With their highly flexible notions of law and their proverbial disdain for commerce, Chinese officials did not really care excessively about such matters as legal jurisdiction or customs tariffs applicable to aliens. Many times in history, when China was militarily defenseless, the Chinese even accepted, without any unbearable sense of calamity, the rule of certain barbarian people over part or all of China itself. Before such a dire situation arose, however, China's rulers would, whenever possible, confer their "benevolence" impartially among different groups of barbarians, "the better to use them against one another." Once they were reconciled to their treaty with Britain in the aftermath of the Opium War, the Ch'ing officials were almost happy to grant similar treaties to the Americans and the French!

Although most-favored-nation treatment must be regarded as Chinese as well as American policy, the fact remains that it was the British who defeated China in the first place and, moreover, created an area of Western freedom at the treaty ports, buttressed by locally devised but essentially Western institutions.[37] In Shanghai and the other treaty ports, it was the energetic British consuls, schooled in the principles of free trade and of Benthamism as well as the harsher aspects of the British imperial administration, that worked out with the rather compliant Ch'ing officials practical arrangements regarding residence, commerce, and shipping. The efforts of George Balfour and his successor as the Shanghai consul, Rutherford Alcock, backed by the successive plenipotentiaries who served also as governors of Hongkong (Sir John Davis, George Bonham, and the pious reformer, Dr. John Bowring) led in the mid-1850's to the creation of two crucial institutions—the Western municipal government with authority to tax and to police in a specified area of Shanghai and the employment of Europeans and Americans as inspectors of the Chinese maritime customs under the protection of the Western consuls. It is true that the American merchant-consul, Edward Cunningham, successfully insisted in 1852 that Americans could buy land in the British settlement without having to register the deeds at the British consulate, and that

37. Since he has been preoccupied with the origins of these institutions, Fairbanks tends to see them as products of "a dual society of a new type, neither wholly native nor wholly foreign." It should perhaps be stressed that certain essentially Western features dominated both the Shanghai municipal government and the inspectorate of customs, and it was such features that accounted for the value of these institutions to the Westerners of the time as well as their far-reaching influence upon China.

Humphrey Marshall, the American commissioner, upbraided the British for prohibiting Chinese domicile in the settlement. Yet the land regulations of 1854 that created the Shanghai Municipal Council were approved by a meeting held at the British consulate; the new American consul, Robert C. Murphy, largely followed the British lead, and the Americans who participated in the meeting were aware of the fact that it was the British who secured from the Chinese the favorable area of town in the first place and did not bar Americans from it. The land regulations of 1854 evolved out of earlier Sino-British regulations of 1845 just as the Municipal Council developed from the British-initiated Committe on Roads and Jetties.[38] The American commissioner, Robert M. McLane, did contribute to the creation of the foreign inspectorate of customs, since it was he and not the British plenipotentiary who in June 1854 was granted an interview by Governor-General I-liang, during which the question of back duties owed by Western merchants was discussed. But it was the British consul, Alcock, who conceived the idea of a foreign inspectorate and who pushed the plan through. The American "equal opportunity" would indeed have been almost meaningless if the British had adopted an exclusive policy in Shanghai, or if the treaty tariff had not come to be administered by an international inspectorate.

The wealth of Chinese and British diplomatic documents has been utilized for only a few topics in the forty years after 1854, but it is plain that the United States continued during this period to rely on Chinese and British impartiality for the maintenance and expansion of American rights in China. The anti-foreignism of the court of Hsien-feng indeed threatened the interests of all treaty powers. But the Anglo-French war against China in 1856–1860 (in which the French contributed a minor part of the forces) compelled the opening of new ports and further concessions to Western trade and proselytism, as well as the real beginning of Sino-Western diplomatic intercourse. The efforts of William B. Reed to obtain the American Treaty of Tientsin (1858) and of John E. Ward to get it ratified in Peking (1859), as discussed in Te-kong Tong's *United States Diplomacy in China, 1844–60*[39] need to be considered in the full context of the British and French military action as described by H. B. Morse, Henri Cordier, and D. Bonner-Smith and E. W. R. Lumby, and in the context of Ch'ing policy as studied by Immanuel

38. A. M. Kotenev, *Shanghai: Its Mixed Court and Council* (Shanghai: North-China Daily News and Herald, 1925), pp. 3–11. See also William C. Johnstone, Jr., *The Shanghai Problem* (Stanford: Stanford University Press, 1937), chaps. 1 and 2.

39. Seattle: University of Washington Press, 1964.

Hsü and Masataka Banno.[40] With the creation of the Tsungli Yamen, one sees the rise of a new Ch'ing policy that adds patriotism to ancient Chinese cultural pride (the Manchus and the Chinese belonged, after all, to the same political entity and shared the same culture). As Mary C. Wright has shown, the Tsungli Yamen's program included resistance to further demands from the powers and a desire to revise at least certain points of the treaties made in the past. In their old-world wisdom, the Manchu and Chinese statesmen saw clearly that until China's "self-strengthening" succeeded, she could not hope to alter the principal treaty provisions. In order to avoid disastrous disputes, the yamen tried, as best it could, to see that the existing treaties were respected throughout the empire.[41] To be sure, with the establishment of the American legation in Peking in 1862, the diplomatic influence of the United States had increased. American ministers, beginning with Burlingame, besides acting in concert with the British and the French—hence his "cooperative policy"—would particularly befriend other colleagues like the Russian and Prussian (later German) ministers and would seek to increase the American leverage by offering to mediate in disputes between China and the other powers. The Tsungli Yamen was apparently persuaded of the good will of the United States, but the fact remains that it was Chinese policy, as well as the pressure of the powers acting in concert, that predisposed the yamen to respect whatever complaints the American minister brought up about the grievances of American nationals.

And it is plain that the United States displayed but little power in China. As late as 1866, when gunboats built for the blockade of the Confederacy were available for service overseas, the American East Asiatic Squadron had only five vessels in Chinese ports, but, during this year, the British had no less than forty-five warships in Chinese waters, including twenty-nine gunboats.[42] The part played

40. Hosea Ballou Morse, *The International Relations of the Chinese Empire*, 3 vols., I (London: Longmans, Green, 1910); Henri Cordier, *L'Expédition de Chine, de 1857–58* (Paris: F. Alcan, 1905), and *L'Expédition de Chine, 1860* (Paris: F. Alcan, 1906); D. Bonner-Smith and E. W. R. Lumby, *The Second China War, 1856–1860* (London: Navy Records Society, 1954); Immanuel C. Y. Hsü, *China's Entrance into the Family of Nations: The Diplomatic Phase, 1858–1880* (Cambridge: Harvard University Press, 1960); Masataka Banno, *China and the West, 1858–1861: The Origins of the Tsungli Yamen* (Cambridge: Harvard University Press, 1964).

41. Mary C. Wright, *The Last Stand of Chinese Conservatism: The T'ung-chih Restoration, 1862–1874* (Stanford: Stanford University Press, 1957), chaps. 10–11.

42. E. Mowbray Tate, "U.S. Gunboats on the Yangtze: History and Political Aspects, 1842–1922," *Studies on Asia*, 7 (1966), 123; Grace Fox, *British Admirals and Chinese Pirates* (London: Kegan, Paul, 1940), app. B.

by the French as well as British naval ships in supporting missionary interests in China is vividly described, for the period 1862–1874, by Paul A. Cohen and Lü Shih-ch'iang.[43] The blatant diplomacy of Walter H. Medhurst and Count Julien de Rochechouart undoubtedly had lightened the duty of American officials regarding the protection of American missionaries. S. T. Wang's *The Margary Affair and the Chefoo Agreement*[44] describes Sir Thomas Wade's threat in 1876 to call for British troops from India to occupy a port in Manchuria and another on the Yangtze, in order to seek redress for the murder of a British interpreter at the China–Burma border. Sir Thomas succeeded in getting Li Hung-chang to sign the Chefoo Convention, which opened more treaty ports and enlarged the provisions of the British Treaty of Tientsin regarding inland taxation of foreign-trade goods. Although George F. Seward, the American minister from 1876 to 1880, played a leading part as a member of the diplomatic corps at Peking in discussing the detailed regulations implementing the several concessions the Chinese made at Chefoo,[45] it was the British that obtained the concessions in the first place.

Although American diplomacy in Peking thus needs to be viewed in the context of European-Chinese relations, does this mean, then, that the American record in this period is less important? I do not think so, for our concern in the study of American policy perhaps should not be confined to the diplomatic background. The United States had committed a minimum of military power to China and was not in a position to initiate the enlargement of treaty rights. Unlike Britain, she did not have an empire in Asia. But the control exercised by the United States over China, as far as it affected the activities of American traders and missionaries, was fully as extensive, at any given time, as that enjoyed by Britain in respect to her nationals. If we should shift our focus from the background to the actual operations of Dennett's most-favored-nation policy, we would get a very different picture—one which centers on the daily endeavor of American consuls and diplomats to bring a piece of the American legal order to China, efforts that were only partly successful but nevertheless real.

43. Paul A. Cohen, *China and Christianity: The Missionary Movement and the Growth of Chinese Antiforeignism, 1860–1870* (Cambridge: Harvard University Press, 1963); Lü Shih-ch'iang, *Chung-kuo kuan-shen fan-chiao ti yüan-yin, 1860–1874* (The causes of the anti-missionary movement among Chinese officials and gentry; Taipei: Academia Sinica, 1966).

44. London: Oxford University Press, 1940.

45. Paul H. Clyde, "Attitudes and Policies of George F. Seward, American Minister at Peking, 1876–1880: Some Phases of the Cooperative Policy," *Pacific Historical Review*, 2 (1933), 387–404.

The early history of American consular jurisdiction in China may be gleaned from Eldon Griffin's *Clippers and Consuls: American Consular and Commercial Relations with Eastern Asia, 1845–1860*,[46] which is a large reference work on the various activities reported in the consular letters to the Department of State during this fifteen-year period; and from Clarence G. Osborn's "American Extraterritorial Jurisdiction in China to 1906: A Study of American Policy,"[47] a dissertation done thirty-five years ago, which is still the best work on the subject. Unlike the British, who had the talent and the experience of the Indian Civil Service on which to draw, the United States was ill prepared to meet the various responsibilities attendant upon her treaty rights. For ten years after 1844, the United States was represented at the treaty ports only by "merchant consuls"— traders who for the sake of its prestige and incidental advantages, and sometimes out of a sense of duty, were willing to assume the consular post for very little in the way of emolument. In Shanghai and Canton, the American consuls up to 1854 were invariably chosen from that "one family of Whigs"—members of Russell and Company. They were replaced, beginning in that year, by men sent out from Washington who were unfortunately the products of the "spoils system" and did not necessarily possess greater legal knowledge or sense of the public good. Consulate scandals were frequent, but it would be unfair to ascribe the failures of American justice in China merely to individuals. It was only in 1848—four years after the Treaty of Wang-hsia—that the Congress authorized the establishment of consular courts in China; for the rowdy Yankee sailors in Shanghai or Canton, there was a "four year period of freedom from legal restraint." The act of 1848 authorized the consular courts to use the common law, as well as United States statutes. Though the jury system was found impractical, the consul as magis-

46. Ann Arbor: Edwards Brothers, 1938. A typewritten "extension volume" in four books, a total of more than eleven hundred pages, was deposited by the author at Baker Library, Harvard Business School, and the library of the University of California, Berkeley. The "extension volume" supplements *Clippers and Consuls* by giving "detailed analyses, illustrative cases from consular courts and administration, and other types of materials of use to research workers in several lines of investigation."

47. Ph.D. diss., Stanford University, 1935. Osborn has made use of the exchanges between the minister at Peking and the successive secretaries of state on the problem of consular jurisdiction, as well as the pertinent congressional records. But he has not attempted to study the extensive consular papers now at the National Archives, nor has he used the reports on the proceedings of the American consular court in the *North-China Herald* (Shanghai, weekly, 1850–   ). For a general view of the American extraterritorial jurisdiction in Turkey as well as East Asia, Frank E. Hinckley, *American Consular Jurisdiction in the Orient* (Washington: W. H. Lowdermilk, 1906) is still valuable.

trate was required to seek the assistance of two to four "associates" from among local American citizens, whose dissenting views could bring the case to the American commissioner in China, in his capacity as appellate judge. Congress failed, however, to make any provisions for marshals and jails, in the mistaken belief that fines and forfeitures available to the courts would suffice to finance an establishment. Consequently, the consuls at the Chinese ports had to depend on the chance of an American naval vessel being in the harbor and its captain being willing to find a place to lock up a culprit and, for longer terms, on the courtesy of Her Majesty's consul, who would accommodate Americans in the local British jail. Whenever such recourse was infeasible (since the British jails were crowded), the American consul would find it pointless to make any arrests at all! As late as 1858, the American Commissioner in China observed: "Every vagabond Englishman, Irishman, Scotchman, anyone who, speaking our language, can make out a *prima facie* case to [his having American] citizenship, commits crime according to his inclination, secure that if he is tried in American courts there is no power of punishment."[48] The lack of restraint on the Americans should also be traced to other defects in American policy and legislation. Although the Cushing treaty declared opium to be contraband, the treaty left the responsibility for controlling smuggling to the Chinese themselves; it was easy therefore for American firms dealing in opium, including Russell and Company, to argue that carrying the drug from India to China in clipper ships did not constitute smuggling, since the drug was always unloaded and stored in receiving ships outside Chinese harbors (whence the Chinese traffickers made their purchases). The consuls did try to prevent American vessels from carrying the slave-like coolies kidnapped into the barracoons of Macao or Amoy across the Pacific to Latin America. But the laws forbidding the overloading of passenger ships were found not applicable to vessels not returning to United States ports, and until 1862, the second year of the Lincoln administration, there was no American law that identified the coolie traffic with the slave trade.[49]

American justice in China did improve in the following decades. The few American ships still carrying "coolies" had to change their flags, and the American connection with the opium trade came almost completely to an end, owing to changes in the trade itself rather than the efforts of the American government. A congressional

48. Quoted in Osborn, "American Extraterritorial Jurisdiction," p. 43 and also in Dennett, *Americans in Eastern Asia,* p. 320.
49. Griffin, *Clippers and Consuls,* pp. 92–100, 194–206.

act of 1860, based partly on William B. Reed's recommendation, provided for four jails in the Chinese ports, as well as attending personnel. George F. Seward (who was William H. Seward's nephew), consul-general in Shanghai from 1862 to 1875, was able to raise further funds from the fines received by his court and to recruit additional staff by examination (held locally in 1864). In the seven years 1862–1869, the American consul in Shanghai tried 597 criminal and 467 civil cases—as many perhaps as the total number of cases heard at all other American consulates in China and Japan during the same seven years.[50] The act of 1860 added "equity and admiralty law" to the consul's legal armory; to guard against his failings, he was required to submit to the United States legation in China a list of local American citizens from among whom the "associates" were to be chosen by him as each case came up. Seward himself confessed that he was not expected by his government to follow "the numerous formalities of the courts at home." But from the reports of the American ministers in Peking on the consular judicial activities under their supervision, Osborn gains the impression that "the formalities of justice, rather than the essentials, were being invaded." Osborn adds, however, that since it was the accustomed duty of the consuls to protect American nationals, they could not be expected to be entirely impartial when non-Americans, especially Chinese, were involved in lawsuits—either as plaintiff or as the injured party in a case brought against an American by the consul himself in his capacity as United States attorney. Further research is needed on the subject, but as is shown in the famous *Huquong* collision case, Seward did at least try to be solicitous toward the Chinese. It had long been the practice of British and American courts in Shanghai not to admit Chinese claims when a junk was run down by a foreign-owned steamer in the harbor, or for that matter, when a Chinese pedestrian was hurt by a foreigner's horse-drawn carriage in the street. But in 1865, when a Russell and Company steamship sank a small junk and drowned three persons, Seward judged in favor of the plaintiffs, although he awarded them only half the indemnity they sought, since he also found "some negligence" on the part of the Chinese vessel's helmsman. S. W. Williams, the missionary author then serving as the American chargé at Peking, commented on this decision that "in this way are

50. Osborn, "American Extraterritorial Jurisdiction," pp. 72 and 440. In his report to Congress in 1872, special inspector DeB. Randolph Keim, who made a trip to East Asia to study consular performance, noted in detail the unsubstantiated rumors in Shanghai that Consul Seward had committed irregularities and had amassed a personal fortune. None of the rumors reported relate to his handling of lawsuits however. See ibid., pp. 446–447.

Western usages in jurisprudence gradually being known and accepted by the Chinese, especially the common people, who are rather disposed to appeal to us."[51]

Whether or not Seward's judicial hairsplitting could assuage Chinese resentment, there were in any case Chinese who appreciated the protection of Western legal order. Because it was a common practice in the treaty ports for Chinese merchants to have their merchandise clear the customs under a foreign name and even to have their firms and vessels registered by foreigners, many of the civil cases the American consuls handled actually involved Chinese defendants as well as plaintiffs. American consuls generally supported the claim of American firms that their native employees could not be freely arrested by Chinese officials. In what must be regarded as a forgotten chapter of American expansionism, Consul Seward secured an agreement from local Chinese officials in June 1863 that no Chinese could be arrested in the American settlement in Shanghai (the Hongkew section in the northern suburb by the river) without the warrant being countersigned by the American consul. The American settlement was soon merged into the British district to form the International Settlement; the arrangement made by Seward regarding Chinese arrests was thereby applied to the larger area.[52]

In 1864 a Mixed Court was created in the International Settlement, to exercise jurisdiction over Chinese inhabitants in all police and criminal cases, as well as civil cases where a Chinese was the defendant and there was a foreign plaintiff. The British consul, Harry Parkes, was principally responsible for this development, and for several years, the Chinese magistrate presided over the Mixed Court in one wing of the British consulate. But the Americans contributed one third of the Western side of the Mixed Court's work. The British "assessor," representing his consul, assisted the Chinese magistrate four days a week, and the American "assessor" performed this duty two days a week. Although in the 1870's the taotai of Shanghai sought to reassert his control over the Mixed Court, the American consul, backed by the minister at Peking and by Washington, formed a common front with the British in supporting the

51. Ibid., pp. 95–96. For contemporary Chinese criticism of consular justice, as well as appreciative remarks on the Western legal system (especially the emphasis on evidence, advocacy by lawyers, and the comparatively light punishment), see the early writings of a Chinese scholarly comprador living in Shanghai, studied in Kwang-Ching Liu, "Cheng Kuan-ying's I-yen (Easy Words): Reform Proposals of the Early Kuang-hsü Period, I, *Tsing Hua Journal of Chinese Studies,* new series 8 (1970), 373–425.

52. Kotenev, *Shanghai: Its Mixed Court and Council,* pp. 47–48.

assessor's role. In cases where an American was the plaintiff, typically for the recovery of debts from the Chinese, the American assessor inevitably introduced Western notions of commercial law. Even in police and criminal cases involving Chinese only, the presence of the assessors at court resulted in the latter's adopting certain Western principles—public trial, advocacy by lawyers, the non-use of torture in the hearings, and reliance on evidence and not confession for the judgment.[53]

Shanghai had the only permanent Mixed Court in China, but in other ports the American consular representative could appear in the regular Chinese tribunal when a case involving Americans was being heard. One of the many known examples is the Chi-mo missionary case of 1874, in which the American Presbyterian, Hunter Corbett, was assaulted by the Chinese for allegedly setting his helper to kidnap Chinese children to be indentured at a mission school. The case was settled by sending the assailants to jail, but not before Eli T. Sheppard, American consul at Tientsin, journeyed to Chefoo to hold with the Chinese officials "joint investigation and joint trial of the accused natives."[54]

The Americans thus exercised a degree of control over Chinese life through consular jurisdiction, but did the Americans in China realize that this jurisdiction was not an exact replica of the legal order at home? The views of American merchants and missionaries on this question have yet to be studied, but Osborn has discovered that the American ministers in Peking in the last forty years of the century, including Seward, who served in that post from 1876 to 1880, were dissatisfied with the quality of American justice in China, and each urged measures of reform. The existing system, according to Burlingame, failed to restrain "some [Americans] in their unlawful and dangerous conduct toward the natives," and, in the words

53. Ibid., pp. 49–99; Mark Elvin, "The Mixed Court of the International Settlement of Shanghai (until 1911)," *Papers on China*, 17 (East Asian Research Center, Harvard University, 1963), 131–159. The assessor system was written into the Sino-American Treaty of 1880 (which was chiefly on immigration matters) negotiated by James B. Angell, minister to Peking, 1880–81. It was provided that in cases involving Chinese as well as Americans, the plaintiff's national officer should have the right "to present, to examine, and to cross-examine witnesses." In 1880, John Hay, as assistant secretary of state, wrote to Angell expressing the hope that presence of the assessor at the Mixed Court would be used to check the Chinese practice of using judicial torture to secure confessions. Angell reported in reply that there had been some amelioration of the severity of Chinese jurisprudence at the Mixed Court, owing at least partly to the presence of foreign assessors in the trial of mixed cases. See Osborn, "American Extraterritorial Jurisdiction," pp. 266–267.

54. Osborn, "American Extraterritorial Jurisdiction," pp. 158–159. Chi-mo is also known as Chi-mi.

of Frederick F. Low (minister to China, 1869–1874), did not provide "the means of carrying out honestly and in good faith our part of the treaty engagements."[55] Various proposals were put forward—better-trained marshals and more court interpreters, greater opportunity for appeal, authority for the minister at Peking to issue regulations dealing with substantive (as opposed to merely procedural) matters with a force equivalent to the state laws in America.

As early as 1865, S. W. Williams recommended that the United States should inaugurate a career consular service for East Asia, and in 1870, Consul Seward was moved by the efficiency of the British Supreme Court for China and Japan (established in 1865 in Shanghai)[56] to suggest to the Secretary of State that Congress be asked to authorize a similar independent judiciary for Shanghai. This idea was later elaborated and proposed to the department by J. Russell Young (minister to China, 1882–1885) and Charles Denby (minister to China, 1885–1898). Such proposals were, however, not enthusiastically entertained by the department and only ineffectively brought before Congress. An act of 1870 did increase the appropriations for the jails in China and designated the ninth circuit in California as the appellate court for serious cases in China and Japan. But major reform of the consular jurisdiction was not debated in Congress until 1880–1883, the same period that exclusion of Chinese laborers from America was considered and acted on. Although two or three senators (Pendleton and Carpenter, joined later by Hoar) sponsored a bill for reform of American consular jurisdiction in East Asia, the scheme was opposed by others on grounds such as the constitutional problem of whether the approval of all the states of the union was not necessary for the creation of a regular court overseas and the financial objection (as Senator Platt put it) to undertaking a ponderous and expensive machinery for "the number of people for whom it is intended."[57] After lasting through three sessions, the bill died in the house in 1883, and the reforms contemplated were not to pass Congress until 1906, in another era of American–East Asian relations. The failure of this reform during the nineteenth century is ascribed by Osborn to the scant awareness on the part of the lawmakers of the responsibility that attended American consular jurisdiction in China; they "simply could not become interested enough in the question to take action." Yet Congress, no less than the State Department, took it for granted

55. Ibid., pp. 72 and 184.
56. See G. W. Keeton, *The Development of Extraterritoriality in China*, 2 vols. (London: Longmans, Green, 1928), vol. I, chap. 5.
57. Osborn, "American Extraterritorial Jurisdiction," pp. 451–470.

that consular jurisdiction was an American right, which the government's representatives in China must scrupulously defend.

The protection of American life and property in China through the most-favored-nation principle was the main objective, but Dennett saw a second and auxiliary objective in America's policy toward China in the nineteenth century. This was the desire to "sustain China"—to uphold her sovereign rights including territorial integrity (subject to the existing treaty commitments) and even to support her internal order and development. Dennett found expressions that were strikingly similar to the language of the Open Door policy in the dispatches of Humphrey Marshall and Anson Burlingame. This evidence led the author to conclude that the two decades before 1870 were crucial to the formation of America's "traditional policy in reference to China" and by inference of American Far Eastern policy in general. Dennett acknowledges that the administration in the mid-1890's had deserted Burlingame's "cooperative policy," but he nevertheless leaves the impression that the United States had been consistently pursuing a policy of upholding China's rights through the second half of the nineteenth century.

Was there ever such a policy? Before one can appraise what the United States did or did not do, one needs obviously to know the Chinese background, including the activities of the European powers there. While it is impossible to review here the entire literature of Chinese history for this period, I find it necessary to hazard a brief survey of the relevant works on Britain's political role in China, as the basis for discussing Dennett's thesis.

Although published more than twenty years ago, Nathan A. Pelcovits' *The Old China Hands and the Foreign Office*[58] is perhaps the first work to read on British policy in China in the second half of the nineteenth century. Pelcovits defends what should be a truism —namely, Britain never had the intention of making China another India. Britain attached great importance to the China trade, of course. Not only was the trade profitable to merchants and manufacturers; as late as 1880 opium produced for China still accounted for approximately one seventh of the revenue of British India.[59] However, the British government—the Board of Trade as well as the Foreign Office—never shared the extravagant optimism with which commercial and industrial groups regarded the China market. To this fact must be added the influence of anti-imperialist sentiment

58. New York: American Institute of Pacific Relations, 1948.
59. David E. Owen, *British Opium Policy in China and India* (New Haven: Yale University Press, 1934).

at home as well as the government's weariness over the financial and administrative burdens already assumed in India.[60] Although the mercantile bodies dominated or inspired by the "old China hands" never ceased demanding economic advantages that would entail British "surveillance" of China, the Foreign Office would work only for the gradual extension of the Western treaty rights in that country, while relying chiefly on the Chinese to make their market safe for the British. This was a classic case of "informal empire"— control exercised indirectly for the sake of trade and of missionary enterprises.

Now whether such a policy would work depended of course on developments within China as well as in her relations with the other powers. First of all, Britain had to have a "collaborator" in a viable Chinese government. Through the 1850's, as J. S. Gregory has emphasized in his *Great Britain and the Taipings*,[61] the British waited patiently for the outcome of the Chinese civil war. For more than seven years after the insurgents had established their capital at Nanking, Britain on the whole observed genuine neutrality toward the combatants, even though British officials continued to deal with the Ch'ing government at the treaty ports and even though the Royal Navy, for the sake of shipping on the South China coast, helped the merchant "convoy vessels" in the hunting of Chinese pirates (who were potentially allies of the rebels).[62] A tentative decision to defend Shanghai with British troops was forced by the Taiping advance to the treaty port in August 1860. However, even though the Manchus accepted the new treaties after the allied occupation of Peking later that year, it was not until early 1862 that the British, now convinced that the Taipings were to fail, began giving military aid to the Ch'ing, by directly defending the thirty-mile radius of Shanghai and by supporting a foreign-officered Chinese force (the so-called Ever-Victorious Army, at first under the American adventurer, Frederick Townsend Ward, and after March 1863 under the famous Charles George Gordon) in its operations against the insurgents. Even then the British still avoided excessive involvement. In 1863, when Horatio Nelson Lay, an Englishman who served as inspector-general of the Chinese maritime customs, wanted personal control over the naval vessels he had purchased for the Ch'ing government, Sir Frederick Bruce (minister to China, 1861–1865), although at first

60. See the illuminating discussion in the introductory chapter of Ronald Robinson, John Gallagher, and Alice Denny, *Africa and the Victorians: The Climax of Imperialism in the Dark Continent* (London: Macmillan, 1961).

61. New York: Praeger, 1969.

62. Fox, *British Admirals and Chinese Pirates*, esp. app. D.

backing Lay, allowed the Chinese to disband the fleet and to dismiss Lay from their service. At least two British commanders in Shanghai, Charles Staveley and W. G. Brown, recommended in 1862–63 that the British forces should fight the rebels inland, beyond the thirty-mile radius of that city. But this course of action was decisively repudiated by London.[63]

By 1862, when the Ch'ing government's ability to restore internal order became more apparent, the emerging British policy, as Mary Wright so vividly shows,[64] was to support this government's authority and its "just rights" in international relations. The Ch'ing central government was held responsible for the scrupulous observation of China's obligations under the treaties. But the British realized that to uphold the treaties it was necessary also to uphold China's rights, for it was after all, her sovereignty that gave validity to the treaties. The British minister, Bruce, opposed the proposal of certain foreign residents of Shanghai that the area within a thirty-mile radius of that port should be converted into a Western-governed "free city."[65] With Whitehall's approval, he argued that the existing municipal councils of the foreign settlements had derived their authority from the Ch'ing government, hence that government's jurisdiction over the *Chinese* living in the settlements, as well as its authority to tax them, should not be questioned. Although in 1864, Bruce approved the establishment of the Shanghai Mixed Court, which soon handled police and criminal cases involving the Chinese residents, it was his insistence on China's rights that resulted in the maintenance of dual authority in the foreign settlements, Chinese as well as Western. At the Mixed Court, the Chinese magistrate and the foreign assessor each exercised influence; while the municipal council collected a poll tax from the Chinese residents, the proceeds were handed over to the Ch'ing government. Meanwhile Bruce's instructions to the British consuls forbade resort to "gunboat policy" except in extremity; and British merchants were enjoined not to flout the Ch'ing regulations—for example by establishing warehouses outside of the treaty ports.

Realizing that the strength of China's polity could only benefit British trade, Bruce and his successor, Rutherford Alcock (minister

63. Richard J. Smith, "Frederick Townsend Ward and the Ever-Victorious Army: Military Innovation in Nineteenth-century China" (M.A. thesis, University of California, Davis, 1968); J. Gerson, "Horatio Nelson Lay: His Role in British Relations with China, 1849–65" (Ph.D. diss., London University, 1966).

64. *The Last Stand of Chinese Conservatism*, chap. 3.

65. Morse, *The International Relations of the Chinese Empire*, II (London: Longmans, Green, 1918), chap. 6.

to China, 1865–1869), sought by indirect means to stimulate Ch'ing reforms. They encouraged growth of the Imperial Maritime Customs under Robert Hart, which not only ensured orderly Western trade but also made possible the efficient collection of duties, as well as accurate reporting of the amounts collected. Hart, who frequently visited Peking even before 1865, when he began residing there regularly, helped arouse the Tsungli Yamen's interest in international law and practices and assisted in the development of the T'ung-wen Kuan, an interpreter's college founded by the yamen in 1862.[66] Bruce and Alcock, as well as Hart, firmly believed that the free flow of commerce, coupled with Western legal influence, could only benefit the Chinese. They felt that Western activities—even including the work of the missionaries, whose zealous desire to go into the Chinese interior they feared would bring unrewarding trouble— were in fact infusing life in China's ancient civilization. They were fascinated, however, by the "tremendous historical significance of a possible gradual modernization" initiated at the top of the Ch'ing government. The British would have liked to see the Ch'ing central government become more powerful. They were sympathetic with the dominant faction at court headed by Prince Kung and Wen-hsiang, who favored China's "self-strengthening" as well as conciliation with the powers and who were under attack by the xenophobic officials whom the Empress Dowager Tz'u-hsi often encouraged. In 1865–66, Hart and Thomas Wade, counsellor of the British legation, each prepared a memorandum for the Tsungli Yamen, warning of the danger in China's international situation and of her need for administrative reforms as well as cooperation with the Westerners. But Alcock, in his negotiations with the yamen, would generally refrain from insisting on such demands which, even if acceptable to Prince Kung and his colleagues, would jeopardize their position at court. Alcock's policy was confirmed by Clarendon's declaration of December 1868 in reply to a letter from Anson Burlingame, visiting London as Chinese envoy. Although treaty port opinion demanded sweeping concessions from the Chinese—including the abolition of the inland taxes and permission for foreigners to build railways and work mines in China—the British government's objective in the treaty revision of 1869 was more modest. As Mrs. Wright emphasizes, the Alcock Convention of that year was remarkable for the concessions made by both sides by mutual consent even though, owing to mercantile criticism, the agreement was never ratified by London.

66. Stanley F. Wright, *Hart and the Chinese Customs* (Belfast: Wm. Mullan, 1950), chaps. 10–13.

Despite the changes in the scene, it may be argued that the pattern of British policy in China, established in the 1860's, persisted in the quarter century that followed. Events in the early 1870's already warned of a heightened international rivalry in the China area: the Tientsin Massacre of 1870 and the French threat of reprisal; the Russian occupation of Ili (Kuldja) in 1871; the Japanese expedition to Taiwan in 1874; the Franco-Annamese Treaty of the same year, which aimed at making all Vietnam a French protectorate. The British continued, however, to work for a gradual extension of treaty rights in China, without hazarding a deeper political commitment. They even refrained from pushing to the limit certain advantages already won by other Western powers—notably the "rights" claimed by France in her conventions with China regarding missionary residence and property ownership in the interior.[67] In the aftermath of serious anti-Christian riots affecting British missionaries—such as the Yangchow case of 1868—the British diplomats did not hesitate to resort to gunboat diplomacy to compel redress for real or alleged grievances. But as Sir Thomas Wade (minister to China 1870–1882) reaffirmed in an 1870 circular to the British consuls, Her Majesty's government would not sanction the permanent residence of missionaries outside the treaty ports. British policy, as Edmund S. Wehrle has suggested, was to avoid vexatious disputes in areas beyond the treaty ports that might necessitate more frequent use of coercion as well as greater political responsibility.[68] Over the issue of A. R. Margary, the British interpreter murdered at the Yunnan border, Wade did threaten to make war, and by the Chefoo Convention concluded in September 1876, he won important rights for the merchants—the opening of new ports, the strengthening of the transit pass system in the interior, and further arrangements concerning justice and taxation at the treaty ports. But it is only fair to say that these concessions were still in the spirit of the earlier treaty settlement; China was still the sovereign nation granting the privileges, which were to be enjoyed

67. The relevant article appeared only in the Chinese text of the Franco-Chinese Convention of 1860 and was believed to have been added on through the duplicity of the French interpreter. However, the Ch'ing government thereafter allowed the missionaries to rent and purchase land in the interior, and in 1865 confirmed the concession with some qualifications in a convention made with the French minister Jules Berthemy. See Cohen, *China and Christianity*, chaps. 2, 5, 6, and 8.

68. Edmund S. Wehrle, *Britain, China, and the Antimissionary Riots, 1891–1900* (Minneapolis: University of Minnesota Press, 1966), chap. 1. Charles A. Litzinger, "Patterns of Missionary Cases Following the Tientsin Massacre, 1870–1875," *Papers on China*, 23 (1970), 87–108.

by the nationals of all treaty powers.[69] Earlier in 1876, Wade, on behalf of a British firm, had pressured the Ch'ing government to permit the operation of a short railway from Wusung to Shanghai, which had been constructed without proper authorization. Departing from Alcock's principle that introduction of the railway and the telegraph should be left to the Chinese themselves, Wade inclined at first to compel the acceptance of the British-owned railway. He retreated from this position, however, and encouraged the Chinese to purchase the road. The provincial authorities bought it in October 1876 and had it dismantled the next year.[70]

If the British government still sought no more than indirect control over China, did it support her when she faced aggression from the other powers? Existing monographs (which have by no means covered the subject exhaustively) suggest two basic elements in Britain's deliberations: for the sake of British trade as well as the delicate international balance in the China area, war on the China coast should be avoided; and although Britain possessed considerable influence in East Asia, this influence varied with the shifting international scene and was often limited. Having acquired Hong Kong during the Opium War and a strip of Kowloon in 1860, Britain could hardly claim Chinese territorial integrity as her doctrine. Moreover, Britain had little concern for the survival of China's tribute system, having completed, in 1862, her absorption of Lower Burma (which traditionally acknowledged Ch'ing suzerainty). Nevertheless, as the several powers encroached upon China's periphery in the 1870's and 1880's, the British used whatever influence they had to prevent war on the China coast. In 1874, when the Japanese landed troops on Taiwan to seek redress for the murder of some Ryukyu sailors, Wade, as Grace Fox has shown, at one point proposed an international guarantee against violation of China's "coasts and rivers."[71] The British minister played a crucial part in persuading the Ch'ing court to accept the Japanese terms for peace, even though the settlement implied Japanese overlordship over Ryukyu, which in China's view owed allegiance to China. In 1874, with the Russians entrenched in Ili, the British, mindful of the security of Afghanistan,

69. Wang, *The Margary Affair.* The principal provisions of the convention were put into effect shortly after its conclusion by the Ch'ing government, although Wade was criticized by the British China-trade interests for failing to obtain more advantageous terms and the convention was not ratified in London until 1885.

70. Blair C. Currie, "The Woosung Railroad (1872–1877)," *Papers on China,* 20 (1966), 49–85.

71. Grace Fox, *Britain and Japan, 1858–1883* (Oxford: Clarendon, 1969), pp. 280–310.

signed a treaty with Yakub Beg, the Kokhandian rebel against the Ch'ing who established a Moslem kingdom to the southwest of Ili. The British mediated between Yakub and the Ch'ing, suggesting that the former be accepted as a vassal under the tribute system. After the Chinese armies advanced toward Ili and the Treaty of Livadia of 1879 (which foolishly conceded to the Russians the control of Ili) was repudiated by the Ch'ing court, the British bent every effort to avoid a Sino-Russian rupture, worried particularly over an imminent Russian invasion of north China. As Immanuel Hsü has emphasized, Wade, transmitting a letter from Queen Victoria to the Empress Dowager, was instrumental in preventing the punishment by death of Ch'ung-hou, the hapless envoy who signed the Treaty of Livadia; and Lord Granville and his ambassador at St. Petersburg were to give valuable advice to the more capable Chinese diplomat, Tseng Chi-tse, who managed to recover Ili through the treaty of St. Petersburg in 1881.[72] In regard to the French designs on Tongking (North Vietnam), the British had been comparatively indifferent, even after the undeclared war between the Chinese and French began there in 1882. Britain had no particular desire to see a Chinese victory in Vietnam, and the English press in China suggested that French victory over the Chinese would make it easier to expand Western commercial privileges in China. As E. V. G. Kiernan has shown, the British became concerned when the French threatened to occupy the island of Chusan at the estuary of the Yangtze and especially after the French navy bombarded Keelung, on Taiwan, in August 1884, this being followed by an assault on the Chinese fleet and navy yard at Foochow. Admiral Amédé Courbet proposed to his government that he should move on to attack the northern coast of China, but this idea was rejected by Jules Ferry; perhaps the French were honoring the pledge they had made to the British that they would not invade the China coast without first declaring war (a step they were unwilling to take, since such a declaration would prevent them from obtaining supplies at the British ports in Asia).[73] Owing to the tension in Egypt and Sudan, Britain had only minimal influence on France at this juncture. In tendering good offices between the two combatants, Lord Granville was willing to

72. Immanuel C. Y. Hsü, *The Ili Crisis: A Study of Sino-Russian Diplomacy, 1871–1881* (Oxford: Clarendon, 1965), Li En-han, *Tseng Chi-tse ti wai-chiao* (The diplomacy of Tseng Chi-tse; Taipei: Academia Sinica, 1966).

73. E. V. G. Kiernan, *British Diplomacy in China, 1880 to 1885* (Cambridge: University Press, 1939), chaps. 6, 8, 9, and 10. Lloyd E. Eastman, *Throne and Mandarin: China's Search for a Policy During the Sino-French Controversy, 1880–1885* (Cambridge, Mass.: Harvard University Press, 1967), esp. pp. 162–173.

transmit France's peace terms, which included her retention "for some years" of the coal mines at Keelung. But the British were relieved that the Sino-French settlement of 1885 did not include the occupation of Keelung, nor any special privilege for the French in the Chinese provinces adjacent to Tongking—even though China was to acknowledge the French protectorate over Vietnam. That the British themselves had scant regard for China's tributary claims is further demonstrated by Britain's annexation of Upper Burma in 1886.

Since the British desired peace and security on the China coast, they were inclined, so long as they could retain China's friendship, to help her in acquiring a diplomatic and military capacity. Beginning in the mid-1860's, Hart and others had been urging the Ch'ing government to establish permanent legations abroad. Wade considered the establishment of Chinese legations in London and other Western capitals the happiest outcome of the Margary affair.[74] The experience Tseng Chi-tse gained in London and Paris contributed to his diplomatic success at St. Petersburg in 1881, although four years later it was not Tseng but Robert Hart's London agent, J. D. Campbell, who arranged the Franco-Chinese peace. Beginning in 1875, Hart, who had won the Tsungli Yamen's confidence by his administration of the maritime customs, arranged with the London government to allow China to purchase British naval vessels. Doing for China what they were doing for Japan, the British not only sold ships but also helped train the new Chinese navy. Wade arranged in 1877 for Chinese cadets to enter naval colleges in England. In 1880 he even suggested to the Tsungli Yamen that Chinese troops be sent to India to be trained with the Indian army—an offer which the Chinese could not accept.[75] Hart himself aspired to become the "naval inspector-general" and the appointment seems to have been considered by the Tsungli Yamen in 1879 and in 1883. But the new Chinese navy remained under the control of Li Hung-chang, the governor-general of Chihli and the commissioner of trade for northern China ports. Although he purchased some dozen British-built warships through Hart, by the 1880's Li was ordering large battleships from the German yards, and he employed a Frenchman to supervise the construction work at the naval base at Port Arthur. Li had, however, accepted in 1880 Hart's candidate, Captain W. M. Lang of the Royal Navy, as the chief instructor of his fleet. British law necessitated Lang's recall during the Sino-French War, but in

74. Hsü, *China's Entrance Into the Family of Nations*, chaps. 10–11. Wang, *The Margary Affair*, p. 126.

75. Kiernan, *British Diplomacy in China*, p. 216.

1886, Lang returned as a Chinese admiral—only to be harassed by his Chinese colleagues and resign in disgust four years later.[76]

In 1880, the Foreign Office rejected a proposal from Wade that Britain should enter into alliance with China to counter Russian expansion. Nevertheless during the next fourteen years, there was a "virtual entente" between Britain and China in reference to Korea.[77] While the Chinese worried about the designs of both Japan and Russia in that peninsula, the British were particularly concerned about Russia's ambitions. Britain not only acceded to the Ch'ing policy of encouraging Korea to establish treaty relations with Western powers but also respected China's claim of suzerainty over the kingdom; after Britain concluded her treaty with Korea in 1883, her minister at Peking served concurrently as the minister to Seoul. In the Sino-Japanese tension that followed the two violent outbreaks in the Korean capital in 1882 and 1884, the British, while urging the avoidance of war with Japan, on the whole backed the Ch'ing. In April 1885, during the Anglo-Russian crisis over Afghanistan, the British, fearful that the Russians might gain naval advantage by occupying a Korean port, themselves occupied the Korean island of Port Hamilton. As Ian H. Nish has suggested, the subsequent British withdrawal from Port Hamilton in 1887 was prompted by balanced calculation of interests: Britain did not want to press Russia too hard in the China area since the latter posed a vital threat to India.[78] After 1887, Britain as well as Russia supported Li Hung-chang's policy in Korea. It was believed that the ascendancy of China, rather than that of Japan, could best serve the stability of the area. China's disastrous defeat by Japan in 1894–1895 was, of course, to alter the entire situation. Britain wanted to stop the war; beginning in October 1894, either directly or together with other European powers, she made at least seven attempts at mediation. But Japan proved adamant, and the British had to be satisfied with the Japanese guarantee that the China coast south of Manchuria would not be disturbed.

After China and Japan signed the Treaty of Shimonoseki, which involved new economic advantages to be enjoyed by all foreign

---

76. John L. Rawlinson, *China's Struggle for Naval Development, 1839–1895* (Cambridge, Mass.: Harvard University Press, 1967), chaps. 4–8; Wright, *Hart and the Chinese Customs,* chap. 16.

77. The phrase is William L. Langer's. See his *The Diplomacy of Imperialism, 1890–1902,* 2nd ed. (New York: Knopf, 1951), pp. 168–75; Kiernan, *British Diplomacy in China,* chaps. 5, 7, 11, and 13.

78. Ian H. Nish, *The Anglo-Japanese Alliance: The Diplomacy of Two Island Empires, 1894–1907* (London: The Athlone Press, 1966), p. 17; Kiernan, *British Diplomacy in China,* chap. 13.

nations in China, as well as the cession of Taiwan and the Liaotung peninsula, the British did not protest. However, they did not advise the Japanese to resist the demand made by Russia, France, and Germany that Liaotung should be returned to China.[79] As Nish has remarked in reference to British policy during the Sino-Japanese War, Britain was "not so much pro-Chinese or anti-Japanese as pro-British." But as the center of European rivalry now moved to China itself, Britain still aimed at preserving the stability of that country, as well as the extension of her treaty rights according to the pattern established in the mid-nineteenth century, in cooperation with an independent Chinese government.

Against the record of the British policy in China, what Dennett describes as the American policy of "sustaining China" may be seen in perspective. Although possessing little military power in the China area during the nineteenth century, the United States was nevertheless diplomatically active and was regarded by the Chinese as the third or fourth most important foreign power. Not all the pronouncements of American diplomats in China were mere rhetoric. In the 1860's, especially, the principles advocated by the American minister in Peking, Anson Burlingame, were specifically approved by the secretary of state; in the American-Chinese treaty of 1868, made by William H. Seward with Burlingame as the Ch'ing envoy, these principles were made into law. However, the question needs to be asked whether this policy produced any effect at the time? Moreover, there is also the question whether the policy lasted through the quarter century after the Andrew Johnson administration? How did American policy in China compare with that of Britain up to the Sino-Japanese War of 1894–95? Even though a few studies on the period have been made since Dennett, these questions obviously need to be further pursued.

It is perhaps not surprising that American representatives in China should make statements in favor of China's sovereignty and independence. Several of the commissioners and ministers who went to China were lawyer-politicians trained in Congress. Their legalistic approach was combined with an instinctive distrust of European powers, particularly Britain. Having less responsibility in China, they could express abstract principles more freely. Humphrey Marshall, a Southern Whig from Louisville, Kentucky, who had once

79. Nish, *Anglo-Japanese Alliance*, pp. 25–35; R. Stanley McCordock, *British Far Eastern Policy, 1894–1900* (New York: Columbia University, 1931), chap. 2.

been considered for a seat on the Supreme Court,[80] interrupted his second term in the House of Representatives to become commissioner in China in 1853. Marshall arrived at Shanghai just after the Taipings had established their capital in Nanking. He lamented that the turmoil in China was damaging American trade and interpreted the British efforts to establish contacts with the rebels as a design for a British "protectorate" in the Yangtze valley; he feared that Britain, as well as Russia, aimed at the "dismemberment of the Chinese Empire." In July 1853, he recommended to the secretary of state unilateral American intervention in China, to help the Ch'ing dynasty suppress the Taipings on the condition that amnesty be granted to the rebels and that greater privileges be granted to Western trade; only when the Ch'ing refused these conditions would the United States deal with the Taipings. Marshall stated what Dennett and Foster Rhea Dulles[81] regard as a precise forecast of John Hay's policy: "It is my opinion that the highest interests of the United States are involved in sustaining China—maintaining order here, and gradually engrafting on this worn-out stock the healthy principles which give life and health to governments, rather than to see China become the theatre of widespread anarchy, and ultimately the prey of European ambition." It is plain, however, that Marshall's plan for American intervention in China was completely unrealistic. He had little knowledge of the actual situation; in 1853 no one could possibly tell whether the Ch'ing dynasty would survive, even with foreign assistance. As is evident in J. S. Gregory's study[82] Marshall had completely misjudged Britain's intentions regarding the Taipings.

Marshall's sentiments were concretely expressed in September 1853, when the Chinese city of Shanghai was occupied by the Triad rebels and the Ch'ing customhouse in that port ceased to exist. The British consul Rutherford Alcock, anxious that trade continue on a legal basis, devised a "provisional system" under which British vessels could be cleared after the traders had handed to the consul promissory notes on the duties owing the Chinese government—the validity of the notes to be determined later by London. Marshall at first adopted this plan for the Americans, omitting only the proviso that the legality of the notes was to be determined later. But in

80. E. Merton Coulter, "Humphrey Marshall," in Dumas Malone, ed., *Dictionary of American Biography*, VI (New York: Charles Scribner's, 1933), pt. 2, pp. 310–311.

81. See his *China and America*, p. 51.

82. See above, note 61.

October, when the Shanghai taotai Wu Chien-chang reappeared in the foreign settlement, Marshall, in an action praised by Dennett and others as showing his concern for China's "territorial integrity,"[83] required that American traders should immediately resume paying duties in specie to the taotai. Actually, the Shanghai foreign settlement was at that moment arming itself to defend its neutrality against both the Ch'ing and the Triad forces; Marshall was oblivious of Britain's general policy in China's domestic conflict. Alcock used a British gunboat to prevent Taotai Wu from establishing a "floating customhouse" on the river by the foreign settlement, partly because the taotai, who had been buying vessels and arms from American firms, was preparing to mount an attack on the Triads from that section of the river. By early January 1854, Marshall, seeing that an increasing number of vessels under continental European flags—and some under American colors—were leaving port without even filing promissory notes, announced that in accordance with the most-favored-nation clause, American traders should now treat Shanghai as a free port. Although he claimed to have legality on his side, each step Marshall took merely disrupted Alcock's plans and weakened the legal claim of the Chinese government—whether Ch'ing or Taiping—on the promissory notes collected.[84]

Marshall's grandiose scheme for American intervention against the Taipings, needless to say, was not heeded by his home government. Recalled by Washington in late 1853, Marshall was replaced early the following year by Robert M. McLane, who was instructed by the secretary of state, William L. Marcy, to use his discretion regarding a possible de facto recognition of the Taipings. McLane visited Nanking in May 1854 on the U.S.S. *Susquehanna* and reported that the rebels were too incompetent and "peculiar" to be accorded de facto recognition.[85] Although the United States had, a few months before, opened Japan to commerce, American expansionism in East Asia was plainly still very limited. The government eschewed both interference in China and encroachment upon her territory. Commodore Matthew C. Perry, a naval strategist who envisioned American competition with the British for "the control of the Pacific," was not satisfied with the treaty with Japan and recommended American possession of the Bonin islands, the Ryukyus, and Taiwan. Some of the Bonin group were briefly occupied, and a treaty with the Ryukyu king, opening Naha to trade, was approved

83. See especially Tong, *United States Diplomacy in China,* chap. 9.
84. See Fairbank, *Trade and Diplomacy on the China Coast,* chap. 22.
85. Tong, *United States Diplomacy in China,* pp. 145–150.

in Washington, but the proposal regarding Taiwan was rejected. Peter Parker, the former missionary who served as American commissioner in China 1855–1857, recommended to Secretary Marcy in December 1856 that pending treaty revision with the Ch'ing government, the United States should occupy Taiwan, while Britain could hoist her flag on the island of Chusan and France in Korea. Parker was advised by his friend Gideon Nye, Jr., a former Canton merchant now engaged in the camphor trade on Taiwan.[86] In early 1857, the commissioner wrote twice to Marcy that regardless of what the British and the French did, the United States should annex Taiwan for the sake of "humanity, civilization, navigation, and commerce." As Huang Chia-mu has emphasized in his history of American relations with Taiwan,[87] Perry and Parker were both American officials; the government of the United States was not free of the imperialist virus. Nevertheless Parker's proposal, like Perry's, was decisively rejected. Replying to the commissioner's dispatch of December 1856, Marcy wrote that the president would consider increasing naval forces in Chinese waters only for the protection of the Americans there and not for "aggressive purposes." Parker's other dispatches on Taiwan did not even receive a reply, and the missionary-diplomat was soon removed from office. Marcy's policy was carried on by Buchanan's secretary of state, Lewis Cass, who instructed William B. Reed, the new envoy to China, to seek treaty revision by peaceful means. Cass believed in the benefits the West could bring to China: "With increased intercourse will come those ameliorations in the moral and physical condition of the people which the Christian and the philanthropist have so long desired." But he reminded Reed that the United States sought no more from China than the "protection of the life and property of its citizens . . . The extension of our commercial intercourse must be the work of individual enterprise, and to this element of our national character we may safely leave it."

If Cass's statement represented actual American policy, a step forward was taken during William H. Seward's secretaryship. The desire to "sustain China" was now translated into some effective diplomacy and was, moreover, solemnly written into a treaty. The man chiefly responsible for this development was Anson Burlingame, a lawyer-politician fond of rhetoric but nevertheless genuinely idealistic. In his three terms as Congressman from Massa-

86. See Harold D. Langley, "Gideon Nye and the Formosa Annexation Scheme," *Pacific Historical Review*, 34 (1965), 397–420.

87. Huang Chia-mu, *Mei-kuo yü T'ai-wan, 1784–1895* (The United States and Taiwan; Taipei: Academia Sinica, 1966).

chusetts, he had consistently advocated the anti-slavery cause, and as a member of the Foreign Relations Committee he had spoken in support of Kossuth and of Sardinian independence.[88] Arriving at the treaty port in 1861, he was struck by the territorial authority the British and French were assuming, and almost as soon as he settled in Peking in the following year, he found himself in sympathy with Prince Kung and Wen-hsiang, the Ch'ing statesmen who strove to restore order in China as well as to cope with the Western powers. Burlingame had little to do with the American role in the Ever-Victorious Army. Frederick Townsend Ward had been active before Burlingame's arrival in China and his force received assistance during the subsequent years from the British, not the Americans. But Burlingame emerged as the most vocal spokesman for China's international rights in Peking's new diplomatic corps. As early as August 1862, when the French were known to have desired an "exclusive concession" in Ningpo, Burlingame protested both to his European colleagues and to the Ch'ing government.[89] Expanding upon Seward's rather casual instruction that he should consult and co-operate with the representatives of the other powers, Burlingame sought to make "consultation and cooperation" a general Western policy. He reported to Seward in June 1863 that he had secured agreement among his European colleagues on what he described as the nonconcession doctrine: "While we claim our treaty rights to buy and sell, and hire, in the treaty ports, subject, in respect to our rights of property and person, to the jurisdiction of our governments, we will not ask for, nor take concession of, territory in the treaty ports, or in any way interfere with the jurisdiction of the Chinese government over its own people, nor ever menace the territorial integrity of the Chinese Empire." Dennett regards Burlingame as the principal formulator of America's traditional policy in China and praises his "unselfish idealism and breadth of statesmanship." A recent dissertation by Samuel Soonki Kim,[90] while designed as a case study of diplomatic techniques, also lauds Burlingame's achievements. Kim particularly stresses the American minister's ability to win the confidence of the Tsungli Yamen, which led to his remarkable appointment in late 1867 as China's first envoy to the Western powers.

88. For biographical data on Burlingame, Telly H. Koo, "The Life of Anson Burlingame" (Ph.D. diss., Harvard University, 1922) is still useful.
89. Morse, *The International Relations of the Chinese Empire*, II, 118–119.
90. "Anson Burlingame: A Study in Personal Diplomacy," (Ph.D. diss., Columbia University, 1966).

Burlingame's idealism seems obvious, but his actual contribution to the so-called "cooperative policy" needs to be further appraised. Even Dennett acknowledges that Burlingame owed his success to the international environment: "In 1863, the foreign powers had secured from China all that they desired and the ground was therefore prepared for Burlingame." The American minister's objective of upholding China's sovereignty was, in fact, British policy to begin with. As early as March 1862, Frederick Bruce had written that he did not consider it "a matter of regret or hostile to our interests that China should be encouraged by a consciousness of her strength, to use bolder language in defending her just rights. The weakness of China, rather than her strength, is likely to create a fresh Eastern Question in these seas."[91] It is true that Bruce's principal dispatches to his treaty-port consuls regarding the status of the foreign settlements were dated subsequent to August 1862, after Burlingame had arrived at Peking and had "thorough and exhaustive" discussions with him. But there is no evidence that he would not have issued these instructions on his own. On the other hand, Kim is persuasive in suggesting that given the conflict of interests between Britain and France especially, Bruce could not always act unilaterally and therefore welcomed Burlingame's self-appointed role as mediator. Kim believes the American minister's "infectious enthusiasm" and tact perfectly suited him for such a role.[92] Even so, it should be stressed that the degree of cooperation achieved among the ministers in Peking was limited.

Jules Berthemy, the French minister who arrived in April 1863, was disposed to follow a temperate policy. He withdrew the French plan for a separate concession in Ningpo, and concerning the Kweichow missionary case involving the death of a Catholic priest, he even consulted the other Western diplomats before presenting his final demands to the Tsungli Yamen. And Bruce on his part was glad to accept Burlingame's suggestions. In the spring of 1864, when Burlingame complained to the British minister about the growth of British police power in the treaty ports, Bruce immediately expressed his agreement and took steps to discourage the trend. On another occasion, Bruce enclosed copies of Burlingame's instructions to George F. Seward, then American consul in Shanghai, in his own instructions to the British consuls, reaffirming the policy of respecting "the jurisdiction of the Chinese government over its own

91. Cited in Kim, "Anson Burlingame," p. 168; also in Gregory, *Great Britain and the Taipings,* p. 112.

92. Kim, "Anson Burlingame," pp. 106–127 and passim.

people."[93] All the powers of course cooperated in Robert Hart's Chinese customs service, in which inspectors of different national- ities administered the treaty tariff impartially. But the principle of dual Chinese-Western authority at the foreign settlements was honored only in the breach. As far as it concerned the French con- cession of Shanghai, this principle had always been disregarded, the French consul there preferring to rule the concession as French territory. Henri de Bellonet, who succeeded Berthemy in 1865, is famous for his high-handed diplomacy regarding the missionary cases; he seldom consulted with the other diplomats on such matters. Although Bellonet was once willing to consider amalgamating the French Concession in Shanghai with the Anglo-American settle- ment, the idea was decisively repudiated by Paris. Burlingame ad- mitted the failure of his efforts when he wrote Secretary Seward in late 1866: "The French prefer a separate municipality, which con- sidering their ideas of administration, may be best for all."[94]

While the effects of the cooperative policy were limited, the case is stronger regarding Burlingame's success as an adviser to the Ch'ing government. As Kim emphasizes, almost from the beginning of his ministry, Burlingame and his Chinese-speaking secretary of the legation, Samuel Wells Williams, repeatedly brought the "non- concession doctrine" to the attention of the Tsungli Yamen, advising it, for example, to resist the French plans for a separate concession in Ningpo.[95] Burlingame was as jealous of foreign rights in China as his European colleagues. In early 1863, Henry Burgevine, an American who succeeded Ward as commander of the Ever-Victorious Army, was dismissed by the Chinese for assaulting the merchant- official, Yang Fang. Burlingame insisted that according to the extra- territorial provisions of the treaty, the case should be examined by the American consul, even though Burgevine had once declared himself a Chinese subject. In June of that year, the American min- ister forced the Tsungli Yamen to accept this interpretation by a sharply worded "ultimatum."[96] But on numerous other occasions, Burlingame convinced the yamen ministers that he was sympathetic with China's rights. In September 1863 he introduced to the yamen

93. Ibid., pp. 123–124, 176–184; Morse, *The International Relations of the Chinese Empire*, II, 129.

94. Kim, "Anson Burlingame," 183–184; Cohen, *China and Christianity*, pp. 203–208.

95. Kim, "Anson Burlingame," pp. 178–179.

96. For the interesting later turn of the Burgevine story and S. W. Williams's decision (while serving as chargé during Burlingame's absence) to turn Burgevine over to the Chinese, see Martin R. Ring, "The Burgevine Case and Extrality in China, 1863–1866," *Papers on China*, 22A (1969), 134–157.

W. A. P. Martin, the American missionary who was then completing a Chinese translation of Wheaton's *Elements of International Law,* which the Yamen subsequently published. In the Lay–Osborn flotilla affair, Burlingame mediated between Bruce and the yamen, the British minister first backing Lay, while Wen-hsiang vowed that his government would rather retreat "beyond the Great Wall" than give in to Lay's demands. At the suggestion of Burlingame (who was also concerned that it might fall into the hands of the Confederacy), the fleet was sent back to England to be sold there.[97]

Burlingame cast himself in the role of an educator of the Chinese: "How hoary is their civilization and how proud they are, and how ignorant of us they have always been, and how little their knowledge of us has tended to create in their minds a desire for change." In October 1863 he persuaded the Tsungli Yamen to employ Raphael Pumpelly, a visiting American geologist, to make a survey of the mines near Peking on behalf of the Chinese. Earlier, in 1862, Burlingame had proposed to Washington that the surplus from the indemnities paid by China for the losses of the Americans during the Anglo-French war should be used to found a college in Peking, where Americans could learn Chinese and the Chinese the "languages, sciences and ethics of Western lands." Burlingame brought up his idea again with Seward in November 1863 and several times in subsequent years; but Seward apparently did not care enough to bring the matter before Congress, which controlled the indemnity funds.[98] Burlingame's most tangible contribution to China remained his diplomatic counsels. In 1863–64, he was intermediary between the yamen and the envoys of Prussia, Denmark, and Sweden, each desiring a treaty with Peking. His good offices between the Prussian envoy and the Chinese in the latter year helped to obtain the release of two Danish ships seized by the Prussian navy in Chinese waters —an event that convinced the Chinese of the value of international law.[99] In March 1865, a few months before Robert Hart established permanent residence in Peking and became a regular adviser to the yamen, Burlingame brought to the latter's attention two general stratagems. He suggested that in rancorous disputes with foreign envoys, copies of the entire correspondence on the issue involved be sent to all the resident ministers in Peking, with the request that they be published by the press in their home countries; he also suggested that China go over the heads of the ministers by sending envoys to Western capitals. The Tsungli Yamen followed Burlin-

97. Kim, "Anson Burlingame," pp. 220–234.
98. Ibid., pp. 213–214.
99. Ibid., pp. 150–157.

game's first advice when in 1866 it published its correspondence with Bellonet concerning Chinese responsibility in the murder of Catholic priests in Korea.[100] And, in late 1867, when the yamen was worried about the forthcoming treaty revision with Britain and other powers—and intimidated particularly by the aggressive demands of the treaty port press for Western railway, telegraph, and mining enterprises—it invited Burlingame, who had indicated his intention to resign as American minister, to be the Chinese envoy to the treaty powers in order to bring China's views before their home governments.

Although Burlingame's diplomacy in Peking was largely on his personal initiative, his embassy for the Chinese, which has been studied by Frederick Wells Williams and Knight Biggerstaff,[101] was to lead to a formal declaration of Washington's policy. Burlingame considered his trip an opportunity to urge his "nonconcession doctrine" on the several powers interested in China. He also genuinely believed in his assignment from the Ch'ing government. While in Peking, he had become increasingly convinced that Prince Kung and his colleagues sincerely desired change. In the spring of 1867 he had forwarded to Seward the Tsungli Yamen's memorials regarding the expansion of the T'ung-wen Kuan's curriculum to include Western sciences: "I marvel as I read [these papers], and call your attention to them with infinite pleasure."[102] Burlingame believed that given time, China would introduce the railway and other innovations on her own; to have Western enterprise force them on her would, however, produce a reaction that would abet the opponents of Prince Kung and Wen-hsiang. In the enthusiastic speeches he delivered on both coasts of the United States, he extolled China's ancient civilization as well as the progress it was capable of making. He asked that the West respect China's rights and leave her alone: "I desire that the autonomy of China may be preserved. I desire that her independence may be secured. I desire that she may have equality, that she may dispense equal privileges to all nations."[103]

This sentiment was written into a new American-Chinese treaty

100. Ibid., pp. 235–238.

101. Frederick W. Williams, *Anson Burlingame and the First Chinese Mission to Foreign Powers* (New York: Charles Scribner's, 1912); Knight Biggerstaff, "The Official Chinese Attitude Toward the Burlingame Mission," *American Historical Review*, 41 (1936), 682–702, and "The Changes in the Attitude of the Chinese Government Toward the Sending of Diplomatic Representatives, 1860–1880" (Ph.D. diss., Harvard University, 1934).

102. Cited in Williams, *Anson Burlingame*, p. 65.

103. Burlingame's speeches, made as Chinese envoy in the United States, and the response from his audience and from the press are cited extensively in Williams and in Koo's dissertation (see note 88 above).

which Burlingame, without explicit authorization from the Tsungli Yamen, concluded with Secretary Seward in July 1868. Since treaty revision between China and the other powers was pending and since Burlingame was soon to visit Europe, he hoped that a commitment on the part of the United States would influence the policy of other powers. The treaty, drafted by Seward in consultation with Burlingame, declared that the emperor of China, in spite of the obligations regarding the treaty ports and extraterritoriality which he had accepted, had "by no means relinquished his right of eminent domain or dominion over the said land and waters." The United States, on her part, disavowed "any intention or right to intervene in the domestic administration of China in regard to the construction of railroads, telegraphs, or other material internal improvements." Seward was perhaps chiefly interested in Article V of the treaty, which committed China as well as the United States to the free flow of Chinese emigrants to this country. Seward believed in cheap labor as well as cheap public land; he had been concerned over the delays in the construction of the Pacific railroads owing to labor shortages.[104] But he also shared Burlingame's views on American policy in China. In 1866 he had defended China's rights against American merchants in Shanghai who wished to extend steam navigation to nontreaty ports. He went on record against the gunboat policy when, during the same year, he censored the American consul at Chefoo for arranging a naval demonstration when a Western-owned cemetery was desecrated, although it was probably with his knowledge that the Navy Department, in 1867, authorized two American warships to land men on Taiwan on a brief "punitive expedition" against the aborigines who murdered the captain and crew of an American bark.[105] Seward must have found clauses of the treaty regarding China's eminent domain at least compatible with the existing American commercial and personal rights in that country.

The immediate effect of the treaty was to give Burlingame moral support in his mission to Europe (although the treaty itself was not ratified by China until November 1869). He arrived in England about the time the first Gladstone ministry took office. Lord Clarendon, perhaps as much out of his own conviction as in response to Burlingame, declared that Britain had no intention of applying "unfriendly pressure" regarding China's foreign relations. In France,

104. Dennett himself wrote of the 1868 treaty: "It was really an immigration treaty to which was attached some declarations of foreign policy." *Americans in Eastern Asia*, p. 410 note.

105. Ibid., p. 411; Wright, *The Last Stand of Chinese Conservatism*, p. 36.

however, Burlingame waited eight months without securing a statement from the Quai d'Orsai. Meanwhile, the Burlingame–Seward policy produced a great furor in the treaty port press in China, and Rutherford Alcock, who was working with the Tsungli Yamen on treaty revision, thought at one time that the Chinese were so encouraged by the Burlingame mission that his negotiations would be futile. As it turned out, the sober-minded ministers of the Tsungli Yamen realized that the new treaty with the United States and even the Clarendon declaration did not give them such advantage that they could avoid dealing with Alcock. From her research on the background of the Alcock Convention of 1869, Mary Wright came to the conclusion that Burlingame's efforts did not create a a great stir at the Ch'ing court: "In retrospect, his mission appears to have been important chiefly for firmly establishing the precedent in China of sending envoys abroad. It was the Alcock Convention and not the Washington treaty that attempted to make cautious improvements in existing conditions."[106]

Viewed as a unilateral statement of abstract principles, the Washington treaty of 1868 is reminiscent of John Hay's notes at the turn of the century. The question is whether the Burlingame–Seward policy had created a tradition, as Dennett implies. Dennett's book deals, in fact, only skimpily with American policy in China in the quarter century after 1869; the outstanding work on the decade that followed is the series of three articles by Paul H. Clyde,[107] which are concerned, however, only with isolated aspects, as a stimulus to research.

The principles behind the Seward–Burlingame treaty were at least acknowledged by Hamilton Fish, Grant's secretary of state. Burlingame's successor in Peking, J. Ross Browne of California, had been criticizing the Seward–Burlingame treaty, but in June 1869 Fish appointed a new minister to replace him.[108] In August 1869 Fish wrote George Bancroft, the historian, then serving as minister to Prussia, apparently with a view to helping Burlingame secure a

106. Ibid., pp. 277–279.
107. These will be cited in the next few paragraphs. See also Clyde's comments on the documents collected in his *United States Policy Toward China*, chaps. 16–21. Shanti Swarup Gandhi's "United States Diplomatic Relations with China, 1869–1882" (Ph.D. diss., Georgetown University, 1953), although a valuable reference, neglects the context of the treaty system in the period dealt with and is further limited by the assumption that American policy toward China was dominated by good will and friendship.
108. Paul H. Clyde, "The China Policy of J. Ross Browne, American Minister to Peking, 1868–1869," *Pacific Historical Review*, 1 (1932), 312–333; Williams, *Anson Burlingame*, pp. 201–214.

pro-Chinese statement from Bismarck. Bancroft was reminded that the United States respected China's "sovereign authority" and "territorial integrity" and would not participate in the cooperative policy in China "so far as that policy was aggressive and attempted to force upon China measures which could not be enforced upon a European state."[109] However, toward the end of the year, when Fish framed his instructions to Frederick F. Low, his new minister to China, his emphasis seems to have shifted. As Clyde has indicated, Fish's instructions to Low presented only a watered-down version of the Seward policy. Low was directed to study the August dispatch to Bancroft, and was specifically told: "You will observe that the President adheres to the policy adopted in 1868 . . . You will, therefore, so shape your private as well as official conversation as to demonstrate to Prince Kung the sincerity of the United States in its wishes for the maintenance of the authority of the central government, . . . and to respect the prejudices and traditions of the people of China when they do not interfere with the rights which have been acquired to the United States by treaty." The secretary stressed, however, not America's good will but China's obligations. "On this point [China's treaty obligations], and in the maintenance of our existing rights to their full extent, you will always be firm and decisive. While you will forward these claims where occasion requires, with prudence and moderation, you will be unyielding in demanding the extreme protection to American citizens, commerce, and property which is conceded by the treaties."[110]

Burlingame's sense of mission, it must be emphasized, was not to be found wanting among his successors; nor did the effects of the treaty of 1868 immediately disappear. For twenty-two years after 1861, the American ministers in Peking were assisted by two former missionaries who served as secretary of the legation, S. W. Williams (secretary, 1861–1876) and Chester Holcombe (secretary, 1876–1883). Their influence remains to be carefully appraised.[111] But as international rivalry arose anew in the China area, the Seward–Burlingame policy was found to be no longer applicable. The American diplomats did not abandon the desire to "sustain China." But more and more, whether by conviction or by rationalization, they tended to regard the interests they were either promoting or simply protecting—economic enterprise and Christian proselytism—as the

109. Williams, *Anson Burlingame*, pp. 315, 318–319.
110. *Papers Relating to the Foreign Relations of the United States* (Washington: Government Printing Office; hereafter cited as *USFR*), 1870, p. 303.
111. See Allen T. Price, "American Missions and American Diplomacy in China, 1830–1900" (Ph.D. diss., Harvard University, 1932), chaps. 9–11.

principal means by which they could contribute to that country's welfare.

Fish's appointment for China, Frederick F. Low (minister to China, 1870–1874), set the new pattern. A New Englander who went to California during the Gold Rush, he had been in business in the Sacramento Valley and in San Francisco and had served as congressman and, in 1863–1867, as governor of California.[112] A few months after he was in Peking, he confessed that most foreigners had been "underestimating the value of Chinese intellect and civilization." He felt, nevertheless, that the Chinese people lacked "a better moral sentiment" and faced, moreover, the serious problem of whether "new sources of industry and wealth can be opened up to replace the losses caused by the use of opium." More pessimistic than Burlingame, Low feared that the Ch'ing government's obstinacy regarding the introduction of Western innovations was likely to exhaust the patience of other nations. But he himself would eschew the use of force to compel progress and saw no alternative to waiting for the West's "educational influence" to take effect among the Chinese. "The masses must be educated through the labors and influence of the Christian missionary chiefly, and the officials must be taught by the wise, judicious and energetic action of foreign governments, through their diplomatic representatives at Peking." The latter must, however, also see that China observed her obligations. "They should insist upon the due fulfillment of treaty engagements, and be prepared to render protection to their own citizens and subjects, whenever the imperial government was either unable or unwilling to do its duty."[113]

Low's general views were only a variation of Burlingame's, but on the other hand, there is no evidence that he was concerned with the principal issue that agitated Burlingame—China's territorial integrity. By 1871 the administrative arrangements of the foreign settlements at Shanghai and other treaty ports had become well established; the Americans had accepted the system of dual Western-Chinese authority at the so-called international settlements and even the exclusive authority of France in *her* settlements. In May 1871, as directed by Fish, Low headed a naval expedition to Korea to seek redress for murdered American sailors and to demand a Perry-style treaty. He was careful enough to have asked the Tsungli Yamen to transmit a message to Korea, ahead of the American expedition; he was satisfied that China regarded her most valued

---

112. See Payson J. Treat, "Frederick Ferdinand Low," in Malone, *Dictionary of American Biography*, vol. VI, pt. 1, pp. 445–446.
   113. *USFR*, 1871, pp. 84–85.

vassal-state as autonomous in foreign as well as domestic affairs.[114] However, in the Russian occupation of Ili during the same year, which was the most serious event since 1860 involving violation of Chinese territory, Low and his government do not seem to have indicated any interest. During his four years in China, the only issue of Chinese sovereignty that concerned him was the position France took regarding the missionaries and their converts. As Clyde has shown,[115] Low was critical of the diplomacy of the French chargé, Julien de Rochechouart in the aftermath of the Tientsin Massacre. The American minister's reading of the treaties further convinced him that the French claims on the missionary's right to reside in the Chinese interior and to enjoy protection over Chinese Christians were "illegal assumptions." Yet because Low himself was charged with the protection of American missionaries in China, he had to take a compromise stand on missionary rights, similar, in fact, to that which the British had adopted. While he would not regard missionary residence in the interior as a treaty right and would remind missions of the possible dangers of venturing into the interior, he would nevertheless permit missionaries to reside inland and supported their claims whenever the evangelists or their churches were harmed in anti-Christian riots. "Missionaries will continue to go into the interior whenever they can gain a safe footing," he wrote Fish in December 1870, "and I have no disposition to embarrass or hinder them." As Charles A. Litzinger[116] has shown, in early 1871, when the Tsungli Yamen proposed regulations that would place the missionaries under the legal and administrative authority of local Chinese officials, Low immediately rejected the proposal, three months before Sir Thomas Wade gave a similar reply. In a communication to Prince Kung dated January 1872 Low did criticize the French policy of encouraging the missionaries to place Chinese converts under their protective wings: "The President [of the United States] would see with regret any attempt to withdraw native Christians from the jurisdiction of the Emperor without his full consent, or to convert the churches founded by the Missions into asylums for the refuge of desperadoes and criminals." Yet Low also warned that the United States expected the Ch'ing

114. *USFR*, 1871, pp. 111–112. See Mary C. Wright, "The Adaptability of Ch'ing Diplomacy; The Case of Korea," *Journal of Asian Studies*, 17 (1958), 371–372.

115. Paul H. Clyde, "Frederick F. Low and the Tientsin Massacre," *Pacific Historical Review*, 2 (1933), 100–108; *United States Policy Toward China*, pp. 107–115.

116. Litzinger, "Patterns of Missionary Cases Following the Tientsin Massacre," pp. 88–91.

government to "afford the full measure of protection guaranteed by Treaty to foreign missionaries and native Christians alike." Whenever there was an anti-Christian riot involving Americans, Low and his consuls would intercede on behalf of the missionaries, regardless of their location and of whether their behavior and that of their converts had been offensive.

That the United States had scant interest in war and peace on the China coast is indicated by its attitude toward the Taiwan affair of 1874. The Japanese, who at the time knew very little about the island, had been advised by Charles W. LeGendre, former American consul at Amoy, who had been on Taiwan on many occasions negotiating with officials and dealing with aborigine chiefs on the question of missing or murdered American sailors. With the encouragement of Charles E. DeLong, the American minister in Tokyo, LeGendre was made a counsellor of the Japanese Foreign Office in 1872, with the promise that the former American consul was to be made "governor of Formosa" should Japan in the future occupy the island.[117] When the Japanese envoy Soejima appeared in Peking in the spring of 1873 with LeGendre in his retinue and brought up with the Tsungli Yamen Japan's claim regarding the Ryukyu islands, as well as her desire to seek redress for the Ryukyu sailors murdered on Taiwan, Minister Low was apprehensive and reported to Secretary Fish that conflict between Japan and China was in the offing. In April 1874, when Japan launched her expedition against Taiwan, John A. Bingham, the new American minister in Tokyo, did lodge a protest. But although LeGendre was restrained from accompanying the expedition, and an American steamship chartered by the Japanese was not allowed to go to Taiwan, two Americans, including one detached from the Navy, did accompany the Japanese force. Huang Chia-mu argues that the Department of State was concerned with the legal and never with the political aspects of the situation. In August, when LeGendre, now a Japanese "general," appeared on the China coast and was believed to be proceeding to Taiwan, George F. Seward, American consul in Shanghai, authorized his arrest in Amoy—only to release him shortly thereafter, neither Seward nor S. W. Williams, the chargé at Peking, being certain of their government's policy. Seward was subsequently criticized by the Department of State for having made the arrest in the first place, since Japan and China had not declared war, and LeGendre's service to the Japanese was not

117. Fox, *Britain and Japan*, pp. 576–578; Dennett, *Americans in Eastern Asia*, pp. 440–443.

illegal.[118] The possibility of Japanese invasion of the China coast, which exercised Sir Thomas Wade, does not seem to have worried the American government. In October 1874, when Benjamin P. Avery, Low's successor as American minister to China, arrived in Tientsin, he was sounded out by Li Hung-chang on American good offices between Japan and China. Avery went only as far as to reply that he would communicate China's plea to Washington, while sending copies of his dispatch on the subject to the representatives of other powers in Peking.[119] Meanwhile, the dispute was settled in Peking on October 31, with the British minister mediating between the Tsungli Yamen and the Japanese envoy.

Avery's short but significant service in Peking (he died in November 1875) reinforced the pattern established during Low's ministry. Avery did not seem to be concerned with the Russian occupation of Ili, nor with a possible Anglo-Chinese conflict arising from the murder of the British interpreter Margary. The American minister's dispatches published in *Foreign Relations of the United States* show that he was preoccupied with Western enterprise in China and with the protection of American missionaries. A noted publisher, editor, and art patron in California, Avery was remembered by the Americans in Peking for his "cultivated mind and refined tastes."[120] He had sympathy for the Chinese efforts at "self-strengthening," being impressed especially by Li Hung-chang's plans to introduce modern methods to China's coal mines. He felt, however, that the United States, in cooperation with the other powers, should try to persuade the Ch-ing government to accept the railway and the telegraph, to be operated either by Western firms or by the government itself. Avery wrote Fish in December 1874 that "the interest in these means of progress is world-wide, and appeals to the humanitarian as well as to the political economist. While the United States justly disclaims any right or purpose to dictate to China how and by what steps she shall advance, that disclaimer surely was not meant to estop us from advising or asking that forward steps be taken when practicable and when demanded by common welfare." Specifically he reported on the short Wusung

118. Huang, *Mei-kuo yü T'ai-wan,* chap. 7. See also Sophia Su-fei Yen, *Taiwan in China's Foreign Relations, 1836–1874* (Hamden, Conn.: The Shoe String Press, 1965).

119. Ernest R. May, "Benjamin Parke Avery; Including a Review of the Office of State Printer, 1850–72," *California Historical Society Quarterly,* 30 (1951), 142–143.

120. Cited in Price, "American Missions and American Diplomacy in China," p. 404.

railway which was initiated by Americans in Shanghai with the encouragement of Consul Seward, as well as the contract to erect telegraph lines between Foochow and Amoy secured by a Danish company, the Great Northern, as a result of the diplomacy of M. M. DeLano, American consul in Foochow.[121] Since the Danish company was seeking Chinese permission to lay shore cables from Vladivostok to Hong Kong, Avery hoped that the secretary of state would approve his having joined with the ministers of other powers in Peking in a representation to the Tsungli Yamen in support of the Danish request. Avery's proposal later received Fish's endorsement, with the proviso that Denmark should not be allowed "exclusive privilege, or monopoly" of the telegraph in China.[122]

While the prospect of China's economic development seems to have captured Avery's imagination, his most difficult task as minister had to do with the missionaries going into the interior. Avery, with Washington's approval, redefined Low's policy as one of distinguishing between "rights which may be claimed as such and the privileges which the missionaries, by their self-sacrificing exertions, may be permitted to enjoy." But whether it was on the basis of right or privilege, whenever the missionaries were victims of Chinese riots, Avery and his consuls would "pursue the business to a just settlement." In July 1875, when American churches were destroyed and missionaries molested or beaten in two places in Kiangsi province, Avery was driven to despair, writing to Fish that "it would probably be impossible by mere suasion to induce the Chinese government to proclaim that it wishes to remain at peace and friendship with foreigners." Avery rejected the proposal of his consul at Hankow that an American gunboat be sent up the Yangtze to compel the settlement of the two cases. But he expressed the hope to Fish that more American naval vessels would be sent to China: "In my judgment, the number and distribution of war vessels on the China coast is inadequate to the service of observation and police to which they are assigned."[123]

Secretary Fish's policy toward China was further developed by George F. Seward (minister to China, 1876–1880), who with his

121. *USFR*, 1875, I, 223, 239–40. Avery congratulated DeLano in March 1875 on the crucial role he played in negotiating with the Chinese on behalf of the Danes: "To such a result, if it comes about, I think we may justly claim that American influence has largely contributed by the disinterested support it has given to initial telegraph effort, no matter by what nationality made, in the interest, solely, of commerce, civilization, and progress." Ibid., p. 279. See Huang Chia-mu, "Chung-kuo tien-hsien ti ch'uang-chien" (The earliest telegraph project in China), *Ta-lu tsa-chih* (Taipei), 36 (1968), 171–187.

122. *USFR*, 1875, I, 274.

123. *USFR*, 1875, I, 383 and 397.

long experience as consul in Shanghai, emerged as the strictest treaty constructionist in Peking's diplomatic corps. Seward shared many of the views of the treaty port merchants. In 1870 he had criticized Burlingame's lack of awareness of the merchants' impatience: "I confess that I should think less of Western civilization and of Western manhood if it were not pushing and aggressive in China."[124] As consul he had backed both the Danish telegraph scheme and the Wusung Railway. Referring to mining in China, he wrote to Fish in February 1876 that "sooner or later the [Chinese] government must learn that its best policy is to encourage enterprises of foreigners as well as those of natives." Early in his ministry, he urged upon the Tsungli Yamen the desirability of establishing a modern mint with a view to instituting currency reform in China. He requested Fish to send along information from the Treasury Department on the cost of a "mint of moderate magnitude."[125] Regarding the missionaries, he acknowledged that the American government had been in fact "the right arm of propagandists of the Christian faith" in China. But he strongly warned the missionaries to avoid moving into hostile areas, and to bring their grievances always to the Chinese magistrate *first* and to the consul only as a last resort. Thanks to this latter policy and to what Seward described as "better feeling among the Chinese generally toward the foreigners," his ministry was comparatively free of major missionary cases involving Americans. Nonetheless, "a considerable number" of incidents did come before the American consuls, and on several occasions Seward himself negotiated with the Tsungli Yamen on their settlement.[126] Seward's great interest lay, however, in the interpretation and improvement of the Sino-Western treaties, which he regarded as the cornerstone of American policy in China. His views on the judicial and fiscal provisions of the treaties were often even more aggressive than Sir Thomas Wade's. When Wade, after having concluded the Chefoo Convention, requested the diplomatic corps at Peking to deliberate on the implementation of some of its provisions, Seward, as Clyde has shown,[127] criticized Wade's policy as either too ambiguous or conceding too much to the Chinese. Regarding extraterritoriality, Wade found that he had to follow

124. Williams, *Anson Burlingame*, p. 331.
125. *USFR*, 1876, pp. 44–46. Cf. Frank H. H. King, *Money and Monetary Policy in China, 1845–1895* (Cambridge, Mass.: Harvard University Press, 1965), pp. 220–222.
126. Price, "American Missions and American Diplomacy in China," pp. 416–423.
127. Clyde, "Attitudes and Policies of George F. Seward, American Minister at Peking, 1876–1880"; *United States Diplomacy in China*, pp. 123–139.

the ruling of the British Supreme Court in China that in *civil* cases, the Chinese magistrate had the right to participate in "joint hearings" even when the defendant was a foreigner. Seward cited the Cushing treaty of 1844 to show that in civil as well as criminal cases, Chinese participation was unnecessary. Wade had wrested the concession from Li Hung-chang at Chefoo that the likin tax was not to be levied at the foreign settlements at the treaty ports. Seward attacked this provision at the conference of ministers, arguing that likin was contrary to the treaties to begin with and that it should be abolished altogether. Although Seward's views were in general backed by Washington, they had no immediate effect, since British ratification of the Chefoo Convention was long delayed and the clauses to which Seward took exception were not among those that the Chinese proceeded to carry out.

While Seward, as Clyde puts it, "derived much enjoyment from debating and defending his ideas on the rights of Americans over whom he presided in China," he made few comments on the political designs of the powers in the China area. On the controversy over the Ryukyus, which brought China and Japan near to war in 1879, Seward did write a long report, explaining the background of Ryukyu's tributary relations with China as well as the island kingdom's obligations to the Satsuma han of Japan. But this dispatch was dated as late as December 1879, nearly six months after former President Grant, who was on a private trip to East Asia, had been invited by the Tsungli Yamen as well as by Li Hung-chang to use his good offices in Sino-Japanese disputes over Ryukyu. Seward approved of Grant's efforts and opined that independence of Ryukyu from both China and Japan might be the best solution. The department, however, instructed the American ministers in Japan and China to make it clear to the two governments that the former president had acted entirely in a personal capacity.[128] Seward did report on the Sino-Russian controversy over Ili in early 1880, when it appeared that the Ch'ing government was inclined to have Ch'ung-hou, the envoy who virtually ceded that Sinkiang outpost to Russia in the treaty of Livadia, pay for the error with his life. The situation was grave, since the Russians were likely to consider Ch'ung-hou's execution an insult and therefore a *casus belli*. But when Seward joined the ministers of other powers to plead for Ch'ung-hou's pardon, he wrote Secretary of State William M. Evarts that "I have been actuated more by a desire to do my duty in a

128. *USFR*, 1880, pp. 194–201; Dennett, *Americans in Eastern Asia*, 444–446; T. F. Tsiang, "Sino-Japanese Diplomatic Relations, 1870–1894," *The Chinese Social and Political Science Review*, 17 (1933), 40–53.

humanitarian point of view than by considerations of danger to our interests." In March, when the crisis worsened as a result of the sentence of decapitation which Ch'ung-hou received and when the British were making every effort to stave off a Russo-Chinese war, Seward wrote complacently: "I see nothing in the situation that requires any change in our attitude. Our policy has been to deal justly with this government, and to do what we can to hold it to the observance of treaty stipulations. I think we could have no better policy. It is possible, in view of it, to feel sympathy for China without descending into the region of sentimentality."[129] It was during the Sino-Russian crisis, in fact, that Seward made some of his chief contributions to Sino-Western relations. In January 1880, the ministers of the powers in Peking accepted Seward's memorandum on judicial matters, reaffirming the practice that in civil as well as criminal cases, when the subject of a treaty power was defendant, he was to be tried by his consul without a Chinese official participating. As a separate issue, Seward, representing the diplomatic body, placed before the Tsungli Yamen in April 1880 a proposal for the reform of the Shanghai Mixed Court which, as we have discussed above, handled mixed cases where a Chinese was defendant, as well as police and criminal cases involving only the Chinese. He proposed that to give the Mixed Court greater authority, the presiding Chinese magistrate should be chosen from among officials of a higher rank (perhaps a circuit intendant); he also recommended improvement of the prisons administered by the court. He rejected, however, Chinese counterproposals that foreign assessors need not be present at the Mixed Court and that attorneys be barred therefrom.[130]

If the American policy in China in the 1870's fell into the pattern described in the preceding paragraphs, then I would suggest that the instructions regarding China from Fish and Evarts and the actions and words of Low, Avery, and George F. Seward in China need to be more thoroughly studied. The United States was actually relying on Britain to maintain the stability of China as a field of American activity—and this had been true even in the decade of Burlingame's "knight-errantry."[131] The substance of American policy in China consisted of the protection of traders and missionaries, whose endeavors were genuinely regarded by diplomats as being in the interest of the Chinese as well as the Americans. The Anglo-Saxon ideal of law, which actually had much to contribute to

129. *USFR*, 1880, pp. 221 and 238.
130. *USFR*, 1880, pp. 214 and 249–254.
131. The phrase is Dennett's; see *Americans in Eastern Asia*, p. 500.

Chinese life, was looked upon as the rationale for American rights in China, even though these rights were, in fact, guaranteed by British power and by the conciliatory side of China's foreign-policy tradition. I would suggest that the American attitudes described above persisted not only through 1895 but well into the twentieth century. Without going into the details of the period from Evarts to Gresham, certain new factors in American policy toward China during this period may be indicated. The task of research, to go beyond the very few studies that are currently available, is surely to examine any signs of a new departure, as well as any patterns that were inherited from the past.

The Chinese exclusion acts and American-Chinese treaties. Mary R. Coolidge's *Chinese Immigration,* which is the basic work on the anti-Chinese movement in California and in Congress, is also the starting point for inquiry into the diplomatic implications of that movement.[132] This latter aspect is of importance, for an integral part of the Seward–Burlingame treaty, concerning "free migration and emigration," was now repeatedly abrogated by Congress, leaving the diplomats the task of salvaging the sanctity of American-Chinese treaties. In 1879 the Congress passed the Fifteen Passenger Bill, which would have limited the number of Chinese coming to the United States to fifteen in any one voyage of a vessel. For the sake of "national faith" (as he remarked in his diary),[133] President Hayes vetoed the bill, and sent a commission to China, headed by President James B. Angell of the University of Michigan, to seek revision of the Seward treaty.[134] The delegation did persuade the Tsungli Yamen to accept a new treaty giving the United States the right to "regulate, limit, or suspend" Chinese labor immigration, but the negotiators of the treaty had taken suspension to mean temporary stoppage of no more than five years. Continued agitation in California and Congress resulted, however, in the first Chinese exclusion act of 1882, which suspended the immigration of Chinese laborers for ten years, and this legislation was reinforced in 1884 by a law providing for a broader definition of the phrase "laborer" and for a visa system for Chinese who went home for a visit and wished to return to this country. The spate of anti-Chinese riots in

132. See also the mechanical but useful account of Tien-lu Li, *Congressional Policy of Chinese Immigration.*

133. Hayes's veto and Arthur's in 1882 (against the bill excluding Chinese for twenty years) are discussed in Gandhi, "United States Diplomatic Relations with China," chap. 8.

134. Ibid.; see also Esson M. Gale, "President James Burrill Angell's Diary as United States Commissioner and Minister to China, 1880–1881," *The Michigan Alumnus Quarterly Review,* 49 (1943), 195–208.

the Western states and territories in the mid-1880's was followed by California's demand that Chinese immigration be stopped altogether. In return for the United States paying indemnity for losses suffered by Chinese in America, the Ch'ing minister in Washington, Chang Yin-huan, making the best of a bad situation, signed a treaty in March 1888, agreeing to suspend Chinese labor immigration for ten years. But while Peking hesitated over the ratification of this compact, Congress took the matter into its own hands and adopted the Scott Act of October 1888, which "absolutely prohibited" the return of any Chinese laborer who had gone to China for a visit— directly contravening a provision of the Angell treaty. The repeated Ch'ing protests were ignored; for many months the communications from the Chinese legation in Washington were left unanswered by the secretary of state.

Ch'ing diplomacy regarding the protection of Chinese in the United States is an obvious topic for research so far neglected by scholars.[135] But the reaction of the Department of State and of American ministers in China to the exclusion acts needs also to be examined. The American representatives in Peking from George F. Seward to Charles Denby (minister to China, 1885–1898) all expressed, at one time or another, disapproval of the particular form the legislation took. John W. Cassey's dissertation, "The Mission of Charles Denby and International Rivalries in the Far East, 1885–1898,"[136] has examined Denby's attitudes in detail, but further work can be done, particularly a study of the record along with the Ch'ing side of the story. The exclusion acts undoubtedly aroused resentment in China, especially in the Canton area and at the Yangtze treaty ports. American commercial and missionary interests in China were adversely affected. However, the business and missionary groups in the United States do not seem to have expressed strong views against Chinese exclusion until the passage of the Scott Act in 1888—although some individual churchmen had been defending the Chinese all along. Research done by Cassey shows that by 1889, articles began to appear in New York business journals discussing specifically how the anti-Chinese legislation would affect shipping and commercial interests, while Methodist,

135. Chinese policy regarding emigration to the United States up to 1880 is briefly reviewed in Li Ting-i, "Tsao-ch'i Hua-jen i-Mei chi 'An-chi li T'iao-yüeh' chih ch'ien-ting" (Early Chinese emigration to the United States and the signing of the "Angell Treaty"), *Lien-ho shu-yüan hsüeh-pao* (Hong Kong), 3 (1964), 1–29. Examples of the reports and communications of the Chinese legation in Washington for the 1880's may be found in Chu Shih-chia, *Mei-kuo po-hai Hua kung shih-liao*, pt. 3.

136. Ph.D. diss., University of Southern California, 1959.

Presbyterian and other church bodies began to submit petitions to Congress, pleading that the immigration laws might prove "well nigh fatal to the missionary enterprises in China."[137] Such opinion did not prevent Congress from passing the Geary Act of 1892, which extended the previous exclusion law for ten years and further stipulated that every Chinese in the United States was to be presumed guilty of illegal residence until he could prove his legitimate status and that Chinese were to be denied bail in habeas corpus proceedings. Allen T. Price believes that the appeals made by church bodies did contribute to the passing of the McCreary amendment of 1893, containing clauses which modified the rigor of the Geary law.[138] Congressional acts on Chinese exclusion did not gain legitimacy, however, until the Ch'ing government consented to a new treaty in March 1894, prohibiting Chinese labor emigration to the United States for ten years, with the vague assurance on the part of the United States that Chinese residents here were to receive "most-favored-nation treatment." The registration which Congress required of the Chinese in this country was also made applicable to Americans in China.

Protection and promotion of American interests in China. During the period of the Chinese exclusion acts, American commercial and missionary interests continued to grow. The total trade of the United States with China and Hong Kong increased from $18,000,000 in 1875 to $28,000,000 in 1895 (within which time exports from the United States grew from $3,500,000 to $10,000,000). The number of American missionaries in China, only 55 men and women in 1858, grew to 150 in 1872, 385 in 1887, 967 by 1898.[139] Although trade was comparatively small in volume, the enterprise of the merchants needed support. John Russell Young (minister to China, 1882–1885) tried, for example, to have the Tsungli Yamen accept an interpretation of a provision in the Sino-Western treaties that would permit Wetmore and Company, an old China-trade firm based in Shanghai, to operate a cotton-spinning factory there. Although the request was rejected, Young hoped that eventually he could persuade the Ch'ing government to accept such enterprises.[140] Among American ministers in the nineteenth century, the most enthusiastic promoter of American economic interests was Charles

137. Ibid., pp. 84–89.
138. Price, "American Missions and American Diplomacy in China," 487–490.
139. Shü-lun Pan, *The Trade of the United States with China*, p. 32; Price, "American Missions and American Diplomacy in China," pp. 391 and 496. The 1887 figure for missionaries is also given as 374.
140. *USFR*, 1883, pp. 129–141; 152–164.

Denby, a lawyer and legislator from Indiana who had been a "railroad director" and who was appointed by President Cleveland to the China post "through the intervention of a New York commercial syndicate."[141] Cassey reveals that during his first two years in China, Denby made a great effort to help General James H. Wilson, who had been encouraged by Secretary Bayard himself in his journey to China to promote railroad building. Denby was irked by the fact that British firms were also offering railway loans to the Chinese and argued with the ministers of the Tsungli Yamen that it was politically safer to use American capital. He wrote to Bayard: "To my mind it is quite certain that the operation of an extended system of railways will destroy the anti-foreign feeling here. Such a system will open the country to foreign trade . . . It will introduce manufactures." He wrote four months later, in October 1886: "It is within the province of duty of the diplomatic agent to show to his countrymen any commercial opening that may occur, to introduce unofficially commercial agents to merchants of China, and perhaps to local authorities . . . It is expected of him to further the promotion of general lawful trade and to uphold the common rights of his fellow citizens, merchants and manufacturers included."[142]

But the American diplomats were called upon even more frequently to uphold the privileges of the missionaries. J. Russell Young and his more religious-minded predecessor, James B. Angell (minister to China, 1880–1881) adhered to what Price terms "the Avery doctrine"—namely, "in case of wrongdoing by American citizens, mob violence was never justified, but rather, redress must be sought from the American officials." Angell is believed to have "lessened, perhaps unconsciously, the emphasis on missionary prudence and on the local settlement of difficulties which had marked [G. F.] Seward's policy." And Angell and Young both subscribed to the view of Chester Holcombe, the former missionary who was secretary of the legation, that the Chinese government, having made no opposition for twenty years to missionary residence in the interior, might be considered "to have positively conceded the right of such residence."[143] The energetic Charles Denby made it a point to visit all the missionary institutions when he visited the treaty ports. He wrote to Bayard in 1886: "To this influence [that of the missionary schools] I ascribe most of the progress in China. I cannot help admiring and respecting the self-devotion which makes these en-

141. Cassey, "The Mission of Charles Denby," pp. vi and 200.
142. Ibid., pp. 172, 200–209.
143. Price, "American Missions and American Diplomacy in China," pp. 424, 437, 442–443.

thusiastic workers give their lives to the Chinese . . . They are directly
benefiting Europe and America by civilizing, instructing, and hu-
manizing a people who must become our customers in the future."[144]
Denby's first years in China coincided with a new wave of missionary incidents (at least some of which were provoked by news about
the anti-Chinese riots in America). Despite his enthusiasm for the
missions' work, Denby valued his good relations with the Tsungli
Yamen and announced that he would support the missionary's
claims on property in the interior only when its acquisition had
been sanctioned by local officials. In the Tsinan property case of
1887, Denby at first considered the Reverend Gilbert Reid's title to
the house he had occupied to be rather weak, since the local magistrate had disapproved.[145] But Reid appealed to Secretary Bayard
in Washington, who endorsed Reid's view on the applicability of the
Catholic practices regarding missionary property-ownership in
China's interior. In the words of the secretary of state, American
missionaries should have "no less a measure of privilege than is
granted by treaty, conferred by favor, or procured through use and
custom for the missionaries of any other nation and creed."[146] Denby
eventually backed Reid's case strongly before the Tsungli Yamen.
Later, during the Yangtze valley anti-Christian riots of 1891, he
recommended to the department that the United States should send
more naval vessels to the China coast, while taking "joint action"
with the British and French to apply pressure on the Chinese government. As Marilyn Young has noted, in the aftermath of the
virulent Chengtu riot of 1895, Denby recommended to Olney that
"even when riots occur in the interior, where the offenders cannot
be reached by a foreign force, the doctrine of reprisals in other
localities might be brought to bear."[147]

   The United States and Sino-Japanese rivalry in Korea. Although,
as suggested above, the United States took little interest in the disputes between China and Japan in the 1870's, she entered upon a
diplomatic venture in Korea during the following decade. The

144. Ibid., p. 500.
145. Philip West, "The Tsinan Property Disputes (1887–1891): Gentry Loss
and Missionary 'Victory'," *Papers on China*, 20 (1966), 119–143.
146. Price, "American Missions and American Diplomacy in China," p. 517.
147. Ibid., 524–558; Cassey, "The Mission of Charles Denby," pp. 143–165;
Marilyn B. Young, *The Rhetoric of Empire: American China Policy, 1895–1901*
(Cambridge, Mass.: Harvard University Press, 1968), p. 21. See also Irwin
Hyatt, "The Chengtu Riots (1895): Myths and Politics," *Papers on China*,
18 (1964), 26–54, and George E. Paulsen, "The Szechwan Riots of 1895 and
American 'Missionary Diplomacy,'" *Journal of Asian Studies*, 28 (1969),
285–298.

American-Korean treaty of 1882, signed by Commodore Robert W. Shufeldt,[148] was in the tradition of Perry and its original purpose was chiefly commercial, with American prestige and the personal fame of the naval officer as added considerations. But by historical accident—just as Burlingame's performance in China and America during the 1860's had owed much to fortuitous circumstances— the United States played a major part in thwarting China's attempt to transform her rather theoretical suzerainty over Korea into a reality. Although often suggesting that "sustaining China" had been a consistent American policy, Dennett acknowledges that in her Korean policy the United States was not cooperating with the European powers or with China but with Japan. "Between Japan and the realization of her program for Korea, Great Britain as well as Russia and China were seen to stand squarely in the way. The United States stood aloof from the contest . . . however, [her policy until 1885] had already been to Japan as helpful as an alliance."[149] Instead of helping to stem Japan and Russia in Korea, as Li Hung-chang had hoped the United States would do when he aided Shufeldt in obtaining the treaty with Seoul, American diplomacy was the principal anti-Chinese influence at the Korean court before the Sino-Japanese War.[150]

A full-scale archival study of the American record in Korea during this period is still awaited. An approach to the subject lies in the two articles Dennett published within two years of the appearance of *Americans in Eastern Asia*.[151] One of these reproduces with com-

148. Charles O. Paullin, *Diplomatic Negotiations of American Naval Officers, 1778–1883* (Baltimore: The Johns Hopkins Press, 1921), chap. 10. On the Korean side of the story, see Pow-Key Sohn, "The Opening of Korea: A Conflict of Traditions," *Transactions of the Korean Branch of the Royal Asiatic Society*, 26 (1960), 101–128. On Chinese policy, see Tsiang, "Sino-Japanese Diplomatic Relations, 1870–1894"; Frederick F. Chien, *The Opening of Korea: A Study of Chinese Diplomacy, 1876–1885* (Hamden, Conn.: The Shoe String Press, 1967); Payson J. Treat, "China and Korea, 1885–1894," *Political Science Quarterly*, 49 (1934), 506–543. On Japanese policy, see esp. Hilary Conroy, *The Japanese Seizure of Korea, 1868–1910* (Philadelphia: University of Pennsylvania Press, 1960).

149. *Americans in Eastern Asia*, p. 482.

150. Selected American documents on the subject are available in George M. McCune and John A. Harrison, eds., *Korean-American Relations: Documents Relating to the Far Eastern Diplomacy of the United States*, vol. I, *The Initial Period, 1883–1886* (Berkeley: University of California Press, 1951), and Spencer J. Palmer, ed., Ibid., vol. II, *The Period of Growing Influence, 1887–1895* (Berkeley: University of California Press, 1963).

151. Tyler Dennett, "Early American Policy in Korea, 1883–7: The Services of Lieutenant George C. Foulk," *Political Science Quarterly*, 38 (1923), 82–103; "American Choices in the Far East in 1882," *American Historical Review*, 30 (1924), 84–108.

mentary a dispatch dated October 1882 from J. Russell Young, minister to Peking, to Secretary of State Frelinghuysen, on the question of whether the Shufeldt treaty should be ratified. His opinion was positive, but he added the thought that some kind of guarantee of Korea's integrity should be worked out at that very juncture, with Japan participating. Friendly to both Japan and China, Young regarded peace between the two countries as a "paramount consideration"; three years before, he had seen them on the verge of war when he accompanied General Grant to East Asia. (Young was a former managing editor of the *New York Tribune* and was recommended by Grant to President Arthur for the Peking ministry.) Young emphasized that "whether Corea is a dependency or a sovereignty, China can never look without natural apprehension upon any infringement of her territorial integrity. The map will show the military importance of Corea. A Russian or a Japanese army in that country would be a grave menace to China." Earlier in the year, China had sent troops to the peninsula after a Korean army mutiny threatened Japanese intervention. Young hoped that Japan could be persuaded to revise her 1876 treaty with Korea, as a basis for a common stand to be taken by Britain, Germany, and the United States, each of them to enter into treaty relations with Korea. Two months later, Young reported that the Japanese minister in Peking suggested in a conversation with him a congress of the powers named above, plus France and Russia, to consider how they could "guarantee the independence of Corea and its neutrality in the event of war"–in other words, to make Korea "another Belgium."

Needless to say, these ideas of Young's were not heeded, and the policy of the United States after the Shufeldt treaty was to uphold unilaterally Korea's independence as well as the newly established treaty relations. But circumstances were to make the now famous Ensign George C. Foulk a more effective Burlingame. Having been assigned as escort to the Korean mission to the United States in 1883, he proceeded to Seoul to become the naval attaché of the American legation, at the request of Min Yong-ik, a high Korean official who led the mission to America. By 1884, when Foulk became the American chargé d'affaires, he had already won the confidence of the Korean monarch, while on the side, he was friendly with the pro-Japanese courtiers who had more modern ideas than the pro-Chinese officials in Korea. Foulk had genuine sympathy for Korea. His growing proficiency in the Korean tongue, his position as head of the only legation of the Western powers in Seoul— these, in addition to the Korean king's resentment of the Chinese and suspicion of the Japanese—gave the young diplomat a chance to assert American influence. On Foulk's advice, the king requested the American government to supply military advisers. None were sent for a few years but meanwhile Foulk, as the trusted adviser of the court, had ranged himself with the Japanese and even the Russians against the Chinese. His influence made Li Hung-chang's task in Korea much more difficult and may even have provoked, after 1885, some of the most despicable political intrigues of the Chinese "resident," Yüan Shih-k'ai.[152]

Since Japan was rapidly becoming stronger and was destined to 'defeat China in war, the policy of Foulk—and of Horace N. Allen who inherited his role in Seoul[153]—perhaps made no difference in the end. But the record of Foulk and Allen is a commentary on the problems of policy on the eve of America's becoming a major power. Dennett suggests that in giving general approval to Foulk's actions at Seoul, the State Department may have been moved by the anti-Chinese sentiment in America.[154] In 1887, at the insistence of the Chinese-dominated Korean Foreign Office, Foulk was recalled.[155] A year later, the United States sent three military advisers to Korea (men who were not members of the Armed Forces and do not appear to have played a significant role in that kingdom). The American policy in Korea should perhaps be compared with the half-hearted American expansionism in the Hawaiian Islands and in Samoa during the same period. The pronouncements about Korea's "*de facto* and *de jure* independence," like such phrases as

152. See in addition to the works on Chinese policy cited above, Dennett, "Early American Policy in Korea"; Harold J. Noble, "The United States and Sino-Korean Relations, 1885–1887," *Pacific Historical Review*, 2 (1933), 292–304.

153. Fred H. Harrington, *God, Mammon, and the Japanese: Dr. Horace N. Allen and Korean-American Relations, 1884–1905* (Madison: University of Wisconsin Press, 1961).

154. Dennett, "Early American Policy in Korea," p. 85 and p. 98 n. 2.

155. Denby had urged in 1885 that Congress authorize the dispatch of military advisers to Korea, as requested by her king. But in the same year, he requested that Korea be transferred to his jurisdiction, just as the British consulate in Seoul was under the British minister to China. He gave as his reason the fear that Korea's loss to another power would lead to the disintegration of China. Later, in 1888, he wrote Bayard: "It is apparent that the citizens of the United States have attained great prominence in the agitation of the subject of Corean independence. Is such prominence desirable? Will it be beneficial to us? Will it compensate us for the loss of the goodwill of China"? Referring to China's claim of suzerainty in Korea, he wrote: "Openly at least, the other powers acquiesce in that relationship and regard it as a safeguard against the absorption of Corea by any other power." Cassey, "The Mission of Charles Denby," pp. 249–250, 252, 257.

"China's territorial integrity" employed by Humphrey Marshall and Anson Burlingame, may have contributed to American–East Asian policy in a later era. But in China, and perhaps also in Korea, it was through their efforts to protect and promote commerce and proselytism that the American diplomats of the nineteenth century did leave a lasting influence, for good or evil.

American Relations with Japan,

1853-1895: Survey and Prospect

In this paper surveying the study of the history of American-Japanese relations from 1853 to 1895 I shall try to make and to illustrate two general points. The first is that scholars ought to broaden the range of their interest beyond traditional diplomatic and political relations to a study of Japanese-American economic and cultural relations as they related to the remarkable process of development and modernization that Japan was undergoing during those years. The second point is that in this type of historical study it is important to use source materials in both Western and Japanese languages, now known to exist or yet to be discovered, in such a way that the two records will illuminate each other.

The advantage of a multi-archival approach to diplomatic topics is, of course, widely recognized. But the same point applies on a much simpler level. The Japanese practice of using their own phonetic syllabary to express foreign words leads to much garbling of names of persons, which can only be rectified by recourse to Western sources. On the other hand, the varying transcriptions of names of Japanese persons and places need to be reduced to one generally accepted system.[1] Since many of the individuals playing important roles spent part of their careers in America, part in Japan, material from both sources needs to be brought together. Indeed, a major project that would be very useful to scholarship in general would be compilation of a set of interlocking biographical accounts of eminent personalities of Meiji Japan, comparable to *Eminent Chinese of the Ch'ing Period*,[2] but including foreign diplomats and advisers as well as leading Japanese in all fields.

---

1. A vivid example is the usefulness of the standard Romanization and the characters added in the Japanese edition of Richard Hildreth's *Japan As It Was and Is*, edited by K. Murakawa (Tokyo: Sanshūsha, 1902).
2. Arthur W. Hummel, ed., *Eminent Chinese of the Ch'ing Period*. 2 vols. (Washington: Government Printing Office, 1943–44).

General Historical Accounts

The positions that the United States and Japan have come to occupy, as two of the major states in the international community, make the early stages of their relations, from 1853 to 1895, both interesting and important. But one must admit at the outset that the history of these relationships is not particularly difficult or controversial. A part of the period is what Thomas A. Bailey has called "the nadir of American diplomacy," a time when the attention and energies of Americans were largely turned inward. The same could be said of the Japanese; their real debut into the world scene did not come until after the Sino-Japanese War of 1894–95. Only by studying American participation in the momentous changes going on within Japan can one get at the most important part of the subject.

Scholars have had difficulty in finding unifying themes for this whole period. Tyler Dennett attempted to do so by claiming that the United States had followed consistently a "cooperative policy." But under this term he included two very different things: the American inclination at times to concert its policy with that of Great Britain, France and Russia, against the Japanese government; and the American tendency to enter, "without any formality or documentary pledge, into cooperation with or support of Japan." Add to this equivocation much admitted inconsistency in American actions, and the claim that "the United States did not retire from cooperation; it merely changed partners" becomes a not very meaningful generalization.[3]

The dean of American scholars concerned with Japanese-American relations in the nineteenth century was, of course, Payson J. Treat of Stanford University. Professor Treat published from his Albert Shaw Lectures on Diplomatic History an intensive study, *The Early Diplomatic Relations between the United States and Japan, 1853–1865*.[4] In later series of lectures given in Japan he covered the whole range of relationships up to the 1920's.[5] Treat's magnum opus is, however, his two-volume study, *Diplomatic Relations between the United States and Japan, 1853–1895*,[6] with a third volume bringing the record down to 1905. This is based on a

3. Tyler Dennett, *Americans in Eastern Asia* (New York: Macmillan, 1922), pp. 663–667, 677–680.

4. Baltimore: Johns Hopkins Press, 1917.

5. *Japan and the United States, 1853–1921* (Boston: Houghton Mifflin Co., 1921; rev. ed.: Stanford University Press, 1928).

6. Stanford: Stanford University Press, 1932; reprint ed.: Gloucester, Mass.: Peter Smith, 1963.

thorough examination of American diplomatic archives. Professor Treat considered this examination essential because out of 2,180 instructions sent to American representatives in Japan between 1855 and 1894 only 194 had been printed in the annual *Foreign Relations* volumes, eight in other official publications; out of 4,433 dispatches sent by American diplomats in Japan from 1856 to 1894 only 599 had appeared in *Foreign Relations*, and 38 in other government documents. Scholars will continue to be grateful for a summarization of diplomatic activity that probably never need be repeated.

Treat's work has two serious shortcomings however, apart from his self-imposed limitations of not attempting to correlate Japanese diplomatic documents or the relevant archives of other Western powers. One is his structuring of his material according to calendar years, which tends to fragment the treatment of many topics. Second, once he gets beyond the mid-1860's he fails to bring to bear much if any other historical material to supplement the archives. The events that happened to get recorded in diplomatic traffic between Tokyo and Washington give a very incomplete picture of what was occurring in Japan during those crucial years of development. If one dares to suggest a doubling of Professor Treat's herculean task, a concurrent examination of the files of the *Japan Weekly Mail* for the same years would have given a fuller context of events. As it is, the rich materials in the English-language press of Japan were noticed only when American diplomats included clippings with their dispatches.[7]

Research by Japanese Scholars

For American historians working in the field of American-Japanese relations it is important to take full advantage of the extensive work that has already been done by Japanese colleagues. Japan has a well-developed historical profession, organized in both general and specialized societies. Japanese historians have enjoyed many opportunities for publication, not only in book form but in historical journals and in series of scholarly papers sponsored by their universities.[8]

7. A subject index to the files of the *Japan Weekly Mail* that are available on microfilm would be a project of great benefit to researchers in many areas of modern Japanese studies.

8. Japanese National Committee of Historical Sciences, *Japan at the XIIth International Congress of Historical Sciences in Vienna: The Development and the Present Stage of Historical Sciences in Japan* (Tokyo: Nihon Gakujutsu Shinkōkai, 1965), gives a complete modern survey of the profession.

Unfortunately, two factors diminish the usefulness of Japanese work. One is that Japanese scholars studying the history of international relations are naturally interested in using publications and materials from abroad. In so doing they often fail to make full use of the published documents, archival materials, and newspaper accounts available in their own country. For the nineteenth and early twentieth centuries a large body of Japanese diplomatic documents has been published in the *Nihon gaikō bunsho* series.[9] But because of their bulk and the difficulty of the forms and the language it is precisely in these materials that foreign scholars most need preliminary sifting and evaluation done by Japanese.

The other unfortunate circumstance is the simple fact that not much of Japanese historical scholarship has been translated into English. Among general accounts of our subject the most accessible is the volume entitled *Japan-American Diplomatic Relations in the Meiji-Taisho Era*, edited by Kamikawa Hikomatsu.[10] But like other volumes in the set covering various aspects of Japanese-American relations, this work was done somewhat hurriedly for publication in connection with the Perry centennial. The topic-by-topic treatment is limited almost entirely to a presentation of the bare facts, with very little interpretation. The treatment of the period through 1867 is the work of Maruyama Kunio, from 1868 to 1895 that of Hanabusa Nagamichi. Professor Hanabusa covers the same ground in broader international context in his *Meiji gaikō shi* (Diplomatic history of the Meiji period).[11] Shimomura Fujio's excellent little volume, *Diplomacy of the Meiji Restoration*, goes well into the 1870's, but does not give equal treatment to all topics.[12] Mention should also be made of Nitobe Inazo's pioneering monograph, *The Intercourse between the United States of America and Japan*[13] and of the *History of Fifty Years of Japanese-American Relations* published in 1909 by the Dai Nihon Bummei Kyōkai.[14]

From among the many Japanese scholars who have devoted themselves to one aspect or another of nineteenth-century Japanese-American relations, two might be given special mention as being representative. One is Tabohashi Kiyoshi (1897–1945), a prewar

9. Tokyo: Nihon Kokusai Rengo Kyōkai, 1936–, in progress. For the Meiji period (1867–1912) there are 91 volumes.

10. Tokyo: Pan-Pacific Press, 1958. This is a translation and adaptation by Kimura Michiko of the second part of *Nichibei bunka kōshō shi*, vol I, *Sōsetsu gaiko hen* (History of Japanese-American cultural relations: general introduction and diplomatic relations) (Tokyo: Yōyōsha, 1956).

11. Tokyo: Shibundō, 1960.

12. *Meiji ishin no gaikō* (Tokyo: Ōyazu Shuppan K.K. 1948).

13. Baltimore: Johns Hopkins Press, 1891.

14. Kitazaki Susumu, *Nichibei kōshō gojūnen shi*.

scholar distinguished for his careful comparison of sources and his lucid and objective presentation. His major works were on the triangular relationship between Japan, China, and Korea, done from his vantage point at the then Keijō Imperial University. In the judgment of Shimomura Fujio, one of the present-day scholars most active in this field, Tabohashi "did not rationalize the attitudes of the Japanese side, but he had full command of the Japanese, Korean, and Chinese materials, and made clear the true situation accurately. His works have become the basis for postwar studies and are highly valued."[15] Tabohashi's excellent *History of Modern Japanese Relations with Foreign Countries* covers the early contacts with American traders, whalers, and naval vessels but unfortunately does not extend beyond the Perry expedition.[16] A separate paper in the Japanese Historical Association's volume of *Studies in the History of the Meiji Restoration* treats selected aspects of Japanese-American relations up to the 1870's.[17] And among his early uncollected papers in journals are several that concern relations with Americans.[18] Because of his objectivity and careful ordering of the facts, American scholars will not have much difficulty in relating to his point of view. On the other hand, Professor Tabohashi does not provide many provocative interpretations of the overall trend and meaning of the events he relates.

Professor Ishii Takashi, by contrast, is representative of that considerable group of Japanese historians whose postwar work has been set in a framework of Marxist theory. His *Theories of the Meiji Restoration* is a fascinating exposition of the varying shades of interpretation that different Japanese scholars have applied to events of that period.[19] His major work *The International Environment of the Meiji Restoration* is a creditable study of diplomatic relations in the period 1860 to 1867. But Ishii feels it important to start with a long prefatory "Summary View of the Political Processes of the Meiji Restoration," which begins with the flat statement that

15. Kokusai Rekishigaku Kaigi Kokunai Iinkai, *Nihon ni okeru rekishigaku no hattatsu to genjō* (Tokyo: Tokyo Daigaku Shuppankai, 1959), p. 166.

16. *Kindai Nihon gaikoku kankei shi* (rev. ed., Tokyo, Tōkō Shoin, 1943).

17. "Bakumatsu ishin shijō no Nichibei kankei," in Shigakkai, *Meiji ishin shi kenkyū* (Tokyo: Fuzambō, 1929), pp. 258–286.

18. "Nasanieru Savorī to Ogasawara shotō" (Nathaniel Savory and the Ogasawara [Bonin] Islands), *Rekishi chiri*, 39 (January 1922), 26–37; (February 1922), 119–137; "Ogasawara shotō no kaishū (The recovery of the Ogasawara Islands), ibid. 39 (May 1922), 361–378; (June 1922), 444–455; 40 (August 1922), 84–95; (October 1922), 255–267; "Edo bakufu no kaigun kakuchō to Beikoku" (The Tokugawa government's expansion of the Navy and the United States, ibid. 41 (May 1923), 387–400; (June 1923), 495–513.

19. *Gakusetsu hihan: Meiji ishin ron* (Tokyo: Yoshikawa Kōbunkan, 1961).

"The Meiji Restoration is a reform marking the shift from the Shogunate-clan system, which was the political form of pure feudalism, to the absolutistic emperor system, which was the political form of the final stage of feudalism."[20] His general view that Japan was being threatened by international capitalism can be seen in his comments on the first American minister, Townsend Harris: "The one who created the basic structure of the commercial treaties was the American representative Townsend Harris. At that time capitalism was not yet established in the United States; what controlled American international trade was not industrial capital but commercial capital. Harris was indeed the representative of this commercial capital, and what he sought in Japan was not so much a sellers' market for the capitalistic products of his home country, but rather a buyers' market for the special products of Japan and a base for vessels sailing the Pacific Ocean route. The policy of this commercially capitalistic America appeared best of all in the tariff rates of the Japanese-American Commercial Treaty. However, these were unsatisfactory to Britain, who sought above all to make Japan a market for capitalistic products. So Britain, who completely grasped the leadership in the diplomacy of various European and American countries toward Japan, took advantage of the Shimonoseki expedition to obtain a revision of the customs rate. Britain's long-cherished desire to get control of Japan as a market under exactly the same conditions as in China was realized."[21] Few American historians would accept fully the assumptions upon which Professor Ishii and like-minded colleagues base their work. But they should be challenged by this thorough-going ideological point of view to go below the surface of events and think about the underlying meaning of historical developments.

Popular Pioneers

The amount of research and writing devoted to different topics within the period is extremely uneven. The proclivity for attention to "firsts" explains a few of the concentrations. The deservedly famous expedition of Commodore Matthew C. Perry has been much written about, and details about even minor participants have been searched out and put into print by both Americans and Japanese. The Japanese have translated the basic American documents and

20. *Meiji ishin no kokusaiteki kankyō* (Tokyo: Yoshikawa Kōbunkan, 1957), p. 1.
21. Ibid., pp. 371–372.

have an extensive periodical literature on the subject. Now that we have a modern reprint edition of the official *Narrative*,[22] Commodore Perry's own personal journals published for the first time,[23] and a modern biography by Samuel Eliot Morison,[24] it is doubtful that further study of the expedition itself will produce much that is new.

American accounts of Perry have tended to emphasize his fine character, his restraint, and his disinterested motives. The commercial interests prompting the expedition are recognized, of course, but these relate more directly to the China trade and to the whaling industry than to Japan itself. Japanese historians of a Marxist inclination have stated his purpose more dogmatically as "the opening of Japan as a market for world capitalism."[25] But on the whole Japanese have shared a high estimate of Perry. Even the rightist leader Ōkawa Shumei, in a radio broadcast a few days after Pearl Harbor, praised the commodore's "spirit," using the term *tamashii* often associated with the *samurai*, and stated that the Franklin Roosevelt and Frank Knox of that time compared unfavorably with Perry.[26]

The career of Townsend Harris, America's first consul and minister in Japan, has attracted almost as much attention as that of Perry. Harris's isolated situation at Shimoda, the uncertainty about his relationship with the servant girl Okichi, his protracted negotiations with the feudal government at Edo, and his brave stance as minister in a dangerous and disorderly capital give the story a natural drama. These elements were given full play in the 1958 movie *The Barbarian and the Geisha* and have been handled more adeptly and accurately in Oliver Statler's new book on *The Shimoda Story*.[27] As a basis for more solid historical fare, we have Harris's own well-written journal and that of his interpreter, Henry Heusken.[28] Hunter Miller has assembled extensive annotations to the two

22. New York: AMS Press, 1967.

23. Roger Pineau, ed., *The Japan Expedition, 1852–1854: The Personal Journal of Commodore Matthew C. Perry* (Washington: Smithsonian Institution Press, 1968).

24. *"Old Bruin": Commodore Matthew C. Perry, 1794–1858* (Boston: Little Brown, 1968).

25. Ishii Takashi, *Bakumatsu no gaikō* (Diplomacy at the end of the shogunate; Tokyo: San'ichi Shobō, 1948), pp. 7–11.

26. Ōkawa Shumei, *Bei-Ei tōa shinryaku shi* (History of Anglo-American aggression in the East; Tokyo: Dai Ichi Shobō, 1942), p. 21.

27. New York: Random House, 1969.

28. Mario Emilio Cosenza, ed., *The Complete Journal of Townsend Harris, First American Consul General and Minister to Japan* (New York: Japan Society, 1930; reprint ed., Tokyo and Rutland, Vt.: Tuttle, 1959): Henry Heusken, *Japan Journal, 1855–1861* (New Brunswick, N.J.: Rutgers University Press, 1964).

treaties that Harris signed.[29] Japanese writers often approach the same events through a study of an equally commanding personality, Lord Ii Naosuke, the chief minister who took the decisive step of signing the commercial treaty with Harris.[30]

Both Japanese and Americans have devoted a great deal of attention to study of the first Japanese official mission to the United States in 1860 and the accompanying voyage of the *Kanrin-maru*, the first modern vessel that the Japanese sailed across the Pacific. Much of the documentation was assembled in a seven-volume set published in Japan in connection with the centennial of that event.[31] The meticulous bibliographical volume lists almost 800 relevant items: publications in both Japanese and English, many manuscripts, and some physical artifacts. One marvels that so much has survived in a country so exposed to the ravages of fire, flood and earthquake! The emphasis on "firsts" is a bit disproportionate, and one hopes at least that in the years immediately ahead similar industry will be devoted to searching out the records of the much larger Iwakura embassy of 1872–73, which was far more significant in seeking knowledge that contributed directly toward modernization in Japan.[32]

Diplomatic Representatives

After Townsend Harris one does not find outstanding personalities among nineteenth-century American ministers to Japan: Robert

29. Hunter Miller, ed., *Treaties and other International Acts of the United States of America,* 8 vols. (Washington: Government Printing Office, 1931–35), VII, 595–648, 947–1170.

30. One of the pioneer modern historical works in Japan, Shimada Saburō's *Kaikoku Shimatsu* (Circumstances of the opening of the country) is built around a biography of Ii. Nakamura Katsumaro's *Ii Tairo to Kaikō* (Lord Ii and the opening of the ports) was partially translated by Akimoto Shunkichi under the title *Lord Ii Naosuke and New Japan* (Tokyo: Japan Times, 1909.) Another popular presentation of the story is Kitamura Jushirō, *Sekai no heiwa o hakaru Ii Tairō to Harisu* (Lord Ii and Harris, who planned the peace of the world; Osaka: Ōmijin Kyōkai, 1934).

31. *Man'en gannen kibei shisetsu shiryō shūsei* (Collection of historical materials on the 1860 embassy to America; Tokyo: Kazama Shobō). This does not entirely supersede the excellent collection of materials in Fumikura Heijirō, ed., *Bakumatsu gunkan Kanrin-maru* (The warship *Kanrin-maru* of the late Tokugawa period; Tokyo: Akamatsu Kan'ichi, 1938).

32. Kume Kunitake, ed., *Tokumei zenken taishi Bei-Ō kairan jikki* (Journal of the observations of the special ambassadors plenipotentiary in Europe and America; 5 vols.; Tokyo: Hakubunsha, 1878) is the basic historical record, and *Kume hakushi kujūnen kaikoroku* (Dr. Kume's reminiscences of ninety years; Tokyo: Waseda Daigaku Shuppanbu, 1934) contains more personal material. Marlene J. Mayo is continuing studies that began with her Columbia University dissertation on "The Iwakura Embassy and the Unequal Treaties" (1961).

H. Pruyn (1862–1865), R. B. Van Valkenburgh (1866–1869), Charles E. DeLong (1869–1873), John A. Bingham (1873–1885), Richard B. Hubbard (1885–1889), John F. Swift (1889–1891), Frank L. Coombs (1892–1893), Edwin Dun (1893–1897), and Alfred E. Buck (1897–1902). Only Hubbard published papers relating to his service in Japan.[33] With the exception of Dun, who had been a resident in Japan for ten years as an agricultural expert, all were political appointees for whom this was their first foreign experience. Judge Bingham's long tenure of office and his previous career as an important Republican politician make him perhaps the best candidate for a thorough biographical study. A useful project would be a volume along the lines of Beckles Wilson's *American Ambassadors to England,* which might give short accounts of each of the envoys and also chronicle the changing physical circumstances of the legation and after 1907 of the embassy.

The corresponding list of Japanese ministers to the United States contains somwhat more illustrious names, because Japan had from the beginning something approaching a career diplomatic service. The first appointee, Mori Arinori, has attracted biographers, but more for his subsequent service as minister of Education than as a diplomat.[34] The papers of Yoshida Kiyonari, who served from 1874 to 1881, are held by the history department of Kyoto University. Terashima Munenori (1882–1883), Kuki Ryuichi (1884–1887), Mutsu Munemitsu (1888–89), Tateno Gōzō (1891–1894) and Kurino Shinichirō (1894–1896) all had later careers of importance. Satō Aimaro, who was later to become ambassador (1916–1918), served as chargé d'affaires during the whole year 1890.[35]

Treaty Revision

Throughout the early part of the Meiji period renegotiation of the commercial treaty with the United States, as well as with other

33. *The United States in the Far East; or Modern Japan and the Orient.* (Richmond, Va.: B. F. Johnson Publishing Co., 1899).

34. Kimura Tadasu, *Mori Sensei Den* (Tokyo, 1899); Ōkubo Toshiaki, *Mori Arinori* (Tokyo, 1944). There is a good short biography and a bibliography in *Kindai bungaku kenkyū sōsho* (Series of studies on modern literature), I, 253–299. Ivan P. Hall has done an extensive study in *Mori Arinori: Maverick Modernizer of Meiji Japan* (Cambridge, Mass.: Harvard University Press, 1972).

35. See Watanabe Ikujirō, *Mutsu Munemitsu den* (Biography of Mutsu Munemitsu; Tokyo: Kaizō-sha, 1934); Hiratsuka Atsushi *Shishaku Kurino Shin'ichirō den* (Biography of Viscount Kurino Shin'ichirō; Tokyo: Kobunsha, 1942). Gaimushō Hyakunen-shi Hensan Iinkai, *Gaimushō no hyakunen* 2 vols. (Tokyo: Hara Shobō, 1969), gives a detailed account of the Japanese Ministry of Foreign Affairs and lists of diplomatic assignments.

foreign powers, was of continuing concern to the Japanese. The existing treaties provided for extraterritorial jurisdiction and put limitations on the tariff duties that Japan could impose. Japan was eager to abolish the "unequal treaties" and to get on an equal basis with Western nations. But the disposition of the foreign powers to concert their action and the fact that the treaties were all linked together through most-favored-nation clauses made it very difficult for the Japanese to get revisions, although there were many negotiations, plans, and conferences. Success was finally achieved in 1894 in a new treaty signed with the United Kingdom and through similar treaties with other powers in the years immediately following.

The tangled history of treaty revision has not been of great interest to American historians. Thorough study of the highly complicated and technical questions would require explorations into many national archives out of proportion to the intrinsic importance of the questions. Apart from Payson J. Treat's chronological treatment, the only extensive study in English is F. C. Jones's *Extraterritoriality in Japan, and the Diplomatic Relations Resulting in its Abolition, 1853–1899.*[36]

To the Japanese the issues involved in treaty revision have seemed more important and worthy of study, partly because they are so closely intertwined with the domestic political history of the period. The pertinent documents have been collected in a special eight-volume set within the *Nihon gaikō bunsho.*[37] Prewar scholars tended to see the negotiations as a struggle for recognition of Japan's national stature and independence. Postwar scholars with a Marxist orientation have interpreted them as an effort to escape from semi-colonialism and imperialist exploitation.[38] Strictly diplomatic historians such as Hanabusa Nagamichi and Shimomura Fujio have been more concerned with setting forth the exact sequence of events.[39]

In general the Japanese have accepted the view that the United

36. New Haven: Yale University Press, 1931.
37. Nihon Gakujutsu Shinkōkai, *Jōyaku kaisei kankei Nihon gaikō bunsho* (Japanese diplomatic documents concerning treaty revision; Tokyo: Nihon Kokusai Kyōkai, 1941 +).
38. Inoue Kiyoshi, *Jōyaku kaisei: Meiji no minzoku mondai* (Treaty revision: A "people's" problem of the Meiji era; Tokyo: Iwanami Shoten, 1955) is representative of this latter point of view.
39. Hanabusa Nagamichi, "Jōyaku kaisei kōshō" (Negotiations for treaty revision), *Kamikawa sensei kanreki kinen: Kindai Nihon gaikōshi no kenkyū* (Studies in recent Japanese diplomatic history on commemoration of Professor Kamikawa's sixty-first birthday; Tokyo: Yuhikaku, 1956), pp. 1–61; Shimomura Fujio, *Meiji shonen jōyaku kaisei shi no kenkyū* (Studies in the history of treaty revision during the early years of Meiji; Tokyo: Yoshikawa Kōbunkan, 1962).

States was basically well-disposed toward Japan and was prepared at certain points to take the lead toward liberalization of the treaties. The more cynical point out that this willingness came from limited vested interests. "Even in the case of the United States," Inoue Kiyoshi writes, "when it came to a case involving its own interest, Buddha quickly turned into a devil." He then cites American resistance to the Japanese attempt in 1881 to forbid importation of kerosene with a flash point under 120° F. "To the American minister, the benefit to American capital was more important than Japan's public safety."[40] Not much is made of the rather complete turnabout in attitude toward the treaties under U.S. ministers John T. Swift and Frank Coombs, primarily out of concern over immigration of Japanese into California. Perhaps this is because the Japanese were at the same time beating a retreat from a commitment to include foreign judges in mixed courts for handling of legal cases involving foreigners.

From the standpoint of Japanese-American relations the most fruitful avenues for further investigation probably lie outside the negotiations. Even if one does not accept the Marxist argument in its simplistic form, it is pertinent to ask what influence American business interests had in determining official policy. Were trading interests benefitting from low tariffs under the existing treaties offset by potential investors desiring the right to own property outside the treaty ports? Did American missionaries take definite stands on the treaty issues? A subsidiary question of considerable interest would be to define more precisely the role of the two American advisers who served the Japanese Foreign Office during the treaty revision negotiations, Henry Williard Denison and Durham W. Stevens.

Immigration

The immigration of Japanese into the United States that was later to raise so many issues between the two countries had only its beginnings before 1895. The scanty information about the pioneer generation recorded in the comprehensive *History of Japanese in America* could undoubtedly be supplemented through a careful search for contemporary personal accounts.[41] The biography of

40. Inoue, *Jōyaku kaisei*, p. 43.
41. *Zaibei Nihonjin shi* (San Francisco: Zaibei Nihonjin Kai, 1940), pp. 31–48. A research project centered at UCLA is collecting information on Japanese in America through interviews as well as documents, but the very first group of immigrants have already passed away.

Wada Toyoji, for example, gives glimpses of a group of young Japanese men working in cigarette factories and retail stores in San Francisco during the years 1885–1892.[42] One subject that certainly deserves closer study is the development of emigration companies in Japan and their relations with employers in the United States and Hawaii.

Although Hawaii was in this period still an independent kingdom, the movement of Japanese emigrants into that area was to have important consequences for later Japanese-American relations. Hilary Conroy has studied this subject in *The Japanese Frontier in Hawaii, 1868–1898*,[43] and there is much detail in Morita Sakae's *Fifty Year History of Hawaii*.[44] Yamashita Sōen and Yoshimori Saneyuki have both published studies of the official relationships between Japan and Hawaii in the years before annexation.[45] The role of Eugene M. Van Reed and Robert W. Irwin as Hawaii's diplomatic representatives and promoters of emigration in Japan might repay further study. But on the whole the story of Japanese immigration as an issue in American domestic politics lies beyond this period.

Relations with China

Although the web of international politics in the Far East is not as tightly knit in this period as after 1895, at several points the United States, or at least individual Americans, did get involved in important ways in the relations between Japan and her Asian neighbors. This is true of Japan's developing relations with China.[46] In the dispute over responsibility for the murder of shipwrecked Ryukyuan sailors by Formosan aborigines the United States became

42. Kita Teikichi, *Wada Toyoji den* (Tokyo: Wada Toyoji Hensankai, 1926), pp. 44–53. Wada and his friend Mutō Sanji soon returned to Japan and became important business leaders.

43. Berkeley: University of California Press, 1953.

44. *Hawaii gojūnen shi* (Waipahu: Shin'eikan, 1919). Matsuda Mitsugu, *The Japanese in Hawaii, 1867–1967: A Bibliography of the First Hundred Years* (Honolulu: Social Science Research Institute, University of Hawaii, 1968) lists 883 items.

45. Yamashita Sōen, *Nihon Hawaii kōryū shi* (History of relations between Japan and Hawaii; Tokyo: Daitō Shuppansha, 1943); Yoshimori Saneyuki, *Hawaii wo meguru Nichibei kankei shi* (Japanese-American relations involving Hawaii; Tokyo: Bungei Shunjū-sha, 1943).

46. The fullest treatment is Wang Yün-shêng's *Liu-shih-nien lai Chung-kuo yü Jih-pen*, 7 vols. (Tientsin: Ta-kung-pao sheh, 1932–34), which has been translated into Japanese by Nagano Iwao and Hatano Kan'ichi, *Nisshi gaikō rokujūnen shi*, 4 vols. (Tokyo: Kensetsusha, 1933–34).

implicated by unauthorized actions on the part of Minister DeLong and through the employment by the Japanese of General C. W. Le Gendre, former American consul at Amoy, as adviser and prospective leader of a military expedition to the island. These complicated events have been studied as part of several dissertations, but no full account has yet been published in English.[47] When the question whether Japan or China had sovereignty over the Ryukyu (Loochoo) Islands remained unsettled and threatened to lead to war in 1879, former President Ulysses S. Grant in the course of a trip around the world served as personal mediator between the two parties. Grant urged that China and Japan themselves come to a settlement, without inviting the interference of Western powers.[48] Grant's role in this episode has always been highly regarded by the Japanese. A full record of his historic meeting with the Meiji Emperor has been published, and there is even a book about the tree that he planted in Ueno Park.[49]

47. Leonard Gordon, "Formosa as an International Prize in the Nineteenth Century," (Ph.D. diss., University of Michigan, 1961), partially published in "Diplomacy of the Japanese Expedition to Formosa, 1874," *Transactions of the International Conference of Orientalists in Japan*, no. 5 (1960), 48–57; Emily H. Atkins, "General Charles Legendre and the Japanese Expedition to Formosa, 1874," (Ph.D. diss. University of Florida, 1954); Sandra Caruthers, "Charles Legendre: American Diplomacy and Expansionism in Meiji Japan, 1868–1893," (Ph.D. diss., University of Colorado, 1966). The American Journalist E. H. House published an eyewitness account of *The Japanese Expedition to Formosa* (Tokyo, 1875). On the Japanese side there are four systematic accounts by diplomatic historians: Hosokawa Kameichi, "Taiwan shōban no tōbu ni kansuru gaikō" (Diplomacy concerning the Pacification of Taiwan natives), in his *Kindai Nihon gaikōshi kenkyū* (Studies in the diplomatic history of modern Japan; Tokyo: Jichōsha, 1942), pp. 181–293; Kiyosawa Kiyoshi, *Gaiseika toshite no Ōkubo Toshimichi* (Ōkubo Toshimichi as a statesman in foreign affairs; Tokyo: Chūō Kōron-sha, 1942); Hanabusa Nagamichi, "Sen happyaku nanajū yonen Taiwan bansha jiken" (The expedition against Formosan aborigines in 1874), *Hōgaku kenkyū*, 24 (September-October 1951), 51–79; and Watanabe Ikujirō, "Taiwan jihen to kindai Nihon no kensetsu" (The Formosa expedition and the construction of modern Japan), *Ōkuma kenkyū*, no. 5 (October 1954), 1–94.

48. John Russell Young, *Around the World with General Grant*, 2 vols. (New York: American News Co., 1879), II, 410–412, 415–416, 545–546, 558–562, 581–582, and John M. Keating, *With General Grant in the East* (Philadelphia: Lippincott, 1879) give extensive accounts. See also Ueda Toshio, "Ryūkyū no kizoku o meguru Nisshin kōshō" (Sino-Japanese negotiations concerning sovereignty over the Ryūkyū Islands), *Tōyō bunka kenkyūjo kiyō*, no. 2 (September 1951), 151–201, and Hyman Kublin, "The Attitude of China during the Liu-ch'iu Controversy, 1871–1881," *Pacific Historical Review*, 18 (May 1949), 213–231.

49. *Guranto shōgun to no go-taiwa hikki* (Notes of His Majesty's interview with General Grant; Tokyo: Kokumin Seishin Bunka Kenkyūjo, 1937); Ikeda Jirōkichi *Ueno Kōen Guranto kinenki* (The Grant commemorative tree in Ueno Park; Tokyo, 1939).

Relations with Korea and the Sino-Japanese War

Americans became similarly involved in the struggle between China and Japan for influence and control in Korea, which led eventually to the Sino-Japanese War of 1894. American representatives in Seoul tended to be sympathetic to the efforts of the Koreans to maintain their independence, but the U.S. government was unwilling to intervene in any decisive way. Two volumes of American diplomatic correspondence from Korea have been published, and Fred Harvey Harrington has studied the American role with emphasis on the part played by the medical missionary and diplomat, Dr. Horace N. Allen.[50] From the Japanese side, relationships with Korea have been treated in three thick volumes by the superb diplomatic historian Tabohashi Kiyoshi, and a large collection of pertinent documents is now in process of publication.[51]

At the outbreak of the Sino-Japanese War the American government was asked to represent Chinese interests in Japan and Japanese interests in China. With Edwin Dun in Tokyo and Charles Denby in Peking the United States had a strong diplomatic team which carried out this role with distinction. When the Chinese government asked the United States to intervene to bring about a peace settlement, good offices for communication between the two capitals were offered but not full mediation. At the peace negotiations at Shimonoseki both sides were served by American advisers acting in their private capacities: Henry Willard Denison for the Japanese, John W. Foster and W. N. Pethick for the Chinese.[52] The negotia-

50. George M. McCune and John A. Harrison, eds., *Korean-American Relations: Documents Pertaining to the Far Eastern Diplomacy of the United States*, vol.I, *The Initial Period, 1883–1886* (Berkeley: University of California Press, 1951); Spencer Palmer, ed., *Korean-American Relations*, vol. II, *Period of Growing Influence, 1887–1895* (Berkeley: University of California Press, 1963). Fred Harvey Harrington, *God, Mammon, and the Japanese: Dr. Horace N. Allen and Korean-American Relations, 1884–1905* (Madison: University of Wisconsin Press, 1944).

51. Tabohashi's works are *Kindai Nissen kankei no kenkyū* (A study of modern Japanese-Korean relations; 2 vols; Keijō: Chōsen Sōtokufu Chūsuin, 1940), and *Nisshin sen'eki gaikōshi no kenkyū* (A study of the diplomatic history of the Sino-Japanese War; Tokyo: Tōkō Shoin, 1951); Kim Chong Myong under the general direction of Kamikawa Hikomatsu is preparing an eight-volume work entitled *Nikkan gaikō shiryō shūsei* (Collection of documents on Japanese-Korean relations; Tokyo: Gannandō, 1964–). The best treatments in English are Hilary Conroy's *The Japanese Seizure of Korea, 1868–1910* (Philadelphia: University of Pennsylvania Press, 1961), and C. I. Eugene Kim and Han-kyo, *Korea and the Politics of Imperialism, 1876–1910* (Berkeley: University of California Press, 1967).

52. See John W. Foster, *Diplomatic Memoirs*, 2 vols. (Boston: Houghton Mifflin Co., 1909), II, 102–146. Payson Treat has a good account of these events in his *Diplomatic Relations between the United States and Japan,*

tions at the end of our period can be taken as a turning point: the United States was about to move from being essentially an interested observer to more intimate involvement in the power struggles in the Far East.

Were we concerned with political and diplomatic relations alone this would bring us to the end of our subject. But it is my contention that the more significant part of the story lies in the economic and cultural relations between Japan and America and the relevance of those relationships to the remarkable economic and social development that Japan was undergoing during this period. Japan's experience as the first non-Western nation successfully to undergo modernization is now being carefully studied for the lessons, positive or negative, it may offer for other late-developing nations. The Conference on Modern Japan of the Association for Asian Studies held a series of meetings on various aspects of this subject, from which came six volumes of papers that are being published by the Princeton University Press.[53] Neither the United States as a nation nor Americans as individuals can claim any decisive role in Japan's modernization, but there are many instances of mutual involvement which if studied more deeply would greatly illuminate the process.

Treaty Port Trade

Trade has certainly been one of the principal interests binding Japan and America together over the past century. Yet surprisingly American historians have given Japanese-American trade little study. Japanese scholars have given it slightly more attention, perhaps because in the nineteenth century the trade was of far more importance to Japan than to the United States. The commercial forces behind Commodore Perry's expedition saw Japan more as a stepping-stone to the China trade than as an end in itself. During the nineteenth century the trade was consistently unbalanced in favor of Japan, the big balancing factor in the form of imports of American raw cotton becoming significant only from 1890 on. To

---

1853–1895, II, 443–544, and in a separate article on "The Good Offices of the United States during the Sino-Japanese War," *Political Science Quarterly* 47 (1932), 547–555.

53. Marius B. Jansen, ed., *Changing Japanese Attitudes toward Modernization* (1965); William W. Lockwood, ed., *The State and Economic Enterprise in Japan* (1965); R. P. Dore, ed., *Aspects of Social Change in Modern Japan* (1967); Robert E. Ward, ed., *Political Development in Modern Japan* (1968); Donald H. Shively, ed., *Tradition and Modernization in Japanese Culture* (1971); and James Morley, ed., *Dilemmas of Growth in Prewar Japan* (1971).

Japan, however, exports of tea and raw silk were of great importance as foreign exchange earners. Through development of these cash crops the agricultural sector in Japan was able to contribute directly to earning the wherewithal for industrialization. Both commodities were heavily dependent on the American market and continued to be so until World War II.

The one historical work in English that examines overall American-Japanese trade relationships during the nineteenth century in detail is *Japanese Trade and Industry in the Meiji-Taisho Era* edited by Ohara Keishi.[54] Professors Yamaguchi Kazuo and Ishii Takashi have devoted much effort and ingenuity to reconstructing the statistics for Japan's foreign trade during the last years of the shogunate.[55] Beginning in 1882 the annual volumes of the *Nihon gaikoku bōeki nempyō* (Yearbook of Japan's trade with foreign countries) published by the Ministry of Finance, provide quite detailed statistics broken down by both commodity and country of destination. The weekly *Supplement* to the *Yokohama Trade Review* published during the 1890's gives the names of importers and exporters and the details of each shipment, information that usually can be obtained only by going into customs house or business records. Files of other English-language newspapers would again be a mine of information.

The nineteenth-century treaty ports of Japan were a special type of commercial community, similar in many ways to the corresponding ports of China but with distinctive features arising out of the Japanese situation.[56] The early development of Yokohama was summed up in 1909, on the occasion of the fiftieth anniversary, and is being given extensive modern treatment in a new *History of Yokohama* still in process of publication.[57] For Kōbe the older *Thirty-year History of the Open Port of Kōbe* gives much detailed information, but not in such a well-organized form.[58] Shigefuji Takeo has

54. Tokyo: Ōbunsha, 1957. This is an adaptation of the *Tsūshō sangyō hen* (Trade and industry volume) in the *Nichibei bunka kōshō shi* (History of Japanese–American cultural relations) series (Tokyo: Yōyōsha, 1956).

55. Yamaguchi Kazuo, *Bakumatsu bōeki shi* (Tokyo: Chūō Kōronsha, 1943); Ishii Takashi, *Bakumatsu bōeki shi no kenkyū* (Tokyo: Nihon Hyōronsha, 1944).

56. Harold S. Williams, *Tales of the Foreign Settlements in Japan* (Tokyo and Rutland, Vt.: Charles E. Tuttle Co., 1958) is a colorful episodic account.

57. Koezuka Ryū, *Yokohama kaikō gojūnen shi* (Fifty-year history of the open port of Yokohama; 2 vols.; Yokohama: Yokohama Shōgyō Kaigisho, 1909); *Yokohama-shi shi* (Yokohama: Yokohama-shi, 1958–; 4 vols. to date).

58. *Kōbe kaikō sanjūnen shi,* 2 vols. (Kōbe: Kaikō Sanjūnen Kinenkai, 1898).

published several studies of the foreign settlement at Nagasaki, which declined steadily in importance as even the trade between Japan and China shifted to other ports, and Unno Fukuju has studied the efforts of the Japanese to recover from the foreigners control of their own foreign trade.[59] It is clear, however, that various aspects of this trade would be a field of research where the interplay of American and Japanese sources could be effectively exploited. To my knowledge, no study has ever been made of any of the American trading firms operating in Japan, in most cases in conjunction with more extensive interests in the China trade.

For the tea trade the Japanese have compiled a compendious *History of a hundred years of export of Japan tea,* and much more detail could be quarried from the three-volume *History of the Japanese tea industry.*[60] A key biography is that of Ōtani Kahei, who rose from a tea buyer for the American firm of Smith, Baker and Co. to become long-time president of the Central Council of Tea Guilds.[61] On the American side the most extensive information I have found is in the chapters on "Tea Trade History of Japan" and "American Tea Trade History" in William H. Ukers, *All About Tea.*[62]

The silk trade is so much at the heart of Japanese-American economic relations that it deserves deeper study. In his *History of the Silk Industry in the United States*[63] Professor Matsui Shichirō has digested a great deal of information and interpreted it from the standpoint of an economist. The five-volume *History of the Japanese Silk Industry* published by the Japan Silk Association in 1935–36 and Sano Ei's earlier *History of Japanese Silk* are wells of information, as is Fujimoto Jitsuya's weighty *The Open Ports and the Raw Silk Trade.* There is also a *History of the Export Silk Industries of*

59. *Meiji shonen Nagasaki no iryuchi gaikoku shōnin to hōshō to no torihiki kankei* (Trading relations between foreign merchants and Japanese merchants of the Nagasaki foreign settlement in early Meiji; Nagasaki: Nagasaki Daigaku Keizai Gakubu, 1956–57); *Nagasaki iryuchi bōeki jidai no kenkyū* (Studies of the period of foreign settlement trade in Nagasaki; Tokyo: Sakai Shoten, n.d.); *Nagasaki iryuchi to gaikoku shōnin* (The Nagasaki foreign settlement and foreign merchants; Tokyo: Kazama Shōbo, 1967); Unno Fukuju, *Meiji no bōeki–iryuchi bōeki to chōken kaifuku* (Foreign trade of the Meiji era: Trade in the foreign settlement and the recovery of commercial rights; Tokyo: Hanawa Shobō, 1967).

60. *Nihoncha yushutsu hyakunen shi* (Shizuoka: Nihoncha Yushutsu Kumiai, 1959); *Nihon chagyō shi,* 3 vols., (Tokyo: Chagyō Kumiai Chūō Kaigisho, 1914, 1936, 1948).

61. Moteki Gentarō, *Ōtani Kahei Ō den* (Biography of Ōtani Kahei; Yokohama: Ōtani Kahei Ō Shōtokukai, 1931).

62. 2 vols.; New York: The Tea and Coffee Trade Journal Co., 1935.

63. New York: Howes Publishing Co., 1930.

Yokohama.[64] A privately printed biography of Horikoshi Zenjurō introduces one of the leading traders in the United States.[65]

Another commodity that deserves special attention is the import of American kerosene into Japan. By 1894 this had reached the level of 887,000 barrels of 42 gallons each.[66] American diplomats were always specially resistant to increases in the duty on kerosene and to Japanese safety regulations that imposed too high a standard. The kerosene lamp was but a passing phase in the march of modernization in Japan, but one that merits closer study. A part of the story is the relationship between Standard Oil's marketing interests and the infant petroleum industry of Japan. Standard itself was to enter the production field in Japan between 1900 and 1906 through the International Oil Company.[67]

Transfer of Technology

Transfer of advanced technology to Japan should be studied more deeply as an important part of the process of modernization. In this Americans played an important but by no means exclusive role, for Japanese drew eclectically from many sources, and it must be remembered that during this period the United States was herself acquiring much machinery and technique from Britain and other European countries. Two large sets assembling Japanese-language materials are a mine of information: the *Industrial History of the Meiji Period* and the *Compendium of the History of Science and Technology in Japan*.[68] Much detailed information about over 1200 foreign technicians who worked in Japan is assembled in a volume entitled *The Westernization of Modern Japanese Industrial*

64. *Nihon sanshigyō shi*, 5 vols. (Tokyo: Dai Nihon Sanshi Kai, 1935–36); Sano Ei, *Dai Nihon sanshi*, 2 vols. (Tokyo: Dai Nihon Sanshi Hensan Jimusho, 1898); Fujimoto Jitsuya, *Kaikō to kiito bōeki*, 3 vols. (Kaikō to Kiito Bōeki Kankōkai, 1939); *Yokohama yushutsu-kinu gyōshi* (Yokohama: Yokohama yushutsu-kinu Gyōshi Kankōkai, 1958).

65. Katō Kiyotoda, *Horikoshi Zenjurō den* (Tokyo, 1939).

66. Harold F. Williamson and Arnold R. Daum, *The American Petroleum Industry, 1859–1899: The Age of Illumination* (Evanston, Ill.: Northwestern University Press, 1959), p. 675.

67. *Sōritsu shichijū-shūnen kinen Nihon sekiyu shi* (Seventieth anniversary history of Japanese petroleum; Tokyo: Nihon Sekiyu K.K., 1958); *Hokuetsu sekiyu-gyō hattatsu-shi* (History of the development of the petroleum industry in the Hokeutsu district; Nagaoka: Ono Tsuyoshi, 1909); "The Echigo Oil Industry," *Japan Weekly Mail*, 38 (August 23, 1902), 200–202.

68. Kōgakkai, *Meiji kōgyō shi*, 13 vols. (Tokyo: Kōgakkai Meiji Kogyō Shi Hakkōsho, 1925–28); Nihon Kagakushi Gakkai, *Nihon kagaku gijutsushi taikei*, 25 vols. (Tokyo: Dai Ichi Hōki Shuppan K.K., 1964–).

Techniques,[69] but there is obvious need to search further for more details about the more important cases. One catches tantalizing glimpses, for instance, of an American named Stevens, who helped to set up the pioneer Kashima cotton mill, of Charles H. Kyle, who introduced tanning and leather making techniques, and of U. S. Treat and W. S. Swat, who helped establish the food canning industry in Hokkaido. Lest we become too euphoric about the achievements of American experts, however, we should recall the case of one Ambrose Dunn, who in the first enthusiasm about petroleum exploration during the 1870's was employed as a driller; even though he proved incompetent, he took legal action to hold his Japanese employers to a handsome contract.

Although capital investment by Americans does not become of great importance until the late 1890's, when revision of the treaties opened the way for foreign ownership of property outside the treaty ports, a few earlier cases can be cited. Here great resources for research are the abundant Japanese company histories, which are widely varying in quality but contain a great deal of detailed information.[70] The pioneer Spring Valley Brewery which the Norwegian-American William Copeland established in Yokohama about 1872 was the forerunner of the present great Kirin Beer Co.[71] The American trading firm of Walsh, Hall & Co. established the Kobe Paper Factory about 1878, but sold out to Mitsubishi interests three years later. The cigarette manufacturing enterprise which Murai Kichibei began in 1891, using techniques and machinery he had acquired in the United States, later had an infusion of capital from the British-American Tobacco Co., a Duke subsidiary, and prospered greatly until absorbed by the Japanese Government Tobacco Monopoly in 1904.[72] In 1894 A. H. Butler and Philip Henry Wheeler transferred the equipment of the bankrupt Otay Pocket Watch Company from the United States to Japan and established the Osaka Watch Manufacturing Co., which had indifferent success until disbanded in 1901.[73] The more significant investments of the General Electric

69. Saegusa Hiroto, Nozaki Shigeru, and Sasaki Shun, *Kindai Nihon sangyō gijutsu no seiōka* (Tokyo: Tōyō Keizai Shimpō-sha, 1960).

70. Kin'yu Keizai Kenkyujō and Ōhara Shakai Mondai Kenkyūjo, *Hompō kaisha-shi mokuroku* (Catalogue of Japanese company histories; Tokyo: Kin'yu Keizai Kenkyūjo, 1962) lists a great number.

71. *Kirin Biiru Kabushiki Kaisha gojūnen shi* (Fifty-year history of the Kirin Beer Co.; Tokyo: Company, 1957), pp. 1–20.

72. The papers of Edward James Parrish, who was vice-president of the Murai Co., are in the Duke University Library.

73. "Industrial Competition of Japan," *Gunton's Magazine*, 10 (March 1896), 206–215. Hirano Mitsuo's *Meiji zenki Tōkyō tokei sangyō no kōrōsha-*

Co. in both the Tokyo Electric Co. (manufacturer of light bulbs) and
the Shibaura Engineering Works (manufacturer of electrical machinery) lie just beyond the end of our period.[74]

Foreign Experts

The technicians mentioned above are but one example of the
widespread use of foreign experts during the early part of the Meiji
period. In an era when there were no foreign aid programs and no
professional technical assistance experts, Japan resolutely sought
out appropriate persons, hired them on direct contracts, and often
paid them what were for the time very handsome salaries. Careful
provision was made for training of what we would now call "native
counterparts," both at home and through study abroad, and as
quickly as possible these foreign employees were "phased out." The
experts and teachers came from all the advanced countries of the
time, but because of proximity and close general relations Americans
played somewhat more than a proportionate role.

Because of both intrinsic interest and obvious relevance to
modern foreign-aid programs, Japan's experience with foreign employees has begun to be studied extensively in recent years. Professor
Umetani Noboru of Osaka University made a general study entitled
Employed Foreigners: Supporting Players in Meiji Japan.[75] Hazel
F. Jones did a dissertation on this subject for the University of
Michigan, based on much research in Japanese government archives.[76] Rutgers University organized a conference around this
theme, April 26–28, 1967, the proceedings of which will eventually
be published. And the Kashima Kenkyūjo Shuppankai in Tokyo is in
the process of publishing a set of sixteen volumes by various authors
on "Foreign Employees," as a project connected with the Meiji
Centennial. The names of several hundred foreigners involved and
the bare facts about their service are now well known; what is

---

tachi (Distinguished persons in the Tokyo clock industry of early Meiji;
Tokyo, 1957) makes clear that Americans were entering an industry where
Japanese were already active with technology derived from Switzerland.

74. Here we have two excellent company histories: *Tōkyō Denki Kabushiki
Kaisha gojūnen shi* (Fifty-year History of the Tokyo Electric Company; Tokyo;
1940) and *Shibaura Seisakusho rokujūgonen shi* (Sixty-year history of the
Shibaura Engineering Works; Tokyo, 1940). See also "Linked with America
in Big Industry: Success of the Shibaura Engineering Works," *Far Eastern
Review*, 18 (November 1922), 665–669.

75. *O-yatoi gaikokujin: Meiji Nihon no wakiyaku-tachi* (Tokyo: Nihon
Keizai Shimbun-sha, 1965).

76. Hazel F. Jones, "The Formulation of the Meiji Government Policy toward
the Employment of Foreigners," *Monumenta Nipponica*, 23 (1968), 9–30.

needed next are some intensive studies of important cases where materials are available from both the American and the Japanese sides. Let me cite two or three good candidates for such study.

David Murray, professor of mathematics at Rutgers College, served the Japanese Department of Education as a general adviser from 1873 to 1879. As such he helped set up many new institutions and plan a fundamental revision of the education law. The manuscripts of his reports to the Japanese are available at the Library of Congress, and the translated texts of most of them have been published in Japan. A wealth of documentary material about educational developments at the time has been published in the voluminous *History of the Development of the Educational System since the Beginning of Meiji*.[77] In addition to other supporting material we have biographies for at least three Japanese who worked closely with Murray: Tanaka Fujimaro, Takahashi Korekiyo, and Egi Senshi.[78] Certainly a monographic study of Murray would be a good entree to the extensive historical relations between Japan and America in the field of education.[79]

William S. Clark's role as first principal of the Sapporo Agricultural College and coiner of the slogan "Boys, be ambitious!" for what has now become Hokkaido University is fairly well known. But Clark was in Japan for only one year, and his influence seems to have been as much charismatic as practical.[80] Perhaps more significant from the standpoint of modernization was the team of American experts who worked in Hokkaido for several years under the direction of General Horace Capron. Their surveys and recommendations had a great deal to do with creating in this northern island a

77. Kyōikushi Hensankai, *Meiji ikō kyoiku seido hattatsu shi*, 12 vols. (Tokyo: Ryūginsha, 1938–39).

78. Nishio Toyosaku, *Shishaku Tanaka Fujimaro den* (Nagoya: Kōsaijuku, 1934); *Takahashi Korekiyo jiden* (Tokyo: Chikura Shōbo, 1936); *Egi Senshi Ō keirekidan* (Tokyo, 1933).

79. Except for the short article by Ernest W. Clement in *Dictionary of American Biography*, XIII 358–359, the only American publication is the brief *In Memoriam: David Murray, Ph.D., LL.D., Superintendent of Educational Affairs in the Empire of Japan, and Adviser to the Japanese Imperial Minister of Education, 1873–1879* (New York: privately printed, 1915). There is a good summary of facts and bibliography in *Kindai bungaku kenkyū sosho* (Tokyo: Shōwa Joshi Daigaku Koyokai, 1958), VIII, 71–118. Unfortunately, the Murray papers in the Library of Congress do not incude much personal correspondence.

80. Ōsaka Shingo in his *Kurāku sensei shōden* (Sapporo: Kurāku Sensei Shōden Kankōkai, 1956) has collected a great deal of information, but his work is poorly organized and uncritical. Hokkaido University has manuscript letters from Clark to Kuroda Kiyotaka and other officials of the Colonization Commission. See also Ōshima Masatake, *Kurāku sensei to sono deshitachi* (Professor Clark and his pupils; Tokyo: Shinkyō Shuppansha, 1948).

pattern of agriculture that still has clearly recognizable American aspects. The personal rivalries within the mission and the difficulties between the Americans and local officials would not seem too unfamiliar to present-day directors of AID missions abroad. The work of Capron and his associates could be very illuminating, if studied against a broad backdrop of the development of Hokkaido, using both Japanese materials and the Capron papers at both the Library of Congress and Yale.[81]

Since teachers are professionally articulate, we have a comparatively full record of the many Americans who taught in Japanese schools and universities during the nineteenth century.[82] Among them Lafcadio Hearn is by far the most widely known, but more for his literary productions than because his teaching experience at Matsue, Kumamoto, and Tokyo Imperial University was unique.[83] Special mention should also be made of William Elliot Griffis, whose book *The Mikado's Empire* gave a combination of description, history, and personal reminiscence about teaching in Fukui and Tokyo that was for successive editions through several decades one of the most popular sources of information about Japan. For a picture of provincial Japan at the turn from feudalism to modernity one

81. Ōsaka Shingo has compiled a rich but rambling book entitled *Kuroda Kiyotaka to Hōresu Kepuron* (Sapporo: Hokkai Taimusu-sha, 1962). David F. Anthony did a Ph.D. dissertation at Yale (1951) on "The Administration of Hokkaido under Kuroda Kiyotaka, 1870–1882" and John A. Harrison has treated the subject briefly in his *Japan's Northern Frontier* (Gainesville: University of Florida Press, 1953). The *Hokkaidō shi Kaitakushi hensan* (History of Hokkaido compiled by the Colonization Commission; Tokyo, 1884) and Horace Capron and his foreign assistants, *Reports and Official Letters to the Kaitakushi* (Tokei [Tokyo]: Kaitakushi, 1875) contain much of the basic material. Herbert H. Gowen wrote about Edward M. Shelton in "An American Pioneer in Japan," *Washington Historical Quarterly*, 20 (January 1929), 12–23. From Edwin Dun there is a manuscript entitled "Reminiscences of Nearly Half a Century in Japan" in the Library of the U.S. Department of Agriculture. Among the general historical studies that might be used are *Shinsen Hokkaidō shi* (New History of Hokkaido; 7 vols.; Tokyo: Hokkaidō Chō, 1937), *Hokkaidō nōgyō hattatsu shi* (History of the development of agriculture in Hokkaido; 2 vols.; Sapporo: Hokkaidō Sōgō Keizai Kenkyūjo, 1963), and Kubota Yoshiteru, *Nihon rakunō shi* (History of dairying in Japan; Tokyo: Chūō Kōron Jigyō Shuppan, 1965).

82. Robert S. Schwantes, "American Influence in the Education of Meiji Japan, 1868–1912 (Ph.D. diss., Harvard University, 1950)," appendix A, compiles information about 227 Americans who taught in nonmission schools in Japan between 1860 and 1912.

83. P. D. and Ione Perkins, *Lafcadio Hearn: A Bibliography of his Writings* (Boston: Houghton Mifflin Co., 1934) and *Literary History of the United States* (New York: Macmillan, 1948), bibliography volume, pp. 556–559, and *Supplement*, p. 137, are the best introductions to the immense bibliography of writings by and about Hearn.

can turn to personal accounts by E. Warren Clark and Arthur Collins Maclay; for a picture of Tokyo University in its early days to Edward S. Morse's delightful *Japan Day by Day, 1877, 1878–79, 1882–83;* for an account of the Peeresses' School in 1888–89 to Alice Mabel Bacon's *A Japanese Interior.* Undoubtedly there are other accounts in magazines or still in manscript that are worth modern publication.

For all their value, such first-person accounts tend to magnify the personal aspects of the experience at the expense of the context in which it occurred. What are needed are studies that assess the contribution of such foreign teachers to the development of a whole discipline in Japan. What did the many individual teachers, not only American but British as well, contribute to the complicated development of English teaching in Japan?[84] How deep and how lasting was the influence of Thomas C. Mendenhall in the field of physics, Frank F. Jewett in chemistry, Henry M. Paul in astronomy, Edward S. Morse and Charles O. Whitman in zoology—all Americans who helped establish the teaching of those sciences in Tokyo University?[85] One could study the succession of Americans— Henry Terry, Charles Bigelow Storrs, Alexander Tison, and James Lee Kauffman—who held the chair of Anglo-American law at Tokyo Imperial University for forty years, to see what counterbalance they constituted to the predominantly German tradition in legal studies.[86]

84. General treatments in Japanese include Takemura Satoru, *Nihon Eigaku hattatsu shi* (History of the development of English studies in Japan; Tokyo: Kenkyūsha, 1933), and Sakurai Tsutome, *Nihon Eigo kyōiku shikō* (Draft history of English language education in Japan; Osaka: Shōbunkan, 1936). In a speech to a convention of English teachers I once attempted a broad-brush treatment: "English Teaching in Japan, from the Standpoint of Japanese-American Cultural Relations," in Zenkoku Eigo Kyōiku Kenkyū Dantai Rengōkai (National League of Research Bodies concerned with English Language Education), *Dai jikkai taikai kiyō* (Proceedings of the tenth meeting; Tokyo: Zen'eiren, 1961), pp. 78–92.

85. For Japanese views see Watanabe Masao, "Meiji shoki no Nihon ni okeru Beikoku kagaku no eikyō" (The influence of American science in Japan of the early Meiji era), in his *Science in the History of Modern Culture* (Tokyo: Miraisha, 1963) and Nakamura Takeshi, "The contributions to foreigners [to the development of science in Japan], *Journal of World History,* 9 (1965), 294–319. Watanabe Masao assembles information about six less well-known teachers in his article "Meiji shoki ni okeru rokunin no Beijin kagaku kyōshi-tachi" (Six American science teachers in the early Meiji period), *Kagaku shi kenkyū,* no. 92 (Winter 1969), 201–209.

86. Takayanagi Kenzō's "Occidental Legal Ideas: Their Reception and Influence," in Nitobe Inazō et al., *Western Influences in Modern Japan* (Chicago: University of Chicago Press, 1931), pp. 70–88. Terry prepared two books specifically for teaching in Japan: *The First Principles of Law* (1878) and *An Elementary Treatise on the Common Law* (1st ed., 1893; 9th ed., 1929).

Japanese Students in America

One of the most important ways in which the United States contributed to Japan's modernization was through the many Japanese who studied here during the late nineteenth century. This phenomenon has never received study comparable to Thomas LaFargue's study of the corresponding pioneer group of Chinese students.[87] For my dissertation and in subsequent research for *Japanese and Americans,* I identified about 300 Japanese who had studied here between 1865 and 1885. The number is not definitive; undoubtedly there were more, but probably not more than another hundred. Of the 300, I was able to trace the later careers of about two thirds. Of these 162 (55 per cent of the total number) came to occupy positions of responsibility and influence in government, academic, and business life.[88]

Several overlapping phases can be discerned in the early history of Japanese study in America. First came those students like Niishima Jō, Yoshida Kiyonari, and Matsumura Junzō, who slipped away despite the shogunate's prohibition against travel abroad. After the Restoration of the new government, as a step toward national unification, invited each of the *han* to choose students to go abroad. About a hundred were sent to the United States. Unfortunately, few had any previous training in English; at places like Monson Academy in Massachusetts and the Preparatory School of Brooklyn Polytechnic Institute they were placed in classes with very young children. After an official investigation revealed that many were not "following the road to learning" but changing their schools and courses of study at will, all below college grade were ordered to return. The Japanese government then substituted a policy of choosing through rigid examinations some of the best students from the new university in Tokyo. Megata Tanetarō was appointed to serve as superintendent of students in the United States. Among those chosen to go to America were Komura Jutarō,

---

87. *China's First Hundred* (Pullman, Washington: State College of Washington, 1942). John W. Bennett, Herbert Passin, and Robert K. McKnight, *In Search of Identity: The Japanese Overseas Scholar in America and Japan* (Minneapolis: University of Minnesota Press, 1958) makes brief historical statements about this early period, but is primarily concerned with persons then living and subject to interview. See also Watanabe Minoru, "Japanese Students Abroad and the Acquisition of Scientific and Technological Knowledge," *Journal of World History,* 9 (1965), 254–293.

88. Robert S. Schwantes, *Japanese and Americans: A Century of Cultural Relations* (New York: Harper, for the Council on Foreign Relations, 1955), pp. 192–214.

Hatoyama Kazuo, and others who later came to occupy prominent positions in the Japanese government. Assignment for a period of study or at least travel abroad became an important part of the Japanese bureaucratic system. In the 1880's a new type of "Japanese schoolboy" began to appear in America: those who were unable to win admission to the limited spaces in Japan's higher schools and universities, often entering less well-known institutions here and working to earn their way. Among this group were Uchimura Kanzō, who became a leader in Japan's "nonchurch" Christian movement, and Katayama Sen, one of Japan's pioneer Socialists.[89]

For study of the impact of the experience in America on these individuals and their subsequent careers in Japan, there is considerable biographical material available.[90] But it is difficult to go beyond surface facts to the mental experiences of this generation of young Japanese. Their American friends did not penetrate far in understanding the continuing concern that the Japanese students had with political and social changes in their own country. The glimpses one gets from letters and diaries written at the time indicate that it would be well worth while to try to recover more of this material and to attempt intellectual biographies of the best documented cases, on the pattern of Eugene Soviak's dissertation on Baba Tatsui.[91] A biographical study of Kaneko Kentarō, for example, could be a cross-cut through a long range of Japanese-American

89. For the general process see Ogata Hiroyasu, "Meiji shoki no kaigai ryugakusei seiritsu katei" (The process of establishing a system of study abroad in early Meiji), Shakai kagaku tōkyū, 2 (November 1957), 377–407; and Kurihara Shin'ishi, Meiji kaika shiron (Historical essays on the Meiji period of enlightenment; Tokyo: Teikoku Tosho K.K., 1944), pp. 139–159.

90. See the references in my Japanese and Americans, pp. 359–362. Additional items of importance are Takahashi Korekiyo jiden (Autobiography of Takahashi Korekiyo; Tokyo: Chigura Shobō, 1936) and Danshaku Megata Tanetarō den (Biography of Baron Megata Tanetarō; Tokyo: Ko Megata Danshaku Denki Hensankai, 1938); Hyman Kublin, Asian Revolutionary: The Life of Sen Katayama (Princeton: Princeton University Press, 1964).

91. "Baba Tatsui: A Study of Intellectual Acculturation in the early Meiji Period," (Ph.D. diss., University of Michigan, 1962). Examples of the more personal type of material are Nitobe Inazō's Kigan no ashi (Reeds of the returning ducks; English title: Student Days Abroad; Tokyo: Kōdōkan, 1907) and the reminiscences of student days in Boston in the 1870's by Kaneko Kentarō in Hara Rokurō Ō den (Biography of Hara Rokurō; 3 vols.; Tokyo: Hara Kunizō, 1937) I, 210–215. Noda Masutaka, ed., Bōkei Tsuda sensei densan (Biographical compilation concerning Bōkei Tsuda; Kumamoto: Tsuda Sei'ichi Sensei Nijūgo-kaiki Tsuitōkai, 1933), pp. 42–68 contains letters written home by a student in America in the early 1870's. Miyase Mutaso, Noguchi Hideyo no tegami (Letters of Noguchi Hideyo; Tokyo: Aia shobō, 1943) contains letters later in date from a Japanese who became an illustrious medical researcher in the United States.

relations: from his student days at Harvard in the 1870's through his participation in drafting the Meiji constitution, his informal negotiations at the time of the Russo-Japanese War, his friendship with Theodore Roosevelt, Justice Holmes, and other prominent Americans, his role as president of the American-Japan Society to his advocacy of a "Monroe Doctrine for Japan" during the 1930's In other cases where a full biography would not be feasible or rewarding, a series of biographical essays could bring out typical aspects of the experience of study in America and subsequent application in Japan.

Intellectual Relations

The transfer of ideas between Americans and Japanese is one of the most difficult, and therefore least explored, facets of the relationship between the two countries. A good deal is known about which American books were read in Japan, either in the original or in translated form.[92] But it is not enough to look for quotations or echoes in writings by Japanese. One must try to discern also the circumstances in Japan or in the life of a particular author that led him to choose and to use a certain American work. Henry C. Carey's *Principles of Social Science* was quite widely read in Japan during the 1880's, for example, because it supplied the protectionist arguments that some Japanese were seeking in order to combat the free-trade doctrines pressed upon them by the British. The relation to the treaty revision issue is obvious.

Among American literary men Emerson attracted the strongest interest during this period; the interest in Whitman was to come after the turn of the century, in connection with the movement toward democracy. But to my knowledge no one has yet studied what elements were selected from Emerson's complex and somewhat ambiguous writings and what interpretation the Japanese gave them.[93] Francis Wayland's *Elements of Moral Science* was much used by Fukuzawa Yukichi in his early teaching, but it would take careful study to determine how deeply the ideas contained therein penetrated the thinking of this important intellectual leader and his

92. The bibliographies at the end of each volume of the *Meiji bunka zenshū* (Collection on Meiji Culture; 24 vols.; Tokyo: Nihon Hyōronsha, 1927–1930) list the most important translations. See also Fukuda Naomi, comp., *Meiji Taishō Shōwa hōyaku Amerika bungaku shomoku* (A bibliography of translations: American literary works into Japanese, 1868–1967; Tokyo: Hara Shobō, 1968).

93. Jugaku Bunshō has compiled *A Bibliography of Ralph Waldo Emerson in Japan from 1878–1935* (Kyoto: Sunward Press, 1947).

disciples. In this realm of intellectual interchange the challenges are many, but the difficulties are great.[94]

The obverse story of the Japanese impact on American thought and taste in the nineteenth century has begun to be studied in Ph.D. dissertations by John Ashmead, Levi M. Cecil, Jr., and James R. Bowditch and in Iriye Akira's stimulating general exploration of the "inner history of American-East Asian relations."[95] Earl Miner has surveyed *The Japanese Tradition in British and American Literature.*[96] Clay Lancaster has done a handsome illustrated work on *The Japanese Influence in America* in the realms of architecture, decoration, and gardening.[97] The story of the collection and appreciation of Japanese art in America is yet to be written.[98] Perhaps among the next steps in this field should be studies of the knowledge and appreciation of Japan in several cultural centers: in the Boston area, in New York, in San Francisco, even in Chicago where a considerable enthusiasm for Japan developed in the wake of the Columbian Exposition of 1893. The total Japanese impact upon the country is to some degree a fusion of these separate regional experiences.

Christianity

Anyone concerned with the intellectual relationship between Japanese and Americans must in the end grapple with the meaning

94. In Japan one of the persons interested in this subject is the prolific writer Kimura Ki, who has published *Nichibei bungaku kōryū shi no kenkyū* (Studies in the history of Japanese-American literary interchange; Tokyo: Kōdansha, 1960). Portions of an earlier version of Kimura's materials have been translated by Philip Yampolsky in *Japanese Literature, Manners and Customs in the Meiji-Taisho Era* (Tokyo: Ōbunsha, 1958).

95. Ashmead, "The Idea of Japan, 1853–1895; Japan as Described by Americans and other Travelers from the West," (Harvard University, 1951); Cecil, "Our Japanese Romance: the Myth of Japan in America, 1853–1905," (Vanderbilt University, 1947); Bowditch, "The impact of Japanese culture on the United States, 1853–1904," (Harvard University, 1964); Iriye, *Across the Pacific: an Inner History of American-East Asian Relations* (New York: Harcourt, Brace & World, 1967).

96. Princeton: Princeton University Press, 1958.

97. New York: Walton H. Rawls, 1963.

98. On Ernest F. Fenollosa, the American teacher of philosophy who stimulated the Japanese to appreciate and preserve their own art, there is Lawrence W. Chisolm's monograph, *Fenollosa: The Far East and American Culture* (New Haven: Yale University Press, 1963). *Yamanaka Sadajirō Den* (Osaka: privately printed, 1939) contains much information about the Yamanaka art firm which facilitated many of the most important American purchases. Yashiro Yukio's *Nihon bijutsu no onjin-tachi* (Benefactors of Japanese art; Tokyo: Bungei shunjū shinsha, 1961) includes essays on Charles Freer, Fenollosa and William Sturgis Bigelow, Richard Fuller, and Langdon Warner.

and the results of the Christian missionary movement. For there the largest total number of people made the most sustained effort at intellectual communication. The foreign missionaries had a message to put across; they consciously sought to replace one set of values with others. The Japanese associating with them also had definite purposes in mind—though not always the same purposes as the missionaries had—the desire to learn a foreign language, to get modern ideas, to have a cosmopolitan experience. What was the outcome, the residue of intellectual effect? One must recognize, of course, that the encounter was between Japanese and the West, rather than between Japanese and Aemircans, though among Protestant missionaries Americans were numerically predominant.

For study of this subject there is an almost embarrassing wealth of material.[99] Several different types of material should be distinguished:

1. Periodic report letters written by missionaries for their mission boards at home. This primary material can be immensely rewarding, but it is sometimes difficult to use because it is inconveniently stored or because the mission boards impose restrictions. Portions of these reports have been published in periodicals put out by churches and mission boards.

2. Published materials produced by the missionary movement at the time. The proceedings of the general conferences of Protestant missionaries held in Osaka in 1883 and in Tokyo in 1900 provide a good starting point.[100] Several libraries in Japan have collections of the tracts and books written by the missionaries and translated into Japanese. Similar materials published in China also had considerable circulation in Japan. By the end of the century there was a considerable number of religious periodicals published in Japan carrying writing by both missionaries and native Christians. The periodic "Review of the Religious Press" carried by the *Japan Weekly Mail* provides a shortcut to this important but hard-to-use material.

3. Biographies of individual missionaries and of leading Japanese

99. Rather than attempting to survey the whole mass, let me mention three bibliographies: Ikao Fujio and James R. McGovern, comps., *A Bibliography of Christianity in Japan: Protestantism in English Sources (1859–1959)* (Tokyo: International Christian University, 1966); *Meiji-ki Kirisutokyō kankei tosho mokuroku* (A catalogue of books concerning Christianity during the Meiji period; Tokyo: Aoyama Gakuin Daigaku Majima Kinen Toshokan, 1954); and Ebisawa Arimichi, comp., *Nihon Kirisutokyō-shi kankei wakansho mokuroku, 1590–1890* (English title: *Bibliotheca Christiana Japonica: Catalogue of Books and Manuscripts relating to the Early Christian Mission in Japan, 1590–1890;* Tokyo: Bunkōdō Shōten, 1954).

100. Yokohama: R. Meiklejohn & Co., 1883; Tokyo: Methodist Publishing House, 1901.

Christians. These exist in considerable numbers, in both English and Japanese languages. They vary widely in quality, of course, from the uncritically complimentary to the truly scholarly.[101] Persons yet unstudied might be fitting subjects for dissertations or monographs. In the case of the pioneer missionary Guido Fridolin Verbeck, for example, there is certainly need for a modern study that will put into perspective his services as adviser to the Japanese government as well as his long career as evangelist and teacher.[102]

4. General histories of Christianity in Japan. For the early Meiji period the old standard work by Otis Cary has not been entirely supplanted by the newer treatments by Charles W. Iglehart and Winburn T. Thomas.[103] The standard history in Japanese is still that by Hiyane Antei,[104] although there was much new writing at the time of the centennial of Protestant missions in 1959.[105]

5. Histories of individual missions and denominations. Either in published or dissertation form, almost every American mission has been treated historically, in some cases several times over by

101. See *Missionary Biography: an Initial Bibliography* (New York: Missionary Research Library, 1965). One of the best in English is Evarts Boutell Greene, *A New-Englander in Japan: Daniel Crosby Greene* (Boston: Houghton Mifflin Co., 1927), by a son who was also a historian. Takaya Michio's *Dokutoru Hebon* (Dr. Hepburn; Tokyo: Makino Shoten, 1954) is an outstanding modern biography in Japanese. Among studies of early Japanese Christians are Kozaki Hiromichi, *Reminiscences of Seventy Years* . . . (Tokyo: Kyōbunkan, 1933); Saba Wataru, *Uemura Masahisa to sono jidai* (Uemura Masahisa and his times; 6 vols; Tokyo: Kyōbunkan, 1937–38) and an extensive literature on Niishima Jō, founder of the Dōshisha.

102. William Elliot Griffis, *Verbeck of Japan* . . . (New York: Fleming H. Revell, 1900) is good but now outdated by our deeper understanding of Meiji political development. The sketch of Verbeck in *Kindai bungaku kenkyū sōsho* (Tokyo: Shōwa Joshi Daigaku Koyōkai) III (1956), 243–289, includes an extensive bibliography.

103. Otis Cary, *A History of Christianity in Japan*, 2 vols. (New York· Fleming H. Revell, 1909); Charles W. Iglehart, *A Century of Protestant Christianity in Japan* (Rutland, Vt. and Tokyo: Tuttle, 1959); Winburn T. Thomas, *Protestant Beginnings in Japan: The First Three Decades, 1859–1889* (Tokyo: Tuttle, 1959).

104. *Nihon Kirisutokyō shi*, 5 vols. (Tokyo: Kyōbunkan 1938–40). Vol. IV covers the period 1844–1889, vol. V 1889 to 1940. His *Meiji ikō no Kirisutokyō dendō* (Christian evangelism since the beginning of the Meiji era; Tokyo: Ōyazu Shuppan K.K., 1947) is somewhat more interpretive.

105. Ebisawa Akira, *Nihon Kirisutokyō hyakunen shi* (Centennial history of Japanese Christianity; (Tokyo: Nihon Kirisuto Kyōdan Shuppanbu, 1959); the *Kirisutokyō Nenkan* (Yearbook of Christianity; 1960; Tokyo: Kirisuto Shimbun-sha), pp. 21–72, contains a good summary history. Good historical articles by Ozawa Saburō have been collected in his *Bakumatsu Meiji yasokyō shi kenkyū* (Studies in the history of Christianity at the end of the shogunate and in Meiji; Tokyo: Ajia Shobō, 1944) and *Nihon Purotesutantu shi kenkyū* (Studies in the history of Japanese Protestantism; Tokyo: Tōkai Daigaku Shuppankai, 1964).

successive generations. These works concentrate on recording and lauding specific accomplishments, but taken together they provide rich materials for comparative studies. The short-lived but influential American Unitarian mission in Japan would be a rewarding subject for investigation, for Arthur May Knapp and Clay Mac-Cauley deliberately took an intellectual rather than an evangelistic approach and as a result had a considerable impact in some of the emerging social movements of the time.[106]

6. Histories of the educational institutions that constituted one of the most important Christian contributions to Japan. One must try, however, to see each stage in their development in the context of the times, not as inevitable progress toward modern-day successors. Some of the early missionary schools that did not survive may have had important influence on the circles of Japanese they touched.[107]

Japanese scholars are using an even broader range of materials to study the total impact of Christianity upon Japanese society. They recognize that though fewer than one per cent of the Japanese people have ever been declared Christian believers, Christianity as an intellectual force has been proportionately far more important. One of the earliest attempts at analysis was *A Study of the Influence of Christianity upon Japanese Culture* that Saitō Sōichi prepared for the 1931 conference of the Institute of Pacific Relations. In post-Occupation years a group of prominent scholars in the Kansai area held a long series of symposia that examined the subject "Modern Japan and Christianity" from a variety of points of view.[108]

Much research on the relationship between Christianity and liberal and labor movements in Japan has been done at Dōshisha University at Kyoto, where a special collection of books on "Christian-

106. The pertinent materials on Unitarianism include Aida Kurakichi's article "Senkyōshi Nappu to Fukuzawa Yukichi (The Missionary Knapp and Fukuzawa Yukichi)," *Shigaku*, 27 (May 1954), 298–348; *The Unitarian Movement in Japan: Sketches of the Lives and Religious Work of Ten Representative Japanese Unitarians* (Tokyo: Nihon Yuniterian Kyōkai, 1900); Clay MacCauley's *Memories and Memorials: Gatherings from an Eventful Life* (Tokyo: Fukuin Printing Co., 1914) and a manuscript account of his work in Japan in the Unitarian Historical Library, Boston.

107. *Nihon ni okeru Kirisutokyō gakkō kyōiku no genjō* (Present status of education in Christian schools in Japan; Tokyo: Kirisutokyō Gakkō Kyōiku Dōmei, 1961) includes much historical material and an extensive bibliography of Japanese-language material on specific institution. The archives of the pertinent American mission boards contain much material. Paul F. Boller did a Ph.D. dissertation on "The American Board and the Doshisha, 1875–1900" (Yale University, 1947).

108. Kuyama Yasushi et al., *Kindai Nihon to Kirisutokyō*, 3 vols. (Tokyo: Kirisutokyō Gakutō Kyōdaidan, 1956–1961.) The first volume covers the Meiji period.

ity and Social Problems" has been assembled and a journal by that name is published. The noted economist Sumiya Etsuji has published a volume entitled *Christianity and Social Problems in Japan*.[109] In a study of the class character of Meiji Christianity, Kudō Ei'ichi of Meiji Gakuin pays particular attention to early successes in rural towns and among samurai. George E. Moore's dissertation studies the conversion of the "Kumamoto Band" of young samurai by Captain L. L. Janes and their subsequent careers as leaders of the Japanese Congregational (*Kumiai*) Church.[110] Irwin Scheiner has made a broader study of *Christian Converts and Social Protest in Meiji Japan*.[111]

Christian missionaries and Japanese converts imbued with the idea of responsibility for the welfare of neighbors, apart from the family system, were in the forefront in introducing to Japan the concepts and institutions of modern social work.[112] Ishii Jūji developed a model orphanage in Okayama, and Tomeoka Kōsuke began counseling work in prisons, both under the influence of the American missionary Dr. John C. Berry.[113] In many modern Japanese social institutions the influence of Christianity is clearly present, but there is danger of claiming too much. What is needed is deeper study of particular cases in order to analyze the combinations of foreign and traditional elements, of the religious and the secular. Likewise, there is need to study more deeply the fusion of Christian and Marxian elements in Japanese socialism, a fascinating subject that lies largely beyond the limits of our time period.

109. *Nihon ni okeru Kirisutokyō to shakai mondai* (Tokyo: Misuzu Shobō, 1963). See the list of library holdings in *Shozō bunken mokuroku* (Kyoto: Dōshisha Daigaku Jimbun Kagaku Kenkyūjo, 1959).

110. Kudō Ei'ichi, *Nihon shakai to Purotesutanto dendō* (Japanese society and Protestant evangelism; Tokyo: Nihon Kirisuto Kyōdan Shuppanbu, 1959). Moore's dissertation entitled "Kozaki Hiromichi and the Kumamoto Band: A Study in Samurai Reaction to the West" was submitted at the University of California, Berkeley, in 1966; part of his material has been published in "Samurai Conversion: The Case of Kumamoto," *Asian Studies* (University of the Philippines), 4 (April 1966), 40–48. The Dōshisha Daigaku Jimbun Kagaku Kenkyūjo has also published a volume of studies concerning the Kumamoto Band: *Kumamoto Bando kenkyū* (Tokyo: Misuzu Shobō, 1965).

111. Berkeley: University of California Press, 1970.

112. Takenaka Katsuo, *Nihon Kirisutokyō shakai jigyō shi* (History of Japanese Christian social work; Tokyo: Chūō Shakai Jigyō Kyōkai Shakai Jigyō Kenkyūjo, 1940) and Matsumiya Kazuya, *Nihon Kirisutokyō shakai bunka shi* (History of the social culture of Japanese Christianity; Tokyo: Shin Shigensha, 1948) are two general studies of this phenomenon.

113. *Tomeoka Kōsuke kun koki kineshū* (Remembrances on Tomeoka Kōsuke's seventieth birthday; Tokyo, 1933); Berry, Katherine Fiske, *A Pioneer Doctor in Old Japan: The Story of John C. Berry, M.D.* (New York: Fleming H. Revell, 1940); Ōkubo Toshitake, *Nihon ni okeru Berī Ō* (Dr. Berry in Japan; Tokyo: Tokyo Hogokai, 1929).

Coda

In the rich but still very incompletely explored history of relationships between Americans and Japanese, future progress in research will lie, I would submit, in two somewhat contradictory directions. The first is to focus on particular cases, particular situations, particular personalities in order to develop a richer factual context out of which meaningful generalizations can eventually be drawn. In most cases this will require bilingual research and a careful matching and cross-checking of sources. The second point is to recognize that by the end of the nineteenth century both Japan and the United States were becoming part of a shared world culture. The dichotomy sometimes assumed between German and American influences in Japanese education is blurred—or one might better say enriched—when one realizes the influence of Herbart on American schools and of German scholarship on American universities. In the area of philosophical and religious thought one must take into account the extensive influence of German philosophy and theology in America rather than positing a clear-cut rivalry between American pragmatism and German idealism. Add to this the problem of assessing the various traditional mind-sets according to which Japanese received and interpreted foreign ideas, and the whole study of relationships becomes more complicated, but in the end more rewarding. Indeed, this approach through study of fusing and interacting perceptions and ideas could be extended to the study of diplomatic and economic contacts as well as to cultural relations.

From the Open Door Notes

to the Washington Treaties

The Quest for Empire

The current quasi-debate about the nature of nineteenth-century American foreign policy is mired in definitional confusion and evasion. The sides are unclear and shifting. On the one hand there are historians who see the Spanish-American War, its origins and consequences, as a coherent bid for "informal empire" by the realistic representatives of hard-pressed but ultimately confident corporate capitalists. Annexationism is played down, the general urge for expansion stressed, and the primacy—though not necessarily the determining force—of economic causes and motives is underlined. In this view, McKinley is generally seen not as an incompetent bungler, nor as a reluctant warrior, but as a calm and certain leader who knew what he wanted and why. William Appleman Williams is perhaps the best representative of this approach whose detailed lineaments are explored by Walter LaFeber and Thomas McCormick.[1] The central thesis of this group has recently been defined by McCormick: "Much of American interest in China —like the Monroe Doctrine in Latin America earlier—sought the preservation of a long-term option there, to see that no combination of nations or circumstances or forces pre-empted that potential market, to keep a foot in the open door to insure that we would not find it closed in our faces at some future point. Any analysis of American Far Eastern policy at this century's beginning that does not come fully to grips with such an interpretation—with what is the very heart of contemporary revisionism—cannot be wholly satisfying."[2]

On the other hand, there are historians who define their subject narrowly as annexationism, separate the issues of origin and consequence and generally avoid taking a stand on what was *most*

1. William Appleman Williams, *The Tragedy of American Diplomacy* (New York: Delta, rev. ed., 1962); *The Contours of American History* Cleveland, World Pub. Co., 1961); *The Roots of the Modern American Empire* (New York: Random House 1969). Walter LaFeber, *The New Empire* (Ithaca: Cornell Univ. Press, 1963); Thomas McCormick, *China Market: America's Quest for Informal Empire, 1893–1901* (Chicago: Quadrangle Press, 1967).

2. Thomas McCormick, "American Expansion in China," *American Historical Review* 75.5 (June 1970), pp. 1395–1396.

basic in a whole bag of basic causes. Here McKinley appears as the victim of mass national hysteria. His competence lay in holding off the war as long as he did; his failure in eventually giving way. Imperialist thinkers—the Adams brothers, Mahan, and others—are discussed at great length while the economics of the situation assumes clearly subordinate importance. The solid *quotidien* nature of decision making is at the heart of much of this view, in direct contrast to the more sweeping efforts of Williams. Ernest R. May's work on the period of the 1890's is the most persuasive example in a very loosely linked group that might also include, with great variations, the work of Richard Hofstadter, Julius Pratt, and Paul Varg.[3] My own work is an effort to bridge the two groups and sometimes suffers the usual fate of those who enjoy balancing on stools.[4]

What has most disappointed me in the work of historians of the late nineteenth century is the way in which clearly differing points of view never meet head on. Views slide past each other and we do not seem to respect each other's work enough really to talk to each other. It is now ten years since Williams published *The Tragedy of American Diplomacy*. Surely he has not converted all American diplomatic historians, yet I have been unable to find any single work which confronts him directly. Professor May, in his recent essay on imperialism, disagrees with Williams in a footnote and then defines the issue so that he need not deal with it. What Professor May does deal with is important, interesting, and illuminating, but how far does it take us? Obviously, if imperialism is defined territorially, America's imperialist career seems, at first glance, brief and, by the standard of other empires, quite modest. If one includes military bases (which do, after all, occupy territory)

3. Ernest R. May, *Imperial Democracy* (New York: Harcourt, Brace & World 1961) and *American Imperialism* (New York: Beacon 1968); Richard Hofstadter, *The Paranoid Style in American Politics and other Essays* (New York: Alfred Knopf 1965); Julius Pratt, *The Expansionists of 1898* (Baltimore: Johns Hopkins Press 1936); Paul Varg, *The Making of a Myth: The U.S. and China, 1897–1912* (East Lansing: Michigan State Univ. Press, 1968); *Missionaries, Chinese and Diplomats* (New Jersey: Princeton Univ. Press, 1958). There is a third group which acknowledges McKinley's skill and calculation but rejects the economism of the Williams interpretation. Although I do not discuss them in this paper, the student should be aware of H. Wayne Morgan's, *America's Road to Empire* (New York: Wiley, 1965), and the essays of John A. S. Grenville and George Berkeley Young in *Politics, Strategy and American Diplomacy* (New Haven: Yale Univ. Press, 1966).

4. Marilyn B. Young, *The Rhetoric of Empire* (Cambridge, Mass.: Harvard University Press, 1968); "American Expansion, 1870–1900: The Far East," in B. Berstein, ed., *Towards a New Past* (New York: Pantheon Press, 1968).

the picture changes. Then the color of the world map becomes spottily but impressively red, white, and blue. Add to bases outright protectorates, disguised protectorates, satellite or client governments, and heavily dependent allies, and the tide of the stars and stripes runs very strongly indeed as the twentieth century progresses. And if we include preponderant economic influence, there would seem to be almost no country, except for the socialist nations, outside the American empire.

What does it mean to talk, as Professor May does, of a "mild case of imperialism"?[5] Is imperialism a curable disease, and if so, what is the prescription? The Platt amendment, the Roosevelt Corollary to the Monroe Doctrine, and the acquisition of the Canal Zone are cited by Professor May as evidence of a continuing infection beyond 1900. While it is true that our expansion as a *colonial* nation ended in that year, what of these other symptoms? How are we to understand them? And how, more significantly, do we understand the litany of interventions which followed 1900: Santo Domingo, Haiti, Nicaragua, Cuba, Mexico, and on through the decades and two world wars to Santo Domingo and Cuba once more. As a nation, worse, as historians, we seem to suffer from historical amnesia of a remarkably virulent kind. We soften the edges of America's behavior in the world by a series of "excepts": except for the Spanish-American War, except for the Taft through Roosevelt Latin American interventions, except for post-World War II intervention in China, Korea, Iran, Guatemala, Lebanon, Laos, Cuba, Vietnam, Cambodia, except for military rule over about one million Okinawans—except for all of these we ceased to be an imperialist power in 1900.

To begin truly to feel, and integrate into our histories, America's aggressive or expansionist role in the world would have an immense impact on the consciousness of all Americans. It might, for example, deeply effect the response of young soldiers in Vietnam. We have all seen them interviewed on television newscasts, their innocence shadowed by a sense of what they are doing. One reporter had a marine read for the viewing audience a poem he had written and put on the back of his flak jacket:

When youth was a soldier and I fought across the sea,
We were young and cold hearts of bloody savagery,

5. Ernest R. May, *American Imperialism: A Speculative Essay* (New York: Atheneum 1968), p. 14.

> Born of indignation, children of our times,
> We were orphans of creation, and dying in our prime.[6]

But when he was asked what he thought about the war, this orphan of creation, like so many of his brothers, answered that it was "better to be fighting the Communists here than fighting them back in San Diego." The lie in the name of which that soldier dies, and worse, kills, is at the heart of the new American empire.

If May does not deal with the central issues raised by Williams, neither does the latter, or more especially, his followers, deal with the concerns of their critics. In an otherwise powerful article on the Spanish-American War, Walter LaFeber asserts that McKinley and his associates emerged from the experience of the 1893 depression and the kaleidoscopic events in Asia "sharing a common conclusion: the nation's economy increasingly depended upon overseas markets including the whole of China; that to develop these markets not only a business-government partnership but also tranquillity was required; and, finally, however paradoxical it might seem, tranquillity could be insured only through war against Spain."[7] Yet the common conclusion reached by the McKinley Administration was quite wrong. The nation's prosperity simply did *not* depend on the Chinese market. Businessmen, in practice, realized it, even if the government did not. In the agricultural field, Williams himself has brought to our attention what has long been obscured—the vigorous support for an aggressive policy of economic expansion by agrarian interests. As Morton Rothstein has pointed out in a recent article, "Virtually every farm leader appearing before the Industrial Commission of 1899 argued that the basic solution to the problem confronting American farmers could be summed up in two words: Asiatic markets."[8] But the argument was a false one, with no foundation in the economic facts of the matter. Europe continued to absorb the bulk of American agricul-

6. Michael J. Arlen, *Living Room War* (New York: Viking Press, 1969), p. 88. Copyright © by Michael J. Arlen. Reprinted by permission of the Viking Press, Inc.

7. Walter LaFeber, "That 'Splendid Little War' in Historical Perspective," *Texas Quarterly* 11.4 (Winter 1968).

8. Morton Rothstein, "The American West and Foreign Markets, 1850–1900," in D. M. Ellis, ed., *The Frontier in American Development: Essays in Honor of Paul Wallace Gates* (Ithaca: Cornell Univ. Press, 1969), p. 405. Testimony before the commission included a rural version of the textile industry's dream of adding an inch to Chinese shirttails: "It is estimated that 40,000,000 bushels of wheat would be less than half a peck for each inhabitant of China . . ." *Report of the Industrial Commission of Agriculture and Agricultural Labor* (Washington, 1901), X, lv.

tural export as it had before the depression. That some (by no means all) business and agricultural leaders believed in the economic analysis they so forcefully presented to the nation and were able to convince politicians to *act* on it is important. But it is no less important that they were wrong. Somewhere in the gap between what was believed and reality lies the explanation for America's fitful, paradoxical, and ultimately brutal involvement in Asia.

Two separate questions seem to divide historians in their approach to America's first venture in asserting its will in Asia. As I indicated earlier, the first has to do with definitions, the second with causes. Is the Open Door part of a unified strategy of expansion or is it best understood in relation to the more limited annexationist approach? Second, whatever one's definition, does the expansionist impulse flow *primarily* from the economic system? I feel there is a tendency, even on the part of those who reject an economic interpretation (and certainly reject economic determinism) to accept the notion that economic imperialism is *really* imperialistic, whereas expansionist policy undertaken for different reasons is somehow exempt from that derogatory denotation. Yet, why is it more of a condemnation of aggression to say it was a product of economic rather than political or strategic causes? Except for a lingering puritanical notion of money as, in itself, a dirtier motive, I am puzzled by this attitude.

For some analyses the direct economic connection is essential. Harry Magdoff, for example, accepts the absolute equation, capitalism equals imperialism, with nothing untidy on either side of the sign. A capitalist society is, of necessity, imperialist; must, of necessity, expand; does, of necessity, fight wars of expansion.[9] An extension of this line of reasoning appears in a recent essay by Gabriel Kolko which argues that the domino theory is no theory but a matter of accurate description. If America does not control the "third world," "they" will. If "they" do, American society as we know and deplore it will collapse.[10] And, it is implied, to deny that all this is necessary is to become an apologist for American imperialism.

I am not at all convinced that things are so very neat. The state is not a simple reflection of the desires and interests of its ruling class, even if one assumes (and in America this is less than certain) a cohesive, self-conscious, and overwhelmingly powerful elite.

9. Harry Magdoff, *The Age of Imperialism* (New York: Monthly Review Press, 1969).

10. Gabriel Kolko, *The Roots of American Foreign Policy* (Boston: Beacon Press 1969).

Rather the state mediates, in complex and often contradictory ways, between powerful and sometimes conflicting interests *it* observes in the world and at home. It should be added that there are also limits within which mediation takes place and lines are set beyond which mediation stops and war begins.

While it would be astonishing to find the government ruling against major corporate interests except by accident or in merely trivial ways, is the reverse necessarily true? Does it always rule for those interests? Can it always, rationally, even determine what those interests are? Obviously not. Vietnam, the pit we have dug for ourselves out of pride and arrogance, is more the product of the political, bureaucratic, and academic mind than the monopoly capitalist one.

In the late nineteenth and early twentieth century, the problem seems to me to be similar. It would be inconceivable for McKinley to have conscientiously set out to work *against* American economic expansion. But what did he do *for* it and how did businessmen respond? How general was the agreement on his policies? Everything depends on the questions we ask and what weight we give to them. Even if we grant that the great debate over annexation of the Philippines was essentially an argument over alternate strategies toward the same goal—economic expansion through overseas markets—the debate remains. We can dismiss it as uninteresting or meaningless only at the risk of falsifying history. For it was clearly a monumental debate at the time and men took seriously the positions they argued and the consequences they predicted. It may be that the senatorial opponents of the ABM system or the Vietnam War differ from the current administration only on the tactics of the matter, that all are equally committed to the American empire. Yet I think we would miss both the reality of contemporary politics and the possibility for change if we simply dismissed them. Tactics matter. They mattered to the Filipinos crushed by American troops in 1900 as they matter to Vietnamese today.

My own view is that, contrary to George Kennan's characterization of them, McKinley, Hay, Rockhill, and the rest were realists responding rationally and concretely to specific international and domestic crises. But an important part of the world they thought they saw was patently unreal. The American economy was not in a state of glut which could only be alleviated by oriental markets. The Open Door notes did not establish America as a balancer of powers in the Far East, nor did it save China from anything, least of all from the European powers. Yet the myth was important domestically—to offset the "unpleasantness" in the Philippines, to reassure a country shaken to its roots by the depression of 1893 and the alleged imminence of Chinese partition, to assert American nationalism, and so forth—and therefore consciously or unconsciously, it was assiduously maintained.

The present offers a useful parallel. In a brilliant article on "American Imperialism and the Peace Movement," Robert Wolfe has noted the "disproportion between the actual pattern of American foreign investment and the global scale and uniform character of American foreign policy."[11] Wolfe argues that the United States, while seeking to "defend real interests, . . . seeks to do so on the basis of a mythological view of the world." Operating mythologically, it is impossible for administrations to distinguish between real and unreal threats. But the importance of the myth is domestic: "The mythology of anti-Communism not only justifies military spending and domestic reaction; it also provides the necessary confirmation for its own distorted perceptions. In this sense one might almost argue that the real goal of American imperialism today is not so much to preserve capitalist holdings abroad as it is to preserve and give substance to the myth upon which capitalism at home now rests."

Why was the myth of China's centrality encouraged by McKinley and sustained by succeeding administrations? Was it, as James Thomson has written in another context, a case of "rhetorical escalation," assumed to be of "crucial significance" to us because we have said that it is of crucial significance?[12] And if so, why did we say it? I doubt if archival research will yield the answer to such questions, but perhaps it will. What I want is a comprehensive grasp of what America was *like* in the late nineteenth century, combined with a constant concern for the possible continuities between that time and the present. To approach Sino-American relations in a more limited framework means only to add to the anarchic production of unconnected scholarly works.

Perhaps historians must begin to look elsewhere for perspective —to literature, for example. On the passionate and contradictory impulses of nineteenth-century imperialism, Joseph Conrad has more to say to us than many historians. Charles Gould, knight errant of material interests in *Nostromo*, justifies his attachment to an inherited concession in the fictional Central American state of Costaguana this way: "What is wanted here is law, good faith,

11. Robert Wolfe, "American Imperialism and the Peace Movement," *Studies on the Left*, 6.3 (May–June 1966), 28–43.

12. James C. Thomson, Jr., "How Could Vietnam Happen? An Autopsy," *The Atlantic* 221.4 (April 1968), p. 51.

order, security. Anyone can declaim about these things, but I pin my faith to material interests. Only let the material interests once get a firm footing, and they are bound to impose the conditions on which alone they can continue to exist. That's how your money-making is justified here in the face of lawlessness and disorder. It is justified because the security which it demands must be shared with an oppressed people. A better justice will come afterwards. That's your ray of hope." To which, several hundred pages later, the cynical Dr. Monygham answers: "No! . . . There is no peace and no rest in the development of material interests. They have their law, and their justice. But it is founded on expediency, and is inhuman; it is without rectitude, without the continuity and the force that can be found only in a moral principle. Mrs. Gould, the time approaches when all that the Gould Concession stands for shall weigh as heavily upon the people as the barbarism, cruelty, and misrule of a few years back."[13] Conrad was able to draw Charles Gould as a whole man, however doomed. To have reduced Gould to his concession would have made a mockery of the novel-ist's grasp of human beings, and the world. To have accepted Gould at his own evaluation would have been no less a travesty. It is this tension, this fullness of understanding, which I should like to see informing our history.

Moreover, we must attempt the much more difficult task of understanding, in all its fullness, the response to American imper-ialism of its far from passive victims. It might be wise, for example, to devote a portion of the scanty funds now available for training American scholars to be bicultural to the translation of significant Chinese works so that the much larger body of uni-lingual students in the field could begin to fight their way out of the slough of parochialism.

Lü Shih-ch'iang's study of the anti-Christian movement should be readily accessible to American students so that we may under-stand, in the greatest possible depth, the *dailiness* of the foreign impact on China.[14] Although Lü's book only goes up to 1874, his perspective, which stresses the political and military rather than the ideological nature of the conflict between Chinese officials and missionaries, is vital. We should have the most complete account-ing of all the missionary cases the Chinese government had to

13. Joseph Conrad, *Nostromo* (New York: New American Library, 1960), pp. 80, 406.

14. Lü Shih-ch'iang, *Chung-kuo kuan-shen fan-chiao ti yüan-yin, 1860–1874* (The cause of the anti-Christian movement among Chinese officials and gentry, 1860–1874; Taipei, Taiwan: Institute of Modern History, Academia Sinica, 1966).

handle, with some estimate of the time, energy, money, and political losses they involved.

It is difficult to think of any nineteenth-century American who did not regard China simply as an object to be manipulated—indeed it is rare enough to find such people even today. As historians of the period we must not fall into the same trap. Hampered as most of us are by the language and the sheer *alien* quality of the country, we must nevertheless try to create, with such secondary works as are available, our own active, living China. This involves a close attention to what is currently being written about China's internal development, alleviating our linguistic poverty by leaning hard on those who are not so impoverished. It also means reading the accounts of contemporary foreign residents of China, especially those sympathetic to its plight and therefore imaginative enough to offer unusual insights.

We need, for example, to look again at the greatest anti-Christian, anti-foreign riot of them all, the Boxer Rebellion. Most accounts focus on the manner in which the powers responded to this complex and confusing popular movement. The Chinese side is usually presented *en bloc* rather than as part of a process. With our invaluable American experience in the genesis of mass disturbances, we might want to look at some of the evidence again. George Lynch, author of an obscure account of the Boxer episode, asserts that in Peking it was a foreign riot.[15] According to Lynch, as soon as Boxers began to appear on the streets of Peking openly, they were captured, shot, and beaten by outraged foreigners. The magnitude of foreign hostility may itself account for the sympathetic attitude Lynch took toward the Boxers. "I have," Lynch wrote in 1901, "the utmost and most complete admiration for the leading motives which actuated the Boxers. If I were a Chinaman I would be a Boxer, and, as I view them, I think that 90% of the vigorous men who love their country . . . would share the ideas of the Boxers."[16] L. L. Seaman, President of the China Society of America, also understood this aspect of the rebellion. "I say," Seaman declared at a symposium on China in 1913, "without fear of contradiction by those who are familiar with that issue (and I was there), that that uprising was one of the most splendid exhibitions of patriotism witnessed in modern times."[17]

15. George Lynch, *The War of the Civilizations, Being a Record of a Foreign Devil's Experiences with the Allies in China* (London: Longmans Green & Co. 1901).

16. Ibid., p. 225.

17. Major L. L. Seaman, "A Plea for Fair Play and the Recognition of the Chinese Republic," *Journal of Race Development* 3 (January 1913), 287.

Neither Lynch nor Seaman saw much to praise in Boxer methods. Still, "the plain fact cannot be gainsaid, nor too strongly emphasized, that the essential motive of that propaganda was the freeing of the land from the hated foreigners, who, in current phrase, had 'robbed the people of their country.' "[18] If it will not do to wax romantic about the Boxers, it is equally unacceptable to make light of their authentic, violent effort to rid China of what they accurately perceived to be an overwhelming threat—the very person of the foreigner backed by state power.

Too often anti-American or anti-foreign attitudes in the Far East, Africa, or Latin America are discussed as if they were slightly pyschotic. We have yet, despite Fanon, to *absorb*, and thus be able to project, a sense of what it meant to be a Chinese set upon by foreign power in his own country. Some nineteenth-century observers were beginning to understand it and we must search out their comments and make good use of them. An official of the Imperial Maritime Customs Service, for example, wrote of his reaction to the vast cry of "Sha! Sha" (Kill! Kill!) coming toward him from a band of approaching Boxers: "It was not the fear of what they could do—most of them, in fact almost all, were armed only with swords; but it was our first dreadful peep into the depths of a Chinaman's heart, and we saw there the deadly, undying wild beast hate of the foreigner that we had barely guessed at before."[19] Amos P. Wilder, American Consul-General at Shanghai, is similarly perceptive. After stressing China's poverty, he praises the strength and capabilities of even the lowest coolie while simultaneously acknowledging a sense of vague uneasiness. "As four chair-bearers, perspiring, panting, yet exulting in their humble task—with no vision of higher employment—as they bear their white burden home luxuriously asleep, up steep inclines at better than four miles an hour, one has an uncomfortable feeling that all their labor may mean storage of power against some day when the law of compensation shall reverse conditions."[20]

18. Ibid.
19. Quoted in Lynch, p. 125.
20. Amos P. Wilder, "Conditions, Favorable and Otherwise, in China's Development," in George H. Blakeslee, ed., *China and the Far East* (New York: T. Y. Crowell & Co. 1910), p. 194.

The notes to this article clearly do not offer the student a comprehensive bibliography for the period. Before listing additional books I have found valuable, I would first urge the student to check such bibliographies as:

The section on foreign policy in "New Radical Historians in the Sixties," *Radical America*, 4.8–9 (November 1970), 92–97.

A history of guilt is as fruitless as a politics of guilt. We must try to discover the nature of China's active resistance to imperialism.

Richard H. Miller's extensive bibliography on the 1890's in *American Imperialism in 1898: The Quest for National Fulfillment* (New York: John Wiley & Sons, Inc., 1970), pp. 191–206.

The superb notes to Philip S. Foner's interesting review article, "Why the United States Went to War with Spain in 1898," *Science and Society* 32.1 (Winter 1968) 39–65.

On the issue of imperialism, I have found the following to be both readable and useful. (The list does not pretend to be complete.)

V. I. Lenin, *Imperialism, The Highest Stage of Capitalism* (New York: International Publishers, 1939).

James O'Connor, "The Meaning of Economic Imperialism," (Detroit: Radical Education Project, n.d.).

D. K. Fieldhouse, " 'Imperialism': A Historiographic Revision," *Economic History Review*, 2nd ser., 14.2 (1961).

John Gallagher and Ronald Robinson, "The Imperialism of Free Trade," *Economic History Review*, 2nd ser. 6.1 (1953).

Oliver MacDonagh, "The Anti-Imperialism of Free Trade," *Economic History Review*, 2nd ser. 14.3 (1962).

George Lichtheim, *Imperialism* (New York: Praeger 1971).

Bernard Semmel, *Imperialism and Social Reform* (Cambridge, Mass.: Harvard University Press, 1960).

S. M. Miller, Roy Bennett, and Cyril Alapatt, "Does the U.S. Economy Require Imperialism?" *Social Policy*, 1.3 (September-October 1970).

Harry Magdoff, "The Logic of Imperialism," *Social Policy*, 1.3 (September-October 1970).

Two useful anthologies should also be mentioned:

K. T. Fann and D. C. Hodges, eds., *Readings in U.S. Imperialism* (Boston: Porter Sargent, 1971).

George H. Nadel and Perry Curtis, eds., *Imperialism and Colonialism* (New York: Macmillan Co. 1964).

The best single volume treatment of American-Chinese relations is Warren I. Cohen's *America's Response to China* (New York: John Wiley, 1971). Students should also consult the relevant chapters of Akira Iriye's interpretive treatment of the whole course of American Far Eastern relations in *Across the Pacific* (New York: Harcourt, Brace and World, 1967).

Focusing on the period of the 1890's, I have found the following to be of particular value (the list is selective, but not random):

Howard K. Beale, *Theodore Roosevelt and the Rise of America to World Power* (Baltimore: Johns Hopkins Press, 1956).

William Braisted, *The United States Navy in the Pacific, 1897–1909* (Austin: University of Texas Press, 1958).

Albert Feuerwerker, "Handicraft and Manufactured Cotton Textiles in China, 1871–1910," *Journal of Economic History*, 30.2 (June 1970).

S. B. Gorelik, *Politka SShA v Man'chzhurii b 1898–1903 GG. I Doktrina "Otkrytkyh Dverei,"* (Policy of the USA in Manchuria, 1898–1903, and the Doctrine of "Open Doors"; Moscow, 1960).

Ralph W. and Muriel E. Hidy, *History of Standard Oil Company (New Jersey): Pioneering in Big Business, 1882–1911* (New York: Harper, 1955).

John Higham, *Strangers in the Land* (New Brunswick, N.J.: Rutgers University Press, 1955).

Through a full understanding both of America's thrust into Asia and of the obstacles it met there we may perhaps do what the Open Door was supposed to do: preserve China's integrity—and thereby contribute toward our own.

John S. Kelly, *A Forgotten Conference: The Negotiations at Peking, 1900–1901* (Geneva: E. Droz, 1962).

Andrew Malozemoff, *Russian Far Eastern Policy, 1881–1904* (Berkeley: University of California Press, 1958).

S. M. Meng, *The Tsungli Yamen: Its Origins and Functions* (Cambridge, Mass.: Harvard University Press, 1962).

H. B. Morse, *The International Relations of the Chinese Empire* (London: Longmans, Green and Co., 1910–1918).

Dana C. Munro, *American Commercial Interests in Manchuria* (Publication no. 654, American Academy of Political and Social Science, reprinted from the *Annals*, January 1912).

Rhodes Murphey, *The Treaty Ports and China's Modernization: What Went Wrong.* (Michigan Papers in Chinese Studies, no. 7, 1970).

William N. Neumann, "Ambiguity and Ambivalence in Ideas of National Interest in Asia," in *Isolation and Security*, Alexander De Conde, ed., (Durham, N.C.: Duke University Press, 1957).

Harvey Pressman, "Hay, Rockhill and China's Integrity: A Reappraisal," *Papers on China*, 13 (Harvard University, East Asian Research Center, 1959).

Victor Purcell, *The Boxer Uprising: A Background Study* (Cambridge, Eng.: Cambridge University Press, 1963).

John Schrecker, *Imperialism and Chinese Nationalism* (Cambridge, Mass.: Harvard University Press, 1971).

E-tu Zen Sun, *Chinese Railways and British Interests, 1898–1911* (New York: King's Crown Press, 1954).

C. C. Tan, *The Boxer Catastrophe* (New York: Columbia University Press, 1955).

Edmund S. Wehrle, *Britain, China and the Anti-Missionary Riots, 1891–1900* (Minneapolis: University of Minnesota Press, 1966).

L. K. Young, *British Policy in China, 1895–1902* (Oxford: Clarendon Press, 1970).

Edward Zabriskie, *American Russian Rivalry in the Far East, 1895–1914* (Philadelphia: University of Pennsylvania Press, 1946).

1901-1906

The half decade from September 1901, when Theodore Roosevelt entered the White House, to the spring of 1906, when China's anti-American boycott ended, witnessed many events that significantly changed the context of U.S.–East Asian relations. In China the boycott against American goods manifested the first stirring of that nationalist sentiment which was soon to overthrow the Ch'ing dynasty and was, in shrill tones, to demand for China something better than second-class citizenship in the international community. In Korea the monarchial regime entered its death throes as Japan moved in to establish a protectorate over the hapless Hermit Kingdom. For Japan the period was of transcendent importance. It brought the Anglo-Japanese Alliance, the successful turning back of the Russian advance in Korea and China, and the establishment of Japanese rights and interests on the continent, a development of great significance for future American–East Asian relations.

The importance of the 1901–1906 period is underscored by the extensive amount of attention that historians have given it. The literature is sufficiently large that no attempt will be made to examine all the periodical material. The primary focus will be on the published books and unpublished doctoral dissertations. The studies are all centered principally on one country rather than the East Asian area, so the survey that follows will take up in turn those relating to China, Korea, and Japan.

Two studies have been made of United States economic relations with China. Morton V. Malin's dissertation, "American Economic Interests in China, 1900–1908," was completed at the University of Maryland in 1954. It is largely a statistical analysis based on the reports of American consular officials, the Treasury Department, and the Department of Commerce and Labor. Trade journals were also consulted. Separate chapters cover such subjects as the cotton goods trade, the kerosene trade, and the tobacco trade. The other study is Barry Lee Knight's "American Trade and Investment in China, 1890–1910," a dissertation completed at Michigan State University in 1968. Knight comes to grips with the thesis expounded by William A. Williams, Thomas McCormick, and others that the

United States pursued imperialism through "informal empire." Basing his study on State Department records, periodicals, and newspapers, Knight tests the rhetoric of American expansionists against the reality of American involvement and achievement. He concludes that the China market was far more accurately identified by its limitations than by its potential. The American business community dealing with China had languid interest and small sales. These conditions resulted in a policy of moderate support for American interests by the government that was fully attuned to the nation's small economic stake.

Two works have analyzed American attitudes toward China in this period: Robert F. McClellan, Jr.'s *The Heathen Chinee: A Study of American Attitudes toward China, 1890–1905;*[1] and Paul A. Varg's *The Making of a Myth: The United States and China, 1897–1912.*[2] McClellan attempts to penetrate public thought through periodical literature, including weeklies, monthlies, and those publications designed to serve special interests. Not surprisingly, he finds American opinion ambivalent with a sympathetic interest in Chinese culture and a violent opposition to Chinese immigration. Varg's brief but perceptive book has chapters which alternate between those on diplomacy and those on nonofficial American attitudes toward China. Both types of chapter are more in the nature of essays than detailed narrative. In analyzing American images of China he draws especially on *The Journal of Commerce and Commercial Bulletin, The Review of Reviews, The Outlook,* and *The Missionary Review of the World.* The chapters on diplomacy emphasize particularly the evidence in the Department of State records and the papers of William W. Rockhill.

China's boycott against American goods in 1905–1906, which grew out of the immigration question, is treated in many studies. Anthony L. Milnar completed a dissertation at Georgetown University in 1949 entitled "Chinese-American Relations with Especial Reference to the Imposition of the Boycott, 1905–1906." It draws some material from the papers of Theodore Roosevelt, John Hay, Elihu Root, and William H. Taft, but more extensive use was made of the unpublished records of the Department of State. The preface states accurately that the account is constructed almost entirely from the day-to-day reports of diplomatic and consular officials. Milnar found that the boycott did no great damage to American trade, that on the contrary exports to China reached a peak in

1. Columbus: Ohio State University Press, 1970.
2. East Lansing: Michigan State University Press, 1968.

1905. He concluded that the boycott had more meaning for Chinese nationalism than for U.S.–China relations. This aspect of the question could not be pursued, however, for Milnar used few sources on the Chinese side other than English language newspapers published on the China coast.

Margaret Field also made a study of the Chinese boycott. It was based on material at Harvard University and was published as an article in *Papers on China*.[3] The principal sources were the State Department records, the papers of William W. Rockhill, the *Foochow Messenger*, the *North China Herald*, and two official publications of Chinese records, the *Ch'ing-chi wai-chiao shih liao* (Historical materials on foreign relations in the latter part of the Ch'ing dynasty)[4] and the *Kuang-hsu i-ssu-nien chiao-she yao-lan* (A digest of negotiations in the year 1905).[5] Field found that the boycott movement had no distinguishable organizational structure, that both Chinese merchants and students supported it, and that the Chinese government sympathized with it but avoided giving it overt support.

Howard K. Beale's treatment of U.S.–China relations in *Theodore Roosevelt and the Rise of America to World Power*[6] focuses in large part on the boycott-immigration problem. Beale did exhaustive research in the private papers of Roosevelt and his associates, though his use of the unpublished State Department records was less thorough. Like Milnar's work, it is written almost exclusively from the American side. It emphasizes the imperialist attitudes of the time and Roosevelt's resort to threats of military action. Beale was not sympathetic to the Roosevelt policy. He stated that Roosevelt could not deal effectively with the Chinese nationalist movement because his contempt for China's weakness made him unable to realize that it was nationalism with which he had to cope. Beale's unsympathetic attitude toward Roosevelt's China policy is also evident in his coverage of the controversy arising out of China's cancellation of the Canton-Hankow railway concession of the American China Development Company. The account emphasizes Roosevelt's role and particularly his belligerent attitude toward the Chinese. A more comprehensive account of this episode was published in an article by William R. Braisted in 1952.[7] It is based upon ex-

3. "The Chinese Boycott of 1905," *Papers on China*, 11 (Cambridge, Mass.: East Asian Research Center, Harvard University, 1957), 63–98.

4. Wang Hsi-yin, ed., Peking, 1932.

5. Foreign Affairs Bureau of the Office of the Commissioner for the Northern Ports, 1907.

6. Baltimore: Johns Hopkins Press, 1956.

7. William R. Braisted, "The United States and the American China Development Company," *Far Eastern Quarterly*, 11 (1951–1952), 147–165.

tensive research in the Department of State records as well as the Roosevelt papers.

The most recent study of the Chinese boycott was published in 1966 in Chinese by the Institute of Modern History of the Academia Sinica at Taipei. Under the sponsorship of that institution Chang Ts'un-wu wrote a detailed, dispassionate, and comprehensive study entitled *Chung Mei Kung-yueh Feng-ch'Ao* (Agitation concerning the Sino-American Labour Treaty of 1905). He draws principally on the archives of the Wai-wu pu, the American consular and diplomatic records, the Chinese press, and source materials published on the mainland since 1949. Chang views the boycott less as an incident in Sino-American relations and more as a Chinese nationalist movement, a prototype of the May Fourth movement.

U.S.–China relations are presently being studied from the American side by Delber L. McKee, a professor at Westminster College in Pennsylvania. The tentative title of his work is "The United States and China, 1900–1906: Chinese Exclusion (and Boycott) versus the Open Door Policy." In addition to research in the usual private papers and Department of State and legation records, McKee has utilized a rich source which has not hitherto been exploited: the "Segregated Chinese Records" of the Bureau of Immigration. McKee emphasizes the dichotomy of the American policy, which was made up of two basically incompatible elements. On the one hand, exclusion was supported by labor, the Californians, the Bureau of Immigration, and probably public opinion generally. On the other hand, the American Asiatic Association, the National Association of Manufacturers, church groups, and university heads sought to preserve an open door for trade, missionary activity, and cultural understanding.

Theodore Roosevelt's Korean policy has been examined in three doctoral dissertations, each of which has a wider scope than the Roosevelt period: Philip L. Bridgham, "American Policy toward Korean Independence, 1866–1910";[8] Dong Hoon Choi, "The United States Policy toward the Japanese Protectorate and Annexation of Korea, 1904–1910"[9] and Jongsuk Chay, "The United States and the Closing Door in Korea: American-Korean Relations, 1894–1905.[10]

Bridgham's work was based on the Department of State records and published sources. The papers of Theodore Roosevelt, Horace N. Allen (the minister at Seoul), and other important personages were not consulted, so the resulting study was not definitive. Bridg-

8. Medford, Mass.: Fletcher School of Law and Diplomacy, 1951.
9. Medford, Mass.: Fletcher School of Law and Diplomacy, 1965.
10. Ann Arbor: University of Michigan, 1965.

ham did come across some evidence in the Department of State records indicating that the Taft–Katsura agreed memorandum of July 27, 1905, might not have been a "secret pact" trading off Korea for a guarantee of the Philippines, as had been alleged by Tyler Dennett in an article in 1924.[11] Bridgham characterized the evidence as enigmatic and did not follow it up. Later I came across the same evidence, and further investigation led to the publication in 1959 of an article on the Taft-Katsura conversation.[12]

Dong Hoon Choi's study of the 1904–1910 period was based upon a wider range of research materials than Bridgham's work. In addition to the official American records, he consulted the papers of Horace N. Allen, Theodore Roosevelt, John Hay, and Philander Knox. The author also drew upon Methodist and Presbyterian missionary correspondence. He concluded that Roosevelt's balance of power concept was the most important determinate of American policy. He observed, however, that Roosevelt had little choice but to let the Japanese take over Korea because of the power of the Anglo-Japanese Alliance. Added to such considerations of power politics was the Korean emperor's negative attitude and unwillingness to carry out reforms. "Of central importance in this episode," says Choi, "is the failure on the part of Korea to reform and modernize in response to the forces of the west." (p. 158)

Jongsuk Chay's dissertation covering the years 1894–1905 draws on a still wider area of source material. On the Roosevelt period the author researched in the official United States records and in the private papers of John Hay, George Kennan, William W. Rockhill, Theodore Roosevelt, Elihu Root, and William H. Taft. The Japanese records were also consulted, including the *Nihon Gaikō Bunsho,*[13] the Foreign Ministry archives microfilm at the Library of Congress, and a microfilm collection at the Hoover Institution on "Japanese Penetration of Korea, 1894–1910." The focus of the study, like those of Bridgham and Choi, is on diplomatic relations. Commercial and cultural aspects are noted only when they have bearing upon the diplomatic side. Chay's interpretation and conclusions are sim-

11. Tyler Dennett, "President Roosevelt's Secret Pact with Japan," *Current History,* 21 (1924–1925), 15–21.

12. Raymond A. Esthus, "The Taft-Katsura Agreement—Reality or Myth," *Journal of Modern History,* 31 (1959), 46–51. The Taft-Katsura conversation is also discussed in Ralph E. Minger, "Taft's Missions to Japan: A Study in Personal Diplomacy," *Pacific Historical Review,* 30 (1961), 279–294, and in Jongsuk Chay, "The Taft-Katsura Memorandum Reconsidered," *Pacific Historical Review,* 37 (1968), 321–326.

13. Japan, Gaimushō, *Nihon Gaikō Bunsho: Meiji Nenkan* (Japanese Diplomatic Documents: Meiji Period), 84 vols. to date (Tokyo: Nihon Kokusai Rengō Kyōkai, 1923–).

ilar to those of Choi. Balance of power considerations, *Realpolitik*, and the corruption of the Korean government loomed large in the determination of American policy. The principal shortcoming of Chay's study is the sketchy coverage of the Russo-Japanese War period.

An examination of the published works dealing with Roosevelt's Korean policy, as well as the unpublished studies, indicates that a definitive study remains to be done. Fred Harvey Harrington's well known *God, Mammon and the Japanese: Dr. Horace N. Allen and Korean-American Relations, 1884–1905*[14] is, as the title indicates, focused sharply on Allen. Only two chapters are devoted to the Roosevelt period, and they tell far more about Allen than about Roosevelt. The story is drawn largely from the official records and the Allen papers. The Rockhill papers were also used, but the Roosevelt and Hay papers were not consulted. My own study, *Theodore Roosevelt and Japan*,[15] has only one chapter on the Korean question. It is drawn principally from the Japanese and American official records and from the papers of Roosevelt, Rockhill, Willard Straight, and George Kennan. The recently published book by Eugene P. Trani, *The Treaty of Portsmouth: An Adventure in American diplomacy*,[16] based upon essentially the same sources, likewise deals only briefly with Roosevelt's Korean policy. When a definitive work on Roosevelt's Korean policy is undertaken, the researcher will have to be prepared to work not only in American records but also in both Japanese and Korean sources. It will be a formidable task, for the Japanese Foreign Ministry telegraphic records on the Russo-Japanese War period alone amount to over 43,000 pages. British Foreign Office records at the Public Record Office in London will need to be consulted also.

Japanese-American relations during the earlier years of the Roosevelt administration have received more attention among scholars than have Sino-American relations and Korean-American relations. The earliest work of note was Tyler Dennett's *Roosevelt and the Russo-Japanese War*.[17] Dennett used only one unpublished source: the Roosevelt papers at the Library of Congress. And in that collection he used only the letters which happened to be filed in a special folder labeled "Russo-Japanese War." Dennett missed one source of great significance, which was available in published form, the Russian records of the Portsmouth Peace Conference. In 1906

14. Madison: University of Wisconsin Press, 1944, reprinted 1961.
15. Seattle: University of Washington Press, 1966.
16. Lexington: University of Kentucky Press, 1969.
17. Garden City, N.Y.: Doubleday, Page & Co., 1925.

the Russian government published the telegrams exchanged between St. Petersburg and the Russian delegation at the peace conference.[18] The existence of this publication was apparently not generally known in the United States. President Roosevelt, who would have been greatly interested in it, never knew of it. As late as the 1950's only one copy existed in the United States, a photostatic reproduction at the New York Public Library. Recently it was microfilmed, and a few scholars and libraries now have copies.

Three years after the appearance of Dennett's work, A. L. P. Dennis published his *Adventures in American Diplomacy, 1896–1906*.[19] Dennis devoted two chapters to Roosevelt and the Far East. He drew heavily upon Dennett's work, but took his own research beyond that of Dennett. He researched in the unpublished Department of State records and the papers of John Hay. He also drew much material from the German documents in *Die grosse Politik*.[20]

Ten years after Dennis's book appeared, Payson J. Treat published the third volume of *Diplomatic Relations between the United States and Japan*. This final volume covered the period 1895–1905.[21] In character it is quite different from the studies of Dennett and Dennis. Treat stated in his preface that the purpose of the book was to make available hitherto unpublished materials in the American diplomatic correspondence. He therefore incorporated liberal extracts of the documents, thus making the book a catalog of dispatches, instructions, and notes. He does add some perceptive comments, however, so the study is more than just a convenient reference work. He attempted to examine every question that had been a subject of diplomatic discussion between the United States and Japan, and he thus gives all the tedious diplomatic exchanges on such matters as the whiskey case, perpetual leases, fur seals, the duty on tea, insurance deposits, the tobacco monopoly, copyright matters, salmon poaching, and so forth.

In the same year that Treat's book appeared, A. Whitney Gris-

18. Russia, Ministerstovo inostrannykh del, *Sbornik diplomaticheskikh dokumentov kasaiushchikhsia perogorvorov mezhdu Rossiei i Iaponiei o zakliuchenii mirnogo dogovora, 24 maia-3 oktiabria 1905* (Collection of Diplomatic Documents Concerning Negotiations between Russia and Japan on the Conclusion of Peace Treaty, May 24–October 3, 1905; St. Petersburg: Ministry of Foreign Affairs, 1906).

19. New York: E. P. Dutton & Co., 1928.

20. Germany, Auswärtiges Amt, *Die grosse Politik der europäischen Kabinette, 1871-1914*, 40 vols. (Berlin: Deutsche verlagsgesellschaft für politik und geschichte, 1922–1927).

21. Stanford: Stanford University Press, 1938.

wold published *The Far Eastern Policy of the United States*.[22] Apart from a separate chapter on the immigration question, Griswold gave only one chapter to Roosevelt's Far Eastern policy. That chapter is devoted primarily to Roosevelt's policy toward Japan, and it has two characteristics which distinguish it from previous interpretations. He attempts to destroy the myth of an Anglo-American cooperative policy in East Asia, and he portrays Roosevelt as a somewhat dull-witted dupe of the German kaiser in the diplomacy of the Russo-Japanese War. Not surprisingly, these and other interpretations of Griswold have been at least partially modified by investigations of later scholars. Griswold undertook to survey four decades and of necessity had to base large sections of his study on secondary sources rather than on original research. In the chapter on Roosevelt he cites the papers of Roosevelt, Rockhill, and Knox, but the bulk of the material is from published sources. Among the published sources, he relied heavily on the diplomatic records of Britain, France, Germany, and Russia.[23]

Almost three decades passed before the story as told by Griswold and his predecessors was significantly revised, though some articles relating to the Russo-Japanese War were published in the interim. Winston B. Thorson published two articles on American public opinion and the Russo-Japanese War. The first, which appeared in 1944, surveyed editorial opinion in the Pacific northwest.[24] The second, published in 1948, analyzed editorial opinion throughout the country concerning the Portsmouth Peace Conference.[25] Thorson found that despite the claims of the Russian delegation to the contrary, there was no significant change in American public opinion, that it was pro-Japanese during the war and remained so during the peace conference.

Two years after Thorson's second article appeared, Robert K. Godwin published an article on Russia and the Portsmouth con-

22. New York: Harcourt, Brace & World, Inc., 1938; reprinted New Haven: Yale University Press, 1962.

23. G. P. Gooch and Harold Temperly, eds., *British Documents on the Origins of the War, 1898–1914,* 11 vols. (London: His Majesty's Stationery Office, 1926–1938); France, Ministère des Affaires Étrangères, *Documents diplomatiques français (1871–1914),* 41 vols. (Paris: Imprimerie National, 1929–1959); Germany, Auswärtiges Amt, *Die grosse Politik der europäischen Kabinette, 1871–1914,* 40 vols. (Berlin: Deutsche verlagsgesellschaft für politik und geschichte, 1922–1927); Russia, *Krasnyi Arkhiv,* 106 *vols.* (Moscow: Gospolitizdat, 1922–1941).

24. Winston B. Thorson, "Pacific Northwest Opinion on the Russo-Japanese War of 1904–1905," *Pacific Northwest Quarterly,* 35 (1944), 305–322.

25. Thorson, "American Public Opinion and the Portsmouth Peace Conference," *American Historical Review,* 53 (1947–1948), 439–464.

ference.[26] Like those who preceded him, Godwin did not use the key Russian records of the Portsmouth negotiations, which the St. Petersburg government had published in 1906, the *Sbornik diplomaticheskikh dokumentov kasaiushchikhsia perogovorov mezhdu Rossiei i Iaponiei o zakliuchenii mirnogo dogovora, 24 maia–3 oktiabria 1905* (Collection of Diplomatic Documents Concerning Negotiations between Russia and Japan on the Conclusion of Peace Treaty, May 24–October 3, 1905). He did nevertheless give some new insights into Serge Witte's role basing his account on some Witte telegrams in the *Krasnyi Arkhiv* which were drawn from the papers of the Russian finance minister, V. N. Kokovtsov.[27] Still more was learned of the Russian side during the war when Ernest R. May published a note in 1957 analyzing revelations in Aleksandr Semenovich Dobrov's study of U.S. Far Eastern policy in the early twentieth century.[28] May found especially significant the material that Dobrov cites from the correspondence between St. Petersburg and Ambassador Arturo Cassini, the Russian representative at Washington. This new information relates to the period February 1902–March 1905. Dobrov rushes over the subsequent period to September 1905 and thus gives nothing new relating to the arrangements for the peace conference or the negotiations at Portsmouth.

A comprehensive rewriting of Roosevelt's role in the Russo-Japanese War came in the 1960's. Between 1964 and 1969 three books were published on the diplomacy of the war. The first to appear was John A. White's *The Diplomacy of the Russo-Japanese War.*[29] For students of U.S. foreign policy, however, White's study was inadequate, for he did not research in the important sources on the American side such as the papers of Roosevelt and Hay and the Department of State records. His study did reveal much on the Japanese and Russian sides, though he did not use the *Sbornik diplomaticheskikh dokumentov.* He used many Japanese records not previously exploited, including the Foreign Ministry's published documents (the *Nihon Gaikō Bunsho*) and the record of Foreign Minister Jūtarō Komura's diplomacy which was also published by

26. Robert K. Godwin, "Russia and the Portsmouth Peace Conference," *American Slavic and East European Review,* 9 (1950), 279–291.

27. "Portsmouth Correspondence of S. Y. Witte and Others," *Krasnyi Arkhiv,* VI, 3–47.

28. Ernest R. May, "The Far Eastern Policy of the United States in the Period of the Russo-Japanese War: A Russian View," *American Historical Review,* 62 (1956–1957), 345-351; Aleksandr Semenovich Dobrov, *Dal'nevostochnaia politika SShA v period Russko-iaponskoi voiny* (The Far Eastern policy of the United States in the period of the Russo-Japanese war; Moscow: Gosudarstvennoe izdatel'stvo politicheskoi literatury, 1952).

29. Princeton: Princeton University Press, 1964.

the Gaimushō (the *Komura Gaikōshi*).[30] White also used the records of Japan's special envoy in the United States during the war, Baron Kentarō Kaneko.[31]

The two other books dealing with the diplomacy of the Russo-Japanese War are written primarily from the American side, though Japanese and Russian records were used. My own work on *Theodore Roosevelt and Japan*,[32] published in 1966, contained five chapters on Roosevelt's role in the diplomacy of the war and the peace conference. Three years after that study appeared, Eugene P, Trani published *The Treaty of Portsmouth: An Adventure in American Diplomacy*.[33] These two books can conveniently be discussed together since they draw upon essentially the same sources and give similar interpretations. On the American side the principal sources are the private papers of Roosevelt, Hay, Taft, Rockhill, Kennan, George von Lengerke Meyer, Whitelaw Reid, Henry White, and the Department of State records. Of the private papers those of Roosevelt and Hay are most important. Next in value are the papers of Meyer, who was ambassador at St. Petersburg in 1905. Least fruitful are the Griscom papers, even though he was minister at Tokyo. The official papers are valuable on the diplomacy of the war but reveal little about the peace conference. On the Japanese side the most valuable sources used are the Telegram Series of the Foreign Ministry records (on microfilm at the Library of Congress) and the *Komura Gaikōshi*. The most valuable Russian source is the collection of documents on the Portsmouth conference which the Russian government published in 1906, the *Sbornik diplomaticheskikh dokumentov*. It makes clear that Roosevelt's principal contribution to the success of the peace conference was that his various appeals to Russia kept the conference going despite the repeated orders of the tsar to break off the negotiations. It also revealed that Witte's own determination to make peace—despite the counterorders of the tsar—and Japan's desperation for peace were more crucial to the success of the conference than any arguments advanced by Roosevelt in his appeals.

The foregoing works on the diplomacy of the Russo-Japanese War do not deal extensively with decision making on the Japanese side,

30. Japan, Gaimushō, *Komura Gaikōshi* (Komura's diplomacy), 2 vols. (Tokyo: Gaimushō, 1953).

31. Kentarō Kaneko, *Beikoku Daitōryō Kaiken Shimatsu* (Interviews with the President of the United States), Foreign Office manuscript, July 9, 1907, and *Nichiro Seneki Beikoku Tairyuki* (Record of sojourn in the United States during the Russo-Japanese war), Foreign Office manuscript, December, 26, 1906.

32. Seattle: University of Washington Press, 1966.

33. Lexington: University of Kentucky Press, 1969.

but that gap is now filled by Shumpei Okamoto's *The Japanese Oligarchy and the Russo-Japanese War*.[34] Okamoto does not recount the diplomacy of the war. He focuses instead on decision making at the most crucial stages of the events preceding the war and of the negotiations ending the war. He draws upon a tremendous quantity of Japanese official records, memoirs, biographies, special studies, articles, and newspapers. The decisions during the prewar negotiations with Russia are analyzed in detail. Wartime decisions relating to diplomacy are dealt with only briefly, but the Japanese context of wartime decision making is given extensive treatment. Okamoto examines the attitudes of the Tairo Dōshikai (Anti-Russian Comrades's Society), the press, the political parties, the Diet, business circles, antiwar activists, and the general public. Once the account moves to the negotiations to end the war, the focus returns to the Genro leadership. Policy decisions relating to the opening of negotiations are discussed at length. On the Portsmouth conference period detailed analysis is given only of the discussions in the crucial last minute negotiations over the indemnity and the cession of Sakhalin. The study ends with two extensive chapters on the anti-peace treaty movement and the Hibiya Park riot.

Okamoto gives the oligarchy high marks. It was capable, cautious, flexible, and realistic. The Genro provided a pillar of unity. The study reveals at the same time that within that circle of unity there was great diversity, both in personalities and opinions. Okamoto has mined the evidence so thoroughly that the contrasting views and attitudes among Japanese leaders come into sharp focus. Our understanding of the diplomacy of the war, including America's role in it, is greatly enhanced by this study of Japan's decision making.

So much work has been done by historians on the 1901–1906 period that it is not easy to suggest additional topics that might be fruitfully pursued at present. In so far as opportunities exist for further studies within the traditional concept of diplomatic relations, U.S.–Korean relations is perhaps the topic most deserving of additional study. An evaluation of what might be done on U.S.–China relations can best be postponed until Professor McKee's study appears. Some topics of a conventional nature which might be investigated are: the role of American advisers like Henry W. Denison and Durham Stevens in Japanese foreign affairs, and the influence of business interests and economic considerations upon decision making at Washington.

34. New York: Columbia University Press, 1970.

For the immediate future the best opportunities for historical investigation lie in the fields of economic and cultural relations defined in their broadest sense. The nonofficial relations between the American people and the peoples of East Asia have hardly been touched on in existing studies. This type of history is, however, more difficult to write than conventional studies, both in terms of finding source material and evaluating it accurately and fairly. When the government policy makers and the influences felt directly by them are studied, there is a definable body of source material which several historians can examine and engage in fruitful debate over. But once the historian moves into the broader area of relations between peoples, the reservoir of source material becomes almost limitless. Every letter of a missionary, every record of an American business establishment in East Asia, every document in a consular archive becomes evidence. This dictates that historians of the future who embark upon studies of economic and cultural relations will face a much more challenging task than that perceived by their predecessors.

1906-1913

In the 1920's historians began to recognize that the years 1906–1913 brought an important transformation in American East Asian policy. Theodore Roosevelt's successor had, quite unexpectedly, adopted a more aggressive policy in China and Manchuria, creating serious complications with the great powers. Tyler Dennett sensed the change more clearly than most other writers in this decade. He judged the diplomacy of Taft and Knox to be a "naive and simple" attempt to pursue a unilateral course in East Asia, one which repudiated Roosevelt's policy of cooperation with the European powers and his commitment of American power to stability in East Asia. According to Dennett, Knox thought "that the question of Manchuria in 1910 could be segregated from world politics and treated as though it were an abstract question of right and wrong."[1]

In the thirties diplomatic historians looked more thoroughly into the nature of this shift in American East Asian policy. They examined Theodore Roosevelt's withdrawal from East Asia during his last years in office and condemned the efforts of Taft and Knox to strengthen the Open Door in China and Manchuria. Some thought the motives of Taft and Knox were both economic and political, that their policy was, as Henry F. Pringle phrased it, "a forced and unhappy marriage between commercialism and idealism."[2] Others, like A. Whitney Griswold, claimed that the hard core of this policy was economic. Griswold saw the Taft-Knox policy as another high point in the cycle of advance and retreat in East Asia. He disapproved of their bold but foolish challenge to Japan, based as it was upon a shallow knowledge of international politics and a serious misreading of the nation's interests in the Orient. Samuel Flagg Bemis agreed. Encouraged by Roosevelt's disengagement from China, Bemis could only deplore the clumsy blunders of Taft and Knox.[3]

1. Tyler Dennett, *Roosevelt and the Russo-Japanese War* (New York: Doubleday, Page and Company, 1925), pp. 320, 335.
2. Henry F. Pringle, *The Life and Times of William Howard Taft*, 2 vols. (New York: Farrar and Rinehart, 1939), I, 686.
3. A. Whitney Griswold, *The Far Eastern Policy of the United States* (New York: Harcourt, Brace and Company, 1938), p. 146. Griswold displayed

Since the thirties historians have disputed some of Griswold's conclusions about Roosevelt's withdrawal from East Asia and have greatly expanded our knowledge of his diplomacy during the Japanese-American crisis of 1906–1909.[4] Some have viewed American policy after 1909 as motivated by both a concern for the integrity of China and a desire for economic expansion; others have continued to emphasize the economic dimension of American East Asian policy. Foster Rhea Dulles, in *America's Rise to World Power*, concludes that Taft and Knox, in contrast to Roosevelt, "tended to interpret the national interest almost exclusively in terms of the interests of the business community." Charles Vevier, in an important monograph on *The United States and China*, claims that "without its verbiage and pretensions of political realism, the China policy of the Taft administration was a shopkeeper diplomacy. Its proponents were aware of swelling inventories at home and mindful of commercial competition in China. They viewed China as a potential customer for American-made goods and demanded that policy be shaped to further this end."[5]

Other recent studies—published and unpublished—have attempted to place the break between the policies of Roosevelt and Taft in a larger context and to explain in more depth the motivations of both men and their advisers. We now have a more subtle understanding of Roosevelt's concept of American interests in China and of the way in which he transformed that concept into policy.

---

originality and clarity in his interpretation of the Root-Takahira Agreement; Samuel Flagg Bemis, *A Diplomatic History of the United States* (New York: Holt, Rhinehart and Winston, 1936), pp. 497–498.

4. Many historians now feel that Griswold read too much into the Root-Takahira Agreement, overemphasizing Roosevelt's disengagement from East Asia. See, for example, Richard W. Leopold, *The Growth of American Foreign Policy: A History* (New York: Alfred A. Knopf, 1962), pp. 275–276, Alexander DeConde, *A History of American Foreign Policy* (New York: Charles Scribner's Sons, 1963), p. 373, and Raymond A. Esthus, "The Changing Concept of the Open Door, 1899–1910," *Mississippi Valley Historical Review*, 46 (December 1959), 448–451, and *Theodore Roosevelt and Japan* (Seattle: University of Washington Press, 1966), pp. 285–286. I state my own position in "Theodore Roosevelt and American Involvement in the Far East, 1901–1909," *Pacific Historical Review*, 35 (November 1966), 433–449, and *An Uncertain Friendship: Theodore Roosevelt and Japan, 1906–1909* (Cambridge, Mass.: Harvard University Press, 1967), pp. 277–284. Though Griswold overdramatized the shift and erred on many details, he caught the essential thrust of Roosevelt's policy during his last three years in office; the most recent studies of Japanese-American relations in this period are Esthus, *Theodore Roosevelt and Japan*, and Neu, *An Uncertain Friendship*.

5. Foster Rhea Dulles, *America's Rise to World Power, 1898–1954* (New York: Harper & Row, 1954), p. 79; Charles Vevier, *The United States and China, 1906–1913: A Study of Finance and Diplomacy* (New Brunswick: Rutgers University Press, 1955), p. 214.

In the case of Taft and Knox, recent scholarship, though inconclusive, suggests that their aims were broader and less concrete than historians have previously indicated.[6] With the coming of the Taft administration, as Akira Iriye notes, "one may date the beginning of a moralistic diplomacy in East Asia."[7] If this is so, then the years 1909–1913 mark a major watershed in the history of American–East Asian relations, one which historians have only begun to comprehend.

The Taft administration's concern over China was a sudden and puzzling development. During their first year in office Taft and Knox demanded the admittance of American financiers into the Hukuang railway loan and also proposed the neutralization of Manchurian railways. The latter plan, which had far-reaching implications for the Japanese and Russian spheres in that region, was an abrupt reversal of Roosevelt's policy toward East Asia. Roosevelt had little sympathy with China and no sense that China's fate involved America's vital interests. Japan, now a great Asian power, seemed a far more immediate problem. In the years following the Russo-Japanese war Roosevelt surmounted many difficulties to achieve an accommodation with that nation. The United States, in effect, recognized Japan's predominance in southern Manchuria, while Japan agreed to control emigration to the United States. Roosevelt's determination to maintain cordial relations with Japan ran so deep that he was willing to see Japan's expansionist thrust absorbed on the mainland of Asia, where there was little risk of serious friction with the United States. It was Japan's task, not America's, to lead China along the road to modernization. Though events after 1905 shook Roosevelt's confidence in Japan, upon leaving office he still believed that Japan would fulfill that respon-

6. For Roosevelt we have books by Esthus and myself, as well as Howard K. Beale's *Theodore Roosevelt and the Rise of America to World Power* (Baltimore: Johns Hopkins Press, 1956), John Morton Blum's *The Republican Roosevelt* (Cambridge, Mass.: Harvard University Press, 1954), William H. Harbaugh's *Power and Responsibility: The Life and Times of Theodore Roosevelt* (New York: Farrar, Straus and Cudahy, 1961), and G. Wallace Chessman's *Theodore Roosevelt and the Politics of Power* (Boston: Little, Brown and Company, 1969); for Taft and Knox the most recent analysis of policy is Walter V. and Marie V. Scholes, *The Foreign Policies of the Taft Administration* (Columbia: University of Missouri Press, 1970), but the best is still Paige Elliott Mulhollan, "Philander C. Knox and Dollar Diplomacy, 1909–1913" (Ph.D. diss., University of Texas, 1966). Akira Iriye's *Across the Pacific: An Inner History of American-East Asian Relations* (New York: Harcourt, Brace and World, 1967) places American policy in a broad comparative perspective, and William L. Neumann's *America Encounters Japan: From Perry to MacArthur* (Baltimore: Johns Hopkins Press, 1963) attempts, with limited success, to trace the evolution of American attitudes.

7. Iriye, *Across the Pacific*, p. 122.

sibility wisely. Immigration and racial tensions, not Japanese expansionism, endangered Japanese-American friendship, and Roosevelt subordinated the vague American stake in China to the control of those explosive issues.[8]

Taft had played an important role in the execution of Roosevelt's East Asian policy. In four trips to Japan he had acquired a first-hand impression of that nation's leaders, and in July 1905 and later in October 1907 he engaged in significant conversations with Japanese statesmen. Throughout the Japanese-American crisis of 1906–1909 Taft seemed less suspicious of Japan than either Roosevelt or Elihu Root. Even before 1909, however, a certain dichotomy appeared in Taft's thought. While loyal to the President's goal of friendship with Japan, his sympathy for China surpassed Roosevelt's, as did his estimate of America's interests there. After visiting China in October 1907 Taft warned Root that "there seems to be a general impression that Japan is determined to secure some undue privileges in China . . . It is quite possible that you will have to assert with considerable stiffness the determination of America to insist on the Open Door policy and not to allow it to be set aside by underhanded methods." In March 1908 Taft sided with those within the administration who favored keeping the battle fleet in the Pacific.[9] The seeds of a different policy were present if only the proper context emerged.

Many forces converged after 1909 to impel the President toward a different course in East Asia. Within the State Department a group of energetic, restless young men wanted to make the Open Door policy a reality. They had been drawn to careers in diplomacy primarily because life in America seemed stale and flat in comparison with the opportunities for adventure in exotic lands. Foreign experience was one way to grapple with that fear of remoteness from real life which affected so many Americans in the early years of this century.[10] Led by Francis M. Huntington Wilson and Willard Straight, they scorned the cautious, skeptical diplomacy of an older generation and conceived bold plans to challenge the status quo in China and Manchuria. They were moved by a variety of considera-

8. These points are developed in much greater detail in Neu, *An Uncertain Friendship*, pp. 6–19, 259–290, 318–319, and Iriye, *Across the Pacific*, pp. 106–110.

9. Taft to Root, October 10, 1907, quoted in Neu, *An Uncertain Friendship*, p. 154; ibid, p. 226.

10. A partial list would include: Lewis Einstein, Henry Fletcher, Francis M. Huntington Wilson, William Phillips, and Willard Straight; Christopher Lasch makes some fascinating comments on this generation's search for experience in *The New Radicalism in America (1889–1963): The Intellectual as a Social Type* (New York: Alfred A. Knopf, 1965), pp. 13, 100–101.

tions—a strong aversion to Japanese culture and policy, a belief in the need for American economic expansion, and, most important, an almost mystical faith in the importance of China. Willard Straight embodied many of these motivations. "In some not very definable way," Herbert Croly writes, "China appealed to his [Straight's] visual and his moral imagination as a world in which there were vast and entrancing vistas to be explored and in which an adventurous spirit without money or position might build marble palaces and shimmering skyscrapers." Straight had, in other words, a "prophetic vision that the frontier of America had crossed the Pacific."[11] A lonely and restless youth, he dreamed of great exploits and at Cornell absorbed the poems of Rudyard Kipling and developed a compelling fascination with China. Upon graduation, Straight entered the Chinese Imperial Maritime Customs Service in search of fame and adventure. He saw himself as the potential Cecil Rhodes of China, a bearer of civilization and progress.[12]

Men with this sort of mission were hard to resist, particularly because of organizational changes in American foreign policy which heightened their influence. Under Roosevelt the President and Secretary of State dominated the decision-making process. Drawing upon a wide range of personal contacts, Roosevelt secured more information from private correspondence than from official dispatches. By 1908, however, this was beginning to change. Prodded by Huntington Wilson, Root in 1908 set up the first of the State Department's geographical divisions, the Division of Far Eastern Affairs. Knox was far more ambitious, instituting an important reorganization which brought three more geographical divisions and a substantial expansion of the State Department's staff.[13] Though we know little about the functioning of these geographical divisions for this or later periods, they did provide an opportunity for policy to move upward from lower bureaucratic levels.

Roosevelt and Root resisted the pressure for a more vigorous East Asian policy because of the strength of their own alternative vision of American–East Asian relations. But the new President was more vulnerable to initiatives from below, as was his secretary of

11. Herbert Croly, *Willard Straight* (New York: The Macmillan Company, 1925), pp. 54, 116.

12. There is interesting biographical information on Straight in Helen Dodson Kahn's "The Great Game of Empire: Willard D. Straight and American Far Eastern Policy" (Ph.D. diss., Cornell University, 1968), pp. 1–13. The general theme of this dissertation—that the goals of American East Asian policy remained unchanged from Roosevelt through Wilson—is unconvincing.

13. Graham H. Stuart, *The Department of State: A History of its Organization, Procedure and Personnel* (New York: The Macmillan Company, 1949), pp. 206–207, 212–215.

state, Philander C. Knox. Taft had been a loyal adviser, dazzled by Roosevelt's intellectual range and quickness, who had never comprehended the full implications of his chief's policy. Without much reflection, he willingly aided in its implementation, glad to be free of the burdens of decision. When Taft was President his lack of confidence combined with the growth of a foreign policy bureaucracy gave subordinates much influence in the formulation of East Asian policy.[14]

Taft, Knox, and State Department professionals seemed to share certain general beliefs about international affairs, which spread among Americans after the turn of the century.[15] Increasing numbers of Americans had become convinced of the decency of modern, civilized man and of the steady improvement of the world. As civilization developed, war would become less likely because the democratization of societies would increase the influence of the people. As backward areas were gradually assimilated into the mainstream of Western civilization, the primary source of international conflict would disappear. Most men agreed with Norman Angell about the futility of war among civilized powers and the world-wide trend toward interdependence and cooperation.[16] There was a tendency to place less emphasis on the role of force and more on a coalescence of mankind into one pacific, international community. In the years 1900–1913 no American statesman escaped the influence of some of these ideas and all thought in terms of creating stability and regularity in international life.

Beyond these common goals, however, the assumptions of Roosevelt, for example, differed greatly from those of Woodrow Wilson. Roosevelt was fascinated with the exercise of power and convinced that conflicting national passions would continue to be an important element in international relations. Wilson became the spokesman for a new era of international life dominated by the desire for a community of power rather than a balance of power. He epitomized

14. Taft's weaknesses as a leader are discussed in: Pringle, *Taft*, I, 339, 367, 399–401, II, 760–761; George E. Mowry, *The Era of Theodore Roosevelt, 1900–1912* (New York: Harper and Row, 1958), pp. 227–236; and Neu, *An Uncertain Friendship,* pp. 15–16.

15. These changes are perceptively discussed in: Henry F. May, *The End of American Innocence: A Study of the First Years of Our Own Time, 1912–1917* (New York: Alfred A. Knopf, 1959), pp. 9–29, 361; Robert Endicott Osgood, *Ideals and Self-Interest in America's Foreign Relations: The Great Transformation of the Twentieth Century* (Chicago: University of Chicago Press, 1953), pp. 71–107; and Robert H. Wiebe, *The Search for Order, 1877–1920* (New York: Hill and Wang, 1967), pp. 235–238.

16. Angell's influential book, *The Great Illusion* (New York: G. P. Putnam's Sons, 1910), elaborated many of these assumptions.

what Robert H. Wiebe describes as the "misty extension of ideas that informed progressivism at home" to world affairs. Wiebe suggests that it was only after 1913 that men in high office accepted these ideas, but one might argue that the shift came in 1909, not 1913, and that the strong strain of idealism in the politics of Taft and Knox pointed more toward the future than the past.[17]

Both men realized that the United States was a world power with heavy responsibilities for the advancement of Anglo-Saxon civilization. As Taft put it, the United States must do its part "in keeping the house of the world in order," and in using its great wealth and power to help weaker, unfortunate nations along the path of progress.[18] The United States, "in the van of Christian civilization," was already performing a "great missionary work" in the Philippines, and in a 1908 address Taft implied that the United States might have a similar role to play in China, which was finally "rousing itself from its sleep of centuries."[19] The President and his secretary of state felt an obligation to employ American power and prestige for humanity's benefit, particularly in Latin America and East Asia. Like Roosevelt, their preeminent concern was the maintenance of stability in the Caribbean and Central America. Taft and Knox devoted far more attention to this task than to any other foreign policy objective. In contrast to Roosevelt, however, they had an intense interest in East Asia but little in Europe. Roosevelt had much insight into the tensions among the great European powers and an acute realization of America's stake in the preservation of the European balance of power. Taft and Knox lacked this consciousness of Europe and went out of their way during pre-war crises concerning Morocco, the Balkans, and Turkey to declare the disinterestedness of the United States.[20] Their idealistic conception of America's mission in backward areas excluded any appreciation of traditional balance of power politics. Both felt that the old, brutal type of world order was passing away. They believed the

17. Wiebe, *The Search for Order,* p. 237.

18. "McKinley and Expansion," address at Cleveland, Ohio, January 29, 1908. Taft expressed this sense of mission with great force in a speech on December 3, 1909, at a mass meeting celebrating the diamond jubilee of the Methodist Episcopal missions in Africa. *Presidential Addresses and State Papers of William Howard Taft* (New York: Doubleday, Page and Company, 1910), pp. 504–505.

19. Address on the ratification of the pending treaties for unlimited arbitration with Great Britain and France, at Denver, Colorado, October 3, 1911; speech of acceptance at Cincinnati, Ohio, July 28, 1908; "McKinley and Expansion," January 29, 1908.

20. William C. Askew and J. Fred Rippy, "The United States and Europe's Strife, 1908–1913," *Journal of Politics,* 4 (February 1942), 68–79.

world was becoming smaller and perceived a growing harmony among nations. Knox foresaw an international federation in which the strong would help the weak and corporate righteousness would destroy injustice. Taft argued that the movement toward interdependence would one day lead to a situation in which all powers could submit their disputes to an international arbitral court. In time a world public opinion would come into being which would enforce the decisions of the court.[21] The Taft–Knox arbitration treaties symbolized the different approach of the Taft and Roosevelt administrations and suggested that Taft and Knox were not reluctant to translate their ideas into more practical policies.[22] So, too, did their China policy.

The administration's justifications for an intensified concern with China always remained elusive. In Latin America idealistic diplomacy had clear strategic roots; in contrast Taft, Knox, and their subordinates were never able to define the precise nature of the nation's interest in China. They largely took that interest for granted and in this, too, they were responding to larger currents of American thought. After 1905 many Americans believed that China had reached a pivotal point in its history; some urged more active guidance of China's transformation.[23] It was an obvious area in which Taft and Knox could practice their new brand of idealistic diplomacy. They did not turn to China because of any substantial pressure from the business community, and, indeed, their attitudes toward economic expansion seemed to vacillate. In 1907 Taft wrote that the domestic market largely absorbed American businessmen, while Knox, in 1909, proclaimed "a new era of international commercial expansion," in which American business was eager to participate.[24] It is likely that both men sensed that the

21. Mulhollan, "Philander C. Knox and Dollar Diplomacy," p. 57. Mulhollan's dissertation contains the first extensive analysis of Knox's foreign policy beliefs. Knox revealed many of his assumptions about international affairs in a speech entitled "International Unity" given before the Pennsylvania Society of New York, December 1909, and reprinted in *International Conciliation*, no. 28 (March 1910), 3–13; Taft, *The United States and Peace* (New York: Charles Scribner's Sons, 1914), pp. 178–180.

22.   John P. Campbell brings out the significance of these treaties and the debate over them in "Taft, Roosevelt, and the Arbitration Treaties of 1911," *Journal of American History*, 53 (September 1966), 279–298.

23. Iriye, *Across the Pacific*, pp. 117–119, and Jessie Ashworth Miller, "China in American Policy and Opinion, 1906–1909" (Ph.D. diss., Clark University, 1940), pp. 6–27. Few wished to see their friendly feelings toward China transformed into forceful policy. Paul A. Varg, *The Making of a Myth: The United States and China, 1897–1912* (East Lansing: Michigan State University Press, 1968), pp. 117–121.

24. Varg, *The Making of a Myth*, pp. 105–111, 126–127, 158. Taft, "China and Her Relations with the United States," address before the American Associa-

China market was more of a future hope than a present reality. Certainly one motive for their policy was to keep that market open for the future, but their impulse to pursue a more aggressive diplomacy in East Asia was primarily stirred by a desire to fulfill America's obligation to a large backward nation and by a desire to maintain America's standing as a world power. Moreover, their basic assumptions about international affairs encouraged Taft and Knox to intervene in Chinese politics, since these assumptions provided little warning of the difficulties ahead.

This important shift in policy was facilitated by the fact that Taft and Knox acted almost intuitively in foreign affairs. So, too, did the State Department professionals upon whom they leaned. In doing so all these men again revealed how much they were a part of their time. Even Roosevelt and other power-oriented thinkers often revelled in an imaginative world with but few connections with reality. As Wiebe remarks, "the fantasies of power, with nations as tokens on a world-wide board, led most of them to dream . . . about shadowy thrusts and counterthrusts."[25] Taft, Knox, and their advisers lacked the imagination to play this game skillfully, as well as a knowledge of world politics which allowed them to discipline their policy against an external reality. Without Roosevelt's redeeming sense of international relationships, they stumbled into an assertion of American power in East Asia.

The administration's two major initiatives in East Asia came in 1909. In May of that year it demanded entry for an American group of financiers into the Hukuang railway loan, and in November, before the first issue was resolved, the administration proposed the neutralization of Manchuria's railways. A strong stimulus for these actions came from diplomats within the State Department and from those stationed in China and Manchuria. In the first instance, William Phillips, Willard Straight, and Francis M. Huntington Wilson argued forcefully for American intervention in the Hukuang loan; in the second, Knox enlarged Straight's plan for the construction of a railway from Chinchow to Aigun into a scheme designed to transform the political situation in Manchuria.[26] The initiatives and rhetoric of State Department profes-

---

tion of China, Shanghai, October 8, 1907, in Taft, *Present Day Problems* (New York: Dodd, Mead and Company, 1908), p. 46; Knox to chairman of the Senate Committee on Appropriations, July 28, 1909, quoted in Charles Chiahwei Chu, "The China Policy of the Taft-Knox Administration, 1909–1913" (Ph.D. diss., University of Chicago, 1956), p. 2.

25. Wiebe, *The Search for Order*, p. 235.

26. Vevier, *The United States and China*, pp. 99–100; Mulhollan, "Philander C. Knox and Dollar Diplomacy," pp. 195–210.

sionals became so intermingled with those of the President and secretary of state that it is difficult, in retrospect, to untangle them.

The President and secretary of state saw themselves as tough, hard-headed men who were solving a difficult problem neglected by their predecessors. They did not, however, see their policy as a bold or controversial break with the past. Knox wrote Taft in August 1909 that America's purposes in China should be accomplished "through a process of steady, healthy and slow development . . . We are not to undertake a quixotically altruistic task for China's benefit." The American government's aim was, as Knox put it, to find a middle path "between silently renouncing our historic policy in China whenever it may cross the interest of another power and being prepared to go to war in defense of that policy." Taft claimed their purpose was to give "new life and practical application to the open door policy."[27] The best way to protect China was to strengthen her through reforms in her systems of currency, taxation, education, and defense, and through the development of communication and transportation facilities. Their hope was to foster internal reform, stability, and republican institutions. Their instrument was the only available one, American investments, which, Knox asserted, would give the United States "more than a moral right to have a voice in all questions affecting China's welfare."[28] Through the penetration of American capital into China on an equal basis with that of the European powers and Japan, the United States could create a base for the expansion of its own trade and, more important, create a concrete interest which would force the other powers to share political decisions with the American government. Thus the United States would have its say in the direction of Chinese reforms. It would seek neither economic nor political supremacy in Manchuria, but rather an equality and cooperation among the powers which would grow out of the internationalization of all projects. Basically Taft and Knox believed that shared investments would produce interdependence, and that a community of interests would develop which the United

27. Knox to Taft, August 26, 1909, quoted in Chu, "The China Policy of the Taft-Knox Administration," p. 72; draft by Knox for Taft's reply to Roosevelt's letter of December 22, 1910, quoted in Elting E. Morison, ed., *The Letters of Theodore Roosevelt*, 8 vols. (Cambridge, Mass.: Harvard University Press, 1951–1954), VII, 190; message of the President, December 3, 1912, in *Papers Relating to the Foreign Relations of the United States, 1912* (Washington, D.C.: Government Printing Office, 1919), p. xi. Mulhollan's "Philander C. Knox and Dollar Diplomacy," pp. 166–190 contains a particularly good discussion of the assumptions behind the administration's China policy.

28. Knox memorandum on "Chinese Railways and Currency Loans," n.d., quoted in Mulhollan, "Philander C. Knox and Dollar Diplomacy," p. 56.

States could direct toward idealistic and humanitarian goals. Time and time again they declared their concern with the fate of China and their determination to use American dollars to secure influence there. "If the American dollar," Knox declared in December 1911, "can aid suffering humanity and lift the burden of financial difficulty from States with which we live on terms of intimate intercourse and earnest friendship, and replace insecurity and devastation by stability and peaceful self-development, all I can say is that it would be hard to find better employment."[29]

The climax of this grandiose vision was the proposal to place Manchuria's railways under the joint supervision of the great powers. To Taft and Knox this was a plan for the "economic, scientific, and impartial administration" of Manchuria, an attempt to systematize and rationalize the development of that chaotic area. If successful, it would take Manchurian development out of East Asian politics, creating "an immense commercial neutral zone," from which all the powers would benefit.[30] It would lessen tensions, spread the burdens of guiding a wayward nation, and quicken the pace of economic growth. While expecting some resistance from Japan and Russia, they apparently assumed that these two nations would find much of the proposal attractive. Japan, after all, had temporarily agreed in 1905 to share the ownership of the South Manchurian railway with Edward H. Harriman, and a faction within the Russian government seemed to favor selling the Chinese Eastern railway.[31]

The failure of the neutralization plan in early 1910 created some bitterness in the State Department, particularly toward Great Britain. Nevertheless, the administration continued to pursue its goals in a more limited way. Knox believed that British public opinion would eventually force a modification of that government's

29. Address before the National Civic Federation, New York City, December 11, 1911, quoted in Herbert F. Wright, "Philander Chase Knox," in Samuel Flagg Bemis, ed., *The American Secretaries of State and Their Diplomacy*, 10 vols. (New York: Alfred A. Knopf, 1927–1929), IX, 326–327.

30. Knox to Sir Edward Grey, November 6, 1909, quoted in *Papers Relating to the Foreign Relations of the United States, 1910*, (Washington, D.C.: Government Printing Office, 1915), p. 234; Knox statement to the press, January 6, 1910,) ibid., p. 245.

31. Washington's knowledge of the powers' attitudes is summarized by Chu, "The China Policy of the Taft-Knox Administration," p. 154. American diplomats in Russia sent misleading reports of that government's position. Paul A. Varg, *Open Door Diplomat: The Life of W. W. Rockhill* (Illinois Studies in the Social Sciences, vol. 33, no. 4, Urbana, Illinois: University of Illinois Press, 1952), pp. 102–103, and Edward H. Zabriskie, *American-Russian Rivalry in the Far East: A Study in Diplomacy and Power Politics, 1895–1914* (Philadelphia: University of Pennsylvania Press, 1946), pp. 148, 151–152.

policy.[32] Later in 1910 the United States took the initiative in a loan to China for currency reform and Manchurian industrial development and approved the formation of a Four Power Consortium; in 1912 the government consented to the expansion of the consortium to include Japan and Russia. Though Taft's and Knox's extravagant hopes for the policy of cooperation diminished, it remained the basis of their approach to China. By late 1912 the American minister in Peking, William J. Calhoun, was pessimistic about the usefulness of the Six Power Consortium, but Knox still believed that American participation would do some good.[33] After the outbreak of the Chinese revolution, the administration adopted a cautious neutrality toward contending factions and hoped that, if intervention was necessary, it would be a cooperative venture. Eventually the American government restrained its own desire to recognize the government of Yuan Shih-k'ai until the other powers concurred. Like most Americans, Taft and Knox had little understanding of the Chinese revolution, and they hesitantly continued a policy dominated by earlier patterns of thought. They left office convinced the United States had accomplished much in China and had followed a policy which was, in Taft's words, "modern, resourceful, magnanimous, and fittingly expressive of the high ideals of a great nation."[34]

Taft and Knox pursued an East Asian policy which often seemed disconnected, as if they were unaware of natural relationships. Knox wrote that he was "unable to see any essential connection between" the Manchurian and immigration questions.[35] By observing its legal obligations to restrict emigration to the United States, Japan could hardly expect concessions in Manchuria. Moreover, both men—unlike some of their subordinates—sought expanded influence in Asia without any apparent sense of hostility toward Japan. Taft admired Japan's achievements and had approved of her absorption of Korea. The President and secretary of state were, to be sure, suspicious of Japanese imperialism, but this did not

32. E. W. Edwards, "Great Britain and the Manchurian Railways Question, 1909–1910," *English Historical Review*, 81 (October 1966), 764; draft by Knox for Taft's reply to Roosevelt's letter of December 22, 1910, quoted in Dennett, *Roosevelt and the Russo-Japanese War*, p. 323.

33. Mulhollan, "Philander C. Knox and Dollar Diplomacy," pp. 236–240.

34. Marilyn Young is now working on a much-needed study of the Taft Administration's attitude toward the Mexican and Chinese revolutions; message of the President, December 3, 1912, in *Papers Relating to the Foreign Relations of the United States, 1912* (Washington, D.C., Government Printing Office, 1919), p. xxvii.

35. Draft by Knox for Taft's reply to Roosevelt's letter of December 22, 1910, quoted in Dennett, *Roosevelt and the Russo-Japanese War*, p. 321.

seem to affect their decisions. A sense of mission rather than antagonism toward Japan inspired their policy toward China, and they showed no reluctance to protect Japanese interests in the United States. In fact, their attitude toward anti-Japanese agitation in California seemed identical to Roosevelt's. Despite Japan's rejection of the neutralization proposal, Taft and Knox in late 1910 and early 1911 intervened strongly in California politics to prevent the passage of anti-Japanese legislation.[36] They won the support of Governor Hiram Johnson and bargained effectively with various anti-Japanese leaders in California. At the same time, they pondered, then rejected, Roosevelt's advice in renegotiating the Japanese-American Treaty of 1894. After some hesitation, the administration accepted Japan's proposal to omit from the new treaty a clause permitting the United States to exclude Japanese laborers, in return for a Japanese memorandum promising to continue emigration restriction. Roosevelt feared that this concession "might bring an outbreak on the Pacific slope or make the Californians feel that the government was not watching their vital interests." He also worried that if, in the future, a failure of the Gentlemen's Agreement should force the United States to pass exclusion legislation, the only alternative of the American government would be to denounce the whole treaty. To Roosevelt it appeared that the administration was insensitive to domestic political considerations.[37] As it turned out, however, Taft and Knox judged political conditions more accurately than Roosevelt. Realizing that Japan would no longer tolerate a discriminatory clause, they convinced Californians to accept the new treaty and worked patiently with the Senate to insure its quick adoption in February 1911.

Whatever the flaws of their East Asian policy, Taft and Knox never lost perspective on their difficulties with Japan. The President did not succumb to any of the fears that agitated Roosevelt

36. The best published account of the administration's efforts to contain anti-Japanese agitation is Roger Daniels' *The Politics of Prejudice: The Anti-Japanese Movement in California and the Struggle for Japanese Exclusion* (Berkeley: University of California Press, 1962), pp. 46–58. The most authoritative and detailed analysis of the whole range of Japanese-American relations during the Taft administration is Teruko Okada Kachi's "The Treaty of 1911 and the Immigration and Alien Land Law Issue between the United States and Japan, 1911–1913," (Ph.D. diss., University of Chicago, 1957).

37. In December 1909 Knox sought British cooperation in treaty negotiations with Japan. He wanted both governments to insist upon the inclusion of an immigrant clause. Britain's rejection of this proposal forced the administration to confront more directly the difficulties of reaching an understanding with Japan and eventually led to substantial American concessions. Kachi, "The Treaty of 1911," pp. 37–38; Roosevelt to Taft, December 22, 1910, Morison, *Letters of Theodore Roosevelt*, VII, 189–192.

during the Japanese-American crisis of 1906–1909. Then Roosevelt had sought a larger naval program to strengthen the nation's Pacific defenses. Taft thought war was impossible and felt reassured by his closeness to important Japanese statesmen. His vigorous advocacy of naval expansion seemed unrelated to his foreign policy, as if he kept diplomacy and strategy in different compartments.[38] Roosevelt's awareness of America's military and naval weakness in the western Pacific had influenced his diplomacy; Taft lacked his predecessor's ability to see the whole rather than its separate parts. Apparently President Taft believed American initiatives in China and Manchuria would appeal to the powers despite the nation's lack of military and naval strength in the Pacific.

The President's calmness did not, however, quiet the concern within the administration over Pacific strategy. In the spring of 1910 the General Board began systematic consideration of war with Japan and by March 1911 had worked out a detailed Orange plan. Somewhat earlier, in November 1909, navy and army planners had finally decided to locate the nation's chief Pacific base at Pearl Harbor. This decision was the culmination of a long and bitter debate between the services and reflected their recognition of American vulnerability in the Philippines. It failed, however, to solve the problem of defending American forces in the Philippines against a Japanese attack. The navy contended that it would soon have a separate battle fleet in the Pacific, operating out of Pearl Harbor, which could protect the Philippines. Army planners, particularly Chief of Staff Leonard Wood, challenged this conclusion and argued that a major naval base should be developed at Corregidor to support the fleet once it reached the western Pacific. These important strategic issues remained confused and unresolved, partly because Taft presided passively over the evolution of the nation's Pacific strategy.[39] In strategy as in diplomacy, Taft's leadership left much to be desired.

This account of the transformation in American East Asian policy raises far more questions than it answers and suggests how frag-

38. The best discussion of naval strategy during the Taft years is William R. Braisted's *The United States Navy in the Pacific, 1909–1922* (Austin: University of Texas Press, 1971).

39. Ibid., pp. 49, 94–118. There is an interesting essay on "The Quest for Security: Admiral Dewey and the General Board, 1900–1917," in John A. S. Grenville and George Berkeley Young, *Politics, Strategy, and American Diplomacy: Studies in Foreign Policy, 1873–1917* (New Haven: Yale University Press, 1966), pp. 297–336.

mentary our knowledge is for the years after 1909. We have always had many more studies of Roosevelt's diplomacy than of that of Taft and Knox, and two recent books explore in depth his policy toward Japan during his final years in office.[40] Gaps remain, but they seem inconsequential compared to those that exist for the 1909–1913 period. Older works by A. Whitney Griswold, Herbert Croly, and Henry F. Pringle utilize only a small portion of the material now available and rest upon a dated interpretive structure. Newer ones, by Charles Vevier, Roger Daniels, and Paul A. Varg still fall short of exhausting the published and unpublished sources. Vevier explores the economic dimension of American diplomacy, claiming, in effect, that it was the primary one. Daniels approaches the anti-Japanese agitation from a Californian perspective, without consulting the manuscript collections of the presidents or secretaries of state or the State Department archives. The most recent of these works, by Paul A. Varg, provides valuable insights into the attitudes of missionaries, businessmen, and diplomats toward China. But it is no more than a sketch, suggesting how rich the possibilities are for further research in this area. There is, of course, Akira Iriye's perceptive survey, full of fresh comparisons, which analyzes the interplay of images among the United States, China, and Japan. And there are four detailed, unpublished studies of the years 1909–1913 by Charles Chia-hwei Chu, Okada Teruko Kachi, Helen Dodson Kahn, and Page Elliott Mulhollan. These dissertations explore a substantial body of archival and manuscript material and often challenge accepted generalizations about this period. Even if they should eventually be published, however, they leave many sources and important interpretive themes untouched.

First of all, we know far too little about some of the major statesmen of these years. Roosevelt and Root have received ample attention from biographers, but for Taft there is only Pringle's dated study, and for Knox only two brief essays.[41] We lack firstrate analyses, then, of the thought of both these men on domestic and foreign affairs. We also need to learn more about secondary

40. Esthus, *Theodore Roosevelt and Japan*, and Neu, *An Uncertain Friendship*.

41. The published studies of Knox are by Herbert F. Wright in Bemis, ed., *The American Secretaries of State and Their Diplomacy*, and by Walter Scholes in Norman A. Graebner, ed., *An Uncertain Tradition: American Secretaries of State in the Twentieth Century* (New York: McGraw-Hill, 1961). Mulhollan's "Philander C. Knox and Dollar Diplomacy" contains a biographical sketch as well as a thoughtful analysis of Knox's concept of international relations.

figures such as Willard Straight, Francis M. Huntington Wilson, and William Phillips—not necessarily biographical studies, but perhaps an analysis focusing on them as a group, one which would attempt to explain their initial involvement in East Asian politics, their differing approaches to China and Japan, and their influence on the formation of policy from 1906 to 1913. Their significance may lie not only in the policies they advocated but also in their role in changing the organizational structure of American foreign policy. Influenced by popular concepts of scientific management and efficiency, they seemed to be well along in the process of developing an identity as professional diplomats.

For the years after 1909 no published or unpublished study has integrated diplomacy, politics, and strategy or has examined the interaction between public opinion and diplomacy. Several books analyze the public's response during the Japanese-American crisis of 1906–1909, but none study the public's reaction to American initiatives in East Asia during the Taft years.[42] Certainly the administration's policy stirred no great enthusiasm, except among missionaries and a few businessmen who were eager to see an active China policy. Paul A. Varg suggests that the widespread faith in the China market weakened after 1906 as more and more Americans recognized the absorption of businessmen in the domestic market and the insuperable obstacles of trading with China. Most members of the foreign policy elite, which weighed so heavily in the formation of the public's response to international events, appeared to react apathetically to the government's intervention in Chinese affairs.[43] In his memoirs, Huntington Wilson bitterly complains about those Americans who "missed the whole point of the Knox policy . . . [and] refused to distinguish between old-fashioned selfish exploitation and the new and sincere and practical effort to help."[44] This complaint raises a number of intriguing questions, for, though intense interest in China existed among only small portions of the foreign policy elite, the idealistic policy of Taft and Knox may have had the potential for arousing great

42. Both Neu, *An Uncertain Friendship,* and Thomas A. Bailey, *Theodore Roosevelt and the Japanese-American Crises* (Stanford: Stanford University Press, 1934), give considerable attention to the role of public opinion.

43. Varg, *The Making of a Myth,* pp. 105–121, 160–163. Editorial opinion, however, initially supported Knox's neutralization proposal. Criticism mounted as the administration failed to achieve any diplomatic success. Eleanor Tupper and George E. McReynolds, *Japan in American Public Opinion* (New York: The Macmillan Company, 1937), p. 87, and Chu, "The China Policy of the Taft-Knox Administration," pp. 180–183, 231–241.

44. Francis M. Huntington Wilson, *Memoirs of an Ex-Diplomat* (Boston: Bruce Humphries, 1945), p. 216.

public enthusiasm. But the administration continually obscured its goals by the means used to achieve them—the intimate collaboration with great American financiers and their institutions. It also displayed political insensitivity by allowing its policy to be labeled "dollar diplomacy." Inevitably progressives were hostile to such a policy, particularly when it emanated from an administration identified with domestic conservatism. Despite the many similarities between Wilson's attitudes toward East Asia and those of Taft and Knox, he took office determined to break away from what seemed a materialistic and selfish policy.[45]

The examination of American East Asian policy during this period should also range beyond the American perspective. We know something about the Japanese response to American diplomacy during the Japanese-American crisis from 1906 to 1909, and Akira Iriye's forthcoming study places the encounter between the two nations in a new context. Iriye probes the interaction of Japanese and American expansionism, emphasizing the attitudes of the foreign policy elite in each nation. In Japan there was a powerful thrust for informal, peaceful expansion extending far beyond continental Asia and centering, for a time, on Hawaii and California. The emergence of anti-Japanese sentiment in the United States after the Russo-Japanese War stunned Japanese leaders, who only painfully and slowly redirected their expansionist aims toward continental Asia. The growing American fears of Japan in both official and nonofficial circles were not, however, matched by similar developments in Japan, though Japan's uncertainty about its own world position and its uneasiness about the United States did increase. Iriye's absorbing study suggests that the years after 1906 mark the beginning of the permanent ideological and psychological estrangement of the two peoples.[46]

Unfortunately there is no full analysis of British East Asian policy after 1906, though Peter Lowe's recent book helps, as does E. W. Edwards' article on "Great Britain and the Manchurian Rail-

45. Arthur S. Link, *Wilson: The New Freedom* (Princeton: Princeton University Press, 1956), pp. 277–288.
46. Neu, *An Uncertain Friendship*, deals with the British, Canadian, and Japanese sides, while Esthus, *Theodore Roosevelt and Japan*, analyzes Japanese policy; Iriye, *Pacific Estrangement: Japanese and American Expansionism, 1897–1911* (Cambridge, Mass.: Harvard University Press, forthcoming). Despite the excellence of Iriye's book, its emphasis on attitudes rather than the formulation of policy leaves many questions unanswered about the behavior of the Japanese government. Shumpei Okamoto's *The Japanese Oligarchy and the Russo-Japanese Way* (New York: Columbia University Press, 1970), with its superb dissection of Japan's ruling elite, suggests how much we can learn from this type of approach.

way Question."[47] The British government, preoccupied with European affairs, was caught between its need to maintain the alliance with Japan and its desire to promote Anglo-American understanding. In early 1908 Great Britain had rejected Roosevelt's overtures to form a coalition against Japanese immigration, a far more modest project than the adventurous diplomacy of the Taft administration in Manchuria. American proposals irritated and embarrassed the British, who could not possibly risk offending Japan and Russia by challenging their spheres of interest in Manchuria.[48] One would like to know much more about the nature of British calculations during these years and what lingering effect their low estimate of American diplomacy may have had.

One may conclude, then, that except for the years 1906–1909, the period between 1906 and 1913 has been neglected in the history of American–East Asian relations. A vast amount of source material remains either sampled or untouched. Only recently have some specialists sensed that these years represent a distinctive shift in the aspirations of American statesmen. The approach of Taft and Knox was the harbinger of a policy that would find its full expression in the Wilson years. Our realization of this is part of a larger awareness that it will no longer do to study the history of American East Asian policy in terms of cyclical movements or rigid continuities. Policy in this period, as in all others, was the expression of attitudes deeply embedded in the flux of American society and thought. The process of rewriting the history of American–East Asian relations from this point of view is already under way, but it will take the labors of many scholars for many years to make the promise a reality.

47. Lowe, *Great Britain and Japan 1911–15: A Study of British Far Eastern Policy* (London: Macmillan, 1969). Other books which touch upon British East Asia policy are: George W. Monger, *The End of Isolation: British Foreign Policy, 1900–1907* (London: Thomas Nelson and Sons, 1963); Ian H. Nish, *The Anglo-Japanese Alliance: The Diplomacy of Two Island Empires, 1894–1907* (London: Athlone Press, 1966); and I-tu Sun, *Chinese Railways and British Interests, 1898–1911* (New York: King's Crown Press, 1954).

48. Edwards, "Great Britain and the Manchurian Railway Question, 1909–1910," pp. 751, 761–769.

1913-1917

A historiographical review of American Far Eastern policy, 1913–1917, may well focus on work of the last twenty years. Prior to World War II, as the foundations of Wilsonian scholarship were laid, American relations with the European belligerents dominated the writing of diplomatic history. Far Eastern policy was relegated to an occasional article, chapters in more extended surveys, or a few paragraphs in presidential biographies.[1] Harley Notter's *The Origins of Woodrow Wilson's Foreign Policies* (Baltimore: Johns Hopkins Press, 1937) was scarcely atypical in assigning to China, Japan, and the Philippines some mention on seventy-four pages out of a total of 654. Compared with this, Tien-yi Li's *Woodrow Wilson's China Policy, 1913–1917* (New York: Twayne Publishers, 1952), and Russell H. Fifield's *Woodrow Wilson and the Far East: The Diplomacy of the Shantung Question* (New York: Thomas Y. Crowell Co., 1952), the first of the postwar studies, appeared exhaustive. Roy W. Curry's doctoral dissertation—more comprehensive than either of the foregoing—was completed in 1952 and was

---

1. Among the older studies, A. Whitney Griswold's, *The Far Eastern Policy of the United States* (New York: Harcourt, Brace, 1938) contains a little more than a chapter on the first Wilson administration. Chapters also are to be found in two popular books by Foster Rhea Dulles: *Forty Years of American-Japanese Relations* (New York: Appleton-Century, 1937); and *China and America: The Story of Their Relations Since 1784* (Princeton: Princeton University Press, 1946). A single chapter, "Japan, America, and the World War," covers Wilson's first and second administrations in Payson Treat's *Japan and the United States, 1853–1921* (*Revised and Continued to 1928*) (Stanford: Stanford University Press, 1928). Thomas E. LaFargue, *China and the World War* (Stanford: Stanford University Press, 1937) presents a sketch of American policy based on documents published on the *Foreign Relations* series. Ray Stannard Baker's *Woodrow Wilson: Life and Letters*, 8 vols. (Garden City, N.Y.: Doubleday, 1927–1929), a monumental authorized biography, has only a scattering of references to Asia. Research on specialized topics before the 1950's was rare. For notable exceptions see two pioneering articles by Paul H. Clyde. "Railway Politics and the Open Door in China, 1916–1917," *American Journal of International Law*, 25 (October 1931), 642–657; and "An Episode in American-Japanese Relations: The Manchurian Freight-Rate Controversy, 1914–1916," *Far Eastern Review*, 26 (August-September 1930), 410–412, 480–483; and Frederick V. Field's *American Participation in the China Consortiums* (Chicago: University of Chicago Press, 1931), is a thorough combing of published documents.

later published as *Woodrow Wilson and Far Eastern Policy, 1913–1921* (New York: Bookman Associates, 1957). These books assumed importance for their revelations in a neglected area of Wilsoniana.[2] The three also were among the earliest entries in a growing list of postwar American Far Eastern policy studies.

Li, Fifield, and Curry were to foreshadow a generation of scholarship. Their books drew heavily on presidential papers and on those of key advisers, like William Jennings Bryan, Robert Lansing, Edward M. House, Breckinridge Long, and Frank Polk. All relied on the State Department's decimal files, the contents of which were far richer than the published sources available to earlier researchers.[3] But they made only limited use of foreign sources: Li cited a few Chinese documents and books; Fifield selected from Japanese archives some key documents for his account of the Shantung controversy; and Curry drew upon published British materials. In a word, these were studies with an essentially American focus. The authors differed in scope and emphasis, but they were alike in viewing Far Eastern problems through Wilson's eyes. They were alike too in the standards by which Wilson's policies were assessed. Each sought to answer much the same questions: What was the nature of presidential policies? What were the sources of those policies? To what extent were they implemented? Or again, given the sources of and restraints upon American policy, did Wilson accomplish all that might have been expected? On the basis of such questions, the three historians formed their estimate of Wilson's achievement. In retrospect, that the three, working at approximately the same time and using much the same materials, should have produced works so broadly similar seems less remarkable than that others should have continued to follow so closely in their paths.[4] By the late 1960's the writing of American Far Eastern

2. Advances in research were aided immeasurably by the opening of State Department archives and significant collections of private papers. Richard L. Watson, Jr., "Woodrow Wilson and His Interpreters, 1947–1957," *Mississippi Valley Historical Review*, 44 (August 1957), 207– 236, views these studies of Far Eastern policy in the context of a vast expansion of scholarship.

3. The key source prior to 1945 were documents published in the *Foreign Relations* series. A listing of titles and publications dates suggests what was available: *Papers Relating to the Foreign Relations of the United States, 1912–1922*, 22 vols. (Washington, 1919–1938); *Papers Relating to the Foreign Relations of the United States: The Lansing Papers, 1914–1920*, 2 vols. (Washington, 1939); *Papers Relating to the Foreign Relations of the United States, 1919: Russia* (Washington, 1937); *and Papers Relating to the Foreign Relations of the United States, 1919: The Paris Peace Conference*, 13 vols. (Washington, 1942–1947).

4. These first studies even influenced foreign scholarship. See, for example, Tamura Kosaka, "The Taisho Era: The Immigration Act and World War One,"

policy, 1913–1917, was still being shaped by administration perspectives; its sources were still mostly American; and historians, while drawing upon fresh American materials, were continuing to ask much the same questions.

If the frame of inquiry remained unchanged, nearly twenty years of research filled out the narrative and produced an increasingly rich array of historical interpretation. These were the results of a scholarship which reached beyond State Department files into the papers of the Commerce, Treasury, and Navy Departments. New perspectives also were offered by studies of such secondary officials as Bryan, Lansing, and the American minister to China, Paul S. Reinsch. And finally, the story of official relationship was supplemented by pioneering works on American commercial and missionary activities. A more detailed examination of this expanding literature will suggest not only what has been accomplished but also some of the tasks ahead.

The Roots of American Involvement

Historians studying the Wilson era have demonstrated fundamental concern with the sources of American conduct. How is the nation's deepening involvement in Asian affairs to be explained? Administration records have not permitted a simple answer. Upon taking office Wilson gave priority to domestic reform. When foreign troubles appeared, they were most acute in the Western hemisphere and in Europe, not in Asia. Yet the years 1913–1917 were marked by a growing American commitment to China and by resistance to Japanese ambitions. Given other problems, why did Wilson allow these Asian involvements? Wilson's own rhetoric emphasized America's "duty" to China, but he also revealed deep interest in the development of a commercial stake. Such tangled evidence has encouraged repeated explorations of the roots of American policy, producing conflicting theories.

On one point historians have agreed: idealism figured importantly in the Wilson administration's approach to Far Eastern questions. According to the President, the United States had a civilizing role to play in world affairs. The American government was to promote human rights, to elevate the moral order, and to cultivate a reign of justice. Given the situation of a revolutionary Asia, these lofty principles were translated by the President into an American

in Kimura Michiko, trans., *Japan–American Diplomatic Relations in the Meiji-Taisho Era* (Tokyo: Pan-Pacific Press, 1958), which derived more from American secondary accounts than from Japanese sources.

duty to assist and defend China while speeding the Philippines toward independence. In a word, Asia became the target of reform impulses which had their source in American domestic problems. "Both men [Wilson and Bryan]," William A. Williams has observed, "were leaders of the secular American reform movement, and both brought to their conduct of foreign affairs a religious intensity and righteousness that was not apparent in earlier administrations and has not been matched since their time."[5]

Interpretive problems have centered on whether these moral and reforming impulses were all that was behind Wilson's diplomacy. How was idealism to be reconciled with the administration's evident concern with the American commercial and investment stake? Some scholars, among whom Wilson's biographer Arthur S. Link is most prominent, have resolved the issue by assigning to nonidealistic factors a subordinate or subconscious role in shaping policy. Thus, Wilson attempted "to serve" Asia through "missionary diplomacy." The ends of such diplomacy were political and social. If Americans profited in more mundane ways, that was fortuitous but profit was not essential to larger purposes.[6] Other historians, while accepting the central thesis of "missionary diplomacy," have found the role of dollars to be more carefully calculated. R. W. Curry, for example, has suggested that Wilson looked upon businessmen and Christian missionaries as apostles of the American way.[7] Thus, American business was not to be encouraged to expand abroad simply for its own sake or even for the benefit of the American economy. Rather, dollars became the means for implementing political and social ends.

These affirmations of Wilson's basic idealism have figured importantly in a second explanation of the origins of American policy. This approach accepts the President's idealistic orientation, but it holds that Wilson alone was not responsible for the content of American policy. Other officials like Lansing and Reinsch were deeply concerned with commercial expansion and the opening of investment opportunities. For Lansing the establishment and protection of an American economic stake in East Asia were the primary ends of policy. He focused less on America's "duty" abroad than on the material needs of an expanding American society. In his view, American interests in East Asia had been historically

---

5. *The Tragedy of American Diplomacy,* rev. ed. (New York: Delta Books, 1961), p. 61.

6. "Missionary Diplomacy," in Link's *Woodrow Wilson and the Progressive Era, 1910–1917* (New York: Harper and Brothers, 1954) outlines the view.

7. *Wilson and Far Eastern Policy,* p. 31.

economic, and they should so remain.[8] Reinsch, on the other hand, combined deep concern for American economic needs with a crusading missionary spirit. As a consequence, he championed economic expansion not only because American society required it but also because—and in this he thought much like Wilson—it would serve the Chinese.[9] Both Lansing and Reinsch were deeply involved in projects calling for the expansion of American investment and trade. It was from these subordinates, not Wilson himself, that policy derived much of its economic content. In other words, Wilson's Far Eastern policy was founded on composite views. This second explanation serves less as an attack on the first than as an amendment.[10]

Such has not been the case with analyses emphasizing the importance of economics in Wilson's ideas. William A. Williams has decried efforts to separate idealism from economics in discussions of the President's motivation. The President's mind, he has argued, did not present neat "moralistic" and "economic" divisions, each "impinging on one another like two billiard balls and pushing the other about." Rather the key issue to Wilson's policy was in his tendency, which was typical of many Progressives, to link American expansion, whether economic or territorial, with moral progress. This wedding of ideas, Williams argued, enabled Robert La Follette to view acquisition of the Philippines as bringing profits to Americans and taking civilization to Filipinos. In Wilson himself these historic tendencies were reinforced in various ways. As a stern Calvinist, Wilson associated political liberty with free enterprise, and from the historian, Frederick Jackson Turner, Wilson learned the importance of expansion to the well-being of American institutions. Such influences combined in Wilson to make him something more than a moralistic crusader who gave little heed to the materialistic aspects of life. On the contrary, according to Williams, in Wilson's ideas was revealed a "keen and sophisticated way" of integrating

8. Burton F. Beers, *Vain Endeavor: Robert Lansing's Attempts to End the American-Japanese Rivalry* (Durham: Duke University Press, 1962), pp. 17–28.

9. Daniel J. Gage, "Paul S. Reinsch and Sino-American Relations" (Ph.D. diss., Stanford University, 1939), the earliest study based largely on the *Foreign Relations* series. Noel H. Pugach, "Progress, Prosperity, and the Open Door: The Ideas and Career of Paul S. Reinsch" (Ph.D. diss., University of Wisconsin, 1967) is a more satisfactory study of motivating ideas.

10. The composite view is advanced most clearly in Beers, *Vain Endeavor.* Pugach's study of Reinsch infers that the President shared the minister's views. Another recent study of the economic concerns of Wilson's subordinates is Jeffrey J. Safford, "Experiment in Containment: The United States Street Embargo and Japan, 1917–1918." *Pacific Historical Review,* 39 (November 1970), 439–451.

"crusading idealism and hard-headed economics." In the pioneering essay which outlined this interpretation, Williams did not assess the relative weights of the idealistic and economic facets of Wilson's motives.[11] Others pursuing this line, however, have produced a fundamentally economic interpretation. By way of example note Lloyd C. Gardner's contention that the "core substance" of American policy was an economic stake in Asia: idealism, though sincerely expressed, served largely as rhetoric presenting American aims in the best possible light. In effect, by holding that ideas served dollars, Gardner reversed the tenets of Link's "missionary diplomacy."[12]

These diverging analyses have in turn been linked with quite different evaluations of Wilson's policy. Historians holding to theories of "missionary diplomacy," have adjudged both the propriety of Wilson's objectives and his chance of achieving them. Curry, the friendliest of Wilson's critics, while applauding Wilson's reforming zeal, has emphasized that slim resources prevented the President from making much headway either in the transformation of China or in protecting that country from Japanese aggression. In the short run Wilson's Far Eastern policy failed. Yet, according to Curry, Wilson's vision of the new China and his struggle to help bring it into being pointed the way to an improved world order. It was for this larger accomplishment that Wilson's policy was to be praised.[13] Link, on the other hand, was critical of Wilson's goals

11. "The Imperialism of Idealism" in *Tragedy of American Diplomacy*, pp. 53–83. The revised version of the essay here cited draws upon Martin J. Sklar's M.A. thesis, the substance of which is published as "Woodrow Wilson and the Political Economy of Modern American Liberalism," *Studies on the Left*, 1 (1960), 17–47. Jerry Israel, "For God, For China and For Yale—The Open Door in Action," *American Historical Review*, 75 (February 1970), 796–807, studies the combination of materialism and idealism as applied to China. The findings of Williams and others was foreshadowed in William Diamond, *The Economic Thought of Woodrow Wilson* (Baltimore: Johns Hopkins Press, 1943). See especially Diamond's observation, pp. 131–132: "Wilson's actions toward . . . foreign nations generally . . . were intrinsically associated with his conception of America and its economy. Though they were shot through with the moral fervor and religious conception of duty which sometimes made Wilson sound more like a missionary than a statesman, Wilson's ideas on the relations of America with the rest of the world were nevertheless related to his conception of what was necessary to keep the American economy running."

12. "American Foreign Policy, 1900–1921: A Second Look at the Realist Critique of American Diplomacy," in Barton J. Bernstein, ed. *Towards a New Past: Dissenting Essays in American History* (New York: Pantheon Books, 1968), pp. 202–231. For an even more recent assessment see Jerry Israel, *Progressivism and the Open Door: America and China, 1905–1921* (Pittsburgh: University of Pittsburgh Press, 1971).

13. "If one agrees that the realities which govern men lie deeply clothed in the emotional caverns of his religious-idealistic nature, Wilson's insistence . . . [on a new order under the League of Nations] can be viewed with apprecia-

themselves. His critique, which echoed the "realist" attack on the legalistic-moralistic tradition in American foreign relations, denied Wilson's assumptions that moral forces controlled international relations, that reason would prevail over ignorance and passion in public opinion, and that men would progress toward an orderly and righteous international society. Thus, the Open Door, standing as a symbol of a transformed China and a new order in East Asian international relations, became a large and imprecise objective, quite beyond the reach of American diplomacy.[14] An entirely different line, on the other hand, has been taken by exponents of economic interpretation. Williams' writings foreshadowed the findings of these scholars in holding that critics of "missionary diplomacy" have missed the crucial point. When stripped of its rhetoric, the American effort to enlarge its economic stake in Asia was not unrealistic. The problem was that materialistic concerns became entangled with an insistence on Asia's social and political transformation. American policy was not to be faulted for its failure to set realistic goals but for its effort to make foreigners over in the American image.[15] In a word, disagreement has marked writings on the fundamentals of policy. There has emerged no broad consensus on questions pertaining to the origins of American conduct and on what was accomplished. It follows, therefore, that research on specific topics in Sino-American relations, 1913–1916, has frequently proceeded from quite dissimilar premises.

tion. If on the other hand man lives solely in the *machtpolitik* reality, divorced from the influence of ethics and value systems, Wilson's idealism assumes all the symptoms of fatal political blindness. We are no longer so sure of the improvability of men, but the challenge is ever present. Nietzsche himself confessed that success is a great liar. Nevertheless, the years of the Wilson administrations marked the first period of outright challenge to a responsible American policy in the Far East. Within the circumstances of the time, the challenge would seem to have been met adequately." Curry, *Wilson and Far Eastern Policy*, p. 332.

14. Arthur S. Link, *Wilson,* vol. II, *The New Freedom* (Princeton: Princeton University Press, 1956). p. 278. Link appears to have drawn heavily upon such writing as George F. Kennan, *American Diplomacy, 1900–1951* (New York: New American Library, 1951), and Robert Osgood, *Ideals and Self-Interest in American Foreign Relations* (Chicago: University of Chicago, 1957).

15. Williams, *Tragedy of American Diplomacy,* pp. 9–13. Williams' view was similar to one advanced in 1925 by Scott Nearing and Joseph Freeman's *Dollar Diplomacy, A Study in American Imperialism* (Reprint ed., New York: Monthly Review Press, 1966), in so far as economic penetration was seen as the "opening wedge" of imperialism. The earlier study, however, associated imperialism with spheres of influence, and political and armed intervention. Williams viewed imperialism as a process that was both more subtle and profound.

American Assistance to China

In the main Wilson's Far Eastern policy was concerned with China. The centrality of this nation was evident even as the President settled into office. Among Wilson's earliest decisions were ones requiring withdrawal of official support from American representatives in the Six Power Consortium and extending diplomatic recognition to the republic under Yuan Shih-k'ai. Subsequently, between 1913 and 1917, the State Department in conjunction with various American business firms proposed to carry out in China three large projects: the Huai River water conservation program; construction of some 1,500 miles of railways in various parts of China; and an administrative loan to the Peking government. Most research has been concentrated upon these American activities and upon foreign competition, especially Japanese competition with the United States in China.

However adjudged, whether as an idealistic pursuit of a transformed China or as expansion of American investments, historians have found only limited accomplishments in Wilson's China policy. Wilson was soon disappointed in the hope that China would be unified under Yuan Shih-k'ai. Disheartening too was the early failure of an American investment program, especially since elaborate preparations sought to insure its success. Reinsch, energetic and imaginative, pinpointed opportunities, the interest of American firms was enlisted, and the State Department facilitated the negotiations of contracts. Indeed, official aid was limited only by the requirement that the American government itself not become a party to a contract, or that the United States not coerce China. Through these restrictions Wilson assured China that her integrity was to be defended. Yet, investments were not forthcoming. As an official of Lee, Higginson, and Company, a Boston firm negotiating with Peking, explained:

> We appreciate fully that the failure to secure a loan for China in the United States at this time may have a far reaching effect on the future trade relations between the two countries, but we are not in any way to blame for the causes which have made it impossible for us . . . to carry on successfully a campaign of education of the American investing public.
>
> [For many months] . . . there has been a steady stream of press cables from China reporting revolutions, rebellions, and friction between China and Japan. At the same time, our security markets have been under pressure to take securities from every

part of the world by nations whose credit is either unquestioned or who could give collateral security of a tangible nature.

Our advice, therefore, to the Chinese Minister has been consistently that unless his Government could give security that the American investing public would be willing to accept, they must wait until the public could be educated to take their bonds and that such a campaign of education could not begin until things had quieted down in China.[16]

Such pessimism was encountered everywhere. By 1917 the United States abandoned efforts to encourage investments independently of other powers and was preparing to urge the reorganization of an international banking consortium.

What were the sources of American failure? Tien-yi Li, who emphasized the moral basis of American policy, found the trouble in Wilson's application to China of idealistic, overly generalized principles. Noting that American recognition of the Yuan government was linked with theories on political evolution dear to the President, Li questioned whether Wilson had thought through the implications of his ideas for a revolutionary China: "Wilson, the champion of democratic self-government in the Western world, the sworn opponent of the Mexican dictator Huerta, never openly criticized Yuan's undemocratic methods. Like Reinsch, . . . [Wilson] thought it justifiable for the Chinese President to assume such great powers as were necessary to strengthen the government and to bring about internal peace."[17] Similar criticisms have been leveled at Wilson's economic program. According to Link, the United States withdrew from the Six Power consortium and launched an independent program without adequate investigation of the consequences. If the consortium presented dangers to China's integrity, these were less than those stemming from competitive international financing. "China," Link has observed, "needed not merely friendship and moral exhortation but aggressive American economic assistance as well. By withdrawing support from the Six Power consortium . . . the President surrendered leadership in that ancient land to the Japanese, who were less concerned with 'moral' principles than he."[18]

Williams, however, has denied that Wilson was either ill-informed or confused. Before deciding upon his China policy in 1913, the

16. To Alvin A. Adee, Sept. 6, 1916, National Archives, State Department Decimal File 893.51/1687.
17. *Wilson's China Policy*, pp. 139–162.
18. Link, *Wilson*, II, 283–288.

President carefully considered the range of alternatives open to him. What he sought was the destruction of barriers to American enterprise. To accomplish this he elected to break away from Taft's policy of international cooperation in matters affecting China. In his view independent American recognition of the Chinese republic and withdrawal from the consortium were first steps in removing inhibitions imposed by other powers. His refusal to support the American banking group was intended to destroy an organization monopolizing China's investment market and to open the field to all American enterprise. In short, Wilson applied new tactics to old purposes. The President in no sense disapproved of his predecessor's desire to enlarge the American economic stake; Taft's program was wrong only in its failure to yield results. That Wilson's efforts also failed, Williams has implied, was due less to the misapplication of idealism than the failure of American capital to seize proffered opportunities.[19]

Williams himself has not investigated the aftermath of the American withdrawal from the consortium, but others emphasizing economic causation have followed the trail of American enterprise. These investigations indicate that in 1913–1916 Americans undertook a number of projects. To cite but a single instance, New York bankers and a giant construction firm joined to form the American International Corporation, a heavily capitalized organization which was intended to operate in China, Latin America, or other developing areas. While this organization contracted for several projects in China, no work was ever done. Noel Pugach, whose study of Reinsch reveals much on American business activities, has attributed the failure to the impact of World War I and to the resumption in 1916 of China's civil war. When Wilson made his first decisions on China, Europe was peaceful; China seemingly was stabilized under the republic; and American businessmen faced stiff competition in foreign markets. Two years later all had changed. Europe's belligerents turned all their resources toward victory, thus opening opportunities seemingly more favorable to American interests than those in China. Moreover, Japan, whose ambitions were inflated by the West's preoccupations, openly challenged American interests. Given these new circumstances, Pugach has argued, the reluctance of American business to enter China was scarcely surprising. Nor in this context was there anything particularly significant about Wilson's later decision to revive the China consortium. This latter decision did not reflect (as Link has maintained) a shift from

19. *Tragedy of American Diplomacy,* pp. 68–74.

"missionary diplomacy" to "dollar diplomacy." Wilson's decision reflected the adoption of new tactics in a continuing effort to encourage the export of American capital.[20]

American-Japanese Rivalry

Research in American-Japanese relations, 1913–1916, has focused mainly on developing tensions. Wilson, scholars have agreed, "never exhibited the same sympathy and tolerance with which he viewed and treated China. Standards of international morality which he held so highly were often waived in judging China but were applied rigidly and without insight in dealing with Japan."[21] This is not to say that the President came into office predisposed against Japan. Histories of the California land tenure question have affirmed without exception the President's determination to allay difficulties. Moreover, this determination has been found to have extended into the early months of World War I, the point at which American-Japanese difficulties over China intensified. Both John V. A. MacMurray's denial that the Root–Takahira notes conveyed to the United States the right to be consulted in advance of the Japanese invasion of Shantung and Robert Lansing's observation that it would be "quixotic in the extreme" to permit the question of China's integrity to involve the United States in international difficulties have been widely noted. Thus, historians have found that it was not until China and Japan were well into the Twenty-One Demands controversy that American policy shifted. In contrast to the Wilson administration's earlier effort to encourage a Sino-Japanese compromise settlement, the American position after mid-April 1915, as the Japanese applied pressure on Peking, was one of opposition to Japan. Wilson directed the State Department to seek reduction of Japanese terms and approved a caveat reserving American approval of whatever understanding might be reached. From this point onward American support of China's territorial and administrative integrity has been seen as the prime source of tension.

Agreement on the foregoing outline, however, has not led to the writing of essentially identical narratives. Differing theories on the objectives of American policy have influenced accounts of American–Japanese relations no less than those of Sino-American dealings. Curry, who, it will be recalled, emphasized Wilson's efforts to safeguard China's integrity, focused on American attempts to con-

20. "Progress, Prosperity, and the Open Door," pp. 316–377.
21. William L. Neuman, *America Encounters Japan: From Perry to MacArthur* (New York: Harper and Row, 1965), pp. 140–141.

tain Japanese expansion. My own research, on the other hand, which stressed Lansing's concern with economic objectives, found that difficulties with Japan were no boon to American trade and investment. In consequence, my narrative dealt, not with containment, but with missed opportunities for the settlement of American-Japanese differences.

On one issue—the California land tenure controversy of 1913—historians have been more nearly agreed than on any other. This episode has not been viewed as presenting a clash of "moralistic-legalistic" and economic concerns. Scholars generally have applauded the President's efforts to reduce tensions on the issue. Differences in historical interpretations have centered on whether he succeeded in his purpose. Thomas A. Bailey, for instance, writing in 1931, advanced interpretations which, on the one hand, were based on research in Wilson's dealings with Japan and, on the other, took into account the President's relations with California's leadership. These combined approaches led to the conclusion that Wilson adroitly managed a potentially dangerous situation. For the President, Bailey has found, the real difficulty was the determination of Californians, Republicans and Democrats alike, to seek partisan advantage in the manipulation of the issue. The governor and legislative leaders were deaf to pleas for delay, even though local problems were not so acute as to require immediate action. The situation was one which did not give Wilson any opportunity to resolve basic issues through, say, a new American-Japanese treaty governing immigration and treatment of nationals. The best the administration could do was to demonstrate its profound sympathies for Japan while the Californians did their worst.[22]

Subsequent research, much of which has been based on materials not available in 1931, has expanded and modified these findings, but it has not produced any fundamentally new approach to the problem. Thus, a reexamination of the domestic side has qualified Bailey's castigation of California officialdom: "The dispassionate observer finds little to justify the conduct of California at this time." Roger Daniels, for example, while agreeing that Republican Governor Hiram Johnson's support of discriminatory legislation was a "wanton act," has found partisanship on levels higher than the state capitol. In Daniels' view, Wilson himself seemed almost as concerned with his party's prospects as with Japanese sensibilities. Shortly after taking office the President headed off anti-Japanese legislation

22. "California, Japan, and the Alien Land Legislation of 1913," *Pacific Historical Review*, 1 (March 1932), 36–59.

in Washington, a state which promised no political embarrassments, but in California, where a firm stand would cost the Democrats votes, Wilson exhibited tender regard for states rights.[23] Still another of Bailey's conclusions—that Wilson did all he could do to satisfy Japan—has been reopened to debate. According to Link, Wilson, disturbed by prospects of trouble over a new treaty and concerned by racial implications of Japanese migration to the United States, chose deliberately to interpret federal powers in the narrowest sense so that he might evade Japan's protests through legalistic arguments.[24] A dissenting view may be found in the writings of Byron's biographer, Paolo E. Coletta. In research which freshly documents Bailey's thesis, Coletta has held that there was no sham in Wilson's entrapment between Japan and California. Confronted with a limited range of alternatives, the President wisely chose "to relieve the tensions . . . by sending Bryan to California as a gesture of friendship."[25]

The more fundamental conflicts in historical interpretations of American-Japanese relations may be illustrated with reference to the Twenty-One Demands. America's role in this episode, the histories agree, was that of an interested party seeking for China the best possible terms. Early in China's negotiation with Japan this American role was confined to backstage advice and encouragement. Later the United States took an official stand. In mid-March 1915 the State Department, by then informed of the full list of demands, objected to a number of Japan's terms. A month later, following Wilson's intervention in the controversy, the department announced that the United States had conceded in China none of its treaty rights; urged Tokyo and Peking to settle their differences peacefully; and sought to organize international support on behalf of China. The final step was the dispatch of the Bryan-Lansing caveat, in which the United States indicated that it would not recognize "any agreement or undertaking . . . impairing the treaty rights of the United States . . . , the political territorial integrity of the Republic of China, or the international policy relative to China commonly known as the open door policy." Except for British objections, which were in no way coordinated with those of the United States, Japan

23. *The Politics of Prejudice: The Anti-Japanese Movement in California and the Struggle for Japanese Exclusion* (Berkeley: University of California Press, 1962), pp. 46–64. See also Spencer C. Olin, Jr., "European Immigrant and Oriental Alien: Acceptance and Rejection by the California Legislature of 1913." *Pacific Historical Review*, 35 (August 1966), 303–315.

24. Link, *Wilson*, II, 289–304.

25. "The Most Thankless Task: Bryan and the California Alien Land Legislation," *Pacific Historical Review*, 36 (May 1967), 163–187.

came under pressure from no other power. Such circumstances, scholars also agree, suggest that the United States exercised only limited influence on the course of negotiations. But did limited American intervention serve any good purpose?

Both Li and Curry have warmly supported the American role. Li has praised Reinsch's sympathetic effort to aid Peking in the early days of crisis, and he has found that the United States defended China's integrity by winning some reduction in Japanese terms.[26] For Curry, the most important result was the involvement of the United States in the struggle to maintain a balance of power in East Asia. Though Wilson's immediate accomplishments were small, his legalistic maneuvers kept Japan's claims in China open for discussion. In Curry's judgment, ". . . the years of the Wilson administration marked the first period of outright challenge to a responsible American policy in the Far East. Within the circumstances of the time, the challenge would seem to have been met adequately."[27]

Link and I have offered dissenting views. Link weighed the presumed concessions won by Wilson's diplomacy against possible damage to American interests. "In view of the future course of events in the Far East," Link observed, "the President was assuming a far larger responsibility than he knew."[28] My own criticism was embodied in the contention that Wilson missed an opportunity to strike a bargain with Japan. The terms were divised by Lansing, who, first as the State Department counsellor and later as secretary of state, urged an American-Japanese accommodation, not a confrontation. Thus, Lansing proposed that the United States would concede Japan's "special interests" in Shantung, Eastern Inner Mongolia, and South Manchuria in return for iron-clad Japanese pledges that she would observe the Open Door elsewhere in China and would concede American terms in settling the immigration and land tenure issues. Lansing's view was that the proposed American concessions simply recognized an existing state of affairs. Since Japan had established" special interests" on the continent and was unlikely to surrender them without a fight, nothing would be lost in trying to make the deal. If it worked, both the United States and China would benefit. Arguing that Lansing's proposal held the potential of protecting American economic interests while limiting

26. *Wilson's China Policy*, pp. 101–129.
27. *Wilson and Far Eastern Policy*, pp. 112–129, 322.
28. *Wilson*, vol. III., *The Struggle for Neutrality, 1914–1915* (Princeton, 1960), p. 308.

the American political commitment, I have held the secretary's view to be sounder than the President's.[29]

The Tasks Ahead

At this point two things should be evident: that a generation of scholarship has greatly expanded our knowledge of the substance and sources of Far Eastern policy, 1913–1916; and that these results have been obtained largely by an examination of the American record. The end of this work is by no means in sight. The biographical approach, which thus far has produced studies of Wilson, Bryan, Lansing, and Reinsch, may be extended to include such figures as George Guthrie, the American ambassador in Tokyo, Edward T. Williams, chief of the State Department's Far Eastern Division, and Frank Polk, the department's counsellor, all of whom participated in shaping Wilson's Far Eastern policy. Nor need the search for relevant material be confined any longer to presidential and State Department files. Enough research has already been conducted in other executive departments to suggest their value. William R. Braisted has recently published a sequel to his earlier volume on the U.S. Navy in the Pacific. Containing eight chapters on the years 1913–1917, this projected volume not only supplements knowledge of the diplomatic record, it also serves as a guide to the exploration of naval records.[30] The War Department's Bureau of Insular Affairs was responsible for colonial administration in the Philippines and a few American troops were maintained on China station, but the records of the War Department have been meagerly used. Some recent research in Treasury and Commerce Departments' files suggests that these ought to be investigated further, especially for additional data on the consortium and Wilson's efforts to encourage the expansion of American economic interests.

While nongovernmental sources have not as yet been fully exploited, their potential value may be surmised. Valentine H. Rabe's "The Drive to Christianize China, 1898–1917" (Ph.D. diss., Harvard University, 1960) has capitalized on missionary materials. Noel Pugach[31] and Harry N. Scheiber[32] have drawn on the papers of

29. Beers, *Vain Endeavor*, pp. 36–51.
30. *The United States Navy in the Pacific, 1909–1922* (Austin: University of Texas Press, 1971).
31. "Progress, Prosperity, and the Open Door," esp. chap. 1.
32. "World War I as Entrepreneurial Opportunity: Willard Straight and the American International Corporation," *Political Science Quarterly*, 74 (September 1969), 486–511.

Willard Straight and Frank A. Vanderlip for data on the American International Corporation's investment plans in China. The chapter "During and After the World War" in Eleanor Tupper and George MacReynolds, *Japan in American Public Opinion* (New York: Macmillan Co., 1937) samples the American press on such issues as the Twenty-One Demands, and a scattering of items on missionary activities, educational exchange, and the like, for the Wilson years are incorporated in Robert S. Schwantes', *Japanese and Americans: A Century of Cultural Relations* (New York: Harper, 1955). Taken together, these studies suggest that there are materials outside government files which will provide new dimensions to the history of Wilson's Far Eastern policy. These materials may be used to document American images of China and Japan; they may also fill out the story of the economic relationships intertwined with American diplomacy. It should be remembered, however, that presently such materials are much less organized and accessible to research than official sources. The collection of such materials and the organization of them for research is one of the larger tasks of the next years.

Finally, it should be evident from the bibliographical review presented earlier that the involvement of the United States in East Asia has been viewed almost exclusively through American eyes. The aims and aspirations of foreign governments that are reflected in the literature have largely been those perceived by American observers. Thus Japanese dealings with north Chinese warlords have frequently been interpreted as aimed at aggrandizement, not—as the Japanese believed—at the establishment of friendly relations.[33] Nor has scholarship based on American materials captured British concern over Japanese ambitions.[34] In a word, the history of Wilson's

33. For the Japanese view of their own policy see Frank C. Langdon, "Japan's Failure to Establish Friendly Relations with China in 1917–1918," *Pacific Historical Review*, 26 (August 1957), 245–258. Another pioneering study drawing on Japanese archives in Sadao Asada, "Japan and the United States, 1915–25" (Ph.D. diss., Yale University, 1963).

34. By 1971 the first studies based on British archival materials had been published. The two most ambitious works were: Peter Lowe, *Great Britain and Japan, 1911–15: A Study of British Far Eastern Policy* (London: St. Martin's Press, 1969), and William Roger Louis, *British Strategy in the Far East, 1919–1939* (London: Oxford University Press, 1971). These two offered the most detailed surveys of British attitudes and activities during the Wilson era. Don Dignan, "New Perspectives on British Far Eastern Policy, 1913–1919," *University of Queensland Papers: Departments of Government and History*, 1.5 (St. Lucia, 1969), 263–312, emphasized London's concern over Japanese ambitions in South Asia and interest in a bargain with Japan which was not unlike the one that Lansing proposed. Robert J. Gowen, "Great Britain and the Twenty-one Demands: Cooperation versus Effacement," *Journal of Modern History*, 63 (March 1971), 76–106, argued that it was Great Britain, not the United States, which restrained Japan in 1915. Like studies of Ameri-

Far Eastern policy is one dimensional. There is nothing in the bibliography for 1913–1917 to compare with the multinational studies that are becoming standard in the history of Western international relations. Yet, British Foreign Office archives are now open to researchers; Japanese and Chinese materials are available in the United States, Japan, and Taiwan.[35] If these materials are linked with the expanding array of American sources, foundations are provided for research surpassing that of the last twenty years.

_____

can policy, all of these recent works offered perspectives which were limited by the authors' reliance upon the sources of a single nation. These pioneering research works, however, documented the assumption that a great deal may be learned through the integration of British and American materials.

35. Participants in the Far Eastern International History Seminar at Yale University have attempted to cope with the linguistic and logistic problems that are presented in multiarchival research by dividing their labors. Professor Louis' study, (noted above) which focuses narrowly on British attitudes and activities for the years 1919–1939, is the first published contribution. Subsequent volumes by others will offer American and Asian comparisons. A final volume synthesizing all research is planned. I am not aware of any similar undertaking for the earlier years of the Wilson era.

1917-1922

The half decade 1917–1922 is not an easy one for the historian of American Far Eastern policy to assess. Punctuated by war and revolution, domestic turmoil and peace, the years of World War I and its immediate aftermath have at once fascinated and baffled historians groping for an explanation of their complexities. Scholars have produced a considerable number of general surveys and monographic studies dealing with the Wilson and Harding Far Eastern policies. Yet, nearly a half century after the events they describe, historians have yet to agree on the place of the 1917–1922 period in the broader history of the American–East Asian relationship.

What kinds of interpretations have scholars shaped for this period in the past? What sorts of specialized researches have their hypotheses produced? And what questions and approaches await the scholars of the 1970's seeking to understand the American role in East Asia during that time?

To answer these questions it would seem appropriate first to look at the interpretive scaffolding built by historians over the past half century. Since their work is essentially a chronicle of the American–East Asian diplomatic encounter, it will then be necessary to analyze their writings in the general order of events as they occurred. Such analysis falls naturally into three parts: the years of war, 1917–18; the postwar settlement and its problems, 1919–1921; and the cluster of issues and problems surrounding the Washington Conference of 1921–22. Having accomplished this, it will then be possible to consider elements of the Wilson and Harding Far Eastern policies—ideas underlying them, political, military, and bureaucratic structures shaping them, and men executing them—that remain less well defined in historical literature. Finally, with a heightened awareness of past historiography, it should be possible to articulate approaches and issues for historians of the future.

A. Whitney Griswold, whose *The Far Eastern Policy of the United States* dominated the historiography of the Wilson and Harding years for a generation, first attempted to construct an interpretive framework in the late 1930's. The Yale historian fitted the war and immediate postwar period into his broader scheme for the history of American Far Eastern policy. He discerned an underlying continuity of principle in it that transcended changes of party and administration. Moving up and down in waves of diplomatic advance and retreat, that policy was, in Griswold's view, steadfast in its friendship and sympathy for China. At times it dashed against the rocks of Japanese imperialism. On other occasions it flowed over the shoals of British diplomatic duplicity in the service of the empire's commercial and strategic interests. But policy consistently sought to contain Japan and constrain European imperialists.[1]

The year 1917 marked the beginning of a wave of Far Eastern policy activism which crested five years later at the Washington Conference. Griswold made Wilson the architect of a policy of containment. Harding and Hughes were carpenters who executed the master's designs. The Democratic President faced Japanese militarism alone during the war, then sought to disarm Nipponese imperialism at the Paris Peace Conference. He was both the "disciplinarian of the Far East" and the loving friend of China. Harding and Hughes then brought Japan to the bar in 1921–22, checking its designs on the Asian mainland. They also restrained wily European powers by forcing them to recognize in treaty form the traditional principles of American Far Eastern policy—the Open Door and respect for Chinese territorial integrity.[2]

The complexities of these years frustrated Griswold's interpretive design. The Yale historian cast Woodrow Wilson in an anti-Japanese mold and placed him in the pantheon of his predecessors as a defender of continuing principles of American Far Eastern policy. Yet he recognized that Wilson backed away from overt clashes with Japan. The President also championed principles for a League of Nations which would include the island empire rather than the precepts of a traditional Far Eastern policy which might contain it. Harding and Hughes were equally contradictory. They somehow were duped by Britain and Japan into agreeing to naval arms limitation, yet proved brilliant and skillful in purely Far Eastern matters. They recognized Japan's naval superiority in the western Pacific yet did not beat a strategic retreat from East Asian affairs. Griswold tried to reconcile these opposites by linking the Five and Nine Power Treaties of Washington. The triumph of principle implicit in the latter's recognition of the Open Door doctrine compensated for the

1. Robert H. Ferrell, "The Griswold Theory of Our Far Eastern Policy," in Dorothy Borg, comp., *Historians and American Far Eastern Policy*, Occasional Papers of The East Asian Institute (New York: East Asian Institute, Columbia University, 1966), pp. 14–21.

2. Griswold, *Far Eastern Policy*, chaps. 5–8. See esp. pp. 207–208, 239, 269, 298, 331.

risks inherent in the former. Griswold thus triumphantly concluded that the Washington Conference, the crest of a Wilsonian wave of activism, was "the apotheosis of the traditional Far Eastern policy of the United States."[3]

Nearly two decades after Griswold formulated his theses, William Appleman Williams offered a far different interpretation of the Wilson and Harding Far Eastern policies. Like Griswold, Williams discerned a continuity of assumptions, objectives, and techniques in all of American diplomatic history. He found that history a tragic mix of humanitarian concern for the welfare of others and national determination to promote overseas economic expansion. Americans wanted to help others but assumed they must become more like themselves. They championed equality of opportunity for overseas economic expansion in the Open Door doctrine. But at the same time, they were blind to the fact that they simultaneously doomed other nations to subserving the needs of American commerce and industry. Thus, in Williams' view, the United States under Wilson and Harding sought to preserve an informal empire no less real than the more formal hegemonial structures Americans had always attacked.[4]

Williams argued that the years 1917–1922 were critical to the development of this informal empire. Wilson and Harding shared a key assumption—the necessity of resisting radical change in the East Asian status quo. This assumption warped their strategic vision so as to shrink China and inflate Japan into the Great Power of Asia. It blinded them to the diplomatic utility of friendship with revolutionary Russia in maintaining the East Asian power balance. At the same time it closed their ears to the pleas of conservative Chinese nationalists for support. Both administrations thus pursued policies that treated China as an object, rather than an actor, on the international stage. This determination to maintain the status quo in spite of "the forces of social and colonial revolt that cracked the barriers of Nineteenth Century imperialism during World War I," not friendship for China or hostility toward Japan, remained the consistent purpose of the Wilson and Harding Far Eastern policies.[5]

Williams held that both Presidents employed a single instrument to maintain empire: the consortium. But he found that they made quite different uses of it. Wilson saw the consortium in political as

3. Ibid., pp. 255, 284, 303, 331.
4. William Appleman Williams, *The Tragedy of American Diplomacy*, Delta Books, 2nd ed. (New York: Dell Publishing Company, 1962), p. 82.
5. William Appleman Williams, "China and Japan: a Challenge and a Choice of the Nineteen Twenties," *Pacific Historical Review*, 26 (August 1957), 260–266.

well as economic terms. A nineteenth century liberal, he wrote it into the international political order as the League of Nations. This structure would constrain imperialist antagonisms in East Asia as well as check Bolshevik revolution. The consortium would also set the bounds of commercial rivalries so as to assure America's triumph in the contest for the great China market. Williams argued that a different philosophical approach underlay Republican use of the consortium. Harding and Hughes cast aside its political restraints, symbolized by the League covenant. They moved, instead, to form a concert of oligarchs for preservation of the status quo and mutual promotion of economic interests in China. In this interpretation, the Washington Conference marked the triumph of cooperation rather than of containment.[6]

The Williams thesis was important in first sounding the theme of cooperation rather than containment as the essence of American Far Eastern policy in 1917–1922. But Williams also identified another critical issue, the link between domestic and diplomatic policies. He found the consortium a technique both useful and dangerous. He recognized that it could moderate Great Power antagonisms in East Asia. At the same time, it might allow private interests to suborn the public good in American Far Eastern policy. This, he argued, is precisely what occurred in 1917–1922. Wilson revived the consortium as a political and economic instrument to deal with China. But the bankers who provided its financial sinews used it to promote trade and capital investment through friendship with Japan. Republican politicians followed their lead, clinching a compact of oligarchs at the Washington Conference. It was in this manner that the means of American Far Eastern policy reshaped its ends.[7]

Akira Iriye built a third interpretation of the Wilson and Harding Far Eastern policies on foundations laid by Griswold and Williams. But his frame of reference was quite different from theirs. Iriye saw 1917–1922 as a period of critical transformations in American Far Eastern policy which amounted to a sharp break with the past. Wilson and Harding, he argued, did not seek simply to contain Japan or to befriend China. Their purpose was not to right the war-disrupted imperialist balance of power in East Asia and still less to protect some new informal empire. Instead, the United States sought to establish a new international political order in East Asia based on cooperation among the Great Powers. It was this cooperationist

6. Williams, *Tragedy*, pp. 86–96, 110–116.
7. Ibid., pp. 70–74 elaborates his thesis on the dangers of the consortium; pp. 123–126 deal with Republican policies.

order, both an objective and a technique of policy, which would best serve American interests in East Asia.

Iriye identified complex international political and attitudinal changes as the source of movement in American Far Eastern policy. He, like Griswold and Williams, pointed to war and revolution in East Asia as important stimuli for change. The former destroyed the pre-war balance of antagonisms in East Asia; but it also re-ordered Japanese-American economic relations, making each nation more important to the other as a trade and financial partner. Revolution did far more than temporarily remove Russia from the East Asian power balance. Iriye found that it triggered important attitudinal changes in the United States, Japan, and China. On one side of the Pacific, Wilson responded to it with the rhetoric of self-determination. On the other, Japanese pressed their government for more Taishō democracy and less bureaucratic control. Even more important, revolution, together with Wilsonian words of self-determination, fed Chinese hopes for the abolition of extraterritoriality and the return of Shantung. When these were shattered, a volcano of nationalist feeling showered antagonisms into Sino-Japanese and Sino-American relations. The result of all this was, for American policy makers no less than their opposites in Tokyo, a reordering of policy priorities. In the wake of war, military and strategic considerations shrunk while economic concern grew larger. In both nations new groups rose to use "new diplomacy" to promote harmony, rather than conflict, between the nations of the Pacific.

The Iriye interpretation, like those offered by Griswold and Williams, ascribed unity and continuity to 1917–1922. But his interpretation differed in substance and structure from theirs. In Iriye's view, the United States was neither disciplinarian nor dupe in East Asia. Instead it was simply a partially successful pupil of experience turned teacher. It did take the initiative, under Wilson, to break with the imperialist past and establish a cooperative international political order in East Asia. Its course was linear and progressive, from the Paris Peace Conference, through the thickets of postwar controversies in East Asia toward the imperfect triumph of Washington. There, American policy makers completed the education of their Japanese and British opposites, sealing the bargain in the treaty structure established in 1922. But Iriye's interpretation went beyond this descriptive function to add a new analytical dimension to the study of American Far Eastern policy during these years. By using the comparative method and by emphasizing shifts in perceptions and priorities, Iriye suggested that American Far Eastern policy was something more than a shuttlecock between friendship for China and containment of Japan or between resistance and embracement of revolution. On the contrary, Wilson and Harding—as imperfect observers of East Asia—were architects of a less than ideal international order there.[8]

Japanese historians, no less than their American counterparts, have been unable to agree on a common interpretation of American Far Eastern policy during 1917–1922. With rare exceptions their accounts have proceeded from either Marxian historiographic axioms or strong nationalist feeling rather than from independent analytical insight. Scholars of both dispositions have agreed with Whitney Griswold that the Wilson and Harding policies were linear in design and anti-Japanese in effect; but they have differed over the underlying motives of that policy. Shinobu Seisaburō, writing late in the 1930's, laid the foundations for the Marxian approach. The Open Door, he concluded, was simply a rhetorical cover for economic and imperialist motives underlying American policies. The United States sought to increase its economic stake and political influence in China during the Wilson and Harding years, and this inevitably brought it into conflict with the imperial Japanese rival. Other scholars have taken up this theme and developed it still further in the postwar years. Inoue Kiyoshi has suggested that America's East Asian policy proceeded from its anti-revolutionary intervention in World War I and the Russian Revolution. This crusade temporarily weakened it and led to collaboration with Japanese imperialists in aggression against the Chinese people. Yet because Japan's imperialism was political and military and America's economic and educational, China proved a fertile ground for Japanese-American imperialist antagonisms. Thus Wilson and Harding added another contradiction to the historical dynamic which reached its apocalyptic conclusion in 1941.[9]

8. Akira Iriye develops his theses in *After Imperialism* (Cambridge: Harvard University Press, 1965), pp. 10–22, and in *Across the Pacific: An Inner History of American-East Asian Relations* (New York: Harcourt, Brace, and World, 1967), pp. 138–145.

9. Shinobu Seisaburō in *Kindai Nihon gaikōshi* (Modern Japanese diplomatic history; Tokyo: Chūō Kōron sha, 1942), pp. 233–258 passim; Inoue Kiyoshi, *Nihon teikoku shugi no keisei* (The structure of Japanese imperialism; Tokyo: Iwanami Shoten, 1968), pp. 381–383, and in his *Nihon kindai shi no mikata* (Interpretations of modern Japanese history; Tokyo: Tabata Shoten, 1968), p. 2/2, reflects the interpretive premises to be found in the many works of this prolific scholar. As the preceding titles suggest, Japanese historians have dealt with American East Asian policy only in connection with other themes more important to them. This chapter does not contain an analysis of all such scholars and their works. Rather the works cited should be regarded as representative samples of Japanese scholarly endeavor.

More nationalistic historians before and after the Pacific War found quite different meanings in American Far Eastern policy in 1917–1922. They suggested that factual misperceptions and mistaken diplomatic strategies carried Japan and the United States a step closer to eventual conflict. In a remarkably perceptive account written just prior to Pearl Harbor Royama Masamichi argued that the Wilson and Harding Administrations had misread the signposts of change in post-World War I East Asia. Overly concerned first with intervention in, then with extrication from, Europe's international political crises, American policy makers slighted the significance of Japan's industrial and cultural growth during the war years. They refused to recognize the island empire's international political importance, and at the Washington Conference they employed a short-sighted, coercive diplomatic strategy against Japan which imposed unrealistic restrictions on its freedom to develop East Asia. More recently, Oka Yoshitake also has argued that misperception distorted the Wilson and Harding Far Eastern policies. Wilson's subordinates misread the history of wartime East Asia to conclude that the Japanese empire sought to establish an Asian Monroe Doctrine, and they determined to oppose it. Wilson then deepened American-Japanese antagonism at the Paris Peace Conference by failing to understand Japan's genuine desire to represent all Asians in writing the principle of racial equality into the League of Nations Covenant. His successors succeeded in establishing a fair Pacific naval and strategic balance of power, but they mistakenly employed a coercive anti-Japanese diplomatic strategy to do so.[10]

Only recently have younger Japanese scholars familiar with modes of political and historical analysis prevalent in the West challenged these earlier interpretations. Mitani Taichirō has argued that changes in America's self image reshaped its Far Eastern policy and Japanese responses to it between 1917 and 1922. Casting aside its traditional role as the preserver of independence from Europe, the United States began to see itself as the protector of democracy, seeking not only to aid China as a "sister republic" but also to promote multi-power diplomatic cooperation and economic development in all East Asia. This changed self-image had a profound impact on the peoples and leaders of Japan and China. It

10. Royama Masamichi, *Foreign Policy of Japan: 1914–1939* (Tokyo: Japanese Council Institute of Pacific Relations, 1941), pp. 23–24, 30, 35; Oka Yoshitake, *Tenkanki no Taishō* (Taishō: A turning point; Tokyo: Tokyo Daigaku Shuppan sha, 1969), pp. 100–104, 112, 181. It should be noted that this is a general study which reflects the conclusions of Professor Oka's other, more thorough, monographic studies of Japan's diplomatic and military history.

provided an impetus to the May Fourth movement in China and reshaped the bases of political power in Japan. America appealed to the Japanese people as a symbol of the "new democracy" and led their leaders to a more idealistic, less self-seeking foreign policy of cooperation with the American republic. Mitani's argument was unique in emphasizing that ideas far more than sheer political influence or economic power reshaped American Far Eastern policy and East Asian responses to it during the Wilson and Harding years.[11]

In contrast to these broad surveys, it is difficult to generalize about more specialized studies. What follows must thus be read with caution. It is clear that monographs written since the late 1930's have focused almost exclusively on the political aspects of American–East Asian relations. They afford the reader an uneven coverage of these years—scarce for the war years, rich for the Paris Peace Conference months, few again for the last months of the Wilson Administration and the first of the Harding regime. They have rarely focused on Far Eastern policy itself. The historian must turn to the political biographer, the historian of East Asia, the chronicler of Anglo- and Russo-American relations, and naval historians for enlightenment. Finally, the history of American Far Eastern policy during the Wilson and Harding years has been, in large part, a search for the key motive or motives behind Presidential statements or actions.

The historiography of the war years well illustrates this last point. Historians of Far Eastern policy have for the most part written within a framework of controversy over motive elaborated in the late 1930's. In 1937, Thomas La Fargue, relying on the published memoirs of former Minister Reinsch, established the theme of America's wartime friendship for China. The differences between President Wilson and his subordinates over Far Eastern policy were those of technique and timing rather than of ends. Whitney Gris-

11. Professor Mitani has put forward this interpretation in two versions of the same essay: "Tenkanki (1918–1921) no gaikō shido" (Foreign policy leadership in a period of change, 1918–1921) in Sunohara Hajime and Mitani Taichirō, eds., *Kindai Nihon no seiji shidō* (Political leadership in modern Japan; Tokyo: Tokyo Daigaku Shuppan sha, 1965), esp. pp. 317, 325–328; and in his *Nihon Seitō seiji no keisei* (The structure of Japanese party politics; Tokyo: Tokyo Daigaku Shuppan sha, 1967), pp. 252–254, 273–297, passim. It should be noted that Mitani's interpretation of the relative impact of America's changed view of its world role on Japan's political leaders has been challenged by Professor Satō Seizaburō of Tokyo University in an essay, "Kyōchō to jiritsu no aida—Nihon" (Japan—Between self-reliance and cooperation), *Nempō seiji gaku* (*Annals of Japanese Political Science*) (Tokyo: Iwanami Shoten, 1970), pp. 99–144.

wold a year later elaborated the corollary to this—mounting Wilsonian suspicion of Japan. He saw presidential determination to contain Japan implicit in the controversy over China's entry into the war. The Ishii-Lansing accord and the revival of the China Consortium in 1917 were stepping stones toward the climax of containment, the decision to intervene in Siberia a year later. Only recently have scholars begun to question these hypotheses. Burton Beers in his study of Secretary of State Lansing has suggested that an alternative policy of accommodation with Japan existed within the administration. Madeleine Chi, in her study of wartime China diplomacy, questions the depth of pro-China sentiment within the Wilson administration and suggests that national self-interest tempered by wartime European exigencies lay at the heart of United States Far Eastern policy.[12]

12. Thomas Edward LaFargue, *China and the World War* (Stanford, Calif.: Stanford University Press, 1937), pp. 78–113, focuses on the problem of China's war entry and chronicles differences between Minister Reinsch and Secretary Lansing; Griswold, *Far Eastern Policy*, pp. 199–204, 208–223; Jeffrey J. Safford, "Experiment in Containment: The United States Steel Embargo and Japan, 1917–1918," *Pacific Historical Review*, 39 (November 1970), pp. 439–451, elaborates on the Griswold thesis but concludes that containment fueled Japanese expansionism; Burton F. Beers, *Vain Endeavor: Robert F. Lansing's Attempts to End the American-Japanese Rivalry* (Durham, N.C.: Duke University Press, 1962). in chaps. 7–9 he elaborates the Lansing alternative for the war years. Madeleine Chi, *China Diplomacy, 1914–1918*, Harvard East Asian Monographs (Cambridge, Mass.: East Asian Research Center, Harvard University, 1970), p. 255, summarizes her critique of wartime American China diplomacy. Chi agrees with the implications of the Griswold thesis in arguing that lack of Anglo-American cooperation shaped much of that diplomacy. Her study is important in drawing upon British, Chinese, and Japanese as well as American archival materials. For other surveys of wartime Far Eastern policy, see Roy Watson Curry, *Woodrow Wilson and Far Eastern Policy 1913–1921* (New York: Bookman Associates, 1957), chap. 6; Russell H. Fifield, *Woodrow Wilson and the Far East* (New York: Crowell, 1952), chap. 2; and William L. Neumann, *America Encounters Japan* (Baltimore: Johns Hopkins University Press, 1963), pp. 135–150. Knowledge of British and Japanese wartime China policy is critical to an understanding of Sino-American relations. Recent studies which make use of newly opened archival materials include Don Dignan, "New Perspectives on British Far Eastern Policy, 1913–1919," *University of Queensland Papers*, 1 (January 1969), 263–302. Peter Lowe, *Great Britain and Japan, 1911–1915* (New York: St. Martin's Press, 1969) deals with the later war years in his concluding chapter. Ian Nish, "Dr. Morrison and China's Entry into the World War," in R. Hatton and M. S. Anderson, eds., *Studies in Diplomatic History* (London: Longmans, 1970) provides comparative insights into Reinsch's problems through use of the manuscripts of the British adviser to the Chinese government. This essay is the harbinger of Nish's *Alliance in Decay*, a broad study of the Anglo-Japanese relationship in 1911–1922. For wartime Japanese policy, see Frank C. Langdon, "Japan's Failure to Establish Friendly Relations with China in 1917–1918," *Pacific Historical Review*, 26 (August 1957), 245–258; Nagaoka Shinjirō, *Dai ichiji taisen to Nihon* (The first world war and Japan; Tokyo: Hara Shobo, forthcoming, promises to be the most thorough scrutiny of Japan's

Two incidents in the wartime American–East Asian dialogue demand special attention here. The first, the Ishii-Lansing agreement, spawned controversy from the moment of its signature. Scholars argued for a generation over whether or not its words really committed the United States to recognition of Japan's "paramount" interests in China. Then they debated whether it was a necessary evil or a positive stroke of containment policy. LaFargue argued the first case, while Griswold took up cudgels for the second argument. It was 1949 before Francis Prescott gained access to key manuscript materials and wrote what remains the most thorough study of the Ishii-Lansing accord. He considered the agreement an element of wartime coalition diplomacy as well as an aspect of Far Eastern policy. Prescott described it as an attempt to resolve immediate wartime problems and an effort to deal with projected postwar difficulties in Pacific shipping, China commerce, and naval competition. His argument made the agreement a necessity. Burton Beers subsequently wrote of it as a lost opportunity. In his view, the agreement was a symbol of the triumph of presidential idealism over Secretary Lansing's desire for a realistic Japanese-American accord.[13]

The Siberian intervention of 1918 is an even more complex illustration of the search for presidential motive in monographic studies. Whitney Griswold was godfather to the only interpretive school which deals with the intervention primarily as an aspect of Far Eastern policy. He forcefully asserted that Wilson's purpose in

---

wartime relations with the Great Powers; Japanese China policy will be dealt with by Usui Katsumi, *Nihon to Chūgoku* (Japan and China; Tokyo: Hara Shobo, forthcoming).

13. Samuel F. Bemis and Grace G. Griffin, eds., *Guide to the Diplomatic History of the United States 1775–1921* (Washington: Government Printing Office, 1935) pp. 501–502, and William F. Langer and Hamilton F. Armstrong, eds., *Foreign Affairs Bibliography* (New York: Council on Foreign Relations, 1933) pp. 482–483, are guides to early literature on the Ishii-Lansing accord; LaFargue, *China and the World War*, pp. 129–139; Griswold, *Far Eastern Policy*, pp. 213–217, suggests that containment was a strong administration motive even though Wilson backed away from a clash with Japan; Francis G. Prescott, "The Lansing-Ishii Agreement," (Ph.D. diss., Yale University, 1949); Beers, *Vain Endeavor*, pp. 102–119, 180–182; Madeleine Chi, *China Diplomacy*, chap. 5, offers a somewhat different interpretation of the negotiations from Beers's. She argues that Lansing was in full control of them and that his talks with Wilson did not substantively modify the outcome of negotiations with Ishii. Asada Sadao, "Japan and the United States, 1915–1925," (Ph.D. diss., Yale University, 1963,) makes extensive use of Japanese archival materials in discussing the Ishii-Lansing talks. Their brief treatment in Gaimushō Hyakunen Shi Hensan Iinkai, ed., *Gaimushō no hyakunen* (The foreign ministry centennial; Tokyo: Hara Shobo, 1969), vol. 1, chronicles the bureaucratic battle in Tokyo over whether or not a broad agreement with the United States was possible.

dispatching American forces "first and last was to resist the Japanese penetration of northern Manchuria and Siberia." John White, in *The Siberian Intervention* (1950), accepted Griswold's containment thesis. Betty Miller Unterberger, in a detailed study of the Siberian episode which appeared six years later, concluded that the desire to constrain Japan ranked first among Wilsonian motives for intervention. In her view Wilson responded to traditional challenges to the East Asian balance of power: shifting antagonisms in northern Manchuria, and the threat of Japanese control of the Chinese Eastern Railroad. The President finally acted to contain Japan's inevitable march into Siberia.[14]

Another school of historians has explained the decision to intervene as an outgrowth of broad non-Far Eastern wartime pressures. Christopher Lasch has argued for the primacy of strategic fears of a German advance to the east in Wilsonian motives. Richard Ullman, on the other hand, has stressed Wilson's relative freedom from such wartime bogeys. George Kennan conceded that Wilson was suspicious of Japan and concerned at Far Eastern international political developments. But he concluded that a complex mix of long range hopes for world peace and immediate misinformation determined the President's choices. As a professional diplomat he demonstrated how the flow of information, true and false, influenced Wilson; and as a student of Russian history he demolished the Stalinist argument that opposition to revolution spelled intervention. Kennan concluded that it was misinformation from Russia, unrelenting pressure from the European Allies, and concern for the fate of Czech forces in Russia that prompted Wilson to act.[15]

14. Griswold, *Far Eastern Policy*, pp. 226–234; John White, *The Siberian Intervention* (Princeton: Princeton University Press, 1950), p. 125; Betty Miller Unterberger, *America's Siberian Expedition, 1918–1920: A Study of National Policy* (Durham: Duke University Press, 1956), pp. 87–88. Other studies which follow this interpretative line include Curry, *Wilson and Far Eastern Policy*, chap. 8; Neumann, *America Encounters Japan*, p. 158, which stresses Japanese-American economic interests in Siberia as a factor in the decision; and Betty Miller Unterberger, comp. *American Intervention in the Russian Civil War* (Lexington, Mass.: Heath and Co:. 1969), which introduces and surveys the literature on intervention.

15. Christopher Lasch, "American Intervention in Siberia: A Reinterpretation," *Political Science Quarterly*, 77 (June 1962), pp. 205–223; Richard H. Ullman, *Anglo-Soviet Relations, 1917–1921, I Intervention and the War*, (Princeton: Princeton University Press, 1961), is the best account of British pressures on Wilson; James W. Morley, *The Japanese Thrust into Siberia, 1918* (New York: Columbia University Press, 1957), deals with the complex Japanese decision to intervene and affords another perspective from which to approach Wilson's decision; Professor Hosoya Chihiro, in the discussion of the Siberian expedition in *Gaimushō no hyakunen*, cited earlier, and in two other studies based on Japanese and Russian as well as American sources,

Historians concerned with the influence of ideology on foreign policy have offered yet another explanation of the Wilsonian decision to intervene. William A. Williams argued that Wilson was a true conservative and that he acted to preserve the Open Door against Soviet revolutionary ideology as well as to check the Japanese threat to the traditional balance of imperial antagonisms in East Asia. Gordon Levin, drawing upon some of the same materials as Williams, recently argued the opposite side of the case. He saw intervention as an attempt to bring Japan into the new international political order rather than a stroke of containment or a reluctant acquiescence to wartime pressures. On the contrary, the intervention was a key element in a broad diplomatic and ideological strategy.[16]

This brief review of the controversies over wartime American–East Asian relations reflects the thought of one generation of historians and points to opportunities for the next. Despite the effort to analyze Presidential motives, the historian of Far Eastern policy still has no broad account of the war period to turn to. No study attempts to see this period in its entirety and to identify its particular characteristics. Scholars have yet to explain in full the dynamics of wartime American-Japanese rivalries in China. They have not yet taken into account the interpretive insights offered by political scientists' studies of Cold War competition to aid revolutionary nations or the fresh perspectives brought to this period by China historians.[17] There is no published account of wartime Sino-Ameri-

stresses the importance of Wilson's attitude in Tokyo's policy debates. His *Shiberia shuppei shiteki kenkyu* (Historical research on the Siberian expedition; Tokyo: Yuhikaku, 1955, deals primarily with the intervention decision; *Roshia Kakumei to Nihon* (The Russian Revolution and Japan; Tokyo: Hara Shobo, forthcoming), promises a broader treatment of the entire Japanese experience with revolutionary Russia. George F. Kennan, *Soviet-American Relations, 1917–1920:* vol. I, *Russia Leaves the War,* and Vol. II, *The Decision to Intervene* (Princeton: Princeton University Press, 1956–1958) is a massively detailed study which must be read in its entirety to be appreciated. Chaps. 13–15 and 23 in the first volume and chaps. 3–4, 15, and 17 in the second deal specifically with Siberia. Robert James Maddox, "Woodrow Wilson, the Russian Embassy, and Siberian Intervention," *Pacific Historical Review,* 36 (November 1967), 435–448, discusses yet another effort to sway Wilson's thinking, and Beers, *Vain Endeavor,* chap. 10, stresses wartime concerns in Lansing's motives for intervention.

16. Williams, *Tragedy,* pp. 110–114. Williams offers a more detailed account of the intervention in *American-Russian Relations 1781–1947* (New York: Rinehart 1952), chaps. 5–6; R. D. Warth, *The Allies and the Russian Revolution* (Durham: Duke University Prses, 1954) stresses the ideological motives underlying intervention; N. Gordon Levin, Jr., *Woodrow Wilson and World Politics* (New York: Oxford University Press, 1968), pp. 104–113.

17. Two studies which approach this period from different perspectives and afford new insights into it are Joseph R. Levenson, *Liang Ch'i-ch'ao and the Mind of Modern China* (Cambridge, Mass.: Harvard University Press, 1953),

can or Japanese-American relations sensitive to the nature of alliance diplomacy or based on multiarchival sources. No one has explored wartime thoughts—except those of the White House and State Department—about postwar East Asian order. Only when these and many other specialized studies have been undertaken will it be possible to understand wartime American Far Eastern policy as part of the larger history of American–East Asian relations.

The months of Wilsonian peacemaking and postwar adjustment, no less than those of war, remain an enigma to the historian. Was this a period of mounting American–East Asian antagonisms or of first gropings toward mutual accommodation? Relatively few specialized studies are available. Those dealing with the Paris Peace Conference reflect, for the most part, the Griswoldian view of it as a Japanese-American confrontation. There is no adequate study of Far Eastern policy preparations for the conference despite the fact that Lawrence Gelfand, the historian of the Inquiry, has pointed out the number and intensity of debates on East Asian problems. Most accounts of the negotiations at Paris, following Griswold, have attempted to understand and assign priorities to the motives in President Wilson's mind as he moved through controversies over Pacific Islands and racial equality toward the excruciating personal decision to accept the Japanese arguments for reversion of Shantung to Chinese control. The history of those choices, like the contemporary debate over them, has been in large part a dialogue between expediency and principle in presidential decision making.[18]

Griswold portrayed Wilson as trapped between Japanese greed and British duplicity in trying to resolve the Pacific Islands, racial equality, and Shantung questions at Paris. He saw application of the mandate principle to the Pacific Islands as a partial victory for Wil-

---

and George T. Yu, *Party Politics in Republican China 1912–1924* (Berkeley: University of California Press, 1966). It might also be noted here that given the growing number of detailed studies of national policy formulation for the war years the time is ripe for comparative multi-national analysis of East Asian International politics in this period.

18. Lawrence E. Gelfand, *The Inquiry: American Preparations for Peace, 1917–1919* (New Haven: Yale University Press, 1963), pp. 228, 260–271. Gelfand's study deals primarily with the Inquiry as an organization and does not discuss at length the policy proposals it generated; Harry L. Harvin, Jr., "The Far East in the Peace Conference of 1919" (Ph.D. diss., Duke University, 1956), makes use of the Inquiry archives and State Department records, but does not discuss American preconference preparations at length. References cited in the following paragraphs would seem to confirm the 1944 interpretation offered by Thomas A. Bailey, *Woodrow Wilson and the Lost Peace* (Chicago: Quadrangle Books, 1963), pp. 26, 279, that Wilson did not go to Paris with firm, well-defined administration-developed policy positions on East Asian problems.

sonian containment. Other scholars have attacked that view and debated the importance of strategic considerations in the minds of Wilson and his advisers. The racial equality issue has received similar treatment from historians. They have argued that domestic political concern, the skill of Wilson's adversaries, personal remnants of racism, and devotion to even more fundamental principles explain his decision not to include racial equality provisions in the League of Nations covenant. They have attacked Wilson's skill as a negotiator on this issue. Roy Watson Curry, like Griswold, linked racial equality with an even more important issue by asserting that "the loss of racial equality (for Japan) made the Shantung settlement inevitable."[19]

Historians have agreed that the Shantung question was the most critical Far Eastern policy problem at Paris. Griswold made it a key element in the Wilsonian offensive against Japan. Fifteen years passed before Russell Fifield explored archival materials dealing with this problem. His study remains the definitive account written from American sources, but it does not differ substantially from the Griswoldian account. Fifield demonstrated that Shantung was truly a case in presidential decision making: the President did not go to

19. Griswold, *Far Eastern Policy,* pp. 241–254; Pacific Islands issue: Edward T. Williams, "Japan's Mandate in the Pacific," *American Journal of International Law* 27 (July 1933), 428–439; Warner Levi, "American Attitudes toward Pacific Islands, 1914–1919," *Pacific Historical Review* 17 (February 1948), 55–64, and Earl S. Pomeroy, *Pacific Outpost: American Strategy in Guam and Micronesia* (Stanford: Stanford University Press, 1951), pp. 51–69, describe pre-Conference attitudes within the administration; Harold and Margaret Sprout, *Towards a New Order of Seapower* (Princeton: Princeton University Press, 1943), p. 92, reverses Griswold to argue that Wilson was insensitive to the strategic implications of giving the mandate to Japan; Fifield, *Wilson and the Far East,* pp. 134–139, pointed out the division among Wilson's advisers and took the Griswoldian view of the President's intentions. Warner Schilling, "Admirals and Foreign Policy, 1913–1919," (Ph.D. diss., Yale University, 1953), pp. 218–229, argues that Wilson was more aware than his professional naval advisers of the strategic consequences of the mandate issue. The controversy is not insignificant, for it deals with one important aspect of the Griswoldian containment thesis. Griswold, *Far Eastern Policy,* pp. 247–252, describes Wilson as trapped on the racial issue by Hughes' ability to exploit it for disruptive purposes both at Paris and in the United States. Paul Birdsall, *Versailles Twenty Years After* (New York: Harcourt and Brace, 1941), pp. 90–101, holds that the race issue was simply a negotiating ploy. Bailey, *Wilson and the Lost Peace* p. 272, argues the opposite case. Neumann, *America Encounters Japan,* p. 154, suggests that Wilson personally was not entirely free of racial prejudices. Seth Tillman, *Anglo-American Relations at the Paris Peace Conference of 1919* (Princeton, N.J.: Princeton University Press, 1961), pp. 301–303, stresses the importance of British opposition on this issue; this study was written, however, entirely from American archival sources. Curry, *Wilson and Far Eastern Policy,* pp. 253–257, lists all the possible motives for Wilson's decision on racial equality.

Paris with firm views on the fate of the former German leased territory. He was impressed by Chinese arguments, angered at Japanese tactics, yet nonetheless limited by the trend of negotiations on other issues at Paris. Left in the critical moment with only unpalatable choices, his decision made more difficult by knowledge that the Japanese threat to quit the conference and the League was real, Wilson ultimately acquiesced before Japanese demands. In this view, Wilson abandoned the immediate goal of containing Japan so as to be better able to constrain it in the League of Nations.[20]

The drama of the Paris Peace Conference attracted many historians, but the tragedy of the last Wilson years left the shelves virtually bare of specialized studies of the immediate postwar era. Shantung after Paris scarcely appears in the literature of Sino-American relations. American historians were quick to describe the domestic repercussions of the Shantung decision on the bitter fight for the Versailles Treaty in the Senate. But they have done little to explain its Far Eastern policy consequences. Griswold criticized Wilson's Shantung diplomacy and suggested that the President did little more than resort to an impotent nonrecognition doctrine. Others have offered different accounts of the denouement of the Shantung issue. But no historian has yet attempted to describe and analyze the protracted post-Paris Sino-American and Japanese-American discussions of the question. Scholars have only begun to analyze the United States' response to the wave of demonstrations and nationalist feeling which the Shantung decision touched off in China. Consequently, Sino-American relations in the immediate postwar era remain a rich field for future historical exploration.[21]

20. Griswold, *Far Eastern Policy*, pp. 252–254, argues that Wilson made his decision on Shantung "in despair." Fifield, *Wilson and the Far East*, chaps. 3–5, is the most detailed account of the negotiations. For a Chinese view of the Shantung issue by a junior member of the delegation, see Wunsz King, *China at the Paris Peace Conference in 1919* (Jamaica, N.Y.: St. John's University Press, 1961). Westel W. Willoughby, *China at the Conference, A Report* (Baltimore: Johns Hopkins University Press, 1922), is a contemporary pro-Chinese view. Japanese scholars have only recently begun to reexamine the history of the Paris Peace Conference. *Gaimushō no hyaknen*, vol. I, pt. 2, chap. 1, is a brief guide to the policy debates in Tokyo preceding and during the conference; Kobayashi Tatsuo, *Pari heiwa kaigi to Nihon* (The Paris Peace Conference and Japan; Tokyo: Hara Shobo, forthcoming) promises a full account based on key archival materials; Ikei Masaru, "Pari kowa kaigi to jinrui sabetsu teppai mondai" (The Paris Peace Conference and the problem of eliminating racial discrimination), *Kikan kokusai seiji* (*International relations;* Autumn 1962), pp. 44–58, argues that the racial equality issue was not simply a negotiating ploy but an attempt by professional diplomats to end a longstanding source of friction with the Anglo-Saxon powers.

21. Robert E. Hosack, "The Shantung Question and the Senate," *South Atlantic Quarterly*, 43 (April, 1944), 181–193, discusses the domestic Shantung

Studies of the immediate postwar Japanese-American encounter are only slightly more numerous than those dealing with Sino-American relations. Griswold argued that Siberia, Yap, racial problems, and naval competition marked increasing Japanese-American tensions during the last days of the Wilson administration. Existing monographic studies neither entirely substantiate nor refute his general arguments. The decision to intervene in Siberia has attracted far more historical attention than that to terminate the expedition. Betty Miller Unterberger describes the intervention itself and chronicles American withdrawal; but her study pays less attention to the conflicting bureaucratic rivalries and motives underlying that choice than to those of the original intervention decision. Other historians have only skirted the interesting and complex issues involved in the decision to withdraw. The controversy over the cable island of Yap has attracted even less attention. Despite the prominence of the Yap problem in Griswold's interpretation and its recurrence in accounts of the coming of the Washington Conference, no historian since L. B. Tribolet, who wrote a dissertation on it in the late 1920's, has made a special study of it using the many archival materials unavailable to him.[22]

----

debate; Griswold, *Far Eastern Policy*, pp. 262–264, reviews the post-Paris effort to get a public Japanese commitment on Shantung; Fifield, *Woodrow Wilson and the Far East*, pp. 345–355, and Curry, *Woodrow Wilson and Far Eastern Policy*, pp. 285–297, describe domestic politics and negotiations in greater detail; Beers, *Vain Endeavor*, pp. 176–177, describes post-Paris Shantung policy in terms of the decline of Lansing's and Wilson's physical and political powers; Chow Tse-tsung, *The May Fourth Movement: Intellectual Revolution in Modern China* (Cambridge, Mass.: Harvard University Press, 1964), pp. 198–207, describes American reactions to the burst of demonstrations in China at this time and argues that businessmen and consular officials were suspicious of the movement but that missionaries and educators were friendly toward it; Warren I. Cohen, "America and the May Fourth Movement: The Response to Chinese Nationalism, 1917–1921," *Pacific Historical Review*, 35 (February 1966), 83–100, reinforces this argument; Cohen holds that this is a key case in which links with the Chinese military and business communities contributed to American misperception of change in East Asia. Charles F. Remer, *A Study of Chinese Boycotts with Special Reference to Their Economic Effectiveness* (Baltimore: Johns Hopkins University Press, 1933), pp. 55–79, discusses the economic dimensions of the Chinese reaction to Shantung.

22. Griswold, *Far Eastern Policy*, p. 271. Griswold held that by the last days of the Wilson Administration "War talk was in the air. At every point Washington and Tokyo were deadlocked"; Unterberger, *America's Siberian Expedition, 1918–1920*, chaps. 6–7; John M. Thompson, *Russia, Bolshevism, and the Versailles Peace* (Princeton: Princeton University Press, 1966), pp. 277–308, discusses the American policy dilemma and points out Wilson's continuing fear that withdrawal would spell Japanese domination; Richard H. Ullman, *Anglo-Soviet Relations, 1917–1920, II, Britain and the Russian Civil War*, (Princeton: Princeton University Press, 1968), describes British policy and affords many insights into the American Siberian problem; Ludor Ben Schranil,

Racial and naval questions pose further problems and opportunities for the historian of this period of American Far Eastern policy. Scholars have described the resurgence of anti-Japanese feeling in postwar America in considerable detail. Roger Daniels identified latent racial and economic antagonisms, a senatorial election, new racist groups, and reaction against nascent pro-Japanese elements as sources of new California discriminatory measures. Other scholars have linked the California controversy with broader anti-immigrant feelings unleashed by the war. But historians have yet to focus on the Wilson administration's dometic and diplomatic efforts to deal with this problem. There is no study of the Morris–Shidehara negotiations for an immigration treaty and the reasons for its failure. Griswold joined contemporary observers in linking these racial tensions with postwar Japanese-American naval competition. During World War II, Harold and Margaret Sprout agreed that the immediate postwar years brought increased naval antagonisms. But they made the decline of British seapower in East Asia the root cause of naval rivalries between the United States and Japan, the world's second and third naval powers. Other scholars have since pointed to this period as the seedbed of strategic assumptions and naval professional attitudes which governed the fighting of a later Pacific war. My own study, in contrast, suggested that policy makers on both sides of the Pacific struggled to find naval security

---

"Japan and the Siberian Expedition, 1919–1920: An Evaluation of Japan's Role in the Allied Intervention," *Columbia University East Asian Institute Researches on the Social Sciences in Japan*, 2 (1959), 77–81, discusses the Japanese post-intervention problem. Various studies have touched on post-intervention American policy motivations and offered different explanations. Curry, *Woodrow Wilson and Far Eastern Policy*, pp. 239–248, chronicles the State-War controversy over the expedition and its aims; Frederick Palmer, *Newton D. Baker: America at War* (New York: Dodd, Mead and Company, 1931), II, 313–322, 394–395, first told of the War secretary's opposition to the expedition. Daniel R. Beaver, *Newton D. Baker and the American War Effort 1917–1919* (Lincoln: University of Nebraska Press, 1966), p. 182, suggests that Baker threatened resignation over the intervention and provides evidence of his continuing strong feelings against it well after the immediate postwar months. *The Siberian Intervention*, pp. 352–357, asserts that the administration had no real explanation for post-Armistice intervention and feared the outbreak of domestic controversy over it. Beers, *Vain Endeavor*, p. 172, argues that Wilson feared to raise the issue in public. Levin, *Woodrow Wilson and World Politics*, p. 227, describes administration policy as an effort to assist Japanese liberals rather than a containment ploy; for a Japanese account which stresses the suspicions and misunderstandings generated by the expedition, see Tamura Kosaka, "The Taishō Era," in Kawakami Hikomatsu, ed., *Japan-American Relations in the Meiji-Taishō Era* (Tokyo: Pan-Pacific Press, 1958), Kimura Michiko, tr., pp. 367–378. See also Leslie B. Tribolet, *The International Aspects of Electrical Communications in the Pacific Area* (Baltimore: Johns Hopkins University Press, 1929), esp. chaps. 3–5.

amidst rapid technological change within a framework of Japanese-American harmony.[23]

23. Roger Daniels, *The Politics of Prejudice: The Anti-Japanese Movement in California and the Struggle for Japanese Exclusion,* University of California Publications in History, 71 (Berkeley: University of California Press, 1962), pp. 79–84; Kell F. Mitchell, Jr., "Diplomacy and Prejudice: The Morris-Shidehara Negotiations 1920–1921," *Pacific Historical Review,* 39 (February 1970), 85–104, analyzes the talks on the basis of American documents only; Bill Hosokawa, *Nisei: The Quiet Americans* (Philadelphia: Morrow, 1969), provides a colorful popular account of Japanese life in America during these years: John Higham, *Strangers in the Land: Patterns of American Nativism 1860–1925* (New Brunswick, N.J.: Rutgers University Press, 1955), chap. 10, is the best description of postwar anti-immigrant feelings. Higham points to a strange mix of heightened nationalism and postwar fears as the source of renewed nativism; Carey McWilliams, *Predjudice: Japanese-Americans, Symbol of Racial Intolerance* (Boston: Little, Brown, 1944), p. 11, argues that failure to solve the domestic racial problem tied the Wilson administration's hands in trying to deal with it internationally; Richard A. Thompson, "The Yellow Peril, 1890–1924," (Ph.D. diss., University of Wisconsin, 1957), deals with the intellectual aspects of postwar racial antagonisms; John R. Stemen, "The Diplomacy of the Immigration Issue: A Study in Japanese-American Relations 1894–1941," (Ph.D. diss., University of Indiana, 1960), surveys the negotiations with Japan in the last Wilson years. A new treatment of the immigration issue is desperately needed. American historians of immigration have tended to pigeonhole anti-Japanese feelings as something apart from more general nativism; and diplomatic historians have not devoted much attention to this, as opposed to earlier, immigration crises. McWilliams, *Prejudice,* p. 94, offers the tantalizing suggestion that the immediate postwar years represented a lost opportunity to permanently resolve this problem in Japanese-American relations; Griswold, *Far Eastern Policy,* pp. 271–274, deals with postwar naval rivalries; Harold and Margaret Sprout, *Toward a New Order,* chaps. 4–6, describe Anglo-American as well as Japanese-American naval antagonisms; Stephen W. Roskill, *Naval Policy Between the Wars,* I, *The Period of Anglo-American Antagonisms, 1919–1929* (New York: Walker and Company, 1968), chap. 7, chronicles British postwar strategic policy developments critical to the development of American and Japanese naval policies; Hector C. Bywater, *Seapower in the Pacific: A Study of the American-Japanese Naval Problem* (Boston: Houghton Mifflin, Co., 1921), is a detailed contemporary study; Richard D. Burns, "Inspection of Mandates, 1919–1941," *Pacific Historical Review,* 37 (November 1968), 445–462, deals with an issue productive of Japanese-American suspicions in these years; Louis Morton, "War Plan Orange: Evolution of a Strategy," *World Politics,* 40 (January 1959), 221–250, describes postwar strategic planning efforts; Roger Dingman, "Power in the Pacific: the Evolution of American and Japanese Naval Policies 1918–1921," (Ph.D. diss., Harvard University, 1969), explores professional and political conflicts over postwar policy and suggests that fears of a postwar armaments race were exaggerated. Japanese studies of the naval problem put much of the onus for the postwar "naval race" on the United States. Oka Yoshitake, *Tenkanki no Taishō,* p. 168, argues that the American 1918 program triggered an inevitable Japanese response. Kobayashi Tatsuo, "Kaigun gushuku joyaku, 1921–1936" (The naval limitation treaties, 1921–1936), chap. 1 in Tsunoda Jun, ed., *Taiheiyō sensō e no michi* (*The Road to the Pacific War;* Tokyo: Asahi shimbun sha, 1963), vol. I, argues that America coerced Japan into the Washington Conference through such "paper program" techniques; Hate Ikuhiko, "Meiji iko ni okeru NichiBei Taiheiyō senryaku no hensen" (Changes in Japanese and American Pacific strategies

Many tasks confront the historian of American Far Eastern policy for this period. Scholars have yet to use British, Chinese, and Japanese archival materials to round out their analyses of presidential decision making at the Paris Peace Conference. They have only begun to explore the attitudes of Wilson's subordinates there, attitudes important to a better understanding of his choices and critical to interpretation of the intra-administration debates over Far Eastern policy problems during the long months of his decline. The historian of the future needs to approach this period with a broader perspective than his predecessors'. Military force, economic pressure, and legal nonrecognition as implements of policy no less than containment and cooperation as its ends were debated in these years as they would be in the future. A heightened sensitivity to these later discussions of American Far Eastern policy might well enable the historian of this era to synthesize a new and more meaningful interpretation of it.

The Washington Conference—dramatic, colorful, and controversial—has attracted historians far more than the last dark months of the Wilson era. A number of specialized studies deal with its domestic and international political sources, policy preparations before it, and negotiators' interplay during it. But no recent multiarchival study has appeared which draws upon these studies to reconcile the conflicting interpretations swirling about the conference. Scholars first studied public opinion as a primary domestic political pressure for the conference. Late in the 1930's Tupper and McReynolds chronicled anti-Japanese and pro-arms limitation sentiments. A few years later Leonard Hoag described in detail the surge of public support behind the Borah campaign for an end to naval construction. J. Chal Vinson, writing in the mid-1950's, offered a broader interpretation of pre-conference politics. He added the theme of struggle between President and Senate for control of all American foreign policy to the story of the conference's origins. But historians have yet to offer further insights into the political struggles of early 1921. Biographers of Harding and Borah have written little of the Far Eastern policy thoughts underlying their actions in this period. Historians have yet to plumb the depths of public opinion on Far Eastern problems or to survey the spectrum of intra-Republican party approaches to East Asia.[24]

---

since the Meiji era), *Kikan kokusai seiji* (Autumn 1968), examines shifting strategic perspectives on both sides of the Pacific in this period.

24. Ernest R. May and Asada Sadao have in preparation studies which should soon remedy the deficiencies described in this period and the following paragraphs; Eleanor Tupper and George E. McReynolds, *Japan in American*

Continuity and coercion rather than conflict mark the historiography of diplomatic preparations for the conference. Griswold described how Hughes picked up tools left by his predecessors—the termination of the Anglo-Japanese alliance, naval arms limitation, and the hoary Irish problem—to bring Britain to the conference table. He argued that coercion was the key element in bringing Japan to Washington as well. Hughes' biographers have happily celebrated the crusty secretary of state's tactical skill in maneuvering his opposites in London and Tokyo to negotiations which he would control. But these accounts leave unanswered major questions about pre-conference diplomacy. Was Hughes the dominant figure? Recently Ernest May has suggested that Harding was much more active in determining and controlling negotiations before the conference. Were Britain and Japan so reluctant to discuss Far Eastern problems at Washington? Akira Iriye's interpretation implied that Hughes' and Harding's opposites were quite ready to cooperate in an endeavor to stabilize postwar East Asia.[25]

Public Opinion (New York: Macmillan, 1937), chap. 5; C. Leonard Hoag, *Preface to Preparedness: The Washington Disarmament Conference and Public Opinion* (Washington, D.C.: Public Affairs Press, 1941); John C. Vinson, *The Parchment Peace* (Athens, Georgia: University of Georgia Press, 1955), esp. chaps. 5–11. The recent revival of interest in Harding has focused far more on his domestic than on his foreign policies. Andrew Sinclair, *The Available Man* (New York: Macmillan, 1965) points up Harding's growing political independence and strength as president: Francis B. Russell, *The Shadow of Blooming Grove: Warren G. Harding in His Times* (New York: McGraw-Hill Book Co., 1968), focuses on Harding the Ohio politician and devotes a scant ten pages to the Washington Conference; Dale E. P. Cottrill, *Conciliator* (Philadelphia: Dorrance, 1968), offers still another interpretation of Harding's presidency; Robert K. Murray, *The Harding Era: Warren G. Harding and His Administration* (Minneapolis: University of Minnesota Press, 1969), pp. 140–166, gives Harding high marks for assuring the success of the Washington Conference. There is no satisfactory biography of Senator Borah. Claudius O. Johnson, *Borah of Idaho* (New York: Longmans, Green and Co., 1936), and Marian C. McKenna, *Borah* (Ann Arbor: University of Michigan Press, 1961), repeat the laudatory account of Borah the champion of disarmament. Robert James Maddox, *William E. Borah and American Foreign Policy* (Baton Rouge: Louisiana State University Press, 1969), described Borah's Far Eastern policies in broad containment and balance of power terms. Maddox argued that the Idaho senator sought to restrain Japan through revived Russo-American relations; despite repeated references to supposed public concern over the Anglo-Japanese alliance, Shantung, and Yap in texts on American diplomatic history, there are no special studies analyzing public opinion on these issues. No study of Republican Far Eastern policy attitudes during the last Wilson years, the campaign of 1920, or the transition to power in 1921 has been made. Laurin L. Henry, *Presidential Transitions* (Washington, D.C.: The Brookings Institute, 1960), pp. 127–269, is the most detailed study of the Wilson-Harding changeover; it simply asserts that Wilson graciously left Far Eastern policy problems to the incoming secretary of state (pp. 244–246).

25. Griswold, *Far Eastern Policy*, pp. 274–282, 298; Merlo J. Pusey, *Charles*

The dramatic story of America's hurried, secret preparations for the conference and its triumph in the negotiations has often been told. But from the perspective of the historian of Far Eastern policy, the account seems lacking in its failure to present Eastern Asian issues in an integrated manner. The Sprouts, relying on the Theodore Roosevelt, Jr. manuscripts, told how Hughes triumphed over professional recalcitrance and went on to win the bulk of the American naval program in the Washington negotiations. In contrast, only a few specialized studies treat Far Eastern aspects of the conference preparations. No single account analyzes perspectives within the State Department or in the White House on the future international political order in East Asia. The actual negotiations, although chronicled many times by journalists and writers of dissertations, have been treated unevenly in specialized studies. Studies on the ending of the Anglo-Japanese alliance, the termination of the Lansing-Ishii agreement, and of modification of extra-territoriality are not as comprehensive as those on the naval aspects of the conference. No one has yet published an account of the conference

---

Evans Hughes (New York: Macmillan, 1951), II 445–449, 455–459. Betty M. Glad, *Charles Evans Hughes and the Illusions of Innocence* (Urbana: University of Illinois Press, 1966), p. 287, criticizes Hughes as a traditionalist who failed to see the gap between means at his disposal and the ends of his Far Eastern policies; Dexter Perkins, *Charles Evans Hughes and American Democratic Statesmanship* (Boston: Little, Brown and Co., 1956), pp. 98–100, offers a more balanced account. Perkins describes Hughes as a skillful tactician who seized upon the opportunity to draw Britain into the conference but does not discuss his actions vis à vis Japan. For a brief, critical portrait of Hughes, see John C. Vinson, "Charles Evans Hughes," in Norman A. Graebner, ed., *An Uncertain Tradition: American Secretaries of States in the Twentieth Century* (New York: McGraw Hill, 1961), pp. 28–148. Special studies of pre-conference diplomacy include Russell Fifield, "Secretary Hughes and the Shantung Question," *Pacific Historical Review* 23 (November 1954), 373–385; M. G. Fry, "The North Atlantic Triangle and the Abrogation of the Anglo-Japanese Alliance," *Journal of Modern History* 39 (March 1967), 46–64, is the most recent study based on Canadian and British archival materials. For British background to this aspect of pre-conference negotiations, see John C. Vinson, "The Imperial Conference of 1921 and the Anglo-Japanese Alliance," *Pacific Historical Review* 31 (August 1962), 257–266; and Ian H. Nish, "Britain and the Ending of the Anglo-Japanese Alliance," *Japan Society of London Bulletin* (October 1967), pp. 2–5; also Malcolm D. Kennedy, *The Estrangement of Great Britain and Japan 1917–1935* (Berkeley: University of California Press, 1969); Nish analyzes Japanese policy in "Japan and the Ending of the Anglo-Japanese Alliance," in K. Bourne and D. C. Watt, eds., *Studies in International History* (Hamden, Conn.: Archon Books, 1967), 369–384. These studies collectively suggest that Britain and Japan were far more willing to come to Washington than the traditional American accounts would indicate. Ernest R. May, in recent Albert Shaw lectures at Johns Hopkins, cited materials in the H. C. Lodge manuscripts that would make Harding far more important in pre-conference diplomacy. See also Iriye, *After Imperialism*, pp. 16–20.

in an attempt to resolve the questions noted earlier. There has been no effort to study Hughes' negotiating techniques to see if they fostered a psychological reaction to coercion among his opposites. Nor has a study of Chinese issues at Washington appeared which might show how and why the powers there collectively missed the impact of China's ongoing, increasingly nationalistic revolution. Consequently the Washington Conference, despite all that has been written about it, remains a critical topic for the historian of American Far Eastern policy.[26]

The literature of presidential decision making in Far Eastern policy for these years is considerable. But what of the ideas underlying, the structures defining, and the men carrying out that policy? The needs and opportunities for the historian of the 1970's concerned with these problems are great indeed. Akira Iriye, virtually alone, has dealt with images and ideas shaping the American–East Asian relationship. His *Across the Pacific* identified the 1917–1922 half decade as a period of transition and flux in the minds of policy makers and public on both sides of the Pacific. But historians

26. Sprouts, *New Order,* chaps. 9–13; see also Gerald F. Wheeler, *Prelude to Pearl Harbor: The United States Navy and the Far East 1921–1931* (Columbia: University of Missouri Press, 1963), pp. 52–65; and Davis, *Navy Second to None,* pp. 270–304. The best contemporary accounts of the conference may be found in Raymond L. Buell, *The Washington Conference* (New York: D. Appleton and Co., 1922); Mark Sullivan, *The Great Adventure at Washington* (Garden City, N.Y.: Doubleday, Page and Co., 1922); and Yamato Ichihashi, *The Washington Conference and After* (Stanford: Stanford University Press, 1928). Ph.D. dissertations dealing with the negotiations include Asada Sadao, "Japan and the United States 1915–1925" (Yale University, 1963); R. G. Burns, Jr., "American-Japanese Relations 1920–1925" (University of Missouri, 1963). Two recent works, Thomas H. Buckley, *The United States and the Washington Conference 1921–1922* (Knoxville: University of Tennessee Press, 1970) and William R. Braisted, *The United States Navy and the Pacific 1909–1922* (Austin: University of Texas, 1971) survey the conference. Braisted makes extensive use of previously unpublished naval documents, and both volumes sample Japanese language materials. But neither book advances new interpretive insights into the first successful strategic arms limitation effort. For details of special aspects of the negotiations, see Merz Tate and F. Foy, "More Light on the Abrogation of the Anglo-Japanese Alliance," *Political Science Quarterly* 74 (1959), 145–152; Choon Sik Hong, "The Termination of the Anglo-Japanese Alliance" (Ph.D. diss., University of Iowa, 1966); Asada Sadao, "Japan's 'Special Interests' and the Washington Conference, 1921–1922," *American Historical Review,* 67 (October 1961), 62–70; John C. Vinson, "The Annulment of the Lansing-Ishii Agreement," *Pacific Historical Review* 27 (February 1958), 57–69; and Wesley R. Fishel, *The End of Extraterritoriality in China* (Berkeley: University of California Press, 1952), pp. 51–68. English language studies of the Chinese position at Washington include A. E. Kane, *China and the Washington Conference* (Shanghai: Kelly and Walsh, 1937); Robert T. Pollard, *China's Foreign Relations 1917–1931* (New York: Macmillan, 1933); and Wunsz King, *China at the Washington Conference 1921–1922* (New York: St. John's University Press, 1963).

have yet to consider in detail what Asians thought of us or we of them in the Wilson and Harding era. Historians of China and Japan have recently offered several interesting insights into what leading East Asians thought of America during these years. Burton Beers has analyzed the intellectual substructure of Robert Lansing and his Far Eastern policies. But scholars have yet to deal with the question of American ideas about Asia during this period on a broader scale. How, for example, did conflicts in America's thought about itself—whether it was a missionary of modernization or isolated exemplar of democracy, disinterested stabilizer of the balance of power or economic and technocratic genius capable of dominating it—shape attitudes and policies toward East Asia?[27]

In asking what Americans' thoughts were, the historian must also consider how and why they took shape. A first step might be to examine which Asians Americans came into contact with. Studies of individuals' interaction with the diverse forms of rural life in East Asia or the more complex elites of government, commerce, and education in China and Japan might tell much of the selection and movement of ideas across the Pacific. A second approach might focus on the more formal instruments of communication. John Hohenberg has shown how vital they have been in

27. Iriye, *Across the Pacific*, pp. 138–145. Chinese perspectives on America and Americans are touched on in Donald G. Gillin, *Warlord: Yen Hsi-shan in Shansi Province 1911–1949* (Princeton: Princeton University Press, 1967), pp. 22, 68, Chun-tu Hsüeh, *Huang Hsing and the Chinese Revolution* (Stanford: Stanford University Press, 1961), pp. 169–184; Joseph R. Levenson, *Liang Ch'i-ch'ao and the Mind of Modern China* (Cambridge, Mass.: Harvard University Press, 1953), pp. 184–189; Hao Chang has written a new study, *Liang Ch'i-ch'ao and Intellectual Transition in China, 1890–1907* (Cambridge, Mass.: Harvard University Press, 1971); Benjamin Schwartz, *In Search of Wealth and Power: Yen Fu and the West* (Cambridge, Mass.: Harvard University Press, 1964), pp. 229–234; Jerome B. Grieder, *Hu Shih and the Chinese Renaissance* (Cambridge, Mass.: Harvard University Press, 1970). Y. C. Wang, *Chinese Intellectuals and the West 1872–1949* (Chapel Hill: University of North Carolina Press, 1966) is a pioneering study important for its statistics, suggested research topics, and introductory surveys of the careers of Chinese educated abroad; see esp. pp. 111–116 for insights into Chinese students in America during the 1917–1922 period. Studies of Japanese ideas about the United States during these years are even fewer. Hyman Kublin discusses the American experiences of an important socialist leader in *Asian Revolutionary: The Life of Katayama Sen* (Princeton University Press, 1964); David J. Lu treats the same subject in his forthcoming biographical study of Matsuoka Yosuke; Miwa Kimitada has written "Japanese Opinions on Woodrow Wilson in War and Peace," *Monumenta Nipponica* 21 (1967), 368–389. American historians writing of the domestic debate over the United States' postwar role have paid little attention to its East Asian aspects. There is no study of "liberal" attitudes on Far Eastern policy despite the fact that leading "Asia hands" like Willard Straight were deeply involved in publishing the progressive *New Republic*.

American–East Asian relations since World War II. The historian concerned with the years of World War I has at his disposal ample materials to study trans-Pacific communications. Periodicals like *Asia* and *Millard's Review* first appeared during the Wilson and Harding years and demand analysis as purveyors of ideas about East Asia. Studies of the wire services, of newspapers and magazines, and of the foreign correspondent during these years might aid in understanding how ideas were selected and translated in moving from East Asia to America. Finally, the historians of the future might well seek to apply theories of communication developed by sociologists and political scientists to this aspect of the study of American Far Eastern policy.[28]

The structures which translated these ideas and impressions into policy demand the attention of future historians of Far Eastern policy. There is no literature that analyzes formal decision-making organizations or their more diffuse counterparts in the American business and missionary communities. The component parts of the Far Eastern diplomatic apparatus have gone unstudied. No monograph deals with the Far Eastern Division in the State Department or the embassies in Tokyo and Peking. No one has analyzed closely the parallel phenomena of nascent professional diplomats' distaste for East Asia and presidential difficulties in securing political figures as American representatives in Tokyo and Peking during the 1917–1922 half decade. Despite their importance, other agencies concerned with East Asia—War, Navy, Treasury, and Commerce— have not received scholarly attention for this period as they have in studies of later Far Eastern policy. Beyond these rather specific needs, scholars must ask how the system itself affected policy outcomes. Did it distort as well as select information about war and revolutionary change in East Asia? This period, with the emotions of war, the tragedy of Wilson's long illness, and the difficulties of

28. John Hohenberg, *Between Two Worlds: Policy, Press and Public Opinion in Asian-American Relations* (New York: Praeger, 1967), offers useful insights on the geneial problem of American-Asian communication as well as details of post-World War II Asian and American journalism; his *Foreign Correspondence: the Great Reporters and Their Times* (New York: Columbia University Press, 1964), chaps. 7–8, deals with the war and postwar era. Frank Luther Mott, *American Journalism: a History of Newspapers in the United States through 260 Years: 1690 to 1950*, 2nd. ed. (New York, Macmillan, 1950), chaps. 36–43, surveys and provides a preliminary bibliographic guide to this topic; Mott studied leading magazines in *A History of American Magazines*, V, *Sketches of Twenty-One Magazines 1905–1920* (Cambridge, Mass.: Harvard University Press, 1968). Kent Cooper, *Kent Cooper and the Associated Press: An Autobiography* (New York: Random House, 1959), deals with wire service competition, as does his earlier *Barriers Down* (New York: Farrar and Rinehart, 1942), pp. 98–99, 120–125, 143–150.

establishing the Harding regime, is rich in comparative situations for the study of this critical question.[29]

Historians have long acknowledged that less formal groupings of businessmen and missionaries had a role in the shaping of American Far Eastern policy. But they have hardly agreed on what the nature and significance of ties between business and government in East Asia were. The controversy has swirled about the China consortium, revived by the Wilson administration and carried over through the Harding. Griswold described it as a European effort to limit American opportunities; Williams wrote of it as a tool against revolution; and Iriye suggested that it was potentially an instrument of cooperation in East Asia. A recent study has fueled the controversy still further by arguing that the attitudes and objectives of private business groups in the consortium differed greatly from those of the Wilson and Harding Administrations. The consortium controversy remains unsettled, but it points to the need for much more careful analysis of American business and businessmen in East Asia during 1917–1922. If this was an era of transition from an imperial to a post-imperial order, how did American businessmen and financiers react and contribute to the changes swirling about them? No study explores in detail the operations of an American firm in China or Japan or considers the reactions of its leaders in comparison with those of native and European competitors. No study has examined how American financiers dealt with Treasury officials and their opposites in East Asia in reordering the postwar international monetary and commercial order. Beyond this, the increasingly important role of the businessman on both sides of the Pacific as negotiator and as shaper of elite opinions remains to be analyzed. Consequently the need remains great to make use of archival sources to examine more carefully the role of the business community in shaping American Far Eastern policy.[30]

29. Waldo H. Heinrichs, Jr., *American Ambassador: Joseph C. Grew and the Development of the United States Diplomatic Tradition* (Boston: Little, Brown, 1966), pp. 96–97, 158, points out the European orientation among aspiring professional diplomats and suggests how, at least in Grew's case, it ill prepared them to deal with the Far Eastern crises of the 1930's. Warren Frederick Illchman, *Professional Diplomacy in the United States, 1779–1939: A Study in Administrative History* (Chicago: University of Chicago Press, 1961), chaps. 3–4, is an initial probe into the diplomatic corps rich in statistics, but it does not deal with questions of geographic competence or preference.

30. Griswold, *Far Eastern Policy*, pp. 211–213, emphasizes European pressures for reestablishment of the consortium in 1917; pp. 223–224 stress its containment objectives; Williams, *Tragedy*, pp. 140–141; Iriye, *After Imperialism*, p. 14. Frederick V. Field, *American Participation in the China Consortiums* (Chicago: University of Chicago Press, 1931), chaps. 9–11, first

The missionary, like the businessman, has long counted as an important figure in the history of American Far Eastern policy, especially that of the Wilson administration. Scholars have termed Wilson's diplomacy "missionary diplomacy" and have identified evangelists in his official and personal entourage. But historians have yet to correlate studies of the missionary movement in East Asia with broader analyses of American Far Eastern policy. From what has been written it would seem that 1917–1922 was a period of unusually intense questioning from within and from without about the mission effort. Paul Varg has noted that the turn from

chronicled the consortium story in detail; he saw the new consortium as a symbol of American failure to understand Chinese nationalism. Fifield, *Woodrow Wilson and the Far East*, pp. 94–95, follows Griswold in making the consortium a tool of containment; Curry, *Woodrow Wilson and Far Eastern Policy*, pp. 190–203, takes up the same theme but located revival initiatives in the Far Eastern Division of the State Department. Beers, *Vain Endeavor*, p. 147, stresses the importance of commercial competition in Lansing's personal thoughts about a Far Eastern order and described the consortium as a return to prewar tactics; Harry N. Scheiber, "World War I as Entrepreneurial Opportunity: Willard Straight and the American International Corporation," *Political Science Quarterly*, 84 (September 1969), 486–511, points out the influence of the war on bankers' thinking. It demonstrates that their objective in postwar East Asian commerce was to attain hegemony rather than mere cooperation in dealing with trade and financial rivals. This theme in a broader context is the subject of Carl P. Parrini, *Heir to Empire: United States Economic Diplomacy 1916–1923* (Pittsburgh: University of Pittsburgh Press, 1969). General studies which touch on the American financial role in China include Charles F. Remer, *Foreign Investments in China* (New York: Macmillan, 1933), useful for its statistics: Frank M. Tamagna, *Banking and Finance in China* (New York: Institute of Pacific Relations, 1942); and Hou Chi-ming, *Foreign Investment and Economic Development in China, 1840–1937* (Cambridge, Mass.: Harvard University Press, 1965), a broad economic survey. Three pioneering studies discuss American investment projects in post-World War I East Asia. Harry W. Kirwin, "The Federal Telegraph Company: a Testing of the Open Door," *Pacific Historical Review*, 22 (August 1953), 271–286, stresses competition rather than cooperation as a motive common to investors and Secretary Hughes alike during the pre-Washington Conference period; Albert Parry, "Washington B. Vanderlip: the 'Khan of Kamchatka,'" *Pacific Historical Review*, 17 (August 1948), 311–330, describes the interests of West Coast oilmen in a project for Siberian oil exploitation which repeatedly bred Japanese suspicions of the United States in this period; Peter Mellish Reed, "Standard Oil in Indonesia," 1898–1928," *Business History Review*, 32 (Autumn 1958), 311–337, discusses another area of Japanese-American antagonism over oil; Thomas W. Lamont, *Across World Frontiers* (privately printed, 1950), tells of his role in the consortium negotiations. Mitani Taichirō and Warren Cohen have in progress studies which should shed light on this important instrument of American East Asian policy. But the need remains for careful analysis of talks among American, Japanese, and Chinese financial leaders at the Paris Peace Conference, the postwar mission of American business leaders to Tokyo, and the financial conversations that paralleled the Washington Conference.

the teens to the twenties was marked by renewed conflict between theologically conservative evangelists and the proponents of the social gospel. China missionaries were questioning their own effectiveness and techniques, turning to education and agriculture as key new fields of endeavor. Americans at home seemed to be questioning the missionary as well. Kenneth Scott Latourette has pointed to the paradox in this half decade of an immense increase in financial support for overseas YMCA work followed by a drastic drop in mission revenues. And from the East Asian side Chinese reformers raised new doubts about the missionary's role in their national revolution. All these clues raise important questions for the historian of American Far Eastern policy. Was the missionary a part of the old "imperialist" order or a spokesman for new Wilsonian idealism? How did he contribute to or figure in changing East Asian attitudes toward America in this period? Finally, how did he serve to interpret to President and public alike the tremendous changes in East Asia in these years?[31]

No discussion of past achievements and future opportunities for this era of American Far Eastern policy would be complete without some discussion of the role individuals played in the American–East Asian encounter. Despite repeated resort to the terminology of human emotions—suspicion, anger, mistrust—to describe American East Asian relations during these years, historians have rarely

31. Paul A. Varg, *Missionaries, Chinese, and Diplomats: The American Protestant Missionary Movement in China, 1890–1952* (Princeton: Princeton University Press, 1958), pp. 147–156, 212–216, 231. Kenneth Scott Latourette, *World Service: A History of the Foreign Work and World Service of the Young Men's Christian Associations of the United States and Canada* (New York: Association Press, 1957), pp. 70–78, is an institutional study; his *A History of Christian Missions in China* (New York: Macmillan, 1929), chaps. 19–20, remains the best survey of American missionary activities in China for this period. Shirley Garrett, *Social Reformers in Urban China: The Chinese Y.M.C.A., 1895–1926* (Cambridge, Mass.: Harvard University Press, 1970) analyzes the YMCA in Shanghai. Special studies dealing with the new importance of education in China mission work include Dwight W. Edwards, *Yenching University* (New York: United Board for Christian Higher Education in Asia, 1959); and Reuben Holden, *Yale in China: The Mainland 1909–1951* (New Haven: Yale in China Association, 1964). The sources for researching the missionary movement have been described elsewhere in this volume. They might well be used in the future to analyze critically the role of the missionary as communicator rather than modernizor or policy aide. Missionary organizations in the United States have not been carefully studied. Despite repeated reference to missionary outrage at the Shantung decision, for example, there is no study of mission efforts to influence American public opinion on it. Similarly special studies have yet to probe divisions in missionary responses to change in East Asia—incidents like the Korean Rebellion of 1919, for example—which were conveyed to public and policy makers at home.

studied men below the presidential level who felt and expressed these feelings. How did such feelings, whether in the hearts of Chinese and Japanese studying in American universities or Americans and East Asians on opposite sides of the conference table at Paris and Washington, develop? The absence of studies of individuals would seem particularly critical in this period of rapid change when shifting personal perspectives on other men and events were all the more important. The fact that 1917–1922 was an era of "new diplomacy" in which unofficial individuals were of particular importance to presidents and prime ministers also demonstrates the need for closer study of persons. The historian cannot neglect the fact, too, that this was a seminal period of impression formulation for politicians Roosevelt and Konoye, diplomats Matsuoka and Hornbeck, and admirals Yarnell and Yamamoto who would figure in the century's greatest American-Asian war. Perhaps by reversing the tendency to view events from the policy-making center, by making use of psychologists' and sociologists' insights into the individual, the historian of the future may come closer to understanding the alchemy of change in American–East Asian relations during these years.[32]

The historian of American Far Eastern policy for the 1917–1922 period is very much "the man in the middle." He is, as always, astride two very different cultures. He confronts war, revolution, and peace and tries to make sense of all. He is caught in a tangle of hypotheses which would carry him from imperialism to something else or from one imperialism to another. Where is he to turn for enlightenment? And what can he use to bring order without distortion to the complex developments of his segment of history? Perhaps there is no single solution to his dilemma. But as this essay has suggested, the routes for him to try are many. He can seek to bring a more sophisticated analysis of policy development to the political record of American–East Asian relations. He can make greater use of the comparative method to understand policy as a whole, the role of institutions in shaping it, and the reaction of

32. The list of individuals who might be subjects of special studies and for whom ample manuscript materials are available is endless. Alone among the diplomats, Paul S. Reinsch has been the subject of a recent dissertation by Noel Pugach; the first fruits of this study have appeared in "Making the Open Door Work: Paul S. Reinsch in China, 1913–1919," *Pacific Historical Review,* 38 (May 1969), 157–175. Others demanding study are diplomats Charles R. Crane, John Van Antwerp MacMurray, Ransford S. Miller, Roland Morris, Jacob Gould Shurman, and E. T. Williams; journalists Thomas F. Millard and Benjamin F. Fleisher; missionaries-turned-interpreters of Japan to America Sidney F. Gulick and George F. Gleason.

individuals to it. He can indulge in a careful, multi-disciplinary probing of the chemistry of individual American–East Asian relations. With courage, sensitivity to the opportunities before him, and an eye to the resources at his command, he may well contribute to a deeper understanding of the American–East Asian encounter.

From the Washington Treaties

to Pearl Harbor

1922–1931

The decade of the 1920's lends itself to some fresh and sophisticated analysis of the nature and problems of American–East Asian relations. There are relatively few documentary gaps. With the opening of the Public Record Office archives, historians who have hitherto relied almost solely on National Archives materials in Washington will have the use of British sources. The few scholars who have utilized these documents have produced significant studies which indicate the promising nature of Foreign Office papers for the investigation of international relations in East Asia.[1] National Archives documents, too, are far from having been exhaustively examined. Consular post files, including communications from Chinese and Japanese officials, often in their languages, have not been systematically looked at, and army and navy records are awaiting scholarly treatment by more historians. In addition, the recently opened-up papers of John V. A. MacMurray and Stanley K. Hornbeck supplement the excellent and well-used Nelson T. Johnson papers.[2] Chinese Foreign Ministry archives still remain closed beyond 1927, but Japanese documentation is constantly being expanded.[3] French published material is very meager for the 1920's, but German papers are now being published, promising some fresh information on German-Chinese relations. The official Soviet series, *Dokumenty vneshnei politiki SSSR* (Documents of Soviet foreign policy), has reached the year 1931.

Beyond providing massive source material, the decade of the twenties challenges the historian, particularly the specialist in

1. E.g., Don Dignan, "New Perspectives on British Far Eastern Policy, 1913–1919," *University of Queensland Papers*, 1.5 (January 1969), 263–302; W. Roger Louis, *British Strategy in the Far East, 1919–1939* (London: Oxford University Press, 1971).

2. For an evaluation of the Johnson and the MacMurray Papers, see Dorothy Borg, *American and the Chinese Revolution, 1925–1928*, 2nd ed. (New York: Octagon Books, 1968), vii–xi. The Hornbeck Papers are utilized in James C. Thomson, "Stanley K. Hornbeck and the State Department," paper presented at the Conference on Japanese-American Relations (1931–1941), July 1969.

3. A good idea of Japanese publications can be gained from the annual issues of *Annals of the Japanese Political Science Association*, which print surveys of current documentation and scholarship.

American–East Asian relations, because of the absence of easily recognizable international crises such as wars and overt aggression that have characterized all other decades of the twentieth century. There were more subtle crises in the 1920's, and to identify and analyze them is to go a long way toward comprehending the complex nature of American–East Asian relations. These relations have too often been studied in terms of aggression and conflict, but the really difficult question of what lies underneath such tangible phenomena has not been adequately explored. At the same time, since the twenties were a decade of relative calm in the entire world, one may be able to put American–East Asian relations in perspective and relate them to other global developments. Only then will it become possible to say just what was unique about America's approaches to East Asia or East Asia's responses to America.

To state these points is to indicate how far one must go before coming to a fuller understanding of the 1920's. Hitherto most historians have been content with treating American–East Asian relations in terms of the foreign policies of the countries involved. Some others have studied public opinion, economic interests, and missionary enterprises. But practically all these authors have adopted a uninational or at most binational approach. While significant strides have been made within the framework of their concern, one yearns for less conventional, more boldly oriented works. The following will be a brief account of past achievements by historians and a discussion of new areas of inquiry and new conceptual frameworks which await attention.

American diplomatic historians have been the trail blazers in the study of the 1920's. The quality of their production can be seen in the very useful bibliographies appended to Robert H. Ferrell, *Frank B. Kellogg—Henry L. Stimson* (New York: Cooper Square Publishers, 1963), and Selig Adler, *The Uncertain Giant, 1921–1941* (New York: Macmillan, 1965). In this chapter it will be unnecessary and meaningless to relist the items that are included in these volumes. Rather, a broad survey of some of the significant works will be made with a view to pointing out scholarly trends and prospects.

First of all, there are good studies of American policy makers. At the top level, recent biographies of Presidents Warren G. Harding and Calvin Coolidge have tried to take a fresh and well-balanced look at these much misunderstood and maligned men. Both Andrew Sinclair, *The Available Man: The Life Behind the Masks of Warren Gamaliel Harding* (New York: Macmillan, 1965), and Donald R. McCoy, *Calvin Coolidge: The Quiet President* (New York: Macmillan, 1967), are objective and well documented studies. But their treatment of foreign affairs is perfunctory, probably reflecting their subjects' lack of serious concern with the question. "Our main problems are domestic problems," said Coolidge, and neither he nor his predecessor saw the need to pay personal and thoughtful attention to external affairs.[4] Since they did so little, it is no wonder that their biographers find little that is not already common knowledge about the two administrations' handling of American diplomacy.

Yet the value of these books lies elsewhere. The very silence of Harding and Coolidge on intricate issues of diplomacy speaks eloquently about American foreign affairs during the 1920's, and for one to understand the decade it becomes essential to examine the intellectual outlook and psychological make-up of the leaders. In this sense the close look the reader gets at the making and functioning of a chief executive enables him to have some sense of the prevailing prejudices, idiosyncracies, and basic assumptions through which men coming out of rural and small-town America related themselves to the challenge of much wider dimensions. International relations are nothing if not relations among men, and if the study of interaction between different value systems and patterns of behavior constitutes a vital part of diplomatic history, it seems obvious that many more biographies like these two are needed.

Herbert Hoover has not been given the kind of good biographical treatment his two predecessors have. There are more autobiographical than monographic accounts.[5] Probably the best work dealing with Hoover's approaches to world problems is a study of him as secretary of commerce: Joseph Brandes, *Herbert Hoover and Economic Foreign Policy* (Pittsburgh: University of Pittsburgh Press, 1962). But the book falls short of treating Hoover's entire foreign policy, both chronologically and topically. It has some interesting data concerning America's search for raw materials in southeast Asia, but no real analysis of Hoover's attitude toward other problems in the East. The only monograph which adequately covers Hoover's first two years as president (before the Manchurian Incident) is Ferrell's *American Diplomacy in the Great Depression: Hoover-Stimson Foreign Policy, 1929–1933* (New Haven: Yale University Press, 1957). Here, however, Hoover is coupled with Stimson, and the only Asian episode before 1931 which is treated is the Chinese Eastern Railway dispute of 1929, in which Hoover does not seem to

4. Sinclair, *The Available Man*, p. 200.
5. See esp. Hoover's *The Cabinet and the Presidency, 1920–1933* (New York: Macmillan, 1951), and *The Great Depression, 1929–1941* (New York: Macmillan, 1952).

have shown much interest. His handling of the world economic crisis, on the other hand, is very ably described in the book. Though East Asia was far from being his central concern as he tried to cope with the crisis, Japan did figure prominently in his mind as he called for naval disarmament as one way of checking the deterioration in the financial picture of the United States. Still, most accounts of the Hoover administration, before it had to bestir itself to cope with an international crisis after 1931, are concerned with domestic economic issues. To the extent that foreign affairs are involved, many writers are content with saying a few words about the European debt and reparations questions.[6] But the years 1929 and 1930 were no less crucial for American–Asian relations than after 1931. It was then that political, economic, and social forces within Japan and China were steadily sundering the fabric of an international system which, though tenuous, had provided the setting for American activities in East Asia. If Hoover had been an architect of postwar economic foreign policy, as Brandes rightly points out, one would want to know much more about his reactions to these changes in Asia which abruptly put an end to an era of American–East Asian relations.

The three secretaries of state in the 1920's—Charles Evans Hughes, Frank B. Kellogg, and Henry L. Stimson—have been given much scholarly attention recently. For Hughes, in addition to the standard documentary history by Merlo J. Pusey and the shorter but wisely reflective account by Dexter Perkins, there is an attempt at psychological analysis by Betty Glad.[7] This last merits serious reading as it is a first of its sort. The author explicitly tries to recapture Hughes' mental image of the world and examine to what successes and errors it led. According to her analysis, Hughes "viewed the world order through the prisms of a nineteenth-century rationalist philosophy," and this optimism was traceable to his socio-ethnic background as well as to the influence of some Brown University professors.[8] Hughes, of course, would not have been alone in holding

6. Among the best works discussing Hoover's domestic economic policies are Harris G. Warren, *Herbert Hoover and the Great Depression* (New York: Oxford University Press, 1959), and Albert Romasco, *The Poverty of Abundance: Hoover, the Nation, and the Depression* (New York: Oxford University Press 1965). See also Edward W. Bennett, *Germany and the Diplomacy of the Financial Crisis, 1931* (Cambridge, Mass.: Harvard University Press 1962).

7. Merlo J. Pusey, *Charles Evans Hughes*, 2 vols. (New York: Macmillan, 1951); Dexter Perkins, *Charles Evans Hughes and American Democratic Statesmanship* (Boston: Little, Brown, 1956); Betty Glad, *Charles Evans Hughes and the Illusions of Innocence: A Study in American Diplomacy* (Urbana: University of Illinois Press, 1966).

8. Glad, *Charles Evans Hughes*, p. 210.

such a philosophy, but the author argues that his rationalism and optimism were reinforced by a puritanical, perfectionist personality. This type of psychological theorizing is risky but illuminating, and one learns a great deal about Charles Evans Hughes. Unfortunately, Glad's discussion of Hughes' foreign policy is so conventional and rudimentary that her fine analysis of the secretary of state as a person seems little related to him as a policy maker. For example, in describing his opposition to American entry into the League of Nations, she writes, "If the United States had assumed a real interest in the status quo of Europe and the Far East and been willing to use its power for that purpose, its membership in the League might have changed the course of interwar politics."[9] Apart from the ambiguities of such terms as "real interest," "status quo," and "power," the statement adds very little to the conventional textbook accounts of interwar diplomacy. Nevertheless, the author's basic approach is refreshing and calls for similar works by others. For American policy toward East Asia after the Washington Conference, however, this book says very little; and since neither Pusey nor Perkins has much information on the subject, one is still mostly in the dark concerning Hughes' handling of the Chinese and Japanese questions between 1922 and 1925.[10]

Secretary Kellogg, on the other hand, has been well studied in connection with his China policy. Dorothy Borg's *American Policy and the Chinese Revolution, 1925–1928* is to a great extent focused on Kellogg and depicts his response to Chinese nationalism. Her ringing conclusion that "his policy was both bold and imaginative in intent and his ideas were considerably in advance of his time" has been challenged by other writers.[11] But every historian of American–East Asian relations in the mid-twenties must start with the book. It remains the most careful and thoughtful analysis of American responses to such issues as treaty revision and the protection of nationals in China. The picture of Kellogg that emerges from this study is that of a liberal who was deeply conscious of his country's task to help channel Chinese nationalism into a constructive course. He was against both imperialism and radicalism and sought to depict the United States as the true friend of China's new aspirations.

L. Ethan Ellis and Robert H. Ferrell have also probed into Kellogg's

9. Ibid., p. 184.

10. See Akira Iriye, *After Imperialism:The Search for a New Order in the Far East, 1921–1931* (Cambridge, Mass.: Harvard University Press, 1965), chap. 1; Akira Iriye, *Across the Pacific: An Inner History of American-East Asian Relations* (New York: Harcourt, Brace & World, 1967), pp. 147–51.

11. Borg, *American Policy*, p. 431.

handling of American diplomacy.[12] Ferrell if anything goes further than Borg in adulation of the secretary, but his interpretation of Kellogg's China policy is essentially the same as hers. He might have looked into a subject which her book does not cover: Kellogg's perception of American–Japanese relations. It is curious that Japan is hardly mentioned in works dealing with America's East Asian diplomacy in the mid-1920's. This again may reflect the fact that neither Kellogg nor Coolidge thought much about Japan, but if so this silence merits study inasmuch as Japan's China policy was often influenced by the Japanese perception of what the United States would do in Asia. Ellis' account of Kellogg's foreign policy, while fuller than Ferrell's, is little better in this respect. Using National Archives materials extensively, Ellis comes to almost identical conclusions with Borg and Ferrell regarding Kellogg's "persistent desire to aid China in her time of trouble."[13] Otherwise the secretary is criticized for lack of courage and imagination in initiating similar policies toward other parts of the world. One wishes that the author himself had shown more imagination in treating American-Japanese relations.

For Stimson there are several excellent biographical studies. The best account, because it traces his youth and career before 1929, is Elting E. Morison, *Turmoil and Tradition: A Study of the Life and Times of Henry L. Stimson* (Boston: Houghton Mifflin, 1960). Beautifully written, the book's contributions lie in the same category of insight as gained from the above-mentioned biographical writings by Sinclair, McCoy, and Glad. As the title indicates, Morison depicts Stimson standing between two worlds and trying to cope with changing situations in the world armed with the ideas and inspirations he had acquired from the American Gemeinschaft. Especially useful in connection with Stimson's relations with East Asia is the description of his tenure as governor of the Philippine Islands. His experiences enabled him to view Asia with some expertise and even self-confidence that he knew something about the "Oriental mind." But one would want to know far more about Stimson's view of East Asia and of America's role in it. His personality is also sketched in the studies by Ferrell, Richard N. Current, and Armin Rappaport.[14] But

12. L. Ethan Ellis, *Frank B. Kellogg and American Foreign Relations, 1925–1929* (New Brunswick, N.J.: Rutgers University Press, 1961); Robert H. Ferrell, *Frank B. Kellogg—Henry L. Stimson* (New York, 1963).

13. Ellis, *Frank B. Kellogg,* p. 152.

14. Ferrell, *Frank B. Kellogg—Henry L. Stimson;* Ferrell, *American Diplomacy in the Great Depression: Hoover-Stimson Foreign Policy, 1929–1933* (New Haven: Yale University Press, 1957); Richard N. Current, *Secretary Stimson: A Study in Statecraft* (New Brunswick: Rutgers University Press,

their focus is on the Manchurian Incident, limiting their usefulness for the study of the 1920's. But it is precisely his ideas and assumptions before 1931 that are in need of investigation if one is to understand better his response to the crisis of that year. In fact the very crisis of the 1930's, if defined to mean something more than a minor railway explosion on September 18, 1931, may be found to have had as an antecedent the kind of emotional estrangement between the United States and Japan in which leading statesmen of the two countries had played a role. All of this is a matter for future study.

Apart from these six top policy makers, there were a number of lower-level decision makers who were more directly involved in day-to-day affairs involving East Asia. Among them the most influential were John. V. A. MacMurray, Nelson T. Johnson, and Stanley K. Hornbeck. These were the top Asian specialists within the U.S. government during the 1920's, and their professional expertise carried them far up the ladder of success in an age which was beginning to institutionalize the career diplomatic and consular services. Thus far, only Johnson has been given scholarly biographical treatment: Russell D. Buhite, *Nelson T. Johnson and American Policy Toward China, 1925–1941* (East Lansing: Michigan State University Press, 1969). This book, however, is fairly thin throughout, and apart from recapitulating Johnson's ideas in his own words, it does not add much to the existing knowledge either of American China policy or of the functioning of American foreign policy in the 1920's. (Fortunately, Buhite's biography of Patrick J. Hurley, to be published by the Cornell University Press, is an impressive piece of work and promises to add much to the literature on U.S.–East Asian relations.) It is to be hoped that the several scholars like James C. Thomson, Gary Ostrower, Christopher Thorne, and Thomas M. Buckley, who have been looking into the MacMurray and Hornbeck Papers will soon add new dimensions to the story of American–East Asian Relations.

Several other public figures have also been subjects of good biographies: Senators William E. Borah, Henry Cabot Lodge, Key Pittman, and Gerald Nye, former Secretary of State Elihu Root, Undersecretary of State Joseph C. Grew, and former Philippine Governor-General Leonard Wood.[15] While they touch East Asia only

1954); Armin Rappaport, *Henry L. Stimson and Japan, 1931–1933* (Chicago: University of Chicago Press, 1963).

15. Claudius O. Johnson, *Borah of Idaho* (New York: Longmans, 1936); Marian C. McKenna, *Borah* (Ann Arbor: University of Michigan Press, 1961); Robert J. Maddox, *William E. Borah and American Foreign Policy* (Baton Rouge: Louisiana State University Press, 1969); John A. Garraty, *Henry Cabot Lodge: A Biography* (New York: Knopf, 1953); Fred Israel, *Nevada's*

peripherally, the portraits of these men help create a picture of official and political minds as they looked at the world. It is not so much their articulate views of China and Japan, which very few of them held, as their assumptions about America's relationship with the rest of the world that merit attention. Senator Borah, for instance, can be usefully looked at as typifying a strand in American thinking exalting "Americanism" and turning to the electorate as the determinant in American foreign affairs.

Apart from these writings, focusing on specific individuals, there are general studies of U.S. policy toward East Asia in the 1920's. Besides Dorothy Borg whose pioneering work has been noted, A. Whitney Griswold, William A. Williams, and William L. Neumann have offered interpretations of American policy.[16] The neglect the decade of the twenties has suffered in historical scholarship is reflected in the fact that Griswold's monumental work, treating the forty-year period (1898–1938) in 500 pages, has a scant thirty pages devoted to American policy in the 1920's. And this is probably the least inspiring part of his otherwise superb book. He sees a gradual erosion of the collective security principle, codified during the Washington Conference, through the challenge of Chinese nationalism and Japan's adherence to what it regarded as its special interests. The view of American-Japanese relations in the interwar period as a conflict between defender and challenger of the status quo has been widely accepted by historians. But this formula itself says little unless it is realized that the United States and Japan had different definitions of the status quo. The need for probing into Japanese psychology regarding the status quo of the 1920's will be further discussed later.

While most historians thus far mentioned follow Griswold's general interpretation of the 1920's, Williams and Neumann, among others, have sought different ways of looking at the decade. Williams

Key Pittman (Lincoln: University of Nebraska Press, 1963); Wayne S. Cole, *Senator Gerald P. Nye and American Foreign Relations* (Minneapolis: University of Minnesota Press, 1962); Richard W. Leopold, *Elihu Root and the Conservative Tradition* (Boston: Little, Brown, 1954); Waldo H. Heinrichs, *American Ambassador: Joseph C. Grew and the Development of the United States Diplomatic Tradition* (Boston: Little, Brown, 1966); Hermann Hagedorn, *Leonard Wood: A Biography*, 2 vols. (New York: Harper, 1931).

16. A. Whitney Griswold, *The Far Eastern Policy of the United States* (New York: Harcourt, Brace, 1938); William A. Williams, *The Tragedy of American Diplomacy* (New York: World, 1959); Williams, "China and Japan: A Challenge and a Choice of the 1920's," *Pacific Historical Review*, 26 (August 1957), 259–279; William L. Neumann, *America Encounters Japan: From Perry to MacArthur* (Baltimore: Johns Hopkins University Press, 1963); Neumann, "Ambiguity and Ambivalence in Ideas of National Interest in Asia," in Alexander DeConde, ed., *Isolation and Security* (Durham, 1957).

sees in it the point of no return for the United States; in his view, America was in a position to stand on the side of revolutionary nationalism in Asia but instead chose to antagonize it by seeking to expand business opportunities in the Japanese empire. There is much to be said for the picture of China and Japan as presenting two radically different sorts of challenge and opportunities for American policy. China was an underdeveloped country trying to modernize itself, Japan was both underdeveloped and modernized, and America was economically the most advanced in the world. The latter could relate itself to either China or Japan, either economically or sentimentally, but some of these relationships would not be compatible with one another. It was no wonder, then, as Neumann argues in his writings, that there were ambiguities and ambivalences in American approaches to Asia, derived from the lack of clearly established policy priorities. I have tried, in my own work, to relate these ambiguities to the uncertain structure of the East Asian international system in the 1920's.[17] It suggests that American policy must be examined not only in terms of what policy makers were saying and doing but also of what other ways they might have contributed to the consolidation of a new order in East Asia.

I have suggested that as the economic variable in the diplomacy of the major powers increased in importance, there grew a wider and wider gap between their foreign and military policies. To substantiate such a hypothesis one needs many more monographic works dealing with naval strategies and attitudes of the 1920's. American naval thinking has been well summarized by Gerald E. Wheeler, *Prelude to Pearl Harbor: The United States Navy and the Far East, 1921–1931* (Columbia, Mo.: University of Missouri Press, 1963), which, however, assumes a rapport between American's foreign policy and military policy. The question of the extent to which the American and Japanese navies retained their sense of rivalry and antagonism while their governments professed friendship may be studied through the episodes of disarmament conferences at Geneva and London. Such authors as Ferrell, George T. Davis, Raymond O'Connor, Merze Tate have written illuminating accounts.[18] But

17. Iriye, *After Imperialism.*
18. Ferrell, *American Diplomacy in the Great Depression;* George T. Davis, *A Navy Second to None: The Development of Modern American Naval Policy* (New York: Harcourt, Brace, 1940); Raymond G. O'Connor, *Perilous Equilibrium: The United States and the London Disarmament Conference of 1930* (Lawrence, Kan.: University of Kansas Press, 1962); Merze Tate, *The United States and Armaments* (Cambridge, Mass.: Harvard University Press, 1948). See also George C. Reinhardt and William R. Kintner, *The Haphazard Years* (New York: Doubleday, 1960), an impressionistic account of military unpreparedness in the 1920's. Two recent studies of the Washington Conference

their uninational orientation makes it necessary to consult works on Japanese naval policy, to be cited below.

Apart from works dealing specifically with American–East Asian relations, there are several that cover other areas of the globe or the entire world and shed light on the 1920's. For example, Alexander DeConde's and Bryce Wood's studies of Latin American policy, Peter G. Filene's perceptive treatment of American-Soviet relations, Waldo Heinrichs' and Laurence Evans' treaties on the Middle East are all relevant to the discussion of American policy toward East Asia.[19] These geographical studies can be put in perspective by more general accounts such as Adler's two books: the above mentioned *Uncertain Giant* and *The Isolationist Impulse: Its Twentieth Century Reaction* (New York: Abelard-Schuman, 1957). This latter, a well documented but conventional treatment of American public opinion in the interwar years, is supplemented by the more analytical works by Robert E. Osgood, Dexter Perkins, and others.[20] The reading of these numerous volumes will enable the historian to test Dorothy Borg's hypothesis that "the motives underlying our policy in Eastern Asia may more often than not have been the same as those which formed the basis of our policies toward the rest of the world."[21]

Surprising as this thesis may appear to some, it is not very different from what non-American writers on U.S. foreign policy have been saying for years. Perhaps reflecting the fact that few of them have specialized in American policy toward East Asia, they have tended to give less attention to the question of the uniqueness of this policy. Rather, they discuss it as just another area in the operation of American foreign policy, which is seen as derived from certain traditional concepts, stylistic peculiarities of decision-making bodies, the country's position in the balance of power, or dictates of

---

offer insights into the naval problems of the twenties: William R. Braisted, *The United States Navy in the Pacific, 1909–1922* (Austin: University of Texas Press, 1971), and Thomas H. Buckley, *The United States and the Washington Conference, 1921–1922* (Knoxville: University of Tennessee Press, 1970).

19. Alexander DeConde, *Herbert Hoover's Latin American Policy* (Stanford: Stanford University Press, 1957); Bryce Wood, *The Making of the Good Neighbor Policy* (New York: Columbia University Press, 1961); Peter G. Filene, *Americans and the Soviet Experiment, 1917–1933* (Cambridge, Mass.: Harvard University Press, 1967); Heinrichs, *American Ambassador;* Laurence Evans, *The United States Policy and the Partition of Turkey, 1914–1924* (Baltimore: Johns Hopkins Press, 1965).

20. Robert E. Osgood, *Ideals and Self-Interest in America's Foreign Relations* (Chicago: University of Chicago Press, 1953); Dexter Perkins, "The Department of State and American Public Opinion," in Gordon A. Craig and Felix Gilbert, eds., *The Diplomats, 1919–1939* (Princeton: Princeton University Press, 1953).

21. Borg, *American Policy,* xiv.

specific interests. Pierre Renouvin, for instance, discusses East Asia as a relatively insignificant aspect of American foreign affairs, an area where America's traditional interests had been primarily economic.[22] E. I. Popova, on the other hand, pays attention to the ideological aspect of American policy, giving due weight to the emotional, noneconomic considerations underlying American approaches to world problems.[23] Her interesting account of American-Asian relations, however, stops in 1922, and few other Soviet writers seem to have worked on the remainder of the decade. This is regrettable because Russian historians have always been interested in international affairs in East Asia and have produced useful monographs dealing with the period before 1922.[24] Christopher Thorne, an English historian, is completing a study of East Asian international relations in the interwar years, focusing on the Manchurian crisis. Its background chapters deal with the 1920's and promise to put American policy in a global, comparative context.

There are a number of Chinese and Japanese studies of American–East Asian policy. I have discussed some of them in my "Far Eastern Scholarship on United States Far Eastern Policy," an essay included in *Historians and American Far Eastern Policy*, edited by Dorothy Borg (New York: Columbia University Press, 1966). Most works by Chinese and Japanese authors tend to view with skepticism any suggestion of a "traditional" American policy in East Asia different in character from policies toward other regions of the world. Rather, they stress either American's economic motives or considerations of power politics. Few writers, however, have dealt specifically with the 1920's, and fewer still have uncovered fresh data on American policy that have not already been known to the readers of American monographs. However, special mention should be made of *Nempō seijigaku 1969* (Annals of the Japanese Political Science Association, 1969; Tokyo, 1970), which is devoted to the discussion of the Washington Conference system. Several authors present excellent studies of U.S. policy, Japanese attitudes, and Chinese nationalism, raising some fresh questions about the meaning of the disarmament agreements and the relationship between expansionism and nationalism. Besides this publication, articles in Japanese on American policy

22. Pierre Renouvin, *La question d'Extreme-Orient, 1840–1940* (Paris, 1947); *Histoire des relations internationales* (Paris, 1957), vol. VII.

23. E. I. Popova, *Politiki SShA na Dal'men Vostoke, 1918–1922* (Moscow, 1967).

24. See the bibliography in the above book. East Asia is barely mentioned in V. K. Furaev, *Sovetsko-Amerikanskie otnosheniia, 1917–1939* (Moscow, 1964), a work which reflects the peaceful-coexistence theme of the Khrushchev era.

and opinion in the 1920's have been written by Asada Sadao, but he is a product of American education, and his interpretations reflect standard American scholarship.[25]

Turning to Japanese foreign policy during the 1920's, one finds an abundance of material on policy makers but as yet little substantial study of policy. Important biographical materials include the published papers (letters, memoirs, diaries, and so forth) of Shidehara Kijūrō, Arita Hachirō, Shigemitsu Mamoru, Yoshizawa Kenkichi, Horiuchi Kanjō, and Nishi Haruhiko among career diplomats, Ugaki Kazushige, Okada Keisuke, and Saitō Makoto among military leaders, and Yamamoto Jōtarō, Harada Kumao, and Matsumoto Gōkichi among politicians. In addition, the "official biographies" of such men as Tanaka Giichi, Shidehara Kijūrō, Gotō Shimpei, and Hirota Kōki contain valuable documentary evidence.[26] These supplement official documents, diplomatic and military, which are mostly unpublished but generally accessible to the researcher. More recently, investigation into the 1920's has been facilitated by the publication of an official history of the Foreign Ministry, and of collections of documents on such subjects as the South Manchurian Railway, the London Naval Conference, and the Kwantung Army.[27]

Unfortunately, the study of Japanese foreign policy lags far behind the publication of primary sources. There are a few monographs dealing primarily with policy toward China but implicitly touching the United States; among them Ikei Masaru's articles on policy toward the Chinese civil war, Usui Katsumi's discussion of Shidehara's and Tanaka's responses to Chinese nationalism, Etō Shinkichi's appraisal of press opinion, Shimada Toshihiko's informative account of the Kwantung Army, and Imai Seiichi's analysis of the "second" Shidehara diplomacy, stand out.[28] But there does not

25. Asada Sadao, "1920-nendai ni okeru America no Nihon-zō" (Images of Japan in America during the 1920's), *Dōshisha America kenkyū* (Doshisha American Studies), no. 2 (1965); Asada, "America no tai-Nichi kan to 'Washington taisei' " (American views of Japan and the 'Washington system'), *Kokusai seiji* (International relations), no. 34 (October 1967), pp. 36–57.

26. For a list of these biographical works, consult Iriye, *Across the Pacific*, p. 344.

27. *Gendaishi shiryō* (Documents of contemporary history), (Tokyo: Misuzu shobō, 1963—) includes three volumes (xxxi–xxxiii) on the South Manchurian Railway and a volume (xi) on the London Naval Conference. The Defence Agency's official history of the Pacific War includes accounts of the Kwantung Army, of which Volume One has just been published.

28. Ikei Masaru, "Dai-ichi-ji Hō-Choku sensō to Nihon (The first Fengtien-Chihli War and Japan), and "Dai-ni-ji Hō-Choku sensō to Nihon" (The second Fengtien-Chihli War and Japan), in Kurihara Ken, ed., *Tai Man-Mō seisaku-shi no ichimen* (Aspects of Japanese policy toward Manchuria and Mongolia)

exist a detailed analysis of any of the key policy makers in the 1920's. The best that one has at present is a product of collective effort: the first volume of the monumental eight-volume *Taiheiyō sensō e no michi* (The road to the Pacific War; Tokyo: Asahi Shimbun, 1962–63), which has fresh, important data on aspects of Japanese foreign affairs after the Washington Conference. In the United States Ralph G. Falconeri and William F. Morton, among others, have written dissertations based on extensive research among Japanese archives. In Japan, however, students of recent history seem to be turning their attention increasingly and primarily to the 1930's. Many more monographs and primary sources are likely to be published on that decade than on the 1920's.

There are even fewer works dealing specifically with Japanese-American relations. Asada Sadao's dissertation at Yale University, "Japan and the United States, 1915–1925" (1962), is the only book-length study, but it is fuller for the period before than after the Washington Conference. Etō Shinkichi has written a model monograph discussing Japanese and American responses to the Nanking Incident of 1927, but it is not a study primarily in Japanese-American relations.[29] The only exception to the rather bleak picture is the naval question, which defined one crucial area of the relations between the two countries. Writings by Itō Masanori, Kobayshi Tatsuo, and Hata Ikuhiko are enormously useful in describing Japanese naval strategy during the 1920's.[30] They serve to underline the fact that the Washington Conference system, which for Foreign Ministry bureaucrats signified an era of good feeling across the Pacific, only convinced naval planners of the inevitable clash between the two navies. It was only in the 1920's that the United States was defined

---

(Tokyo, 1966); Usui Katsumi, "Shidehara gaikō oboegaki" (A memorandum on the Shidehara diplomacy), *Nihon rekishi* (Japanese history), no. 126 (December 1958) pp. 62–68; Usui, "Tanaka gaikō ni tsuite no oboegaki" (A memorandum on the Tanaka diplomacy), *Kokusai seiji,* no. 11 (January 1960) pp. 26–35; Etō Shinkichi, "Nik-Ka kinchō to Nihonjin" (The Sino-Japanese tension and the Japanese), in Banno Masataka and Etō Shinkichi, eds., *Chūgoku o meguru kokusai seiji* (International politics revolving around China; Tokyo, 1968); Shimada Toshihiko, *Kantōgun* (The Kwantung Army; Tokyo, 1965); Imai Seiichi, "Shidehara gaikō ni okeru seisaku kettei" (Decision making in the Shidehara diplomacy), *Nenpō seijigaku* (Annals of the Japanese Political Science Association; 1959), pp. 92–112.

29. Etō Shinkichi, "Nanking jiken to Nichi-Bei" (The Nanking Incident, Japan, and the United States), in Saitō Makoto, ed., *Gendai America no naisei to gaikō* (Politics and foreign policy of contemporary America; Tokyo, 1959).

30. Itō Masanori, *Gunbatsu kōbōshi* (The rise and fall of military cliques; Tokyo, 1958) 3 vols.; Kobayashi Tatsuo, introduction to *Gendaishi shiryō,* (Tokyo, 1964) VII; Hata Ikuhiko, "Meiji-ki ikō ni okeru Nichi-Bei Taiheiyō senryaku no hensen" (Changing Japanese and American strategies in the Pacific after the Meiji era), *Kokusai seiji,* no. 37 (October 1968), pp. 96–115.

as the most likely enemy, necessitating the initiation of detailed strategic planning. The gap between civilian policy and military thinking continued to widen until, in 1930, the conflict came out into the open following the signing of the London disarmament treaty. Itō Takashi's recent and excellent monograph gives massive documentation on this episode and traces the domestic implications of the treaty.[31] He, as well as some others, points out that the United States had come to symbolize the existing order of international and national life in Japan. To oppose the Japanese-American agreement in London was not only to protest against specific disarmament arrangements but also to challenge the structure of the Washington system which, it was widely believed, provided the framework for the continuation of a cooperative foreign policy and a conservative fiscal and social policy at home.[32]

Though meager in comparison with works on American policy, these writings on Japanese policy enrich our understanding of the decade by enlarging the perspective on the subject. They also indicate the kinds of questions that await further investigation. The most important of these questions are ones related to China. In what way did the United States and Japan react to one another in China? Were their interests at odds, and if so was this clearly recognized by policy makers and the public? Did the American perception of Japanese policy correspond to reality? Was the Japanese image of American behavior in China more (or less) accurate than the American perception of itself? In what way did the two countries aid or impede developments in China toward unity and modernization?

None of these questions has been explored in depth, and most of them will remain only partially answered until the Chinese side of the picture is examined more closely. Here the record is even more meager. Chinese authorities in neither Peking nor Taipei have shown much interest in publishing diplomatic documents for the 1920's; most of the printed material consists of papers relating to domestic developments such as warlordism, the Nationalist northern expedition, and Soviet activities in China. In addition there is biographical material on and by such figures as Chiang Kai-shek, Sun Yat-sen, and Mao Tse-tung.[33] Some of the available material has

31. Itō Takashi, *Shōwa shoki seiji-shi kenkyū* (A Study of Japanese politics during the early Showa era; Tokyo, 1968).

32. See also James B. Crowley, *Japan's Quest for Autonomy: National Security and Foreign Policy, 1930–1938* (Princeton: Princeton University Press, 1966).

33. Mao Szu-ch'eng, ed., *Min-kuo shih-wu-nien i-ch'ien chih Chiang Chieh-shih hsien-sheng* (Chiang Kai-shek before 1926) (n.p., n.d.) 20 vols.; *Sun*

been translated into English.[34] All this, however, is pitiably inadequate when one considers the immensely complex configurations of political-military structures, patterns of opinion-making, and combinations of traditional ideas and modern symbols in Republican China. In the absence of massive documentation in Chinese, one will continue to have to turn to diplomatic dispatches and consular reports by American, British, Japanese, and German officials in China. Since they contain newspaper clippings and official and non-official communications, and since some of the foreign representatives were proficient in Chinese, their reports contain a mine of information, which has been tapped only superficially.

The result is that an extensive treatment of Chinese foreign policy in the 1920's is virtually nonexistent. Some historians at the Academia Sinica have been diligently reading *Wai-chiao-pu* documents housed there, but their monographs have tended to cover the late Ch'ing and the early republican periods. General accounts of Chinese foreign policy, such as those by Fu Ch'i-hsüeh and Liu Yen, offer standard chronological treatments.[35] The broad surveys by Robert T. Pollard and Werner Levi are based on Western sources and unexciting, although Pollard's book is still a good introduction to the powers' policies toward China in the 1920's.[36] The same holds for Wesley R. Fishel's careful study of the extraterritoriality question and Stanley F. Wright's monumental volume dealing with the tariff autonomy problem.[37] China's revolutionary nationalism has been well analyzed in the context of the May Thirtieth movement by Banno Masataka, Nakamura Takahide, and Charles F. Remer.[38]

Chung-shan hsüan-chi (Collected works of Sun Yat-sen; Peking, 1956); 2 vols., *Mao Tse-tung hsüan-chi* (Collected works of Mao Tse-tung; Peking, 1951–1964), 4 vols.

34. Conrad Brandt, Benjamin I. Schwartz, and John K. Fairbank, *A Documentary History of Chinese Communism* (Cambridge, Mass.: Harvard University Press, 1952); C. Martin Wilbur and Julie Lien-ying How, *Documents on Communism, Nationalism, and Soviet Advisers in China, 1918–1927* (New York: Columbia University Press, 1956); Stuart Schram, *The Political Thought of Mao Tse-tung* (New York: Praeger, 1963).

35. Fu Ch'i-hsüeh, *Chung-Kuo wai-chiao-shih* (Diplomatic history of China; Taipei, 1957); Liu Yen, *Chung-kuo wai-chiao shih* (Diplomatic history of China), revised and expanded by Li Fang-ch'en (Taipei, 1962).

36. Robert T. Pollard, *China's Foreign Relations, 1917–1931* (New York Macmillan 1933); Werner Levi, *Modern China's Foreign Policy* (Minneapolis University of Minnesota Press, 1953).

37. Wesley R. Fishel, *The End of Extraterritoriality in China* (Berkeley: University of California Press, 1952); Stanley F. Wright, *China's Struggle for Tariff Autonomy, 1843–1938* (Shanghai: Kelly and Walsh, 1938).

38. Banno Masataka, "Dai-ichi-ji taisen kara go-sanjū made: Kokken kaifuku undō-shi oboegaki" (From World War I to the May 30th incident: A study of the rights recovery movement), in Ueda Toshio, ed., *Gendai Chūgoku o*

But the whole field is crying out for more monographs.

It is not surprising that there have as yet been very few works dealing specifically with Chinese-American relations from the Chinese side. Nor would it be particularly useful to have general interpretations of the subjects before further empirical studies are undertaken. One promising sign in this direction is the publication of a number of excellent biographical analyses. Sun Yat-sen has been extensively studied, enabling the historian to have some sense of Sun's views of the world including his attitude toward the United States.[39] Even if one did not have an explicit view of America, it is still valuable to look at his mental equipment and intellectual orientation. Warloads Feng Yü-hsiang and Yen Hsi-shan, for example, have been subjects of recent biographies; and while they had little specific to say on external affairs, their behavior tells a great deal about one stratum of the Chinese mind, just as studies of Presidents Harding and Coolidge reveal a strand of American thinking.[40] In this sense the studies by Y. C. Wang and Jerome Grieder, among others, of some Chinese students who studied in the United States and then returned to China to emerge as intellectual leaders of the country are extremely illuminating.[41] If these "returned students" were not always explicitly aware of or willing to talk about what they had learned from and thought of America, their whole lives are demonstrations of the kinds of subtle influences that work on a person transplanted into a different cultural environment.

meguru sekai no gaikō (World diplomacy and China; Tokyo, 1951); Nakamura Takahide, "Go-sanjū jiken to zai-Ka-bō" (The May 30th incident and the cotton spinning industry in China), in *Kindai Chūgoku kenkyū* (Studies on modern China; Tokyo, 1964), Vol. VI; Charles F. Remer, *A Study of Chinese Boycotts* (Baltimore: Johns Hopkins Press, 1935). See also Kikuchi Takaharu, *Chūgoku minzoku undō no kihon kōzō* (The substructure of the Chinese nationalistic movement; Tokyo, 1966).

39. Leng Shao Chuan and Norman D. Palmer, *Sun Yat-sen and Communism* (New York: Praeger, 1960); Marius B. Jensen, *The Japanese and Sun Yat-sen* (Cambridge, Mass.: Harvard University Press, 1954); Nozawa Yutaka, *Son Bun* (Sun Yat-sen; Tokyo, 1962); Fujii Shōzō, *Son Bun no kenkyū* (A study of Sun Yat-sen; Tokyo, 1966).

40. James F. Sheridan, *Chinese Warlord: The Career of Feng Yü-hsiang* (Stanford: Stanford University Press, 1966); Donald G. Gillin, *Warlord: Yen Hsi-shan in Shansi Province, 1911–1949* (Princeton: Princeton University Press, 1967). See also Donald W. Klein and Anne B. Clark, *Biographic Dictionary of Chinese Communism, 1921–1965* (Cambridge, Mass.: Harvard University Press, 1971).

41. Y. C. Wang, *Chinese Intellectuals and the West, 1872–1949* (Chapel Hill: North Carolina University Press, 1966); Jerome Grieder, *Hu Shih and the Chinese Renaissance: Liberalism in the Chinese Revolution, 1917–1937* (Cambridge, Mass.: Harvard University Press, 1970).

The area of individual relations is, after all, the most intriguing aspect of contact between the United States and East Asia. The story of American–East Asian relations would be quite uninspiring were it to concern itself merely with formal policies and opinions conceived and expressed separately in various countries. For instance, one would be only scratching the surface of American-Chinese relations if one were only to discuss how policy was made in Washington or Nanking, or what the public in the two countries thought of each other. An American sitting in a middle-class suburban home may have all sorts of images about China, and these may determine how he votes in an election. But it will be difficult to assess the interaction of these ideas with developments in China. Much more fundamental and interesting will be the direct encounter between Chinese and Americans, either in China, the United States, or a third country. American-Chinese relations are after all a sum total of direct and indirect relations between individual Americans and Chinese, but the direct encounter has not been given the attention it deserves. The same is true of Japanese-American relations.

Some of the works already cited do go into this question. Dorothy Borg's book, for example, has a fine chapter dealing with the responses of the American community in China to the Nanking Incident. Conflicting currents of opinion among Americans are presented through their publications. Paul A. Varg's *Missionaries, Chinese and Diplomats: The American Protestant Missionary Movement in China, 1890–1952* (Princeton: Princeton University Press, 1958) is also rich in data concerning American missionaries' disagreement with Minister MacMurray's handling of the crisis in the mid-1920's. This was the time when basic assumptions that had guided liberal Christian enterprises were seriously questioned, not only by Chinese nationalists but also by American missionaries in China, and the episode provides a classic example of two value systems meeting at a crossroads. More positive contributions by Americans in China to the latter's modernization have been sketched in the recent studies by Arthur N. Young, James C. Thomson, and Jonathan Spence.[42] They describe how certain Americans applied their expertise to help China solve its administrative, financial, and

42. Arthur N. Young, *China and the Helping Hand, 1937–1945* (Cambridge, Mass.: Harvard University Press, 1963); James C. Thomson, *While China Faced West: American Reformers in Nationalist China, 1928–1937* (Cambridge, Mass.: Harvard University Press, 1969); Jonathan Spence, *To Change China: Western Advisers in China, 1620–1960* (Boston: Little, Brown, 1969).

social problems. China in the 1920's was crying out for "relevant" reforms, a need which could be partially filled by American specialists trained in flood control, bridge construction, monetary policy, and bureaucratic administration. Even so, this was a period when Chinese, rather than foreigners, determined what was "relevant" to the country's needs, and Americans often experienced a feeling of severe self-doubt as they were working in a Chinese setting guided by their professional training, which was solely Western. As Spence quotes Edward H. Hume, president of Yale-in-China, "In 20 years I have never felt so humble, so utterly weak and so completely puzzled about the future."[43]

Extremely valuable as these studies are, one would want to know more about what happened to the Americans after they returned to the United States. The impact of a person's experience abroad upon the totality of his personal development should be an immensely fascinating though difficult subject to pursue in discussing American–East Asian relations. Americans who went to China in the 1920's as students, missionaries, or journalists later emerged as China specialists in the United States, as spokesmen for or against Communist China, or as interpreters of things oriental to the American layman. Their sojourn in China enabled them to form a certain coherent picture of that country, and through their writings and speeches their views of China influenced the thinking of Americans who had never been to Asia. This interaction has been vividly portrayed in Harold Isaacs' study of how Americans form their images of China and India.[44] What is equally interesting is to trace the impact of one's first-hand acquaintance with China upon oneself. Whether he likes it or not, a man has to live with his experiences, and the extent to which he is willing to be articulate about them tells a great deal about the impact of these experiences upon his personal and intellectual growth. Kenneth E. Shewmaker has written a very interesting monograph tracing the direct encounter between Americans and Chinese Communists, a work which suggests one direction that further research might take.[45]

Unfortunately, there are no comparable studies dealing with Americans who went to Japan in the decade. One has to fall back upon personal reminiscences by Pearl Buck, Thomas W. Lamont, and others to gain some understanding of their encounter with the

43. Spence, *To Change China*, p. 175.
44. Harold Isaacs, *Scratches on Our Minds: American Images of China and India* (New York: J. Day, 1958).
45. Kenneth E. Shewmaker, *Americans and Chinese Communists, 1927–1945: A Persuading Encounter* (Ithaca: Cornell University Press, 1971).

Japanese. It is to be hoped that private papers will be examined with this question in mind. One finds, for instance, among the papers of Edgar A. Bancroft (ambassador to Japan during 1924–25), evidence of how a Chicago lawyer who went to Japan without much enthusiasm was overwhelmed by the first impressions of the country and tried to influence his countrymen's attitude toward it. His contacts were limited to the court circle and businessmen who assured him that the masses and mass media of Japan had little influence on the governing group but that the latter shared the former's resentment of the Japanese exclusion act. "My conclusions are," he wrote, "that the Japanese people, with substantial unanimity, keenly felt that a humiliating slight was put upon their race by the form of the Immigration Act; that this feeling of insult was intensified by the friendship of the Japanese toward America, and their confidence that America was their friend. . . . It is this attitude of suppressed sadness and deep disappointment coupled with a gracious courtesy, that is very appealing to me."[46] Thus began the intimate relationship between the families of Ambassador Bancroft and Count Kabayama Aisuke that has continued to this day.

"There are so many graduates of American universities and colleges in positions of power and influence here," wrote Bancroft to his friend, Silas Strawn, "that it only requires a sympathetic handling of relations between the two nations to make Japan an absolutely devoted and perpetual friend of America."[47] Thus the ambassador was mentioning another crucial aspect of Japanese-American relations which bears further investigation: Japanese who had studied in the United States. Two of them, Nitobe Inazō and Uchimura Kanzō, top leaders in Japan's religious and educational life, had first gone to America in the 1890's. They left personally repudiated by anti-Japanese laws, but their responses to the immigration crisis differed, as Miwa Kimitada's manuscript in preparation reminds us anew.[48] Others, like Nagai Kafū, had also studied in the United States but remained unmoved by the question.[49] What caused these differences? What place did their American experiences occupy in their respective mental pictures and whole personalities? These

46. Edgar A. Bancroft to Charles Evans Hughes, Jan. 5, 1925, Bancroft Papers (Cambridge, Mass.).

47. Bancroft to Silas Strawn, Feb. 25, 1925, ibid.

48. Kimitada Miwa, "Crossroads of Prewar Japanese Patriotism: Uchimura Kanzō, Niobe Inazō, and Shiga Shigetaka" (Ph.D. diss., Princeton University, 1968). See also Miwa's excellent study of another American-educated Japanese: *Matsuoka Yōseki* (Tokyo, 1971).

49. Edward Seidensticker, *Kafū the Scribbler: The Life and Letters of Nagai Kafū, 1879–1959* (Stanford: Stanford University Press, 1965).

questions await investigation by specialists in literature and psychology as well as history.

There is no doubt, however, that the immigration episode revealed one central aspect of American–East Asian relations. The question was whether Japanese and Americans could coexist, not only as two separate nations across the Pacific but also living together in the United States. There are some good studies on the direct encounter in California, from both the American and the Japanese points of view.[50] But one has to know a great deal more about general American attitudes toward race on the one hand, and Japanese visions of expansion toward the American continent on the other. Oscar Handlin, John Higham, Richard A. Thompson, and others have blazed the path.[51] The recent preoccupation of American historians with the subject of racism can be expected to produce further illuminating accounts. On the Japanese side, I have tried to explain the intellectual and psychological reality of the racial crisis by linking it to the ideology of postwar expansionism.[52] Only by looking at these areas of inquiry will it become possible to understand the "failure" of the Washington Conference system. It was not simply or even primarily that the United States was not "prepared" to back up the new status quo by force that brought about the ascendancy of Japanese militarism. Had America taken a more conciliatory stand on the immigration question, scores of prominent Japanese would have found sufficient courage and intellectual honesty to speak out against the exponents of forceful expansionism. On the eve of the Mukden incident, the respected former diplomat, Ishii Kikujirō, privately penned his thoughts on Japanese-American relations. He said that there was no possibility of war

50. Roger Daniels, *The Politics of Prejudice: The Anti-Japanese Movement in California and the Struggle for Japanese Exclusion* (Berkeley: University of California Press, 1962); Yamato Ichihashi, *Japanese in the United States* (Stanford: Stanford University Press, 1932); Carey McWilliams, *Prejudice: Japanese-Americans, Symbol of Racial Intolerance* (Boston: Little, Brown, 1944).

51. Oscar Handlin, *The American People in the Twentieth Century* (Cambridge, Mass.: Harvard University Press, 1954); John Higham, *Strangers in the Land: Patterns of American Nativism, 1860–1925* (New Brunswick, N.J.: Rutgers University Press, 1955); Richard A. Thompson, "The Yellow Peril, 1890–1924" (Ph.D. diss., University of Wisconsin, 1957).

52. Iriye, "The Failure of Economic Expansionism, 1918–1931" (paper presented at the Conference on Taisho Japan; Durham, N.C., Jan. 1969); Iriye, "Heiwateki hattenshugi to Nihon" (Peaceful expansionism and Japan), *Chūōkōron*, 84.10 (October 1969), pp. 74–94. Japanese psychology, especially the sense of isolation in international society, in the 1920's is well described in an autobiographical study by Captain Malcolm D. Kennedy, *The Estrangement of Great Britain and Japan, 1917–1935* (Berkeley: University of California Press, 1969).

between the two countries but that there was one serious problem; it was not the naval question, nor the problem of the Pacific or China, nor the Open Door. It was the racial question. Real danger existed if the United States was made to stand for the white race and Japan for the colored races.[53] Such observations serve to connect Ishii's known personal integrity and his defense of aggression in Manchuria soon afterwards.

Finally, another equally fascinating theater of direct encounter was the meeting of Americans, Chinese, and Japanese in China. Americans and Japanese took with them certain conceptions and expectations about China as well as notions about each other. The antagonism between Japanese and Americans in China seems to have increased in the 1920's, but this needs documentation. In the absence of an obvious diplomatic crisis between Washington and Tokyo, it was precisely this sort of antagonism which, in addition to the immigration question, revealed the complex nature of American–East Asian relations. To investigate this subject one will have to study the Japanese-language press in China and the newspapers edited by Americans there. The *Peking shūhō* (Peking weekly), for instance, abounded in references to America, most of them derogatory, reciprocating the cordial dislike of Japan expressed in the pages of the *China Weekly Review*. Often Americans suspected Japanese of fomenting pan-Asianism among Chinese, a reaction which dates back to the 1890's. The Japanese in China, on the other hand, considered that Americans were actively instigating the Chinese to turn against Japanese goods and services in order to reap their own benefits. This extremely interesting phenomenon has never been sufficiently studied.[54]

These issues lead to further problems. To understand why Japanese and Americans behaved the way they did in China, we must know more about the kinds of Japanese and Americans who went to China—their socio-economic background, their education, and their relationship to the official establishment. Why did they go to China rather than somewhere else? What images did they have of their being in China, and of their countrymen's view of their life

53. Ishii Kikujirō, "Gaikō zuisō" (Essays on diplomacy) (July 14, 1931), in *Kokusai seiji*, no. 29 (October 1965) pp. 109–149.

54. Some discussion of Japanese-American antagonism shortly after World War I is given in Mitani Taichirō, *Nihon seitō seiji no kenkyū* (A study of Japanese party politics: Tokyo, 1967). Institute of Pacific Relations conferences gave an opportunity for responsible Chinese, Japanese, and Americans to get together to air their views. This phenomenon is discussed in Sadako Ogata, "Non-Governmental Organizations in Japan" (paper presented at the Conference on Japanese-American Relations; Japan, 1969).

in China? While the 1920's saw little outright aggression on their part backed up by military force, this was the time when the Chinese were demanding an end not only to formal colonialism and imperialism but even to peaceful expansionism within the framework of the treaty system. But how could China achieve its goals, such as unification and modernization, without reckoning with the presence of foreigners on its soil, some of them potential helpers and advisers in this task? How could foreigners help China without exerting subtle or overt political and economic influences upon Chinese life and thought? How were Americans and Japanese to safeguard their own interests and maintain self-respect?

It is evident that we are raising questions not only of American–East Asian relations during the 1920's but of world history throughout the modern era. Various forms of expansion have taken place and given way to others, bringing peoples of diverse races and cultures closer together and producing conflict and tension in the process. In this process Asia has been transformed, but the transformation has also had its repercussions on the rest of the world. The encounter between the United States and East Asia has been part of the global phenomenon of expanding contact among peoples. Whether the mutual expansion and encounter have changed man is the crucial problem of modern history. Karl Marx wrote, "The whole of history is nothing but a continual transformation of human nature."[55] To identify changes in Chinese, Japanese, and American life as a result of their interaction, to indicate what meaning this story has had for their respective national histories, and above all to trace subtle influences which the three peoples have exerted upon the ideas and habits of one another, provide a meaningful area of historical inquiry.

All diplomatic history is hyphenated history. It deals with relations, direct and indirect, between two or more states and peoples. But American–East Asian relations should be hyphenated in more than one way. To make positive contributions to scholarship, its study should not simply be diplomatic history; it should be diplomatic-intellectual-psychological history.

55. Quoted in Tang Tsou, "The Cultural Revolution and the Chinese Political System," *China Quarterly* (April–June 1969), p. 64.

1931–1937

The years 1931–1937 are a hazy interval in world history. It lies uncertainly between the illusive internationalism of the twenties and the downhill plunge to war of the late thirties. Full of outcomes and preludes, it lacks a character of its own and with some notable exceptions receives superficial and passing attention. This is a dangerous condition encouraging overemphasis on events related to periods which precede or follow. We need a clearer perception of the nature of international relations in the early and middle thirties.

It is especially tempting to view these years as prelude, as the time when the great storm of World War II was brewing. The habit of chopping history into decades and the fairly consistent character of the twenties suggest a unitary conception of the thirties. The world economic crisis and the Manchurian crisis of 1931 marked a sharp break with the past and portended the dismal events to come. Hitler and Roosevelt, major actors in the world drama, made their entrances in the early thirties. Japan's road to the Pacific War beginning at Mukden and ending at Pearl Harbor has no small attraction as an historical unit. Many paths leading to the cataclysmic events of the forties seem to have convenient starting points at the beginning of the thirties.

An equally plausible case can be made for assigning a retrospective quality to the period. Most of the noteworthy events of 1931–1937 involved repudiation of the internationalism of the twenties. The London Economic Conference ended any common approach to currency stabilization and trade enlargement. The weary search for European disarmament formulas petered out at Geneva and the painfully wrought system of naval limitation collapsed at London in 1935. League sanctions failed over Abyssinia, and the United States rejected a most qualified membership in the World Court. Regional security pacts fared no better. The Locarno Pact dissolved with the occupation of the Rhineland and the Brussels Conference marked the demise of the Nine Power Treaty. Versailles, Washington, the Covenant, Kellogg Briand: one by one the symbols of the New Diplomacy came down. The universalism and multilateral-

ism of the twenties died not abruptly with Manchuria but linger-
ingly, year by year, over the whole course of this period. So these
years are closely intertwined with neighboring periods and lack a
character of their own. We tend to look backward or forward for
the regnant events and characteristics, missing perhaps the underlying reasons why internationalism ended and the law of the jungle
supervened.

A starting point in defining the character of international relations in the early thirties is the salient fact that national energies
and concerns were directed inward toward resolution of domestic
problems. The world economic crisis was a powerful solvent of
international cooperation. Economic autarky was the most obvious
result. No less destructive were the social and political tensions
and upheavals induced by the depression. Contending with industrial paralysis and unemployment, regimes faced the even more
fundamental problems of retaining power and holding the polity
together. Fiscal orthodoxy and stubborn pacifism ruled England,
while France under shaky coalitions settled into cynicism and
despair. Franklin Roosevelt concentrated almost exclusively on pro-
pelling the United States toward economic recovery, Chiang Kai-
shek on extending the sway of Kuomintang and modernizing the
army. For Hitler the early thirties were a time for arming and
legitimizing and consolidating Nazi power.

Foreign policy took a back seat. Diplomatic initiatives—the Stresa
Front, the Eastern Locarno, the Anglo-German naval agreement,
the Franco-Soviet rapprochement, American overtures to Britain
during the Manchurian crisis—were desultory and inconclusive.
Imperial ventures confined themselves to remote East Africa and
Northeast Asia with minimum abrasion of the vital interests of other
great powers. The Japanese army was riven with factionalism and
indiscipline. Its best minds contemplated general war only after
a period of national mobilization and industrial development. Generally external affairs lacked the immediate urgency of internal and
governments lacked the necessary margin of political power to undertake initiatives abroad.

Diplomacy in the early thirties lacked any clearcut character.
International relations were atomized and featureless. Such faith
as existed in the old formulas and arrangements drained away.
The world drifted as the weather changed.

At some point the drift stopped. Let me suggest that the year was
1936. That year Hitler reoccupied the Rhineland, established accord
with Mussolini, and joined him in internationalizing the civil war
in Spain. In China the subjugation of the Kwangtung and Kwangsi

generals, victory over Japanese puppet troops in Suiyuan, and the Sian Incident paved the way for internal truce and common action against the foreign aggressor. In Japan the February 26 Incident ended factionalism and indiscipline in the army. The following August the army and navy agreed upon certain "Fundamentals of National Policy" which, however overreaching and contradictory, reflected a programmatic approach to external affairs. Soon after, Japan signed the Anti-Comintern Pact, her first political treaty with a western power since the founding of the Anglo-Japanese Alliance, and thereby reconnected European and East Asian diplomacy. In November, after his overwhelming triumph at the polls, President Roosevelt journeyed abroad for the first time to inaugurate a new hemispheric security policy.

The year 1936 would seem to have been the time when the process of recouping from internal crisis and of consolidating power had reached the point where governments found the necessary margin to undertake external initiatives or at least found external circumstances for once more demanding than internal problems. The result was new strategic thinking and the reactivation of diplomacy. Appeasement, however misguided, was a departure from the quiescence of British diplomacy in the early thirties. The shape of coming coalitions was obscure in 1937 but the new mode of international politics was evident in the play for position and tentative alignments that ensued.

If this characterization of the period has any validity, it raises some new questions. In the conventional view World War II originated in the aggression of totalitarian, "have not" powers and the belated response of the democratic, status-quo powers and the Soviet Union. Neat, vertical dichotomies, geographical and to some extent ideological, lead to a straightforward cause–effect explanation. However, if we assume that a phase of national introversion occurred between 1931 and 1936, ending with reactivation of international politics on a new basis, then we are led to ask whether internal histories do not in themselves provide some part of the explanation for the world crisis of the late thirties and the war. The measures taken by regimes to maintain or consolidate power and cure depression, in "have" as well as "have not" countries, may well have heightened international insecurity and tensions. For example, the Roosevelt administration was hardly pursuing a vigorous foreign policy, and yet its naval programs of 1933 and 1934 had a disquieting effect on Japan and provided the rationalization for Japanese naval increases. Roosevelt was responding within treaty limits to earlier Japanese increases, but he was also helping to resolve the problem of unemployment and gaining political dividends in the process. In Germany and Japan aggressive designs could be strongly affected in tempo and direction by decisions as to which groups and interests needed to be placated in order to make the regimes secure. In other words it may be useful to consider international relations in this period of national autonomy from the inside out, that is, by way of domestic political histories.

The traditional focus on the formal aspects of relations would seem in any event to have yielded about as much as can be expected. Exhaustive studies of the Manchurian crisis exist for the Japanese side, both in Japanese and English, as well as for the American.[1] A much needed study of British policy based on recently opened archives will undoubtedly be forthcoming soon and then an international history of the crisis will be in order. But enlargement of scope and enrichment of official sources is not likely to change the main outlines of the story. Dorothy Borg's comprehensive and judicious book, though by no means limited to formal aspects of relations, will long remain the standard treatment of American Far Eastern policy and diplomacy for the half-dozen years following the Manchurian crisis.[2] It seems convenient to leave the formal side of relations for the time being and explore the foreign implications of domestic policy.

On the American side a number of questions come to mind. We need to learn about the politics of naval building, in particular about the emergency PWA appropriation of 1933 and the Vinson–Trammell program of 1934.[3] An adequate treatment of the Silver Purchase

1. The best of these are: Sadako N. Ogata, *Defiance in Manchuria; The Making of Japanese Foreign Policy, 1931–1932* (Berkeley: University of California Press, 1964); Armin Rappaport, *Henry L. Stimson and Japan, 1931–1933* (Chicago: University of Chicago Press, 1963); James B. Crowley, *Japan's Quest for Autonomy: National Security and Foreign Policy, 1930-1938* (Princeton: Princeton University Press, 1966). For Japanese multivolume studies and documents relating to the Manchurian crisis see review articles by Akira Iriye in *Journal of Asian Studies*, 23 (November 1963), 103–113, and 26 (August 1967), 677–682. John E. Wiltz, *From Isolation to War, 1931–1941* (New York: Crowell, 1968) provides an up-to-date survey of the literature on the Manchurian crisis and the period as a whole.

2. Dorothy Borg, *The United States and the Far Eastern Crisis of 1933–1938: From the Manchurian Incident through the Initial Stage of the Undeclared Sino-Japanese War* (Cambridge, Mass.: Harvard University Press, 1964).

3. On the navy in the thirties see Stephen Ernest Pelz, "Race to Pearl Harbor: The Failure of the Second London Naval Conference and the Coming of World War II" (Ph.D. diss., Harvard University, 1970). The only available account in print is Thaddeus V. Tuleja, *Statesmen and Admirals: Quest for a Far Eastern Naval Policy* (New York: Norton, 1963). My forthcoming essay is, I hope, suggestive of possible lines of inquiry: "The Role of the U.S. Navy,"

Act of 1934 and its impact on China is in order.[4] The effect of administration policies on trade relations with Japan begs attention. Indeed, so does the whole area of American-Japanese economic relations; little has been done since the valuable study by William W. Lockwood, Jr., published in 1936, though Mira Wilkins' recent essay paves the way for intensive investigations.[5] We should find out how the administration responded to domestic pressures for import restrictions, particularly from the cotton textile industry. How much did it resist and how far placate, and why? How did New Deal recovery programs seeking to protect the domestic market and raise prices affect Japanese imports? What effect did the New Deal policy of reducing farm surpluses have on hopes for market expansion abroad, especially among influential cotton congressmen? The ancient illusion of a great China market animated New Dealers like Henry Morgenthau, as Lloyd Gardner shows, but recovery and reform measures seem generally to have discouraged trade outside the hemisphere.[6] And however determined the administration was to avoid provoking Japan, it was narrowing trade outlets for Japan in the western hemisphere and the Philippines and thereby reinforcing her movement toward imperial isolation.

Japanese internal developments pose a different problem. Thus far scholarship has emphasized the army and navy and undoubtedly they were the dynamic elements in Japanese expansionism, while civilians in and outside government followed, willingly or not, in their wake. But the fact that democratic, parliamentary forces failed to control or restrain the military does not mean that political processes ceased. On the contrary, given the contradictory imperial

Conference on Japanese-American Relations, 1931–1941, Lake Kawaguchi, Japan, July, 1969. The Lake Kawaguchi Conference papers, frequently cited below, are due to be published shortly.

4. Allan Seymour Everest, *Morgenthau, the New Deal, and Silver: A Story of Pressure Politics* (New York: King's Crown Press, 1950), though making use of the Morgenthau Diary, is limited in other sources. See also: Fred L. Israel, *Nevada's Key Pittman* (Lincoln, Nebraska: University of Nebraska Press, 1963); John Morton Blum, *From the Morgenthau Diaries: Years of Crisis, 1928–1938* (Boston: Houghton Mifflin, 1959).

5. William W. Lockwood, Jr., "Trade and Trade Rivalry between the United States and Japan," document 1, *Problems of the Pacific, 1936: Aims and Results of Social and Economic Policies in Pacific Countries,* Proceedings of the Sixth Conference of the Institute of Pacific Relations, Yosemite National Park, California, 15–29, August 1936, W. L. Holland and Kate L. Mitchell, eds. (Chicago, n.d.), pp. 211–262; Mira Wilkins, "The Role of U.S. Business," Lake Kawaguchi Conference Papers.

6. Lloyd C. Gardner, "The Role of the Commerce and Treasury Departments," Lake Kawaguchi Conference Papers. See also his *Economic Aspects of New Deal Diplomacy* (Madison, Wisconsin: University of Wisconsin Press, 1964), pp. 77–78.

ambitions of the army and navy and their tug-of-war for available national resources, one would suppose competitive solicitation by both services of politicians, publicists, intellectuals, and businessmen. Did Mitsui, Mitsubishi, Sumitomo, and Asano invest in the army's enterprises or the navy's, or did they nicely calculate a mixed portfolio? Which right-wing groups leaned toward the army, a continental policy, and war with the Soviet Union, and which toward the navy, southern advance and possible confrontation with Britain and the United States? Which way did the wind blow in the circles surrounding such key figures as Baron Hiranuma and Prince Konoe? The outcome, embracing both northern and southern expansion, may well have resulted not simply from interservice rivalry but from that rivalry played out in a broad political context. The ideas and interests of civilians cannot be ignored in explaining Japan's increasingly threatening posture in Pacific and Asian affairs.

Japanese interservice rivalry over the direction of expansion at least offered two outcomes for Japanese-American relations, one of which was bound to be less unattractive than the other. Of the two thrusts, the army's was less immediately threatening to the United States and in fact the army was anxious to attract American capital to Manchuria and recognized Japan's dependence on American resources. If this was the case, why was American trade and investment not more significant as a constructive factor in Japanese-American relations? Obviously the depression provides one set of answers. Another set may lie in the conditions afforded American trade and investment in Japan. Some American companies, oil and automobile for example, remained keenly interested in doing business in Japan and yet they faced stringent regulations which made their efforts unprofitable.[7] Singer Sewing Machine and National City Bank suffered official harassment. American businesses undoubtedly offered convenient targets for government-inspired popular wrath and xenophobia. But at a more fundamental level there existed a contradiction between economic partnership with the United States and the objective of creating a modern, self-sufficient, industrial foundation for total war. This duality in Japanese economic policy remains to be explored.

In the case of China, the lack of sources makes it difficult even to ask questions let alone find answers. To this nonspecialist one central question might be framed as follows: was the object of the Nanking government at this time the unification, control, and

7. Wilkins, "Role of U.S. Business," pp. 20–31.

strengthening of China as a means to ultimate expulsion of the Japanese, or, reversing priorities, was a war of liberation against the Japanese seen as the means to national unification? It would seem that the former was the case before Sian and the latter thereafter, and yet the design of the new Central Army which Chiang and his German military advisers were creating, with its armor and anti-aircraft guns, suggests that war with Japan was the first order of business. On the other hand it may be more profitable to think in terms of power rather than program and consider whether Chiang's overriding objective was not to build a warfare state ensuring his control, and whether he was not less occupied with the thought of using his army against any particular enemy, thereby risking it, than with simply having such an army. These considerations bear directly on the Far Eastern crisis of 1937, and again suggest the foreign implications of domestic history.

This is one area where experience in American foreign relations can assist the China specialist. The scarcity of Chinese sources for the Kuomintang period makes Western sources all the more important. The archives of the State Department relating to the internal affairs of China have by no means been fully exploited: Americanists tend to cream off material on American policy and ignore the bulk of information on Chinese conditions. The correspondence and reports of Western missionaries, journalists, educators, businessmen, and travelers will continue to provide rich monograph and dissertation material, and now that we are familiar with the tendency of Americans to project their values on Chinese realities, we might filter out the cultural distortion and find more useful what these voyagers were reporting from China. The dispatches of German, Japanese, British, and American military observers should be particularly valuable in describing the militaristic regime in China. Arrangements for use of the military archives of the United States are far from ideal but most records for this period are available and provide systematic coverage of many events and conditions in China. They include, besides military and naval attaché reports, intelligence gathered by marine detachments in north China and destroyer and gunboat captains of the Yangtze and South China Patrols, as well as evaluations by the Asiatic fleet commander and his intelligence officer. The value of these reports lies in their wealth of concrete detail, which is in short supply for the China hands of history.

So far this paper has suggested a research strategy that skirts the traditional, formal aspects of foreign relations to probe the foreign implications of domestic political history. Taking the same round-about route by way of internal history within a much narrower context, we can learn much about international relations by examining governmental institutions involved in external affairs, not primarily in terms of what they did but rather how they did it. What I am suggesting is greater attention to bureaucratic behavior and politics.

American Far Eastern policy, as Dorothy Borg has so convincingly demonstrated, was extraordinarily passive during the early Roosevelt years. Respecting Japan, the administration pursued a course of nonprovocation and yet noncondonement. Precisely why this was so should be explored more fully. Explanations confined to the issues can show little more than the prevalence of negative opinion. But why was activist, innovative opinion so feeble? Why did the nay-sayers usually win out? To say that any system is weighted against change merely begs the question. We need to know in what ways and how much.

The most important element in the State Department was the geographical division. It is high time that this basic operating unit of the department received scholarly attention. Originating before World War I, the Divisions of Far Eastern, Western European (later European), Near Eastern, and Latin American Affairs dominated the policy-making process until the middle of Warld War II. They enjoyed a number of advantages. Large enough to quarter the globe (by 1937), yet small enough to be dominated by an individual, they disposed of the routine business of the department case by case. Cases became precedents and precedents in that most staid of government bureaucracies hardened into policy. In addition they had the advantage of holding the initiative: they had cognizance of all incoming intelligence for their areas, the opportunity of making the first evaluations by memoranda, and responsibility for drafting instructions. They represented the expert knowledge of the department and no secretary of state would lightly consider neglecting or overruling them. Efforts to formulate policy the other way, from the top down, were sporadic. The assignment of assistant secretaries to geographic areas in the late twenties did not survive as a rule and that echelon in the thirties was left with miscellaneous duties that failed to provide continuous, substantive control. Division chiefs such as Wallace Murray, Stanley K. Hornbeck, and Jay Pierrepont Moffat proved indispensable, and with each new administration tightened their hold on policy. They fiercely resisted incursions on their bureaucratic territory and worked out informal pacts that reduced infighting to a minimum. Thus each division in the thirties enjoyed considerable autonomy. To Dean Acheson they seemed like feudal baronies.[8]

The most powerful and self-conscious of these baronies was the Far Eastern Division under the firm direction of Stanley Kuhl Hornbeck.[9] An argumentative, didactic, in many ways difficult personality, Hornbeck was a most tenacious bureaucratic chieftain. He seemed obsessed with the need for consistency and continuity in Far Eastern policy, pounding away with memoranda as if to embed it permanently in national doctrine. He saw himself only carrying forward the work of his mentors Paul Reinsch and E. T. Williams, and they and John Hay only giving concrete expression to fundamental traits in the national character, but he could not have been unaware that a distinctive, traditional Far Eastern policy was his division's best guarantee of autonomy and influence. Thus, while flexible as to implementation and adaptable to prevailing opinion, Hornbeck indefatiguably reminded his superiors of essential principles to be upheld at all cost. Policy was skewed toward China by Hornbeck's predilections and also by the fact that the bulk of the division's routine business related to China and was conducted by China hands. Specialization may have strengthened orthodoxy: Chinese and Japanese language officers in the Foreign Service made heavy career investments in their area and were conceivably the more inclined to defer to divisional doctrine. Later in the decade as Europe gained more and more attention, the division became increasingly isolated and jostled aside in national policy formulation, but in the years under consideration "FE" was seldom crossed.

The preoccupations, presuppositions, and administrative habits of Presidents and secretaries of state in this period generally reinforced divisional autonomy. What little time the White House found for sustained attention to foreign affairs was more often directed toward Latin American and European problems than Far Eastern, except during the Manchurian crisis. A gloomy, harassed Herbert Hoover, his ideas increasingly irrelevant, exercised only a negative, cautionary influence on policy. No more innovative in regard to the Far East was his successor. Recent studies and the publication of Roosevelt's foreign affairs papers for 1933–1937 suggest that he gave little thought to the Far East and was indifferent to diplomacy, at least

8. Dean Acheson, *Present at the Creation: My Years in the State Department* (New York: Norton, 1969), p. 15.

9. For an incisive portrayal of Hornbeck and the State Department bureaucracy in the thirties see James C. Thomson Jr., "The Role of the Department of State," Lake Kawaguchi Conference Papers.

before 1936.[10] He judged that China, in the grip of a prolonged and obscure process of change, had best be left alone. However obstreperous Japan might be, she remained dependent on foreign raw materials, and awareness of America's preponderant industrial capacity and enlarging navy should keep her within bounds.[11] Roosevelt did take a persistent interest in appointments and was responsible for an extensive reshuffling of high officials in 1936–37 but most of the new team he installed in State were veteran diplomats, one old guard replacing another, and the division chiefs remained. All three undersecretaries from 1931 to 1937 had close personal relations with the President, and tensions resulted between the two principal officers of the department that enterprising divisions could make good use of. Henry Stimson was of course a forceful secretary, but he operated with a tight little group of advisers somewhat removed from the permanent hierarchy of the department, while Cordell Hull, a diffident and hypersensitive man, so heavily depended on his "associates," including division chiefs, that he largely became their prisoner.

Now if these observations have any merit, they suggest that in the absence of forceful leadership, of reorganization and rethinking, American Far Eastern policy was left largely in the hands of those whose interests as well as ideas strongly leaned toward a perpetuation of past policy. This is perhaps one reason why, at a time of relative quiescence in the Far East, when Congress set the Philippines on the road to independence, trade with the Far East was at a minimum, and American will to engage actively in world affairs was weakest, a policy aimed at easing tensions and conciliation, on a pattern designed for a smaller cloth of means and interests, did not arise.

Consideration of the autonomy of the Far Eastern Division does not exhaust the possibilities for new insights by way of the study

10. Edgar B. Nixon, ed., *Franklin D. Roosevelt and Foreign Affairs, 1933–1937*, 3 vols. (Cambridge, Mass.: Harvard University Press, 1969). Recent studies of Rooseveltian diplomacy include: Arnold A. Offner, *American Appeasement: United States Foreign Policy and Germany, 1933–1938* (Cambridge, Mass.: Harvard University Press, 1969); Robert A. Divine, *The Illusion of Neutrality* (Chicago: University of Chicago Press, 1962); Brice Harris Jr., *The United States and the Italo-Ethiopian Crisis* (Stanford: Stanford University Press, 1964); Richard P. Traina, *American Diplomacy and the Spanish Civil War* (Bloomington: Indiana University Press, 1968); Beatrice Farnsworth, *William C. Bullitt and the Soviet Union* (Bloomington: Indiana University Press, 1967); Bernard Sternsher, "The Stimson Doctrine: F.D.R. *versus* Moley and Tugwell," *Pacific Historical Review*, 31 (August 1962), 281–289.

11. Gardner, *Economic Aspects of New Deal Diplomacy*, 74–75; Franklin D. Roosevelt, "Shall We Trust Japan?," *Asia*, 23 (July 1923), 475ff.

of organization. To take another example, this period coincided with a serious slump in the fortunes and morale of the Foreign Service on account of the rigid, unimaginative administration of Assistant Secretary Wilbur Carr as well as budget cutting that brought a halt to promotions, reductions in force, cutting of allowances, and even withholding of salaries. The impairment of morale and shortage of staff may have significantly affected the quality and quantity of advice and information received from Far Eastern posts.

The U.S. Navy was scarcely less influential than the State Department in Far Eastern policy, and here too bureaucratic interest played a part. The navy held that the United States had a great stake in the Far East which was threatened by a historically expansionist Japan and that to protect that stake the nation required a fleet capable of moving into the western Pacific to defeat the Japanese navy. This view of the national interest was subtly affected by the navy's conception of its own interest. Thus, while a transoceanic mission required a great navy, from the bureaucratic perspective the reverse was equally true, namely that a great navy required a transoceanic mission. Concern for at least maintaining if not increasing budgetary allocations led the navy to stress the importance of American Far Eastern interests and the threat posed by Japan. Arguing from the conception of a large policy for the Far East, naval leaders persisted in the outdated and unrealistic Orange Plan strategy of a main fleet engagement in the western Pacific, sought to prevent a decision against retention of bases in the Philippines after independence, and insisted on maintenance of the Washington Conference naval ratios for the London Conference of 1935. The navy was by no means encouraging immediate opposition to Japan, but nonetheless it had the effect of making traditional policies somewhat more absolute and dogmatic and of weakening options involving settlement by concession.[12]

Scholars are gaining valuable insights by directing their attention to the roles of subunits of government, as illustrated by the recent Conference on Japanese-American Relations, 1931–1941, held at Lake Kawaguchi, Japan. There Russell Weigley described a very different disposition toward the Far East in the U.S. Army than appeared in the navy.[13] Highly conscious of the vulnerability of the

12. This argument is set forth more fully in my Lake Kawaguchi Conference paper, "The Role of the U.S. Navy."

13. "The Role of the War Department and the Army," Lake Kawaguchi Conference Papers. See also Louis Morton, "Army and Marines on the China Station: A Study in Military and Political Rivalry," *Pacific Historical Review*, 29 (February 1960), 51–73, and "War Plan Orange: Evolution of a Strategy," *World Politics*, II (January 1959), 245–249.

Philippines, the army favored withdrawal from the Far East but was constrained by tradition from meddling in national policy formulation and blocked from a strategic reappraisal by the navy veto power on the Joint Army–Navy Board. The papers of General Douglas MacArthur at Norfolk may reveal contrary opinion in the army, views more closely attuned to the navy's. Of course Mac-Arthur, as Weigley points out, was a maverick, but he was also chief of staff at this time. Further, it might prove interesting to learn about early Army Air Corps conceptions of air power as it related to the American position in the Far East. After all, it was confidence in air power that led the army ultimately to reverse itself and invest heavily in the defense of the Philippines.

Lloyd Gardner dealt with the Commerce and Treasury Departments at the Kawaguchi Conference.[14] Commerce encouraged enlargement of trade with China but was "programmed," as Gardner puts it, to outdated conceptions of international trade and lacked forceful leadership, so it had little influence on policy. Treasury, on the contrary, although having little institutional interest in the Far East, played a significant role because of the aggressive leadership and strong convictions of Secretary Henry Morgenthau. Gardner portrays Morgenthau as another captive of the China market myth, envisaging it as the great prize in a vast struggle among the dollar, yen, and sterling blocs. The Treasury secretary repeatedly clashed with the State Department as he sought ways of assisting China unilaterally even at the cost of provoking Japan. Finally in May 1936 the Morgenthau–Chen scheme for currency stabilization by American purchases of Chinese silver met State's insistence on nonprovocation of Japan as well as Morgenthau's objective of befriending and assisting China.

Examination of the departments involved in external affairs somewhat modifies our picture of American Far Eastern policy in this period. True, the outcome was do-nothing diplomacy. Only the army urged withdrawal and only the Treasury a forward policy. At the same time, in the key State and Navy Departments institutional bias weighed heavily toward maintaining America's role as a Far Eastern power. The formal expression of this concern was repeated invocation of the Open Door and the international treaties relating to the Far East. Thus in a sense this was an activist period. American policy emerged from the tunnel of depression years into the years of international crisis as a reinforced legacy.

Studies of Japanese bureaucracies in this period offer interesting

14. "The Role of the Commerce and Treasury Departments," Lake Kawaguchi Conference Papers.

comparisons with the American experience. In spite of vast differences between the two systems, a not entirely dissimilar process of decision making was at work. In Japan, as we all know, the failure of institutional restraints outside the military services left them wide latitude in the determination of policy. In the United States Roosevelt retained the final say and ensured that departmental activities proceeded within broad guidelines. Nevertheless, he seldom chose to exercise his prerogatives, leaving his subordinates free to deal with most issues and fight out differences among themselves. Thus in both cases we find some degree of devolution of authority and decentralization of decision making, and in both cases a serious problem of reconciling differences and achieving consensus. Occasionally, for example in setting policy for the London Conference, the White House held an American version of the Imperial Conference where all concerned were represented and registered prior agreement. Most often problems in both countries had to be worked out by informal liason between departments or, in the American case, within the unsatisfactory format of the Joint Army–Navy Board.

One can detect factionalism in the American as well as Japanese bureaucracies, but here the similarity is superficial. American examples are the "Gun Club" that allegedly controlled high appointments in the navy, China hands who were veterans of the old Consular Service, and old school diplomats like Joseph C. Grew and Hugh R. Wilson, who had served together in Europe and had a common tendency to depreciate the importance of American Far Eastern interests. But these groupings were not as persistent, closely knit, or influential in policy as the Japanese factions were. In Japan any shared occupational experience, as between classmates, shipmates, or colleagues in a foreign post, could produce permanent ties that emerged as policy alignments. In the American case, personal associations and policy views rarely coincided, and where they did, rarely carried over from one issue to the next. Organizational behavior was fundamentally different in the two countries, the Japanese reflecting a culture that assigned high value to cultivation of personal associations, the American reflecting a pluralistic, fluid society where clubbiness was unproductive and a highly rationalistic system of government.

Some of the most valuable Kawaguchi papers dealt with factionalism in the Japanese government. The work of James B. Crowley and others has already introduced us to the complex perspectives and interests that went into Japanese army expansionism in the early and middle thirties, but we had only a dim notion of the forces at work in the navy and Foreign Ministry.[15] I, at least, was under the impression that liberal and moderate forces retained some foothold in these ministries, undoubtedly less than Ambassador Grew supposed, but still some influence countering expansionism, some significant worldly wisdom and caution.[16] Usui Katsumi and Asada Sadao have shaken that idea. In his excellent paper on the Foreign Ministry, Usui has shown that the moderates, the Europe–America faction, lost their influence during the Manchuria crisis. Control gradually passed to the faction headed by Arita Hachirō, who, with Foreign Minister and Prime Minister Hirota Kōki, though opposing reckless adventures, favored a policy of progressive domination of China and the ultimate exclusion of Western interests. Thus the Amō doctrine was an accurate reflection of mainstream Foreign Ministry thinking.[17] Asada described a similar shift of factions in the navy. The "administrative" faction, centering on the Navy Ministry and carrying on the conservative Katō Tomosaburō tradition in the Japanese navy, gave way to the Katō Kanji "fleet" faction, which pressed for an end to naval limitation and preparation for the southward advance, even at the risk of war with the United States.[18]

In this chapter I have stressed some new areas of research and modes of inquiry partly because they seem particularly relevant for this period and partly because more familiar approaches appear to me fairly well covered for the present or unproductive. To this last category of the unproductive it is tempting to consign the study of public opinion. For the period as a whole, excepting the Manchurian crisis, indications are that the American foreign policy public shrank to minimum size. Domestic crisis dominated the popular consciousness and when the world strayed onto page one it was likely to be the European world. Even the Mukden Incident was outplayed on the front pages of the *New York Times*. The public was of course deeply averse to an active role in world affairs but so, at the time, were both Presidents; public opinion may have been a limiting factor to Stimson but not to Hoover.

Nevertheless, public attitudes cannot be ignored. Definition of the foreign policy public in this period, when it was minimal in size and

15. Crowley, *Japan's Quest for Autonomy;* Fujiwara Akira statement, "Conference on Japanese-American Relations, 1931–1941, Proceedings," Michael K. Blaker and Dale K. Anderson, comps., pp. 38–41.

16. On Grew in these years see my *American Ambassador: Joseph C. Grew and the Development of the United States Diplomatic Tradition* (Boston: Little, Brown, 1966), chaps. 12–15.

17. Usui Katsumi, "The Role of the Foreign Ministry," Lake Kawaguchi Conference Papers.

18. Asada Sadao, "The Role of the Japanese Navy," Lake Kawaguchi Conference Papers.

impact, is indispensable as a base point in describing and explaining the upswing of public involvement in the late thirties. Adopting Ernest R. May's approach to opinion in an earlier decade, we can search out the internationalist elites of this period.[19] Whom did Americans look to nationally and locally for guidance on foreign affairs? What were the world views of these opinion leaders and how were these affected by fascism, militarism, world economic crisis, and tension and change at home?

Researchers must also investigate the role of private groups and organizations. James C. Thomson Jr. has provided a model for this sort of inquiry in his recent study of American missionary and philanthropic endeavors in China during the Kuomintang decade, 1928–1937. His moving account of the efforts of American reformers to provide a gradualist alternative for China's reconstruction, and their ultimate failure, illuminates fundamental problems in the Sino-American relationship.[20] Warren Cohen has shown the value of studying private organizations interested in foreign affairs in his Kawaguchi paper, which describes the leadership and objectives of various peace groups and how they responded to successive Far Eastern crises.[21] About the time of the Sian Incident Americans began taking an interest in China which they saw finally on the road to unification and independence, and we need to know who these new friends of China were. We might begin by collecting lists of people from organization letterheads and then dig away to find out whom and what they represented. For the much smaller public interested in Japan a good starting point would be the membership list of the Japan–America Society, a copy of which has been found in, of all places, the records of the War Department.

Delineation of group attributes and interests must not detract from the force and value of ideas themselves. Ideas are not simply the function of interests. We would do well to heed the warning of Dorothy Borg that historians have tended to neglect the intrinsic importance of internationalist convictions in the interwar period.[22] Many Americans, including Stimson, Hull, and Hornbeck, believed that the world had taken the only possible road toward peace in developing a working international peace structure and were pro-

19. Ernest R. May, *American Imperialism: A Speculative Essay* (New York: Atheneum, 1968).

20. James C. Thomson Jr., *While China Faced West: American Reformers in Nationalist China, 1928–1937* (Cambridge, Mass.: Harvard University Press, 1969).

21. "The Role of Private Groups," Lake Kawaguchi Conference Papers.

22. Lake Kawaguchi Conference "Proceedings," p. 99.

foundly motivated by that faith in extending it or at least in keeping it from being torn down.

In the more traditional vein of diplomatic history, the events of 1936 merit close attention. Surely it was not entirely coincidental that turning points occurred around the world in close succession that year. The problem is to determine where the chain reaction started and the cause-effect order of events. American and captured enemy archives have yielded studies of several segments of the global network and the British archives and publication of French and Italian documents will yield more. Unfortunately few feel equipped to attempt diplomatic history in the grand manner of William L. Langer and little documentation on Chinese and Soviet foreign policy will be available in the foreseeable future. One project that could be attempted right now is a study of American–British Commonwealth relations for the period as they bore on the Far East. Raymond Esthus has explored the slow and painful improvement of relations between the United States and Australia during the decade and Francis Holbrook has touched on the problem of British mid-Pacific islands in his study of American development of trans-Pacific air routes.[23] Naval policy, financial assistance to China, the President's Pacific neutralization proposal of 1936–37, and British inclinations toward rapprochement with Japan all merit special attention. From 1931 to 1937 the Anglo-Saxon powers made repeated advances to each other but somehow never at the right time or the same time. The question is why they failed to form a common front.

Surveying what has been done and thinking about what might be done leaves a distinct impression about the relation of the early and middle thirties to the coming of war in 1941. The stormy years after 1937 give an alluring quality to the earlier years of the decade suggestive of peaceful alternatives. Yet the closer we examine these years the less hopeful they appear. War was never inevitable; it did not come like two trains rocketing toward each other on a single track, as Hornbeck liked to say in retrospect. Choices always existed and decisions were complex. What seems so remarkably absent in the 1931–1937 period was any significant disposition toward peace-

23. Raymond A. Esthus, *From Enmity to Alliance: U.S.-Australian Relations, 1931–1941* (Seattle: University of Washington Press, 1964); Francis X. Holbrook, "United States National Defense and Trans-Pacific Air Routes, 1933–1941" (Ph.D. diss., Fordham University, 1969). See also Gerald Wheeler, "Isolated Japan: Anglo-American Diplomatic Cooperation, 1927–1936," *Pacific Historical Review*, 30 (May 1961), 165–178; Robert A. Hecht, "Great Britain and the Stimson Note of January 7, 1932," ibid., 38 (May 1969), 177–191. A useful study of relations with another Pacific power is Judith R. Papachristou, "American-Soviet Relations and United States Policy in the Pacific, 1933–1941" (Ph.D. diss., University of Colorado, 1968).

ful solutions. Economic crisis and its remedies tended to increase autarky and dissipate remnants of the spirit of cooperation. Institutional biases either reinforced the status quo on the American side or leaned against it on the Japanese side. Leaders and followers, whether by conviction or indifference, were not disposed to reach out for solutions while time remained. The drift lay toward confrontation and contrary currents were weaker than I supposed.

1937–1941

The sequence of events that led to Pearl Harbor and the questions they raised have attracted historians ever since that fateful day. On the American side, few periods have been as closely studied or as fully documented as the years immediately preceding World War II.[1] In part, this interest is the product of the controversy over the wisdom of the policies the United States pursued during these years. Political considerations played a part also in the interpretation of these events. To brand the foreign policy of the Roosevelt administration as short-sighted or to assert that a Democratic president deliberately maneuvered the nation into war was not without benefit to the Republican opposition. Moreover, a general interest in the way wars begin is a subject of considerable concern in a world of nuclear weapons. Finally, events since 1945 in China and Southeast Asia have focused attention on the background of American Far Eastern policy and have increased the importance of a better understanding of the nations in that part of the world.

On the Japanese side, the literature on the events that led to war with the United States is also large. For the Japanese, the war and their subsequent defeat and occupation are the central events in their recent history. It is only natural, therefore, that they should seek to understand them better. Early postwar studies in Japan took their cue largely from American historians, but more recently a group of

1. For background on the period 1937–1941, see George F. Kennan, *American Diplomacy, 1900–1950* (Chicago: Chicago University Press, 1951); William Appleman Williams, *The Tragedy of American Foreign Policy* (Cleveland: World Publishing Co., 1959) and *American-Russian Relations* (New York: Rinehart, 1952); John K. Fairbank, *The United States and China* (Cambridge, Mass.: Harvard University Press, 1971); Edwin O. Reischauer, *The United States and Japan*, 3rd ed. (Cambridge, Mass.: Harvard University Press, 1965); A. Whitney Griswold, *The Far Eastern Policy of the United States* (New York: Harcourt, Brace and Company, 1938); T. A. Bisson, *American Policy in the Far East, 1931–1940* (New York: Institute of Pacific Relations, 1940); William L. Neumann, *America Encounters Japan* (Baltimore: Johns Hopkins Press, 1963); Paul Clyde, *The Far East* (Englewood Cliffs, N.J.: Prentice Hall, 1958); H. S. Quigley, *Far Eastern War, 1937–1941* (Boston: World Peace Foundation, 1942); Selig Adler, *The Isolationist Impulse* (New York: Abelard-Schuman, 1957); Paul Varg, *Missionaries, Chinese and Diplomats* (Princeton: Princeton University Press, 1958); John Toland, *The Rising Sun: The Decline and Fall of the Japanese Empire, 1936–1945* (New York: Random House, 1970).

young Japanese scholars have turned their attention to the prewar years in an attempt to explain why the nation went to war. Their work as well as the documents they have uncovered are, unfortunately, not available in English.

Wars bring few blessings, chief of which for the historian is the flood of primary sources—records of foreign ministries and war offices—released by the victor to prove the justice of his cause and the guilt of the enemy. Statesmen and soldiers hasten into print to record for posterity their version of the great events in which they played, as they see it, a leading role. Thus, even while hostilities were still in progress, documents setting forth the American case began to appear. By the end of the decade, large quantities of official documents from the American archives had been published, as had an equally large collection of Japanese documents produced as evidence in the Tokyo war crime trials. More recently, the American state papers for the period have been opened and additional Japanese documents, produced less with an eye to proving the guilt of Japanese officials than to illuminating the course of Japanese policy, have been published. In addition, private collections of papers and official files have been made available to historians. The result is a vast storehouse of primary sources on American and Japanese policy during the 1930's.

Chronologically, the first collections of documents to appear and the ones on which the earliest accounts of the prewar period were based were the two-volume *Foreign Relations: Japan, 1931–1941* and *Peace and War: United States Foreign Policy, 1931–1941*, published by the State Department in 1943 and presenting the American case. It was six years before the State Department published any more documents on the Far East. The occasion was the Chinese Communist victory in 1949, when it issued the so-called *China White Paper*.[2] Though the "White Paper" dealt primarily with the period after 1941, it covered briefly America's prewar China policy, which it described as consisting of "the twin principles of (1) equality of commercial opportunity, and (2) the maintenance of the territorial and administrative integrity and political independence of China." In view of the continuing debate over the role of China in the events that led to the Pacific War, this statement of official policy, which is

2. U.S. Department of State, *United States Relations with China* (Washington, 1949; reissued by Stanford University Press, 1968), with an intro. by Lyman P. Van Slyke. At the annual meeting of the American Historical Association in Washington, December 1969, an entire session was devoted to the *White Paper*, with papers by John F. Melby, O. Edmund Clubb, and James Peck, and comments by Norman A. Graebner.

reflected in most of the traditional interpretations of the period, is of particular interest.

The State Department's regular volumes in the Foreign Relations series covering the years 1937 to 1941 appeared between 1954 and 1963.[3] While these volumes contained additional documentation to supplement earlier publications, they contained little that was new. More important were the State Department files for the period, most of which are now open to scholars. They constitute an indispensable source for all students of American foreign policy, as do the files of the War and Navy Departments, the Department of Commerce and the Treasury.

The official files hardly exhaust the archival material. Almost as important for a study of the period are the papers of President Roosevelt and of his principal civilian and military advisers. These are to be found at various locations, placing on the scholar the burden and expense of considerable travel. In addition to Hyde Park, the scholar must visit the Houghton Library at Harvard to see the Grew and Moffat diaries; the Sterling Library at Yale for Stimson's diary; the Library of Congress for the papers of Nelson T. Johnson, and Admirals Leahy and Yarnell; the Hoover Institution for Stanley Hornbeck's paper; and Lexington, Virginia, to consult General Marshall's papers.[4]

Comparable to this latter category of material is the memoir literature, including biographies. They vary widely in quality and importance, but remain a prime source. On the American side, virtually every member of Roosevelt's official family and some of the leading congressional figures have told their side of the story, or have had it told for them.[5] Lesser officials who played an impor-

---

3. U.S. Department of State, *Foreign Relations of the United States: Diplomatic Papers, 1937–1941* (Washington, 1954–1963). The British and German Foreign Office records have also been published: *Documents on German Foreign Policy, 1918–1945*, Series D, 13 vols. (Washington, 1949–1964); Great Britain, *Documents on British Foreign Policy, 1919–1939* 3rd series, E. L. Woodward and Rohan Butler, eds., 9 vols. (London, 1949–1955). Useful also are the unofficial *Documents on International Affairs* published by the Royal Institute of International Affairs and the Council on Foreign Relations' annual survey *The United States in World Affairs*. See also Richard W. Leopold, "The Foreign Relations Series: A Centennial Estimate," *Mississippi Valley Historical Review*, 49 (March 1963), 595–612.

4. Selections from some of these have been published. The specific titles of the published selections from Stimson, Hull, Grew, and others are noted below. The papers of Jay Pierrepont Moffat have been edited by Nancy H. Hooker (Cambridge, Mass.: Harvard University Press, 1956).

5. Although Roosevelt himself did not write any memoirs, his correspondence and public papers have been published and there are a number of excellent studies and biographies, notably those by Arthur Schlesinger, Jr., Frank Fridel, James McG. Burns, William Leuchtenberg, Basil Rauch, and others. Most

tant role in the shaping of policy, like Stanley Hornbeck and Joseph Ballantine, also contributed their version of events.[6]

The Japanese have been almost as prolific as the Americans in their output of memoirs, and there are biographies in English of many of the key officials of the period.[7] Probably the best of these is Robert J. C. Butow's study of General Tojo, a work of real scholarship based on an intimate knowledge of Japanese as well as American materials.[8]

Particularly important for the study of American–East Asian relations, are the memoirs of Hull, Stimson, Morgenthau and Grew. As secretary of state, Cordell Hull, in his memoirs, stated the administration case for its Far Eastern policy and provided a detailed account of his discussions with Nomura from April to December 1941. Julius W. Pratt's biography of Hull is somewhat more critical of American policy and, though generally sympathetic to Hull, criticizes him for his moralism and inflexibility in dealing with Japan.[9]

Stimson's task as secretary of war was to prepare the country for war, but he was also an active participant in the formulation of

---

recently, Edgar B. Nixon has edited Roosevelt correspondence on foreign affairs to 1938 in *Franklin D. Roosevelt and Foreign Affairs*, 3 vols. (Cambridge, Mass.: Harvard University Press, 1969). Schlesinger's review in *The New York Times*, Sunday Book Review, July 6, 1969, is helpful also. Hopkins, Hull, Stimson, Morgenthau, Ickes, Grew, and others as noted below, have written their memoirs and, in addition, are the subject of biographies.

6. Those memoirs not described elsewhere in this paper are: Wayne S. Cole, *Senator Gerald P. Nye and American Foreign Relations* (Minneapolis: University of Minnesota Press, 1962); Fred L. Israel, *Nevada's Key Pittman* (Lincoln, Nebraska: University of Nebraska Press, 1963); M. C. McKenna, *Borah* (Ann Arbor, Michigan: University of Michigan Press, 1961); Sumner Welles, *The Time for Decision* (New York: Harper and Brothers, 1944); Stanley K. Hornbeck, *The U.S. and the Far East: Certain Fundamentals of Policy* (Boston: World Peace Foundation, 1942); Joseph W. Ballantine, "The Foreign Policies of Japan," *Foreign Affairs*, 27 (July 1949), 651–664; Sir Robert L. Craigie, *Behind the Japanese Mask* (London: Hutchinson and Company, 1945). Craigie was British ambassador to Japan. There are several relevant essays in Gordon A. Craig and Felix Gilbert, eds., *The Diplomats, 1919–1939*, 2 vols. (Princeton: Princeton University Press, 1953).

7. Shigenori Togo, *The Cause of Japan* (New York: Simon and Schuster, 1956); Shigeru Yoshida, *The Yoshida Memoirs: The Story of Japan in Crisis* (Boston: Houghton Mifflin, 1962); Leonard Mosley, *Hirohito, Emperor of Japan* (Englewood Cliffs, N.J.: Prentice Hall, 1966); Frederick Moore, *With Japan's Leaders* (New York: C. Scribner's Sons, 1942); Mamoru Shigemitsu, *Japan and Her Destiny* (New York: Dutton, 1958); Toshikasu Kaze, *Journey to the Missouri* (New Haven: Yale University Press, 1950).

8. *Tojo and the Coming of the War* (Princeton: Princeton University Press, 1961)

9. Cordell Hull, *The Memoirs of Cordell Hull*, 2 vols. (New York: Macmillan, 1948); Julius W. Pratt, *Cordell Hull*, 2 vols. (New York: Cooper Square, 1964).

American policy. His views had been shaped during the Manchurian crisis when he had been secretary of state, and he, with Morgenthau and Ickes, formed a militant group in the cabinet that advocated a firm policy toward Japan. There are also several important biographies of Stimson: one by Richard N. Current, which places a large share of responsibility for the war on Stimson's insistence on strong economic sanctions; the other by Elting Morison, which is more sympathetic to Stimson.[10]

Secretary Morgenthau's role comes through clearly in the second volume of John M. Blum's *From the Morgenthau Diaries*, covering the years 1938 to 1941 which shows Morgenthau exerting a strong influence over foreign policy in favor of economic sanctions against Japan.[11] *The Secret Diary of Harold L. Ickes* reveals a man who sought with only slight success to play an important role in policy making on the eve of the war. But Ickes has much to say about members of the administration and offers a refreshing glimpse of Roosevelt's close advisers.[12]

Distant from the Washington scene but playing a vital role in the unfolding drama of Japanese-American relations was the American ambassador in Tokyo, Joseph C. Grew. In his memoirs, as well as in his two wartime volumes, Grew generally supported Roosevelt's Far East policy and argued that the war had come because the Japanese extremists in control had been bent on conquest.[13] More recently, Waldo Heinrichs has published a full-length biography of Grew which skillfully combines an account of the prewar years with the role played by the ambassador in representing his nation to the Japanese while assessing for his superiors in Washington the situation in Japan. Except for a brief biography, we have nothing comparable for the American ambassador to China, Nelson T. Johnson.[14]

10. Henry L. Stimson and McGeorge Bundy, *On Active Service in Peace and War* (New York: Harper and Brothers, 1948). Stimson kept a detailed diary, portions of which are published in *Hearings on the Pearl Harbor Attack*, pp. 5416–5441. See also Armin Rappaport, *Henry L. Stimson and Japan* (Chicago: University of Chicago Press, 1963); Richard N. Current, *Secretary Stimson: A Study in Statecraft* (New Brunswick, N.J.: Rutgers University Press, 1954); Elting Morison, *Turmoil and Tradition: A Study of the Life and Time of Henry L. Stimson*, 2 vols. (Boston: Houghton Mifflin, 1960). See also Stimson's *The Far Eastern Crisis* (New York: Harper and Brothers, 1936).

11. John M. Blum, *From the Diaries of Henry Morgenthau, Jr., II, Years of Urgency, 1938–1941*, 2 vols. (Boston: Houghton Mifflin, 1965).

12. Vol. III, *The Lowering Clouds* (New York: Simon and Schuster, 1954).

13. Joseph C. Grew, *The Turbulent Era*, ed. Walter Johnson, 2 vols. (Boston: Houghton Mifflin, 1952); Joseph C. Grew, *Report from Tokyo* (New York: Simon and Schuster, 1942) and *Ten Years in Japan* (New York: Simon and Schuster, 1944).

14. Waldo H. Heinrichs, *American Ambassador: Joseph C. Grew and the Development of the United States Diplomatic Tradition* (Boston: Little, Brown

The most extensive and important collections of primary source materials published in the immediate postwar period were the results of two separate investigations, one of the Pearl Harbor attack and the other of 25 high-ranking Japanese military and civilian figures as war criminals. The first was conducted by a joint committee of the Congress in 1945 and 1946 and recorded in 39 volumes, nineteen of which consisted of exhibits (including Japanese documents), eleven of testimony and nine more of the proceedings of earlier wartime investigations. The report of the committee was published separately.[15]

Even more voluminous and valuable were the products of the International Military Tribunal for the Far East, which met in Tokyo from 1946 to 1948. The great mass of material assembled for the trial covers all aspects of Japanese foreign and domestic affairs over a twenty-year period and virtually defies easy description. Fortunately the work of the scholar has been facilitated by checklists and indices prepared by both the prosecution and the defense and published descriptions of the material.[16]

The documents assembled for the Tokyo trials were only part of the fruits of victory. American authorities also hauled off large bodies of Japanese Army and Navy files, altogether some 30,000 volumes of official records.[17] The Japanese Foreign Office records seized by the occupation authorities were not brought to the United States but were microfilmed by the State Department in cooperation

---

and Company 1966). The biography of the ambassador to China appeared at the time this paper was written, Russel D. Buhite, *Nelson T. Johnson and American Policy toward China, 1925–1941* (East Lansing: Michigan State University Press, 1969).

15. U.S. Congress, Joint Committee on the Investigation of the Pearl Harbor Attack, Hearings before the Joint Committee, 79th Cong., 1st sess., 39 parts in 15 vols.; *Report of the Joint Committee,* 79th Cong., 2nd sess., (Washington, 1945–1946). The minority report is separately published as Senate Executive Document 244 (Washington, 1946).

16. International Military Tribunal for the Far East, *Record of the Proceedings, Documents, Exhibits, Judgements, Dissenting Judgements, Interrogations, etc.* (Mimeographed, Tokyo, 1946–1949.) Copies or microfilm are available in Library of Congress and various other libraries. For a description of this material, see Delmer M. Brown, "Recent Japanese Political and Historical Materials," *American Political Science Review,* 43 (October 1949), 1010–1017; Dull and Umemura, *The Tokyo Trials: A Functional Index to the Proceedings of the International Military Tribune for the Far East* (Ann Arbor: University of Michigan Press, 1957); James T. C. Liu, "The Tokyo Trial: Source Materials," *Far Eastern Survey,* 17 (July 28, 1948), 168–170.

17. These records were turned over to the National Archives. See James W. Morley, "Checklist of Seized Japanese Records in the National Archives," *Far Eastern Quarterly,* 9 (May 1950), 306–333; John Young, comp., *Checklist of Microfilm Reproductions of Selected Archives of the Japanese Army, Navy . . . 1868–1945* (Washington: Georgetown University Press, 1959).

with the Library of Congress.[18] Other Japanese records were collected by the Strategic Bombing Survey, which published two volumes of *Interrogations* as well as a series of documents relating to the military aspects of the Pacific War.[19] Finally, former high-ranking Japanese Army and Navy officers, working under the supervision of General MacArthur's headquarters, prepared a large number of monographs on all aspects of the war, including operations in Manchuria from 1931, in China from 1937, prewar planning and political strategy.[20] Out of this effort came the four-volume Japanese history of the war by Tatsuhiro Hattori, a former chief of the powerful operations section of the General Staff and one of the officers who worked on the project.[21]

This brief description hardly does justice to the richness of the Japanese material available to the scholar. Included among the exhibits of the Tokyo trials are the diaries of Marquis Kido, Lord Privy Seal, and Prince Konoye who was thrice premier of Japan during the prewar years. Of particular value are the memoirs of Prince Saionji, last of the Japanese genro, prepared by his private secretary, Baron Harada.[22] The exhibits of the trials included affidavits, interrogrations, testimony of the witnesses, and documents of all types running to more than 50,000 pages, and these constitute only a small part of the documentation assembled.

The Japanese records collected by the occupying authorities by no means exhausted the material available in Japan. There were still memories to be tapped, private papers that had eluded the authorities, and, after the peace, archives assembled by the Japanese themselves. Starting in the mid-1950's the Japanese began pub-

18. Cecil H. Uyehara, comp., *Checklist of Archives in the Japanese Ministry of Foreign Affairs, Tokyo, Japan, 1868–1945.* Microfilmed for the Library of Congress (Washington: Library of Congress, 1954).

19. U.S. Strategic Bombing Survey, *Interrogation of Japanese Officials,* 2 vols. (Washington, 1946); *The Campaigns of the Pacific War* (Washington, 1946). The full file of documents and interrogations collected by U.S.S.B.S. is in the National Archives, Washington, D.C.

20. These monographs, together with personal history statements and a narrative history, were translated and deposited in the Office of the Chief of Military History, U.S. Department of the Army, Washington, D.C.

21. *Dai-Toa Senso Zenshi* (History of the Greater East Asia War; 4 vols.; Tokyo: Masu Shobo, 1953).

22. The memoirs are available in microfilm at the Library of Congress. They have recently been published in Japanese, *Saionji Ko to seikyoku,* (Saionji Ko and the Political Situation), 8 vols. (Tokyo, 1951–1952). The Kido diary has not been published, but microfilm copies are available at various libraries. Konoye's diary is available in English in *Pearl Harbor Attack: Hearings . . . ,* exhibit 173, part 20, pp. 3985–4029. A Japanese version was published in Japan and later translated and published in the United States, but it is reputed to be less accurate than the version in the *Pearl Harbor Attack.*

lishing their own records. In 1954 the Japanese Ministry of Foreign Affairs issued two volumes of chronology and key documents covering the period 1840–1945.[23] In 1963 the Japanese Association of International Relations published a volume of documents which included the records of the Liaison and Imperial Conferences of 1940–41.[24] The same group, about four years later, published a seven-volume collection, *Documents on Contemporary History*, for the period 1931–1941.[25] Comprising some 50,000 pages, most of them related to Sino-Japanese relations, this multi-volume work has been described as "probably the most formidable collection of Japanese source materials to date," and "a treasure of genuine value" for the student of prewar Japanese history.[26]

The existence of this body of material in Japanese raises the problem of language competence for the student of foreign policy and international relations. There is little need to argue the case here. Professor Fairbank stated it persuasively and eloquently in his presidential address at the annual meeting of the American Historical Association, and those who must take their Japanese (or Chinese) in translation can only look with envy on those who can use these records in the original.

During the war and for the first decade after its close, most of the accounts of the prewar period fell into two general groups, categorized by Wayne S. Cole, largely with reference to Europe, as "internationalist" and "isolationist," terms that link the postwar interpretations to the prewar debate over foreign policy.[27] The internationalist or traditionalist position may be summarized as follows: President Roosevelt and many of his principal advisers recognized the threat presented by Japanese aggression to world order, to the territorial integrity of China, and to American interests in the Far

23. Gaimushō (Ministry of Foreign Affairs), *Nihon gaikō nenpyo narabi ni shuyo bunsho* (Chronological tables of Japanese diplomacy together with important documents), 2 vols. (Tokyo, 1955).

24. Nihon Kokusai Seiji Gakkai, *Taiheiyō sensō e no michi* (The Road to the Pacific War), 8 vols., VIII, *Betsukan shiryohen* (Documents) (Tokyo: Asahi 1963). It was from this work that Nobutaka Ike largely drew for his documentary collection, *Japan's Decision for War: Records of the 1941 Policy Conferences* (Stanford: Stanford University Press, 1966).

25. *Gendaishi shiryō*, VIII–XIII (Tokyo, 1964–1966).

26. Akira Iriye, "Japanese Foreign Policies Between World Wars: Sources and Interpretations," *Journal of Asian Studies*, 26 (August 1967), 677–682.

27. Wayne S. Cole, "American Entry into World War II: A Historiographical Appraisal," *The Mississippi Valley Historical Review*, 48 (March 1957), 596–617. See also Louis Morton, "Pearl Harbor in Perspective: A Bibliographical Survey," U.S. Naval Institute, *Proceedings*, 81 (April 1955), 461–468; Robert Ferrell, "Pearl Harbor and the Revisionists," *Historian* (1955), 215–233.

East but they were forced to proceed cautiously because of strong isolationist sentiment, America's military unpreparedness, and the growing crisis in Europe. As the situation in Europe worsened, resulting finally in war, the scale of Japanese aggression mounted. Moderation failing, the United States adopted a stronger policy, moving from diplomatic protest to open aid to China and finally to economic sanctions against Japan in the hope that firmness might prevail where persuasion had not. At the same time, the administration undertook to educate the American people to the dangers of noninvolvement. In its negotiations with Tokyo and conversations with the Japanese emmissaries in 1941, the State Department and the President acted in good faith, making every effort to preserve the peace. These efforts failed because of Japanese obduracy and insistence on continuing the war in China and expanding into Southeast Asia. The sudden and unexpected attack on Pearl Harbor which brought negotiations to a close was therefore, in the traditional view, an unprovoked act of treachery by Japan. Reduced to its essentials, the internationalist position is that war came because of Japanese aggression in China. It was China that constituted the most significant obstacle to peace. For nearly half a century, wrote Joseph Ballantine in 1952, the Japanese military leaders remained committed to a single objective, domination of China. The United States, on its part, was as firmly committed to equal opportunity for all and the territorial integrity of China.[28]

The isolationist historians, who may loosely be termed revisionists, found much to criticize in the policies of the Roosevelt administration.[29] In general, they argued that American participation in the war had been avoidable and had been brought about either through blundering or sinister intention by a policy that deceived the American public and provoked Japan. Roosevelt had erred in his

28. Ballantine, "American Policy in Eastern Asia," pp. 195–203. See also his "Mukden to Pearl Harbor: The Foreign Policies of Japan," *Foreign Affairs*, 27 (July 1949), 651–664.

29. The major revisionist works of this period are: Charles A. Beard, *American Foreign Policy in the Making, 1932–1940* (New Haven: Yale University Press, 1946) and *President Roosevelt and the Coming of War, 1941* (New Haven: Yale University Press, 1948); George Morgenstern, *Pearl Harbor: The Story of the Secret War* (New York: Devin-Adair Company, 1947); Charles Tansill, *Back Door to War: The Roosevelt Foreign Policies, 1937–1941* (Chicago: H. Regnery Company, 1952); William Henry Chamberlin, *America's Second Crusade* (Chicago: H. Regnery Company, 1950); Frederick R. Sanborn, *Design for War: A Study of Secret Power Politics, 1937–1941* (New York: Devin-Adair Company, 1951); Harry Elmer Barnes, *Perpetual War for Perpetual Peace* (Caldwall, Idaho: Caxton Printers, 1953); Current, *Secretary Stimson,* and most recently T. R. Fehrenbach, *F.D.R's Undeclared War* (New York: McKay Company, 1967).

support of Nationalist China and by imposing on Japan intolerable economic pressure. During the negotiations with Japan, the revisionists argued, Roosevelt and the State Department had made unreasonable demands and had rejected reasonable proposals for a settlement. Hull's reply in November 1941 to the last Japanese proposal, they termed an ultimatum. Deliberately or unintentionally, Roosevelt had invited the attack at Pearl Harbor by a series of moves that left Japan little choice but war. America's prewar policies, according to some revisionists, were short-sighted at best and disastrous at worst. They had unnecessarily involved the United States in a long and costly war on two fronts, cut off a lucrative trade with Japan, committed the United States to a decadent and corrupt regime in China and the defense of colonial interests in Southeast Asia, and finally had permitted the Soviet Union to gain a stronger foothold in the Far East.

The internationalist interpretation of American policy, derived in large part from Western sources and reflecting the judgment of the International Military Tribunal of the Far East, virtually dominated historical writing about the prewar period in the decade after the war. It found powerful expression in the two volumes of Langer and Gleason, still perhaps the most complete work on the diplomacy of the period, in S. E. Morison's *Rising Sun in the Pacific*, in Walter Millis', *This Is Pearl*, in the memoirs of the leading figures in the Roosevelt administration and in numerous other works.[30] An integral part of this interpretation was the restriction imposed on the policy makers by the isolationists, a subject covered most recently by Manfred Jonas in his study of the isolationist movement from 1939 to 1941. Relevant to this question is Dorothy Borg's analysis of the origins and reactions to Roosevelt's "quarantine" speech.[31]

30. William L. Langer and S. Everett Gleason, *The Challenge to Isolation, 1937–1940* (New York: Harper, 1952); *The Undeclared War, 1940–1941* (New York: Harper, 1953); Basil Rauch, *Roosevelt: From Munich to Pearl Harbor* (New York: Creative Age Press, 1950); Ernest K. Lindley, *How War Came* (New York: Simon and Schuster, 1942); S. F. Bemis, "First Gun of a Revisionist: Historiography for the Second World War," *Journal of Modern History,* 19 (March 1947), 55–59; S. E. Morison, "Did Roosevelt Start the War? History Through a Beard," *Atlantic Monthly,* 182 (August 1948), 91–97; Herbert Feis, "War Came at Pearl Harbor: Suspicions Considered," *Yale Review,* 45 (March 1956), 378–390; Dexter Perkins, "Was Roosevelt Wrong?" *Virginia Quarterly Review,* 30 (Summer 1954), 355–372.

31. Manfred Jonas, *Isolationism in America, 1935–1941* (Ithaca, N.Y.: Cornell University Press, 1966); Dorothy Borg, "Notes on Roosevelt's Quarantine Speech," *Political Science Quarterly,* 72 (May 1965) 141–161. See also Wayne S. Cole, "The Role of the U.S. Congress and Political Parties," a paper prepared for the conference on Japanese-American Relations, 1931–1941, Hakone, Japan, July 14–18, 1969.

Other aspects of New Deal diplomacy supporting the traditional view have been dealt with by Robert Divine in his study of American neutrality and by Lloyd Gardner, A. S. Everest, and Arthur N. Young on the economic side.[32] The role of organized pressure groups, an area that deserves further study, has been dealt with by Walter Johnson, Wayne S. Cole, and Donald J. Friedman.[33]

The major reassessment of American Far East policy and the best single work for the period covered is Dorothy Borg's study of the years 1933 to 1938.[34] Miss Borg views the Marco Polo Bridge Incident in July 1937 as a turning point, not so much because U.S. policy altered sharply at that time but because Japan by this move created a new situation that challenged world peace. She rejects the idea that President Roosevelt wanted to take strong action but was prevented from doing so by isolationist sentiment. Although the United States failed to take a firm stand against Japanese aggression in 1937, Secretary Hull condemned the move in strong moral terms, stressing the sanctity of treaties and the necessity of abstaining from force. Linking the Japanese move to world peace he invited other nations to take a similar position but avoided collective action. The Panay Incident, says Borg, did not materially alter America's cautious attitude in the Far East, but by the end of the year 1938 the aims of policy had changed significantly. In the American view, Borg asserts, the Japanese attack on China was regarded as involving larger issues than the dispute between China and Japan, issues, she writes, "which were intimately connected with the welfare of

32. Robert A. Divine, *The Illusion of Neutrality* (Chicago: University of Chicago Press, 1962); Lloyd Gardner, *Economic Aspects of New Deal Diplomacy* (Madison, Wisconsin: University of Wisconsin Press, 1964); A. S. Everest, *Morgenthau, the New Deal and Silver: A Study of Pressure Politics* (New York: King's Crown Press, 1950); Arthur N. Young, *China and the Helping Hand, 1937–1945* (Cambridge, Mass.: Harvard University Press, 1963); Wayne S. Cole, "Senator Key Pittman and American Neutrality Policies, 1933–1940," *The Mississippi Valley Historical Review*, 46 (March 1960), 644–662. R. N. Stromberg, "American Business and Approach to War," *Journal of Economic History*, 13 (New York University Press, 1953), 58; J. C. Donovan, "Congressional Isolationists and the Roosevelt Foreign Policy," *World Politics*, 3 (April 1951), 299.

33. Walter Johnson, *The Battle Against Isolation* (Chicago: University of Chicago Press, 1944); Wayne S. Cole, *America First: The Battle Against Intervention, 1940–1941* (Madison: University of Wisconsin Press, 1953); Robert A. Divine, *The Reluctant Belligerent: American Entry into World War II* (New York: Wiley and Sons, 1965). Donald Friedman, *The Road from Isolation: The Campaign of the American Committee for Non-Participation in Japanese Aggression, 1938–1941* (Cambridge, Mass.: Harvard University Press, 1968).

34. *The United States and the Far Eastern Crisis of 1933–1938* (Cambridge, Mass.: Harvard University Press, 1964).

all nations, and might precipitate a concerted effort on the part of the Axis powers to overwhelm the European democracies."[35]

The revisionist interpretation encompasses a wide variety of views of the prewar period, ranging from scholarly criticism of America's Far East policy to charges of a conspiracy by high officials to bring the United States into the war. Among the former is Paul W. Schroeder's study of the Axis alliance and its effect on Japanese-American relations.[36] Schroeder is extremely critical of Hull's legalistic and moralistic approach to Japan and argues that a more conciliatory attitude with respect to China could have produced a settlement and avoided war. Nicholas R. Clifford takes a different tack in his study of British policy during these years.[37] He criticizes the British for appeasement of Japan, but also the Americans for their unwillingness to join with Britain to oppose Japanese aggression. After 1938, Clifford asserts, economic measures and a show of force were inadequate to deter the Japanese and should have been abandoned.

William L. Neumann presents a survey of American policy toward Japan that is broader than that of the conventional revisionists, although he accepts many of the basic criticisms of Roosevelt's Far East Policy.[38] He explains America's China policy in terms of public attitudes, asserting that the American people had traditionally looked upon China as a fertile area for Christian missionary work and as a potentially profitable market. Roosevelt and his advisers, says Neumann, were motivated by the militant idealism of the Wilson era and the conviction that the United States had a moral obligation to play a major role in the maintenance of world peace.

Criticism of America's prewar China policy is fairly common in revisionist writing. Frederick R. Sanborn termed it hypocritical and Charles Tansill asserted that it could be traced to the fact that Roosevelt's Delano inheritance had come from smuggling in China.[39] He also suggested that Russian intrigue might have had an effect

35. Borg, *The United States and the Far Eastern Crisis*, p. 543; for the Panay Incident, see the recent study of Manny T. Koginos, *The Panay Incident, Prelude to War* (Lafayette, Ind.: Purdue University Studies, 1967). See also Frederick C. Adams, "The Road to Pearl Harbor: A Reexamination of American Far Eastern Policy, July 1937–December 1938," *Journal of American History*, 58, No. 1 (Spring 1970), 61–72.

36. *The Axis Alliance and Japanese-American Relaions, 1941* (Ithaca, N. Y.: Cornell University Press, 1958).

37. *Retreat from China: British Policy in the Far East, 1940–1941* (Seattle: University of Washington Press, 1967).

38. *America Encounters Japan.*

39. Sanborn, *Design for War;* Tansill, *Back Door to War.*

on American policy. Even the internationalists were critical, and Whitney Griswold, in a prewar article in *Harper's* argued that the American commitment to the Open Door and the territorial integrity of China could not be justified if it jeopardized more vital American interests, such as the support of Britain.[40] He wanted to limit American liabilities in the Far East and seek a reapprochement with Japan. In the words of one historian, the United States had "pursued its will-o-the-wisp China policy to the tragic end."[41]

Criticism from another point of view is advanced by Anthony Kubek,[42] who argues in cold war terms that American prewar policy was responsible for the victory of the Chinese Communists in 1949. In his view Japanese expansion was a response to the threat of Russian communism. The economic sanctions imposed by the United States forced Japan to move southward and finally to go to war, leaving the Communists a free hand in China. American policy during and after the war, concluded Kubek, only aided the final Communist takeover. Tang Tsou, on the other hand, contends that the Communist victory was the result not so much of diplomatic blunders as of certain basic unrealistic American attitudes toward the East Asian countries, an observation that is emphasized in a more contemporary setting by a number of Far Eastern scholars.[43]

In the summer of 1938, the United States instituted a "moral embargo" on aircraft parts. This was the first tentative step in a program designed to restrain Japanese aggression through economic pressure. In July 1939 Hull gave Japan the requisite six months' notice that the 1911 American-Japanese commercial treaty was to be abrogated, and in January 1940 the treaty was permitted to lapse. Successively, aviation fuel, scrap iron, and other items were placed on the embargo list. The final step in this deliberately escalated economic pressure was taken in the summer of 1941. On July 25 Roosevelt issued an executive order freezing Chinese and Japanese assets in the United States and on August 1 placed a complete embargo on the export of petroleum to Japan.

40. "Our Policy in the Far East," *Harper's*, 181 (August 1940), 259–267.

41. Waldo H. Heinrichs, "The Griswold Theory of Our Far Eastern Policy: A Commentary," in Dorothy Borg, comp., *Historians and American Far Eastern Policy* (New York: Columbian University, Occasional Papers of the East Asian Institute, 1960), p. 39.

42. *How the Far East Was Lost: American Policy and the Creation of Communist China, 1941–1949* (Chicago: H. Regnery Company, 1963). See Richard Leopold's excellent review of this and other volumes dealing with this question in "American Policy in China, 1937–1950: A Review," *The Journal of Conflict Resolution*, 8 (December 1964), 505–510.

43. Tang Tsou, *America's Failure in China, 1941–1950* (Chicago: University of Chicago Press, 1963).

These moves constitute one of the most controversial issues in America's prewar policy and at the time were hotly debated within the inner councils of the government. Herbert Feis states that Hull, backed by Sumner Welles and Far Eastern expert Maxwell Hamilton, urged caution in the application of economic pressure, while a faction led by Treasury Secretary Morgenthau (and after 1940 Secretary Stimson), supported by Stanley Hornbeck and Norman Davis, called for more drastic measures.[44] Hull and Welles have explained their reluctance to apply economic pressure before 1941 on the ground that the risk of war was too high. Welles particularly noted his successful battle against the proposal of the War, Navy, and Treasury Departments in July 1940 for a complete trade embargo.[45] Ambassador Grew also urged caution until the signing of the Tripartite Pact, when he sent his "green light" message recommending a greater show of strength.[46]

The role of the U.S. Navy in the imposition of the oil embargo in 1941 has been explored by James H. Herzog.[47] The Navy Department, Herzog asserts, was split on the issue. Admiral Stark joined Hull and Welles in opposing the embargo because of America's increasing involvement in Europe, the Navy's unpreparedness, and the possibility that Japan might react by moving into the Netherland Indies. On the other hand, Secretary of the Navy Frank Knox and several high ranking officers, says Herzog, supported the position taken by Morgenthau, Stimson, and Ickes.

Critics of the Roosevelt administration emphasize these economic measures as a prime cause and even a justification for the Japanese attack. William Neumann characterized them as a "war of economic attrition" designed to bring Japan to its knees. Charles Tansill went a step further. He interpreted these measures as a deliberate attempt to force Japan to attack the United States, and Harry Elmer Barnes viewed them as an indefensible provocation on the part of President Roosevelt.[48]

Revisionist writers have made much of the failure of the Hull–

44. Feis, *Road to Pearl Harbor* (Princeton: Princeton University Press, 1950), pp. 4–12, 40–54.

45. Welles, "Roosevelt and the Far East," *Harper Magazine*, 202 (February 1951), 32–33; Hull, *Memoirs*, I, 570–571.

46. Grew, *Turbulent Era*, II, 1229–1231.

47. "Influence of the United States navy in the Embargo of Oil to Japan," *Pacific Historical Review*, 35 (August 1966), 317–328. See also John McVickar Haight, Jr., "Franklin Delano Roosevelt and a Naval Quarantine of Japan," *Pacific Historical Review*, 40, No. 2 (May 1971), 203–226.

48. William L. Neumann, *The Genesis of Pearl Harbor* (Philadelphia: Pacifist Research Bureau, 1945); Tansill, *Back Door to War*; Harry Barnes, ed., *Perpetual War for Perpetual Peace*.

Nomura conversations in 1941, charging Hull with rigidity and a lack of realism in dealing with the Japanese emissaries, and Roosevelt with a lack of sincerity. Robert Butow traces the conversations in detail and argues that there was from the beginning a fundamental misconception between the two parties.[49] In this connection, Kurusu's role in the conversation, characterized by Sumner Welles as that of a "goat tethered as bait for the tiger," is covered fully and in sympathetic fashion by Immanuel C. K. Hsu.[50]

Hull's response to the final Japanese proposal of November 20, 1941, the so-called modus vivendi, has been described by revisionists as an ultimatum to Japan. Charles Beard charged that it left Japan with only two possible courses: abject surrender or war, and even Hull's usually sympathetic biographer called it a "petulant response by a tired and angry man."[51]

The rejection of the Japanese proposal for a meeting between Roosevelt and Konoye has also been criticized by many as a lost opportunity that might have averted the disaster. Roosevelt seems to have been favorable to the suggestion initially and Grew urged it strongly. Herbert Feis and David Lu argue that the meeting should have been held, but neither charges Hull or Roosevelt, as Beard does, with a secret desire to avoid any action that might result in a settlement.[52]

Another revisionist charge is that Roosevelt had entered into a secret agreement with Great Britain to come to her aid in the event of a Japanese attack on British possessions in Southeast Asia. Langer, Gleason, Bemis, Dexter Perkins, Feis, and others have asserted the evidence was insufficient to support the charge, or dismissed the charge as groundless. Sir Llewellyn Woodward gave further substance to the charge in 1962 in his study of British policy in World War II, and the following year, in a probing analysis of the question, Raymond Esthus concluded that Roosevelt had indeed committed the United States to come to Britain's aid but tempered

49. Hull, *Memoirs*, II, 998–1037; Butow, "The Hull-Nomura Conversations: A Fundamental Misconception," *American Historical Review*, 65 (July 1960), 822–836. See also Feis, *Road to Pearl Harbor*, 171–179, 199–212. For earlier informal conversations, see John H. Boyle, "The Drought-Walsh Mission," *Pacific Hisorical Review*, 36 (May 1965), 141–161.

50. Welles, *Time for Decision*, p. 295; Immanuel C. K. Hsu, "Kurusu's Mission to the United States and the Abortive *Modus Vivendi*," *Journal of Modern History*, 24 (September 1952), 301–307.

51. Beard, *President Roosevelt and the Coming of War, 1941*, pp. 238–239, 556–559; Pratt, *Cordell Hull*, II, 515.

52. Feis, "War Came at Pearl Harbor," pp. 385–386; Beard, *Roosevelt and the Coming of War*, pp. 483–516; Tansill, *Back Door to War*.

this judgment with the qualification that Roosevelt did so in the belief that Congress would quickly declare war in the event Japan attacked.[53]

No other issue has been as emotionally debated as the question of responsibility for the Pearl Harbor attack, involving on one level the entire foreign policy of the Roosevelt administration and on another personal culpability for the heaviest naval loss in American history. The conclusion of the majority of the Joint Congressional Committee that investigated the attack was that ultimate responsibility for the attack rested with Japan. The committee also exonerated the President and other high officials in Washington of charges that they had "tricked, provoked, incited, or coerced Japan . . . in order that a declaration of war might be more easily obtained from the Congress"—a frequent revisionist accusation.[54] It placed the blame for inadequate preparation and faulty intelligence on the Hawaiian commanders, Admiral Kimmel and General Short, and on Army and Navy staff officers in Washington, but specified they had committed "errors of judgement and not dereliction of duty." The minority members of the committee, however, placed responsibility for the disaster on Roosevelt, Stimson, Knox, Marshall, and Stark, as well as the Hawaiian commanders.

The revisionist argument followed closely the finding of the minority judgment, although some writers relieved Kimmel and Short of any guilt. In its more extreme form the revisionist position, as stated by Admiral Theobold, was that Roosevelt had deliberately placed the Pacific Fleet at Pearl Harbor as bait for the Japanese attack which he knew about through Magic, the name given to the interpreted and decoded Japanese messages, but the knowledge of which he purposely withheld from the Hawaiian commanders.[55] In Theobold's version, General Marshall and Admiral Stark were actively involved in this conspiracy. Admiral Kimmel's version, while not quite so bold, held that vital information that would have alerted

53. Raymond A. Esthus, "President Roosevelt's Commitment to Britain to Intervene in a Pacific War," *The Mississippi Valley Historical Review*, 50 (June 1963), 28–38; M. L. Hill, "Was There an Ultimatum Before Pearl Harbor?" *American Journal of International Law*, 42 (April 1948), 355–367; Llewellyn Woodward, *British Foreign Policy in the Second World War*, London: H. M. Stationery Office, 1962).

54. *Pearl Harbor Report*, pp. 251–252.

55. Robert A. Theobold, *The Final Secret of Pearl Harbor* (New York: Devin-Adair, 1954). See also Louis Morton, "Pearl Harbor in Perspective: A Bibliographical Survey," U.S. Naval Institute, *Proceedings*, 81, (April 1955), 461–468.

him to the attack in time to take preventive measures had been withheld on orders from high officials in Washington.[56]

A critical element in the revisionist case against Roosevelt and his close advisers was the Magic file. Ladislas Farago, who had served during the war in the Office of Naval Intelligence published what purported to be a full account of this top secret operation.[57] Many Japanese clues to the attack, he claimed, were missed by American intelligence, but he concluded that the failure was due to technical and human error and not to a conspiracy. Undoubtedly the best work on the Japanese attack is Roberta Wohlstetter's *Pearl Harbor: Warning and Decision*.[58] Tracing the information that came into Washington through Magic during the final months before Pearl Harbor, Mrs. Wohlstetter concludes that while "signals" of the Japanese intention could be read into these messages from hindsight, the signals had been distorted by contradictory "background noises" and could have been interpreted in several ways. The merits of Mrs. Wohlstetter's study are many, but chief among them is her close analysis of the process by which decisions were made by the small group of men who were privileged to read the Magic messages.

American and Japanese military planning for war, a subject usually hidden from the public gaze, has been carefully researched, thanks to the decision to publish a full and authentic history of the war. With virtually unlimited access to the files of the strategic planners, a group of professionally trained civilian historians have reconstructed the military planning for the prewar years. American planning for war with Japan centered around the various revisions to 1938 of War Plan Orange, described in a separate essay by the present writer.[59] Planning for the period after 1938, involving the various Rainbow plans as well as preparations for war and military participation in policy, are covered by the present author in his study of the strategy of the Pacific War in the army's official history of World War II and in two other excellent volumes of that series: Mark S. Watson's account of General Marshall's office in the prewar period and Matloff and Snell's volume on strategic planning. The best description of the machinery for military planning before and

56. Husband E. Kimmell, *Admiral Kimmel's Story* (Chicago: H. Regnery Company, 1955).

57. *The Broken Seal: The Story of "Operation Magic" and the Pearl Harbor Disaster* (New York: Random House, 1967).

58. Stanford: Stanford University Press, 1962.

59. Louis Morton, "War Plan Orange: Evolution of a Strategy," *World Politics*, 11 (January 1959), 221–250. Reports of the military attaches during this period are summarized by Russell F. Weigley, "The Role of the War Department and the Army." The U.S. Navy's role is described by Waldo H. Heinrichs, Jr. in "The Role of the U.S. Navy," delivered at the same conference.

during the war is Ray Cline's *Washington Command Post,* also a volume in the army series.[60]

Unlike most senior military officers of World War II, the strategic planners were not given to self-justifying memoirs. It is worth noting, however, that Generals Eisenhower and Wedemeyer, before they assumed command of active theaters of operation, were members of the army's strategic planning staff and their memoirs contain material on this subject, mostly for the wartime period.[61] Neither George Marshall nor Harold R. Stark, chief of naval operations before the war, has written memoirs. But Marshall's biographer, Forrest C. Pogue, interviewed the general extensively before his death, and his second volume covers the prewar years. On the naval side, the memoirs of Admiral William Leahy and Ernest J. King, though they deal mostly with the war years, contain useful material on prewar planning and policy.[62]

Of the extensive memoir literature by military commanders, two are useful for the Far East: General Claire L. Chennault's *Way of a Fighter* and *The Stilwell Papers,* edited by Theodore H. White. As adviser to the Chinese Air Force and commander of the American Volunteer Group, the "Flying Tigers," between 1937 and 1941, Chennault came to know China and Chiang Kai-shek very well. He had high praise for the Generalissimo and was critical of the limited aid furnished China in its struggle against Japan during these early years. Stilwell has little favorable to say about Chiang Kai-shek or for the Chinese military effort, and his relations with the Generalissimo finally became so strained that he had to be relieved. His experiences in China are fully recounted in two volumes of the army series, *Stilwell's Mission to China* and *Stilwell's Command Problems,* both by Charles F. Romanus and Riley Sunderland.

60. Louis Morton, *The War in the Pacific: Strategy and Command* (Washington, 1961); Mark S. Watson, *Chief of Staff: Prewar Plans and Preparations* (Washington: U.S. Department of the Army, 1950); Maurice Matloff and Edwin M. Snell, *Strategic Planning for Coalition Warfare, 1941–1942* (Washington: U.S. Department of the Army, 1953); Ray S. Cline, *Washington Command Post: The Operations Division* (Washington: U.S. Department of the Army, 1951).

61. Dwight D. Eisenhower, *Crusade in Europe* (Garden City, N.Y.: Doubleday, 1948); A. C. Wedemeyer, *Wedemeyer Reports* (New York: Holt, 1958). See also the various biographies of General Eisenhower and *The Papers of Dwight David Eisenhower: The War Years,* 5 vols., Alfred D. Chandler, Jr., ed. (Baltimore: The Johns Hopkins University Press, 1970).

62. Forrest C. Pogue, *George C. Marshall,* 2 vols. (New York: Viking Press, 1963–1966); Ernest J. King and Walter Muir Whitehill, *Fleet Admiral King: A Naval Record* (New York: W. W. Norton, 1952); William D. Leahy, *I Was There: The Personal Story of the Chief of Staff to Presidents Roosevelt and Truman* (New York: Whittlesey House, 1950).

Japanese planning for war is covered in considered detail in the *Pearl Harbor Attack Hearings,* which includes a copy of the final plan for war, and in the records of the Tokyo war crimes trial. Drawing on these sources, Robert E. Ward described the development of the Japanese plan for the attack on Pearl Harbor. The steps by which the leaders of Japan made the decision for war is described in several studies and is summarized in an essay by the present author.[63]

Because of the role played by the military in Japanese internal and foreign affairs, historians have devoted considerable attention to Japanese military organization and activities—more so than to the American military. But there are few memoirs or biographies in English of Japanese army and navy officers. Butow's study of Tojo has already been mentioned; of interest also is John Dean Potter's recent biography of Admiral Yamamoto, commander-in-chief of the Japanese fleet in 1941 and originator of the plan for the Pearl Harbor attack.[64]

The picture of a Japanese conspiracy led by the military clique to dominate East Asia, so strongly presented by the International Military Tribunal, was an essential part of the traditional interpretation of the origins of the war. It found most eloquent expression in Herbert Feis' *Road to Pearl Harbor,* which remains the standard work on the subject, and is developed in considerable detail in a number of other works on Japan. The British historian F. C. Jones, in his study of the period, traces the internal struggles of rival groups in Japan for control, and the gradual drift of Japan into the Axis camp after the outbreak of the war in Europe. Y. C. Maxon, using the material assembled for the Tokyo war crimes trial, traced in great detail the rise of military influence in the Japanese government and the conflict within the military itself over policy. A more complex picture of Japanese leadership is presented by Richard Storry. His explanation of Japan's policy in Asia is based on the rise of a nationalist spirit aroused by civilian and military agitators working with cliques of junior officers in organized terrorist societies.[65]

63. U.S. Naval Institute, *Proceedings,* 77 (December 1951), 1271–1283; Louis Morton, "The Japanese Decision for War," in K. R. Greenfield, ed., *Command Decisions* (Washington: U.S. Department of the Army 1960).

64. *Yamamoto: The Man Who Menaced America* (New York: Viking Press, 1965).

65. *Japan's New Order in East Asia: Its Rise and Fall, 1938–1945* (London, 1954); Yale Candee Maxon, *Control of Japanese Foreign Policy: A Study of Civilian-Military Rivalry, 1930–1945* (Berkeley: University of California Press, 1957). For a recent work that seeks to prove the Emperor's complicity and re-

Japanese historical writing on the origins of the Pacific War until recently tended to follow the American lead, translating or paraphrasing those studies that held greatest appeal for them.[66] Most accepted the dominant American view that war with the United States had come as a result of Japanese aggression in China. Others found the work of such revisionists as Beard and Tansill more attractive and took solace in studies, such as those by William A. Williams and several of his students, that were critical of American policies in general.[67] Most Japanese historical writing during these years displayed a preoccupation with the role of the military and naval officers in Japanese politics and their influence in taking the nation into war.

Within the past few years, a new generation of Japanese and American scholars have begun to reexamine Japanese and Chinese policy during the 1930's. The result has been a reinterpretation of many of the accepted views of the immediate postwar years. The most complete Japanese account of the entire period is *Road to the Pacific War*, prepared by a group of scholars working under the aegis of the Japanese International Relations Association.[68] Based on the records of the former military agencies, the archives of the Foreign Office and other government agencies, unpublished private papers, and interviews with many Japanese leaders, these volumes cover Japanese foreign policy from the invasion of Manchuria to the attack on Pearl Harbor. Altogether, fourteen authors, among whom

---

sponsibility, see David Bergamini, *Japan's Imperial Conspiracy* (New York: William Merrow, 1971).

66. This survey of Japanese historical writing is based on Akira Iriye's admirable essay, "Far Eastern Scholarship on United States Far Eastern Policy," in Borg, *Historians and American Far Eastern Policy*, pp. 22–31, and the papers prepared by a number of Japanese historians for the Conference on Japanese-American Relations, 1931–1941 held at Hakone, Japan, July 14–18, 1969. Among the Japanese papers used by the author were Seiichi Imai, "Cabinet, Emperor, and Senior Statesmen"; Katsumi Usui, "The Role of the Foreign Ministry"; Taichiro Mitani, "Contemporary Japanese Studies of Japan's Foreign Policy With Special Reference to China"; Sadao Asada, "The Japanese Navy and the United States."

67. Williams, *The Tragedy of American Foreign Policy*; Beard, *President Roosevelt and the Coming of the War*; Tansill, *Back Door to War*; Gardner, *Economic Aspects of New Deal Diplomacy*; Neumann, *America Encounters Japan*.

68. Nihon Kokusai Seiji Gakkai, *Taiheiyō sensō e no michi*. This discussion is based on Akira Iriye's "Japanese Imperialism and Aggression: Reconsiderations, II," *The Journal of Asian Studies*, 23 (November 1963), 103–113. The separate volumes are as follows: I, *Eve of the Manchurian Incident*; II, *Manchurian Incident*; III, *Sino-Japanese War, Part I*; IV, *Sino-Japanese War, Part II*; V, *Tripartite Alliance; Soviet Japanese Neutrality Pact*; VI, *The Southward Advance*; VII, *The Outbreak of War between Japan and the United States*; VIII, *Documents*.

were some of the ablest diplomatic historians in Japan, participated in the project. Throughout there is an emphasis on military matters, a concern with the role of the military in decision making—one of the major problems that confronts the student of prewar Japanese policy.[69]

Some American scholars of the postwar generation, equipped with the ability to use Japanese sources began, like their Japanese colleagues, to dispute the traditional interpretation presented by the International Military Tribunal of the Far East. In a sense they were revisionists, but the arguments of the early revisionist writers like Beard and Tansill, held little appeal for them. Instead of picturing Japan as a country under a totalitarian regime dominated by a conspiratorial military clique pursuing an aggressive program of expansion, they saw Japanese policy as an effort to achieve and maintain security and economic self-sufficiency. For a country as poor as Japan, the only way to achieve this goal, the leaders of Japan believed, was through control of strategic areas necessary for the defense of the homeland and of territories capable of supplying the resources required to maintain its military forces in peace and war —in short a program of expansion. Thus Japanese policy was, in the view of these revisionists, not the result of a military conspiracy but a pursuit of legitimate national aims by the leaders of the Japanese government, civilian as well as military. Representing the basic aims of the nation for survival and economic well-being, this policy could not be compromised or negotiated.

David J. Lu was one of the first, with Robert Butow, to review Japanese policy in the light of Japanese as well as Western materials. The former traced the Japanese path from the Marco Polo Bridge to Pearl Harbor and concluded that the immediate cause of the war was "Japan's unwillingness to withdraw its troops from China and America's uncompromising stand on the freezing order and oil embargo."[70] Lu asserted also that the Japanese army, which pressed for an expansionist policy, totalitarian control and a planned economy, was largely to blame for the conflict. To the army, he claimed, China represented a power base which made possible its control of the nation. And like others who had studied Japanese policy, Lu found that the machinery for decision making in Japan was inflexible and cumbersome, failing to provide the means for reconciling

69. See Professor Iriye's review cited in note 68. James Morley is currently translating and editing these volumes.
70. David J. Lu, *From the Marco Polo Bridge to Pearl Harbor: Japan's Entry into World War II* (*New York: Public Affairs Press,* 1961), p. 238.

contradictory views. But he did not blame the military alone for prewar Japanese policy. The conservative wing of the business community, he said, willingly supported the aggressive policies of the military, as did other elements of the ruling class.

Unlike most other students of the period, Lu argued that evaluation was really directed against the Soviet Union, not the United States, and was used by the American policy makers simply to identify Japan with Hitler and the hated Nazis. It was, he said, never really an issue and was only made so by Roosevelt and Hull to manipulate American public opinion. With respect to the effect of economic sanctions on Japan's decision for war, Lu agreed they were of first importance, but believed that their imposition was unfortunate and the timing wrong. Had the embargo been imposed on Japan in July 1937, he wrote, "the result might have been entirely different."[71]

Lu's analysis was not far from the traditional Western interpretation. Feis, who wrote an introduction to the volume, regarded Lu's work as "thorough and considered," and "estimable diplomatic history."[72] He took exception only to Lu's estimate of Matsuoka and his interpretation of the Tripartite Pact. Feis especially noted that Lu had made excellent use of the Japanese archives, and his comment recalls a remark Feis had made earlier in reference to Japanese records, that "though they might provide more details they do not change the fundamental view of this experience [the events that led to Pearl Harbor] or its main features."[73] He also expressed doubts at the time that there were in secret British or American archives any information that might alter our understanding of these events.

Robert Butow's study of Tojo, published the same year as Lu's volume, focused on the responsibility of the military for the Japanese decision to go to war. Skillfully blending history and biography, Butow, who had earlier written perhaps the best analysis of Japan's decision to surrender, briefly traced the role of the Japanese army in the events leading to war through the career of General Tojo. While not denying the important part played by the military in the formulation of foreign policy, Butow held that figures of lesser rank, the middle echelon officers in the general staff and War Ministry, working behind the scenes, often played a decisive role in the unfolding drama. Alvin D. Coox, in his study of the military in the year 1937–38 came to virtually the same conclusion. Hostilities in China, he asserted, resulted from a corrosion of discipline within the army,

71. Ibid., p. 245.
72. Ibid., p. 111.
73. Feis, "War Came at Pearl Harbor."

which opened the way for subordinate officers to wield considerable influence.[74]

James B. Crowley dealt with the Japanese military also but in a broader context than either Butow or Coox. His work was concerned primarily with the roots of Japanese foreign policy from 1930 to 1938 and dealt, therefore, with policy making as well as policy, that is with "the political process by which these policies were formulated and implemented."[75] Boldly, Crowley challenged two of the hallowed generalizations of the traditional interpretation of the origins of the Pacific War: that the basic cause of the war was Japan's aggressive foreign policy after 1931; and that this policy was the work of a military clique that seized political power after 1931 through a program of terror, political assassinations, and conspiracies. Crowley found this explanation unsatisfactory. The Japanese quest for hegemony in East Asia to achieve national security and economic strength, he argued, led to an increasingly authoritarian government, a new style of imperialism, and ultimately to the war in China. In a separate article Crowley reviewed the Marco Polo Bridge Incident and rejected the contention that it was the result of a conspiracy of army officers.[76] Rather, he said, it was the result largely of "the interaction" of the policies and acts of the two governments. Far from provoking renewed fighting in the aftermath of the clash at the Marco Polo Bridge, the military commands had effected a local settlement. It was the overreaction of officials in Nanking and Tokyo, said Crowley, that escalated the conflict.

One of the most perceptive and broad-ranging analyses of the prewar period is Akira Iriye's *Across the Pacific*.[77] The distinguishing characteristic of Iriye's work was his treatment of the subject as a four-way relationship involving the domestic and foreign policies of the major powers in the Far East—China, Japan, Russia, and the United States—based upon a knowledge of the sources and languages of these countries. The result of this kind of comparative history was revealing and suggestive. It was the Treasury Department under Morgenthau, Iriye pointed out, that took the lead in aid to China through its purchases of silver after 1937, while Hull assumed a moral stance, arguing that Japan's actions would lead to further

74. Butow, *Tojo and the Coming of the War;* Alvin D. Coox, *Year of the Tiger* (Tokyo: Orient/West Incorporated, 1954).

75. *Japan's Quest for Autonomy: National Security and Foreign Policy, 1930–1938* (Princeton: Princeton University Press, 1966), p. xiv.

76. "A Reconsideration of the Marco Polo Bridge Incident," *Journal of Asian Studies,* 22 (May 1963), 227–291.

77. *Across the Pacific: An Inner History of American-East Asian Relations* (New York: Harcourt, Brace, and World, 1967).

aggression and possibly a world conflict. American concern, said Iriye, was less with China than with Japanese aggression and its global implications, coupling "moral globalism" with "political universalism." The Japanese, he argued further, though they recognized the possibility of a war with the United States, did not believe their actions in China would precipitate hostilities.

The Chinese, for their part, said Iriye, looked to a Japanese-American war as a solution to their difficulties and maintained this belief even when American aid was not forthcoming. Some Chinese, however, as Werner Levi noted, were disappointed at the small amount of assistance they received from the United States, and as late as the eve of Pearl Harbor, feared an American betrayal.[78]

All three views—the American, the Japanese, and the Chinese— were correct, and not at all inconsistent. But unlike the traditionalist historians, Iriye denied that Japanese aggression in China was the root cause of the Pacific War, satisfying as this thesis is psychologically and in other ways. Rather, it was Japan's decision to move southward in 1938, that brought the United States and Japan into sharp conflict.

There was a connection, of course, between Japan's policy in China and Southeast Asia. Japan required the resources of Southeast Asia to carry the war in China to a successful conclusion, which, once accomplished, would release additional forces for expansion to the south. Japan's leaders, said Iriye, recognized that the southward advance posed real risks but felt they were necessary to secure the resources needed for such a conflict. After 1939, with the outbreak of war in Europe, the risks seemed less; German victories in Europe and Britain's struggle for survival thus opened the way for the southward advance.

For the Americans, who regarded British and American security as interdependent, Japanese expansion to the south meant ultimately the destruction of Britain's position in Asia and the weakening of British security. Thus, after 1938, the United States began to take a stronger stand in opposition to Japanese efforts to establish a new order in Asia. It was at that time, Iriye points out, that American strategic planners moved away from the Orange concept of a United States–Japanese war fought without allies on either side and developed the Rainbow plans based on a more realistic assumption of the international situation. It was also at this time that the United States, linking the war in Asia with developments in Europe, began to aid the victims of aggression and to apply economic sanctions

78. *Modern China's Foreign Policy* (Minneapolis: University of Minnesota Press, 1953).

against Japan. The Tripartite Pact, Iriye believed, confirmed the American view that Japanese aggression in Asia was one with Nazi aggression in Europe and represented a threat to the free world—an alliance for conquest of the world.

American policy during the years 1940–41, according to Iriye, was based on the view that the only way to stop Japanese aggression was through strong action. Force was the only language the Japanese understood; concessions, it was argued, would only lead to further demands. Despite Ambassador Grew's warning that the Japanese might act irrationally out of desperation, American policy makers believed that a firm attitude backed by superior military strength and industrial resources was the only way to stop Japan and avoid war. Both sides indulged in wishful thinking and both sides, says Iriye, based their policies on what they wanted to believe the other side would do.

In December 1966, on the 25th anniversary of Pearl Harbor, the American Historical Association devoted a session of its annual meeting to a discussion of the events leading to the attack. The speaker was Chihiro Hosoya, one of the new generation of historical scholars in Japan. Hosoya identified two factions in the American government involved in the making of policy in the period preceding the war: a "hard-line" group consisting of Hornbeck, Stimson, Morgenthau; and a "soft-line" group, among whom he placed Hull and Sumner Welles.[79] The hard-line faction, he stated, argued for forceful measures against Japan and the imposition of economic sanctions to deter Japan from aggression. This group won out over the soft-line faction. This was not exactly an original observation, but Hosoya's point was that the policy urged by the hard-line faction had the opposite effect from that intended; instead of deterring the Japanese, it stiffened them in their determination to move south. Believing they had no choice but submission or war, they opted for war. Thus, the Americans, because of a mistaken policy, had forced Japan into war. Hosoya recognized the Japanese decision as irrational and attributed it in large part to the influence of the middle-echelon officers, who were less responsible than their superiors, and to the weakness of the decision-making process.

Hosoya's argument was deliberately framed in contemporary cold war terms. His characterization of American policy makers as hard-liners and soft-liners carried unmistakable connotations to his

79. The paper was published under the title "Miscalculations in Deterent Policy: Japanese-United States Relations, 1938–1941," *Journal of Peace Research*, no. 2 (1968), 97–115. I was chairman of the session and have based this discussion of the paper on papers in his personal possession.

audience of hawks and doves. Even more interesting was his description of American policy as a policy of deterrence. For Hosoya, the lesson of 1941 was plain: the hawks had failed. Instead of deterring the Japanese, the hard-line policy had escalated the conflict and led finally to war.

The analogy between 1941 and the postwar period is not an unreasonable one; others have noted it and drawn a similar lesson. Nobutaka Ike also describes American policy in the prewar period as a policy of deterrence. That it failed to deter the Japanese in 1941 seemed to him to demonstrate that there are definite limits to the effectiveness of threats as a deterrent against one nation by another and he thought the experience of 1941 cast serious doubts on the validity of the theory of deterrence developed during the 1950's. "Against those who are willing to take great risks," he warned, "deterrence may not be effective."[80]

Russian and Chinese historiography, as well as much Japanese historical writing on the 1930's is, as one would expect, Marxist in character, although Marxist interpretations of the period are by no means limited to the historians of these countries. Whatever the nationality of the author, Marxist writers share certain common characteristics: they view foreign policy in terms of economic interests and the various stages of capitalism; they read history backwards, interpreting the past in the light of future events to demonstrate the inevitability of socialist victory; they select from capitalist historians only that which supports their thesis.

In Marxist works, the United States is pictured as one of a number of capitalist nations, albeit the most powerful, exploiting China for its own ends. Inevitably, the capitalist countries struggle for supremacy in China, and during the 1930's, according to the Marxist view, this struggle narrowed to a contest between Japan and the United States. Some Marxist historians assert that the United States encouraged Chiang Kai-shek to submit to Japan so that the two could divide China between them; others that the United States encouraged Chinese resistance to Japan to gain the Chinese market for itself. Another line is that the United States opposed Japan's advance to the south because it wanted the Japanese to move north against the Soviet Union.[81]

80. *Japan's Decision for War* (Stanford: Stanford University Press, 1967), p. xxvi.

81. Taichiro Mitani, "Contemporary Japanese Studies of Japanese Foreign Policy With Special Reference to China, 1931–1941," Conference on Japanese-American Relations, 1931–1941, pp. 26–33; Iriye, "Far Eastern Scholarship on United States Far Eastern Policy," in Borg, *Historians and Far Eastern Policy*.

Typical of Marxist interpretations is D. J. Goldberg's *Japan's Foreign Policy, September 1939–December 1959*, published in Moscow in 1959.[82] The driving force behind Japanese aggressions, says Goldberg, was pressure from the "monopoly bourgeoisie," whose aspirations were fueled by concessions made by Western powers, usually at the expense of China and the Soviet Union. When these concessions were no longer forthcoming, Japanese capitalists pushed for a program that would give them what they wanted even at the risk of war. The United States, he says, hoped to profit from a long war between China and Japan, which would weaken the latter and give American capitalism a monopoly of the Chinese market—the real aim of American policy in China. Goldberg ignored Western and Japanese source materials, but quoted from American revisionists when it suited his purpose. In one respect—the inevitability of the clash between American policy in China and Japanese imperialism —this interpretation was not very different from that of some American writers.

Criticism of American prewar policy in the Far East has come also from the New Left. Non-Marxist in nature, this leftist interpretation comes very close to the right-wing revisionist interpretation of some of the Republican critics of President Roosevelt. Illustrative of this point of view is Noam Chomsky's tribute to A. J. Muste in *American Power and the New Mandarins*.[83] The immediate cause of the Pacific War, says Chomsky was the recognition by the military elements in Japan that it was "now or never," that if it did not resist by force while it still had the capability of doing so, it would be doomed to second power status and never again be in a position to challenge the United States. According to Chomsky, Japan was being denied the materials it needed for its very existence as punishment for what it was doing in China and for associating itself with Germany and Italy in the Tripartite Pact. It had no choice but to submit to American domination or fight.

In expanding her influence on the Continent, Chomsky asserts, Japan was merely following the traditional policies of Western powers. When this policy challenged America's position in Asia, the Roosevelt administration took ever more stringent measures to protect American economic and political hegemony in China. Opposed

82. The discussion of Goldberg's book is drawn from Paul E. Sanger's review in *The Journal of Asian Studies*, 22 (1963), 107–108. See also the review of another Soviet history in ibid., p. 201.

83. "The Revolutionary Pacifism of A. J. Muste," in *American Power and the New Mandarins* (New York: Pantheon Books, 1969), pp. 159–220; Lionel Abel, "The Position of Noam Chomsky," *Commentary* (May 1969), and the exchange between Chomsky and Abel in ibid. (October 1969), pp. 12–43.

at every turn by the Americans, the Japanese turned to Germany and Italy, and, when denied oil and iron, turned southward. During the conversations with Japan's emissaries in 1941, the United States, he says, made the Tripartite Pact a major issue when, in fact, it was not. American terms for a settlement were such that Japan would have had to abandon its legitimate interests and aims in Asia and become "a mere subcontractor in the emerging American world system."[84] Aware that it could not win but hoping for a negotiated peace, Japan chose war rather than accept American domination.

Chomsky's work is based on a wide reading of the secondary literature on the subject, but he places heavy reliance on Paul W. Schroeder's study of the Axis alliance and its effect on relations between the United States and Japan. His real target is American policy in the 1960's and the liberal intellectuals, the "new mandarins" who support and profit from it. A. J. Muste, he writes, foresaw in 1941 that out of World War II would emerge " 'a new American empire' incorporating a subservient Britain," that would seek world domination, as Hitler was trying to do.[85]

It would seem that with a literature so large for a period so short, there would be little left for the historian to do. Actually that is not the case; there are still many questions to which we do not have the answers, and many new questions to ask. For example, we know comparatively little about the relationship of events in Europe and elsewhere to American and Japanese policy. There are several excellent studies of German policy in the Far East, but there is certainly room for more work in this field.[86] Nicholas Clifford has recently published a study of British policy in the Far East, and there may be a rich harvest for enterprising students in the recently opened British archives for the period.[87] The Far Eastern policy of the Soviet Union has been studied extensively, but the effect of this policy on American relations in the area remains obscure.[88] As for

84. Ibid., p. 204.
85. Ibid., p. 165.
86. In addition to Schroeder's study cited above, there is Ernest L. Presseisen, *Germany and Japan* (The Hague: M. Nishoff, 1958); Frank W. Ikle, *German-Japanese Relations, 1936–1940* (New York: Bookman Associates, 1956); Johanna Menzel Meskill, *Hitler and Japan: The Hollow Alliance* (New York: Atherton Press, 1966); Hans L. Trefosse, *Germany and American Neutrality, 1939–1941* (New York: Bookman Associates, 1951), and "Germany and Pearl Harbor," *Far Eastern Quarterly*, 11 (November 1951), 35–50; James T. C. Liu, "German Mediation in the Sino-Japanese War, 1937–1938," *Far Eastern Quarterly*, 8.4 (1949), 157–171.
87. Clifford, *Retreat From China*; also, Irving S. Friedman, *British Relations with China, 1931–1939* (New York: Institute of Pacific Relations, 1940); Craigie, *Behind the Japanese Mask*.
88. Harriet L. Moore, *Soviet Far Eastern Policy 1935–1945* (Princeton:

France and other European nations, there is little available.[89] Certainly it is reasonable to assume that the relations between the United States and Japan were not conducted in a vacuum and that their policies in East and Southeast Asia were affected by larger considerations and by their policies toward other countries.

China is a special problem. The language presents special difficulties for Western scholars and the victory of the Chinese communists in 1949 has made difficult any historical writing in China that does not conform to a Marxist-Leninist interpretation. Finally, records comparable to those we have for the Western countries and Japan are not available for China, and it is doubtful that they will be in the foreseeable future.[90]

Additional research is needed on the relationship between domestic affairs, public opinion, and foreign policy. For the United States we have studies of various groups, such as the isolationists, the business community, peace groups, and organized pressure groups and their efforts to influence public opinion and officials in policy-making positions.[91] But the subject needs further investigation. There were literally scores of organizations and groups attempting to influence American public opinion, Congress, the State Department, and other governmental agencies concerned with foreign policy in the years before the war. With the recent advance in research methods of com-

---

Princeton University Press, 1945); Pauline Tompkins, *American-Russian Relations in the Far East* (New York: Macmillan, 1949); Henry Wei, *China and Soviet Russia* (Princeton: Princeton University Press, 1956); David J. Dallin, *Soviet Russia and the Far East* (New Haven: Yale University Press, 1948).

89. Roger Levy, *French Interest and Policies in the Far East* (New York: Institute of Pacific Relations, 1941); Hubertus J. van Mook, *The Netherlands Indies and Japan: Battle on Paper, 1940–1941* (New York: W. W. Norton and Company, 1944); Frank M. Tamagna, *Italy's Interests and Policies in the Far East* (New York: Institute of Pacific Relations, 1941).

90. See Iriye, "Far Eastern Scholarship on United States Far Eastern Policy," in Borg, *Historians and Far Eastern Policy;* Warren Cohen, "The Study of Sino-American Relations." Paper read at the National Archives, June 17, 1969. Leopold, "American Policy and China," *The Journal of Conflict Resolution,* 8 (December 1964), 505–506; Taichiro Mitani, "Contemporary Japanese Studies . . . With Special Reference to China," Conference on Japanese-American Relations.

91. In addition to the studies already cited, see Hadley Cantril, ed., *Public Opinion 1935–1946* (Princeton: Princeton University Press, 1951); Bernard C. Cohen, *The Influence of Non-Governmental Groups on Foreign Policy Making* (Boston: World Peace Foundation, 1959); John W. Masland, "American Attitudes Towards Japan," *Annals of the American Academy of Political and Social Science* 215 (May 1941), 160–165; "Pressure Groups and American Foreign Policy, *Public Opinion Quarterly,* 6.1 (Spring 1942), 115–122 and "The Peace Groups Join Battle," ibid. 4 (December 1940), 664–673, Eleanor Tupper and George McReynolds, *Japan in American Public Opinion* (New York: Macmillan, 1937).

munication techniques, such study might well produce significant results, not only for American policy but for other countries as well. And perhaps the techniques of research employed by the behavioral scientists, such as model building and quantitative studies made possible by the computer, could be used with profit by historians of American foreign policy as they have by others.

We need to know also more of what was happening inside the governments of China and Japan. The study of Japanese records has already yielded significant results, but there is more yet to learn, and we have nothing comparable for China. What were the pressures on the policy makers? How much influence did organized groups and economic interests exert? What policies did they favor and why? These and other questions are still to be answered fully.

The role of the military in Japan has been extensively researched,[92] but not that of the American military—apparently on the assumption that the military in the United States played only a subordinate role in policy formulation. Was this actually the case? Thanks to the historical programs of the services we have a number of excellent studies of prewar planning, but little except indirect evidence to indicate to what extent they were able to influence executive and congressional decisions. During the 1920's and 1930's, the military planners complained frequently that they lacked policy guidance on which to base their plans and offered schemes from time to time to remedy this lack.[93] After 1935 such complaints are rarely heard and by 1939 they had virtually ceased despite the fact that formal mechanisms for coordination were limited largely to the Standing Liaison Committee, which dealt mostly with Latin-American affairs. Were there other ways in which the military influenced policy? What policies did they favor and why? Were there internal struggles in the services over policy, cliques with differing views of strategy that competed for influence? How about interservice competition? To what extent did strategic plans reflect a particular

92. In addition to the works already cited, see Hugh Byas, *Government by Assassination* (New York: A. A. Knopf, 1942); E. E. N. Causton, *Militarism and Foreign Policy in Japan* (London: G. Allen & Unwin Limited, 1936); Mark Gayn, *Japan Diary* (New York: Sloan Associates, 1948); Kenneth W. Colegrove, *Militarism in Japan* (Boston: World Peace Foundation, 1936); John Maki, *Japanese Militarism* (New York: A. A. Knopf, 1945). See the transcript of Session IV (July 15, 1969) of the Conference on Japanese-American Relations for an interesting discussion comparing the Japanese and American military.

93. See Louis Morton, "Interservice Cooperation and Political-Military Collaboration," in Harry L. Coles, ed., *Total War and Cold War* (Columbus: Ohio State University Press, 1962); Ernest R. May, "Development of Political-Military Consultation in the United States," *Political Science Quarterly*, 70 (June 1955).

view of the world or a particular policy? Were particular strategic plans, such as Orange, formulated and supported, as Waldo Heinrichs has suggested, as much with an eye to congressional appropriation or the needs of the service as to political and strategic requirements.[94] We know something, not nearly enough, about the role of the navy in the Pacific for the early period, but very little for the years immediately preceding the Pearl Harbor attack and less about the army's role.[95]

This survey illustrates the depth and richness of research and scholarship and the diversity of interpretation that have characterized the study of American–East Asian relations in the years preceding Pearl Harbor. Despite the great amount of research in the United States and Japan, there still remain a number of important areas of disagreement among scholars in the field—disagreements that may never be resolved—as well as areas that have not yet been fully explored. These disagreements reflect the differences in interpretation that appeared in the immediate postwar period between those who had supported President Roosevelt's Far East policy and those who had opposed it, between an internationalist or traditional interpretation and a revisionist interpretation. But with the passage of time and the appearance of additional sources, these terms have begun to lose their meaning. A new generation of historians in Japan and the United States, viewing these events with more detachment and in broader perspective than their elders, have produced fresh and challenging interpretations of the period. They may yet settle the outstanding controversies and answer the questions that have not yet been answered.

94. See his paper "The Role of the U.S. Navy" read at the Conference held in Japan, summer 1969, as well as the paper read at the National Archives Conference, June 17, 1969. Not much has been done on the question of fortification of the Japanese (or American) islands, or the relationship between possession of the Pacific Islands and policy. See Earl S. Pomeroy, "American Policy Respecting the Marshalls, Carolines, and Marianas, 1898–1941," *Pacific Historial Review* XVII (February 1948), 43–53, and his *Pacific Outpost* (Stanford: Stanford University Press, 1951).

95. O. J. Clinard, *Japan's Influence on American Naval Power, 1897–1917* (Berkeley: University of California Press, 1947); Gerald E. Wheeler, *Prelude to Pearl Harbor: The United States Navy and the Far East, 1921–1931* (Columbia, Mo.: University of Missouri Press, 1963); Armin Rappaport, *The Navy League of the United States* (Detroit, Wayne State University Press, 1962); William R. Braisted, *The United States Navy in the Pacific, 1897–1909* (Austin: University of Texas Press, 1958).

The Forgotten Philippines,

1790–1946

The beginning of America's direct contact with the Philippine Islands antedated by more than a century its acquisition of sovereignty there in 1898. Vessels trading principally with some other part of Asia may have called in the archipelago as early as 1790; and in 1796 the Salem ship *Astrea* opened direct trade between the two countries, exchanging hats, wooden compasses, and Madeira for sugar, indigo, pepper, and hides. By the latter date there was already an American commission merchant living in Manila. These early American visitors to the islands came during the first stages of the development of an export economy in the Philippines; and their successors, who fueled that development, contributed by doing so to the social and cultural changes in Philippine life that undermined Spanish authority and gave rise to the revolutions of 1896 and 1898. It should be evident, therefore, that the study of American-Philippine relations concerns not only what is widely called the American period, but also its antecedent, the Spanish period of Philippine history. For American-Philippine relations not only follow upon the Spanish period and involve a people whose character and institutions had been affected by three and a third centuries of Spanish rule; they also took place during and helped give shape to the last of those centuries.

In spite of this, the study of American-Philippine relations has been addressed almost exclusively to the years since 1898. In part, this reflects the political orientation of the scholars involved, who for the most part have been either Americans or Filipinos trained in the American-designed schools of the islands. It also reflects a characteristic of Philippine historiography, the definition of periods of the islands' history by reference to the external forces affecting them and a tendency in each of these periods to write off the preceding stage.[1] The pre-Hispanic past of the people would probably

1. For notable exceptions among modern works, see Onofre D. Corpuz, *The Philippines* (Englewood Cliffs, N.J.: Prentice-Hall, 1965), and Gregorio F.

have been lost during the Spanish period had it not been for accounts left by early Spaniards.[2] As it was, these accounts were avidly seized upon near the end of Spain's rule by Filipino nationalists who, in their frustration and disgust over what their people had been brought to in the course of Spanish rule, sought knowledge of the achievements Filipinos had once wrought on their own. Early in this century, the Spanish period was downgraded by Filipino commentators, because so seemingly negative and destructive an experience was painful and presumably of little relevance to their hopes for the future. At the present time, one prominent Filipino historian is given to observing that there is no Philippine history prior to 1872—only Spanish history;[3] others are engaged in intensive study of the pre-Hispanic past. Whatever the reason, students of the relations between our two countries and peoples have regularly ignored the full complexity of their topic and denied themselves important elements of perspective and dimension.

The first permanent Spanish settlement in the Philippines was established on the island of Cebu in 1565, and within a decade of that date most of the populated parts of the archipelago outside the mountainous regions of Luzon and the Muslim, or Moro, strongholds in the south had been brought under Spanish sovereignty. For the next two centuries Spain deliberately isolated the islands and their inhabitants from contacts with other Westerners. Part of the motivation for doing so, of course, was strategic and commercial; but to a large extent the Spaniards hoped by closing the islands to rival powers to ensure that Filipinos would become hispanized and Catholicized. Their success in meeting this essentially missionary responsibility has been analyzed by John Leddy Phelan in a short, bracing book, *The Hispanization of the Philippines: Spanish Aims and Filipino Responses, 1565–1700.*[4] Phelan, an American whose interests run also to Spanish colonial history in this hemisphere, argues persuasively that Spain's cultural impact upon the Filipinos, elaborate

---

Zaide, *Philippine Political and Cultural History*, 2 vols. (Manila: Philippine Education Company, 1949).

2. For a discussion of this literature, see the footnotes to chapter 2 of John Leddy Phelan, *The Hispanization of the Philippines: Spanish Aims and Filipino Responses, 1565–1700* (Madison: University of Wisconsin Press, 1959). For new light on the pre-Hispanic past and a droll debunking of the so-called Marco manuscripts, see William Henry Scott, *A Critical Study of the Pre-Hispanic Source Materials for the Study of Philippine History* (Manila: University of Sto. Tomas Press, 1968).

3. Teodoro A. Agoncillo, whose recent book, *A Short History of the Philippines* (New York: Mentor Books, 1969), devotes 55 of its 300 pages of text to the more than 330 years when Spain ruled the islands.

4. Madison: University of Wisconsin Press, 1959.

and intensive in design, was in fact sparse and uneven. His thesis bears summarization here.

The Philippines were remote: administratively they were part of the viceroyalty of Mexico, with which they made contact once a year through the voyage of the celebrated Manila galleon. It took two years, in normal times, for officials in Madrid to get an answer from their government at Manila. The Spanish population of the archipelago was never large; and, partly because the clergy made heroic efforts to discourage laymen from living among the natives and corrupting or exploiting them, contact between Spaniards and Filipinos within the islands was minimal. These conditions, complemented by rugged geography and a decentralized population pattern, prevented the implementation of the government's hopes for rigorous hispanization. What emerged was a selectively or unevenly altered version of traditional pre-Hispanic culture. Even in the case of religion, the aspect of Spanish civilization that most consistently and intensively touched the lives of Filipinos, the outcome of Spanish efforts was a highly syncretistic folk Catholicism.

Phelan's thesis is arguable in certain respects.[5] It is, to some tastes, unduly approbatory toward the hybrid culture that emerged; and it supposes a large amount of purposefulness and selectivity on the part of Filipinos where some think they discern helplessness either to preserve the existing culture or switch to an integral approximation of an occidental model. Was Hispano-Philippine culture basically a successful *because limited* form of acculturation—a matter, as Phelan puts it, of "freedom in selecting their responses to Hispanization," of "creative social adjustment"[6]—or was it stultifying?[7]

Early in the second half of the eighteenth century the Philippines'

5. Certain of his facts are disputed and he is charged with inadequate knowledge of the Philippines (which he did not visit in the preparation of his book) in a review by Zaide in *Journal of Southeast Asian History*, 2 (March 1961), 104–108.

6. Phelan, *Hispanization of the Philippines*, p. viii.

7. Phelan's book contains an excellent bibliography, listing the great depositories of source materials for the Spanish period, some of which are in the United States or Mexico. Before repairing to archives, however, students should mine the 55 volumes of source materials for the Spanish years collected and translated by Emma Helen Blair and James A. Robertson under the appropriately inclusive title, *The Philippine Islands* (Cleveland: Arthur H. Clark, 1903–1909). For secondary sources, see Nicholas P. Cushner, *Spain in the Philippines* (Rutland: Tuttle, 1972); José Montero y Vidal, *Historia general de Filipinas desde el descubrimiento de dichas islas hasta nuestros días*, 3 vols. (Madrid: M. Tello, 1887–95); Horacio de la Costa, *The Jesuits in the Philippines, 1581–1768* (Cambridge: Harvard University Press, 1961); and Corpuz, *The Philippines.*

isolation was pierced. British forces occupied Manila from 1762 to 1764, and during their stay Philippine commerce was opened for the first time to Europeans from outside Spain. When the British withdrew, the commercial interest which had begun under their administration remained. Bribing and smuggling when necessary, Europeans from outside the Peninsula entered the market for Philippine agricultural products and pushed up land values by making it profitable for landowners to specialize and produce for the export market. Partly in response to this challenge and partly as an outgrowth of the new efficiency of the government at Madrid under the rule of Charles III (1757–1788), Spain itself launched a program of economic development and subsequently opened the islands legally to foreign trade and alien residents. As a result of this commercial penetration, new wealth appeared in the provinces in the hands of Filipinos; and with it came new aspirations to lead a more Western style of life. Foreign influences and some secular thought invaded regions long isolated under the domination of Spanish friars. Crop specialization, urbanization, the appearance of a middle class of Filipinos, the increased number of Filipinos who traveled or were educated abroad were signs of the change. Old notions concerning the division of the islands' population into *indios, mestizos, chinos, insulares* (or *creoles*), and *peninsulares* gave way; the use of the term Filipino in its present inclusive meaning acquires its validity from nineteenth-century social changes.[8]

Americans were not the first to penetrate Philippine commerce; but during parts of the nineteenth century, after Spanish efforts at development had bogged down, they were second in importance only to the English as catalysts of social and economic change. The American trading houses Russell and Sturgis and Peele, Hubbell and Co., the former coming to be known simply as "the great company," not only acted as commission merchants, but as bankers, investors, shipping and insurance agents, and landowners. In a country lack-

8. Eliodoro G. Robles, *The Philippines in the Nineteenth Century* (Quezon City: Malaya Books, 1969); Benito Legarda, Jr., "Foreign Trade, Economic Change, and Entrepreneurship in the Nineteenth Century Philippines" (Ph.D. diss., Harvard University, 1955); Horacio de la Costa, "The Formative Century, 1760–1870," and Legarda, "The Colonial Economy," in *Philippine Perspective: Lectures on the Prehistory and History of the Philippines*, 2 vols. (Manila: Ateneo de Manila, 1964), sess. 1, part 2, lectures 4 and 6; Edgar Wickberg, *The Chinese in Philippine Life, 1850–1898* (New Haven: Yale University Press, 1965); María Lourdes Díaz-Trechuelo, *La real compañía de Filipinas* (Seville: Escuela de Estudios Hispano-Americanos de Sevilla, 1965); M[aria] L[ourdes] Díaz-Trechuelo, "The Economic Development of the Philippines in the Second Half of the Eighteenth Century," *Philippine Studies*, 11 (April 1963), 195–231; James F. Cloghessy, "The Philippines and the Royal Philippine Company," *Mid-America*, 42 (April 1960), 80–104.

ing modern banking and credit facilities, among a people disinclined to assume entrepreneurial responsibilities, they and their foreign counterparts were the locus of economic initiative. It was a rewarding but risky business; and in the end both failed, Russell and Sturgis in 1876, when Visayan sugar planters failed to produce crops against which the company had made advances, and Peele, Hubbell and Co. in 1887, when its investments in the inefficient sugar industry depreciated because of competition from European beet-root sugar on the world market.[9]

A great deal can be learned about nineteenth-century Philippine life and the tensions produced in it by economic changes from a discreet reading of the travel literature that sprang up with the removal of impediments to foreign visitors. Much of this literature, however, is invidious. Travelers from more modern, liberal, and secular places often exaggerated both the iniquities and oppressiveness of insular Spaniards in general and friars in particular, and also the alleged perversity and indolence of Filipinos.[10] A different, but only slightly more favorable point of view may be seen in reports by official Spanish observers, among whom the most penetrating were perhaps Sinibaldo de Mas and Juan Manuel de la Matta.[11] In a

9. Benito Legarda, Jr., "American Entrepreneurs in the Nineteenth Century Philippines," *Explorations in Entrepreneurial History*, 9 (1957), 142–59; Nathaniel Bowditch, *Early American-Philippine Trade: The Journal of Nathaniel Bowditch in Manila, 1796*, Thomas R. and Mary C. McHale, eds. (New Haven: Yale University, Southeast Asia Studies, Monograph Series no. 2, 1962); John H. Reinoehl, "Jacob Crowinshield, 'Some Remarks on the American Trade,'" *William and Mary Quarterly*, series 3, 16 (1959), 104. See also the works cited in notes 8 and 10. Antonio Maria Regidor y Jurado and J. Warren T. Mason, *Commercial Progress in the Philippine Islands* (London: Dunn & Chidzey, 1905) was an erratic early account.

10. The most reliable and perceptive of these books are Tomás de Comyn, *Estado de las islas Filipinas en 1810* (Madrid: Repullés, 1820); Henry Piddington, *Remarks on the Philippine Islands, and on Their Capital Manila, 1819 to 1822* (Calcutta: Baptist Mission Press, 1828); Robert MacMicking, *Recollections of Manila and the Philippines, during 1848, 1849, and 1850* (London: Richard Bentley, 1851); Feodor Jagor, *Travels in the Philippines* (Manila: Filipiniana Book Guild, 1965); Frederick Sawyer, *The Inhabitants of the Philippines* (London: Sampson, Low, Marston and Co, 1900). John Foreman, *The Philippine Islands,* 2nd ed. (New York: Scribner's, 1899), widely used, is captious in tone, credulous toward rumor, and misinformed about many historical matters. It is valuable, however, for first-hand observations. Much of the nineteenth century literature is appearing in modern editions in the Filipiniana Book Guild Series.

11. Sinibaldo de Mas, *Informe Secreto* [*Report on the Conditions of the Philippines in 1842*], Carlos Botor and Alfonso Felix, Jr., trans. (Manila: Historical Conservation Society, 1963), also in Blair and Robertson, *The Philippine Islands*, LII, 29–90; Juan Manuel de la Matta, "Communication from the Intendant of the army and treasury of the Filipinas Islands . . . in regard to the moral condition of the country . . . ," in Blair and Robertson, *The Philippine Islands*, LII, 91–111.

class by themselves are the works of the highly hispanized Filipino nationalists José Rizal and Trinidad H. Pardo de Tavera. One may wish to argue with the traditional Filipino estimate of Rizal's literary achievement, but his novels *Noli me tángere* and *El filibusterismo* are social documents of the first importance.[12] Pardo de Tavera, a distinguished bibliographer, a landowner and physician, an advocate of modernization, and the leader of the pro-annexationist Federal Party in the first years of American rule, gave a learned synthesis of his country's history from the viewpoint of one who had lived through the final years of the nineteenth century in his *Reseña histórica*.[13]

The Philippine Revolution concerns us here only insofar as it touches upon Philippine-American relations.[14] There has been a tendency since the Huk uprisings of the late 1940's and early 1950's to de-emphasize traditional explanations of the revolution as the product of the frustrations of reform-minded patricians in the so-called propaganda movement, and to emphasize the element of class struggle and racial assertion that obviously played a role. Teodoro A. Agoncillo gave a melodramatic but impressive example of the class interpretation in his *Revolt of the Masses: The Story of Bonifacio and the Katipunan*. In a second book, *Malolos: Crisis of the Republic*, he took the same attitude toward the Philippine Republic and its war against the United States. Agoncillo's account has striking similarities to the Beard and Becker views of the American Revolution: upper class reformers losing control to true revolutionaries con-

12. José Rizal, *Noli me Tángere*, III, *Escritos de José Rizal*, (Quezon City: Martinez, 1958), and *El filibusterismo*, II, *Escritos de José Rizal* (Quezon City: Martinez, 1958). There are English translations by Charles Derbyshire, published as *The Social Cancer* and *The Reign of Greed* (Manila: Philippine Education Co., 1912); and by León Ma. Guerrero, entitled *The Lost Eden* (Bloomington: University of Indiana Press, 1961) and *The Subversive* (Bloomington: University of Indiana Press, 1962). See also Rizal, *The Philippines a Century Hence*, Charles Derbyshire, trans. (Manila: Philippine Education Co., 1912) and *Rizal's Political Writings*, Austin Craig, ed. (Manila: Oriental Commercial Co., 1933).

13. An English version appears in *Census of the Philippine Islands, 1903*, I, 309–388.

14. The classic accounts of the revolution are Leandro H. Fernandez, *The Philippine Republic* (New York: Columbia University Press, 1926), and Teodoro M. Kalaw, *The Philippine Revolution* (Manila: Manila Book Co., 1925). Carlos Quirino elegantly summarized the contribution of *ilustrado* publicists and reformers in "Propaganda and Revolution, 1870–1899," in *Philippine Perspective*, sess. 1, part 2, lecture 7, and recently treated the principal military figure in *The Young Aguinaldo: From Kawit to Biyak-na-bato* (Manila: Bookmark, 1969). See also John N. Schumacher, "The Filipino Nationalists' Propaganda Campaign in Europe, 1880–1895" (Ph.D. diss., Georgetown University, 1965); and Maximo M. Kalaw, *The Development of Philippine Politics, 1872–1920* (Manila: Oriental Commercial Co., 1926).

cerned not only with metropolitan relations and power distribution within the establishment but also with basic social and economic reform; a counterattack by conservatives, hoping to make the new government their own; and, in the Philippine case, the eventual desertion of the upper class conservative reformers to the Americans once the latter had demonstrated their military power and their willingness to recognize and protect basic civil liberties.[15] Contemporaneously with Agoncillo, Cesar Adib Majul has been exploring the intellectual history of the revolution in a series of books.[16] Majul's studies demonstrate the familiarity of Filipino revolutionary leaders with Western political thought, and in doing so suggest not only that the intellectual foundations of the revolution should be taken seriously (they have not always been) but also that they may explain many ideas to which Filipinos recurred after years of American tutelage.

In 1899, after collaborating with Filipino revolutionaries during the previous year to end Spanish rule, the United States acquired sovereignty over the Philippines.[17] Coincident with the institution

15. Teodoro A. Agoncillo, *Revolt of the Masses: The Story of Bonifacio and the Katipunan* (Quezon City: University of the Philippines, 1956), and *Malolos: Crisis of the Republic* (Quezon City: University of the Philippines, 1960).

16. Cesar Adib Majul, *The Political and Constitutional Ideas of the Philippine Revolution* (Quezon City: University of the Philippines, 1957), and *Mabini and the Philippine Revolution* (Quezon City: University of the Philippines, 1960). See also his *A Critique of Rizal's Concept of a Filipino Nation* (Diliman [Detroit: dist. Cellar Book Shop, 1959]), and his article "The Historical Background of Philippine Nationalism," *Asia*, 9 (Fall 1967), 51–66.

17. American imperialism, defined in terms of the motivation and expectations of those who advocated a "large" policy in the 1890's or were concerned specifically with the decision to annex the Philippines, is a topic in itself, and the literature on the subject is immense. On the phenomenon of territorial acquisition and the motivation for it, see in particular Ernest R. May, *Imperial Democracy: The Emergence of America as a Great Power* (New York: Harcourt, Brace & World, 1961), and *American Imperialism: A Speculative Essay* (New York: Atheneum, 1968); Julius W. Pratt, *Expansionists of 1898* (Baltimore: The Johns Hopkins Press, 1936); David Healy, *U.S. Expansionism: The Imperialist Urge in the 1890s* (Madison: University of Wisconsin Press, 1970); Richard Hofstadter, "Manifest Destiny and the Philippines," in Daniel Aaron, ed., *America in Crisis* (New York: Alfred A. Knopf, 1952); Walter LaFeber, *The New Empire: An Interpretation of American Expansion, 1860–1898* (Ithaca: Cornell University Press, 1963); Thomas McCormick, "Insular Imperialism and the Open Door: The China Market and the Spanish-American War," *Pacific Historical Review*, 32 (May 1963), 155–169; Howard K. Beale, *Theodore Roosevelt and the Rise of America to World Power* (Baltimore: The Johns Hopkins Press, 1956); Frederick Merk, *Manifest Destiny and Mission in American History* (New York: Alfred A. Knopf, 1963); and William Appleman Williams, *The Tragedy of American Diplomacy* (Cleveland: World Publishing Co., 1959). For treatments of anti-imperialism, see Robert L. Beisner, *Twelve Against Empire: The Anti-Imperialists, 1898–1900* (New York: McGraw-

of American government in the islands there is a marked change in the character and the amount of source materials available for the study of American-Philippine relations. Whereas prior to 1898 students are dependent upon scattered business records, diaries, travel accounts, erratic Spanish statistics and reports, and inferential conclusions drawn from frequently contradictory sources having to do with domestic Philippine history, after that date materials concerned specifically with the topic at hand abound.[18] Incomparably the richest source of primary materials on the topic for the years up to the mid-1930's is the files of the Bureau of Insular Affairs in the National Archives in Washington.[19] Almost all contact between the governments in Manila and Washington took place through the bureau, which collected and catalogued originals or copies. It also kept files on legislative developments and on many other aspects of Philippine government, economy, and society; and biographical files on official and unofficial persons prominent in Philippine affairs. Staff members have left scattered through its files informative and sometimes startlingly frank and revealing memoranda of their views

Hill, 1968); E. Berkeley Tompkins, *Anti-Imperialism in the United States: The Great Debate, 1890–1920* (Philadelphia: University of Pennsylvania Press, 1970); Fred H. Harrington, "The Anti-Imperialist Movement in the United States, 1898–1900," *Mississippi Valley Historical Review,* 22 (1935), 211–230; Christopher Lasch, "Anti-Imperialists, the Philippines, and the Inequality of Man," *Journal of Southern History,* 24 (1958), 319–331; John W. Rollins, "The Anti-Imperialists and Twentieth Century American Foreign Policy," *Studies on the Left,* 3 (1962), 9–24; E. Berkeley Tompkins, "Scylla and Charybdis: the Anti-Imperialist Dilemma in the Election of 1900," *Pacific Historical Review,* 36 (1967), 143–61; William George Whittaker, "Samuel Gompers, Anti-Imperialist," *Pacific Historical Review,* 38 (1969), 429–445; and Ronald Radosh and Horace B. Davies, "American Labor and the Anti-Imperialist Movement: A Discussion," *Science and Society,* 28 (Winter 1964), 91–104.

18. Among published official sources, the most useful are the annual reports of the Philippine Commission (1900–1916), the governor-general of the Philippine Islands (1917–1935), and the high commissioner to the Philippine Commonwealth (1936–42, 1946). Apart from these, Philippine-American relations figure occasionally in a host of government reports and documents, including the *Congressional Record;* the *Annual Report of the Chief of Staff, United States Army; Foreign Relations of the United States* (particularly the supplement *Japan, 1931–1941*); and reports of the United States Tariff Commission. Statistical information is available in the *Census of the Philippine Islands* taken in 1903, 1918, and 1939, and in the *Statistical Bulletin of the Philippine Islands* issued by the Bureau of Commerce and Industry, Manila. A wide spectrum of official and unofficial opinion on governmental, economic, and cultural aspects of the relationship may be found in the annual reports of the Lake Mohonk Conference on the Indian and Other Dependent Peoples.

19. Guides to the holdings are Richard S. Maxwell, *Records of the Bureau of Insular Affairs* (Washington: The National Archives, Preliminary Inventories, no. 130, 1960), and Kenneth Munden, *Records of the Bureau of Insular Affairs Relating to the Philippine Islands, 1898–1935: A List of Selected Files* (Washington: The National Archives, October 1942).

and those of leading figures in the making of Philippine policy. All these holdings are cross-referenced and, generally, abstracted in a card file. Whether the BIA was a policy-making body or primarily only an organ of coordination and communication is a question that has never been systematically studied; evidence from its files suggests that at least during the Wilson years, when no high official in the government had personal knowledge of the Philippines, the bureau conceived of itself as a source of initiative and exercised a considerable influence in Congress and the Cabinet. Beginning in 1935, the most important materials concerning American-Philippine relations are to be found in the files of the U.S. High Commissioner.[20]

Important collections of personal papers in the United States include those of William Howard Taft, Francis Burton Harrison, Woodrow Wilson, Leonard Wood, Elihu Root, Theodore Roosevelt, Francis B. Sayre, and Theodore Roosevelt, Jr., at the Library of Congress; Dean C. Worcester, Frank Murphy, and Joseph Ralston Hayden in the Harlan Hatcher Library and the Michigan Historical Collections, University of Michigan;[21] James A. LeRoy at Duke and the University of Michigan; Franklin D. Roosevelt at Hyde Park; Henry L. Stimson at Yale; Clarence R. Edwards at the Massachusetts Historical Society, Boston; Bernard Moses and David Barrows at the University of California, Berkeley; and James F. Smith at the Washington State Historical Society and Museum, Tacoma. W. Cameron Forbes, who was secretary of commerce and police in the insular government from 1904 to 1909, and governor-general from 1909 to 1913, kept a colorful and revealing journal, which he subsequently annotated; copies are deposited in the Library of Congress and in the Houghton Library at Harvard University. Forbes also accumulated voluminous quantities of newspaper clippings from the Spanish, English, and Tagalog press of Manila, and personal and official correspondence and reports. Much of this, too, he later annotated. This material, one of the great sources for the study of official aims and achievements up to 1913, of the excursions and alarums of retentionists out of power from 1913 to 1921, and of the background and progress of the Wood–Forbes Mission to the islands in 1921 is also deposited in the Houghton Library.

Galley proofs for John R. M. Taylor's monumental unpublished

20. Richard Maxwell, *Records of the Office of the U.S. High Commissioner to the Philippine Islands* (Washington: The National Archives, Preliminary Inventories, no. 151, 1963).

21. For a detailed description of the unusually rich Philippine collections at Michigan, see "Balita mula Maynila," *Michigan Historical Collections Bulletin* No. 19 (February 1971).

work, "The Philippine Insurrection against the United States," are available at the Library of Congress and the University of Michigan.

Many of the most important sources located in the Philippines were lost during World War II, most notably many of the personal papers of Sergio Osmeña and the official records housed in the former Legislative Building or in the executive offices in Malacañan Palace. The papers of Manuel Quezon survived, however, and are now kept in the National Library in Manila. (Fifty-four reels of microfilms from the Quezon Papers are now available for viewing at the Michigan Historical Collections.) The collection is large and fascinating, containing personal and official correspondence, cables, and drafts of speeches and legislation. From it there emerges a compelling picture of a dramatic personality and brilliant tactician confronting almost every aspect of his country's political and economic life. Students of the independence movement may profitably compare what Quezon told Filipinos with what the BIA files show him telling certain Americans. Unless currently unknown materials are someday made public, Quezon's exchanges with Osmeña and the documents from Osmeña's presidency which have been added to the collection will remain our principal source for understanding that enigmatic, but appealing figure. Papers of Manuel Roxas from the years 1937 to 1948 are also in the National Library, and the papers of José P. Laurel are at the Lyceum of the Philippines.

For many years, the study of relations between the United States and the Philippines in the period after 1898 was dominated by books written by participants in those relations. Their accounts are revealing if read comparatively. Chronologically the first of these books, in terms of subject matter, are James A. LeRoy's *The Americans in the Philippines* and Daniel R. Williams' *The Odyssey of the Philippine Commission*.[22] LeRoy and Williams went to the Philippines as secretaries to members of the original Taft Commission. Both developed a repertory of feelings and ideas common in the higher echelons of what was then termed the Civil Government: shock, tending in time toward irritation, over the backwardness of Philippine life; certitude that, owing both to their alternately childish and dangerous characteristics and also to the perverse and demoralizing effects of Spanish rule, Filipinos could not successfully govern themselves; confidence, therefore, that America's acquisition of the islands was honorable, and her retention of them at least potentially

22. James A. LeRoy, *The Americans in the Philippines*, 2 vols. (Boston: Houghton Mifflin, 1914); Daniel Roderick Williams, *The Odyssey of the Philippine Commission* (Chicago: A. C. McClurg, 1913).

beneficial; frustration that uncomprehending and intractable army officers were alienating Filipinos through continuing an iron-fisted policy after it had ceased to be necessary; and determination, instead, to "attract" the natural leaders of the people—Agoncillo's conservative reformers—to cooperate with civilian American authorities in pacifying the country and beginning its modernization. Their books, however, are very different; and each illuminates the other. LeRoy, afflicted with terminal tuberculosis and believing that his having been passed over for higher position signaled a change in policy, returned to the United States, accumulated all the books and official documents he could lay hands on, and, having ensconced himself in the American consulship at Durango, Mexico, devoted the last years of his life to proving through a massive and rigorous book that he and his country had wrought well. Williams stayed in the Philippines and went into practice as a lawyer, specializing in business and land cases. He, too, kept the faith; and in 1913, fearing Wilson would release the islands, he published the letters he had written to his family in America while serving with the Commission. Immediate and emotional, choked at times with pride in his country and its men, they show something LeRoy's documents omit about the spirit of the endeavor.

One year earlier, James H. Blount, a former army officer and judge in the Philippines, whose resignation from the insular judiciary had been involuntary, had published *The American Occupation of the Philippines, 1898–1912*.[23] Blount's loyalty was to the United States Army, and he resented both the Taft Commission's displacement of the military government and also its pretension to be able to win by a policy of attraction a people whom the army had been unable fully to break by a policy of coercion. The deprecatory view of Filipinos' capacities in vogue in the Civil Government seemed to him to imply deprecation as well of the American army that had so bitterly fought them. Blount wrote his book with the encouragement and financial backing of the Philippine resident commissioner at the time, Manuel Quezon; but it is not, properly speaking, anti-imperialist in sentiment. He argued for the courage and capability of the Filipinos and imputed ignorance, expediency, and in some cases bad faith to leaders of the Civil Government. But he also celebrated the campaigns of American soldiers, and the corollaries to his defense of Filipinos' capability and determination to be independent, were prolonged military control of the islands and more rigorous impressment of America's will

23. New York: Putnam's, 1912.

upon the people. In his opinion, the fundamental error of granting civil government too soon had prevented Americans from establishing their control. Filipinos, far from being coopted by Taft, had recognized him for a soft mark and shifted their energies from armed resistance to penetration and subversion of the new government. Wherefore Blount was led to the all-or-nothing position that having failed to persevere to a definitive triumph over Filipino revolutionaries, the United States ought to end the farce and let them take open responsibility for their government. Blount is only the most obvious of a number of former combatants, Filipino as well as American, who acquired for one or another reason considerable respect for their enemies. One of the minor curiosities of Philippine history for at least two decades after the so-called insurrection is the occasional appearance of such men, former enemies currently committed to conflicting views of the future, in alliances to achieve specific goals. The Noriel case and the Philippine National Guard episode are cases in point.

Blount was pointedly answered in 1914 by Dean C. Worcester, a member of both the Schurman and Taft commissions and insular secretary of the interior from 1901 to 1913. Worcester, a truculent man who had unnecessarily alienated countless Americans and Filipinos by his brusk personality and tendency to overkill, was granted the use of official files by Governor-General Forbes in the hope that this, when combined with Worcester's extensive personal knowledge of the islands and their people, would lead to a definitive work in the defense of the American record. *The Philippines Past and Present*[24] turned out, however, to be a rambling and polemical work. Worcester knew as much as any American about the goals and achievements of the insular government in health, sanitation, science, and the treatment of the non-Christian minority of Filipinos; and there is justifiable pride in his highly personal, lavishly colorful account of this work. Like many other Americans concerned with developmental or humanitarian tasks, he bitterly resented the agitation of nationalistic politicians. But in Worcester, as in a few others, there is an additional dimension, something close to contempt for the majority of Filipinos and especially those who were articulate and politically conscious. In his book he amassed almost every conceivable argument against Filipino capacity and character and concluded that the Filipino was incapable of responsible government and possibly might always be. Indefinitely prolonged American tutelage would be necessary to save the people from themselves.

24. 2 vols., New York: Macmillan, 1914.

A different view of the same period may be gleaned from two volumes by one of Worcester's colleagues, Charles B. Elliott.[25] A former justice of the Philippine Supreme Court and briefly secretary of commerce and police, Elliott had been unceremoniously fired after intriguing against Governor-General Forbes. His books have a kind of judicial thoroughness, but the second is embarrassingly self-defensive and suffers from ambivalence of tone in combining charges that Forbes' government was autocratic and that ambitious Filipinos were too much humored by it. Elliott's conflicts with Forbes reveal worlds about the tensions built into relations between the executive and the legislature by the structure of the Philippine Commission.

From 1913 to 1921, Governor-General Francis Burton Harrison labored with a Wilsonian combination of elegance, zeal, and pettiness to prepare the Philippines for early independence and to secure it. In 1922 he published *The Corner-stone of Philippine Independence: A Narrative of Seven Years*.[26] Even Filipino nationalists sometimes felt that Harrison's devotion to their country's cause was naive. In December 1913, after attending Harrison's inauguration and observing his immediate steps to clean out many high-ranking American officials and speedily filipinize the government, Quezon hurried back to Washington and expostulated to the chief of the Bureau of Insular Affairs: "My God . . . I think he believes in independence. He thinks he can turn us loose in about four years. He believes in it."[27] In the end, his achievement was difficult to assess. By forcing the issue, he succeeded in committing Americans and Filipinos alike to early independence; in the short run, however, his pace may have been too brisk. He left behind a government mired in a major financial crisis and plagued with inefficiency, graft, and nepotism. His book, more frankly personal and less pretentious than those of most participants, captures something of his vision, defends his achievements, and occasionally betrays his almost paranoid sensitivity to opposition. It should be read alongside Daniel R. Williams' *The United States and the Philippines,* written during the ensuing Wood administration, which is sharply critical of the Harrison period; Maximo M. Kalaw's *Self-Government in the Philippines,* a Filipino contemporary's defense of Filipinos'

25. *The Philippines to the End of the Military Regime* (Indianapolis: Bobbs-Merrill, 1916), and *The Philippines to the End of the Commission Government* (Indianapolis: Bobbs-Merrill, 1917).

26. New York: Century, 1922.

27. General Frank McIntyre, memorandum, 29 December 1913, Bureau of Insular Affairs 4325–158.

achievements under Harrison; and Rafael Palma's "Our Campaign for Independence from Taft to Harrison."[28]

In 1919, towards the end of Harrison's New Era in the Philippines, Cameron Forbes began to sift his enormous holdings of Philippine materials and think about the future of the islands if, as he hoped, Republicans captured the presidency the following year. A bachelor who had ruined his health in the islands and felt that his service there had been his "life's work," he had been deeply stung by overt or implied criticisms of his administration during his successor's term, and he wanted to set the record straight. He went on sifting and annotating for several years, during which time he revisited the Philippines as part of the Wood–Forbes Mission, and then called his former executive secretary in the islands to his side and set out to write the book Worcester had failed to write in 1913. The resulting work, *The Philippine Islands*,[29] while by no means free from bias, especially in its chapters on Harrison and the independence movement, accurately reflects in its excellent, detailed coverage of the promotion of infrastructure, good health, widespread education, and efficient government the developmental and professedly apolitical emphasis of its author's service in the insular government. It also conveys his love both of the islands and, in a paternalistic way, of the people. In 1944, a condensed version was published at the request of Forbes' old friend President Osmeña, who considered it a prime source of knowledge about the Philippines for Americans.

The most ambitious of the participants' books, and by far the most scholarly, is Joseph Ralston Hayden's classic, *The Philippines: A Study in National Development*.[30] Hayden, a professor of political science at the University of Michigan, served as vice-governor from 1933 to 1935, during the controversies over the Hare–Hawes–Cutting and Tydings–McDuffie acts, the last great showdown between Quezon and Osmeña, and the preparations for inaugurating the Philippine Commonwealth. He was the foremost student of the modern Philippines of his day, a judicious heir to the developmental emphasis found in Worcester and Forbes;[31] and his thoughtful,

28. Daniel R. Williams, *The United States and the Philippines* (Garden City, N.Y.: Doubleday, Page and Company, 1924); Maximo M. Kalaw, *Self-Government in the Philippines* (New York: Century, 1919); Rafael Palma, "Our Campaign for Independence from Taft to Harrison" (Manila: Bureau of Printing, 1928).

29. W. Cameron Forbes, *The Philippine Islands*, 2 vols. (Boston: Houghton Mifflin, 1928).

30. New York: Macmillan, 1942.

31. In 1930 he brought out a new edition of Worcester's *The Philippines*

superbly documented book is of special value both as a description of political development under the Americans and an evaluation and analysis of it.

In addition to Palma and Kalaw, two prominent Filipino participants have left memoirs. Teodoro M. Kalaw's *Aide-de-Camp to Freedom*,[32] while self-serving and imprecise, suggests the tone and motivation behind Filipino encounters with Americans as seen by a sometime cabinet officer and intellectual adviser to Osmeña. Manuel Quezon's *The Good Fight*[33] was written in the United States during World War II, when the author was deprived of access to his papers, and was published posthumously by his friend W. Morgan Shuster. It is of little use for specifics or details but does capture the author's dramatic flair and is disarmingly frank in spots.

With one exception, this participants' literature dominated the study of Philippine-American relations until after World War II.[34] The exception was Grayson L. Kirk's *Philippine Independence: Motives, Problems, and Prospects*,[35] which Quezon in a personal letter to Kirk called the best work yet published on the subject. Writing between the passage of the Tydings–McDuffie Act and the inauguration of the Commonwealth, Kirk asserted that independence was coming at the wrong time, for wrong reasons, and in a wrong way. In his view, the United States had not fulfilled the tutelary responsibility it had voluntarily assumed towards Filipinos, but had, by means of free trade, distorted the islands' economic growth and created a dependent economy. Having ignored independence demands for three decades, it had granted them in the early thirties because "American dairy interests, cottonseed oil interests, cane and beet sugar growers, organized labor, the Cuban sugar interests, the cordage manufacturers, the patriotic societies, and the senators and congressmen who were aligned with these groups,"[36] frightened by the depression, had sought protection against Philip-

Past and Present (New York: Macmillan) with a warm biographical sketch of its author, four new chapters, and numerous annotations.

32. Maria Kalaw Katigbak, trans. (Manila: Teodoro M. Kalaw Society, 1965).

33. New York: D. Appleton-Century, 1946.

34. American anti-imperialist literature was never a major factor. It may be sampled at its best in Moorfield Storey and Marcial P. Lichauco, *The Conquest of the Philippines by the United States, 1898–1925* (New York: Putnam, 1926); Henry Parker Willis, *Our Philippine Problem: A Study of American Colonial Policy* (New York: H. Holt and Co., 1905); and Charles Edward Russell, *The Outlook for the Philippines* (New York: Century, 1922). The first and last of these were subsidized by Filipino officials.

35. New York: Farrar & Rinehart, 1936.

36. Ibid., p. 100.

pine imports. Independence legislation establishing for the Commonwealth period import quotas below the level of existing Philippine imports to the United States and applying the full U.S. tariff after independence, seemed to Kirk a selfish and ruinous blow to an economy weakened by our own past actions. His solution was reciprocal free trade and, if Filipinos would accept it, establishment of a permanent "semi-protectorate" to guard them against Japan.

Kirk's volume was a turning point in the literature concerning American-Philippine relations. The participants' accounts had been for the most part massive, omnibus treatises of a character that, despite some pettiness and invidiousness, approached the magisterial. Together, they marked out a body of themes that seemed for many years to be inclusive. Among these perhaps the most pregnant have been the following: the character of the revolutionary government—whether it was broadly based, representative in its institutions or aspirations, capable of maintaining stable government over a period of time; the ethics of America's legal acquisition and military conquest of the islands; the wisdom and intent of the policy of attraction and the early establishment of civil government with Filipino participation; the legitimacy of the avowedly nationalistic leaders like Osmeña, Quezon, Palma, and DeVeyra, who began to appear as national figures as early as 1906—the number and nature of their ideological constituents, whether these visible leaders followed or led public opinion, indeed, whether there was any meaningful public opinion and whether the leaders meant what they said; the relationship of economic development and social modernization to independence—whether the former took priority over the latter, whether one could have both, whether pursuit of either was likely to result in compromising the other; the American tutors' responsibilities, if any, to reform a social order dominated by *caciques,* to protect or reconcile the non-Christian minorities, and to spread education and opportunity; the commercial and strategic value of the Philippines to the United States and vice versa—who profited from the association and how much this affected policy; the motives, tactics, and good faith (or lack of it) of American political leaders. Much of the postwar literature, by contrast, has been monographic and has confined itself to amplifying or revising these themes and their several corollaries.[37]

37. All along, of course, there has been a growing body of biographies treating the various participants. For Elihu Root, see Philip C. Jessup, *Elihu Root,* 2 vols. (New York: Dodd, Mead, 1938), and Richard Leopold, *Elihu Root and the Conservative Tradition* (Boston: Little, Brown and Co., 1954); for Lodge, see John A. Garraty, *Henry Cabot Lodge* (New York: Alfred A. Knopf, 1953); for Leonard Wood, see Herman Hagedorn, *Leonard Wood: A Biography,* 2 vols.

Garel A. Grunder and William E. Livezey provided a starting point for postwar scholarship in *The Philippines and the United States*, a summary of political and legislative history that contains a useful list of U.S. government publications from 1898 to 1951; they were, however, shallow in their treatment of events in the islands.[38] Suppression of the insurrection has come under new scrutiny in the aftermath of the Huk uprisings in the Philippines and the growing involvement of the United States in Vietnam during the 1960's.[39] The most provocative, though not the most

---

(New York: Harper & Brothers, 1931); for Stimson, see Elting E. Morison, *Turmoil and Tradition: A Study of the Life and Times of Henry L. Stimson* (Boston: Houghton Mifflin Co., 1960); for Wilson, see the multivolume work by Arthur S. Link, still in progress. Henry F. Pringle's *The Life and Times of William Howard Taft*, 2 vols. (New York: Farrar & Rinehart, 1939), should be supplemented by Oscar M. Alfonso, "Taft's Early Views on the Filipinos," *Solidarity*, 4 (June 1969), 52–58. The most illuminating exposure of Theodore Roosevelt's views remains Howard K. Beale, *Theodore Roosevelt and the Rise of America to World Power* (Baltimore: The Johns Hopkins Press, 1956), but this should be supplemented by *The Letters of Theodore Roosevelt*, Elting E. Morison and John M. Blum, eds., 8 vols. (Cambridge, Mass.: Harvard University Press, 1951–1954), by Forbes' "Recollections of Theodore Roosevelt" in series 2 of the Forbes Journal, and by Oscar M. Alfonso, *Theodore Roosevelt and the Philippines, 1897–1909* (Quezon City: University of the Philippines Press, 1970). Douglas MacArthur is the subject of John Gunther, *The Riddle of MacArthur: Japan, Korea, and the Far East* (New York: Harper & Brothers, 1950); Frazier Hunt, *The Untold Story of Douglas MacArthur* (New York: Deven-Adair, 1954); D. Clayton James, *The Years of MacArthur*, I, *1880–1941* (Boston: Houghton Mifflin Co., 1970). On the Filipino side, a great deal remains to be done. Manuel Quezon is treated in Carlos Quirino, *Quezon, Paladin of Philippine Freedom*, (Manila: Filipiniana Book Guild, 1971) and also in a sketch I have written for the forthcoming *Dictionary of American Biography*, supp. 3, as well as in Sol H. Gwekoh, *Manuel L. Quezon: His Life and Career* (Manila: University Publishing Co., 1948); and Isabello P. Caballero and M. de Gracia Concepcion, *Quezon* (Manila: International Publishers, 1935). For Manuel Roxas, see Marcial P. Lichauco, *Roxas* (Manila: n.p., 1952). There is no biography of Sergio Osmeña, although Vicente Pacis is currently at work on one. Renato Constantino in *The Making of a Filipino: A Story of Philippine Colonial Politics* (Quezon City: University of the Philippines, 1969), has studied the career of Claro M. Recto and drawn from it the lesson that one is not truly Filipino until freed from the colonial mentality.

38. Norman: University of Oklahoma Press, 1951. For other early surveys, see Julius W. Pratt, *America's Colonial Experiment* (New York: Prentice-Hall, 1950); Whitney T. Perkins, *Denial of Empire: The United States and its Dependencies* (Leyden: A. W. Sythoff, 1962); and David Bernstein, *The Philippine Story* (New York: Farrar, Straus and Co., 1947).

39. John Gates, "An Experiment in Benevolent Pacification: The U.S. Army in the Philippines, 1898–1902" (Ph.D. diss., Duke University, 1967); Leon Wolff, *Little Brown Brother* (Garden City, N.Y.: Doubleday & Co., 1960); Kenneth E. Hendrickson, Jr., "Reluctant Expansionist—Jacob Gould Schurman and the Philippine Question," *Pacific Historical Review*, 36 (November 1967), 405–421, Ralph Eldin Minger, "Taft, MacArthur, and the Establishment of Civil Government in the Philippines," *The Ohio Historical Quarterly*, 70 (1961), 308–331.

scholarly, of these examinations was provided by an American who fought with the Huks, William J. Pomeroy. His "Pacification in the Philippines, 1898–1913" is a tale of American duplicity, brutality, stupidity, and racism, well and earnestly told, but marred throughout by omissions of inconvenient facts.[40] The Taft era, so-called, has been probed by Bonifacio Salamanca in *The Filipino Reaction to American Rule, 1901–1913,* which ironically is based on American sources.[41] Salamanca returned to the question whether Filipino leaders had been coopted by Taft's policy of attraction and concluded that in fact the conservative Filipino elite, by making itself indispensable to Taft, was able to control aspects of American policy and stultify hopes for many types of modernization and social change. There is more than a hint in this of parallels to the condition Phelan describes in the sixteenth and seventeenth centuries. Roy W. Curry's *Woodrow Wilson and Far Eastern Policy, 1913–1921* has a sensible, detailed chapter on Philippine policy, showing than American officialdom was aware of Quezon's private desire to postpone, rather than hasten independence.[42] Traditional interpretations of Leonard Wood, picturing him as an intractable, reactionary figure who needlessly embittered Philippine-American relations while presiding over the adjustments of the 1920's, have been sharply challenged by Michael P. Onorato;[43] but the implications of Wood's economic and racial views have not been thoroughly examined and a wholly plausible alternative interpretation has not yet been offered. J. Woodford Howard, Jr., portrayed Frank Murphy as an American who brought to the islands the perspective of an Irish-American Progressive, championing economic development, social reform, and early independence.[44] Gerald Wheeler, improving upon the implications of Kirk's argument, explored suggestively but inconclusively the willingness of some Filipino and American leaders to abort independence in the late 1930's.[45] Apart from

40. *France Asie/Asia,* 21 (1967), 427–446.

41. Norwich, Connecticut: The Shoe String Press, 1968.

42. New York: Bookman Associates, 1957. For the surface contours of Quezon's independence campaign in these years, see John A. Beadles, "The Debate in the United States Concerning Philippine Independence, 1912–1916," *Philippine Studies,* 16 (1968), 421–441.

43. Michael P. Onorato, *A Brief Review of American Interest in Philippine Development and Other Essays* (Berkeley: McCutchan Publishing Corp., 1968).

44. J. Woodford Howard, Jr., "Frank Murphy and the Philippine Commonwealth," *Pacific Historical Review,* 33 (1964), 45–68.

45. Gerald Wheeler, "The Movement to Reverse Philippine Independence," *Pacific Historical Review,* 33 (1964), 167–181.

these essentially political studies, there is a host of monographs on special topics.[46]

With the passage of time, new interpretive syntheses have begun to appear.[47] The authors of the first two, G. I. Levinson and Georges Fischer, were agreed that the United States had made the Philippines economically and culturally dependent, thereby frustrating modernization and reform even in the years after the achievement of political independence.[48] Levinson, a rigid Marxist and a xenophobic Russian, attributed this to a malevolent design to make the Philippines part of America's apparatus for fighting capitalist rivals

46. On the emergence of a Philippine bureaucracy, see Onofre D. Corpuz, *The Bureaucracy in the Philippines* (Quezon City: University of the Philippines Institute of Public Administration, Studies in Public Administration, no. 4, 1957). For studies of the evolution of economic policy toward the Philippines, see Pedro E. Abelarde, *American Tariff Policy towards the Philippines, 1898–1946* (New York: King's Crown Press, 1947); Amado A. Castro, "The Philippines: A Study in Economic Dependence" (Ph.D. diss., Harvard University, 1954); José S. Reyes, *Legislative History of American Economic Policy toward the Philippines* (New York: Columbia University Press, 1923). The American influence upon Philippine education is treated at length in Hayden, *The Philippines;* and in Carl H. Landé, "The Philippines," *Education and Political Development*, James S. Coleman, ed. (Princeton: Princeton University Press, 1965); Encarnacion Alzona, *A History of Education in the Philippines* (Manila: University of the Philippines Press, 1932); and Manuel G. Lacuesta, "Foundations of an American Educational System in the Philippines," *Philippine Social Science and Humanities Review*, 23 (June–December 1958): 115–140. Various aspects of church–state relations under the United States are discussed in Gerald Anderson, ed., *Studies in Philippine Church History* (Ithaca: Cornell University Press, 1969); and Frank T. Reuter, *Catholic Influence on American Colonial Policies, 1898–1904* (Austin: University of Texas Press, 1967). Immigration policy is the subject of Bruno Lasker, *Filipino Immigration to the Continental United States and to Hawaii* (Chicago: University of Chicago Press, 1931), and of Josefa M. Saniel, ed., *The Filipino Exclusion Movement, 1927–1935* (Quezon City: University of the Philippines, Institute of Asian Studies, 1967). The government of the Moros is treated in Peter Gordon Gowing, "Mandate in Moroland: The American Government of Muslim Filipinos, 1899–1920" (Ph.D. diss., Syracuse University, 1968). World War II in its Philippine aspect is the subject of three volumes in the series *The United States Army in World War II: The War in the Pacific:* Louis Morton, *The Fall of the Philippines* (Washington: Department of the Army, 1953); M. Hamlin Cannon, *Leyte: The Return to the Philippines* (Washington: Department of the Army, 1954); and Robert Ross Smith, *Triumph in the Philippines* (Washington: Department of the Army, 1963).

47. For a brief but scintillating treatment, see Theodore Friend, "Goodbye, Mother America: An Overview of Philippine-American Relations, 1899–1969," *Asia*, no. 15 (Summer 1969), 1–12. See also the Rōyama and Takéuchi work, edited by Friend, cited in footnote 53.

48. G. I. Levinson, *Filippiny Mezhdu Pervoy i Vtoroy Mirovymi Voynami* (Moscow: Izdatel'stvo Vostochnoy Literatury Akademii Nauk USSR, 1958); Georges Fischer, *Un Cas de décolonisation: Les États-Unis et les Philippines* (Paris: Pichon & Durand-Auzias, 1960). Both have been reviewed by Theodore Friend in *Journal of Asian Studies*, 22 (1962), 89–94.

and destroying the Soviet Union. Fischer, by contrast, saw it as an anachronistic survival of patterns incompatible with the postwar interests of the United States. During the sixties, these European studies were supplemented by American works. George E. Taylor gave a sympathetic account of American-Philippine relations before and after independence, arguing that the United States had largely fulfilled the goals of the Philippine revolution.[49] In *American Neo-Colonialism,* on the other hand, William J. Pomeroy portrayed America's conduct toward the Philippines as cynical and exploitive.[50] Having destroyed an agrarian revolution so that powerful economic interests might possess themselves of Philippine resources and strengthen their position in the China market, Pomeroy argued, American leaders had second thoughts and backed away from accepting the responsibilities attendant upon the sovereignty they had usurped. Instead, the danger of conflict with Japan, the powerful opposition of racists and various domestic economic interests to full incorporation of the Philippines into the American polity and economy, and the reluctance of investors to involve themselves in Asia led to a tactical adjustment. Cuba, a model often invoked by "anti-imperialists," showed the way. By imposing a "stable" (that is, nonrevolutionary) social order on the Philippines, exacting preferential trade agreements, and reserving the use of military and naval facilities in the islands, the United States was able to grant Filipinos formal independence and rid itself of the cost and risk of sovereignty while retaining all the advantages of imperial domination. The Philippine experience, Pomeroy concluded, prefigured America's mid-century wars of "aggression" in Korea and Vietnam, its suppression of national liberation movements throughout Asia, and its economic colonization of the third world. My own view, argued in a recent dissertation,[51] has been that economic interests were only one of a variety of forces behind acquisition and retention of the Philippines, but that retentionists in office, finding themselves with weak political support in the United States, seized upon economic development and social reform as a program that would both justify retention and also, if properly carried out, dispose Filipinos to maintain their links with the United States. In adopting this approach, Americans responded to two of the central

49. George E. Taylor, *The Philippines and the United States: Problems of Partnership* (New York: Praeger, 1964).

50. William J. Pomeroy, *American Neo-Colonialism: Its Emergence in the Philippines and Asia* (New York: International Publishers, 1970).

51. Peter W. Stanley, "A Nation in the Making: The Philippines and the United States, 1899–1921" (Ph.D. diss., Harvard University, 1970).

thrusts behind the Philippine revolution; and for this reason, many Filipinos, prominent nationalists among them, were willing to cooperate in the pursuit of short- and intermediate- range goals and even to postpone independence while doing so. Few were willing to forgo independence altogether, however; and the scarcely veiled political designs of retentionists, the racism of Americans in general, and the agitation of the independence issue for various reasons by Americans braced up the backsliders and saved them from real cooptation in most cases. Hence, in this formulation, the ambiguities of the Philippine-American relationship: its tone of altruism and nation building and the large amount of good will felt on both sides, along with the distrust and sense of betrayal sometimes evident beneath the surface.

Scholarly treatments of American-Philippine relations in an Asian context, analyzing the ways in which they affected and were affected by other nations and movements in East Asia, have been surprisingly rare.[52] Prior to the war, the subject was virtually the property of retentionist propagandists, who depicted the threat from Japan in a fearsome light and asserted America's obligations to defend the Philippines through her continued presence there. Since the war, the subject has opened up. Theodore Friend studied the Philippine-Japanese-American triangle of the thirties and forties in a book which measurably sharpened our understanding of the relationship between foreign or metropolitan affairs and domestic politics in the islands.[53] He followed this by editing an unusually cogent wartime analysis of Philippine history by two Japanese scholars[54] and is presently at work on a comparative study of the Japanese occupation in the Philippines and Indonesia. David Joel Steinberg analyzed Filipino responses to the Japanese occupation as a crisis of loyalties, juxtaposing the reciprocal values of Philippine society at large against the survival ethic and patronal pretensions of the

52. For exceptions to the rule, see Alleyne Ireland, *The Far Eastern Tropics: Studies in the Administration of Tropical Dependencies* (Boston: Houghton, Mifflin, 1905); Edward A. Powell, *Asia at the Crossroads: Japan, Korea, China, Philippine Islands* (New York: Century, 1922); George M. Dutcher, *The Political Awakening of the East: Studies of Political Progress in Egypt, India, China, Japan, and the Philippines* (New York: The Abingdon Press, 1925); Vangala Siva Ram, *Comparative Colonial Policy with Special Reference to the American Colonial Policy* (New York: Longmans, Green, 1926); Andre Labrouquère, *L'Independence des Philippines* (Paris: Domat-Mont Chretien, 1936).

53. Theodore Friend, *Between Two Empires: The Ordeal of the Philippines, 1929–1946* (New Haven: Yale University Press, 1965).

54. Rōyama Masamichi and Takéuchi Tatsuji, *The Philippine Polity: A Japanese View*, Theodore Friend, ed. (New Haven: Yale University Southeast Asia Studies, Monograph Series, no. 12, 1967).

elite.[55] More recently, he has assayed the islands' past in the context of modern Southeast Asian history.[56] Other scholars have treated the effect upon Philippine-American relations of Japan's prewar economic penetration of the islands and of maneuvers by both Filipino and Japanese leaders during the thirties to establish a satisfactory relationship prior to Philippine independence.[57] Karl J. Pelzer's two books, *An Economic Survey of the Pacific Area* and *Pioneer Settlement in the Asiatic Tropics*, while not oriented toward American-Philippine relations, touch upon them and suggest ways in which the narrow perspective usually employed could fruitfully be broadened.[58] David Wurfel contributed a section on the Philippines to the omnibus *Governments and Politics of Southeast Asia*, which has in a different way a similar virtue.[59] Numerous studies of American–East Asian relations oriented toward Japan or China touch upon the Philippines in passing.[60]

Since the war, there has been a growth of studies of the Philippines based upon sociological findings.[61] Carl Landé amplified and system-

55. David Joel Steinberg, *Philippine Collaboration in World War II* (Ann Arbor: University of Michigan Press, 1967).

56. David Joel Steinberg, ed., *In Search of Southeast Asia* (New York: Prager, 1971).

57. Grant K. Goodman, *Four Aspects of Philippine-Japanese Relations, 1930–1940* (New Haven: Yale University Southeast Asia Studies, Monograph Series, no. 9, 1967); Goodman, *Davao: A Case Study in Japanese-Philippine Relations* (Lawrence: University of Kansas, Center for East Asian Studies: International Studies, East Asian Series research publication no. 1, 1967); Goodman, "Japanese Penetration of the Philippines, 1899–1941" (Ph.D. diss., University of Kansas, 1965); Milagros C. Guerrero, "A Survey of Japanese Trade and Investments in the Philippines, with Special Reference to Philippine-American Relations, 1900–1941," *Philippine Social Sciences and Humanities Review*, 31 (March 1966).

58. Karl J. Pelzer, *An Economic Survey of the Pacific Area* (New York: Institute of Pacific Relations, 1941), and *Pioneer Settlement in the Asiatic Tropics* (New York: American Geographical Society, 1945).

59. David Wurfel, "The Philippines," in George McTurnan Kahin, ed., *Governments and Politics of Southeast Asia* (Ithaca: Cornell University Press, 1959).

60. Akira Iriye, *Across the Pacific: An Inner History of American-East Asian Relations* (New York: Harcourt, Brace & World, 1967); Charles E. Neu, *An Uncertain Friendship: Theodore Roosevelt and Japan, 1906–1909* (Cambridge, Mass.: Harvard University Press, 1967); Marilyn B. Young, *The Rhetoric of Empire: American China Policy, 1895–1901* (Cambridge, Mass.: Harvard University Press, 1968); A. Whitney Griswold, *The Far Eastern Policy of the United States* (New York: Harcourt, Brace and Co. 1938).

61. In addition to Landé's work, cited in note 60, see Jean Grossholtz, *Politics in the Philippines* (Boston: Little, Brown, and Co., 1964); Mary R. Hollnsteiner, *The Dynamics of Power in a Philippine Municipality* (Quezon City: University of the Philippines, 1963); Jaime C. Bulatao, "Hiyâ," *Philippine Studies*, 12 (1964), 424–438; Charles Kaut, "Contingency in a Tagalog Society," *Asian Studies*, 3 (1965), 1–15 and "Utang na loob: A System of Contractual Obligations among Tagalogs," *Southwest Journal of Anthropology*,

atized the widely held impression that Philippine politics turns on personal, dyadic loyalties, rather than class or ideological alignments.[62] If Landé is right, and the evidence suggests he is, at least as to postwar politics, then earlier histories, which assumed Filipino politics was akin to our own and emphasized the independence issue and economic considerations in explaining Filipino attitudes toward America, will need revision. An illustration of the form such revision might take may be found in Friend's *Between Two Empires*, which places the not unfamiliar story of the duel between OsRox and Quezon over independence legislation, and the history of Quezon's presidency, in a context shaped less by policies or principles than by shifting personal balances and intricate maneuvers in a competition of quasi-caciques. The difficulty in historical application of the insights of Landé and others is that common to most attempts to read back into history the findings of modern sociology. As one moves farther into the past, the types of evidence available less perfectly suit the requirements of proof than they do in the recent past; and what may be taken fairly confidently as a tool for analysis of the present becomes a potentially misleading hypothesis. Moreover, there are special dangers of two kinds inherent in the nature of these particular insights—namely, that the appeal our age finds in the McLuhanesque conclusion that goals are illusory and process is all may lead to a reductionistic deprecation of the role of issues and principles in Philippine history and that interpretations stressing what is to Western eyes anomalous in Philippine life may take on invidious and condescending tones.[63]

It will be apparent from what has been said here that the study of American-Philippine relations has been carried out largely by Americans. This may have been inevitable, since the richest collections of official records and personal papers are located in the United States; but it has not been entirely a happy development.

17 (1961) 256–272; Frank Lynch, "Philippine Values II: Social Acceptance," *Philippine Studies*, 10 (1962), 82–99; Socorro C. Espiritu and Chester L. Hunt, *Social Foundations of Community Development—Readings on the Philippines* (Manila: R. M. Garcia, 1964).

62. Carl Landé, *Leaders, Factions, and Parties: The Structure of Philippine Politics* (New Haven: Yale University Southeast Asia Studies, Monograph Series, no. 6, 1965).

63. Westerners have often been pleased to suppose that there is no intellectual substance in Philippine life and culture. Not a few have explained Filipino statecraft and governmental institutions as extensions of rural cultural patterns. For a distinguished Filipino's rejoinder, see Onofre D. Corpuz's barbed remarks in his "Realities of Philippine Foreign Policy," in Frank H. Golay, ed., *Philippine-American Relations* (Englewood Cliffs, N.J.: Prentice-Hall, 1966), pp. 59–60.

For the most part, American scholars have been concerned to support a point of view as to the wisdom, legitimacy, or credibility of America's undertaking a professedly tutelary mission in the islands; but they have generally been unequipped to do so in a socially or culturally perceptive way. Few of the authors mentioned in this paper were tri-lingual in English, Spanish, and Tagalog; and none of the Americans, so far as I know, understood Visayan, Ilokano, or any of the other important dialects of the Filipino people. Given the nature of their interest and the limitations imposed upon them by lack of familiarity with Philippine languages and society, they have tended to emphasize what the West in fact or in myth imported into the islands, placing initiative in relations between the American and Filipino peoples exclusively with the former. Until after World War II, and to some degree even now, most historical writing about the Philippines was in effect devoted to explaining what other nations or peoples (for example, overseas Chinese) had done in or to the islands and how a relatively small number of highly visible Filipinos such as traditional leaders in the early Spanish period and the new rich and nationalist leaders of later years had reacted to these initiatives.[64]

Wherefore we have an abundance of studies treating American policy and Philippine politics, the latter defined as the activities and announced platforms of parties and leaders and the proceedings of the Philippine legislature. Doubtless we shall have more. The Harrison years have received no modern, detailed study;[65] and the filipinization of parts of the economy during that period is of great importance, coming as it did just when American capital finally became interested in the Philippines as a source of raw materials and as a trading base for China.[66] Comparative studies of imperial

64. For a discussion of this point, see Onofre D. Corpuz, "Western Colonisation and the Filipino Response," *Journal of Southeast Asian History,* 3 (1962), 1–23.

65. A start has been made in Napoleon J. Casambre, "Francis Burton Harrison: His Administration in the Philippines, 1913–1921" (Ph.D. diss., Stanford University, 1968).

66. BIA file 4958 deals with "China, Trade with, etc." The first reference in it to the Philippines as a trading base for China is to a speech given by a Manila promoter in 1909; the bureau did not begin to receive copies of State Department reports on trade with China until 1910. On 6 February of that year, the chief of the bureau wrote to a Congressman: "while . . . statements as to the future possibilities of the Islands seem to be logical, and it is hoped that they will prove true in the end, it is a fact that up to the present time the Philippines have had little or no influence on American trade in that region outside of the Islands themselves." (Clarence R. Edwards to Joseph V. Graff, 6 February 1910, BIA 3432–15.) There is no evidence of significant trade between the Philippines and China in non-Philippine goods until after World

policy in the Philippines and other colonies are notably lacking; and the importance of Egyptian, Puerto Rican, and Cuban models at various stages of the Philippines' colonial administration is evident to those who have read the sources. Indeed, the definition of policy needs refinement. It is simplistic and has often been misleading in previous studies to assume that there was an American policy, a Republican policy, or even a Republican policy during the Taft years with regard to the Philippines. Great rewards await the scholar diligent enough to break through such formulas and expose the tensions and divisions out of which any given policy or action arose.

Useful though such studies may prove to be, however, the field will remain deceptively unbalanced until the study of Philippine history has both broadened and deepened our knowledge of the Philippine side in American-Philippine relations. Work is now in progress on urbanization and other aspects of the islands' political geography; and there is at least one doctoral dissertation treating the technological impact of America upon the Philippines.[67] Materials touching the social, cultural, and technological history of the islands turn up from time to time in the *University of Manila Journal of East Asiatic Studies*, whose editor, Charles Houston, has regularly encouraged Philippine historians to diversify their interests. These are only beginnings, however; and it has proven hard even for Filipino historians to break out of the esablished working assumptions that Filipinos responded, but did not initiate.

Ultimately, one places great hope in the inclusion of the Philippines in the study of East Asia. This inclusion does not come naturally to some circles. Spanish Catholicism and American democracy have been held to separate Filipinos from inhabitants both of the Asian mainland and of the Indonesian archipelago; and Filipinos themselves have often spoken and written as if being the faithful in a region peopled with the unconverted, or being "democracy's bridgehead in Asia," was more central in the definition of their identity than being a Malay people with centuries of contact and exchange with China. They may, of course, have been right. But it will do historians no harm to examine the question. At the least, inclusion of the Philippines in the East Asian field will invite comparative studies and encourage the application to the Philippines of sociological approaches derived from Eastern rather than Western

War I, at which time a major program was launched to make Manila a trading base and possibly a free port.

67. Joseph Van Hise, "American Contributions to Philippine Science and Technology" (Ph.D. diss., University of Wisconsin, 1957).

expectations. It should remind us that Americans did not deal with the Philippines in a vacuum but as part of their Asian policy; and that Filipinos did not lack alternative models for development and modernization.

From Pearl Harbor to the Present

America and the Chinese

Revolution, 1942–1946:

An Interpretation

China during World War II provides all the ingredients for a drama of epic proportions—the disintegration of Nationalist China, the death throes of an archaic social system, the birth of the most monumental revolution of the century, a people rising, armed guerrilla bands, Japanese imperialism and Kuomintang reaction, the collapse of British power, the rise of America to dominance in the Pacific. And always there is the suffering—such black corruption and oppression, such bleak, unrelieved misery for millions upon millions of China's peasants that the imagination falters and sensitivities numb. Underneath it all, shaking the puppet generals, collaborators, smugglers, the warlords, and the corrupt Kuomintang was an enormous force arising from cleaving social and class struggle. China was preparing to shake the world.

For America, the war itself was a climactic event—the victory of American power over all its enemies; the collapse of the imperial systems of its allies; and the settlement of the Pacific War largely on its terms. The United States, its technology and science unsurpassed, its economic strength unequalled, its hopes and visions global, had suddenly become the most powerful force in a charred and leveled world. Yet in China a force was already coalescing which would shatter the unity of that vision and spread the first doubts about American capabilities (though these doubts were to be quickly submerged in the ideological cold war of the 1950's).

To Americans the war years appeared to mark a new stage in our relationship with the Chinese—a large-scale involvement significantly funneled through the U.S. government. Yet for China it was only another stage in a much broader episode, a final stage in which yet one more Western power had arrived to persuade, assist, and guide. In the relations between China and America in the 1940's can be seen a conflict growing and deepening, revealing in the process much about both. In China, for the first time, but without really realizing it, Americans collided with a force that adamantly and successfully refused to accept the Eurocentric framework of world politics. It was in China that American power had early to confront those vast revolutionary forces that have ever since baffled, frightened, and challenged the American government. It was there for the first time that the United States was faced with questions about the limits of power it tried so hard to avoid until Vietnam. And there, too, was challenged the very ability of the American system to promote any progressive changes, to find any alternative to forms of imperial control, or to adapt to a revolutionary world.

The American Bull in the China Shop: War Aims and Chinese Politics

> The Chinese government is a structure based on fear and favor, in the hands of an ignorant, arbitrary, stubborn man. . . . Only outside influence can do anything for China—either enemy action will smash her or some regenerative idea must be formed and put into effect at once.
> —General Joseph Stilwell

From the beginning, the American-Nationalist alliance was torn by a series of bitter cross purposes. With Pearl Harbor, Chiang and the Americans became allies. But China was always only a peripheral part of America's global effort—its Europe-first, Russia-second, and Pacific-third strategy. The United States could only defer greater assistance to the Chinese "until victory over Germany would enable us and our allies, without dangerous strain, to beat a way into China, and along with the Chinese to expel the Japanese." Nonetheless, Chiang was expected to redouble his efforts and prepare for the day when his armies could move against the Japanese. At the very least, Chiang could tie up large numbers of Japanese troops, Chinese air bases might be built to harass the Japanese, and China might help counterbalance the Japanese propoganda of "Asia for the Asiatics."[1]

1: Herbert Feis, *The China Tangle: The American Effort in China from Pearl Harbor to the Marshall Mission* (Princeton: Princeton University Press, 1953), p. 74. On the specific military implications of America's role in China see Charles F. Romanus and Riley Sunderland, *Stilwell's Mission to China* (Washington: Department of the Army, Historical Division, 1953); *Stilwell's Command Problems* (Washington: Department of the Army, Historical Division, 1956); *Time Runs out in CBI* (Washington: Department of the Army, Historical Division, 1959).

However, while the United States burst upon the scene urging Chiang to fight on, Chiang realized any major military actions in China itself "might mean the end of the government."[2] For him, America's entry into the battle appeared to guarantee the allies' ultimate victory, so the Nationalist government began preparations to sit out the remainder of the war. The American war effort to Chiang, then, was only one part of his broader political world; for the Americans it was initially the totality. Chiang's world was seen only through American war concerns—a prism which blocked out the process of accommodation which had developed between Chinese and Japanese lines, the vast smuggling trade between occupied and unoccupied China, and the intricately balanced military power constellation that was the source of Chiang's power. Most important, the American preoccupation with the defeat of fascism led them to ignore the growing polarization in the Chinese revolution, even though Chiang more and more acted as though the major threat to his power were the Chinese Communists, not the Japanese.

Onto this political stage walked General Joseph Stilwell. Long acquainted with Chinese realities, he was assigned to "increase the effectiveness of U.S. aid to the prosecution of the war and to improve the combat efficiency of the Chinese army." His mission was to organize the one thing China had in quantity—manpower. He labored under few illusions. His attitude toward Chiang's armies was little different from Luddendorf's classic summation of Austria's fighting potential: "We are allied to a corpse."[3]

That Chiang was weak, his armies disorganized, his problems growing is hardly in dispute in the historical works on this period. Indeed, several basic assumptions are accepted—that the Kuomintang had been savagely weakened by the Japanese onslaught, forced to retreat from the centers of the "progressive commercial" circles, and isolated in a remote, primitive area of China; that the party consequently became even more dependent on the highly conservative landlord elements of the interior; and that the Nationalists were increasingly worried about the Communists.

General agreement on these few assumptions, however, simply points toward the broad areas of disagreement that divided observers at the time and historians ever since—the relative strength of the central government and the Communists, the real nature of the two main Chinese antagonists, the wartime military role of each against Japan, the long-term prospects of the American-Soviet alli-

2. Feis, *The China Tangle,* p. 74.
3. Joseph W. Stilwell, *The Stilwell Papers* (New York: W. Sloane Associates, 1948).

ance, and the outlook for American-Chinese postwar relations. In general, two trends of analysis are evident. One group concludes that though a reform movement in the Kuomintang was desirable, the Nationalists would have had little difficulty maintaining themselves if sufficient military force had been available. At the center of this perspective is a belief in a basically dedicated and victimized Chiang Kai-shek. However weakened the Nationalists, certainly, they say, it was not his fault. Was it not the blockade which caused the runaway inflation? Were not his best troops lost in the heroic struggles against the Japanese at Nanking and Shanghai? Was he not isolated from his traditional sources of wealth? Was not America, because of its Europe-first policies, preventing Chiang from obtaining the arms he needed to renew the struggle?[4]

Another view of the situation, developed in a series of competent works describing the operations of America's military mission in China, the debate over allocation of lend-lease supplies, the campaign in Burma, and the controversies among the allies in the China-Burma-India theater, concentrates upon various American reform proposals, usually military, the structure of the Kuomintang, and the personality of its leader. It was not simply the war which was the source of the Kuomintang's weakness. The Chinese army, they sug-

---

4. This "apologetics" approach was prevalent among many American diplomats during the war and formed the core of the later position of the China Lobby. Stanley Hornbeck's memoranda in U.S. Department of State, *Foreign Relations of the United States: China, 1942* (Washington: Government Printing Office, 1956), are among the more classic examples. Harold Isaac's *Images of Asia: American Views of China and India* (New York: Capricorn, 1962) offers samples of the news media and the growing glorification of Chiang in the late 1930's and early 1940's, and A. T. Steele's *The American People and China* (New York: McGraw Hill, 1966) tends to criticize those so harsh on Chiang. Anthony Kubek's *How the Far East Was Lost: American Policy and the Creation of Communist China* (Chicago: Henry Regnery Co., 1963) presents a case for Chiang's collapse in terms of American failures. Freda Utley's *Last Chance in China* (Indianapolis: Bobbs-Merrill, 1952) is a masterful polemic against any and all of Chiang's critics. Hollington Tong's *China and the World Press* (Nanking?:1948) is a smooth explanation of the censorship system he operated for Chiang during the war. Claire Lee Chennault, *Way of a Fighter: The Memoirs of Claire Lee Chennault* (New York: G. P. Putnam's Sons, 1949) provides a defense of Chiang and a plea for air power. Ross Koen's *The China Lobby in American Politics* (New York: MacMillan Co., 1960) was never officially released by MacMillan, though a copy is tentatively scheduled for publication in 1971 by Harper & Row. The story of its suppression is told by Koen in his "McCarthyism and our Asian Policy," *Bulletin of Concerned Asian Scholars*, 1.4 (May 1969), 27–31). His book remains the best introduction to the issues used by the China Lobby to reinforce Chiang's image and explain his defeat—the Yalta Agreements, the Amerasia Affair, the resignation of Ambassador Hurley, the failure of the Marshall mission, the "spy ring" revelations of the ex-Communists and the conviction of Hiss, and the Korean War.

gest, could only mirror the regime of which it was a part. Hence, when Stilwell sought to tackle military weakness, he found himself entangled in the power and leadership structure of the Kuomintang. To "increase the combat effectiveness of the Chinese army" required a minimal control over American aid to build a reliable, well-fed, patriotic, national army for China out of the coterie of warlords, feudal chieftains, and military cliques carefully controlled through Chiang's political balancing act. That made Stilwell a "reformer," which, fundamentally, was why he came into such irreconcilable conflict with the Generalissimo. To apply Western expertise to the problems of logistics and military organization threatened to undermine Chiang's political power, ousting his favorites, weakening his authority, and exposing him to dangers of defection to the Japanese.[5]

Between these two camps of opinion there is little disagreement over the disruptive impact of American power on Chiang's political world. Nor is there much debate about its growing weakness as the war continued. But debate about the meaning of such conclusions and other topics was rampant. And there is a wealth of material available on the divisions at the time within the American community in Chungking and in Washington over Chiang and his "reformist" prospects. The often perceptive writings of a brilliant group of young Foreign Service officers, the often underrated ambassador, Clarence Gauss, numerous talented journalists, and various military personnel all reflect an increasing fear that the Nationalists were collapsing.[6] By 1944 the Communists appeared stronger than ever.

Given this situation, it is hardly surprising that the Communists moved more and more toward being and have ever since remained the center of debate over America's China policy. Was a coalition

5. Both Herbert Feis and Romanus and Sunderland share this view. A brutally concise statement of this position is in Harold Issacs's excellent *No Peace for Asia* (Cambridge: M.I.T. Press, 1947), pp. 43–80. For two observers views see Theodore White and A. Jacoby, *Thunder Out of China* (New York: William Sloane Associates, 1946), and Lawrence Rossinger, *China's Crisis* (New York: Alfred A. Knopf, 1945).

6. All the U.S. Department of State, *Foreign Relations of the United States: China* have been released for the war years. They provide a wealth of materials. Some of the best work ever done by American Foreign Service officers is to be found in the perceptive reporting of John Service, John Davies, George Atcheson, John Melby, John Carter Vincent, Ambassador Gauss, and many others. The *Morgenthau Diary (China)*, vol. II, (Washington: Washington Government Printing Office, 1965) has numerous incisive and colorful accounts of the Kuomintang. Besides the various military accounts of the period, it is noteworthy that a community of reporters remained in Chungking throughout the war. They provide, in microcosm, the disputes, debates, and changing perceptions of Americans toward the Kuomintang, Chiang, and the Communists. Especially important are Harold Issacs, Theodore White, Brooks Atkinson, Israel Epstein, A. T. Steele, Gunther Stein, and Jack Belden.

government feasible and in American interests? Could American power force Chiang to make reforms or find another leader to support? Or were the Communists such a fact of life that they should be recognized as such and cultivated as a group not inherently hostile to the United States? Around such questions lies the debate over American China policy. They raise the central problems about the possible uses of American power and its impact. Among the various perspectives and styles of evaluation are the following:

"If Asia were Clay in the Hands of the West." How is it that America, so powerful and important to the Nationalist government's future, could not force Chiang to make the reforms essential for its survival, or find another leader who would? Since Chiang was "utterly dependent on American support for victory in the war against Japan and for survival after the war in their struggle with the Communists,"[7] why was American power not used to demand reform and sweeping changes? To Tang Tsou, in his *America's Failure in China*, "failure" meant rejecting the use of a quid pro quo ("tactics of pressure") strategy on Chiang. It meant rejecting the Stilwell strategy of "everything we do *for* him, we should exact a commitment *from* him."[8] But, concludes Tang Tsou, official Washington, far more worried about other theaters of action, fearful of rejecting an established allied wartime government, sometimes worried about a separate peace with the Japanese and occasionally struck with a guilty conscience for its pre-1941 policy, refused to exert such pressures. Consequently, the United States was unwilling "either to persuade Chiang to undertake the reform necessary for the survival of his regime or to help fashion a new political force to replace him."[9] American aid was not only wasted; but, worse than that, it entangled America disastrously in Chiang's "inevitable defeat." In the end, it was a policy that combined operation rathole with operation booby trap.

An interpretation of General Stilwell, the strongest advocate of quid pro quo, is central to this type of questioning. His recall in 1944 was a crucial event. For in the fall of that year, as Chiang's armies collapsed, with Chungking threatened, President Roosevelt had demanded Stilwell's appointment as commander-in-chief of the Chinese armies. Thus, for a moment, it seemed that Washington might

7. Tang Tsou, *America's Failure in China, 1941–1950* (Chicago: University of Chicago Press, 1963), p. 89. This work has often been regarded as the most thorough and critical study of the 1940's. It is emphasized here as indicative of the dominant approach to American-Chinese relations that developed in the 1950's and 1960's.

8. Ibid., p. 89.

9. Ibid., p. 90.

march all the way down the road with Stilwell to the total acceptance of quid pro quo tactics. When Roosevelt relented soon after, though, it seemed to convince Chiang that America's commitment to him was so strong that he would have free rein to do as he pleased. For Tang Tsou, the implications of this "weakness of will" were catastrophic. It meant the United States would not promote reforms among the non-Communist groups (even without Chiang) in order to prepare them to "compete successfully with the CCP both on the battlefield and in the realms of political, economic, and social reforms."[10] Nor could it believably use talk of "coalition government" with the Chinese Communist Party to threaten Chiang into needed reforms. And what made this defeat and failure so pitiful for the United States was that it was due to a failure of judgment and will rather than the objective weakness of its political position.

Tang Tsou's analysis, however, reflects a basic postulate about the war years—that Stilwell was essentially correct in his analysis of Chiang's regime, while General Chennault, the leader of the American air force in China, a strong supporter of Chiang and a believer that the Communists, closely linked with Moscow, were the major threat to postwar American interests, was generally accurate about the Communists.[11] The "appropriate" policy, in this case, was seen to fall somewhere between these two insights. It should have sought, in short, to rebuild the "social and political foundations of the Nationalist Government" through "a series of sweeping reforms."[12] Such a policy was the "indispensable condition for the success of a program of active support to the government." American power was to force China to change. The vast forces demanding change were to be molded by American hands, set in motion according to American plans, and supervised by American personnel. America not only had the power, apparently, but the wisdom to restructure a political world in which the Chinese would be pleased to dwell. Few other historical works on this period reflect such a faith in America's ability to control China. Nor is there even a hint of what Jonathan Spence concludes about Stilwell's attempt to become commander of the Chinese armies—"that it was the most ambitious and most arrogant of all attempts by Western advisers in China [throughout history] to gain power."[13]

10. Ibid., p. 56.
11. An excellent example of this type of argumentation is Richard Rovere and Arthur Schlesinger, Jr., *The General and the President, and the Future of American Foreign Policy* (New York: Farrar, Straus, and Young 1951), pp. 192–220.
12. Tang Tsou, *America's Failure*, 146.
13. Jonathan Spence, *To Change China: Western Advisers in China, 1620–*

To Change China or Accept a Changing China? Though his recall symbolizes for Tang Tsou the crucial defeat of American attempts to reform the Kuomintang and build up the anti-Communist forces, Stilwell's role is not nearly so clear when robbed of Tsou's cold war framework. For, by 1944, Stilwell could almost be viewed as an anachronism, almost the only leading figure in Chungking who really wanted to prosecute the war against the Japanese or who thought the Chinese (if not the Nationalist government) could successfully fight the Japanese. Increasingly, others worried about the postwar fate of the Kuomintang. Not Stilwell. And this made him among the last of the great non-cold war reformers in China's long history of Western penetration. His deep respect for the Chinese people was rivaled only by his near total disgust with the Kuomintang. He would fight with those willing to fight.

Stilwell's attempt to become commander of China's armies was certainly audacious as well as indicative, at best, of that realm where altruism and imperial attitudes meet. It was a demand for a foreigner to assume enormous power in Chinese political life. But it is hardly clear that the success of such a scheme would have forced the Kuomintang to reform itself. Another path was possible. That would have been a closer relationship with the Chinese Communists, the only group Stilwell thought was really fighting the Japanese by 1944. And they did it, he concluded, because they obtained support from the peasantry by offering them a better life. What critics often overlook in the Stilwell controversy is his desire to construct a national army independent of Kuomintang control and to arm all elements willing to fight. Either aspect of the strategy left little room for the Kuomintang.

While Stilwell neglected the possible ramifications of his position, others were already beginning to face the problem of dealing with the Communists. Roughly speaking, this approach can be associated with the telegram various Foreign Service officers sent to Washington in February 1945.[14] President Roosevelt, they urged, should inform Chiang that the United States was going to cooperate with and supply the Communists and other suitable groups (because of the requirements of "military necessity") in the war against Japan. Part of the intention, however, was a postwar hope. Convinced that the Chinese Communists were here to stay, indeed were the most dynamic, if not yet the most powerful force in China, they hoped to "hold the Communists to our side instead of throwing them into the

---

1960 (Boston: Little, Brown, 1969), p. 259, an enjoyable, readable work with a good chapter on Chennault and Stilwell.

14. *Foreign Relations of the United States: China, 1945*, pp. 242–246.

hands of the Soviet Union." This did not necessarily mean the end of support for the Kuomintang, but Chiang would either reform or collapse while the Communists were supplied and treated as a force independent of Russia. As John Davies cabled from Moscow in April 1945, "What can be concluded at this juncture is that if any communist regime is susceptible to political 'capture' by the U.S., it is Yenan."[15] Optimism was not a notable trait, however, among those who suggested this approach. Nor was it based, as Feis wrongly concludes, on the premise that "if shown friendship by us, the Communists would align their actions to the policies of the West."[16] China would be independent, controlled and dominated neither by Russia nor by the United States. Such an attitude seemed the only plausible one—"the Communists are in China to stay. And China's destiny is not Chiang's but theirs"[17]—because the attitudes of the CCP would be partly formed in response to American actions; because reforming the corrupt, reactionary Kuomintang seemed almost hopeless; because commiting American power to such a task was a blatant disregard for its limits; and because with the likely forthcoming Russian participation in the war, it was essential to develop contacts quickly, to build a minimal basis of trust, to establish the American interest in an independent China. This line of argument did not preclude a coalition government (indeed it was often spoken of under this rubric). However, these men realized the paramount fact about China at that time—it was in the midst of an enormous revolutionary upheaval. No plan or policy was plausible if this paramount fact were neglected.[18]

15. Ibid., p. 338.
16. Feis, *The China Tangle*, p. 263.
17. Davies Memorandum in *Foreign Relations of the United States: China, 1945*, p. 671.
18. This approach has been so widely ridiculed that it is almost forgotten that some of the most perceptive observers felt it was a plausible, or at least possible, course of action for the American government. See, for example, Mary Wright's excellent review of the *China White Paper* in the *Far Eastern Quarterly*, 10 (1950–51), pp. 99–104; Derk Bodde's *Peking: A Year of Revolution* (Boston: Henry Schuman, Inc. 1950); Owen Lattimore's *The Situation in Asia* (Boston: Little, Brown and Company, 1949), pp. 161–180; Nathaniel Peffer, "The Dangerous Choice We Face in China," *The New York Times Magazine* (Jan. 25, 1948). One of the best statements of this view is John Fairbank's "Our Chances in China," *Atlantic* 178.3 (September 1946), pp. 37–42.

Warren Cohen's "The Development of Chinese Communist Policy toward the United States, 1934–1945," *Orbis*, II (Summer 1967), suggests that during the war years the interests of the CCP were distinct from, sometimes in conflict with, the Russians. This was evident on the ideological level, too. It was reasonable to assume a flexibility on their part, both tactically and in terms of long-range policy. In short, an "open historical situation" existed.

This "paramount fact," of course, was either neglected or distorted by almost all later historians and critics of American policy in the 1940's. For years, American academics from right to liberal have elaborated perspectives which refused to take such an approach seriously. At best, they claim, it was naive, certainly ignorant of the way "Communist parties" operate or the great pull of "international Communist" ideology. Even though many defended those condemned in the McCarthy period for such views, they usually did so by insisting upon the "loyalty" and "honesty" of the men under attack. Yet because they could provide no framework in which this approach toward Chinese-American relations made sense, their defense probably reinforced the position that here was a stupidity so great that it bordered on treason.[19]

Was it not obvious, as Tang Tsou so unquestioningly assumes, that the formation of "Communist" foreign policy, unlike that of other systems, is a largely unilateral process relatively unaffected (except tactically) by the past or present policies of other countries? Of course, those so deeply involved in Chinese affairs and lacking time to study the methods of communism and the operations of Leninist parties could easily be fooled. Unless properly "initiated," apparently, it was difficult to see present policy governed by the "ultimate objective" or to know that Communist foreign policies are always "tactical." If only these individuals had observed more closely, they would have seen the ideological (some add organizational) tie with Moscow. To advocate a policy of American flexibility was wrong, concludes Tang Tsou, because it "underestimated" the role of ideology in Chinese Communist affairs. "Once they had come into power or felt strong enough to defy the US with impunity, the power-political calculations from which professions of friendship for the US apparently stemmed would have lost much of their weight. Correspondingly, ideological considerations and the organizational ties with the international Communist movement would have exercised greater influence."[20] Herbert Feis adds another dimension. Such an approach toward the Communists resulted partly from individuals allowing their view of Chiang as hopelessly corrupt to

19. Individuals who study Chinese-American relations in either the 1940's or the 1950's should read, I think, the IPR Hearings. It is crucial to recapture the atmosphere of the early 1950's and its effect on the way the Chinese revolution was understood. U.S., Congress, Senate, Committee on the Judiciary, Internal Security Subcommittee, *Institute of Pacific Relations: Hearings.* 15 parts. 82nd Cong., 1951 and 1952. For a case study of one victim of the 1950's, see Ross Terrill, "John Carter Vincent and the American 'Loss' of China," in Ross Terrill and Bruce Douglas (eds), *China and Ourselves* (Boston: Beacon Press, 1970).

20. Tang Tsou, *America's Failure,* p. 217.

"color their view of official action," thus "weaken(ing) faith in the power of the Generalissimo and his group to govern China."[21] An additional twist to the argument is added by Benjamin Schwartz who, though long a proponent of the disintegration of the Marxist faith, argued in 1968 that "to maintain that it should always have been obvious that the ideological authority of Moscow was not real and would not endure is to engage in what might be called fraudulent hindsight"[22]—truly a remarkable feat for those at the time.

Many conservative critics simply concluded that the Communists were aggressive; indeed it was an inherent trait of a "totalitarian" system or "Leninist" party organization. Others provided different arguments. China's hostility reflected the centuries-long "humiliation" at the hands of the West (now symbolized by America), the lack of experience in dealing with other states as equals (the center of the world syndrome), China's pride ("Chinese are probably the proudest people in the world and may still find it difficult to accept the rest of us as equals"),[23] the nature of the Communist system which requires an enemy for internal reasons ("One wonders if the CCP could survive without us; our role as enemy seems essential to Chairman Mao's morality play")[24] or the revolutionary zeal and romanticism of China's first generation leaders (a more moderate, rational, second generation will "adapt" to the "international community"). Almost always, the *fundamental* obstacles to improved relations were Chinese—a result of their history, culture, or problems of revolutionary adjustment. And while some of these explanations may have value in very broad terms, they have tended to exclude serious consideration of the actual course of American policy since 1941.[25]

Approaches toward Unconditional Support: Hodgepodge and Zany. On November 7, 1944, the new American ambassador, Patrick J. Hurley, arrived in Yenan—his uniform dazzling, his greeting to the Communists warm, his Indian war whoop loud. Such was the man chosen by Franklin Roosevelt to help patch up China through a coali-

21. Feis, *The China Tangle*, p. 259.

22. Benjamin Schwartz, *Communism and China: Ideology in Flux* (Cambridge, Mass.: Harvard University Press, 1968), p. 33.

23. Edwin Reischauer, *Beyond Vietnam: The United States and Asia* (New York: Alfred Knopf, 1967), p. 170.

24. John K. Fairbank, "New Thinking About China," in *China: The People's Middle Kingdom and the U.S.A.* (Cambridge, Mass.: Harvard University Press, 1967), p. 96.

25. For an approach toward understanding the ideological orientations in Chinese studies, see my "The Roots of Rhetoric: The Professional Ideology of America's China Watchers." *Bulletin of Concerned Asian Scholars*, 2.1, pp. 59–69 and the exchange with John Fairbank in 2.3, pp. 51–71.

tion government. Stilwell's lack of diplomatic skills was finally surpassed.

Hurley's policy, now almost universally criticized, sought to promote a "united and democratic" China under the leadership of Chiang Kai-shek. His role, as he saw it, was to advise Chiang to reach a settlement with the Communists, though only persuasion, not force, could be used. Continued American support and Russian acquiescence, would allow the Nationalist government to reach an agreement that would bring Chinese Communist armies into a unified command structure. Hurley's program was based on a belief in the political viability of the Kuomintang, his faith in Chiang's leadership, an underestimation of Communist strength, and his belief that Russia would intervene to control Yenan while cooperating with Chungking. It is indeed striking that Hurley, who repeatedly claimed that the Communists were not true communists, was "convinced that the influence of the Soviets will control the action of the CCP," while those Foreign Service officers who recognized the Chinese Communist commitment to communism and the power of the revolutionary forces it represented, concluded that it was "useless to try to persuade the USSR to hold back Yenan."[26]

In any case, Hurley's approach—significantly dependent upon great power influence to mold China's government—was widely shared. The various debates over Yalta, the possible role of Russia, the efforts to create stability in China based on postwar unity among the great powers (perhaps Roosevelt's hope after the Stilwell affair), are still relatively unexplored. But certainly it was a hodgepodge, makeshift approach, attempting constantly to patch up the political world Americans knew best—seeking here to gain a concession from the Chinese Communists; there, a sign from the Russians that they would support Chiang; hoping Chiang would reform. Few critics argue that it was a realistic policy, but its longevity was never based on its inherent logic. Those who went along with Hurley, and there were many, did not want to reject Chiang and the Nationalists; but even more important, this policy was always the easiest way. A crisis in China was the last thing Washington wanted. The future was bleak; but one could stumble down the path with Chiang just a bit longer. There would be time—tomorrow.

A different perspective on unconditional support for Chiang Kai-shek had roots in the 1940's but became more prominent in the 1950's. It was an odd assortment of "poisonous weeds" that bloomed into the China lobby. Ross Koen's long suppressed *The China Lobby*

26. *Foreign Relations of the United States: China, 1945*, pp. 431, 517.

in American Politics is a good first step toward understanding the impact and operation of this influential group. Its actual understanding of events in China may have been nil. Yet it largely framed the way such events were viewed in America. It certainly was not Chiang Kai-shek, they argued—that sturdy Christian hero of the war against Japan, that dedicated servant striving to create a unified, democratic China, that fervent foe of atheistic communism—who was at fault for the success of the Chinese Communists. No, it was America. It was the U.S. government which had fought a Europe-first war, failed to understand that the future was in Asia, refused to stand by Chiang as he grew weaker from the blockade and the lack of supplies, and even allowed harping criticism from Americans to undercut his regime. And then the United States tried to force Chiang into an unholy alliance with the CCP, deprived him of essential weapons and ammunition, and sabotaged his final hopes through the Marshall mission. No other explanation would suffice to explain why the peasantry had turned to an "external force"—and to a ruthless, totalitarian Communist regime. Surely only in America could the fundamental explanation be uncovered, again by exposing stupidity at the top, treason just below.

The success which this group had in defining the terms of debate over the Chinese revolution is still imbedded in most American scholarship. Volumes have been written to carefully and laboriously refute the charges of the right. Questioning about the People's Republic of China, at best, was done in a defensive, unsympathetic tone. "How were such positive improvements—education, health, industry—undertaken by a ruthless, manipulative, cruel system, one that denied individuality or dignity?"

There is another, less explored aspect to the forties and fifties—the widespread belief in the unlimited capacity of American power. Those who accepted the "tactics of pressure" approach, who believed in America's capacity and right to involve itself in the most intricate internal affairs of other nations in order to bring about sweeping, U.S.-approved changes, and those on the right each, in their own way, joined in an anti-communist crusade. Beneath all the bitterness of those years, such views formed into a subtle consensus about America that lasted until Vietnam. Liberals spoke of globalism. The right spoke the language of inverted globalism and saw the international struggle focused on the home front. Both accepted a view of American society as the unambiguous leader of the "free world." Both shared an almost unlimited faith in American power. Both generally came to accept a Manichean bipolar world, with liberals launching an international crusade as the right launched a domestic ideological campaign. Globalism abroad and McCarthyism at home proved compatible if not complementary. The latter ensured that the consequences of the former would not be fundamentally examined. This was a crucial development. It meant that America's involvement in the internal affairs of other countries would be seen as progressive and well intentioned. Some stressed the techniques of involvement overseas; others, cleansing the process of government at home. Neither were to explore critically the limits of power.

Inside the Peanut Shell

Any evaluation of these various approaches toward American policy will reflect certain assumptions about China. Were the major obstacles to the transformation of Chinese society the result of leadership incompetence, of the stupidity, greed, and inadequacy of Chiang's cohorts? Or was there a structural barrier implicit in the very composition of the Kuomintang—its lack of roots among the peasantry, the reliance on landlord hegemony, and the pattern of urban development which linked them in the 1930's to foreign powers? Was the structural barrier always present, but so aggravated by the war that the Kuomintang had no future? Or were the central problems war-induced, capable of being overcome by Chiang with sufficient American assistance? The answers are actually implicit in a part of the work that concentrates on the 1940's. For while most work at the policy level stresses the leadership problems of the Kuomintang, almost all studies of the rise to power of the Chinese Communists emphasize the structural aspects of Chiang's collapse.

Though there are many disagreements about Chiang, a very general picture of his political world can be suggested. Through a cautious mixture of military force and conciliatory tactics, Chiang had gradually brought power into a system that revolved around his own person in the late 1920's and early 1930's. Alliances were made with those he could not defeat, and through a shrewd process of manipulation and deception of political leaders, he successfully raised himself to the position of the central figure in Chinese political life. Throughout the 1930's Chiang had sought to build his delicate system of power balances by turning his back on Japan. To bargain for time in which to strengthen his system, he turned over more and more Chinese territory. However much the Chinese patriot (and he was a Chinese patriot), he realized that "his" China might not survive the onslaught. He, perhaps more than anyone else, understood the fragility of the political structure he had built.

Though no good biography of Chiang exists, most agree that he survived in politics through his skilled political balancing acts, playing off one potential opponent against another: right against left, reactionary against liberal, warlords against businessmen, secret service against students, T. V. Soong against H. H. Kung, and later, Stilwell against Chennault, the United States against Russia. His was indeed a formidable talent and one wedded to the desperate times in which he was born. Such traditional talents made him dominate Chinese politics for a quarter of a century.

But times changed. When the Japanese armies swept across China, destroying his military forces and obliterating his administrative system, the weaknesses of that system became apparent. Chiang's administrators had not been inculcated with the desire to form ties with the peasantry simply because the peasantry was not the central factor in Chinese politics before 1937—Chiang's political world, like traditional China, was one in which the Chinese peasantry was not an active force. Chou En-lai was right when he told Edgar Snow that "the first day of the anti-Japanese war will mean the beginning of the end for Chiang Kai-shek."[27] Confined to Chungking after 1938, Chiang found himself at a disadvantage with the CCP, who had lost a generation learning how to develop ties to the peasantry and organize it in a way Chiang's power constellation was simply incapable of doing. In this new political world, a vision of society and the related politicization of the masses shifted the very locus of power from a tiny elite based on urban and feudal rural conditions to a mass-based revolutionary movement, from the cities to the rural areas. And this new situation Chiang could not understand. When Americans arrived in Chungking in 1941, they found a regime which no longer offered a vision that could give meaning to the struggling, indescribable suffering of the Chinese people.[28]

27. Chou En-lai quoted by Edgar Snow, *Journey to the Beginning* (New York: Random House, 1958).

28. For an analysis of the fate of gradualism during the Nanking decade, see James C. Thomson Jr., *While China Faced West: American Reformers in Nationalist China, 1928–1937* (Cambridge, Mass.: Harvard University Press, 1969). In the controversy over "peasant nationalism" the dispute over nationalistic vs. a program of immediate socio-economic reform should not conceal the wide agreement over the structural aspects of Chiang's weakness and the new role (or the vastly expanded role) the peasant played after 1937. See Chalmers Johnson, *Peasant Nationalism and Communist Power: The Emergence of Revolutionary China* (Stanford: Stanford University Press, 1962), and an earlier exposition of much the same thesis in George Taylor, *The Struggle in North China* (New York: Institute of Pacific Relations, 1940). For a refutation of Johnson's thesis and a continued emphasis on the structural aspects of Chiang's failure, see Mark Selden, "People's War and the Transformation of Peasant Society: China and Vietnam," in Edward Friedman

Some of the most moving and graphic works from this period describe the internal collapse of Kuomintang China—the archaic social system not quite able to die sitting on a people barely able to live. Graham Peck's *Two Kinds of Time* is just an introduction to the sheer horror of peasant life in China during World War II. Nowhere does the notion of the wretched of the earth seem more appropriate than here—in the merciless, ruthless governmental and landlord exploitation of the peasantry; in the slaughter of Chinese peasants in the endlessly corrupt Nationalist conscription system; in the brutality of local "traditions" which supported landlord power; in the massive famines induced as much by man as by nature. This was not simply the world the Kuomintang was forced to put up with because of the war. It was, I think, the essence of the Kuomintang's system of government during the 1940's. If much of this brutality and butchery is absent in American scholarship, one need only return to some of those perceptive observers at the time.

Wrote Theodore White in his tour through Honan in 1944: "The peasants, as we saw them, were dying. They were dying on the roads, in the mountains, by the railway station, in their mud huts, in the fields. And as they died, the government continued to wring from them the last possible ounce of tax . . . The government in county after county was demanding of the peasant more actual poundage of grain than he had raised on his acres. No excuses were allowed; peasants who were eating elm bark and dried leaves had to haul their last sack of seed grain to the tax collector's office. Peasants who were so weak they could barely walk had to collect fodder for the army's horses, fodder that was more nourishing than the filth they were cramming into their own mouths. Peasants who could not pay were forced to the wall; they sold their cattle, their furniture, and even their land to raise money to buy grain to meet the tax quotas. One of the most macabre touches of all was the flurry of land speculation. Merchants from Sian and Chengchow, small government officials, army officials, and rich landowners who still had food were engaged in purchasing the peasants' ancestral areas at criminally low figures. Concentration and dispossession were pro-

---

and Mark Selden, eds., *America's Asia* (New York: Pantheon, 1969). Also, see Donald Gillin, " 'Peasant Nationalism' in the History of Chinese Communism," *Journal of Asian Studies*, 23.2 (February 1964). Little work has been done on the Nationalist attempts to organize guerrilla forces or to combat the spread of the Communists' appeal. Laurance Tipton's *Chinese Escapade* (London: Macmillan, 1949) provides an account of an Englishman's experiences with Kuomintang guerrillas operating in Shantung and reveals through their problems why the Communists succeeded where the Nationalists failed.

ceeding hand in hand, in direct proportion to the intensity of hunger . . . Bitter of heart, we returned to Chungking. The bland equanimity of the capital was unruffled . . . The dead bodies were lies; the dogs digging cadavers from the loess were figments of our imagination. We knew that there was a fury, as cold and relentless as death itself, in the bosom of the peasants of Honan, that their loyalty had been hollowed to nothingness by the extortion of their government."[29] White simply found that this Honan famine reflected the reality in extremis of the Kuomintang regime. And Jack Belden, in his *Still Time to Die*, describes the "overwhelming nature of this hideous mass hopelessness" in his travels through China in the late 1930's.[30]

Perhaps the very realities of this China defy description. How is one to describe the millions and millions of deaths, the staggering suffering of the poor, their lack of hope, and complete destitution? How is one to then dispassionately describe the role of the Kuomintang in this situation? Of course, almost all historical work on this period succeeds nicely. Such realities slip comfortably into the background, covered quickly in a few appropriate phrases. China is treated as though it were composed of Chungking and Yenan. An unsuspecting reader would hardly know of the collapse of Chinese society. No wonder. It would have been difficult indeed to graphically portray even glimpses of this rotting society and then recommend continued American support for the Nationalist government or for a gradual process of "reform." Surely it is long since time to insist that "reform" be defined in the context of this general collapse. Surely just a portion of the time spent tracing ideological debates can be devoted to trying to see what was happening among the wretched of China. Why not, as Owen Lattimore suggested, view American actions from China looking outward, instead of primarily through the prism of American policy debates?[31] Why not evaluate American actions as to whether they simply prolonged this agony? Could they have done anything progressive in this situation by 1945 if they intended to oppose the Communists? From the Chinese revolution outward, in short, an image of America and an understanding of its power may emerge far more accurate than that possessed by Americans themselves. A step in this direction is involved in an analysis of the Chinese Communists.

29. White and Jacoby, *Thunder Out of China*, pp. 174–175.
30. Jack Belden, *Still Time to Die* (New York: Harper and Brothers, 1944)
31. Owen Lattimore, *From China, Looking Outward* (Leeds: Leeds University Press, 1964).

The China that Stood Up

> The movement for social revolution in China may suffer defeats, may temporarily retreat, may for a time seem to languish, may make wide changes in tactics to fit immediate necessities and aims, may even for a period be submerged, be forced underground, but it will not only continue to mature; in one mutation or another it will eventually win, simply because (as this book proves, if it proves anything) the basic conditions which have given it birth carry within themselves the dynamic necessity for its triumph. And that triumph when it comes will be so mighty, so irresistible in its discharge of catabolic energy, that it will consign to oblivion the last barbarities of imperialism which now enthral the Eastern world.
> —Edgar Snow, *Red Star over China* (1937)

As Japanese armies swept over China in 1937, knocking the props from under Chiang's world, Edgar Snow's journalistic classic revealed that there was another China. In the backlands of north China, Snow described the dedication of the Communists to social revolution and resistance to the Japanese. Never before had Snow seen a Chinese force of such potential magnitude, so deeply rooted in the peasantry, so capable of radically improving their lives, and so guided by a meaningful vision of society. Here was a new China. Its story remains captured in the titles of three of the greatest writings of the time—from *Red Star Over China* (1937), to *Thunder Out of China* (1946), to *China Shakes the World* (1949).

Not until 1944 were Americans again able to closely observe the Chinese Communists. The various writings of journalists and governmental personnel describe a regime, ultimately authoritarian perhaps, but in many ways "democratic," cooperating with most classes, distributing land, promoting education, working efficiently and honestly, and inspiring enthusiasm and support. Instead of war weariness, observers found the "fighting enthusiasm of a primitive pioneer community" whose "tough, well-fed, hardened troops" any "allied commander would be proud to command." Instead of accommodation, they found a "hatred of the Japanese and a determination to defend their achievements against all interference."[32]

Yenan, moreover, seemed the fountainhead of an immense revolutionary force, one which held genuine promise of justice for the peasants. Concluded Theodore White, "There is only one certainty in Communist politics in China: the leaders' interests are bound up

32. The quotes are from *The New York Times* and *Christian Science Monitor* stories in July and August 1944.

with those of the masses of poverty stricken, suffering peasants, from whom they have always drawn their greatest support. They, and they alone, have given effective leadership to the peasant's irresistible longing for justice in his daily life. In great areas of North China the Communists have established a new way of life."[33] Example after example of this new way of life was noted: the close relationship between peasants and soldiers, the participation of the peasants in decisions that affected their lives at the local level, experimentation and initiative at all levels in the liberated areas.

Later criticisms of such perceptions of Yenan were so intense that they all but obscure this period as the only one of intimate contact between Americans and the Chinese revolution. In these critics the alleged "romanticism" of some of these early observers, their "ignorance" regarding the operations of "Communist" parties, even psychological explanations (a frustration complex with decadent, foggy Chungking prepared a favorable projection on youthful, sunny Yenan) created a framework that discredited any basically favorable accounts. And two of the greatest classics of the 1940's—Jack Belden's *China Shakes the World* and William Hinton's *Fanshen*— are still largely ignored. Yet what is actually involved in such criticisms are basic assumptions about revolutionary transformation, peasant liberation, and the consciousness of the oppressed.

The basic criticism against all those favorably impressed by the Chinese Communists is that they looked at the body of the movement rather than its core.[34] They observed support for various reforms, but failed to realize that the leadership was all important. They overlooked the Leninist party structure and its inherent logic of totalitarianism. Consequently, they failed to understand the drive toward total domination and the effort to reorganize society under conscious direction from above. Concluded Benjamin Schwartz in one of the standard works on the rise of Chinese communism, "This totalitarian tendency is part of the vital core of Chinese Communism inhibited only by the force of external circumstances and softened until recently by the party's sparing use of force."[35]

Though there was room for a wide range of argument within such a "critical" perspective, several crucial assumptions generally guided most research. Social change and revolutionary transformation were essentially understood through leadership techniques of con-

33. White and Jacoby, *Thunder Out of China*, p. 314.
34. Tang Tsou's chapter, "The American Image of Chinese Communism and the American Political Tradition," *America's Failure*, pp. 176–236, is an excellent example of this style of criticism.
35. Benjamin Schwartz, *Chinese Communism and the Rise of Mao* (Cambridge, Mass.: Harvard University Press, 1951), p. 203.

trol and domination. Revolutionary spirit becomes the fuel for an effective, responsive party apparatus; political subjects become malleable, manipulated objects. The revolutionary process was understood through the concept of the party, rather than the party in the context of a vast revolutionary transformation. In such a perspective, Mao emerges more as a systems builder than as the leader of a vast historical revolution.

It is true that some of the most gifted observers of the 1940's stressed the revolutionary spirit, growing popular support, and the new forms of community and political participation which made organizations work. They wrote of the new sense of dignity, the breaking down of the old forces of oppression which allowed a real freedom for individuals to respond creatively to their immediate circumstances. But it is simply wrong to assert that such writers as Jack Belden, Edgar Snow, William Hinton, John Service, and Theodore White ignored the organizational discipline, unity, and dedication of purpose in the CCP. Their focus was less on organizational devices and control techniques than a sensitivity to a complex dialectic between leaders and led, party and populace, consciousness and inchoate demands for change—all of which formed a part of peasant liberation.

The key word is liberation. However much some observers at the time struggled to find appropriate words to describe what they saw, the process appeared to be "liberating" the majority of the Chinese people in the areas they observed. The very definitions of leader and led were being recast, the basis of a new social order created. Wrote Jack Belden: "Peasant and cadre were like a two-man patrol into enemy territory; they went forward into the unknown by a process of mutual encouragement, first one holding back, then the other, then both rushing forward together."[36] Between leaders

36. Jack Belden, *China Shakes the World* (New York: Harper & Brothers, 1949. Other outstanding books by observers are William Hinton, *Fanshen: A Documentary of Revolution in a Chinese Village* (New York: Monthly Review Press, 1968); Edgar Snow, *Red Star over China* (New York: Garden City Publishing Company, 1939); and Graham Peck, *Two Kinds of Time* (Boston, Mass.: Houghton Mifflin, 1950). During the last decade, however, work on the rise of the Chinese Communists has sought to quantify the Chinese revolution, to reject "grand causes" or "sweeping theory" and to concentrate on "reality in all its complexity." Rejecting the "mechanical" theories that understand the development of Chinese communism as the result of such forces as "imperialism," "organized indignation," and "rural impoverishment," various studies have undertaken detailed work on innumerable factors in China's 2,000-odd counties. While the reliability of the data is open to serious question, the problems in the methodology serious, and the choice of variables questionable, the more notable consequence of this approach so far has been a marked inability of those who quantify to deal with the qualitative, often

and led, in short, there seemed to be a relationship of mutuality, identification, and coperformance that released the creative energies and rage so essential for revolutionary struggle and increased political consciousness. Mark Selden's excellent work reveals this process well.[37] The peasants had to be brought to consciousness of their situation; the cadres had to be under sufficient popular influence to ensure the relevance of their leadership to local needs. Cadres could be effective only if their ideas and plans pointed the way for peasants themselves to act to overcome the existing exploitive situation. Belden's work provides a graphic illustration of this approach in his descriptions of "accusation, speak bitterness and struggle" meetings. Communist power could break the external restraints, the formal power, of the feudal society. But the peasants themselves had to participate fully, speak out, rid themselves of all the internalized repression. "Scarface, Crooked Head, Lop Ear—the number of these nameless creatures was legion in the land. For such a man to stand up and speak before his fellow villagers, both rich and poor, constituted by its very nature a revolutionary break with the past. In the same moment that he burst through the walls of silence that had enveloped him all his life, the peasant also tore asunder the chains that had bound him to feudalism. Awkwardly at first the words crawled from his throat, but once the first word passed his lips, there came gushing forth, not only an unarrestable torrent of speech, but the peasant's soul.

By such methods, the typically selfish peasant began to identify himself with other men. He began to generalize politically, to see himself both as an individual and as a part of society."[38] Must such a process as this be constantly squeezed primarily through a vision of control, manipulation, and indoctrination? Must scholars continue to use such vocabulary as "strongly indoctrinated in the importance of honesty"? Is it really just a process of leadership control and domination when cadres seek to show peasants aspects of their collective interests so that they can become more aware

elusive, factors that observers in the 1940's took for granted. The flood of detail has so far been rivaled only by the paucity of theoretical results. And there remains a recurring refusal to ask the broad questions about the West that ultimately are a part of any analysis of China. Several essays in A. Doak Barnett, ed., *Chinese Communist Politics in Action* (Seattle: University of Washington Press, 1969), exemplify these tendencies. One of the better examples is Roy Hofheinz, "The Ecology of Chinese Communist Success: Rural Influence Patterns, 1923–45," pp. 3–78.

37. Mark Selden, *The Yenan Way in Revolutionary China* (Cambridge, Mass.: Harvard University Press, 1971).

38. Belden, *China Shakes the World*, pp. 169–170.

through their own actions of any given plan? Hinton's brilliant work on one village in north China should at least give the critics pause. Liberation, he concluded, meant a constant mutual education (not control) of leaders and led, maximum participation of the majority in political action at the local level, and local initiative undertaken within an ideology that provided a meaning for the effort. It is this notion of liberation—with all its contradictions and failures, to be sure, but also with its successes and the hope it offered for the future—which has rarely received serious consideration.

Just as crucial is another theme in the American literature—that revolution is the failure of other means. Revolution results from the breakdown of the normal pattern of development. There is nothing inherently positive or unique in revolutionary action, nothing of value which could not more appropriately be "injected" into the "system" through a reformist leadership. Theodore White echoed this theme well: "There is no brutality more ferocious than that of a mass of people who have the chance to work primitive justice on men who have oppressed them. The spectacle of loot and massacre, of temples in flames, of muddy sandals trampling over silken brocades, is awesome; but there is scant mercy or discrimination in any revolution, large or small. The great question of China is whether any democratic form of government can ease these tensions by wise laws peacefully, *before* the peasant takes the law into his own hands and sets the countryside to flame.[39] It is as though the changes that could be brought about through a "reformist" leadership in China, through some "peaceful" means, were not qualitatively different from those brought about through revolution. This was a crucial assumption.

It meant that the process of "modernization" and "development" could be separated from the act of revolution. Questions about the creative thrust and inherent justice in the revolutionary act were carefully set aside. And this despite the overwhelming evidence in the Chinese revolution of the creative mobilization of the peasantry, the enormous programs of experimentation, the new forms of organization and self-expression, and the speed with which improvements could be made. Surely this revolutionary process could have suggested just a few of the unique possibilities mass-based revolutionary movements possessed in China for overcoming institutionalized violence in the 1940's. All those whose work concludes that America's "failure" in China was the inability to force reform

39. White and Jacoby, *Thunder Out of China*, p. 32.

must be asked whether its slowness, if it came through the elite at all, could ever have matched the attack led by the Communists on the inordinate costs and horrors of the existing order. Could it ever have allowed for the role of politically active peasantry with all the consequences involved in increasing consciousness of the sources and causes of exploitation in rural life?

The assumption meant that revolution was seen as the failure of a more desirable process of "gradual" change, a break from the normal, hoped-for pattern, a breakdown of safer means. Some critics simply underestimate the 100 years of rebellion and violent conflict in China. Surely this was more "normal" than those who have argued for a "third path" in the 1940's and ever since. Such analysis of China proceeds as though reform measures could have brought about the achievements of revolution, too, though more humanely. Change becomes a question of tactics and method— whether applicable from above through the established elite, or from below in a mass-based movement. Change is reduced to a technical question, almost outside the broadest socio-economic context in which it is undertaken. And it is here that one sees a blurring together of the results of "orderly" and "gradual" change with revolutionary transformation, just as a similar process is evident in the blurring of revolutionary and counterrevolutionary forms of politicization in totalitarian theory.

The assumption meant that an elite closely linked with the West might lead the economic and social transformation of the country. Involved in this assumption are two key questions. First, did the revolutionary process require action against the dominance of the Euro-American system in the educational, techno-economic sphere just as in the political arena, or was American involvement in educating China's elite, providing industrial, financial, and military assistance, both well intentioned and progressive? Second, if the process of revolutionary transformation is inherently hostile to Western forms of penetration, does this sufficiently explain hostility at the level of state to state relations?

To explore this last point, so essential for evaluating in broad terms American-Chinese relations, it is helpful, I think, to recognize that the Chinese revolution had two distinct currents. One arose in the villages of inland China. The other was modern and urban centered. The first current, dependent upon military force, was intricately interwoven with class warfare in the villages. The second, the development of a middle class in response to the impact of imperialism and colonialism, was decisively linked to Western education. After 1927, this urban group played the dominant role in nationalist movements in coastal politics. Though some members of the higher bourgeoisie wished to follow a policy of accommodation with Japan, the hatred of Japan and other foreign powers was too deeply rooted to be destroyed. As the Kuomintang continued its campaigns against the CCP in the 1930's, opposition to appeasement of Japan flared more and more openly, reaching a fever pitch when the Japanese invaded Manchuria.

The revolutionary current in the rural areas, simply put, was anti-traditional (hatred of the gentry and the traditional system), and that of the cities was intensely nationalistic and often anti-colonialist. This the Chinese Communists well understood. China was a semi-feudal, semi-colonial country. The struggle was not for immediate socialism, but for the liquidation of feudalism, to achieve social democracy on the one hand and the achievement of national emancipation on the other.

Many Americans who urged reform in the 1940's and since were essentially asking, it seems to me, for this urban centered middle class to lead the fight against feudal rural conditions. This middle group was the China Americans knew, the one through which their interests were expressed. In a sense, Americans felt so at home with the "liberal" and professional groups precisely because they had constructed their dwelling. "Chinese officials have studied our Anglo-Saxon institutions. Chinese leaders in education, journalism, banking, and industry have followed our example. Modern China as we know it has been built by men who have used our experience."[40] Conservatives in the mid-1940's often saw China's problems as the result of the weakness of the capitalist revolution that the Japanese had aborted.[41] Decimated by the war, it became threatened by the Communists and weakened further by the increased influence of feudal elements in the Kuomintang. The only answer (however implausible by 1945) was, they felt, to revitalize the capitalist revolution. Liberals spoke another language to be sure.[42] Their key hope was to find a path between reaction and revolution. But their agency of change was the same, in essence,

40. John K. Fairbank, "Our Chances in China," *Atlantic* 178.3 (September 1946), p. 39. For an introduction to the impact of Western education, particularly American, on Chinese life see Y. C. Wang, *Chinese Intellectuals and the West, 1872–1949* (Durham: University of North Carolina Press, 1966).

41. George Taylor, "An Effective Approach in Asia," *Virginia Quarterly Review* 30.3 (Winter 1950), pp. 342–54 presents a concise statement of the conservative view in terms of capitalism.

42. An example of the liberal approach is in John Fairbank's articles, "Can We Compete in China," *Far Eastern Survey* 17 (May 19, 1948), pp. 113–117 and "Toward a Dynamic Far Eastern Policy," *Far Eastern Survey* 18 (Sept. 7, 1949), pp. 209–212.

as for the conservatives—they spoke of the Western trained technicians, bureaucrats, engineers, and scientists who would build the new China and of the American educated liberals who could provide a "humane" conception of development. This group was the receptacle of America's "good intentions," the very key to a middle way.

What shocked and bewildered some of those sensitive, often extremely perceptive people in the 1940's were the blatant contradictions in their hopes—they found an American government backing a corrupt, brutal, reactionary regime, the very incarnation of the status quo. The middle class seemed impotent, powerless, unable to provide any alternative to the life and hope in the liberated areas. Instead of a progressive role for American power, the agonies of the Chinese after 1945 seemed only to increase with its use. In this polarized context, between revolution and counter-revolution, there seemed nothing progressive the United States could do.

Some individuals genuinely grappled with the very viability of rapid change through the middle class. Was it not perhaps their Western education and outlook, their position as part of a nascent, frightfully weak bourgeoisie, which made them "lose their ability to communicate with the masses of China which alone could have galvanized them to convert plans into reality"?[43] Was it the lack of an independent indigenous industrial sector that made them too weak to play a dynamic role, while the fear of revolutionary consciousness among the peasantry and the workers made them concerned about challenging too strongly the reactionary elements? Was it that "having divorced itself from the workers in the cities and particularly from the peasant masses in the countryside, the Chinese bourgeoisie lost the capacity for political action"?[44] To say that the Chinese middle class could not have led a movement capable of rapidly and radically improving the lives of the peasantry is not to say they could not have clung to power. But was American support for such groups, had it succeeded, something which would not have simply prolonged the agonies of the status quo? Had not those highly educated intellectuals, so close to American "ideals," lost touch with their own people? Concluded one frustrated State Department officer: "They could know what had

43. John Melby, "Review of *The East and West Must Meet: A Symposium*," *Far Eastern Survey* 28 (December 1959), pp. 188–189.

44. Belden, *China Shakes The World*, p. 143. Belden's chapters on "Contradictions in China's Development" and "The Last Rules of Old China" superbly pose this problem.

to be done and still feel more at home in the Faculty Club at Harvard or the International Club in Shanghai than they could in the villages where the work of China is done. There is no society which would not have welcomed them—except their own."[45] In such a situation, is it surprising that a revolutionary movement reacted against America's "outpost" in China and defined a new role for the modern professionals? Was it essential, then, for American involvement to be rejected in order for China to stand up? Instead of viewing opposition to American penetration of Chinese society as slightly paranoic, instead of the accepted assumption that development in the world capitalist system could have allowed China to rapidly face its rural problems, it is time to question whether the middle class, even in better circumstances, had the power or ability to lead the Chinese population toward a better life.

America in Postwar Asia

> Writing a history of the Second World War will be like "trying to capture a great dream before it dies."
> —FDR to Archibald MacLeish, 1943

American policy was undoubtedly guided by a series of immediate military objectives from 1941 to 1945. But there were also broader, more inarticulate visions of economic and political goals which were seen as important end products of the struggle. In Asia, China was at the center of a vision of postwar Asia. Though little work has been done on the role American officials hoped China might play, there are bits and pieces from different accounts which, taken together, suggest some of the crucial factors involved in post-1945 policy.

Alone among the big three, Franklin Roosevelt spoke of China as a great power. Until the Stilwell affair, it was to be second only to the United States in Asia and the Pacific. Though Churchill constantly muttered about the American obsession with China, he could not dissuade Roosevelt. As James Burns argues, "Roosevelt saw China as the kingpin in an Asiatic structure of newly independent and self-governing nations and hence as the supreme example and test of his strategy of freedom."[46] Though the difficulties in this hope were apparent to those in the China-Burma-India theater (and perhaps to Roosevelt himself), the emphasis on China

45. John Melby, *The Mandate of Heaven: A Record of Civil War—China, 1945–1949* (Toronto: University of Toronto Press, 1968), p. 302.

46. James MacGregor Burns, *Roosevelt: Soldier of Freedom* (New York: Harcourt Brace Jovanovich, 1970), p. 378.

should not be reduced to a naive or romantic gesture on Roosevelt's part. A stable, "democratic" (pro-Western) China was almost a prerequisite for a stable, peaceful Asia *if* Japan were to be demilitarized, dominated by the United States, and prevented from building a new economic empire. American policy had long been based on either Japan or China as its gateway to the Asian mainland. If China emerged from the war hostile to the United States, it would be hard indeed to continue planning for a disarmed, neutral Japan. A stable, nonaggressive China would also allow for the transition from European colonialism to nationalism in other countries. "By concentrating our Asiatic effort on operations in and from China," wrote one presidential adviser in Tehran, "we keep to the minimum our involvement in colonial imperialism."[47] Chinese-American friendship, it was hoped, would provide the necessary security and stability in which the anticolonialist struggle would triumph, thus reducing danger of great turmoil. A united China would also suggest an Asia relatively free of Russian power.

The harshest criticism of China as a great power, not surprisingly, came from those who wanted a "soft peace" with Japan. Those who sought a harsher peace (the controversy over the emperor is a case in point), yet knowing of China's disastrous internal conditions, floundered around in search of a less murky concept of postwar Asia. To Herbert Feis, the President's faith in China was based on a series of serious misconceptions—that China would emerge from the war "friendly to the West," that the government could emerge united and properly administer the country, that the Chinese had the "latent qualities to become a great nation." With such assumptions, Roosevelt "risked the whole future of the Far East." Feis clearly faces the implications of a weak China in his own perception of Asia. One of the "really important faults" of the Cairo and Yalta accords was "the decision to reduce Japan to a dependent power in the Pacific." Indeed, the crucial decision about postwar Asia for Feis was made at Cairo—"that Japan was to forfeit its whole Empire and position on the continent of Asia."[48] Here is clearly a crucial

47. *Foreign Relations of the United States: Cairo and Tehran, 1943*, p. 372.
48. Herbert Feis, *Roosevelt, Churchill, and Stalin: The War They Waged and the Peace They Sought* (Princeton: Princeton University Press, 1957), pp. 517, 253. With Gabriel Kolko's *The Politics of War: The World and United States Foreign Policy, 1943–1945* (New York: Random House, 1968), Feis attempts to understand some of the broader political implications of global strategy and the nature of the decisions involved in postponing actions in China. Feis, in a rare display of imagination, suggests the consequences that might have resulted if Asia had been the primary theater of action (p. 46). What is lacking in the broad range of books on this subject is a detailed analysis of the groups which wanted an Asia-first policy, the divisions within

theme of the postwar period—that growing awareness of the death of a pro-American China which deeply influenced developments in occupied Japan and the rest of "liberated" Asia.[49] A changing perception of China thus implied a shifting position on the dangers of the anticolonialist movements and a broader role for America in many Asian countries and for Japan as a "junior" partner.

Besides the explosive emergence of a nuclear armed America into Asia, an understanding of three other macroevents, I think, make up the main threads of how one looks at post-World War II China. Of the three events, one has been largely ignored and two are distorted. The three events: the death of the European colonial systems; the reemergence of Russia as an Asian power; and the spread of revolutionary movements and the widespread demands for radical change.

The collapse of the Japanese empire meant not just the temporary eclipse of an Asian power seeking imperial prominence, but also the collapse of the European colonial system. America exploded onto the scene as the great global, capitalist power, replacing the British. One perspective on this change, still generally ignored, is the British reaction to America's new role in Asia.

Gabriel Kolko's excellent work, *The Politics of War* (New York Random House, 1968) does suggest a wide range of conflicts between the United States and Great Britain in Europe and over Britain's role in the war against Japan. China, however, remains largely untouched. Yet the British view of the American "take-over" could provide a most provocative insight into American actions. The official history of the British Foreign Office bluntly states that Britain "wanted closer Anglo-American cooperation in China, but realized that American opinion generally—including official opinion —continued to distrust British motives . . . America seemed still to be more suspicious of British than Russian policy."[50] ("All the

---

the military establishment, particularly as it related to initial postwar planning, and the relationship of "Asia firsters" to the conservative, neo-isolationist strain in American domestic politics.

49. The relationship between events in China and American occupation policy in Japan is almost completely neglected. Most work on Japan proceeds as though it were in an international vacuum. John Dower's "Occupied Japan and the American Lake, 1945–1950," in Friedman and Selden, eds., *America's Asia,* and "The Eye of the Beholder: Background Notes on the U.S.–Japan Military Relationship" *Bulletin of Concerned Asian Scholars,* 2.1 (October 1969), pp. 15–31, provide an excellent corrective to the prevailing interpretation.

50. Ernest Llewellyn Woodward, *British Foreign Policy in the Second World War* (London, H.M. Stationery Office, 1962), p. 427. Feis, *Roosevelt,*

British are interested in," concluded Representative Mansfield after a tour of Asia for Roosevelt in late 1944, "is Singapore, Hongkong, a restoration of prestige, and a weak China.")[51] Numerous other officials warned of the future threat of Russia in the same breath with which they condemned British imperialism.

Even more, as America's "protectorate" developed in the initial postwar years, concludes Brian Porter in his *Britain and the Rise of Communist China,* conservative and business opinion was decidedly unsympathetic to American attempts to "dam the tide" of communism. Why? "When, after granting facilities to American businessmen, the KMT Government refused to open its ports to British ships, failed to restore British property on the Yangtze, and delayed resuming payments on British loans, fears which had already been expressed in parliament and the press that the U.S. was bent upon creating an exclusive economic empire in China appeared to be confirmed. Thus, from the commercial point of view, the establishment of an efficient Chinese government with whom it would be possible to trade, even though that government should be Communist, seemed to British merchants preferable to a situation from which they benefited little.[52]

America, long Britain's understudy, apparently wanted to write its own script. And the British just couldn't see the benevolent motives and lack of imperial objectives. Perhaps they were too practiced in recognizing them. Britain undoubtedly wished to restore its imperial prerogatives in Asia and was displeased with American policy on this score. But such an objective does not negate British perceptions and may provide yet another counter to the arguments about America's uniqueness. Britain, with far more investment in China than America, evidently preferred to deal with a strong Communist regime rather than an American dominated Kuomintang.

Russia's re-emergence as an Asian power was viewed from the late 1940's until the Sino-Soviet split in terms of a bipolar world. The two superpowers faced each other across the ruins of the Japanese "new order." Events in such countries as China came to be interpreted primarily in terms of "Russian interests" or "American interests." By the time Secretary Acheson wrote his letter of trans-

---

Churchill, and Stalin makes a similar point and refers to the repeated and deep divisions between the Americans and the British.

51. *Foreign Relations of the United States: China, 1945,* p. 16.

52. Brian Porter, *Britain and the Rise of Communist China: A Study of British Attitudes, 1945–1954* (London: Oxford University Press, 1967), pp. 13–14. Porter's work has various suggestions for following this subject in parliamentary debates.

mittal to the *China White Paper*, China was almost reduced to a passive, buffeted object in an ideological struggle between two powers and two ways of life.

Recent work on Russia's actual objectives in China, however, suggests how limited they were. Anxious to preserve their influence in Manchuria and to a lesser degree in north China through a weak Nationalist government, perpetually worried by the threat of a fairly potent Communist movement it sought unsuccessfully to control, the Soviet Union essentially sought to prevent *any* combination of power capable of challenging their position.[53] The relationship between the Soviets and the CCP in Manchuria is at last being explored in depth.[54] Clearly there was military assistance. The Chinese Communists were able to gain strategic footholds and to acquire Japanese materials in Manchuria. However, the Russians initially gave political assistance to the Nationalist government, signing the 1945 Treaty of Friendship. Economic "assistance" was limited to stripping Manchuria of its industrial assets, an act that proved most embarrassing to the CCP. Raymond Garthoff concludes, as does Charles McLane, that Soviet looting was clearly inconsistent with the U.S. contention that Russia handed Manchuria over to the CCP so that they could have a base against the Nationalists.[55] Indeed, the Russians and the Nationalists may have been far more involved with each other through secret negotiations than either could have admitted since 1949.

Above all else, Adam Ulam and Charles McLane contend that the Russians most feared a greater American control over China. Though some may argue that Russia hoped only to draw America into a civil war that would exhaust U.S. resources, Russian press reactions, closely followed by McLane, revealed their concern over American policy debates in late 1945 when the Marshall mission took shape. It is also probable that Stalin sharply underestimated the strength of the CCP, found the Marshall mission initially compatible with Russian interests, and worried over how to control the CCP. Ulam adds his voice to a growing chorus who now doubt that the CCP was even closely toeing the Russian ideological line. It

53. See Adam Ulam, *Expansion and Coexistence: The History of Soviet Foreign Policy, 1917–1967* (New York: Frederick A. Praeger, Inc., 1968), and Charles B. McLane, *Soviet Policy and the Chinese Communists* (New York: Columbia University Press, 1958).

54. Dissertation work in progress by Steven I. Levine, Harvard University, on "Political Integration in Manchuria, 1945–1948."

55. Raymond Garthoff, "Soviet Intervention in Manchuria, 1945–46," in R. Garthoff ed., *Sino-Soviet Military Relations* (New York: Frederick A. Praeger, 1966) McLane, 239. Also see Edmund Clubb, "Manchuria in the Balance, 1945–46," *Pacific Historical Review*, 26.4 (November 1957), pp. 377–391.

hardly provided them with the best justification for gaining power in China.

Gar Alperovitz's *Atomic Diplomacy: Hiroshima and Potsdam* analyzes the impact of the nuclear dimension on the American bipolar world view.[56] Among its many merits, the book shows how uneasiness among Washington officials over Russia's postwar intentions in Europe and Manchuria was brought to a climactic head by reflections on the consequences of atomic power.

The demand for radical social change in Asia at the end of World War II is noted by numerous American scholars.[57] This awareness, however, was increasingly blurred by the fear of Russia. Elites within many societies had fought for political independence from their colonial overlords, but many were at the same time engaged in a struggle against revolutionary forces in their own societies. The war had led to a decisive rupture between leaders and led. It was this struggle within societies which was so distorted by the standard American interpretations. The struggle between elites and popular movements became a microcosm of an international struggle between Russia and the United States, between "communism" and "democracy." Consequently, tolerance, even appreciation of revolutionary movements, became less and less apparent by the late 1940's and early 1950's.

In practice, America's response to the collapse of the traditional imperial system was to try to reinforce the elites within societies who were attempting to hold the line against insurgency movements.[58] This was justified in terms of anti-communism and the Russian threat. But this meant opposition to revolutionary movements and an American intention to intervene in internal conflicts. Truman's letter of instruction to Marshall states this bluntly: "Events of this century . . . would indicate that a breach of peace anywhere in the world threatens the peace of the entire world. China has a clear responsibility . . . to eliminate armed conflict within its territory as constituting a threat to world stability and

56. Gar Alperovitz, *Atomic Diplomacy: Hiroshima and Potsdam, The Use of the Atomic Bomb and the American Confrontation with Soviet Power* (New York: Random House, 1965).

57. Numerous American observers constantly stated the widespread demands in Asia for revolutionary change. It seems important to reread some of the on-the-scene accounts, for in later years the demand for revolutionary transformation slips out of most books, particularly in terms of the emotional urgency with which the problem was felt at the end of World War II. Harold Issac's *No Peace for Asia* (Cambridge, Mass.: M.I.T. Press, 1947) is one of the best of these works.

58. Gabriel Kolko's *The Politics of War* develops this theme on a global scale in a provocative and skillful way.

peace." True, the roots of disorder among states, to a degree, are the result of instability within states. But Truman's statement reflects a constant trait of postwar American policy—the belief that an attempt to maintain a certain type of order among states required a certain type of order (and change) within states.[59] More and more this meant support for the established elite as the only alternative to insurgency movements "Communists" would exploit. American power, faced with the collapse of the traditional colonial system and the widespread demand for radical change, came to support numerous elites against revolutionary movements—and to understand and justify such a development in terms of anticommunism and the threat of Russia.

Such macroevents, however, do not necessarily explain specific policies or their consequences, though they provide an ultimate framework in which some sense can be made of them. The particular development of Chinese-American relations was certainly related to a series of American decisions to involve itself in the Chinese civil war on the Nationalist side.[60] These decisions, often taken in moments of crisis, acquired their own momentum. So many American historians conclude that U.S. policy was relatively neutral in the civil war that the growth of Chinese Communist opposition to the United States seems a result only of their ideology, not American actions. Yet even a brief survey of a few of the major decisions in the postwar period suggests otherwise. For the period from V-J day through the Marshall mission may have had a marked effect on long-term relations, setting the stage for an American-Chinese ice age later capped by the Korean War. Among these decisions were:

The Japanese Surrender and the American Airlift. Officially, American policy was "neutrality." Yet from the day General Order

59. Robert Tucker, "The American Outlook" in Robert Osgood, Robert Tucker and others, *America and the World: From the Truman Doctrine to Vietnam* (Baltimore: Johns Hopkins Press, 1970) develops this theme in a broad postwar context.

60. John Gittings provides a good overview of this period of increased American commitment to the Nationalist cause. See his "Origins of Chinese Foreign Policy," in David Horowitz, ed., *Containment and Revolution* (Boston: Beacon Press, 1967). Among the most easily usable but often overlooked source materials on this period are the extensive American government translation series. Though not published, the U.S. Office of War Information *China Daily Digest*, pp. 1–111, provides the day by day account of key radio and newspaper reports for both Communist and Nationalist China during the crucial post V-J period. Many of the radio broadcasts in the *Daily Digest* are now all but impossible to locate in Chinese. *The Chinese Press Review*, compiled for limited circulation by the American Counsel-General in Shanghai, is available for the years from 1946 to 1950.

No. 1 was promulgated (August 14), most works on the period reveal that the United States made a massive commitment to Chiang —by the decision that Japanese troops in China would surrender only to Chiang, that an American airlift would transport his troops throughout the country in order for him to reestablish control, and by the use of Japanese troops to hold the line against the Communists until Chiang could arrive with sufficient force.

Herbert Feis concludes that General Order No. 1 was written with China specifically in mind. Both MacArthur and Marshall strongly warned the Japanese of the consequences of surrendering to the Chinese Communists. And Hurley, in line with this policy, urged on August 11 that "the terms should penalize Japan for any attempt to arm any belligerent forces within China against the National Government of the Republic of China."[61]

The decision to use Japanese troops to hold the line against the Communists in China was complemented by the decision to airlift Chiang's troops to the key centers of China, to commit American forces to hold several ports and cities, and in the repeated instructions to American units to deal only with the Nationalists. This was not "neutrality," as many at the time fully understood. Truman was only too accurate when he described this strategy in his memoirs: "It was perfectly clear to us that if we told the Japanese to lay down their arms immediately and march to the seaboard the entire country would be taken over by the Communists. We therefore had to take the step of using the enemy as a garrison until we could airlift Chinese Nationalist troops to South China and send marines to guard the seaports. In due course Japanese troops would surrender to them, march to the seaports, and we would send them back to Japan. This operation of using the Japanese to hold off the Communists was a joint decision of the State and Defense Departments which I approved."[62]

The American government, concludes Feis, committed itself to establishing the authority of the Nationalist government throughout China. ("And to do these things first—before the Communists interfered and possibly against their armed opposition.")[63] The results of America's effort are impressive. Within a few months of V-J day, close to half a million Nationalist troops were airlifted—the largest airlift in history up to then, and an action that surprised the Russians and angered the Chinese Communists.

61. Hurley in *Foreign Relations of the United States: China, 1945*, p. 529.
62. Harry S. Truman, *Memoirs*, II, *Years of Trial and Hope* (New York: Doubleday, 1956), 113–114.
63. Feis, *The China Tangle*, p. 305.

Throughout 1945 (and reports exist that such was the case until at least the end of 1948), sizable numbers of Japanese troops were used by the Nationalist government "to protect lines of communication and installations against depredation and attack by Chinese Communists."[64] It was the airlift which enabled Chiang to implement his strategy of cooperation with the puppet troops in vast areas of China. It should be remembered as well that most of the military operations launched by Chiang until 1948 were in north China and Manchuria, territory the Kuomintang could never have reached without the fleet of American planes and ships. Concludes Tang Tsou, such efforts "swung the balance in favor of the Nationalist Government and averted an imminent Communist victory." If Tang Tsou is correct, it meant additional years of civil war—thanks to the Americans.[65]

The American Troop Commitment. Both the extent of America's involvement in the civil war as well as some of the limitations on American power are evident in the official marine history's account of the 60,000 marines in north China.[66] Wedemeyer's task was officially to "advise and assist the Chinese Nationalist Government in the disarmament and deportation of Japanese from the China theater" without involving himself in the civil war. Wedemeyer himself constantly argued that his instructions were contradictory, and in dispatch after dispatch pleaded for some coherency in his orders. Just about every other official connected with the problem knew his instructions were contradictory (though some were more practiced in the art of self-deception). The marines, concludes the marine history, were of "incalculable help to the Central Government." By their very presence they were a "force for stability," standing for American power and its commitment to Chiang. "The very presence of the Marines in North China, holding open the major ports of entry, the coal mines, and the railways was an incalculably strong military asset to the Central Government. And the fact that the U.S. had provided a good part of the arms of the troops scheduled to take over North China and Manchuria made the situation even more explosive. The supply of ammunition and replacement parts for these weapons, even though they were now used

64. General Wedemeyer to Army Chief of Staff Eisenhower, *Foreign Relations of the United States, China, 1945*, p. 662.
65. Tang Tsou, *America's Failure*, p. 305. Tang Tsou provides a fairly good description of this period.
66. Benis M. Frank and Henry Shaw, Jr., *History of the U.S. Marine Corps: Operations in World War II*, vol. V *Victory and Occupation* (Washington, D.C.: Government Printing Office, 1968). Also see the extensive documentation in *Foreign Relations of the United States: China, 1945* on this subject.

to fight the Communists rather than the Japanese, was a charge upon the American government."[67]

So, too, was the American decision to work with the Japanese troops. This story has yet to be told.[68] But it hardly requires an inordinate amount of imagination to guess the response of the Communists to the degree of "mutual trust" spoken of in the marine history between the Japanese and the Americans when it "extended to the point where they mounted guard over the railways of Hopeh together," where Americans used over 10,000 Japanese troops just to guard the bridges and isolated stretches of railway track between Chinwangtao and Peking throughout 1945.[69] Let it also not be forgotten that it was the American marines who "liberated" Peking over the violent objections of the Chinese Communists. When Chou En-lai personally protested to General Worton outside Peking in October 1945, he was told: "The Marines most certainly would move in, that they would come by rail and road . . . Further, that II corps was combat experienced and ready, that it would have overwhelming aerial support, and that it was quite capable of driving straight on through any force that the Communists mustered in its path." All in all, concludes the marine history, such tasks "savored much of the duties which fell to Marine expeditionary forces in the Caribbean islands in the '20s and '30s."[70]

In addition, the debates among the military and the diplomatic advisers to Truman in 1945 are becoming available. The diplomatic papers on China, for example, reveal the various debates over building up the Nationalist air force and navy so China could obtain "internal security" and meet its "international obligations." Repeatedly the Joint Chiefs of Staff argued that before the China theater was deactivated, a U.S. military advisory group should be established. The plan, argued over for months, called for the exemption of all personnel from Chinese legal jurisdiction, complete exemption from any import duty on goods used and consumed in China, China's agreement not to purchase military equipment from another power without prior U.S. consultation, and preferential treatment for American commercial organizations in China. Events in China and the rapid demobilization demanded by the American public tended to constantly interrupt such planning. The situation

67. Frank and Shaw, *Victory and Occupation*, pp. 578–579.

68. American diplomats reported seeing Japanese troops used by the Nationalist government at least through 1948. An example is John Melby's *Mandate of Heaven*.

69. Frank and Shaw, *Victory and Occupation*, p. 649.

70. Ibid., pp. 547–548.

was deteriorating too rapidly; commitments throughout the world appeared more pressing. The objective, however, was always clear— all economic and political assistance would be "carefully integrated at all times with military assistance provided China." Such ideas found general approval. The question was one of available power. Only a few raised strenuous objections, and these were often from the China desk in the State Department. Some pointed out the obvious—that, as the director of Far Eastern Affairs, John Carter Vincent concluded, such plans had all the characteristics of "a de facto protectorate with a semi-colonial Chinese army under our direction."[71]

The background of the Marshall mission. Surely, though, the Marshall mission is a sign of American neutrality. Yet here again the standard works reveal the facts, while downplaying the conclusion. It was clear in the debate over the drafting of Marshall's instructions that a "neutral" position would have meant Americans dealing directly with the Communists in the repatriation of the Japanese where the CCP was dominant. To do otherwise was support for the Kuomintang alone and opposition to the Communists. Marshall and Truman clearly chose this later course as the basis for the mission. In the unwritten part of the directive, it was decided that if the Communists refused to cooperate with the American initiative, the United States would continue to transport Chiang's troops into north China and Manchuria. But if Chiang was uncooperative, America would support him anyway and move his troops. To this Vincent and Byrnes protested, insisting that should Chiang refuse to cooperate "no assistance to move the troops would be provided and that we would be forced to deal directly with the Communists in repatriating the Japanese from North China."[72] Such was clearly a feasible military possibility—according to the military commander in north China and the under secretary of tlᴢ navy. Yet Byrnes and Vincent were overruled, and on this "neutral" basis the mission began. Truman was not just speaking from cold war hindsight when he wrote in his memoirs that the mission was designed to save the non-Communist groups in China. It was "the only way by which Chiang Kai-shek might have saved himself without full scale military intervention from the United States."[73]

71. *Foreign Relations of the United States, China, 1945*, p. 615.
72. Dean Acheson, *Present At the Creation* (New York, 1969), p. 143. Vincent argued in a similar manner, see *Foreign Relations of the United States, China, 1945*, 760. See Feis for background information.
73. Truman, p. 114.

It was necessary to reiterate these various examples of American involvement in China's civil war because of the firm conviction that it was not U.S. policy which was instrumental in the collapse of American-Chinese relations. Most historians still conclude, as does Edwin Reischauer, that "it should, of course, be recognized that the Chinese Communists would almost certainly have developed a strong hostility toward us no matter what we did."[74]

Such a view fits snugly into the normal American cold war ideology—of U.S. "neutrality" in the internal affairs of other nations, the benevolence of American power, the refusal to ask even the most elemental questions about capitalism, American imperialism, and the counterrevolutionary zeal that marks American policy. Against the background of American globalism confronting the most sweeping process of revolutionary transformation in history, the twenty-year avoidance of these questions takes on additional dimensions. This is particularly true given the nature of the brutal problems evident throughout the 1940's, yet ignored in the United States because of the blanket of ideological conformity. No more provocative and stirring story is to be found, nor one quite so illustrative of the various aspects of American character and society. Few stories are quite as dramatic as this collapse of one Chinese political world and the rise of another. Against the background of this sheer disaster for the American government, and the success of the Chinese revolutionaries, the issues and questions are posed about as clearly as they will ever be.

74. Edwin O. Reischauer, *Beyond Vietnam* (New York, 1967), p. 168.

The Truman Era

If there are such things as turning points in history, the seven years in American–East Asian relations after World War II richly deserve the title. During this time Chinese-American friendship, indifference to Korea, and troubled relations with Japan turned into Chinese-American enmity, massive involvement in Korea, and Japanese-American accord. Generally the subject of an unsatisfying polemical literature, this transformation in American–East Asian affairs needs attention from scholars ready to address the complex questions surrounding these events. To do so successfully, however, scholars will need an understanding of both American and East Asian culture, history, and politics. For in spite of the fact that the United States became the dominant power in East Asia at the end of the war, it is clear that indigenous forces remained central in determining the course of Chinese, Japanese and Korean affairs.

The logical starting point in the study of American–East Asian relations, 1946–1952, is Washington's role in China's civil war. Aside from Vietnam, no issue in post-1945 United States foreign relations has stirred more controversy. On the one side stands the official Washington explanation known as the *China White Paper*. Published in August 1949, eight weeks before the declaration of the Chinese People's Republic, the 1054-page volume of narrative and documents emphatically declared the United States free from responsibility for Kuomintang defeat and Communist victory. In the words of Secretary of State Dean Acheson, "The ominous result of the civil war in China was beyond the control of the government of the United States. Nothing that this country did or could have done within the reasonable limits of its capabilities could have changed that result; nothing that was left undone by this country has contributed to it." The chief cause of Nationalist defeat was Nationalist political, economic, and military failure; corruption and loss of popular confidence, runaway inflation, and the "world's worst [military] leadership" were all cited in the *White Paper* as central to Kuomintang collapse.[1]

1. *China White Paper: August 1949*, 2 vols. (Stanford: Stanford University

At an opposite pole from official Washington's view is the picture of Communist success resulting from naiveté and betrayal in the American government. Voiced first in November 1945 by General Patrick J. Hurley, restated in 1947 by Congressman Walter Judd, elaborated in 1950–1952 by Freda Utley and particularly Senator Joseph McCarthy, this thesis found its most systematic expression in Anthony Kubek's How the Far East Was Lost.[2] Arguing that Chiang Kai-shek's Nationalist government was perfectly capable of maintaining itself in power with American aid, Kubek attributes the "loss" of China to Soviet agents in key State and Treasury Department posts, pro-Soviet control of the most influential elements of the American press and "top American officials who sought to buy Soviet co-operation at any price." In short, events in Washington rather than in China gave birth to the unfriendly Peking regime.[3]

Between these contentions that America bore either no or primary responsibility for Chinese events stands the argument that America played a limited part in Chiang's defeat and that this was the result of honest mistakes. During World War II, for example, Washington failed to tie its military help to political demands which might have transformed the Nationalist government into a more popular and stable regime. Further, after the war when an all-out American effort in behalf of Nanking or a willingness to abandon it for a Third Force was needed to prevent Communist success, the Truman administration did neither. Instead, it first pressed Chiang into unsuccessful negotiatons with the Communists and then provided him with enough aid to be identified with his defeat but not enough to assure his continued presence on the mainland.[4]

Press, 1967), pp. iii-xvii, the quote is from p. xvi. It was originally published by the Department of State under the title, United States Relations with China, With Special Reference to the Period 1944–1949 (Washington: Government Printing Office, 1949). See also Dean Acheson, Present at the Creation: My Years in the State Department (New York: W. W. Norton & Co., 1969), chaps. 16 and 23, and pp. 302–307.

2. For the history of this interpretation, see Tang Tsou, America's Failure in China, 1941–1950 (Chicago: University of Chicago Press, 1963), pp. 234, 343–344, 538–546. See also Akira Iriye, Across the Pacific: An Inner History of American-East Asian Relations (New York: Harcourt, Brace & World, Inc., 1967), p. 269.

3. Anthony Kubek, How the Far East Was Lost: American Policy and the Creation of Communist China, 1941–1949 (Chicago: Henry Regnery Co., 1963), esp. pp. 287, 404–410.

4. The fullest statement of this argument is in Tang Tsou's America's Failure. It also provides the best available account of the interaction between Nationalists, Communists, and Americans in China after 1945. For other expressions of this argument, see John K. Fairbank, "Toward A Dynamic Far Eastern Policy," Far Eastern Survey, 18 (Sept. 7, 1949), 209–212; Walter Lippmann, Commentaries on American Far Eastern Policy (New York: Insti-

More than twenty years after their first expression, these views look more like examples of traditional attitudes toward China than convincing explanations of America's part in the civil war: the *White Paper* may be described as another statement of the Open Door policy or the American idea that China was a country for which we had ends but not means; while the other interpretations seem to spring in varying degrees from traditional convictions that a weak, exploited China relied on America to shape her domestic life.

The trouble with all these explanations is that they start from the wrong question: what could America have done in China? Before we can judge America's influence in China, we need to know what happened among the Chinese. Indeed, if we are to extend our knowledge of American behavior in postwar China, we must first have a full-scale study of recent Chinese history. Moreover, it must carry back to at least the beginning of China's all-out struggle with Japan in 1937, if not to 1931, taking account of the war's impact on China's contending factions. How, in short, did the eight years of fighting affect Nationalist and Communist strength? And what then happened after the war? Considering political, economic, and military action, how did the Nationalists fail and the Communists succeed? What were Nationalist and Communist assumptions about the United States? And what did the Soviets contribute to Mao's victory? It is only at this point that it seems useful to inquire about the impact of American actions and, more specifically, the likely consequence of greater aid to Chiang.

A fair assessment of America's China policy requires not only that we study events in China but also that we answer questions primarily on the American side—namely, who were the American policy makers and what motivated them? The public debate of the early 1950's, for example, showed that the State Department and its East Asian experts in particular had a major say in China policy, but it obscured the substantial role played by the defense chiefs. Indeed, the fact that the State Department was blamed for the "loss" of China probably had less to do with the actual division of responsibility for policy than with a reluctance on the part of Americans to indict the single most important authority on foreign policy—the military. If one does well to look at both the State

tute of Pacific Relations, 1950); Edwin O. Reischauer, *Wanted: An Asian Policy* (New York: Alfred A. Knopf, 1955), pp. 12–14, 130–133; John K. Fairbank, *The United States and China* (2d ed. rev.; New York: The Viking Press, 1962), chaps. 13 and 15.

Department and the military for architects of China policy, what can he conclude about their ideas and aims? How, for example, did policy makers view the Nationalists and Communists and what was the basis for their belief in a negotiated settlement? Did it have much to do with a picture of the Communists as essentially "agrarian reformers" and the Nationalists as increasingly unable to assert popular control? Or was the impulse to negotiate a settlement chiefly the product of convictions that American resources and public opinion would not allow substantial help to the Nationalists in a civil war? Further, to what extent was continued American involvement with Chiang the result of international as opposed to domestic considerations? Which was uppermost in administration minds: a concern to keep China out of Communist hands or fear that ending aid to Chiang would give the Republicans an effective point of attack?[5] Moreover, if the administration were so concerned to prevent China policy from growing into a political liability, why did it become so great a matter of public debate? Did the establishment of a hostile Communist government form too sharp a break with long-term assumptions about Chinese-American affairs? Was it chiefly a case of one too many Communist successes, of the "loss" of China coming too hard on the heels of Soviet atomic capability and American spy trials? Or was it primarily the consequence of the administration's inability to enunciate or follow a clear line of policy? Did reactions to China bloc critics in 1947–1949, such as resuming interrupted aid to Chiang, replacing the chief of the State Department's Office of Far Eastern Affairs and publishing the *China White Paper*, make administration leaders appear unsure and defensive about China policy, opening them to Republican attack? And did this in turn bring China to the attention of normally inattentive citizens, permitting Senator Joseph McCarthy to agitate them with a simple but seemingly authoritative explanation of how China was "lost"? Or, as Michael Paul Rogin suggests, did the loss of China fail to arouse mass concern until the Korean War?

5. Though Tang Tsou addressed himself to these questions in *America's Failure*, his answers were based chiefly on printed sources rather than on the papers of the policy makers. A study in progress which will help us to respond more confidently to these questions is being done by Gary May, a doctoral candidate at the University of California, Los Angeles, on "John Carter Vincent and the American Foreign Service in China, 1924–1953." Also of value here are: John F. Melby, *The Mandate of Heaven: Record of a Civil War: China, 1945–1949* (Toronto: University of Toronto Press, 1968); and John S. Service, *The Amerasia Papers: Some Problems in the History of U.S.-China Relations* (Berkeley: University of California Press, 1971).

It will be no simple matter responding to these questions. This is particularly true for the Chinese side of the story. Since Peking is not likely to open its archives to Western scholars, studies of Communist behavior in, say, the extremely complex negotiations mediated by General Marshall from December 1945 to January 1947 or in the political maneuvering and fighting which lasted from the autumn of 1945 to the occupation of Hainan Island in May 1950 can at present only be pieced together from published Chinese materials and American observers on the scene, a kind of shrewd guesswork on the order of Allen Whiting's analysis of Chinese intervention in the Korean War.[6]

One side of the Communist story, though, which seems already to have been worked out as fully as possible from available materials is the Soviet role in the Chinese revolution. The opinion of those who have scrutinized Russian publications and actions is that Soviet connections with China's Communists were far more complicated than the picture drawn by some Nationalists and Americans of a revolution strictly directed from Moscow. Indeed, though it is contended that Russian-Chinese Communist ties were closer than Stalin wanted Americans to believe when he dismissed Mao's followers as " 'margarine' Communists," it is the consensus of these Russian experts that Yenan rather than Moscow was the driving force in the revolution. Soviet fears of American intervention and exaggerated ideas of Nationalist strength inclined Moscow to deal with Chiang, hoping first only for Communist representation in the Nationalist government and later, after Mao's armies occupied all of northern China in early 1949, for Communist control over just a part of the mainland. A close look at how scholars have reached these conclusions from limited sources provides another model of how Chinese Communist behavior may be assessed.[7]

A study of the Nationalists should be a somewhat easier task. With a substantial body of U.S. diplomatic and military reports from American representatives, who were much closer to the Nationalists than the Communists, and with published recollections and judgments from a handful of officials like Arthur N. Young, F. F. Liu, and Carsun Chang, who were knowledgeable about Kuomintang policies, it should be possible to work out a representative

6. Allen S. Whiting, *China Crosses the Yalu: The Decision to Enter the Korean War* (New York: The Macmillan Co., 1960).

7. See Max Beloff, *Soviet Policy in the Far East, 1944–1951* (London: Oxford University Press, 1953), chaps. 2 and 3; Robert C. North, *Moscow and Chinese Communists*, 2d ed. (Stanford: Stanford University Press, 1963), chap. 13; Adam B. Ulam, *Expansion and Coexistence: The History of Soviet Foreign Policy, 1917–1967* (New York: Frederick A. Praeger, 1968), pp. 470–495.

picture of Nationalist political, economic, and military actions before and during the Civil War.[8]

The fullest account of what happened, though, is likely to come from the American side. U.S. Army, State and Treasury Department records should give us a good idea of both who determined policy in Washington and how it was carried out in China. For the pressures and motives influencing policy makers, however, it will be necessary to turn to their public speeches, memoirs, substantial private papers, and, wherever possible, recollections given in interviews. Unfortunately, these government and private manuscripts have been closed to scholars, and consequently, no qualified historian has had the chance to blunt the bitter political debate over the "loss" of China with a dispassionate research study like the Herbert Feis and William L. Langer, S. Everett Gleason volumes on the prewar and war years.[9] Some work, however, has already been accomplished with the use of printed materials and interviews, and as unpublished records become more available in the future, it will be increasingly possible to do this work.[10]

8. These reports of American officials are not yet available. Examples of published accounts by officials knowledgeable about the Nationalists are: Arthur N. Young, *China and the Helping Hand, 1937–1945* (Cambridge, Mass.: Harvard University Press, 1963); *China's Wartime Finance and Inflation, 1937–1945* (Cambridge, Mass.: Harvard University Press, 1965); Chang Kia-ngau, *The Inflationary Spiral: The Experience in China, 1939–1950* (Cambridge, Mass.: The M.I.T. Press, 1958); F. F. Liu, *A Military History of Modern China, 1924–1949* (Princeton: Princeton University Press, 1956); Carsun Chang, *The Third Force in China* (New York: Bookman Associates, 1952).

9. See Herbert Feis, *The Road to Pearl Harbor: The Coming of the War Between the United States and Japan* (Princeton: Princeton University Press, 1950); *The China Tangle: The American Effort in China from Pearl Harbor t̩ the Marshall Mission* (Princeton: Princeton University Press, 1953); William L. Langer and S. Everett Gleason, *The Challenge to Isolation, 1937–1940* (New York: Harper Brothers, Publishers, 1952); *The Undeclared Wa , ᵀ940–1941* (New York: Harper Brothers, Publishers, 1953). Though these volume. have been criticized as "court" histories, they are first-rate works of scholarship which remain unsurpassed.

10. Unfortunately, U.S. government records are still closed for the post-World War II period. State Department records, for example, are not "available to nonofficial researchers in advance of the publication of the 'Foreign Relations' volumes." According to the most recent information, two volumes in this series dealing with China in 1946 and the Marshall mission in particular are scheduled for publication in 1971. The Historical Office of the State Department is unable to predict when the "Foreign Relations" volumes for 1947 will appear. I am indebted to Dr. William M. Franklin, Director, Historical Office, Department of State, for this information. Dr. Franklin to author, September 15, 1969.

Since Treasury Department "records for the period 1946–1952 contain materials of a sensitive nature," the director of the Department's Office of Administration writes, ". . . we cannot permit general examination." The

Questions about why and how China became a major public issue, though, seem open to study at once. The extensive survey data available from the early 1950's and the substantial attention already given to McCarthyism suggest the possibility of effectively analyzing the China question in domestic politics.[11]

A study of American public reaction to the Chinese upheaval would be an important step toward a broader understanding of Chinese-American relations after World War II. But until we have specialized studies on everything from Nationalist military performance to the effects of American aid, we can not hope to get a balanced overall picture of what happened between China and the United States in the postwar years.

---

availability of specific materials, however, will be determined upon request. Leonard S. Dixon to author, October 24, 1969.

As for Department of the Army manuscripts, the Office of the Chief of Military History indicates that an 800-page classified manuscript, "History of the China Theater," by Captain Fenton Keyes and First Lieutenant Charles F. Romanus, is available for examination in his office "providing the researcher obtains an unofficial researcher's clearance." The manuscript includes discussions of "Japanese Surrender to China," "Russia and the Far East," "Recovery of Manchuria," "Military Advisory Group," and "Repatriation." It is listed on page ninety-five of "Historical Manuscript Accession List (Selected Subjects) No. 5, Office of the Chief of Military History." Colonel Robert H Fechtman to author, November 25, 1969.

White House Files on the President's papers are sealed. An inquiry to the Harry S. Truman Library, Independence, Missouri, brings the reply that the library "has, at present, very little material in its files relating to American policy toward China, Korea and Japan during the Truman Administration. There may be significant documents in this area among the small quantity of Truman papers not yet in our possession. While these files will eventually be turned over to the Library, they are not presently available for either our staff or to researchers." Philip D. Lagerquist, Research Archivist to author, September 9, 1969.

For a wide-ranging discussion of research opportunities in the Truman period, see Richard S. Kirkendall, ed., *The Truman Period as a Research Field* (Columbia: University of Missouri Press, 1957).

11. Discussions of domestic politics and public attitudes toward the China issue can be found in H. Bradford Westerfield, *Foreign Policy and Party Politics: Pearl Harbor to Korea* (New Haven: Yale University Press, 1955), chap. 16; Norman A. Graebner, *The New Isolationism: A Study in Politics and Foreign Policy Since 1950* (New York: The Roland Press, 1956), chaps. 1–3; Eric F. Goldman, *The Crucial Decade—and After: America, 1945–1960*, rev. ed. (New York: Vintage Books, 1960), chaps. 6–7.

On McCarthyism, see Daniel Bell, ed., *The Radical Right* (New York: Doubleday & Co., 1963), esp. chap. 9 by Talcott Parsons which suggests the central importance of foreign affairs to McCarthyism; Michael Paul Rogin, *The Intellectuals and McCarthy: The Radical Specter* (Cambridge, Mass.: The M.I.T. Press, 1967), esp. p. 243.

For a model of how past opinion on a foreign question can be reconstructed, see Ernest R. May, *American Imperialism: A Speculative Essay* (New York: Atheneum, 1968), especially chap. 9.

If learning about Chinese-American relations after the war seems to be a formidable task, it appears modest beside the job of understanding Korean-American affairs. This work is complicated by the fact that knowledge of Korean domestic history is woefully limited, apparently in East Asia as well as in the United States. According to Gregory Henderson, the author of a recent study of Korea's political tradition, "Koreans habitually interpret the history of their nation in terms of foreign invasion . . . To such agencies and causes is often imputed blame for loss of independence, failure of the independence movement, inability to 'protect' democracy, failure to make economic progress and so forth." To Henderson, though, "external factors are for Korea and her internal courses of secondary importance." In his estimate, domestic rather than foreign influences are central to the "fundamental operation" of Korean affairs.[12]

The body of English literature on Korea is small. But what does exist seems to be an offshoot of this Korean self-image, focusing almost exclusively on what was done to the Koreans rather than by them. Just as "the Chinese sense of central uniqueness . . . [about] the Chinese record has rubbed off on Western students of that record," so have Korean assumptions about an externally dominated history taken stage center in Western descriptions of that history.[13]

Take, for example, the handful of books on Korean-American relations after World War II: they uniformly relate how Americans of limited understanding and sympathy prevented the creation of a modern, unified, democratic state. According to these accounts, Washington failed to prepare for the occupation of Korea with trained personnel and detailed political and economic plans. Instead, it left most matters to its military representatives who "were so often uncertain and cautious about inaugurating definite policies as to appear dominated by the situation." Moreover, the occupation rebuffed healthy first steps toward self-rule, kept Japanese in administrative posts, antagonizing Koreans, favored conservative anticommunists over moderate and left-wing political groups, undermining democratic development, and refused to institute fundamental economic and social reforms. Finally, Roosevelt and Truman contributed to Korea's division when the former established neither a time limit for the occupation nor the nature of the interim government, while Truman neglected opportunities to bring about a

12. Gregory Henderson, *Korea: The Politics of the Vortex* (Cambridge: Harvard University Press, 1968), intro., esp. pp. 6–7.
13. The quote is from John K. Fairbank, "The American Approach to China, ca. 1840–1860," chap. 1 in this book.

north-south coalition government whose sovereignty and neutrality could have been guaranteed by the powers.[14]

Most striking in these histories is the extent to which they share the shortcoming of which they complain—the failure to take account of indigenous forces. Indeed, if we are to make rational judgments on postwar American actions in Korea, we need to know how traditional Korean political, economic, and social patterns affected what the United States did. In brief, we must learn whether Korean habits made democracy and modernization a realistic goal and whether the Koreans themselves were prepared to patch up differences for the sake of a unified nation–state.[15]

A similar problem exists in trying to explain the outbreak of the Korean War. North Korea's attack on the south is set down as Moscow's response to American mistakes: assuming that Korea was strategically insignificant in an all-out war, that air and naval units would provide a better defense than ground forces and that South Korea could see to its own security with a constabulary force, the United States shifted responsibility for Syngman Rhee's republic to a powerless United Nations, withdrew its infantry units, refused tanks and antitank weapons to South Korea's defenders, and made known its unwillingness to include the republic in an East Asian defense perimeter. The result, it is generally agreed, was Moscow's attempt to dominate all Korea and neutralize Japan.[16] Is it possible, as a few have suggested, that the war may have been the consequence of chiefly "local factors . . . the weakness of Rhee's repressive government, his threats to march on the North, [and] the belief of the North Koreans that they could unify the country easily"?[17] Despite almost universal agreement that it was a Soviet-inspired attack and that it is impossible for the time being to prove

14. George M. McCune, *Korea Today* (Cambridge: Harvard University Press, 1950), esp. pp. 268–270; Edwin O. Reischauer, *Wanted: An Asian Policy* (New York: Alfred A. Knopf, 1955), pp. 14–23; Soon Sung Cho, *Korea in World Politics, 1940–1950* (Berkeley: University of California Press, 1967), chaps. 4 and 12, and esp. pp. 34, 88–91.

15. For an attempt to explain postwar Korea developments this way, see Henderson, *Korea*, chap. 5.

16. Leland M. Goodrich, *Korea: A Study of U.S. Policy in the United Nations* (New York: Council on Foreign Relations, 1956), chaps. 1–4; Carl Berger, *The Korea Knot: A Military-Political History* (Philadelphia: University of Pennsylvania Press, 1957), chaps. 1–7; Ulam, *Expansion and Coexistence*, pp. 514–521; Marshall D. Shulman, *Stalin's Foreign Policy Reappraised* (Cambridge: Harvard University Press, 1963), pp. 139–144; Whiting, *China Crosses the Yalu*, chap. 3.

17. Ronald Steel, "Commissar of the Cold War," *The New York Review of Books*, 14 (Feb. 12, 1970), 18. See also Wilbur W. Hitchcock, "North Korea Jumps the Gun," *Current History*, 20 (March 1951), 136–144.

otherwise, one should not dismiss "local factors" out of hand.

It would be gratifying if we could have as full a knowledge of what touched off the Korean War as we already have about Washington's response. Indeed, we currently know more about the American reaction to the Korean conflict than about anything else in postwar American–East Asian affairs. The subject of several articles and a full-length book, the Truman administration's decision to defend South Korea has been reconstructed from firsthand information given by participants. This work has already been so thorough that, as one expert on decision making suggests, it is unlikely that the opening of the archives will do more than add details to what we know about the discussions of June 24–30.[18]

Still, there are problems to be solved. While all writers agree that the administration saw its decision to meet force with force in Korea as applying the lesson of the 1930's—namely, collective security measures to discourage future aggressions—the extent to which domestic political considerations played a role in the decision is unclear. Some scholars have argued that Harry Truman's decisions on major foreign policy issues were made without attention to political advantage or presidential standing. In the opinion of one writer, Truman "shunned ideas and interventions which might lay him open, *in his own mind*, to the charge that he 'played politics with national security.' "[19] At the first Blair House conference on June 25, for example, he rejected Undersecretary of State James Webb's request that they "talk about the political aspects of the situation," saying, "We're not going to talk about politics. I'll handle the political affairs." "The available record of the Korean decision," the most careful student of the subject writes, "reveals that apparently no explicit consideration was given to the domestic political implications of an American military engagement in Korea."[20]

Yet this same writer believes that Truman's action was in line with what he anticipated as popularly acceptable. Further, conserva-

18. Two early articles are: Albert L. Warner, "How the Korean Decision Was Made," *Harper's Magazine*, 202 (June 1951), 99–106; Beverly Smith, "The White House Story: Why We Went to War in Korea," *The Saturday Evening Post* (Nov. 10, 1951), 22–23 et passim. The best article on the subject is: Alexander L. George, "American Policy-making and the North Korean Aggression," *World Politics*, 7 (January 1955), 209–232. The full-length study is: Glenn D. Paige, *The Korean Decision: June 24–30, 1950* (New York: The Free Press, 1968). The observation is from the introduction by Richard C. Snyder, p. xii.

19. Richard E. Neustadt, *Presidential Power: The Politics of Leadership* (New York: John Wiley & Sons, 1960), pp. 176–179.

20. Paige, *The Korean Decision*, pp. 141, 304. See also Samuel P. Huntington, *The Soldier and the State: The Theory and Politics of Civil-Military Relations* (Cambridge, Mass.: Harvard University Press, 1964), pp. 382–384.

tive Republicans at the time felt that they deserved much of the credit for the decisions to fight in Korea and defend Formosa from the Chinese Communists. Having agitated for a tougher Far Eastern policy for several months, they assumed that the President was doing no more than adopting their suggestions. Finally, it is the opinion of the author of one recent study that if Truman and his advisers "stressed the excessively flagrant character of the North Korean assault as the principal reason for the reversal" of their policy, "the Republican party's prolonged pressure on the Administration for being soft on Communism in the Far East obviously also contributed to the Administration's fear of further loss of prestige should it fail to act." Indeed, it is hard to see how the charges against the Democrats of losing China and of allowing Communists or Communist sympathizers to shape East Asian policy did not have an impact on the decisions to fight in Korea and save Formosa for the Nationalists. The extent to which this was a consideration, though, must await the opening of the private manuscripts of the decision makers, especially of Secretary of State Acheson and other members of the State Department who bore the brunt of the Republican attacks.[21]

There are other, more speculative questions about the Korean decision. Was it concern with collective security or national interest which led the administration to take up arms? And was American intervention the best answer to the North Korean attack or were there other alternatives? The first question has been raised and effectively answered by Arnold Wolfers, who says that, despite claims to the contrary, America's response represented no radical departure from traditional power politics. Collective security, which Wolfers defines as "a policy of defense directed against . . . any aggressor anywhere," was not the motivating force behind the Korean action. Instead, it was a case of collective defense or of protecting "strong American national interests": proving "to its [America's] European allies that they could rely on American military assistance in case of Soviet attack"; and making the United Nations "serve as a substitute for a formal alliance of the free world." It has been suggested that the administration's failure to appreciate and publicize these selfish reasons for American intervention "deepened public confusion and anxiety" about the war. It remains to be shown

21. Paige, *The Korean Decision*, pp. 304–305; John W. Spanier, *The Truman-MacArthur Controversy and the Korean War* (Cambridge: Harvard University Press, 1959), pp. 58–64; Trumbull Higgins, *Korea and the Fall of MacArthur: A Précis in Limited War* (New York: Oxford University Press, 1960), pp. 21–23; Ulam, *Expansion and Coexistence*, p. 522.

in detail, however, how this emphasis on selfless causes for fighting undermined pulic confidence and whether appeals to self-interest would have been as effective in winning public backing.[22]

The question of whether American intervention was the best response to North Korean aggression is also open to discussion. On one side is the argument that if the United States had stood aside, "Peking and the Kremlin would have been encouraged to engineer other attacks at vulnerable points along the Sino-Soviet periphery." Such a response, it is also said, "might have fatally weakened the NATO coalition" and "would certainly have encouraged neutralism in Japan and Germany and a massive swing to the Communist bloc throughout the defenseless areas of Asia."[23] A contrasting view suggests that traditional Soviet caution would have discouraged Moscow from taking success in Korea as an inducement to bolder actions. Was there, the question is therefore raised, no means of minimizing the demoralizing effects on the free world of the loss of South Korea? Was not protecting Formosa, increasing military aid to Indochina and the Philippines, stepping up rearmament and mobilization at home, and deciding to rearm Germany enough to shore up morale and discourage Communist moves elsewhere in the world?[24] The answers to these questions, it would appear, can only be worked out from studying attitudes toward the war in Japan, the NATO states, West Germany, and the U.S.S.R.

American conduct in the war poses equally challenging problems. There is a major gap in our knowledge about the decision to cross the 38th parallel. Having entered the war to repel the North Korean attack and restore the South Korean state, the movement across the border signified a determination to pursue the original postwar aim of unifying Korea. The outcome, of course, was Chinese intervention and almost two years of indecisive fighting or "the least popular war in American history." How did this change in American war aims take place? Why did the Chinese intervene? And why did American intelligence fail to foresee the consequences of carrying the war to the north?

There have been strong differences of opinion on why the United States crossed the parallel. After the crossing proved to be a mistake, the idea took hold that General Douglas MacArthur "had forced a reluctant Civil Administration into a dubious political

22. Arnold Wolfers, "Collective Security and the War in Korea," *The Yale Review*, 43 (June 1954), 481–496, esp. pp. 482, 489–490. Robert E. Osgood, *Limited War: The Challenge to American Strategy* (Chicago: The University of Chicago Press, 1957), pp. 165–167, 192–193.

23. Osgood, *Limited War*, p. 178.

24. George, "*American Policymaking*," pp. 220–226.

adventure" by appealing to military necessity. It was also said that the general engineered the crossing by exceeding his orders. But MacArthur's sharpest critics have rejected this explanation. "At no time during his tenure as UN Commander," one of them writes, "did General MacArthur and the authorities in Washington, both civil and military, agree so fully on operations in Korea." The decision to cross the parallel, then, has been put squarely on the administration in most unflattering terms. This possibly "most critical decision of the Korean War," Walter Millis writes, was the product of "blurred and fuzzy processes." It was made in "the worst way, for confused reasons, on deficient intelligence and with an inadequate appreciation of the risks." One student who has tried to make sense of the decision has attributed it to a failure to anticipate Chinese intervention, the momentum of the Inchon victory, the conviction that a possible Chinese response could be easily handled, and the "desire to re-establish the Democratic Administration's prestige in its Far Eastern policies."[25]

It may also be suggested that crossing the parallel represented no change in thinking at all. If one assumes that the original intention in countering the North Korean assault had as much to do with recouping American losses in East Asia as with preventing World War III, the argument follows that Washington was predisposed to use the war to bring the north under Seoul's control. It is interesting of course that American leaders partly explained Pyongyang's attack as Moscow's effort to make up for defeats in Europe and Japan. Is it possible that these leaders were in fact expressing their own unarticulated wish to make up in part for China lost? One will have to read carefully between the lines of the decision to move north to see if there were unspoken assumptions which the decision makers themselves did not confront.

Explaining why the Chinese intervened can only be, as so much else about Communist China, a matter of conjecture. Among the early speculations on Chinese motives was the suggestion of General MacArthur's chief aide, General Courtney Whitney, that the

25. Walter Millis, *Arms and the State: Civil-Military Elements in National Policy* (New York: The Twentieth Century Fund, 1958), pp. 272–279; Martin Lichterman, *To the Yalu and Back* (University: University of Alabama Press, 1963), pp. 24–27. See also Richard H. Rovere, and Arthur M. Schlesinger, Jr., *The General and the President* (New York: Farrar, Straus and Young, 1951), pp. 146–152; Harry S. Truman, *Memoirs*, II, *Years of Trial and Hope, 1946–1952* (New York: Doubleday & Co., 1956), pp. 383–384. For the argument that crossing the parallel was chiefly a tactical move to defeat enemy forces, see Acheson, *Present at the Creation*, pp. 445–455. For the opposing argument that "the advance into North Korea reflected a political decision," see Spanier, *The Truman–MacArthur Controversy*, pp. 87–91.

Chinese decision came after the British defectors Burgess and MacLean told Peking that the United States would not strike across the Yalu into Manchuria It is difficult to believe that the Chinese committed themselves to fight the United States on the sole strength of this uncertain intelligence. A far more persuasive analysis of Chinese motives argues that Peking's intervention was a reluctant last resort to prevent several developments: the establishment of a Northeast Asian anti-Communist coalition of Japan, Korea, and the United States; the undermining of Chinese prestige through the loss of a Communist neighbor and an inability to conquer Taiwan; and the threat to the People's Republic from a determined enemy on China's border encouraging internal dissenters to overturn the new regime. Yet this picture says nothing about how the Russians could "get away with . . . steering the Chinese into a dangerous conflict" which was designed to "retrieve what was their own blunder." "The detailed answer," a Soviet expert explains, "must await future revelations as to the communications that passed between Moscow and Peking . . . But the main factor was undoubtedly the Soviet Union's dominant position in world Communism." Indeed, as this author puts it, "if China had to react to the American advance to her borders, could she afford at the same time the slightest hint of dissonances with the U.S.S.R.?"[26]

The uncertainties about Chinese and Russian behavior are matched by the unresolved questions about America's failure to anticipate China's resort to arms. There has been substantial controversy over who was to blame. As was the case with Pearl Harbor, Washington put the responsibility for its surprise on its field commander, MacArthur, who assured it that Peking would not come into the war. MacArthur, meanwhile, attributed his miscalculation of Chinese intentions to incompetence and disloyalty at home, or more specifically, to Washington's refusal to let him attack across the Yalu and to Peking's advance knowledge of this through Burgess and MacLean. Both explanations have been justly challenged. MacArthur defended himself by arguing that he had given no foolproof guarantee and that the highest government agencies, including the State Department, the Defense Department, and the Central Intelligence Agency, apparently shared his estimates of Peking's plans. On the other side, MacArthur's explanation of the surprise has been set down as "unsubstantiated speculation."

Writers trying to lift the discussion above the level of polemic

26. Courtney Whitney, *MacArthur: His Rendezvous with History* (New York: Alfred A. Knopf, 1956), pp. 393–395; 455–457; Whiting, *China Crosses the Yalu*, chap. 8; Ulam, *Expansion and Coexistence*, pp. 525–530.

have concluded that MacArthur and the administration shared in the failure to anticipate the Chinese attack. Both knew that China had 300,000 troops in Manchuria, giving it the capability to enter the war. Yet neither predicted this result. Why? Washington's failure was apparently the result of a self-righteous conviction that Peking knew we were China's friend or of an inability to accept the Chinese Communist image of America as her chief enemy, assuming that the Chinese would naturally assign that role to the U.S.S.R. MacArthur's failure to anticipate Chinese intervention apparently stemmed from the belief that America's advance to the Yalu would intimidate Peking. Whether these in fact were the assumptions that misled the administration and MacArthur needs to be fully explored. But even if they were, this does not explain why the entire American intelligence establishment miscalculatd Chinese intentions. An analysis, therefore, of the amount and kind of information coming to intelligence officers and, most important, its impact, or lack of it, on them would seem to make good sense. As with Roberta Wohlstetter's *Pearl Harbor: Warning and Decision,* such an analysis should allow us to see the sort of fundamental misconceptions about Chinese intentions, capabilities, and behavior which caused Americans not to foresee and prepare for "an entirely new war."[27]

The story of the Chinese-American confrontation in Korea from Peking's intervention in November 1950 to the start of armistice talks in July 1951 may be taken in three parts: the grand conflict within the American government and the NATO Alliance over how to end the war; the state of American domestic opinion; and Communist attitudes.

Like the administration's decision to fight in Korea, the first subject has been fairly well reconstructed. Though many details will no doubt come to light from study in the archives, the general outlines of the Truman–MacArthur controversy and of American-European relations have already been garnered from the United States Senate hearings on the military situation in the Far East and from other printed documents. In brief, the argument over America's response to the Chinese intervention set MacArthur and Republican senators at opposite poles from the allies, with Truman and Acheson in the middle. MacArthur pressed for a unified Korea through an expanded war, including air strikes against Manchuria, a blockade of the Chinese mainland and an "unleashing" of Nationalist forces

27. See Spanier, *The Truman–MacArthur Controversy,* pp. 91–103; Lichterman, *To The Yalu and Back,* pp. 41–44. Roberta Wohlstetter, *Pearl Harbor: Warning and Decision* (Stanford: Stanford University Press, 1962).

on Formosa; the allies led by Britain counseled a speedy end to the war through conciliation of Communist China with de facto recognition, United Nations membership and abandonment of Chiang's regime; the Truman administration rejected both an expanded military effort and concessions to the Chinese for military operations to restore the South Korean state.

The motives for these attitudes seem reasonably clear. There has been some speculation that MacArthur sought to turn his differences with the administration into a bid for the Republican presidential nomination in 1952. But there has been no substantive support for this charge so far, and it seems likely that the general's public challenge to Truman's policy came from the conviction that Asia rather than Europe was the center of the Communist threat and that there could be no compromise with Communist aggression. The allies' attitude apparently arose from the fear than an expanded war would produce an all-out conflict with the Soviet Union, or at the very least a reduction in America's commitment in Europe which would make the continent more vulnerable to Soviet attack. The forces behind Truman's policy seem to have been a desire to avoid the consequences envisioned by the allies, and a wish to prevent both injury to national prestige and intensified quarrels at home through appeasement of Peking. In positive terms, the administration apparently viewed further military efforts to save South Korea as a signal of continued determination to stand with allies against external threats.[28]

The state of American public opinion is less easy to ascertain. On the one hand, the administration's reverses in the congressional elections of 1950 show that "the electorate had apparently listened attentively to those who attributed the loss of China and other gains of Communism to a conspiracy within the American government and voted for candidates who advocated a more vigorous anti-Mao policy, a reduction of economic aid, less deference to our allies in Western Europe, and a thorough 'housecleaning' of the State Department, beginning of course with the Secretary of State." On the other hand, there is evidence that the appeal of MacArthur's victory program waned in the spring of 1951 and that the public would have been delighted to escape altogether from the Korean War. Would it have been acceptable then for the administra-

28. The Senate hearings have been published under the title: *Military Situation in the Far East: Hearings before the Committee on Armed Services and the Committee on Foreign Relations*, 5 vols. (Washington: Government Printing Office, 1951). Rovere and Schlesinger, Jr., *The General and the President*, pp. 152–175; Spanier, *The Truman–MacArthur Controversy*, chaps. 8–10; Higgins, *Korea and the Fall of MacArthur*, chaps. 7–8.

tion to have struck a quick bargain with Peking which would have preserved South Korea and ended the fighting? A response to this question requires some close attention to shifting public attitudes between November 1950 and June 1951.[29]

The answer also depends, however, on what the Chinese were ready to do and what Moscow cared to allow. Would the Chinese have exchanged a cease-fire along the 38th parallel for the concessions Britain wished to give? And would the Soviets have been willing to see an end to the war early in 1951? It is worth considering these matters, for until we do it will remain difficult to make satisfactory judgments on the administration's Korean policy.

The same conclusion may be drawn about the truce negotiations of 1951–1953. Until we have a clearer picture of Chinese and Russian thinking, it will be difficult to make sound assumptions about American strategy. For example, there has been substantial criticism of the fact that Washington adopted a defensive military posture once the talks began. Only continued heavy military pressure, critics have said, was likely to force the Communists into an agreement. In its absence, the negotiations dragged on for two years and became a forum for enemy propaganda. Yet in one writer's opinion, since the Communists "did not greatly care how many lives they expended in pursuit of" their political objectives, "they presented the United States and the other Western democracies with policy and military issues of extraordinary difficulty. In such a situation the generals could give no more expert advice than anyone else on how to utilize military force in accomplishing political ends." In other words, since we can not be sure of the Communists' response to battlefield losses from another U.N. drive into North Korea or even of its success, it seems unjustified to conclude that a defensive posture frustrated American efforts to halt the war.[30]

All this is not to suggest that we should defer work on administration policy in the truce talks until we can appraise Communist mo-

29. The quote is from Spanier, *The Truman–MacArthur Controversy*, pp. 151–152. For discussions of the state of public opinion, 1950–1952, see ibid., pp. 217–220, 268–270; Goldman, *The Crucial Decade*, pp. 202–218; Ronald J. Caridi, *The Korean War and American Politics: The Republican Party as a Case Study* (Philadelphia: University of Pennsylvania Press, 1968), pp. 209–213; Warren E. Miller, "Voting and Foreign Policy," and Kenneth N. Waltz, "Electoral Punishment and Foreign Policy Crises," both in James N. Rosenau, ed., *Domestic Sources of Foreign Policy* (New York: The Free Press, 1967), 213–230, 263–293.

30. Criticisms of the administration's approach to the negotiations are summarized in David Rees, *Korea: The Limited War* (London: Macmillan & Co., 1964), chap. 16. The last third of the book, chaps. 16–23, deals with the armistice talks. The quote is from Millis and his argument is given in *Arms and the State*, pp. 363–368.

tives. On the contrary, it would be gratifying to have a study of American policy formulation, but this, like so much else about the Korean War, must await the opening of the archives.[31]

The least discussed side of postwar American–East Asian relations is the American occupation of Japan. Indeed, for the student coming fresh to the literature on the post-1945 American–East Asian encounter, there is a picture of unrelieved failure—failure to preserve China from Communist control, failure to unify Korea and failure to prevent or win the Korean War. Yet the story of how the most powerful East Asian nation was transformed from a totalitarian enemy into a generally democratic friend goes all but untold. There is probably no more important task in setting the record straight on American–East Asian relations after World War II than to give these events their proper weight.[32]

What explains this neglect of Japanese-American relations? Probably the fact that the drama of events in China and Korea and the controversy over our policies there excited much more interest than the comparatively placid story of American success in Japan. Yet there is much that remains to be told about "Japan's American inter-

31. The only full-scale works we have on the negotiations are the recollections of two participants: Admiral C. Turner Joy, *How Communists Negotiate* (New York: The Macmillan Co., 1955); and William H. Vatcher, Jr., *Panmunjom: The Story of the Korean Military Armistice Negotiations* (New York: Frederick A. Praeger, 1958). The transcript of the negotiations is at the Hoover Institute, Stanford University. The Washington record of policy making is unavailable.

32. See Herbert Passin's comment that "this seminal experience [the occupation] has been virtually disregarded by Americans. It is a curious commentary on American political thought that twenty years after the war we still have no important systematic studies of the occupation, and that the educated public has so little idea of what it was all about." The American Assembly, *The United States and Japan* (Englewood Cliffs, N.J.: Prentice-Hall, 1966), pp. 2–3. The best surveys of the occupation are: Kazuo Kawai, *Japan's American Interlude* (Chicago: University of Chicago Press, 1960); Edwin O. Reischauer, *The United States and Japan*, 3d ed., rev. (New York: The Viking Press, 1965); Robert E. Ward, "The Legacy of the Occupation," in the American Assembly volume, chap. 2; and Hugh Borton, *American Presurrender Planning for Postwar Japan* (New York: Columbia University, Occasional Papers of the East Asian Institute, 1967). Some early works on the occupation are: Edwin M. Martin, *The Allied Occupation of Japan* (Stanford: Stanford University Press, 1948); Robert A. Fearey, *Occupation of Japan: Second Phase, 1948–1950* (New York: The Macmillan Co., 1950); *Political Reorientation of Japan: September 1945 to September 1948: Report of Government Section, Supreme Commander for the Allied Powers* (Washington: Government Printing Office, 1949); Robert B. Textor, *Failure in Japan* (New York: John Day Co., 1951); Harry E. Wildes, *Typhoon in Tokyo; The Occupation and Its Aftermath* (New York: The Macmillan Co., 1954). Professor Robert E. Ward of the University of Michigan is at work on a study of the occupation and its aftermath. Professor Robert E. Ward to author, June 4, 1971.

lude." For one, there is the question of the occupation's success in setting Japan upon a democratic course. While most students of Japanese history would probably agree that "Japan emerged from the Occupation a reasonably well organized democratic nation, strongly inclined to peace and at long last starting to regain its economic legs," they would all probably add that the test of Japan's democratic commitments must await the passage of time.[33]

Second, there is the question of the occupation's role in reforming Japan. One view has it that everything in postwar Japan flowed from what the United States did and did not do. Opposed to this is the contention that " 'East is East and West is West.' Japan is and always will be essentially Japanese," this argument runs, ". . . and reform measures imposed from without are therefore essentially meaningless. The whole occupation effort to reform Japan was sheer folly."

Common sense alone suggests that neither argument rings true and that both Japanese and American forces, in that order, determined postwar developments. In the words of Professor Edwin Reischauer, "Most of the truly important postwar changes seem to be simply the acceleration of changes that were already taking place in prewar Japan . . . The war and the occupation between them seem to have swept away certain barriers to the forward motion of these currents . . . Herein may be the true significance of the war and the occupation for Japan. Instead of diverting Japan into a new channel, it cleared the old one of the obstruction of militaristic reaction and changed a slow and meandering flow into a rushing torrent."[34]

What one would like now is a more exact accounting of Japanese and American influences on specific reforms. The best we have been able to obtain so far are approximations of the forces at work. For example, the detailed operations of the Supreme Commander for the Allied Powers (SCAP) and the role and influence of General MacArthur in particular are still essentially unstudied.[35] A more specific example is the case of land reform where the most careful study in English to date, by R. P. Dore, offers but limited support for

33. Reischauer, *The United States and Japan*, pp. 288–289.

34. Ibid., pp. 283–286, 291–292. See also Kawai, *Japan's American Interlude*, chap. 12.

35. "Many of the records of SCAP have been reproduced on 35 mm. microfilm. *The History of the Non-Military Activities of the Occupation of Japan, 1945–1951*, Monographs 1 through 55 in particular cover nearly every activity or reform which occurred during the American occupation of Japan." Edwin R. Flatequal, Chief, Archives Branch, National Archives and Records Service, to author, Oct. 31, 1969. MacArthur's personal papers are available for research purposes in the Bureau of Archives, MacArthur Memorial, 198 Band Street, Norfolk, Virginia 23510.

the conclusion, drawn from the unpublished manuscript of one American official, that the occupation's "principal role was that of a midwife to a healthy reform which had been in its pre-natal stage. The reform idea was Japanese in origin; it was not a policy imposed by a conqueror on the conquered." Similarly, an attempt to piece together the story of the origins of the Japanese constitution yields, by the author's own reckoning, only an incomplete account. Whether one considers business, educational, family, political, or trade union reform, the story is the same: while we have a general idea of what happened, the full record of how the war and occupation interacted with Japanese traditions and postwar actions remains to be gathered from the sources.[36]

More directly on the American side, we need some careful work on the changing nature of the occupation. We already know that after 1947 SCAP became more concerned with rehabilitating than with reforming Japan. The extent and motives for this shift, how-ever, are a matter of keen debate. Japanese and American "liberals," for example, argue that the cold war moved American policy makers to abandon plans for a "moderately socialistic" Japan, substituting instead commitments to a "bourgeois capitalist democracy" partly built along prewar lines. Other commentators dispute that SCAP ever envisioned a socialistic Japan, asserting that the change in policy was one more of degree than of kind. Moreover, it is the belief of these writers that between 1947 and 1950 this shift in emphasis had less to do with hopes for an East Asian "capitalist" ally than with convictions about America's limited capacity either to bear the costs of the occupation or to continue influencing Japanese domestic life. If we are to decide between these contending views, we shall have to look first at what happened in Tokyo, where, as George Kennan says, "Washington did not loom very large on the horizons of this highly self-centered occupational command."[37]

The place of Japan in postwar Soviet-American relations is an-other incomplete story. The extent to which American policy, 1946–

36. R. P. Dore, *Land Reform in Japan* (London: Oxford University Press, 1959), esp. Part II; the conclusion is on pp. 147–148. Robert E. Ward, "The Origins of the Present Japanese Constitution," *American Political Science Review*, 50 (December 1956), 980–1010. The Japanese side of the occupation has been the subject of many specialized studies which are too numerous to list here. For the most important, see Reischauer, *The United States and Japan*, pp. 383–384. An important volume not mentioned by Reischauer is Shigeru Yoshida, *The Yoshida Memoirs* (London: Heinemann, 1961).

37. See Ward, "The Legacy of the Occupation," pp. 30–33, 45, 48–51; George F. Kennan, *Memoirs, 1925–1950* (Boston: Little, Brown & Co., 1967), chap. 16, especially pp. 413–414; Edwin O. Reischauer to author, October 29, 1969.

1952, produced a contest with Moscow over Japan is a vital untold chapter in the history of the cold war. This tale can be taken in two parts: whether American actions in the Allied Council in Tokyo and the Far Eastern Commission in Washington, 1946–1948, were responses to or causes of Soviet behavior; and whether the peace settlement and security arrangements with Japan, 1949–1952, were the result of internal administrative difficulties and "primitive" cold war reasoning in Washington, as George Kennan says, or of the objective situation we had before us, as Dean Acheson contends.[38]

It is perhaps not too much to suggest that a host of both apprentice and seasoned scholars could devote the better part of their careers to the study of American–East Asian relations, 1946–1952, and still not satisfy our curiosity about all its dimensions. That scholars will have this chance in the near future is apparently unlikely. For until the United States government, and the State Department and leading officials in particular, release their papers to researchers, the prospects for serious study are dim.

For the time being, therefore, it is perhaps enough to hope that the story of America's postwar East Asian encounter can be rescued from the polemical debate into which it fell in the 1950's. If a synthetic volume could be constructed in the near future on the whole range of American relations with China, Korea, Japan and Russia, it would at least allow us to see that the Truman administration's record was one of more than unrelieved failure. Indeed, if Americans could be brought to appreciate that the movement of Japan into the Western camp and the preservation of the South Korean state were as important as Communism's rise to power in Peking, and that the last was not an event over which we necessarily ruled, it would be a major contribution to rational hopes and plans for what we may accomplish in our future East Asian affairs.

---

38. Kennan, *Memoirs,* pp. 414–418; Acheson, *Present at the Creation,* pp. 426–435 and chap. 56.

Chapter 14 of Herbert Feis, *Contest Over Japan* (New York: W. W. Norton & Co., 1967), surveys post-1945 Soviet-American relations over Japan. Bernard C. Cohen has dissected the domestic processes of American policymaking, emphasizing the fundamental effects of "the climate of public opinion," "organized and unorganized political interest groups" and "the media of mass communication" on the decisions relating to the Japanese peace agreements of 1951. *The Political Process and Foreign Policy: The Making of the Japanese Peace Settlement* (Princeton: Princeton University Press, 1957). Frederick S. Dunn has given us an account, drawn from still classified and uncited State Department papers, of how the United States government moved toward the settlement with Japan. His book stands as a good introduction until more work can be done. *Peace Making and the Settlement with Japan* (Princeton: Princeton University Press, 1963).

The Eisenhower Years

A review of the literature of the period is made easier by a preliminary survey of some of the major events and themes. The Eisenhower period was marked by increased concern with Asia. However, U.S. interest in Asia was seen within the context of the Soviet-U.S. cold war in which primary attention continued to be focused on Western Europe. Against this background East Asia was viewed as a theater in a worldwide struggle to halt the spread of communism. In this view China and the Soviets represented a communist bloc in Asia, and United States–East Asian relations during the Eisenhower administration were characterized by U.S. attempts to isolate the Chinese and, concomitantly, to foster dependent military and economic relationships with her neighbors.

One of Eisenhower's first moves was to remove the buffer of the Seventh Fleet between Formosa and the mainland in a move that came to be known as the "unleashing of Chiang." The United States rebuffed Peking's efforts to improve relations after agreeing to open ambassadorial talks. The United States blocked China's entrance into the United Nations. In addition, mutual defense pacts were concluded between the United States and the nations surrounding the Chinese, while Dulles proclaimed a policy of "massive retaliation" to back up these local forces.

Eisenhower rode to office on a wave of popular disenchantment with the Democrats' handling of the war in Korea, and a commitment to peace in Korea. After extensive negotiations, primarily on prisoner-of-war exchanges and the new demarcation line—and subsequent difficulties in persuading Rhee to go along with the agreement—an armistice was signed in July 1953, including an agreement to discuss a final settlement at Geneva. During the remainder of the decade, the United States concluded a Mutual Security Treaty with the South Koreans and provided extensive financial support to the Rhee government totaling approximately 75 percent of the military budget and 50 percent of the civil budget. Such massive funding, however, did little to effect real political or economic change in South Korea. In 1960, following widespread rioting protesting the character of his latest election, Rhee was forced to resign, with another pro-Western government replacing him.

Governing U.S.-Japanese relations during the Eisenhower administration was a Mutual Security Agreement which Japan had entered into in 1951 as an occupied nation. Many of the factors which made acceptance of the treaty a foregone conclusion in 1951 were not at work in Japanese society when the treaty was renegotiated in 1960. In extensive rioting against the treaty a scheduled Eisenhower visit to Japan was canceled. (He did visit Korea and Taiwan.) When the treaty was later successfully ratified, Kishi Nobusuke, the Conservative prime minister, resigned, satisfying some of the opposition's demands.

The general theme of hostility in the triangular relationship between China, Taiwan, and the United States was acted out in the controversies over the Offshore Islands in 1954 and again in 1958. Responding to the U.S. policy of encirclement, coupled with the Nationalists' harassment of her coast and "return to the mainland" policy, the Chinese began the shelling of Quemoy, an offshore island, in September 1954, just prior to the conclusion of the U.S.-Nationalist Mutual Defense Pact. At the President's request, the United States Congress passed the Formosa resolution empowering the President to defend Quemoy if necessary for the defense of Taiwan.

In early 1955 the Nationalists evacuated the Tachen Islands, and the Communists occupied them. The crisis over Quemoy temporarily abated, recurring in August 1958, when the shelling of the island began again. The Chinese hoped to persuade the United States to remain aloof so that they could capture the island. However, Eisenhower was prepared to defend Quemoy using nuclear weapons and, after a brief probe, the Chinese slowly disengaged. Visiting Taiwan several weeks later, Dulles secured an agreement that no force would be used against the mainland.

The fear of Chinese expansion into Southeast Asia, especially after the Korean aggression, and the desire to cement France more firmly into the Atlantic Alliance, led the United States to aid the French in reestablishing colonial rule in Indochina. American aid totaling an average of $500 million annually went to a French force that was rapidly losing its determination to continue the futile and protracted conflict. Dulles' "united action" proposal to aid the French in 1954 was rejected by Eisenhower, and the French secured a Soviet agreement to seek peace in Indochina. At the Geneva conference the participants agreed to a neutral Vietnam, Laos, and Cambodia, with Vietnam to be temporarily divided at the 17th parallel and elections to be held there within two years. While not signing the accord, the

United States agreed not to use force to disrupt it. Dulles then moved ahead with plans for a Southeast Asia security pact, and SEATO was created at the Manila conference of September 1954. The United States now became active in Indochina on its own, moving to shore up the Diem regime in South Vietnam and sponsoring a right wing coup in Laos.

General

Much of the general literature focuses appropriately on the two principal architects of American policy toward the Far East— Eisenhower and Dulles. The Eisenhower memoirs, *Mandate for Change*, and *Waging Peace*[1] shed little light on the construction of overall policy but are useful in providing insight into the American response to some of the crises of the period. They provide detail on his secret trip to Korea before the inauguration, on some of the discussions at the Panmunjom talks, and Eisenhower's alarm at Rhee's undercutting of the negotiations. In the chapter on the Indochina crisis he discusses some of the considerations in his decisions surrounding American action to limit aid to France. Eisenhower also discusses his reactions in the Quemoy crises, making clear his willingness to use nuclear weapons if necessary. His remarks about the cancellation of his Japanese trip are remarkable for the simplicity with which Eisenhower viewed the situation.

Sherman Adams' *Firsthand Report*[2] provides some further insight on the 1954 Offshore Islands crisis, the Formosa resolution, and the situation in Indochina. Emmett Hughes' *Ordeal and Hope*[3] tells us almost nothing specific about U.S. policy in the Far East, but it is an interesting portrayal of the tone of the Eisenhower administration, the nature of the man, and especially the Eisenhower–Dulles relationship—all of which are necessary for an understanding of the U.S.–Far Eastern relationship during this period. *Eisenhower: The Inside Story*[4] by Robert Donovan is the biography of Eisenhower which deals most extensively with Eisenhower and Far Eastern affairs.

John Foster Dulles published no memoirs, but the Dulles Library at Princeton has collected his papers. In the unclassified materials there is not much material pertaining to Far Eastern questions; but

1. Dwight D. Eisenhower, *Mandate for Change, 1953–1956* (New York: Doubleday, 1963). *Waging Peace, 1956–1961* (New York: Doubleday, 1965).
2. Sherman Adams, *Firsthand Report* (New York: Harper, 1961).
3. Emmett Hughes, *Ordeal and Hope* (New York: Atheneum, 1963).
4. Robert Donovan, *Eisenhower: The Inside Story* (New York: Harper, 1956).

there are a few very interesting items, including a paper in Dulles' handwriting prepared for his use when talking to the Chinese Nationalists and indicating his belief that the Nationalists should abandon the Offshore Islands, as well as any hope of returning to the mainland by force. Dulles' biographers provide little information on our relations with East Asia. The Korean truce and the Indochina and Formosan crises are dealt with, although superficially, in John Beal's work *John Foster Dulles*.[5] Eleanor Lansing Dulles, the secretary's sister, however, has provided in *John Foster Dulles: The Last Year*[6] the only Dulles biography to give a fairly useful and highly personal account of Dulles and his activities in the second Quemoy crisis.

Some insight into American military strategy and the thinking of some of the men who were advising the President on military and strategic concepts in the Far East, particularly on the Korean question and the concept of massive retaliation, is provided in the memoirs of the generals—Mark Clark's *From the Danube to the Yalu*,[7] Maxwell Taylor's *The Uncertain Trumpet*,[8] and Ridgway's *The Korean War*[9] and *Soldier: the Memoirs of Matthew Ridgway*.[10] Perhaps the most interesting aspects of the books are the extent to which they disagree with the policy makers—Taylor, for example, arguing that the doctrine of massive retaliation does not buy the "little peace" and Ridgway's firm insistence that the Quemoy–Matsu Islands were not the place to take a stand against the Chinese. Some information on the China question, as viewed from Taipei, is provided by Karl Lott Rankin's memoirs *China Assignment*.[11] Rankin, ambassador to China during most of the Eisenhower administration, reports on his vigorous opposition to proposals to force the Nationalists off the Offshore Islands. Official unclassified documents dealing with our foreign policy toward any of the countries are not numerous. Foreign Relations Committee hearings on the various mutual security treaties concluded provide some official viewpoints on the U.S. side.[12]

5. John Beal, *John Foster Dulles* (New York: Harper, 1957).

6. Eleanor Lansing Dulles, *John Foster Dulles: The Last Year* (New York: Harcourt, Brace & World, 1963).

7. Mark Clark, *From the Danube to the Yalu* (New York: Harper, 1954).

8. Maxwell Taylor, *The Uncertain Trumpet* (New York: Harper, 1959).

9. Matthew Ridgway, *The Korean War* (New York: Doubleday, 1967).

10. Mathew Ridgway, *Soldier: The Memoirs of Matthew Ridgway* (New York: Harper, 1956).

11. Karl Lott Rankin, *China Assignment* (Seattle: University of Washington Press, 1964).

12. U.S. Congress, Senate, Committee on Foreign Relations, *Mutual Defense Treaty With The Republic of China*, 84th Cong. 1st Sess. U.S. Congress, Senate,

A word ought to be said here about the more general cold war histories which are not specifically dealt with in this paper. Their contribution to our understanding of this period is primarily in placing the Far Eastern aspects in perspective as a segment of a larger conflict. Louis Halle's *The Cold War as History*[13] is especially interesting. Finally, in dealing with history as recent as the Eisenhower period, research need not be limited to the literature. Interviews with available participants are a valuable source of information and should be conducted wherever possible.

Korea

As might be expected, the literature on Korea is relatively extensive regarding the armistice but tapers off to almost nothing of significance for the remainder of the decade. As a result, the nature of the postwar military and economic relationship between the United States and South Korea has received almost no treatment. This, despite the fact that Korea might well serve as a model for U.S. efforts to assist a developing economy, complete with such features as an extensive U.S. commitment, an ancient society resistant to change, and U.S. support of an intransigent local dictator whose popularity was highly questionable.

Literature on North Korea is scarce. *North Korea Today*,[14] edited by Robert Scalopino, contains essays on a number of aspects of postwar North Korean society, including its industrial development and foreign policy. Glenn D. Paige has also analyzed North Korea's foreign policy in terms of its alternate emulation of Russian and Chinese behavior.[15]

The Republic of Korea has received more extensive treatment. The personification of postwar American influence in South Korea, Syngman Rhee, has been examined by a number of biographers. The best is Richard Allen's *Korea's Syngman Rhee*,[16] which is relatively good in the immediate postwar period.

The question of U.S. involvement in the shaping of the postwar economy has received some treatment in W.D. Reeves' work *The*

Committee on Foreign Relations, *Treaty of Mutual Cooperation With Japan*, 86th Cong. 2nd Sess. U.S. Congress, House, Committee on Foreign Affairs, *Mutual Security Programs With Korea*, 86th Cong. 2nd Sess.

13. Louis Halle, *The Cold War as History* (New York: Harper, 1967).

14. Robert A. Scalopino, ed., *North Korea Today* (New York: Praeger, 1963).

15. Glenn Paige, "North Korea and the Emulation of Russian and Chinese Behavior" in A. Doak Barnett, ed., *Communist Strategies in Asia* (New York: Praeger, 1963), pp. 228–261.

16. Richard Allen, *Korea's Syngman Rhee* (Vermont: C. E. Tuttle Co., 1960).

Republic of Korea: A Political and Economic Study.[17] Reeves' study, however, is little more than a data collection on the extent of foreign aid and some aspects of economic development. What is needed in this area is an analysis of real economic change in Korea in terms of U.S. foreign aid and foreign policy objectives. Of particular interest is the problem of Rhee, who consistently refused to concentrate on economic development, opting instead for the maintenance of one of the largest standing armies in the world.

The most comprehensive explanation of Korean society available is Gregory Henderson's *Korea: the Politics of the Vortex.*[18] Henderson views Korea, for centuries a homogeneous society with a highly centralized government, as having a mid-level power vacuum and weak political party structure. He examines the political patterns and economic consequences growing out of this structure and looks at some of the new forces in Korean society, such as the army, that may alter some of these traditional patterns.

For the crisis-oriented, the focus of the Eisenhower period is the Korean armistice talks. *Panmunjom*[19] by William Vatcher, an American official at the armistice talks, provides a detailed accounting of the bargaining session but little insight into the meaning of these events as an instance of a local limited war in a nuclear age.

In *Korea: the Limited War,*[20] David Rees examines the limiting factors of the war and the problems accompanying the fighting of a war that "was not a crusade." Rees demonstrates that the problems facing the American governments were not merely with the enemy, but with the generals, the American people, and the South Korean government. In part 3 Rees studies the paradox of a "war for peace" and gives an excellent account of the armistice.

Japan

The decade of the fifties was a period of social and economic reconstruction for Japan at a time when the U.S. military presence there was enormous. This period has received surprisingly little treatment, however, and a number of important research areas have not been explored.

Since Japan's natural resources are limited, foreign trade is vital

17. W. D. Reeves, *The Republic of Korea: A Political and Economic Study* (London: Oxford University Press, 1963).

18. Gregory Henderson, *Korea: The Politics of the Vortex* (Cambridge, Mass.: Harvard University Press, 1968).

19. William Vatcher, *Panmunjom: The Story of the Korean Military Armistice* (New York: Praeger, 1958).

20. David Rees, *Korea: The Limited War* (London: Macmillan, 1964).

to her economy. Cut off from her traditionally close economic ties to Northeast Asia, the Japanese were largely dependent on the American market. In the rebuilding process the American business and economic interests in Japan grew to sizable proportions. Richard Allen's *Japan's Economic Recovery*[21] and Jerome Cohen's *Japan's Postwar Economy*[22] treat her economic development during this period, but a fresh analysis of Japan's economic growth, its political implications, and the influence of the American presence on the direction of that growth is needed for an understanding of U.S.–Japanese relations during this and subsequent periods. The growing strength and durability of the Japanese economy was a fact that often went unappreciated in the United States with a tendency to dismiss it as temporary good fortune, and both these early studies (1958) reflect that bias.

Similarly unappreciated in the United States was the growth of Japanese nationalism and the extreme sensitivity of the Japanese on the question of weaponry (particularly nuclear arms) in the face of an extensive U.S. military presence. Both these elements surfaced, most notably in the security treaty crisis of 1960, but little work has been done on the period preceding the crisis. Particularly useful, for example, would be an examination of the question of how important the U.S. military continued to be in the shaping of U.S. policy toward Japan after the Japanese resumed control of their own government.

Most of the studies of the Eisenhower–Kishi period in U.S.–Japanese relations, however, focus on the security treaty crisis of 1960, with its implications about evolving Japanese independence and U.S. defense needs in the Far East. Scalopino and Mosumi use the security treaty crisis as a case study in their analysis of factionalism and Japanese politics in *Parties and Politics in Contemporary Japan*.[23] James Cary in *Japan Today: Reluctant Ally*[24] provides a narrative history of the treaty crisis and related U.S.–Japanese problems during the same period. Edwin Reischauer, in "Broken Dialogue With Japan,"[25] examines the security treaty episode and the communications crisis between the United States and Japan.

21. G. C. Allen, *Japan's Economic Recovery* (London: Oxford University Press, 1958).

22. Jerome Cohen, *Japan's Postwar Economy* (Bloomington: Indiana University Press, 1958).

23. Robert Scalopino and Jinnosuke Mosumi, *Parties and Politics in Contemporary Japan* (Berkeley: University of California Press, 1962).

24. James Cary, *Japan Today: Reluctant Ally* (New York: Praeger, 1962).

25. Edwin Reischauer, "Broken Dialogue with Japan," *Foreign Affairs*, 39 (October 1960), 11–26.

By far the most extensive study of the crisis is George Packard's *Protest in Tokyo: The Security Treaty Crisis of 1960*.[26] Packard dismisses simplistic explanations of the events of 1960—for example, Eisenhower's view that it was the work of international communism —and contrasts popular Japanese attitudes toward the 1951 and 1960 agreements. He examines the campaign against the ratification of the treaty in the light of the unpopularity of U.S. military bases, the specific shortcomings of the treaty, the strong anti-Kishi feeling, the serious questions of many Japanese about the relative military and technological power of the United States and, finally, the Japanese fear of fighting a war "for Chiang" against the mainland Chinese. He demonstrates how such apparently unrelated incidents as the shooting down of the U-2 and the overthrow of Rhee in South Korea heightened opposition to the treaty. Against this background Packard examines the popular demonstrations and the party activities (including Kishi's willingness to sacrifice himself) that surrounded the crisis.

Packard's analysis provides evidence of the importance of understanding domestic political considerations in an analysis of any such crisis. He also illuminates the wide gap which can develop in the perceptions held by people in two countries about the same events. In this instance, the "protected" nation, Japan, saw herself as being manipulated by a powerful nation who might very well engage her in wars unrelated to Japanese national security. The "protecting" nation, the United States, saw herself as extending security guarantees at a great cost to an ungrateful Japanese people who prospered at her expense.

An analysis of domestic political considerations also figures importantly in Donald Hellmann's recent study of the Soviet-Japanese peace settlement.[27] Hellmann concludes that in this instance the Japanese decision was controlled by the Liberal Democratic Party, but a number of other factors are considered in his decision-making model—including public opinion, the press, the institutional framework, and the traditional insulation of Japanese bureaucrats.

Neither Packard's nor Hellmann's study, however, considers the interplay of domestic political process between countries. For example, apart from one passing reference to Eisenhower's need for a successful visit after the abortive Paris summit conference, Packard does not discuss U.S. domestic or bureaucratic politics. What is

26. George Packard, *Protest in Tokyo: The Security Treaty Crisis of 1960* (Princeton: Princeton University Press, 1966).

27. Donald C. Hellmann, *Japanese Foreign Policy and Domestic Politics* (Berkeley: University of California Press, 1969).

needed is a study which builds on this work but extends the time frame and considers the interaction of domestic imperatives in the two countries. Such a study would provide useful comparison and contrast with Richard Neustadt's study of two U.S.–British crises.[28]

Southeast Asia

As the major foreign policy problem area for the United States in the sixties, Southeast Asia, particularly Vietnam, has recently received much attention from scholars. Since much of the current U.S. involvement there is rooted in the Geneva accord and the subsequent American assumption of the French colonial burden, the Eisenhower–Dulles era has been studied extensively.

Works on the politics of Southeast Asia for the period include two general studies by O. E. Clubb[29] and Russell Fifield.[30] Clubb's book is an interesting analysis of the events in Southeast Asia in terms of Soviet and U.S. strategy and provides a concise and objective history of the United States' involvement there. Fifield, who has written extensively on Southeast Asia, provides a more detailed accounting of U.S. military and economic posture in the area, but his political analysis is sometimes simplistic in its portrayal of U.S. action in Southeast Asia as almost inevitably a response to aggressive Communist action. Clubb's presentation of U.S. activities is more useful in its portrayal of American initiative.

Much has been written on U.S. policy in Vietnam; only a few major works will be discussed. In large part the studies on U.S. activity in Vietnam are variations on a theme perhaps best expressed in some of Bernard Fall's writings on Vietnam—that the United States stepped into the vacuum created by France's failure and learned little from the French experience. Fall's *The Two Vietnams*[31] is a political and military analysis of the participants in "the second Indochina war." Joseph Buttinger's *Vietnam: A Dragon Embattled*[32] is another extensive study of the events in Vietnam and contains a selected and annotated bibliography of works on Vietnam that would be valuable to anyone researching the area.

Other works on Vietnam focus on the events of 1954–1955 as

28. Richard Neustadt, Alliance Politics, (New York: Columbia University Press, 1970).

29. Oliver E. Clubb, Jr., *The United States and the Sino-Soviet Bloc in Southeast Asia* (Brookings: Washington, D.C., 1962).

30. Russell H. Fifield, *Southeast Asia in United States Policy* (New York: Praeger, 1963).

31. Bernard Fall, *The Two Vietnams* (New York: Praeger, 1967).

32. Joseph Buttinger, *Vietnam: A Dragon Embattled,* II (New York: Praeger, 1967).

crucial. Victor Bator's *Vietnam: A Diplomatic Tragedy*[33] and Melvin Gurtov's *The First Vietnam Crisis*[34] are essentially diplomatic histories of the Geneva agreement and the SEATO pact. Bator argues that it was the Eisenhower–Dulles militancy that broadened the scope of the Southeast Asian crisis. Philippe Devillers' and Jean Lacouture's misnamed study, *The End of a War*[35] first published in 1960 is the most complete study of the events surrounding the Geneva conference. The revised edition argues that rather than ending the war, the Geneva conference merely marked the transfer of the French burden to the Americans.

Despite the number of works on Vietnam, gaps do exist. Where the literature is weakest is in the domestic political and bureaucratic origins of U.S. involvement, particularly in the Eisenhower period. The Gurtov and Bator books, for example, only touch on this aspect of the subject. Arthur Schlesinger's *The Bitter Heritage*[36] is perhaps the best domestic analysis. In this regard, the bureaucratic momentum created by U.S. military and CIA activities in Indochina in the 1950's needs to be considered, as well as the political implication of, for example, Eisenhower's warning to Kennedy during the transition that a non-Communist Laos was vital to American security.[37]

The other countries of Southeast Asia—Laos, Cambodia, and Thailand—have received much less attention, and incisive analyses of U.S. relations with them are almost nonexistent. Arthur Dommen's *Conflict in Laos*[38] is a historical narrative of events in Laos from 1945 to the early 1960's. Dommen's work is perhaps the best available on Laos, placing heavy emphasis on the U.S. involvement in the various coups.

Cambodia has received the least attention of any of the Southeast Asian nations, despite her ability to deal effectively with internal opposition with a minimum of foreign involvement. Countering the frequent charge that Cambodia is inconsistent in her foreign policy toward the United States, Roger Smith's work on Cambodia, *Cam-*

33. Victor Bator, *Vietnam: A Diplomatic Tragedy* (New York: Oceana, 1965).

34. Melvin Gurtov, *The First Vietnam Crisis* (New York: Columbia University Press, 1967).

35. Philippe Devillers and Jean LaCouture, *End of a War: Indo-China 1954* (New York, Praeger, 1969).

36. Arthur M. Schlesinger, Jr., *The Bitter Heritage* (Boston: Houghton Mifflin Co., 1967).

37. Clark Clifford, "A Vietnam Reappraisal," *Foreign Affairs*, 47.4 (July 1969), pp. 601–622.

38. Arthur Dommen, *Conflict in Laos* (New York: Praeger, 1964).

bodia's Foreign Policy[39] argues that Cambodia's foreign policy toward the United States (and China) is almost totally dependent on how the two great powers affect the threat posed by Cambodia's two traditional enemies—Thailand and Vietnam.

Finally, in the case of Thailand, the only Southeast Asian power not to have been under colonial rule, there is an important study by Frank Darling, *Thailand and the United States*,[40] who attempts to assess the impact of American aid on domestic politics in Thailand. Darling's study would be a useful model to apply to other Southeast Asian nations.

China

Currently there exist two significant but abbreviated studies of the Offshore Islands crises. One, O. E. Clubb's *Formosa and the Offshore Islands*,[41] focuses primarily on U.S. domestic moves culminating in her reactions in 1955. The other, by Tang Tsou, *Embroilment over Quemoy*,[42] focuses on the three principal actors in the crisis, Mao, Chiang, and Dulles. A. Doak Barnett has reviewed the background of the Offshore Islands crises and the implications of the defense of the islands in the context of a larger study on the Chinese challenge to American policy in Asia.[43] A forthcoming book on the crises by Tang Tsou and the author will be discussed below.

Economic performance figures importantly in Chinese foreign relations as a constraint on the regime, and a number of studies have been made on the economy of mainland China. The principal ones are: Dwight Perkins, *Market Control and Planning in Communist China*,[44] Alexander Eckstein, *Communist China's Economic Growth and Foreign Trade*,[45] and Ta Chung Liu and K. C. Yeh,

39. Roger M. Smith, *Cambodia's Foreign Policy* (Ithaca: Cornell University Press, 1965).

40. Frank Darling, *Thailand and the United States* (Washington: Public Affairs Press, 1965).

41. O. E. Clubb, "Formosa and the Offshore Islands in American Policy, 1950–55," *Political Science Quarterly*, 74 (December 1959), 517–531.

42. Tang Tsou, *Embroilment Over Quemoy* (Utah: University of Utah Press, 1959).

43. A. Doak Barnett, *Communist China and Asia* (New York: Random House, 1960).

44. Dwight Perkins, *Market Control and Planning for Communist China* (Cambridge, Mass.: Harvard University Press, 1966).

45. Alexander Eckstein, *Communist China's Economic Growth and Foreign Trade* (New York: McGraw-Hill, 1966).

Economy of the Chinese Mainland.[46] Not one of these works, however, attempts to investigate the relationship between economy and foreign policy in any systematic way. In the case of Taiwan, Neil Jacoby's *U.S. Aid to Taiwan*[47] is an evaluation of the effectiveness of U.S. aid to Formosa, focusing more on administrative difficulties than policy implications.

The question of the nuclear element and its effect on Chinese foreign policy has been treated in two works: Alice Hsieh's *Communist China's Strategy in the Nuclear Era*[48] and my *China and the Bomb.*[49]

An examination of the diplomatic aspect of U.S.–Chinese relations is contained in Kenneth Young's *Negotiating with the Chinese Communists.*[50] Young, a former U.S. diplomatic official, gives the Geneva–Warsaw ambassadorial talks central importance in shaping U.S.–Chinese relations. For a detailed accounting of events at the talks the book is useful, but on the broader question of U.S.–Chinese relations it tells us little. Young's treatment is handicapped by an attitude common to semiofficial discussions of such issues—the assumption of moral rectitude. Implicitly, and at times explicitly, he proceeds as if the United States were seeking to improve relations, acting from noble purposes, and negotiating "sincerely." At the same time, Young points out Chinese acts of duplicity, the unreasonableness of Chinese behavior, and their constant efforts to use the talks for their own ends. At one point, in discussing the period 1954–1955, when the Chinese were seeking limited steps to improve relations and the United States was resisting them, Young does allow that the United States may not have acted as forthrightly as it might have in seeking to improve relations. Most outside observers would argue that a major change to improve relations was deliberately passed over. In writing from this perspective, Young gives an accurate picture of the attitude with which bureaucracies approach their relations with "hostile" countries.

Bureaucrats assume that the objectives of their nations are consistent with a higher good and that the other side's sincerity is open to question. More important, they resist analyzing the other side's

46. Ta Chung Liu and K. C. Yeh, *Economy of the Chinese Mainland: National Income and Economic Development, 1933–1959* (Princeton: Princeton University Press, 1965).

47. Neil Jacoby, *U.S. Aid to Taiwan* (New York: Praeger, 1966).

48. Alice Langley Hsieh, *Communist China's Strategy in the Nuclear Era* (New Jersey: Prentice Hall, 1962).

49. Morton H. Halperin, *China and the Bomb* (New York: Praeger, 1965).

50. Kenneth T. Young, *Negotiating with the Chinese Communists* (New York: McGraw-Hill, 1968).

behavior, taking into account what its officials believe about the world. An understanding of overall U.S.–Chinese relations requires an analysis of the policies of each nation as an outgrowth of their images of the world and domestic imperatives. We need to understand how China has viewed the relation and to assess as objectively as we can why each nation comes to see the other as a threat to its security.

A forthcoming work on the period by Tang Tsou and myself focuses on the Offshore Islands crises in the context of overall relations between the two nations and attempts to provide an understanding of how leaders in each capital viewed the intention of the other. China's perception of the United States, particularly her fears of encirclement, and her Great Leap Forward plan for her domestic economy, for example, are some of the factors that provide the background for a discussion of the events of the Offshore Islands crises. Additional studies are needed of particular aspects of U.S.–Chinese relations and on the overall relations.

The Nineteen Sixties as History:

A Preliminary Overview

What should one tell an apprentice scholar about accomplishments, problems, and prospects in the history of American–East Asian relations during the years 1961–1970? That the accomplishments are so far minimal; that the problems are enormous; and that the prospects are exhilarating.

We deal here with current history, the domain of the journalist, the bureaucrat, the polemicist, the premature memoirist, and, of course, the political scientist. We deal, furthermore, with terrain out of context: we know what came before but not what happened next, so we can't begin to judge the decade's significance. Was Vietnam the last battle of the Cold War; or was it the prelude to something worse? We lack the historian's great virtue, perspective, and are afflicted, as usual, by the profession's limitation, one's parochial vantage point.[1]

An essay on the history of the sixties is necessarily, therefore, an act of bravado and an exercise in sheer speculation. At best it can only detect themes and raise questions that might be of interest to future researchers. In the present case, the focus will be largely on the American end of the relationship and on English language materials.

The Terrain

The decade begins with the victory of Kennedy over Nixon; it closes with the end of Nixon's first year in the presidency. Like the thirties, it is a period overcast with a "Far Eastern Crisis"; and again like the thirties, East Asia is by no means the whole show. American–East Asian relations have the wider context of Soviet-American con-

---

1. For some thoughtful essays on the problem of vantage point in American-East Asian relations, see Dorothy Borg, ed., *Historians and American Far Eastern Policy* (New York: East Asian Institute, Columbia University, 1966).

flict and gingerly accommodation, NATO diplomacy, Middle East hostilities, and concern for hemispheric security. Far Eastern policy may have its own dynamics and momentum; but it can never be fully divorced from considerations beyond that region.

One constant throughout these years is the Washington–Peking stalemate; despite minor adjustments in rhetoric and action—a slight thaw on the American side, a bit more frost on China's part for much of the period–the essentials of mutual containment and isolation, inherited in 1961, remain intact in 1970. Equally intact is one chief producer of the stalemate, Taiwan. There is hardly a hint of the Sino-American breakthrough to come in 1971–1972.

Central to the decade is Japan, and here things have changed in American–East Asian relations. The crisis of 1960 between great power and restive client has given way—through deft diplomacy and shared affluence—to something more like partnership. With the Okinawa problem nearly resolved, the Tokyo–Washington relationship is already listed as a "success story" of the decade. Again, there is minimal forewarning of the shocks that 1971 will hold for Japanese–American partnership.

As for the Korean peninsula, here again "success" will be alleged by many: a shift in South Korea from riots, instability, and a military coup in 1961, to apparent political stability under "legitimized" military rule, and a shift from economic stagnation to economic boom—owing largely to the Vietnam War and the American-induced settlement with Japan. The peninsula remains fragile, however, artificially divided between two intensely hostile regimes.

But American–East Asian relations, by 1961, can no longer be viewed in traditional pre-World War II terms that excluded that one-time colonial appendage, Southeast Asia. The interdependence of the broader region, and its relationship to wider world politics, is underscored by an American presence in South Vietnam and Laos and a Soviet presence in Laos and North Vietnam. When one moves, as one must, to insular and peninsular Southeast Asia, the picture becomes more troubled. Despite its share in Vietnam profiteering, our traditional ward, the Philippines, emerges from the decade much as it entered it: an economic swamp and political jungle; the ambivalent relationship with Washington remains a constant, so far muting spasms of insurgency and nationalist frustration. To the south, Southeast Asia's largest prize in terms of potential wealth, Indonesia, is still in a state of recovery from economic profligacy and a convulsive bloodletting; if stolid acquiescence–America's failure to panic over Sukarno's march to the left and its failure to bear-hug his military successors—is a hallmark of mature diplomacy, Indonesian–American relations might be judged "successful" over the sixties.

On the continent itself, the scene is darker. Washington's relations with Malaya, Singapore, and eventually the new Malaysia are fairly satisfactory through the decade, despite the perils of first, "confrontation" and later, communal strife; and indeed they improve markedly with Singapore's Lee Kuan Yew. With Burma they are, in a sense, even more satisfactory, to the extent that a xenophobic state with a foreign policy strictly neutral on all significant issues can be said to have a foreign policy at all. As for Cambodia, relations begin rather poorly, move sharply downward, return to quiet poorliness— and then, with Sihanouk's overthrow and the U.S.–Vietnamese invasion of May 1970, become subsumed in a widened, ongoing Indochina War.

It is with Thailand, Laos, and Vietnam that the sharp transformations are most obvious. The increase in the American presence in all three countries between 1961 and 1969 is staggering in terms of money, materiel, and manpower. Here is the heart of the "Far Eastern Crisis," in the 1960's version: an unresolved civil war on a Cold War Frontier in one portion of former French Indochina (South Vietnam), an inevitable early spillover into the "march" that separates Vietnamese from Thais (Laos and, much later, Cambodia), and a rising degree of alarm and alignment on the other side of that march (Thailand).

President Kennedy inherited a Laos crisis plus a renewed civil war in Vietnam plus anxiety in Thailand. President Nixon inherited a massive though "covert" Laos war plus a spectacularly Americanized Vietnam war plus continued anxiety in an Americanized Thailand. Add to this the fact that one upshot of the American–East Asian experience in the sixties seems to have been the gravest domestic crisis the United States had faced since the Civil War, and one is forcibly reminded that "American–East Asian" relations are more than ever a two-way street. These days each trans-Pacific party impacts heavily upon the other.

The Sources

Except for traditions of leakage, indiscretion, and court histories, scholars would have to wait a good many years to get at relevant materials beyond those found in official documents, press conferences, and the hearings of Congressional committees. Fortunately, such traditions persist, more vigorous than ever in times of ruptured consensus–indeed, dramatically so in the case of the so-called "Pentagon Papers." Already, by the end of the decade, one finds available at least four categories of additional sources with which to work: memoirs and histories by those who served in the Kennedy and Johnson administrations; prematurely released documentary collections; articles and books by journalists and other outside analysts who have sought to provide accounts both from Washington and from Asia; and early interpretive efforts by academics who seek to place our Asian involvement of the sixties in the wider context of American foreign policy since World War II or even before that war. A fifth category of "official history," of which Lyndon Johnson's *The Vantage Point* is an early example, should eventually be forthcoming on the basis of the presidential archives and oral history projects associated with Kennedy Papers in Waltham, Massachusetts (awaiting the construction of the Kennedy Library in Cambridge), and the Johnson Papers in Austin, Texas.[2] In addition, further personal memoirs will undoubtedly emerge from some of those who left Washington in early 1969 as well as others who have not yet departed.[3]

Among the first and most notable of the works by former Kennedy Administration officials are, of course, the accounts by Arthur Schlesinger, Jr., Theodore Sorensen, and Roger Hilsman.[4] Of these three, Hilsman provides the most extensive narrative and analysis of East Asian relations. His book, deplored by some at the time as a

2. On Kennedy, see Alfred B. Rollins, *Report on the Oral History Project of the John F. Kennedy Library* (Cambridge, Mass.: 1965). The Johnson Oral History Project is directed by Professor Joe B. Frantz of the University of Texas. See Lyndon B. Johnson, *The Vantage Point: Perspectives of the Presidency, 1963–1969* (New York: Holt, Rinehart and Winston, 1971).

3. Among recent officials who are writing books pertinent to policy making in the sixties is former Far East Assistant Secretary of State William P. Bundy. Former Undersecretary and Ambassador to India Chester Bowles has contributed some useful insights into East Asian decision making in his *Promises to Keep: My Years in Public Life* (New York: Harper & Row, 1971). Although former Undersecretary George Ball's book, *The Discipline of Power* (Boston: Atlantic-Little, Brown, 1968), reveals little about the inner workings of the Kennedy–Johnson years, some of Ball's Vietnam papers were apparently made available to the journalist Henry Brandon, whose book is cited below (note 13).

4. See Arthur M. Schlesinger, Jr., *A Thousand Days* (Boston: Houghton Mifflin, 1965); Theodore C. Sorensen, *Kennedy* (New York: Harper and Row, 1965); and Roger Hilsman, *To Move a Nation: The Politics of Foreign Policy in the Administration of John F. Kennedy* (Garden City, N.Y.: Doubleday, 1967). Another work that relates, in part, to Southeast as well as South Asia is John Kenneth Galbraith, *Ambassador's Journal: A Personal Account of the Kennedy Years* (Boston: Houghton Mifflin, 1969). See also Richard Goodwin, *Triumph or Tragedy: Reflections on Vietnam* (New York: Vintage, 1966). I have offered my own preliminary and impressionistic account of Vietnam policy making in "How Could Vietnam Happen?—An Autopsy," *Atlantic* 221 (April 1968), 47–53.

kiss-and-tell memoir,[5] is a pioneering study of "the politics of policy making" in foreign affairs; seldom has the veil that shrouds the decision-making process been removed so completely and the process analyzed so fully by a recent participant. Whatever its many flaws, largely products of the author's vantage point within the government, this work should remain a primary source for the Kennedy period. The Hilsman tradition is followed late in the decade by the former Defense Department official, Townsend Hoopes, whose focus is much narrower, that is, the critical decisions of the Johnson Administration in the spring of 1968.[6] (The tradition is also followed, with less pertinence to this paper, by a temporary White House observer, historian Eric F. Goldman.)[7] If nothing else, Hilsman and Hoopes demonstrate that current history *can* be written, to the benefit of the scholar and citizen, by literate and perceptive decision makers. Furthermore, their inevitably one-sided accounts provide a stimulus to corrective writings by other participants—all to the benefit of researchers and the public. For the present, perhaps the most dispassionate effort by a recent participant to analyze the history of America's Indochina involvement is that of Chester L. Cooper, a former CIA and NSC official.[8]

The second category of materials on the sixties is the massive and highly classified documentary study of Vietnam decision making, 1945–1967, which Defense Secretary Robert S. McNamara authorized in 1967.[9] The unauthorized release of these materials to the press and certain congressmen in 1971 has resulted in a boon to scholars—but also in a complex research problem, since these "Pentagon Papers" not only come in three variegated and incomplete editions but also present, inevitably, only one large piece of the whole. It may be hoped that the existence of this narrative and archive of documents will force earlier-than-usual release of presi-

5. See Meg Greenfield, "Kiss and Tell Memoirs," *Reporter* 37 (November 1967), 14–19. Similar views were also attributed to Secretary Rusk.

6. Townsend Hoopes, *The Limits of Intervention* (New York: David McKay, 1969). The Hoopes account has been disputed and further refined by other participants and observers.

7. Eric F. Goldman, *The Tragedy of Lyndon Johnson* (New York: Knopf, 1969).

8. Chester L. Cooper, *The Lost Crusade: America in Vietnam* (New York: Dodd, Mead, 1970).

9. See *The Pentagon Papers, As Published by the New York Times*, written by N. Sheehan, H. Smith, E. W. Kenworthy, and F. Butterfield (New York: Quadrangle, 1971); *The Pentagon Papers: The Defense Department History of U.S. Decisionmaking on Vietnam. The Senator Gravel Edition* (Boston: Beacon, 1971); and *United States-Vietnam Relations, 1945–1967: Study Prepared by the Department of Defense*. Printed for the use of the House Committee on Armed Services (Washington, D.C.: U.S. Government Printing Office, 1971).

dential and other pertinent papers to provide a fuller understanding of America's Indochina involvement.

When one shifts to a third category, the works of the fourth estate, the pertinent literature is voluminous but necessarily still thin; leakage, gossip, and careful observation in Washington and Asian capitals provide shafts of useful light but never the whole picture. One of the best of the observers, more scholar than journalist, is Theodore Draper, whose *Abuse of Power* makes brilliant use of unclassified sources on the early escalation of the Vietnam war;[10] of often the same quality, though more exuberantly polemical, are the writings of I. F. Stone, a relentless and usually well-informed inconoclast.[11] Both Draper and Stone focus on the Vietnam crisis, as do scores of their journalistic brethren. A partial listing of the most useful analyses of this crisis would include the works of the late Bernard Fall, David Halberstam, Malcolm Browne, Robert Shaplen, Ward Just, Frances FitzGerald, Wilfred G. Burchett, Jonathan Schell, Don Oberdorfer, and John Mecklin (a bureaucrat as well as a reporter), all on the American impact upon Vietnam;[12] David Kraslow and Stuart H. Loory, and also Henry Brandon, on the elusive search for peace in Vietnam;[13] and Marvin Kalb and

10. Theodore Draper, *Abuse of Power* (New York: Viking, 1967).

11. See almost any issue of *I. F. Stone's Weekly* (Washington, D.C.); see also his several essays on the Vietnam war in *The New York Review of Books*, 1967–1969.

12. Bernard B. Fall, *Vietnam Witness 1953–66* (New York: Praeger, 1966); David Halberstam, *The Making of a Quagmire* (New York: Random House, 1965); Malcolm W. Browne, *The New Face of War*, rev. ed. (Indianapolis: Bobbs-Merrill, 1968); Robert Shaplen, *The Lost Revolution* (New York: Harper and Row, 1965), *Time Out of Hand: Revolution and Reaction in Southeast Asia* (New York: Harper and Row, 1969), and *The Road From War, Vietnam 1965–1970* (New York: Harper and Row, 1970); Ward S. Just, *To What End— Report from Vietnam* (Boston: Houghton Mifflin, 1968); Frances FitzGerald, "Struggle and the War," *Atlantic* 220 (August 1967), 72–82; Wilfred G. Burchett, *Vietnam: Inside Story of the Guerrilla War*, 3rd ed. (New York: International, 1968); Jonathan Schell, *The Village of Ben Suc* (New York: Knopf, 1967), and *The Military Half: An Account of Destruction in Quang Ngai and Quang Tin* (New York: Knopf, 1968); Don Oberdorfer, *Tet! The Story of a Battle and its Historic Aftermath* (New York: Doubleday, 1971); and John Mecklin, *Mission in Torment* (Garden City, N.Y.: Doubleday, 1965). See also Arthur J. Dommen, *Conflict in Laos: The Politics of Neutralization* (New York: Praeger, 1964). Halberstam has now completed an important study of Vietnam decision makers of the sixties; Miss FitzGerald is writing an account of the American impact upon the culture of Vietnam.

13. David Kraslow and Stuart H. Loory, *The Secret Search for Peace in Vietnam* (New York: Random House, 1968); and Henry Brandon, *Anatomy of Error: The Inside Story of the Asian War on the Potomac, 1954–1969* (Boston: Gambit, 1969), which is notable for its use of some of George Ball's papers.

Elie Abel on the "roots" of American involvement in Asia.[14] Two help-ful collections of documents have been compiled by Marcus G. Ras-kin and Bernard Fall as well as Marvin E. Gettleman.[15] Significant pieces by some of the above and others are found in the *Atlantic Monthly's* anthology, *Who We Are*.[16] Books by foreign journalists besides Burchett, Fall, and Brandon are also, of course, plentiful.

Other aspects of American–East Asian relations in the decade have so far received minimal attention from the journalistic com-munity. Thanks to the Council on Foreign Relations, the veteran reporter A. T. Steele produced in mid-decade a study of American attitudes toward China;[17] but there is little on the Japanese-Ameri-can relationship since George R. Packard's book on the 1960 crisis, and still less on U.S. relations with the rest of East Asia.[18]

Some effort has been made, to be sure, to study the overall foreign policies of Kennedy and Johnson. Philip Geyelin's *Lyndon B. Johnson and the World* and Tom Wicker's *JFK and LBJ: The Influence of Personality upon Politics* are the most durable of several premature political biographies.[19] But they are thin fare for the scholar.

It is in the fourth category of sources that one confronts some fundamental questions that will surely dominate the future his-toriography of the era. Here one finds a mix of scholars and other analysts who variously describe, or interpret, or, at times, preach about, the American–East Asian relationship. Here again, Vietnam is the central obsession: Why are we there and what does it mean? Is the war a costly but necessary undertaking in terms of the national interests? Is it a tragic mistake but an aberration? Is it a logical extension of traditional American aims and activities in East Asia?

14. Marvin Kalb and Elie Abel, *Roots of Involvement: The U.S. in Asia, 1784–1971* (New York: W. W. Norton, 1971).

15. Marcus G. Raskin and Bernard B. Fall, eds., *The Vietnam Reader*, rev. ed. (New York: Vintage, 1967); and Marvin E. Gettleman, ed., *Vietnam: History, Documents and Opinions on a Major World Crisis* (Greenwich, Conn.: Fawcett, 1966).

16. Robert Manning and Michael Janeway, eds., *Who We Are: An Atlantic Chronicle of the United States and Vietnam* (Boston: Atlantic–Little, Brown, 1969).

17. A. T. Steele, *The American People and China* (New York: McGraw-Hill, 1966).

18. See George R. Packard, *Protest in Tokyo: The Security Treaty Crisis of 1960* (Princeton: Princeton University Press, 1966).

19. Philip Geyelin, *Lyndon B. Johnson and the World* (New York: Praeger, 1966); and Tom Wicker, *JFK and LBJ: The Influence of Personality upon Politics* (New York: Morrow, 1968). See also Hugh Sidey, *John F. Kennedy, President* (New York: Atheneum, 1964), and *A Very Personal Presidency: Lyndon Johnson in the White House* (New York: Atheneum, 1968); and Row-land Evans and Robert Novak, *Lyndon B. Johnson: The Exercise of Power, A Political Biography* (New York: New American Library, 1966).

Or is it part and parcel of a larger American world view, only the most flagrant and recent example of a continuing imperialist thrust?

The literary output of scholars, by no means all of them East Asia specialists or historians, is already very great. Much of it originated in the campus teach-in movement of 1965–66; much, though not all, has been polemical, and as the crisis has intensified, so have the polemics. One need cite here only a handful of representative works. Among those who regard the war as necessary, if costly, are Frank N. Trager, Wesley R. Fishel, and Chester A. Bain;[20] similar views are offered in the articles of Ithiel de Sola Pool and Samuel P. Huntington as well as CIA analyst George Carver.[21] Proponents of the "tragic error" approach—"the politics of inadvertence"—would seem to include Arthur Schlesinger, Jr., John Kenneth Galbraith, Hans Morgenthau, and East Asia specialists George McT. Kahin and John W. Lewis in *The United States in Vietnam*.[22] Concepts of inadvertent moves into an unperceived "quagmire" have been disputed more recently by Daniel Ellsberg and others who distill from their reading of the "Pentagon Papers" patterns of executive advertence and deception—and hence greater executive culpability.[23]

The tendency to view the Vietnam War as a logical consequence of America's longer-term and iniquitous involvement in East Asia is a fairly recent development among scholars, although its ideological godfather would appear to be historian William A. Williams;[24] the primary effort, so far, as seen in the works of Noam Chomsky and younger contributors to the *Bulletin of Concerned Asian*

20. Frank N. Trager, *Why Vietnam?* (New York: Praeger, 1967); Wesley R. Fishel, ed., *Vietnam: Anatomy of a Conflict* (Itasca, Ill.: Peacock, 1968); and Chester A. Bain, *Vietnam: The Roots of Conflict* (Englewood Cliffs, N.J.: Prentice-Hall, 1967).

21. See, for instance, Ithiel de Sola Pool, *Village Violence and Pacification in Vietnam* (Urbana, Ill.: University of Illinois, 1968); Samuel P. Huntington, "The Bases of Accommodation," *Foreign Affairs* 46 (July 1968), 642–656; and George A. Carver, Jr., "Real Revolution in South Vietnam," *Foreign Affairs* 43 (April 1965), 387–408. See also the contributions by Pool and Huntington in *No More Vietnams?* (note 27).

22. See Arthur M. Schlesinger, Jr., *The Bitter Heritage: Vietnam and American Diplomacy, 1941–1966* (Boston: Houghton Mifflin, 1967); John Kenneth Galbraith, *How to Get Out of Vietnam* (New York: New American Library, 1967); Hans J. Morgenthau, *Vietnam and the United States* (Washington: Public Affairs, 1965); and especially, George McT. Kahin and John W. Lewis, *The United States in Vietnam*, rev. ed., (New York: Dial, 1969).

23. See Daniel Ellsberg, "The Quagmire Myth and the Stalemate Machine," *Public Policy* 19 (Spring 1971), 217–274; also, Leslie H. Gelb, "Vietnam: The System Worked," *Foreign Policy* 3 (Summer 1971), 140–167; also the exchanges involving Ellsberg, Gelb, and Arthur M. Schlesinger, Jr., in *The New York Review of Books* 17 (October 21 and December 2, 1971).

24. William A. Williams, *The Tragedy of American Diplomacy*, rev. ed., (New York: Delta, 1962).

Scholars, is to reinvestigate past relations between the United States and China during and after World War II and between the United States and Japan, all done in the light of national habits and qualities that the Vietnam crisis is said to have revealed.[25] When one moves across the barely visible line that separates some of these neorevisionists from analysts who view the war as the quintessence of a global and not merely regional tradition in foreign affairs—a "radical" analysis of American history and foreign policy—one encounters the works not only of Chomsky again, but of Howard Zinn, Carl Oglesby, and most notably, Gabriel Kolko.[26] Such writers move well beyond Vietnam to other parts of Asia and, of course, to other times and places, to chronicle and indict "American imperialism." The preceding spectrum of viewpoints is reflected in the proceedings of a 1968 Chicago conference on the war's lessons (or nonlessons) edited by Richard M. Pfeffer under the title, *No More Vietnams?*[27] Predictably, no consensus emerges.

Although Vietnam has dominated academic analysis of the decade, Sino-American relations have received some attention as a result primarily of the Council on Foreign Relations' series on "The United States and China in World Affairs." Most pertinent in this series, besides the Steele book previously cited, are the late Robert Blum's chronicle of the Washington–Peking relationship and Kenneth T. Young's study of the specifics of negotiations between the two parties.[28] In the same series Fred Greene presents a heavily conventional analysis of American security policy in the region.[29] Fur-

25. See Noam Chomsky, *American Power and the New Mandarins* (New York: Pantheon, 1969), and *At War with Asia* (New York: Pantheon, 1970); also the articles by James L. Peck, John Dower, and others in the *Bulletin of Concerned Asian Scholars*, 2 and 3. For a provocative collection of revisionist essays, see Edward Friedman and Mark Selden, eds., *America's Asia: Dissenting Essays on Asian–American Relations* (New York: Pantheon, 1971).

26. Howard Zinn, *Vietnam: The Logic of Withdrawal* (Boston: Beacon, 1967); Carl Oglesby and Richard Shaull, *Containment and Change* (New York: Macmillan, 1967); and Gabriel Kolko, *The Roots of American Foreign Policy* (Boston: Beacon, 1969). See also David Horowitz, ed., *Containment and Revolution* (Boston: Beacon, 1967).

27. Richard M. Pfeffer, ed., *No More Vietnams? The War and the Future of American Foreign Policy* (New York: Harper and Row, 1968). For a highly critical but well-documented study of America in Vietnam, see Committee of Concerned Asian Scholars, *The Indochina Story* (New York: Pantheon, 1970). For a similar study of the Laos conflict, see Nina S. Adams and Alfred W. McCoy, eds., *Laos: War and Revolution* (New York: Harper and Row, 1970).

28. Robert Blum, *The United States and China in World Affairs*, A. Doak Barnett, ed. (New York: McGraw-Hill, 1966); and Kenneth T. Young, *Negotiating with the Chinese Communists: The United States Experience, 1953–1967* (New York: McGraw-Hill, 1968).

29. Fred Greene, *United States Policy and the Security of Asia* (New York: McGraw-Hill, 1968).

ther reflections on the Sino-American relationship are also found in the collected essays of John K. Fairbank, as well as his updated *The United States and China*, in the articles of John Gittings and David Mozingo, in portions of Edwin O. Reischauer's *Beyond Vietnam*, and most notably, with extensive analysis by a number of specialists, in the second volume of *China in Crisis*, edited by Tang Tsou.[30]

As for scholarly studies of American relations with the rest of Asia, the fare here is once again thin. Except for the Reischauer work, the third edition of his *United States and Japan*, and a collection of essays under an identical title edited by Herbert Passin, Japanese-American relations in the sixties have yet to be explored in depth.[31] The same can be said for Korea and also for Southeast Asia, with the exception of Russell H. Fifield's study early in the decade.[32]

Of course no bibliographical review, however abbreviated, can neglect congressional sources. In addition to the records of hearings on authorization and appropriations for departmental budgets and for military and economic assistance programs in East Asia, the researcher will find a wealth of material in the published hearings of the Senate Foreign Relations Committee on Communist China

30. John K. Fairbank, *China: The People's Middle Kingdom and the USA* (Cambridge, Mass.: Harvard University Press, 1967) and *The United States and China*, 3rd ed. (Cambridge, Mass.: Harvard University Press, 1971); John Gittings, "China and the Cold War," *Survey* 58 (January 1966), 196–208; David P. Mozingo, *Containment in Asia Reconsidered* (Santa Monica, Calif.: Rand Corp., 1966); Edwin O. Reischauer, *Beyond Vietnam: The United States and Asia* (New York: Knopf, 1967); and Tang Tsou, ed., *China in Crisis* II, *China's Policies in Asia and America's Alternatives* (Chicago: University of Chicago Press, 1968). See also Ishwer C. Ohja, *Chinese Foreign Policy in an Age of Transition: The Diplomacy of Cultural Despair* (Boston: Beacon, 1969); Bruce Douglass and Ross Terrill, eds., *China and Ourselves: Explorations and Revisions by a New Generation* (Boston: Beacon, 1970); and the latter sections of Warren I. Cohen, *America's Response to China* (New York: John Wiley, 1971).

31. Edwin O. Reischauer, *The United States and Japan*, 3rd ed., (Cambridge, Mass.: Harvard University Press, 1965); and Herbert Passin, ed., *The United States and Japan* (Englewood Cliffs, N.J.: Prentice-Hall, 1966). See also Warren S. Hunsberger, *Japan and the United States in World Trade* (New York: Harper and Row, 1964), and Lawrence Olson, *Japan in Postwar Asia* (New York: Praeger, 1970).

32. Russell H. Fifield, *Southeast Asia in United States Policy* (New York: Praeger, 1963); aspects of the Taiwan problem are treated in Mark Mancall, ed., *Formosa Today* (New York: Praeger, 1964), and in Jerome A. Cohen, et al., *Taiwan and American Policy* (New York: Praeger, 1971). On the Philippines, see Frank Golay, ed. *The United States and the Philippines* (Englewood Cliffs, N.J.: Prentice-Hall, 1966). On one aspect of the region as a whole, see John Hohenberg, *Between Two Worlds: Policy, Press and Public Opinion on Asian–American Relations* (New York: Praeger, 1967).

in 1966 and on Vietnam in both 1966 and 1968.[33] More recently, the Senate Subcommittee on United States Security Agreements and Commitments Abroad (Symington Subcommittee) has held hearings—and published their record—which provide invaluable data on America's relations with the Philippines, Laos, Thailand, Korea, and other Asian allies during the decade of the sixties.[34]

Finally, it must be stressed that there are other readily available indicators of the American–East Asian relationship beyond the narrow confines of governmental ties: the statistics of burgeoning trade, investment, publications, air travel, mass communications, and educational, scientific, and cultural exchange—a process that has brought more Americans and Asians in touch with each other and with each other's cultures in this decade than ever before. The transformations recorded in these data, particularly the data of economic and cultural ties, may well be of far greater long-term significance to the region and the relationship than the more visible political and military confrontations.

For instance, the paucity of analyses, by scholars, journalists, or others, of the Japanese–American relationship in the sixties is strikingly at odds with the nature of the relationship. Japan's spiraling economic growth and Japan's vast importance as a trading partner are overshadowed by crises elsewhere in the region. Yet the fact of Japanese economic power encourages American strategists to press for a sharing of Asian responsibilities, particularly in the aid-giving area. It also poses problems for an increasingly troubled American economy. And it leaves the decade overcast by the unavoidable question, Whither Japan?

Some Themes and Questions

As the nineteen sixties recede in East Asia, it is hard not to view their passing with relief. The impact of our East Asian involvement

33. U.S. Senate, 89th Congress, 2nd sess., Committee on Foreign Relations, *Hearings on U.S. Policy with Respect to Mainland China* (Washington: U.S. Government Printing Office, 1966); *The Vietnam Hearings* (New York: Vintage, 1966); and U.S. House of Representatives, 91st Congress, 2nd sess., Subcommittee on Asian and Pacific Affairs of the Committee on Foreign Affairs, *Hearings on United States–China Relations: A Strategy for the Future* (Washington, D.C.: U.S. Government Printing Office, 1970). See also Akira Iriye, ed., *United States Policy Toward China* (Boston: Little, Brown, 1968).

34. U.S. Senate, 91st Congress, 1st sess., Subcommittee on United States Security Agreements and Commitments Abroad of the Committee on Foreign Relations, Hearings: pt. 1, *The Republic of the Philippines* (Washington, D.C.: U.S. Government Printing Office, 1969). See also pt. 2, *Kingdom of Laos*; pt. 3, *Kingdom of Thailand*; pt. 4, *Republic of China*; pt. 5, *Japan and Okinawa*; and pt. 6, *Republic of Korea* (Washington, D.C.: U.S. Government Printing Office, 1970).

seems devastating, both at home and abroad. Few serious students of the region would argue that the stakes, if any, were worth the cumulative costs.

And yet there are other ways of looking at the period. For instance, nuclear war was avoided. So was war with Communist China. Curiously, Sino-American relations, frozen solid in 1961, showed signs of thaw in the multi-polar world of 1970—and suddenly broke loose in 1971. In addition, Japanese-American relations improved and matured, despite points of sharp and continuing contention and an uncertain future. Furthermore, economic growth and political stability were greater on portions of China's East Asian periphery at the decade's end than at the beginning. As for Vietnam, the war was sharply escalated; but then it was de-escalated—no mean feat for a great and proud power—and the momentum of ground-force de-escalation and American withdrawal persists. Finally, the Vietnam experience appeared to have chastened the American people and also their officialdom; "low posture," "low profile," "Asian self-help," "Asian initiatives," "decreased American presence," "no more Vietnams"—all became part of an evolving conventional wisdom enshrined in the so-called Nixon Doctrine. If American mistakes (or expansionism, or imperialism) crested in Vietnam, some cresting somewhere was probably the prerequisite to the receding of the wave and the development of a healthier relationship.

Much of the foregoing analysis would be accepted by recent public servants, defensive about the fruits of their labors. Radical critics would accept far less, if any, of it. Yet even radical analysis might logically perceive some virtues in the recent decade. Not merely has the wave apparently crested; the soul searching at home about the meaning of Vietnam has opened the eyes of new sections of the public to the imperfections of American society and institutions. It has thereby at least increased the possibility of radical social and political change at home and a less interventionist role abroad.

However tempting it may be, then, to view the sixties in East Asia as unmitigated tragedy and error, the apprentice scholar would probably do well to resist that temptation for the time being. The key questions to be probed concern less the rightness or wrongness of America's East Asian involvement in these years than the hows and whys of what happened: what men thought they were doing, how they did it, and why, on both sides of the Pacific.

Any effort to understand the decade must grapple eventually, and probably initially, with the problem of American national interests or stakes in the west Pacific region. This is at the same time both fundamental and elusive; it is difficult to separate rhetoric from political reality and further difficult to separate domestic political reality, as perceived by policy makers, from the international politics of the region, as perceived by the same men.

How did President Kennedy and his chief advisers define America's East Asian interests in 1961? To what extent was a definition—or definitions—actually articulated, rather than assumed as a "given," and to what extent was the accepted definition challenged from within—and on what grounds? One asks such questions about the region as a whole; but one must ask them at once, more specifically, about Southeast Asia, since the inherited Laos crisis and then Vietnam consumed the immediate attention and energies of the incoming administration.

The answers, of course, are extraordinarily difficult to find—despite the "Pentagon Papers" and other revelations. This is hardly surprising, since the federal government, even at its upper reaches, is a highly pluralistic institution; and each of its senior members is subject to a mix of forces from within and without, personal and political, domestic and foreign.

What was the relative importance to our East Asian policy, for instance, of a number of such forces or factors that are now clearly identifiable in the climate of 1961 and later? What follows is merely a suggestive and illustrative list, by no means a definitive one; the items occur in no particular order.

1. *The shift in politico-military thinking, with the advent of the new administration, from a policy of "massive retaliation" to one of "flexible response."* Such a shift from the much denounced Dulles doctrine pulled back from brinkmanship; but it gave a new lease on life to specialized conventional forces; and it found a civilian and largely academic constituency among social science critics of Dulles, whose studies of "political development" and "modernization" had imbued them with enthusiasm for techniques of "counter-insurgency." What precisely was the motivation and influence of these latter-day technocratic Wilsonians?

2. *Early crises in foreign policy quite extraneous to East Asia.* Many have written that the Bay of Pigs fiasco made Khrushchev misjudge Kennedy and that the Soviet challenge at the Vienna summit and in Berlin convinced the President that he must "stand firm" at the next place of challenge (Vietnam) to maintain his balance in Soviet-American relations. Was this actually central? And in later years, how did the external realities of Soviet-American confrontation and then detente affect East Asian decision making in regard to China as well as Vietnam?

3. *The legacy of McCarthyism.* The Democratic party, charged in the early fifties with "softness on communism" and the "loss of China," could ill afford to permit a further square foot of "Free World" territory to fall under Communist rule (despite Kennedy's position on the Offshore Islands in the television debates of the 1960 campaign). The bureaucracy that it inherited had been similarly seared by McCarthyism. To what extent did such constraints affect the reporting, recommendations, and decision making of the early Vietnam years?

4. *The domino theory.* This Eisenhower seedling has been hard to uproot among citizens and policy makers, in large part because it is only disprovable if you take certain risks—and the consequences of having it prove correct once you take those risks are usually viewed as unacceptable. It is difficult to determine the extent to which dominoism was a rhetorical shorthand to assure public support as opposed to a serious factor in policy calculation. One suspects that the answer would vary from person to person and from year to year. It is also worth asking if the one significant "domino" (and perhaps the only one) was not the administration in power in Washington; in other words, if you lost Saigon, you would very soon lose Washington to the opposition party.

5. *Monolithic communism: the "Sino-Soviet Bloc."* There is an apparent time lag between the actuality of Sino-Soviet tensions leading to rift, the perception of tensions and rift among outside and inside specialists, and the gradual understanding of that new reality among top policy makers. Once China was seen as a separate entity and once Moscow–Peking tensions began to affect Communist parties elsewhere in Asia, including Vietnam, a multiple, flexible strategy was increasingly attractive. But such an awareness came only slowly, haltingly, and unevenly to key officials. Hence the tendency for Rusk and even Humphrey to refer to "Asian Communism" long after the term had been judged meaningless among regional specialists within the government.

6. *Fear of Communist China's potential expansionism.* Here the emphasis is on China's "Chineseness" and alleged imperial aspirations rather that the world-wide threat of communism. To what extent did policy makers, particularly those who held office during the Korean War, misread Chinese intervention in that war, in retrospect, and fear a Chinese spillover into Indochina and Southeast Asia? Even such a progressive thinker as Chester Bowles was obsessed by the relationship between China's food–population dilemma and Southeast Asia's food production potential; similarly, W. W.

Rostow thought that some food-for-peace *quid pro quo* might be arranged on the basis of Southeast Asian rice exports in return for a renunciation of force by Peking.

7. *Benevolence, altruism, and humanitarian aims.* The internal as well as external rhetoric of the period is replete with expressed desires to help modernize the "fragile new nations" on China's periphery and to protect these nations from external threats during the inevitably difficult process of modernization. How central were such sentiments to American decision making, both in Washington and in Asia? To what extent were they rooted in previous traditions of intended benevolence (for example, the mission movement, particularly in its social gospel phase; expressions of concern, primarily for China, emanating from aspects of the Open Door doctrine)? To what extent were they infused with a conscious or unconscious desire to impose an American model on Asian societies, and were therefore hostile or insensitive to alternative models much closer to Asia?

8. *Fear of instability in East Asia.* It is hardly surprising that nuclear powers are concerned lest regional instability anywhere lead to wider hostilities and, eventually, to the possibility of nuclear confrontation. Obsession with stability in regions undergoing great change can lead to the evils of premature intervention and over-intervention. Efforts to mute instability can also lead, less dramatically, to embracement of the status quo and to counterembracement by local elites. To what extent did the desire to keep the region stable—in order perhaps to free attention for greater problems elsewhere (for example, U.S.–U.S.S.R. relations) or to resolve one major local problem (for example, Vietnam)—persuade policy makers to accommodate themselves to transitory "stability" (for example, Taiwan, South Korea, Thailand, and earlier, Diemist Vietnam) in the decade? Were there those who argued that a higher level of instability in East Asia was inevitable and therefore must be tolerated?

9. *Desire to control present or future raw materials or markets in the region.* Traditional Marxist-Leninist views of the nature of imperialism have been rehabilitated, in one form or another, by some critics of America's East Asian involvement in the sixties. Spurred by such hypotheses, researchers should seek to investigate the economic underpinnings of policy and policy makers in the region in this period and their formal and informal relationship to private American firms—to probe the alleged existence and workings of a military-industrial complex or perhaps a civilian-industrial complex. What was the precise economic objective, as manifested in the

writings and actions of the officials, and which countries, markets, and raw materials figured in this objective? What evidence of pressure from American industry and finance, and of response to that pressure, can be found? As an important related question, to what extent was the Vietnam War fueled by a weapons or supply industry in complicity with military or civilian bureaucrats?

10. *Denial of territorial hegemony to others, regardless of the U.S. national stake.* Was there, perhaps, a paramount negative theme in these years, as at times previously: the theme of simple denial (one key factor, it seems, in the decisions to annex the Philippines in 1898, to freeze Japanese assets in 1941, to aid the French in Indochina in 1949, and to support Diem in 1954)? Did denial to others need to be based on any clear definition of U.S. interests, economic or political, present or future? The writings of some participants already indicate far greater clarity on the nature of the *threat* to Southeast Asia than on the nature of any American national *stake* there.

11. *Containment of Communist China, with or without isolation.* This factor is implied earlier in both the concept of monolithic communism and the fear of China. In many officials, we must assume, the desire remained strong—from the preceding decade—to apply to a militant and bellicose Peking regime the same strategy that had seemed appropriate to Stalinist Russia: a regional network of defensive alliances as the groundwork for collective security. To what extent was the appropriateness of close-in containment and isolation accepted or disputed within the government, and what alternative strategies were proposed—with what results? How much was the eventually evolved Kennedy–Johnson strategy of slightly modified containment affected by Chinese rhetoric and behavior, by other foreign policy considerations (for example, of the U.S.S.R., Taiwan, Japan), and by assumed domestic constraints?

12. *The quest for collective security and world order.* Much of the rhetoric of our East Asian involvement in this decade contains such terms and phrases as "our commitments," "our pledged word," "our allies," "the appetite of the aggressor," "the defeat of aggression," and "aggression through subversion." Many who used these terms had served in the government during and after World War II; they had matured in the thirties; they remembered the Manchurian Incident and, of course, Munich. To what extent was the East Asian outlook of key decision makers affected by an extraregional dedication to the creation and maintenance of a viable system of international order buttressed by collective security agreements—a system in which territorial demarcations (drawn lines)

were crucial, for example, West Berlin, the 38th parallel in Korea, and in the 17th parallel in Vietnam, and in which the violation of one line might endanger the whole system? In some minds, a nuclear world was simply too dangerous for any but "peaceful change"; change by force, once successful and therefore legitimized, would destroy the delicate balance.

There are, of course, a host of other questions, beyond those raised in the preceding paragraphs, that must also concern the student of the sixties. Here are a few of them:

What, for example, was the continuing force and influence of "China," both the mainland and Taiwan, in the minds of policy makers and in the American public in this period? (Can one discern, for instance, any proprietary sense, nostalgia, or excessive fear or hatred that would support the hypothesis of a continuing concern?) What was the role of East Asian expertise, both inside and outside the government? (The role of China experts, outside and inside, had been drastically curtailed and even severed in 1953. What effect had this curtailment had on policy; and with what consequences were the government's ties with academic Asian specialists gradually reestablished after 1961?)

What was the role of Japan in the minds of policy makers and the public? This is clearly a question of crucial significance for the seventies. Japan emerges from this decade fully rehabilitated as a major industrial power and, second only to Canada, America's foremost trade partner. Japan is therefore at the point of political and, perhaps, military "take-off" in the region and the international arena. How were Japan's evolving role and the complexities of Japanese-American relations perceived and appraised? One logical point of departure, for the inquiring historian, would be the record of Okinawa planning and negotiations from the 1961 Kaysen mission through the 1969 Sato visit.

Further, what knowledge and understanding of both Vietnams was available within the government, and outside, from 1961 onward, and how was it used, if at all? Similar questions may be asked in regard to Korea, Indonesia, Thailand, and other nations.

Or a deeper and much more elusive kind of question: what was the role of race, and of "racism," in the approach of policy makers to East Asia and, in particular, to the Vietnam War? Is it possible to identify certain decisions men took and tactics they applied against an Asian enemy that would not have been palatable against a Caucasian enemy? What perceptions or myths about "Asians" seem to have affected the minds of policy makers?

Or, in terms of institutional analysis: What were the roles of

State, Treasury, Defense, the White House, the CIA, and other agencies, and of individuals and enclaves within these agencies, in key decisions regarding East Asia (most significantly, the escalatory decision of 1964–65)? And externally, what was the role of pressure groups (including the peace movement), of Congress and political parties, of the press and especially television, and of "public opinion," in our East Asian involvement during the sixties?

And further, there are always questions to be asked about continuities with the past, and discontinuities: regarding rhetoric, definitions of national interest, perceptions of Asia and Asians, and uses of national power. Lyndon Johnson sounds sometimes like Theodore Roosevelt and Alfred T. Mahan, Rusk like Stanley K. Hornbeck, others like Henry L. Stimson or Woodrow Wilson. Yet at least two discontinuities are also striking: America's paramountcy in the west Pacific since the defeat of Japan, and the fantastic growth and proliferation of the postwar governmental apparatus.

And then there is always the fundamental factor of people. The sixties are a well-stocked hunting ground for Asian-oriented biographers, sooner or later: two Presidents, plus a year of Nixon's term; Rusk as a central figure of elusiveness but of long East Asian experience, increasing strength, and formidable obstinacy; McNamara, part computer, part poet, loyal supply master for a war in which he ceases to believe; the brothers Bundy, heirs to the patrician tradition of Colonel Stimson in East Asia; the irrepressible global technocrat Rostow; the indefatigable negotiator Averell Harriman; the fatigable negotiator Cabot Lodge; the professor-turned-ambassador Edwin Reischauer; and undoubtedly several others.

And, of course, there is the Asian side of the relationship: who *they* were, what they sought, how and why, and how they viewed *us*, in Tokyo, Peking, Hanoi, Saigon, and many other places. Here again the same types of questions must be asked—but in each case from a very different vantage point.

Conclusion

For the apprentice scholar, then, the task is very difficult. But it can also be exhilarating. For he is dealing with a time of high drama and change in the long history of East–West collision, a time when the trans-Pacific relationship has begun to be more equal.

The greatest hazard in studying the sixties remains the hazard of vantage point; and vantage point means, for the next few years, Vietnam.

For the teacher, Vietnam is a great boon. It is immediate, dramatic, and enraging, both microcosm and macrocosm of other blunders, tragedies, and evils (one takes one's pick) in America's relations with East Asia over a very long period of time—or even, some would say, in America's relations with much of the rest of the world, at least since World War II. It is vividly instructive.

But the pedagogical usefulness of Vietnam as an object lesson—and the cathartic value of believing and preaching the war's stupidity, illegality, immorality, and indeed, its exposure of American iniquity—is no substitute for scholarship on American–East Asian relations in the sixties.

It will take much digging to move beyond the hyperbolic rhetoric of many defenders and critics of the war; but that digging must be done. It might begin, one hopes, with an effort to put aside the global dominoism of both camps: of those of the left *and* the right who say that America stands or falls on the Vietnam outcome; of those self-styled radicals *and* social-science technocrats who, moving out from Vietnam, see the "Third World" as a meaningful cohesive unit; of those who look for similarity and unity rather than diversity and diviseness in approaching international relations.

Synthesis—the discovery or creation of unities—is an admirable and appropriate objective for the scholar. But synthesis requires prior command of detail. And what is lacking, more than ever, in the study of American–East Asian relations during the past decade is professionally analyzed detail. We are flooded, of course, with detail about Vietnam. And Vietnam has raised important questions about American power, America's Asian and global role, and even the tradition of Asian studies in America.

But what is needed and so far absent is scholarly analysis of American–East Asian relations beyond the Vietnam debate, ideally a series of case studies: not only those probings of American decision making suggested earlier in this paper, but studies, specifically, of the U.S. relationship with Laos, Thailand, Cambodia, and even Burma throughout the decade; most important, with Indonesia, and with Malaysia, Singapore, and the Philippines; with the Chinese Communists, at Warsaw and elsewhere, and with Taiwan; imperatively, with Japan; and also with Korea. (A further footnote could even be written on the interplay of domestic, East Asian, and Soviet relations by focusing on the U.S. non-relationship with Mongolia.) Such studies should weigh the degree of American understanding and official and private involvement in each situation, the nature of the local government and its opposition, American and Asian stakes in the relationship, who was using whom for what purposes, why, and when—and, of course, what it all means. From such studies there might eventually evolve a full and fair appraisal of American–East Asian relations in the sixties. It is just possible that, out of such studies, the sixties might emerge as a highly significant watershed when American misapprehensions of the post-World War II era were belatedly if brutally corrected and, simultaneously, the groundwork was laid for something less violent and destructive in both the region and the relationship.

In any event, only on the basis of such scholarly analysis can the assumptions, intuitions, and moral outrage of the present about the latest stage of trans-Pacific interaction give way to something more useful and more durable. Until such things are done, those who seek to rewrite the past in the klieg lights of the recent present proceed at their own considerable risk.

Notes on Contributors

BURTON F. BEERS
Professor of History, North Carolina State University. Co-author of *The Far East: A History of the Western Impact and the Eastern Response*, 1830–1970, 5th rev. ed. (Englewood Cliffs, N.J.: Prentice-Hall, 1971).

ROBERT DALLEK
Associate Professor at the University of California, Los Angeles, where he teaches American diplomatic history. He is the author of *Democrat and Diplomat: The Life of William E. Dodd* (New York: Oxford University Press, 1968), and he is currently working on a study of Franklin D. Roosevelt's conduct of foreign policy.

ROGER DINGMAN
Assistant Professor of History at the University of Southern California. He is preparing for publication a study of the origins of naval strategic arms limitation in the Pacific, 1914–1922.

RAYMOND A. ESTHUS
Professor of History, Tulane University; author of *Theodore Roosevelt and Japan* (Seattle: University of Washington Press, 1966) and other works.

JOHN K. FAIRBANK
Francis Lee Higginson Professor of History, Harvard University; author of *The United States and China*, 3rd ed. (Cambridge, Mass.: Harvard University Press, 1971) and other writings on Chinese history and foreign relations.

EDWARD D. GRAHAM
Associate Professor of Humanities and in the Justin Morrill College, Michigan State University.

MORTON H. HALPERIN
Senior Fellow of the Brookings Institution and a former Deputy Assistant Secretary of Defense.

WALDO H. HEINRICHS, JR.
Professor of History, University of Illinois, Urbana-Champaign; author of *American Ambassador: Joseph C. Grew and the Development of the U.S. Diplomatic Tradition* (Boston: Little, Brown and Company, 1966).

AKIRA IRIYE
Professor of American History, The University of Chicago. Author of *After Imperialism: The Search for a New Order in the Far East, 1921–1931* (Cambridge, Mass.: Harvard University Press, 1965), *Across the Pacific: An Inner History of American-East Asian Relations* (New York: Harcourt, Brace & World, 1967), and *Pacific Estrangement: The Interaction Between American and Japanese Expansion, 1897–1911* (Cambridge, Mass.: Harvard University Press, 1972).

KWANG-CHING LIU
Professor of History, University of California, Davis. A specialist in Chinese history of the late Ch'ing period, he maintains an interest in the history of America's relations with China.

ERNEST R. MAY
Professor of History and Director of the Institute of Politics, Harvard University. Author of *The World War and American Isolation, 1914–1917* (Cambridge, Massachusetts: Harvard University Press, 1959), *Imperial Democracy; The Emergence of America as a Great Power* (New York: Harcourt Brace and World, 1961), *American Imperialism: A Speculative Essay* (New York: Atheneum, 1968), and other works. Chairman, American Historical Association Committee on American-East Asian Relations.

LOUIS MORTON
Provost, Daniel Webster Professor of History, Dartmouth College, Hanover, New Hampshire.

CHARLES E. NEU
Associate Professor of History at Brown University. He is the author of *An Uncertain Friendship: Theodore Roosevelt and Japan, 1906–1909* (Cambridge, Mass.: Harvard University Press, 1967), and "The Changing Interpretive Structure of American Foreign Policy" in John Braeman, Robert H. Bremner, and David Brody, eds., *Twentieth-Century American Foreign Policy* (Columbus: Ohio State University Press, 1971).

JIM PECK
Ph.D. candidate in sociology at Harvard University; co-director, Bay Area Institute, San Francisco; editor Pantheon Books.

ROBERT S. SCHWANTES
Vice President for Programs, The Asia Foundation; author of *Japanese and Americans: A Century of Cultural Relations* (New York: Harper and Brothers, 1955).

PETER W. STANLEY
Assistant Professor of History at the University of Illinois at Chicago Circle. He is presently completing a study of the American-Philippine encounter.

JAMES C. THOMSON, JR.
Lecturer on History at Harvard University; he teaches the history of American-East Asian relations. From 1961–1966 he was a Far East specialist at the State Department and White House. He is the author of *While China Faced West: American Reformers in Nationalist China, 1928–1937* (Cambridge, Mass.: Harvard University Press, 1969).

MARILYN B. YOUNG
Lecturer in the History Department of the University of Michigan, teaching at the Residential College. She is on the editorial board of the Bulletin of Concerned Asian Scholars and the author of *Rhetoric of Empire: American China Policy, 1895–1901* (Cambridge, Mass.: Harvard University Press, 1968).

Index